ROAD ATLAS

2022 EASY TO BRITAIN

G000298160

Papworth Rd
Trumpington
CB2 0AY

CONTENTS

Inside front cover: **Key to map pages**

II **Route planning maps**

XII **Distances and journey times**

XIII **Key to map symbols**

2 **Road maps of Britain**

289 **Index to road maps of Britain**

Inside back cover: **County and unitary authority boundaries**

www.philips-maps.co.uk

First published in 2020 by Philip's
a division of Octopus Publishing Group Ltd
www.octopusbooks.co.uk
Carmelite House, 50 Victoria Embankment
London EC4Y 0DZ
An Hachette UK Company
www.hachette.co.uk
Second edition 2021
First impression 2021
ISBN 978-1-84907-562-6
Cartography by Philip's
Copyright © 2021 Philip's

Map data

This product includes mapping data licensed from Ordnance Survey®, with the permission of the Controller of Her Majesty's Stationery Office. © Crown copyright 2021 All rights reserved. Licence number 100011710.

Information for National Parks, Areas of Outstanding Natural Beauty, National Trails and Country Parks in Wales supplied by the Countryside Council for Wales.

Information for National Parks, Areas of Outstanding Natural Beauty, National Trails and Country Parks in England supplied by Natural England. Data for Regional Parks, Long Distance Footpaths and Country Parks in Scotland provided by Scottish Natural Heritage.

Gaelic name forms used in the Western Isles provided by Comhairle nan Eilean.

Data for the National Nature Reserves in England provided by Natural England. Data for the National Nature Reserves in Wales provided by Countryside Council for Wales. Darparwyd data'n ymwneud â Gwarchodfeydd Natur Cenedlaethol Cymru gan Gyngor Cefn Gwlad Cymru.

Information on the location of National Nature Reserves in Scotland was provided by Scottish Natural Heritage.

Data for National Scenic Areas in Scotland provided by the Scottish Executive Office. Crown copyright material is reproduced with the permission of the Controller of HMSO and the Queen's Printer for Scotland. Licence number C02W0003960.

Printed in China

*Data from Nielsen Total Consumer Market 2020 weeks 27-39

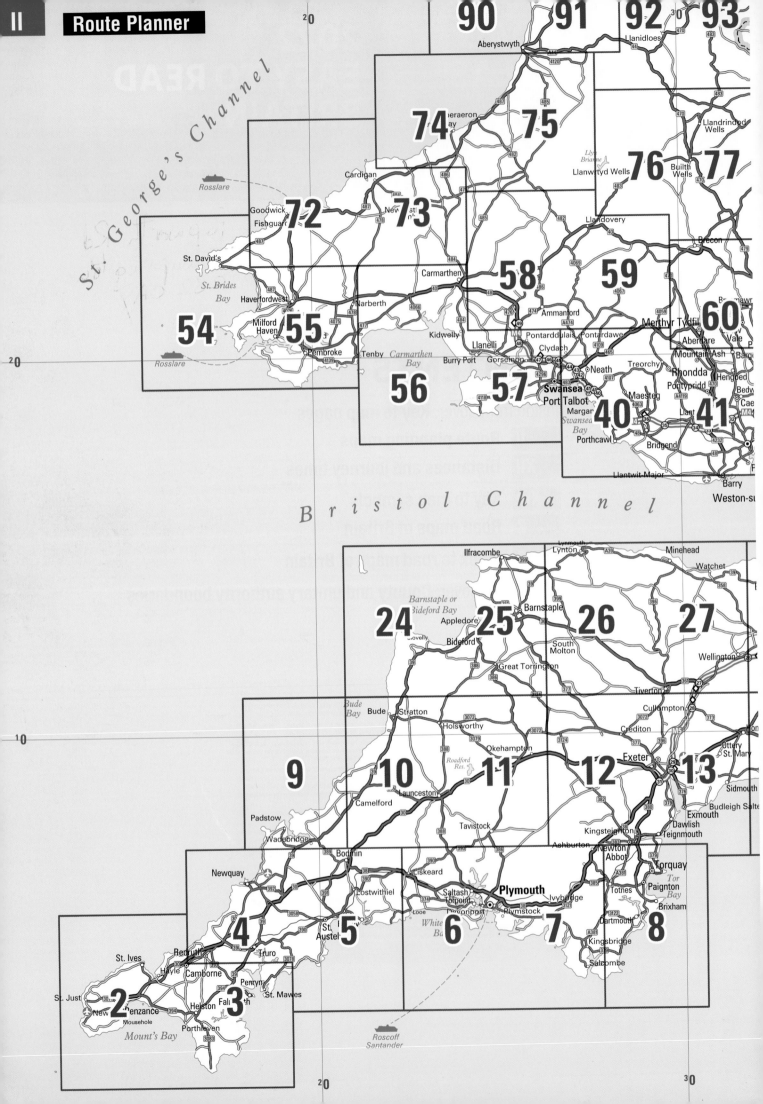

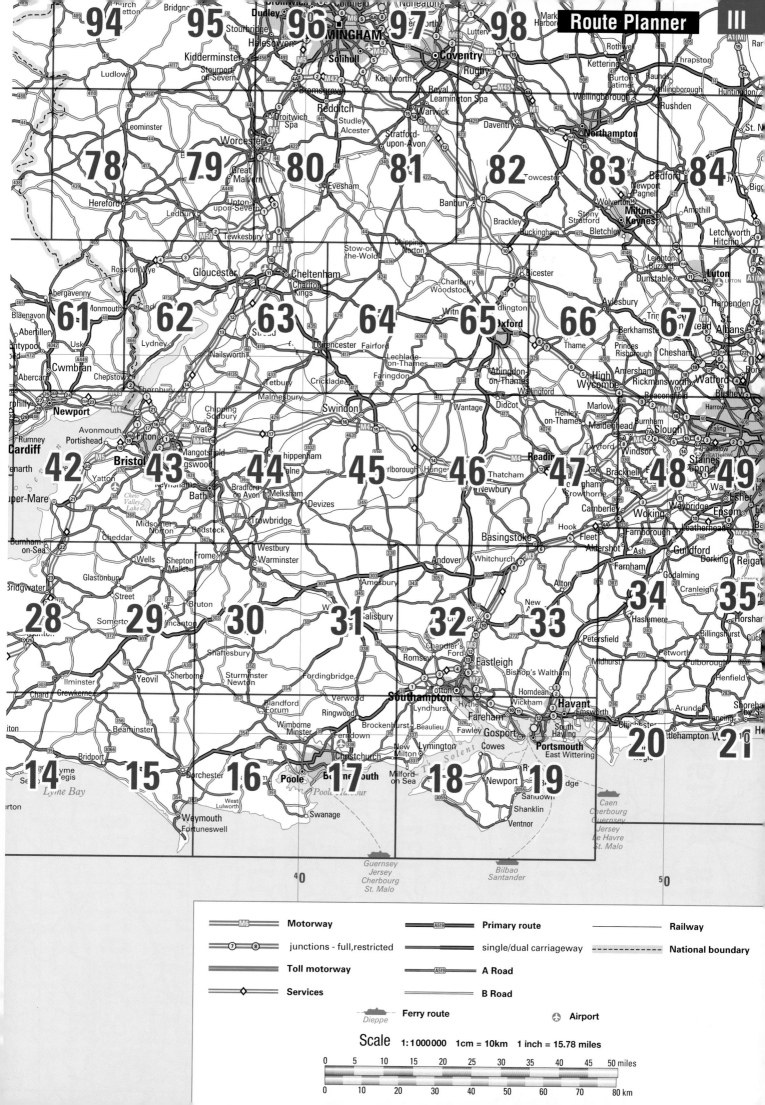

Scale

1:1000000   1cm = 10km   1 inch = 15.78 miles

	Motorway
⑦ ⑧	junctions - full, restricted
	Toll motorway
◇	Services

	Primary route
A519	single/dual carriageway
A519	A Road
	B Road

	Railway
	National boundary

Dieppe	Ferry route
✈	Airport

0   5   10   15   20   25   30   35   40   45   50 miles

0   10   20   30   40   50   60   70   80 km

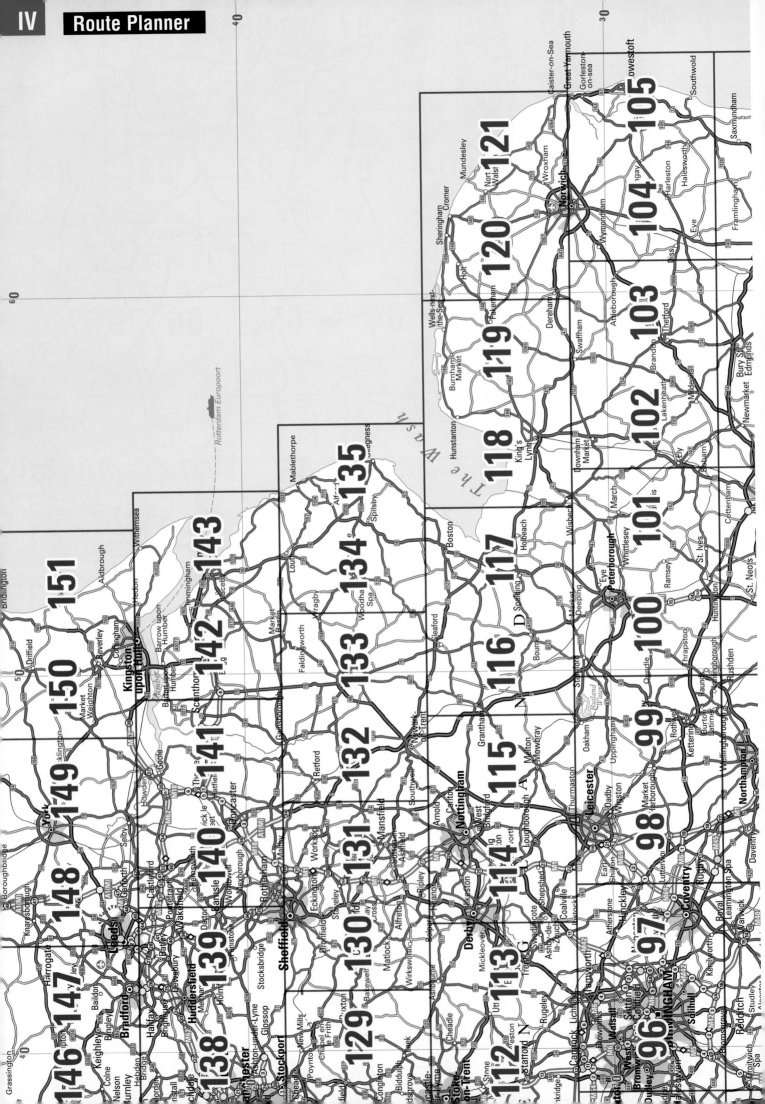

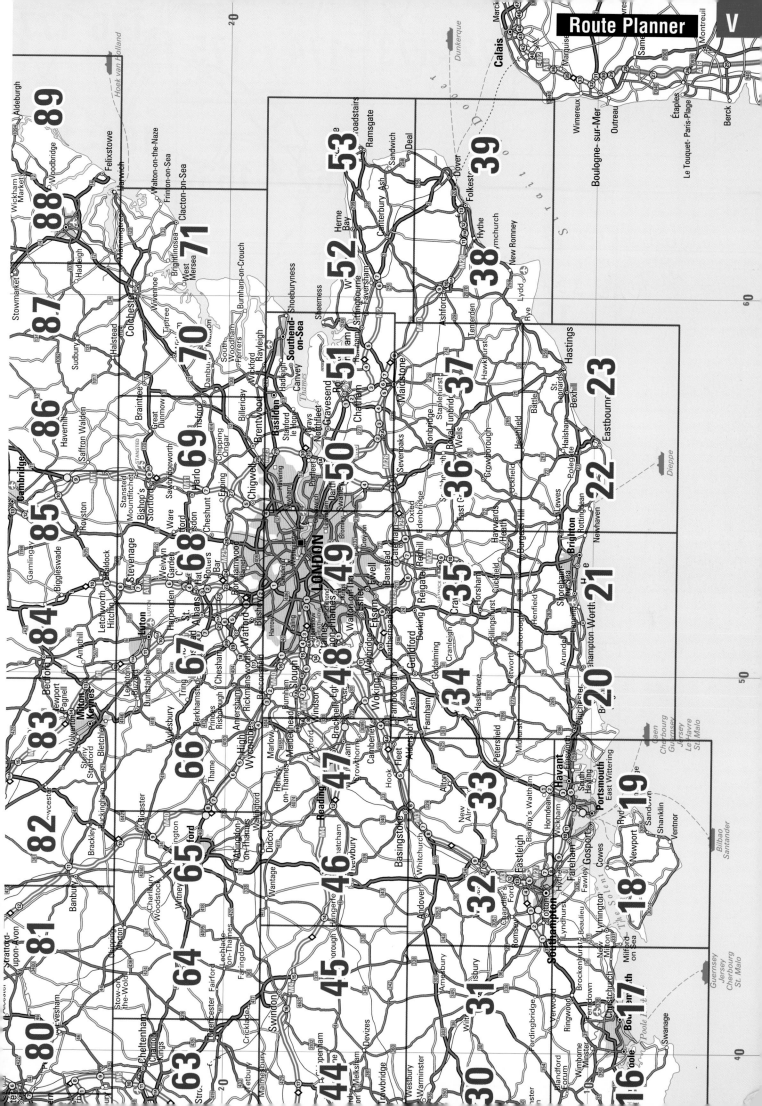

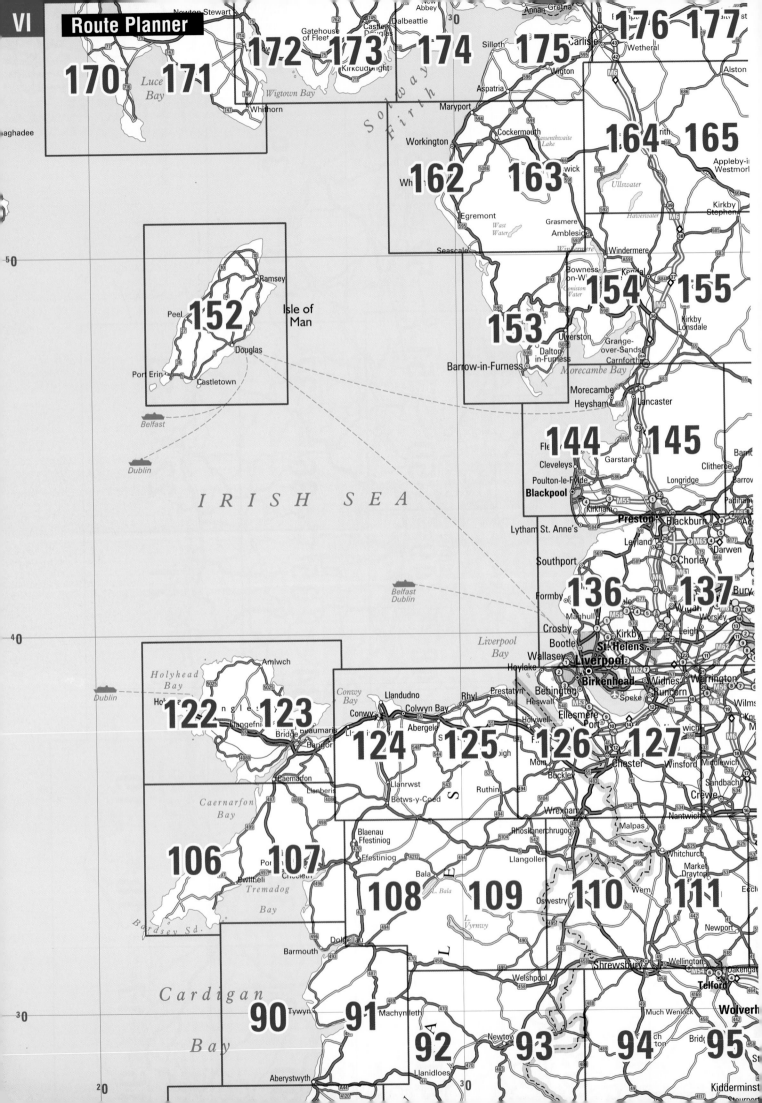

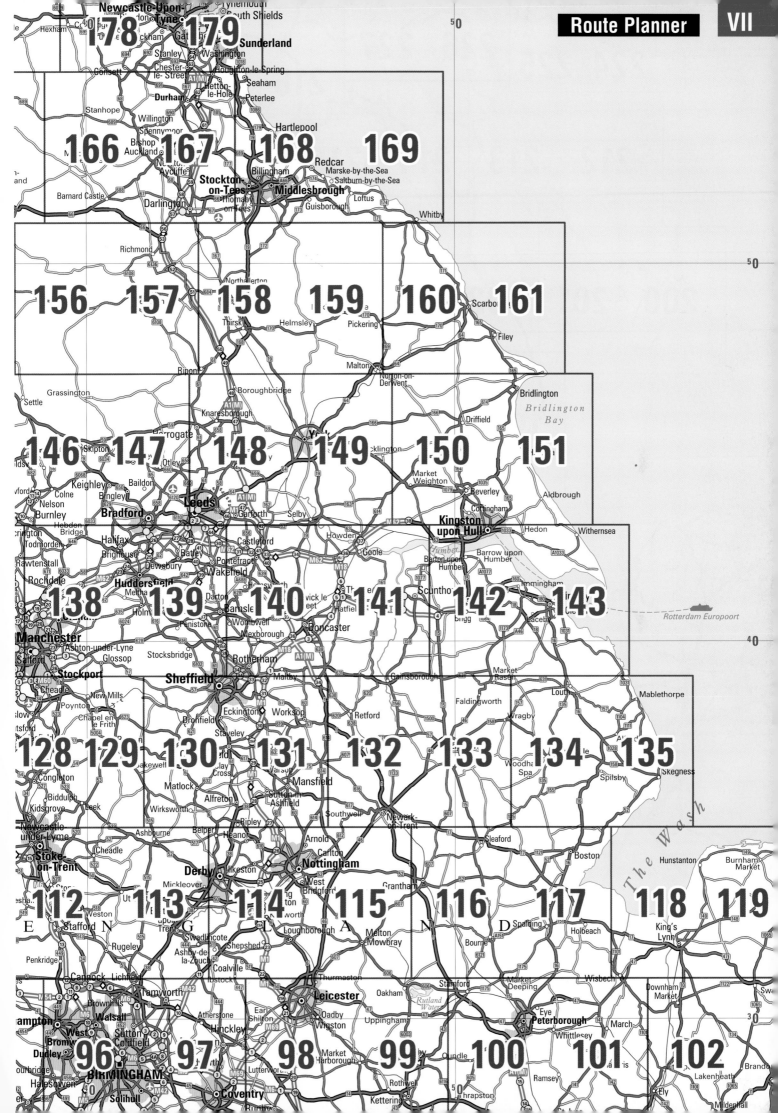

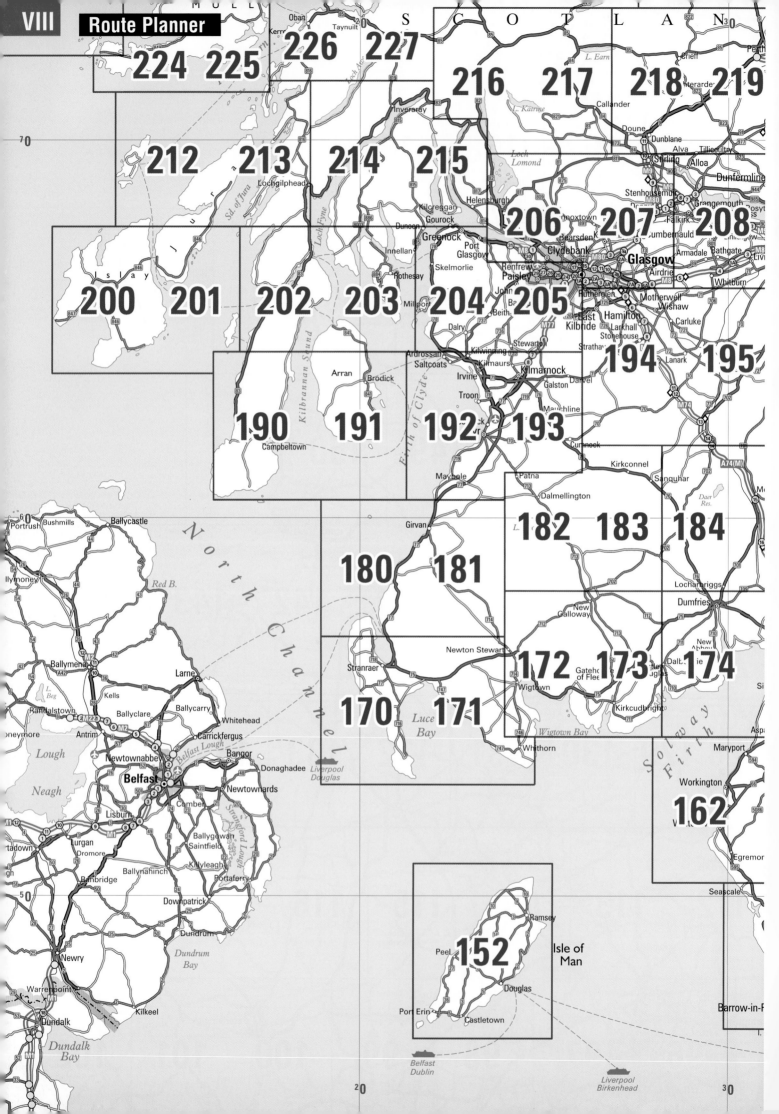

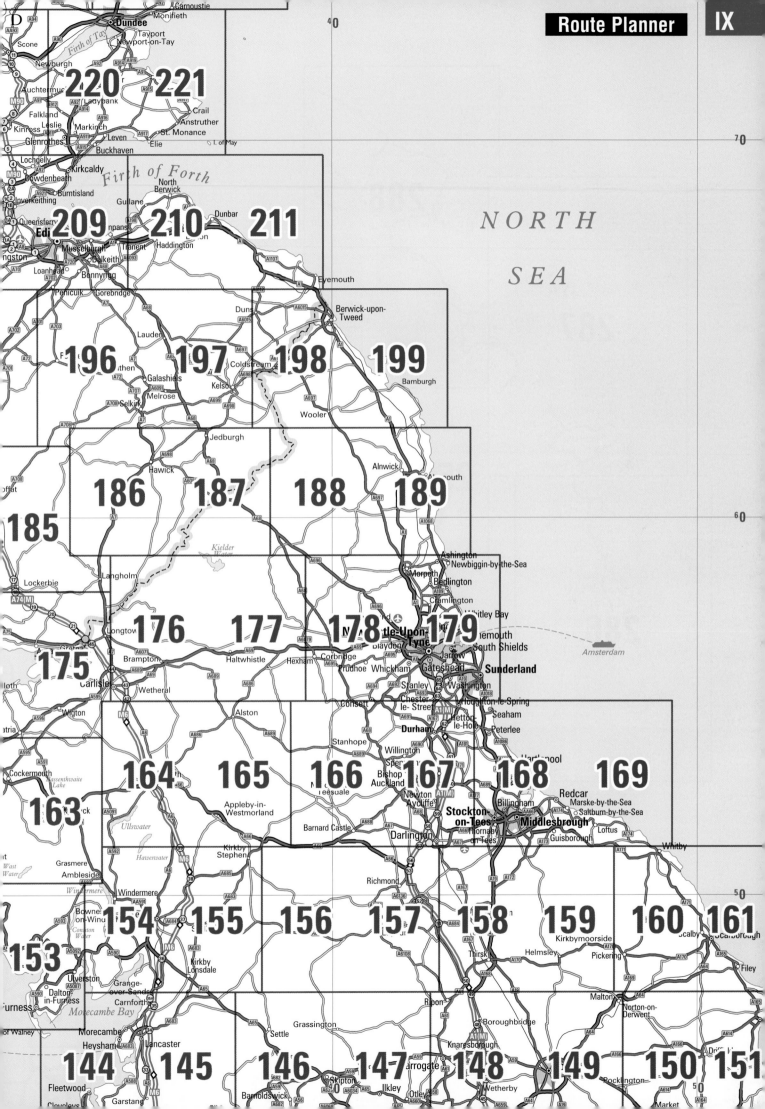

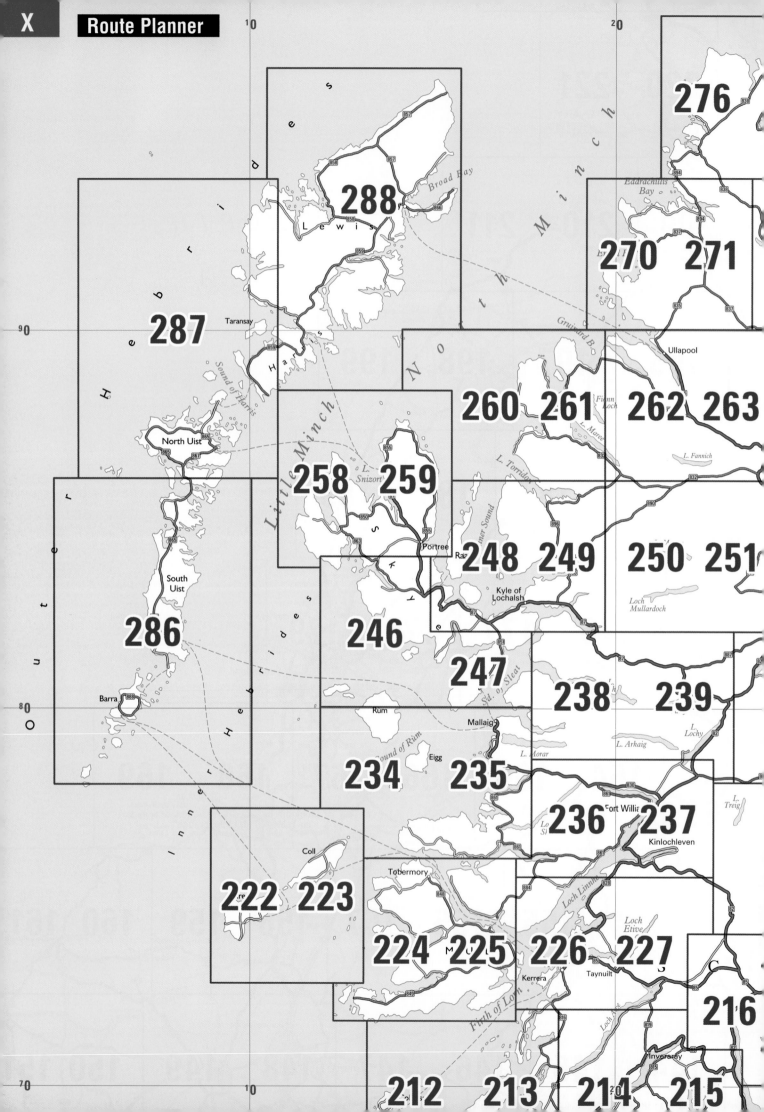

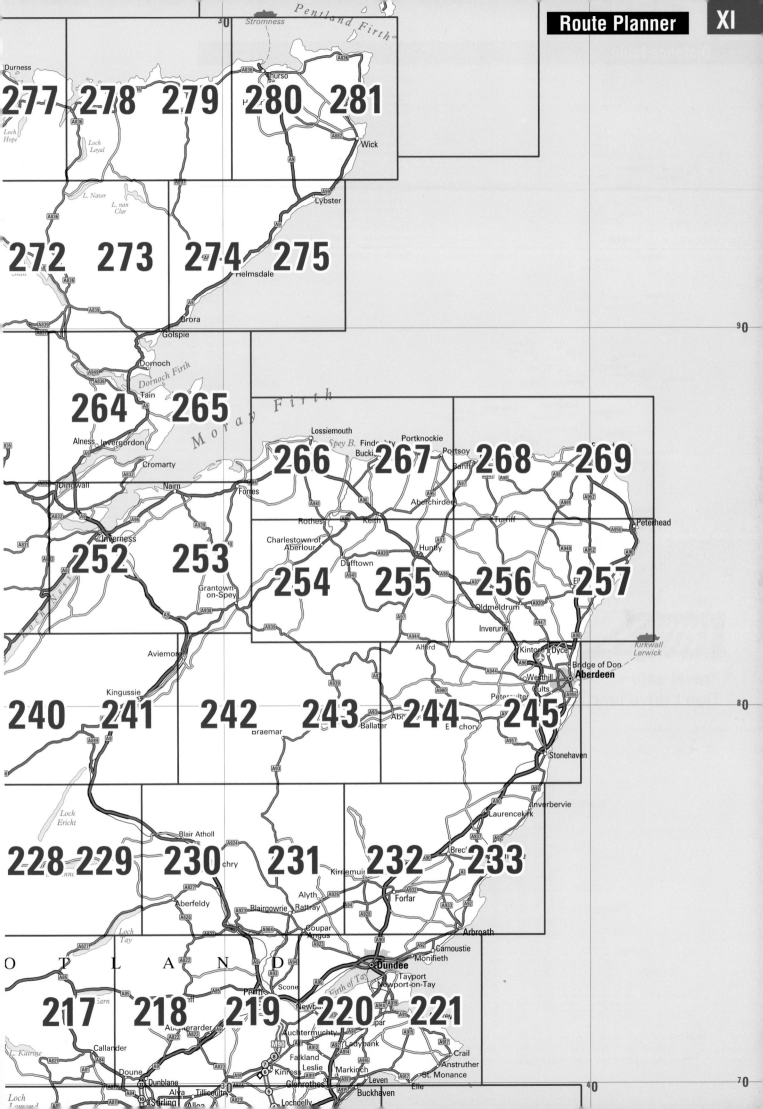

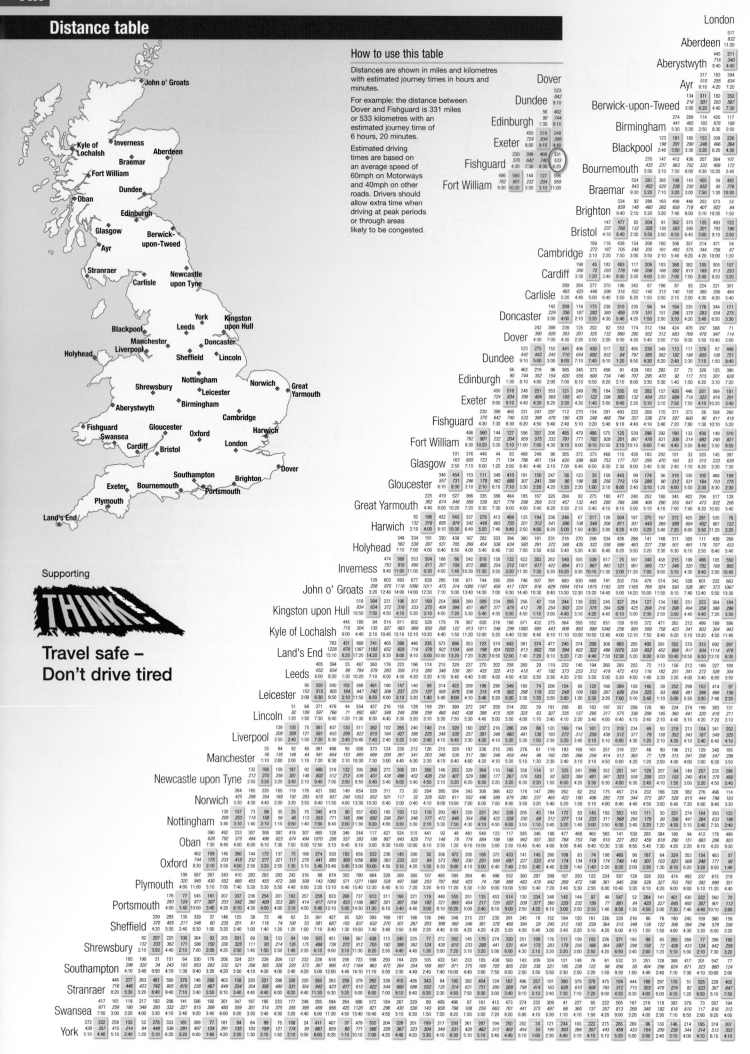

Distance table

How to use this table

Distances are shown in miles and kilometres with estimated journey times in hours and minutes.

For example: the distance between Dover and Fishguard is 331 miles or 533 kilometres with an estimated journey time of 6 hours, 20 minutes.

Estimated driving times are based on an average speed of 60mph on Motorways and 40mph on other roads. Drivers should allow extra time when driving at peak periods or through areas likely to be congested.

Supporting

THINK!

Travel safe –
Don't drive tired

Road map symbols

Motorway, toll motorway
Motorway junction – full, restricted access
Motorway service area – full, restricted access
Motorway under construction

Primary route – dual, single carriageway
Service area, roundabout, multi-level junction
Numbered junction – full, restricted access
Primary route under construction
Narrow primary route
Primary destination

A road – dual, single carriageway
A road under construction, narrow A road

B road – dual, single carriageway
B road under construction, narrow B road

Minor road – over 4 metres, under 4 metres wide
Minor road with restricted access

Distance in miles
Scenic route
Toll, steep gradient – arrow points downhill
Tunnel

National trail – England and Wales

Long distance footpath – Scotland

Railway with station
Level crossing, tunnel
Preserved railway with station

National boundary
County / unitary authority boundary

Car ferry, catamaran
Passenger ferry, catamaran
Hovercraft
Ferry destination
Car ferry – river crossing
Principal airport, other airport

National Park, Area of Outstanding Natural Beauty – England and Wales National Scenic Area – Scotland
forest park / regional park / national forest

Beach
Linear antiquity
Roman road
Hillfort, battlefield – with date
Viewpoint, nature reserve, spot height – in metres
Golf course, youth hostel, sporting venue
Camp site, caravan site, camping and caravan site
Shopping village, park and ride

Adjoining page number – road maps

Tourist information

† Abbey, cathedral or priory
Ancient monument
Aquarium
Art gallery
Bird collection or aviary
Castle
Church
Country park
England and Wales
Scotland
Farm park
Garden
Historic ship
House

House and garden
Motor racing circuit
Museum
Picnic area
Preserved railway
Race course
Roman antiquity
Safari park
Theme park
Tourist information
Zoo
Other place of interest

Road map scale
1: 150 000 • 1 cm = 1.5 km • 1 inch = 2·37 miles

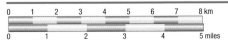

Outer Hebrides, Orkney and Shetland:
1: 303 000 • 1 cm = 3.0 km • 1 inch = 4.78 miles

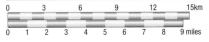

1   4   2   3

5

A

CORNWALL

SW

Nav
Pt.

Godrevy Island
Godrevy Pt.

The Carracks

Clodgy
Pt.
TATE ST IVES
BARBARA HEPWORTH MUSEUM

The
Island
St Ives
Bay
SOUTH WEST
COAST PATH
Gwithia

Gurnard's
Head
Zennor
B3306
St Ives
Carbis Bay
Phillack
Con
Dov
Copperhouse

Porthmeor
247
Towednack
Halsetown
A3074
Lelant
Frad

SOUTH WEST
COAST PATH
B3306
252
Cripplesease
PARADISE PARK
Hayle
Leedstow

B

GEEVOR TIN
MINE MUSEUM
Morvah
Bojewyan
Pendeen
Higher
Boscaswell
Trewellard
Carnyorth
B3318
Nancledra
Newmill
B3311
Canon's Town
B3309
St Erth
A30
4
Hayle
Townshend
Frad

CHYSAUSTER
ANCIENT VILLAGE
Madron
P&R
Ludgvan
Crowlas
Relubbus
B3302
GODOLPHIN
HOUSE
Trescowe

Botallack
Cape
Cornwall
St Just
A3071 TRENGWAINTON
Heamoor
PENZANCE
Gulval
A30
B3280

The Brisons
BALLOWALL BARROW
LAND'S END
Bosavern
Newbridge
6
Chyandour
Marazion
A394
St Hilary
Goldsithney
Germoe

Kelynack
224 Sancreed
CARN EUNY
ANCIENT VILLAGE
Res.
Tredavoe
Penzance
ST MICHAEL'S
MOUNT
Perranuthnoe
Praa
Sands

C

Whitesand
Bay
Brane
Lower Drift
Catchall
8
Newlyn
NEWLYN
ART GALLERY
SOUTH WEST
COAST PATH
Cudden Pt.

Longships
Sennen Cove
Crows-
an-wra
B3283
Kerris
Paul
Mousehole
Trewa
Hd.

Sennen
A30
St Buryan
Trewoofe
St Clement's
Island
SOUTH WEST
COAST PATH
Ri

LAND'S
END
LAND'S
END
Polgigga
B3315
Boskenna
B3315
Lamorna
Lamorna Cove
MOUNT'S   BAY

Porthcurno
Treen
TREGIFFIAN
BURIAL CHAMBER

TELEGRAPH
MUSEUM
PORTHCURNO
St Levan
MINACK OPEN
AIR THEATRE
ISLES OF SCILLY
(Mar-Nov)
3

Gwennap Hd.
Runnel
Stone

Isles of Scilly
3 miles to 1 inch

3   9   4   2

White Island

St Helens
KING CHARLES CASTLE
Bryher
CROMWELL'S CASTLE
Bryher
41
New Grimsby
St Martin's
47
Higher Town

E

Tresco
TRESCO ABBEY
GARDENS
Eastern Isles

North West Passage
Samson
The Road
BANT'S
CARN
Newford
51
INNISIDGEN CAIRNS
Maypole
Crow Sound

D

Crim
Rocks
GARRISON WALLS
Hugh Town
A3110
ST MARY'S
Old Town
St Mary's
1

Broad Sound
Annet
St Mary's Sound
Gugh
Smith Sound
PENZANCE
(Mar-Nov)

St Agnes
St Agnes

0   1   2   3 miles
0 1 2 3 4 5 km

Bishop
Rock

4   2   9

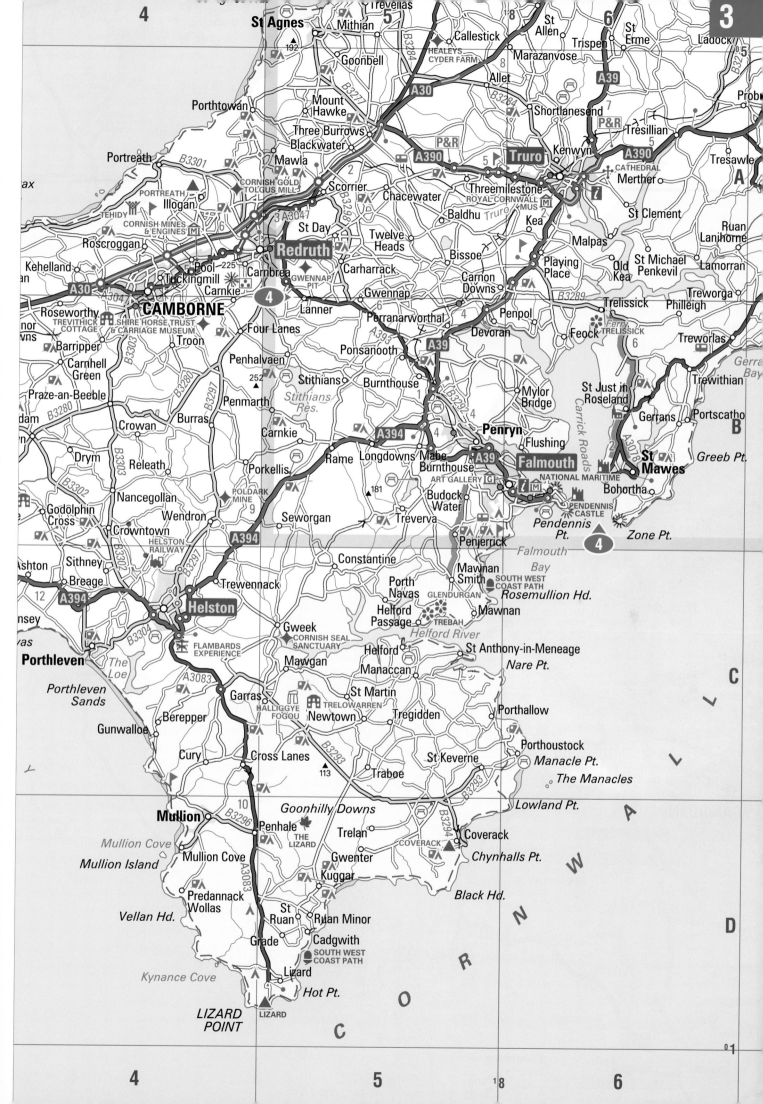

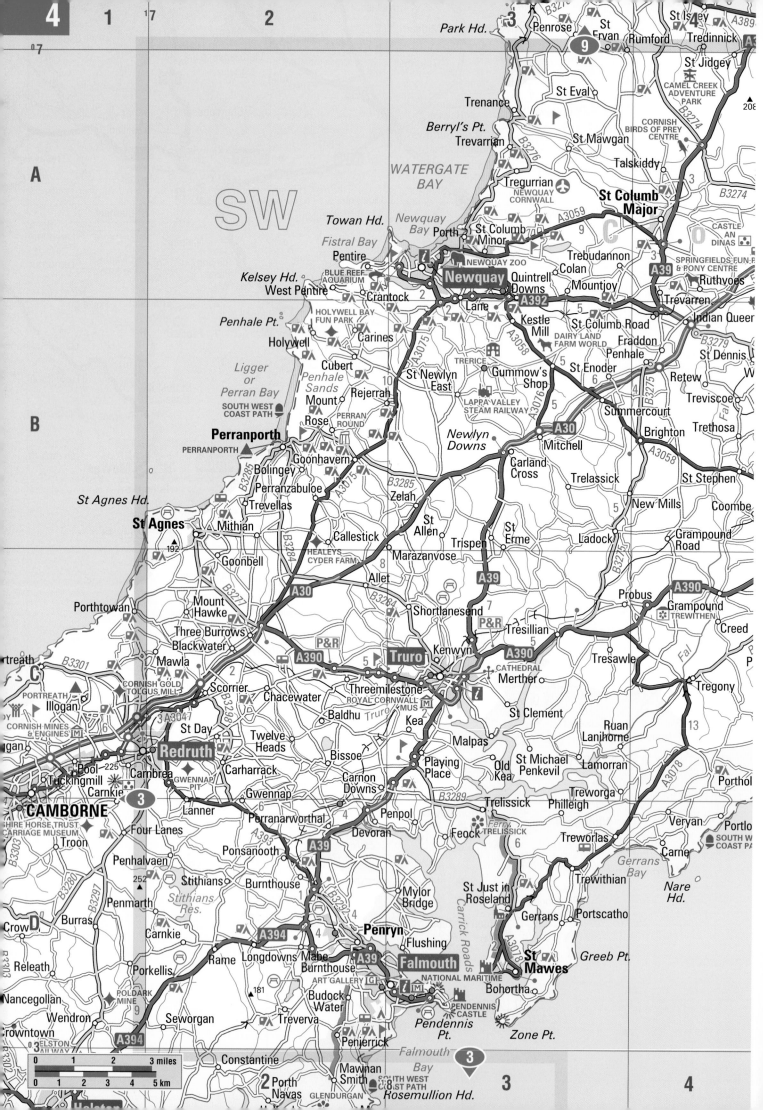

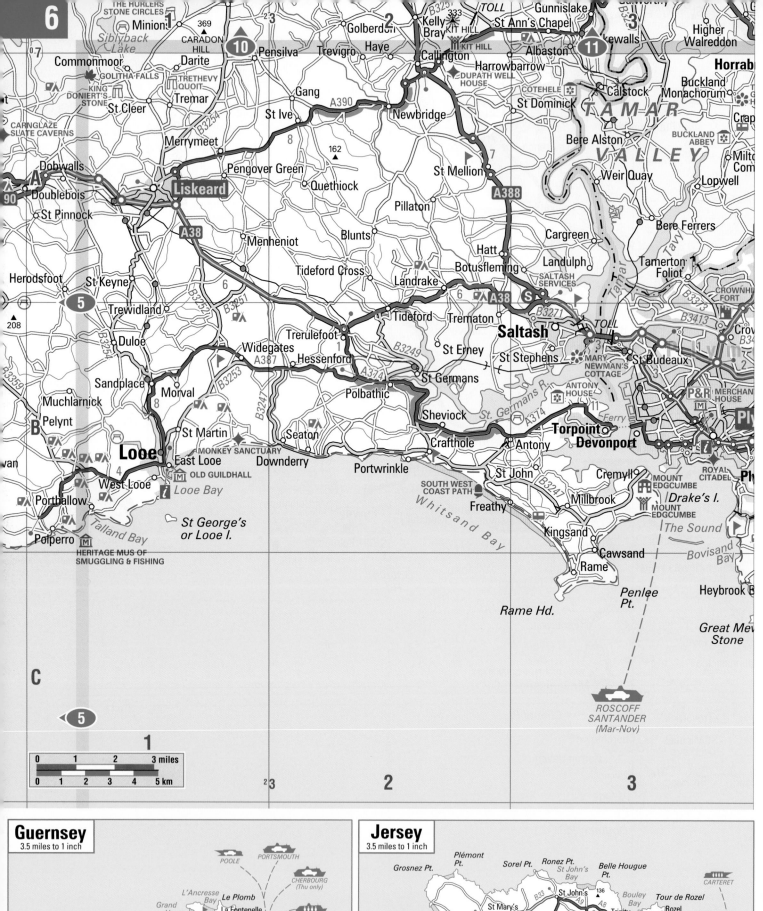
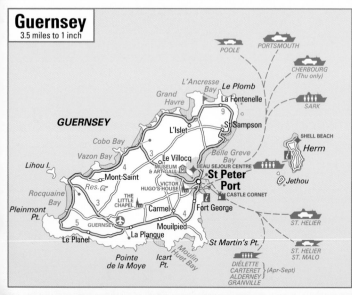
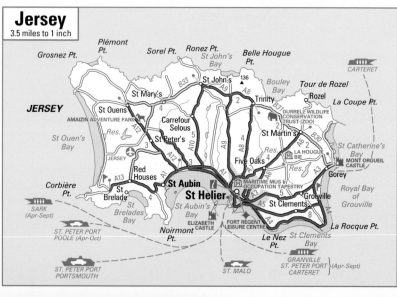

4   **5**   20   **6**

11   11

A   **A**

SR   SS

10   10

SW   SX

B   **B**

Fire Beacon Pt.   Be

BOSCASTLE

Trevalga   Bosc

CASTLE

Tintagel Hd.   3

OLD POST OFFICE   Bossiney

TINTAGEL   Tintagel   308   B3266

Treknow   Trewarmett   THE

Start Pt.   B3263

Trebarwith   B33

C   Treligga   **C**

SOUTH WEST COAST PATH   Delabole   i

Port Isaac Bay   Valley Truckle

B3314   Helstone

Port Isaac   B3267

Pentire Pt.   *Port Quin Bay*   Port Quin   Port Gaverne   St Teath

New Polzeath   B3267   LONG CROSS   Pendoggett   Treveighan

Gulland Rock   *Padstow Bay*   Trelights   10   Michaelstow

Trebetherick   Polzeath   St Endellion   Trelill   A39

Gunver Hd.   Crugmeer   St Minver   Trewethern   St Kew   St Tudy   Row

TREVOSE HEAD   Pityme   B3314   Chapel Amble   St Kew

PRIDEAUX PLACE   Rock

Constantine Bay   Trevone   NATIONAL LOBSTER HATCHERY   St Kew Highway   We Dordbri

D   TREYARNON   Constantine Bay   St Merryn   **Padstow**   *Camel*   Bodieve   **D**   Blis

Treyarnon   Trevanson   St Mabyn

SOUTH WEST COAST PATH   Shop   Little Petherick   Whitecross   **Wadebridge**   PENCARROW HOUSE   Helland

Porthcothan   B3276   8   St Breock   Egloshayle   A389

Park Hd.   Penrose   St Ervan   St Issey   A389   6   *Camel*

07   Rumford   Tredinnick   A39   Burlawn   *Bodmin Forest*   A30   07

St Eval   St Jidgey   5   Washaway   Card

CAMEL CREEK ADVENTURE PARK   ST BREOCK DOWNS MONOLITH

4   **5**   20   **6**

CORNWALL

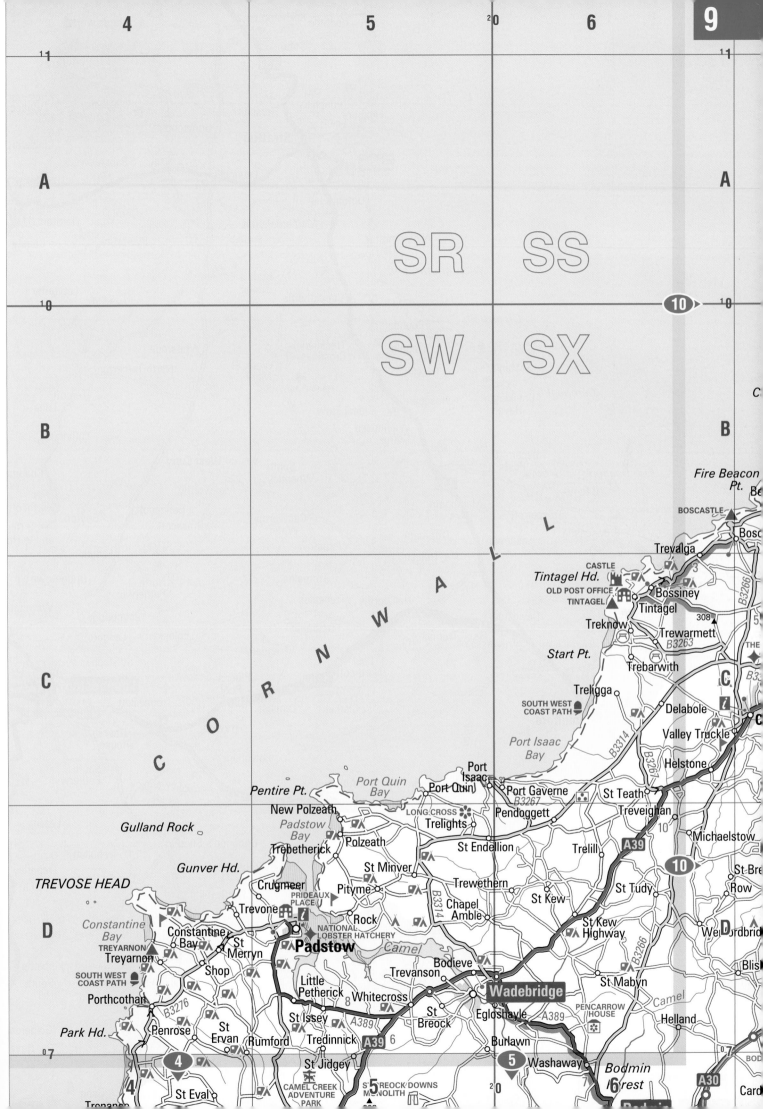

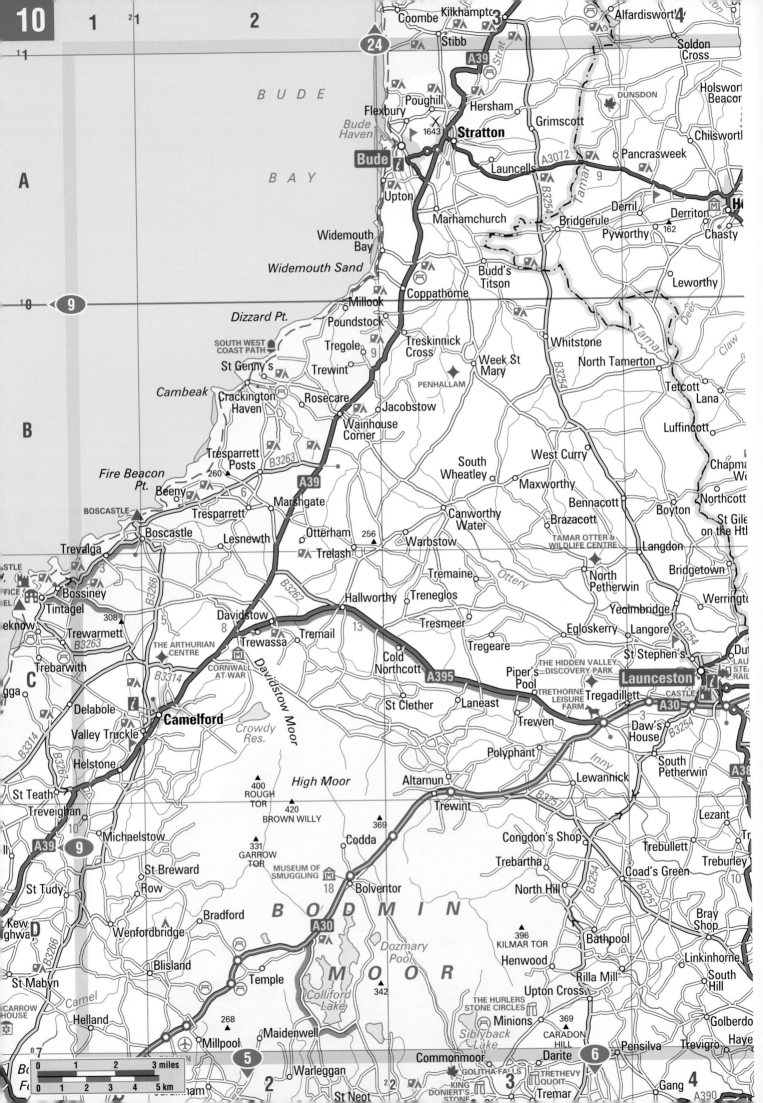

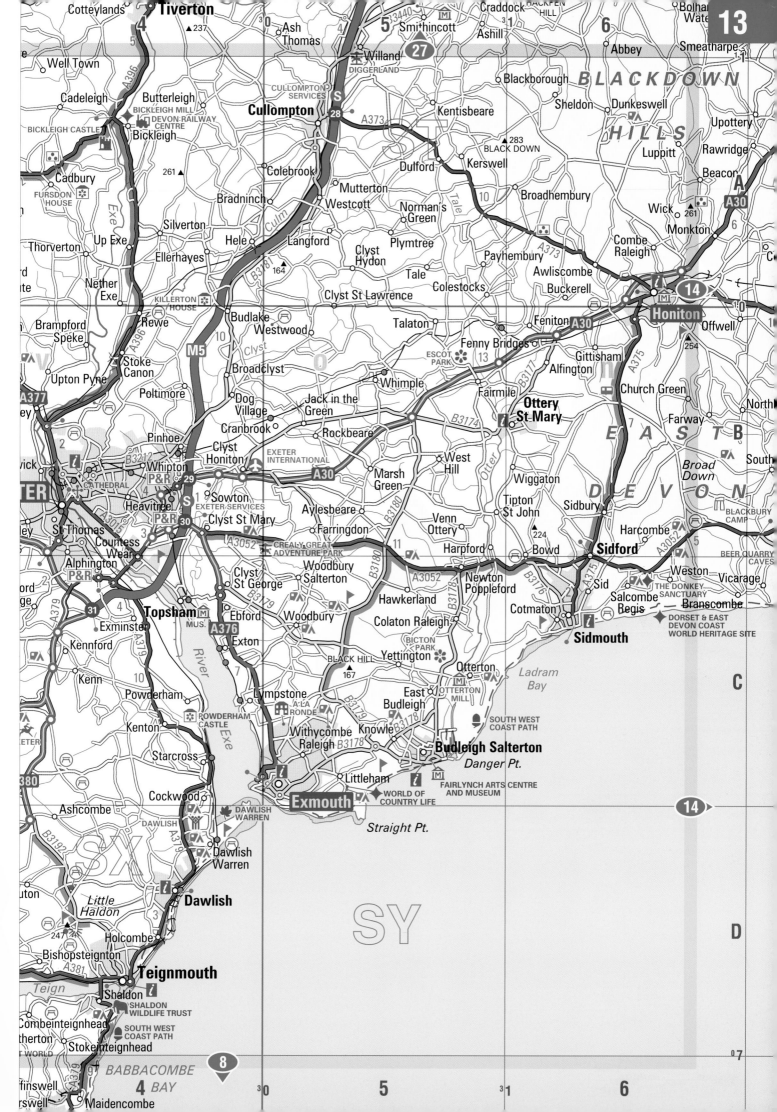

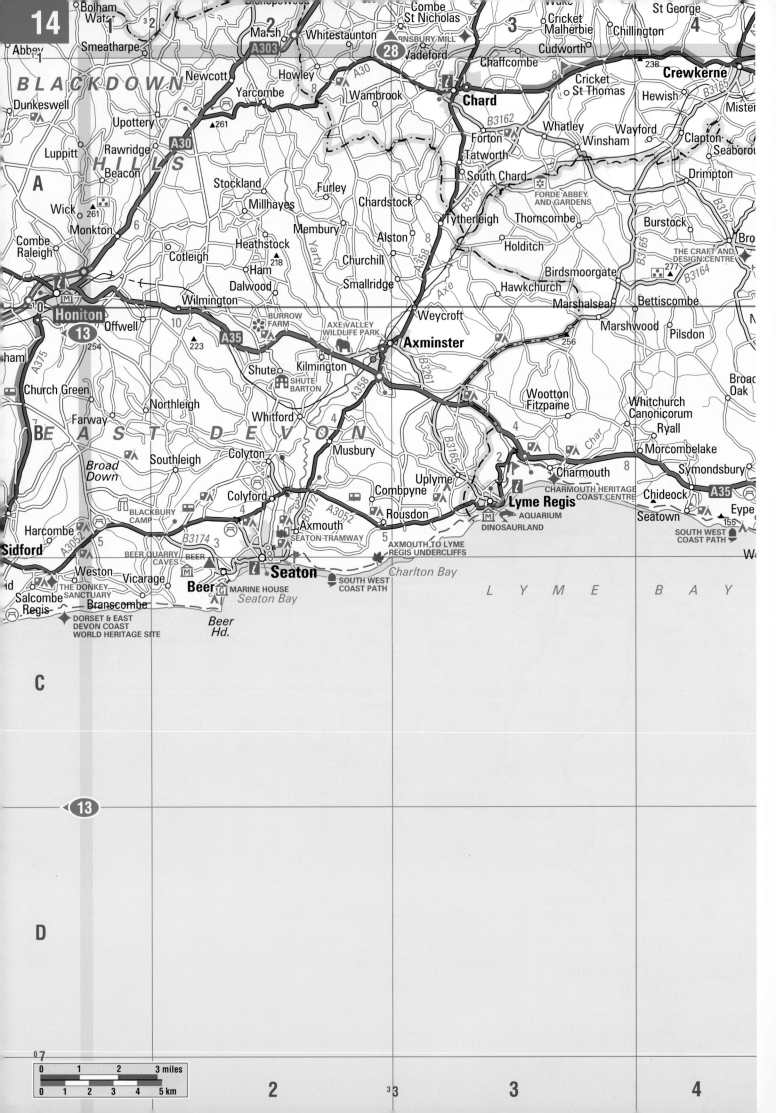

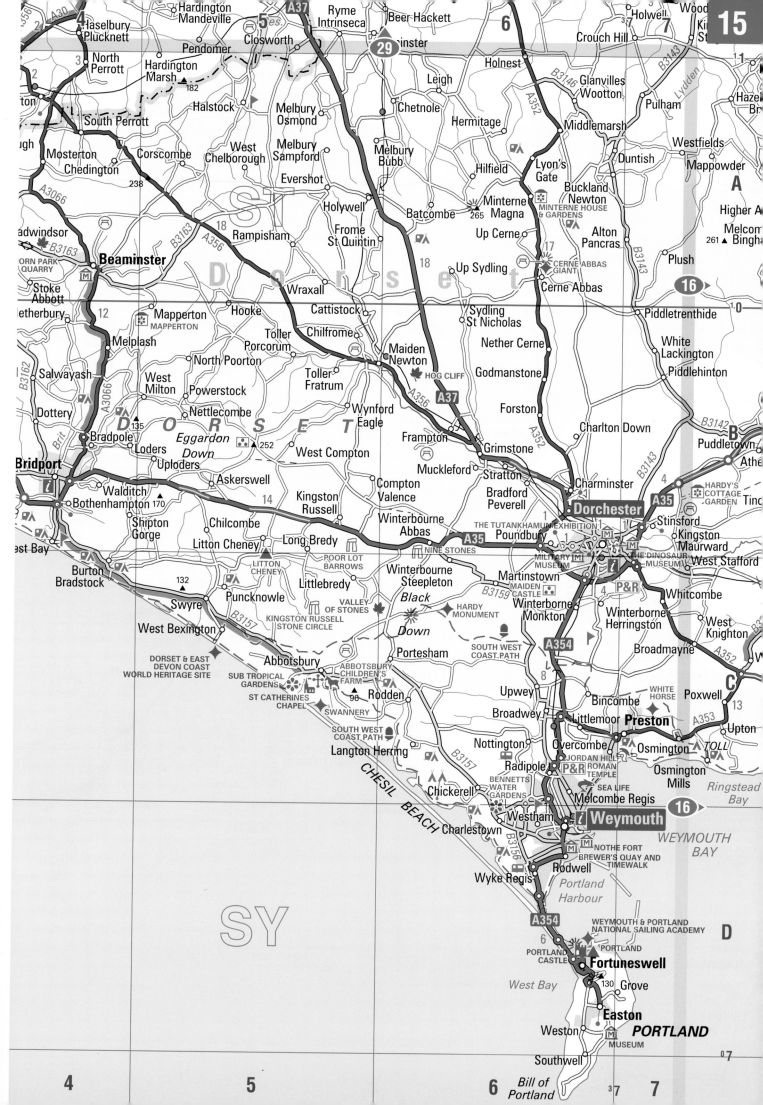

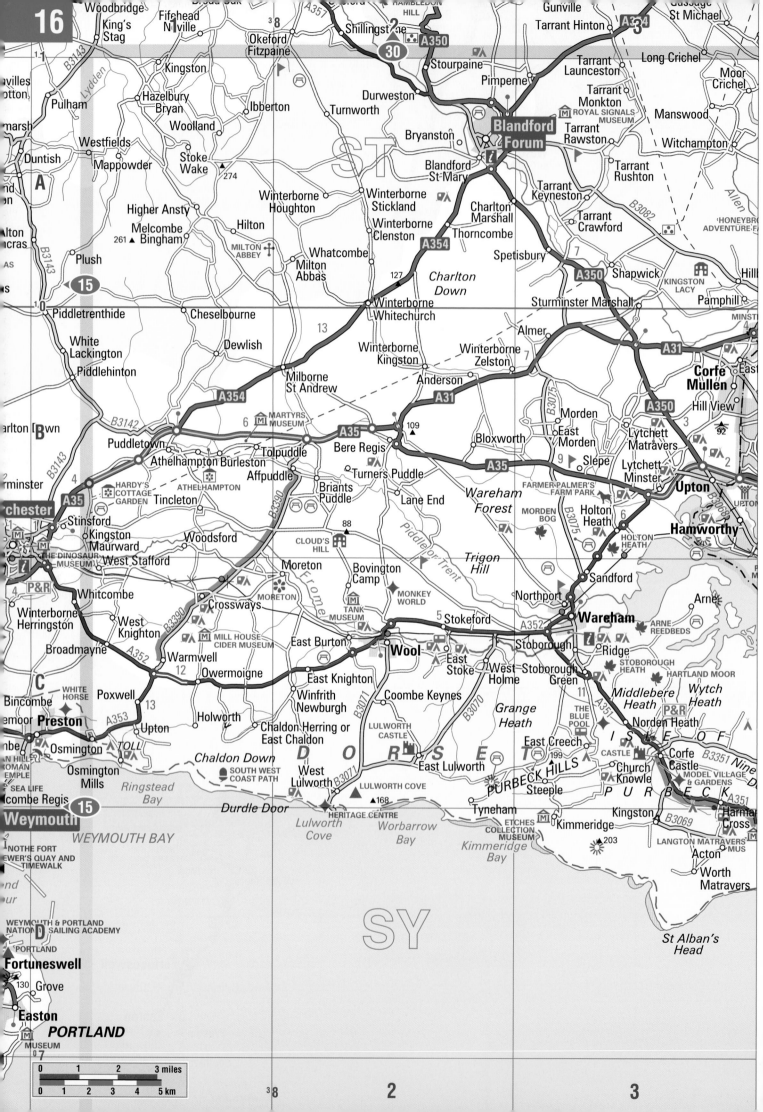

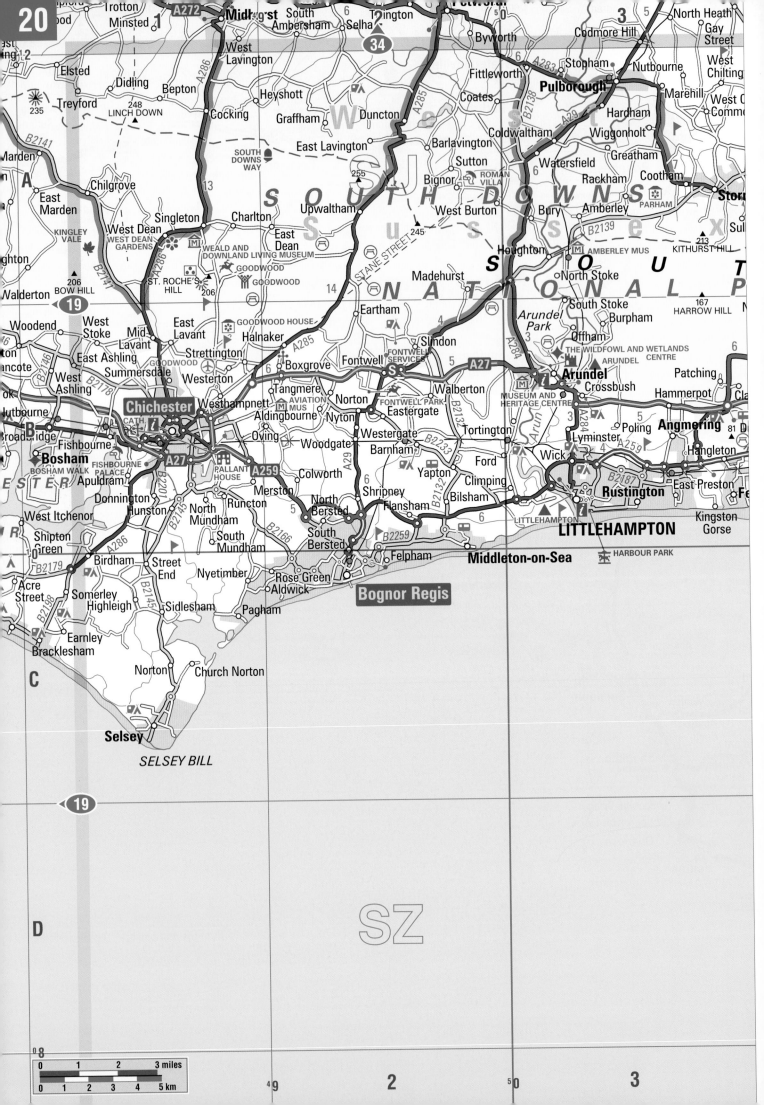

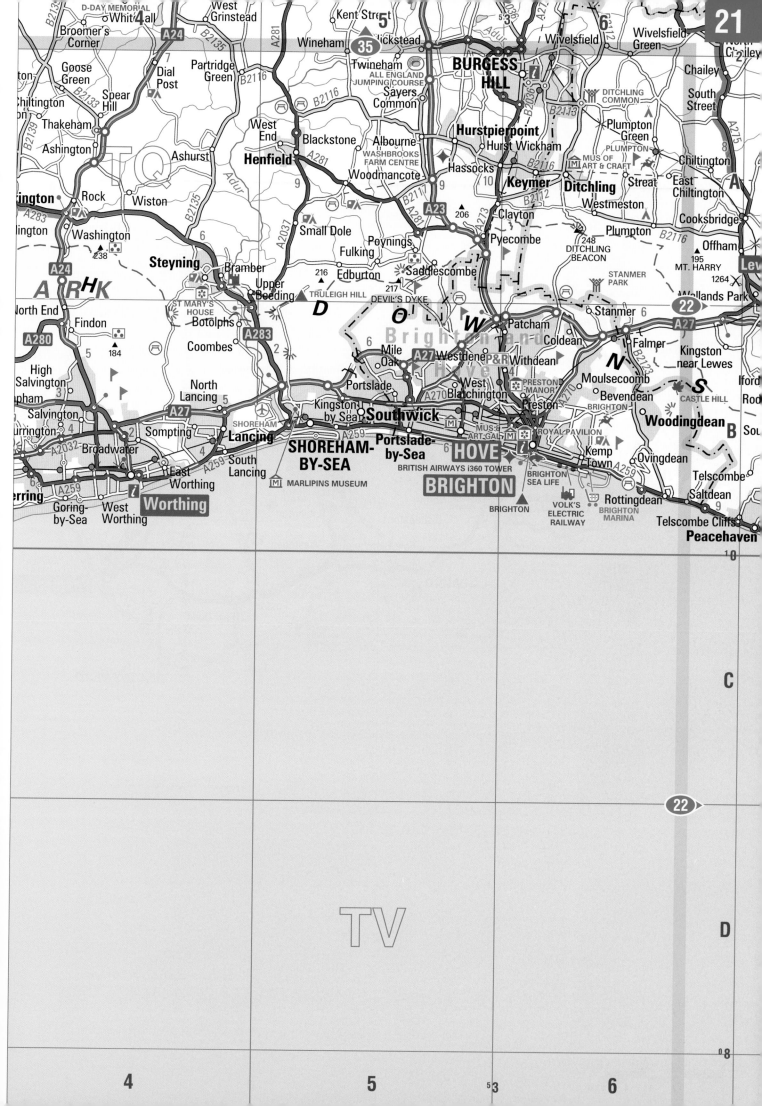

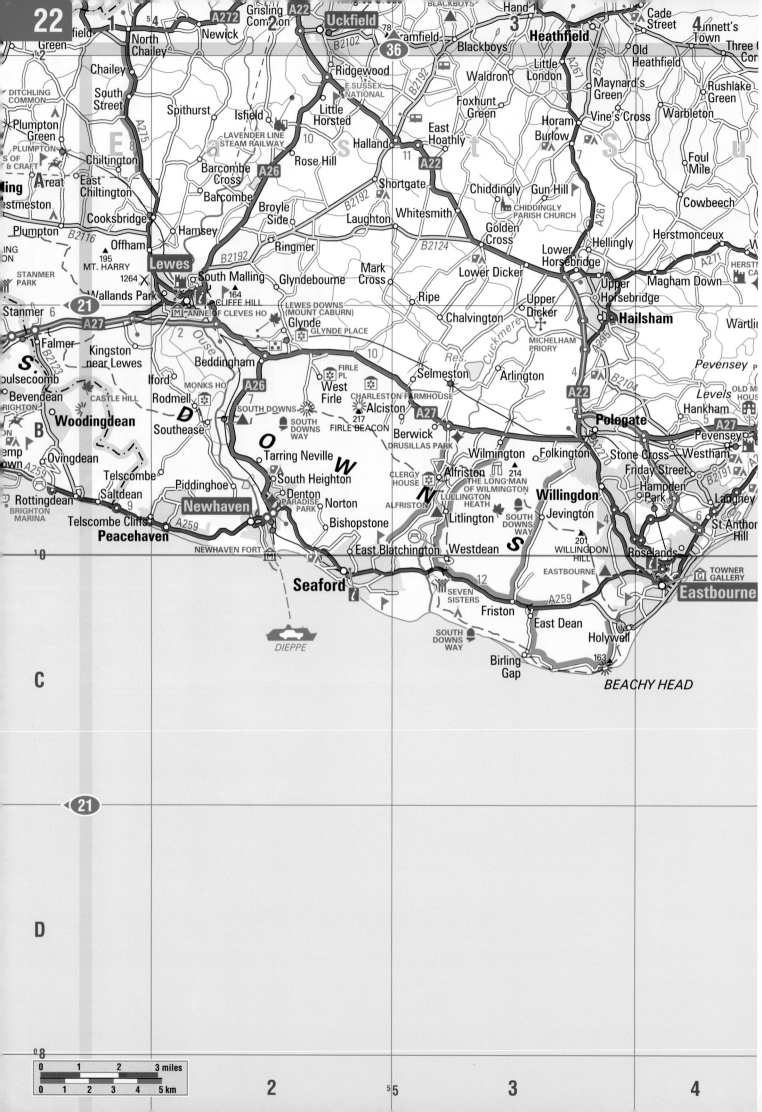

1 2 3 4

Uckfield
Heathfield

Grisling Common
A272
A22
North Chailey
Newick
78
ramfield
Blackboys
Hand
Cade Street
unnett's Town
Three Co
Green
B2102
36
Old Heathfield
Chailey
Ridgewood
Blackboys
B2203
2
South Street
Waldron
Little London
Maynard's Green
Rushlake Green
DITCHLING COMMON
E.SUSSEX NATIONAL
Foxhunt Green
A261
Plumpton Green
Spithurst
Isfield
Little Horsted
East Hoathly
Horam
Vine's Cross
Warbleton
PLUMPTON
A275
LAVENDER LINE STEAM RAILWAY
A26
Burlow
A267
Foul Mile
S OF & Craft
Chiltington
Barcombe Cross
10
Halland
Cowbeech
A
Great
East Chiltington
11
A22
Chiddingly
Gun Hill
estmeston
Cooksbridge
Barcombe
Rose Hill
Shortgate
Whitesmith
CHIDDINGLY PARISH CHURCH
Herstmonceux
Plumpton
B2116
Hamsey
Broyle Side
B2192
Laughton
Golden Cross
Hellingly
HERST
ING
Offham
Ringmer
B2124
Lower Horsebridge
Magham Down
CA
ON
195 MT. HARRY
Lewes
South Malling
Glyndebourne
Mark Cross
Lower Dicker
Upper Horsebridge
A271
1264
Wallands Park
164
CLIFFE HILL
Ripe
Upper Dicker
MICHELHAM PRIORY
Hailsham
Wartli
Stanmer
21
ANNE OF CLEVES HO
LEWES DOWNS (MOUNT CABURN)
Glynde
Chalvington
Res.
A295
B2104
Pevensey
STANMER PARK
A27
Ouse
GLYNDE PLACE
Selmeston
Arlington
A22
OLD M HOUS
Stanmer 6
Falmer
Kingston near Lewes
Beddingham
10
Cuckmere
Levels
Hankham
S
B2123
Iford
MONKS HO
FIRLE PL
A27
Michelham
A27
oulsecoomb
CASTLE HILL
Rodmell
A26
West Firle
CHARLESTON FARMHOUSE
Berwick
Polegate
A22
Stone Cross
Pevensey
Bevendean
SOUTH DOWNS
7
Alciston
DRUSILLAS PARK
Westham
BRIGHTON
Southease
217 FIRLE BEACON
Wilmington
Folkington
A27
D
Tarring Neville
SOUTH DOWNS WAY
Friday Street
Langney
B2191
Woodingdean
O
CLERGY HOUSE
Alfriston
214
Willingdon
Hampden Park
B
Ovingdean
W
THE LONG MAN OF WILMINGTON
St Anthor
own
A259
South Heighton
ALFRISTON
LULLINGTON HEATH
Jevington
Hill
Telscombe
N
Litlington
SOUTH DOWNS WAY
4
Rottingdean
Piddinghoe
Denton
Bishopstone
201 WILLINGDON HILL
Roselands
BRIGHTON MARINA
Saltdean
9
Newhaven
PARADISE PARK
Norton
S
EASTBOURNE
TOWNER GALLERY
Telscombe Cliffs
A259
East Blatchington
Westdean
A259
Eastbourne
Peacehaven
NEWHAVEN FORT
Seaford
12
0
M
Friston
Rottingdean
SEVEN SISTERS
East Dean
Holywell
DIEPPE
SOUTH DOWNS WAY
163
Birling Gap
BEACHY HEAD
C

21

D

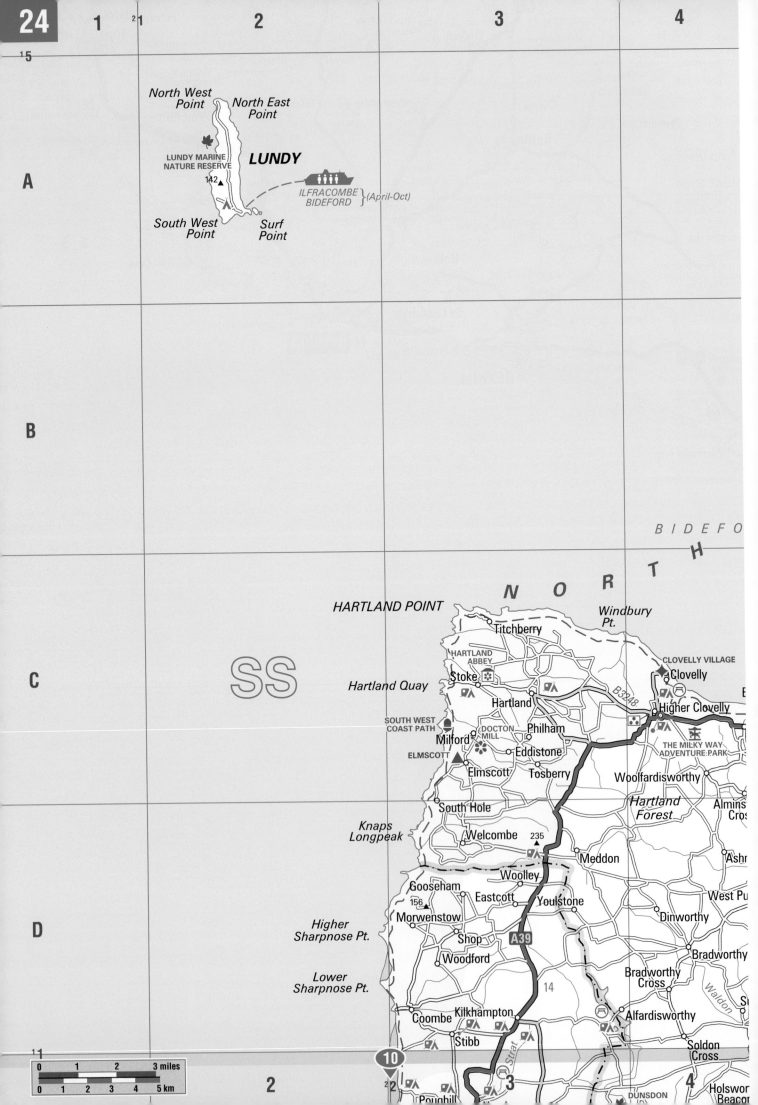

North West Point

North East Point

LUNDY

LUNDY MARINE NATURE RESERVE

142▲

South West Point

Surf Point

ILFRACOMBE
BIDEFORD } *(April-Oct)*

B I D E F O

N O R T H

HARTLAND POINT

Windbury Pt.

Titchberry

HARTLAND ABBEY

CLOVELLY VILLAGE

◆ Clovelly

Hartland Quay

Stoke ❀

B3248

Hartland

Higher Clovelly

SOUTH WEST COAST PATH

DOCTON MILL

Philham

THE MILKY WAY ADVENTURE PARK

Milford

ELMSCOTT

❀

Eddistone

Elmscott ▲

Tosberry

Woolfardisworthy

Hartland Forest

Almins Cros

South Hole

Knaps Longpeak

Welcombe

235▲

Meddon

Ashr

Woolley

Gooseham

Eastcott

Youlstone

West Pu

156▲

Morwenstow

Dinworthy

Higher Sharpnose Pt.

Shop

A39

Woodford

Bradworthy

Lower Sharpnose Pt.

14

Bradworthy Cross

Waldon

Coombe

Kilkhampton

Alfardisworthy

10

Stibb

Soldon Cross

0 1 2 3 miles
0 1 2 3 4 5 km

SS

DUNSDON

Holswor Beacon

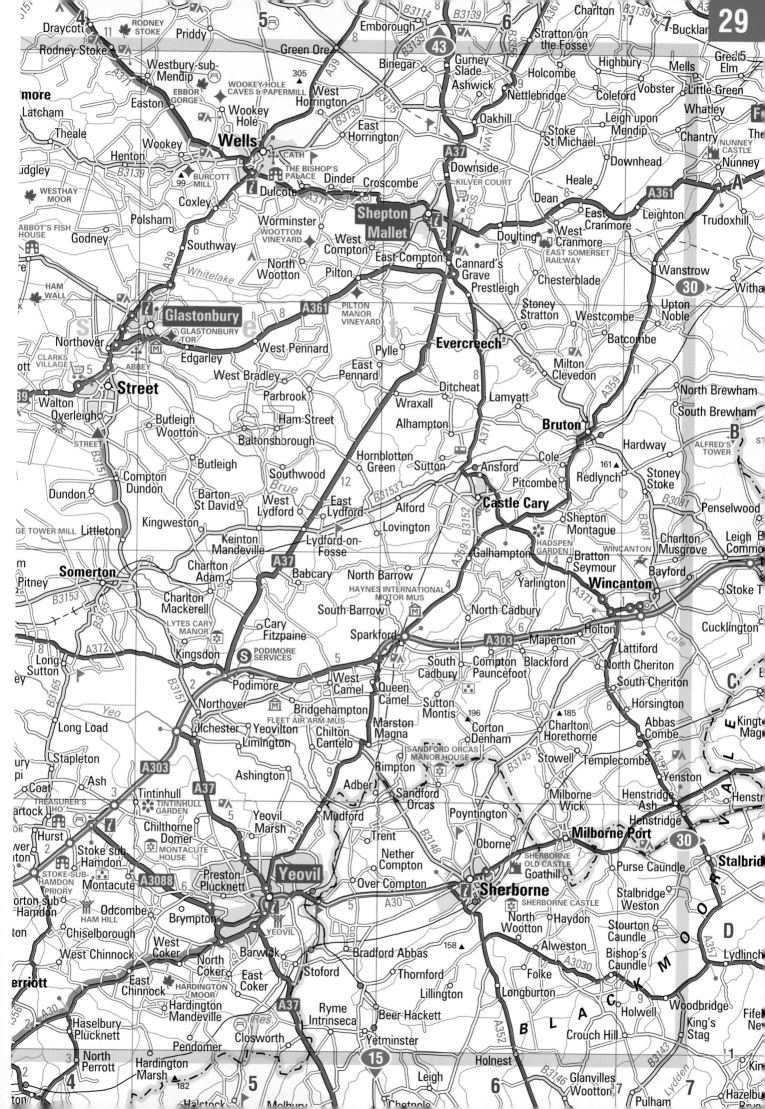

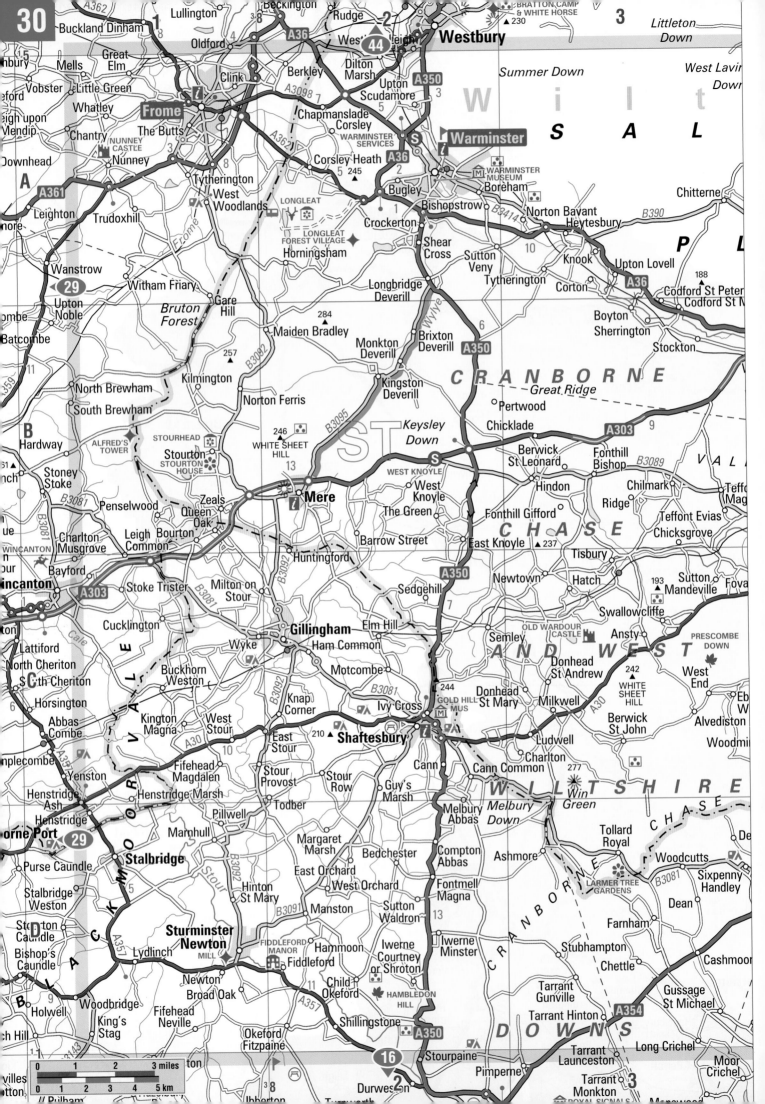

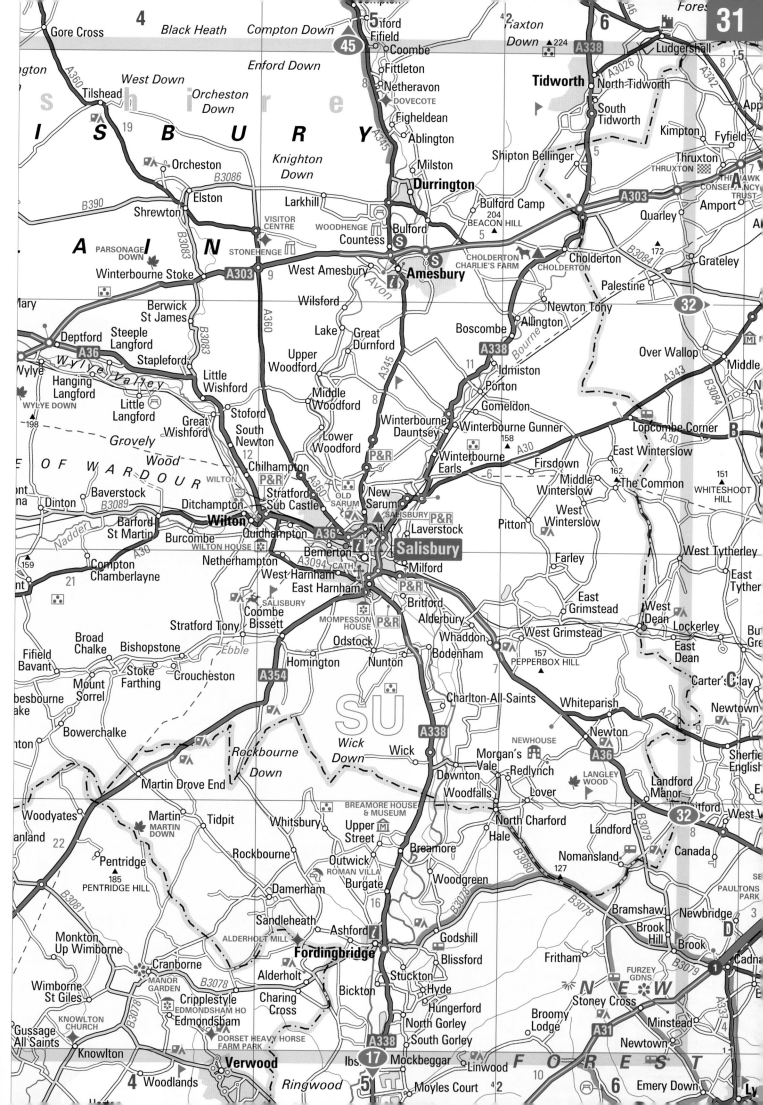

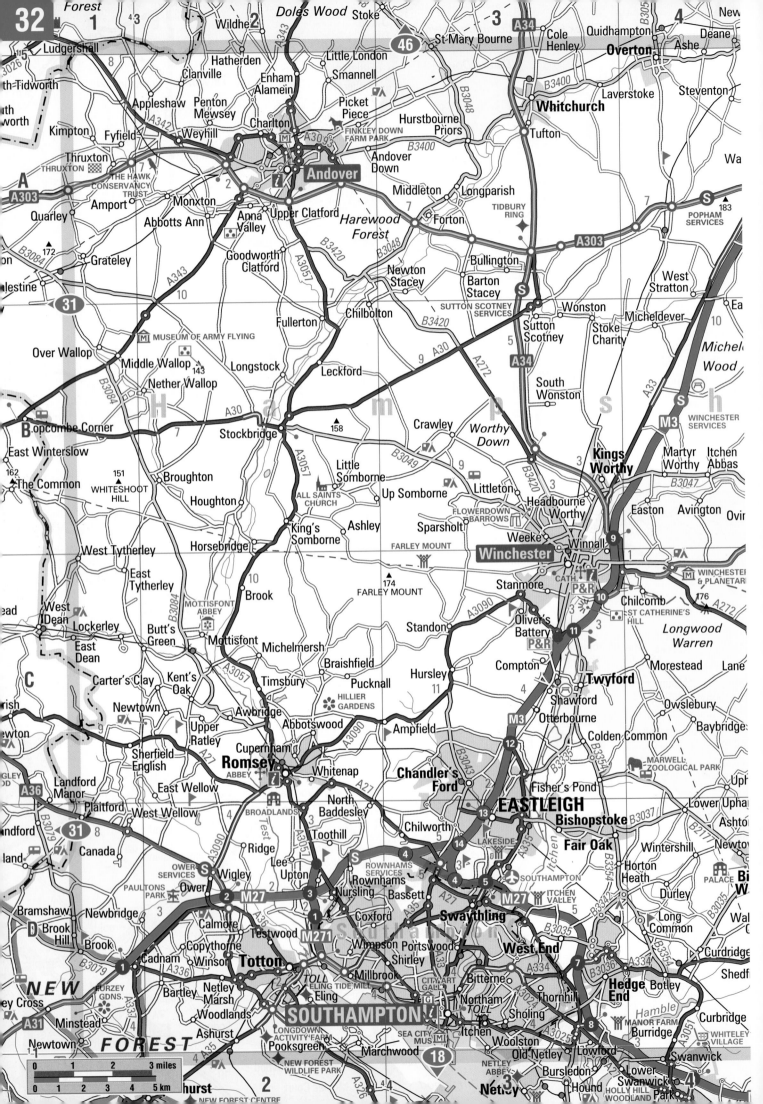

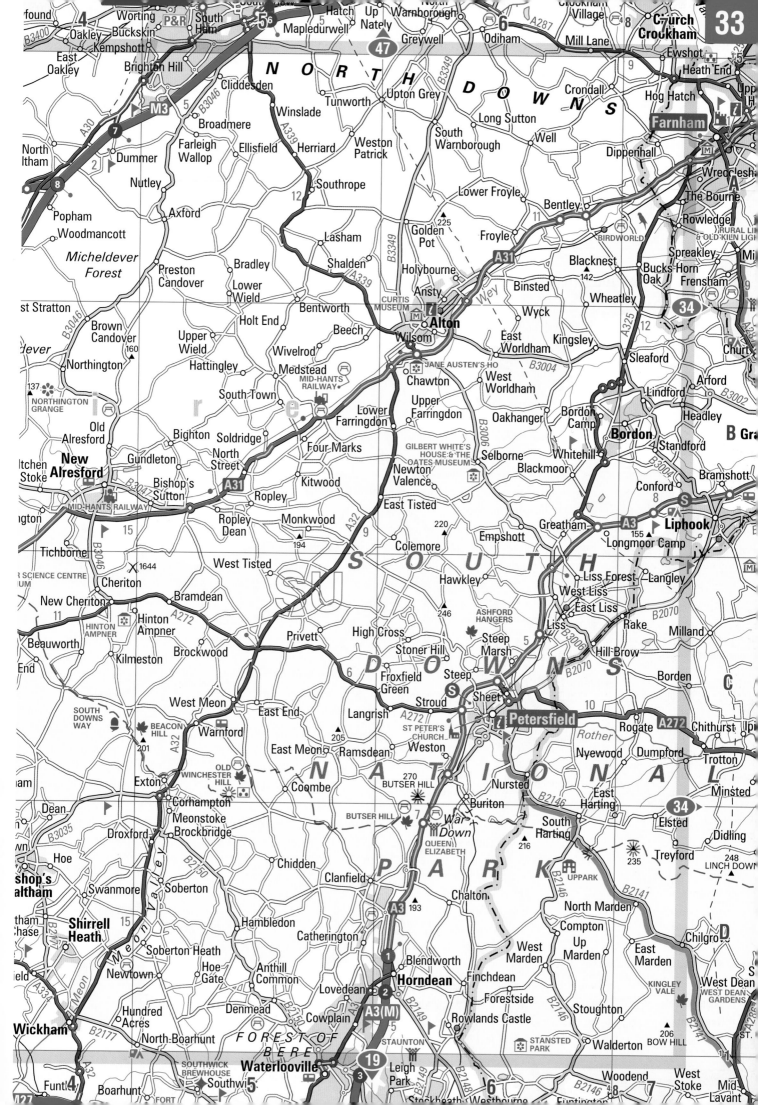

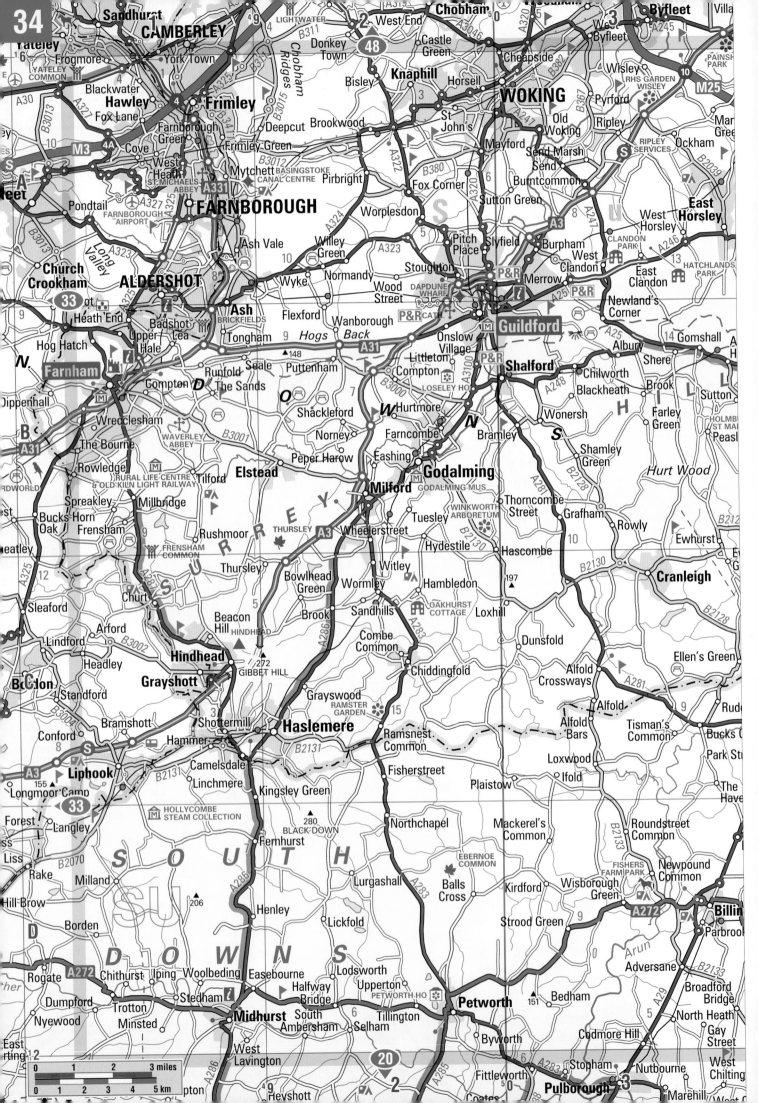

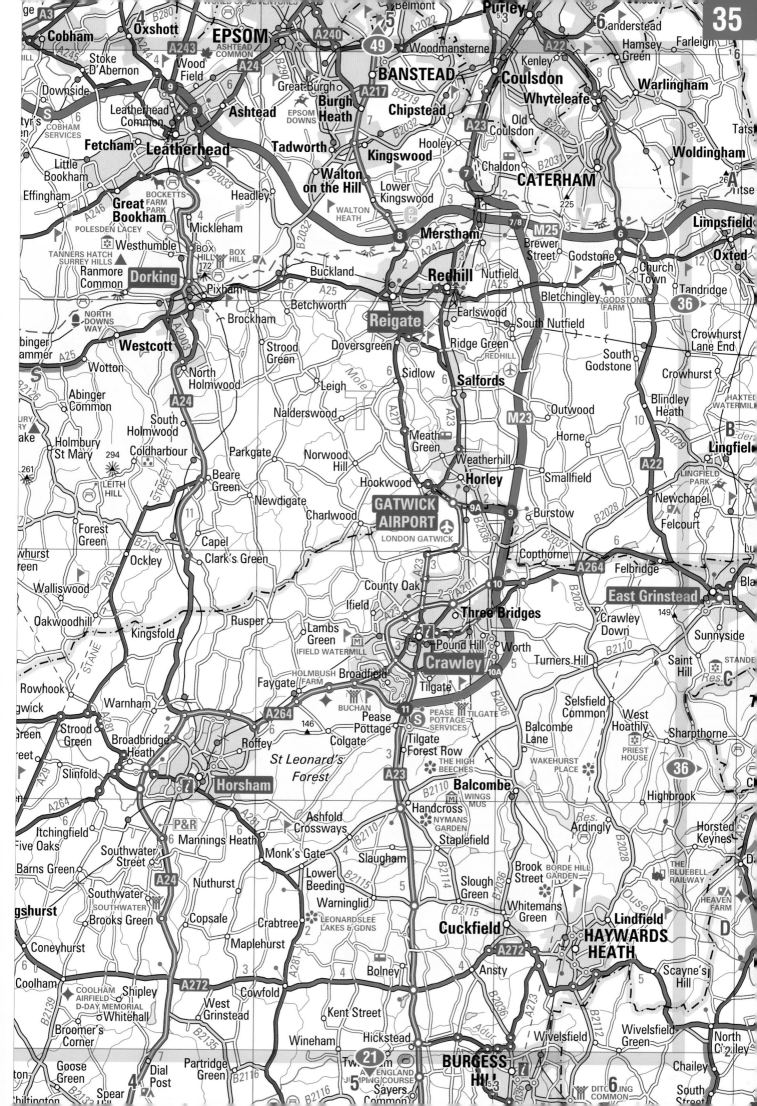

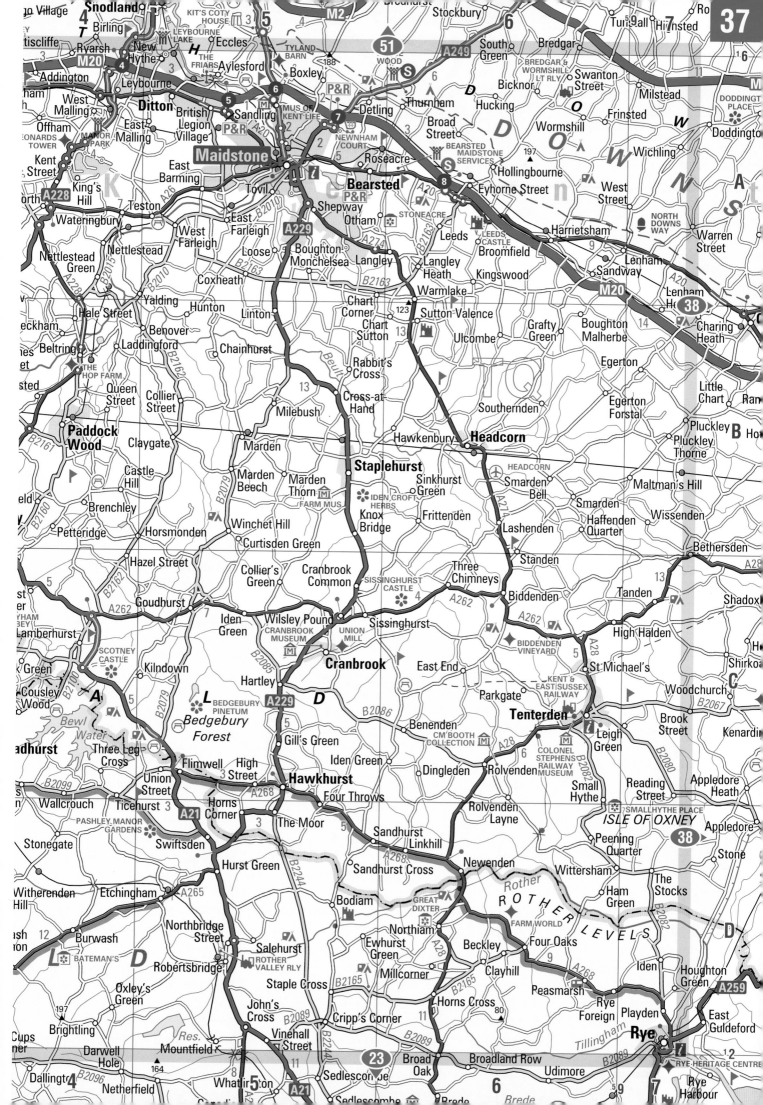

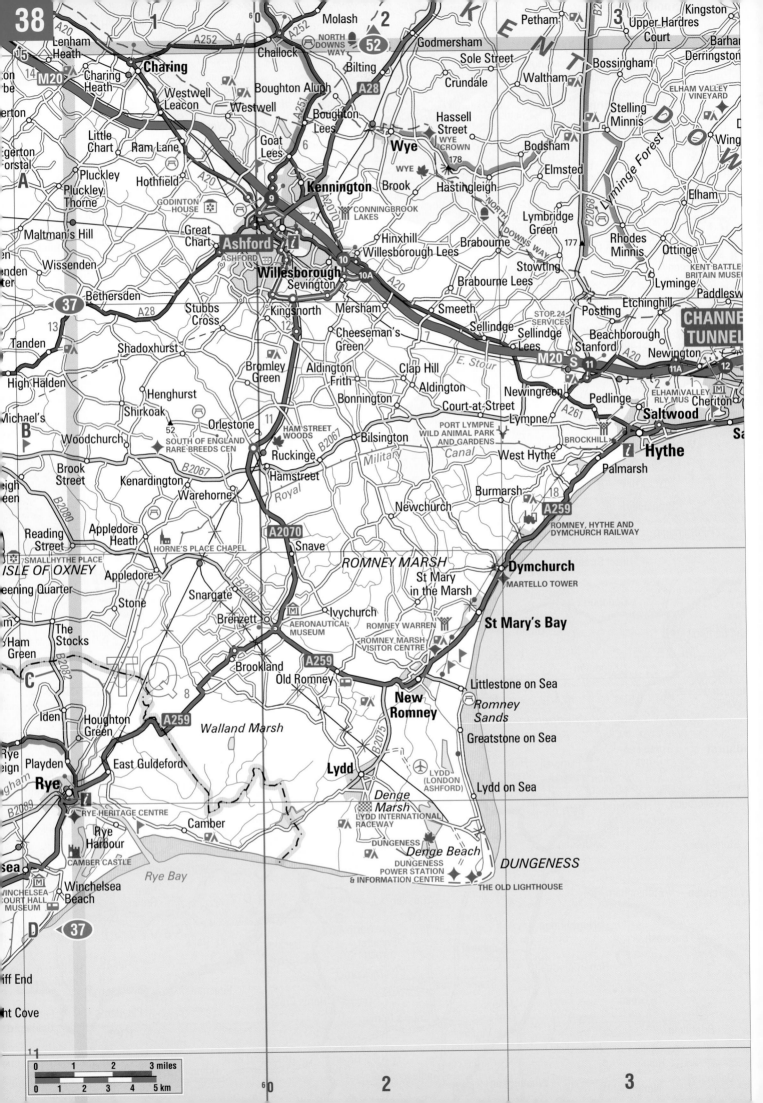

THE DOWNS

6

DEAL CASTLE

Walmer
WALMER CASTLE
AND GARDENS

Kingsdown

Martin

Martin Mill

St Margaret's at Cliffe

West
Cliffe

THE BAY MUSEUM

St Margaret's Bay

THE PINES
GARDEN

SOUTH
FORELAND

CALAIS
DUNKERQUE

WHITE
CLIFFS

CASTLE & HELLFIRE CORNER

DOVER

DE BRADELEI
WHARF

Aycliff

SAMPHIRE
HOE

EAST CLIFF &
WARREN

East Wear
Bay

Folkestone

CLIFF LIFT

andgate

CHANNEL TUNNEL

TR

ENGLISH CHANNEL

Nonington

Sowdown

Tilmanstone

Elvington

Great
Mongeham

53

Ripple

Sutton

Ringwould

East
Studdal

West
Langdon

East
Langdon

Guston

Whitfield

Womenswold

Barfrestone

Eythorne

EAST KENT
RLY

Woolage
Green

Shepherdswell

Coxhill

Coldred

A256

Denton

more

LYDDEN

Wootton

Selsted

ST JOHN'S
COMMANDERY

LYDDEN
TEMPLE EWELL

Ewell
Minnis

Temple
Ewell

CRABBLE
CORN MILL

Buckland

ROMAN PAINTED
HOUSE

Maxton

Swingfield
Street

Swingfield
Minnis

Alkham

Drellingore

West
Hougham

Farthingloe

Densole

Hawkinge

Capel le
Ferne

B2011

A20

13

1

2

3

A2

A260

A258

A2

A256

A256

4

5

6

4

5

6

A

B

C

D

15

11

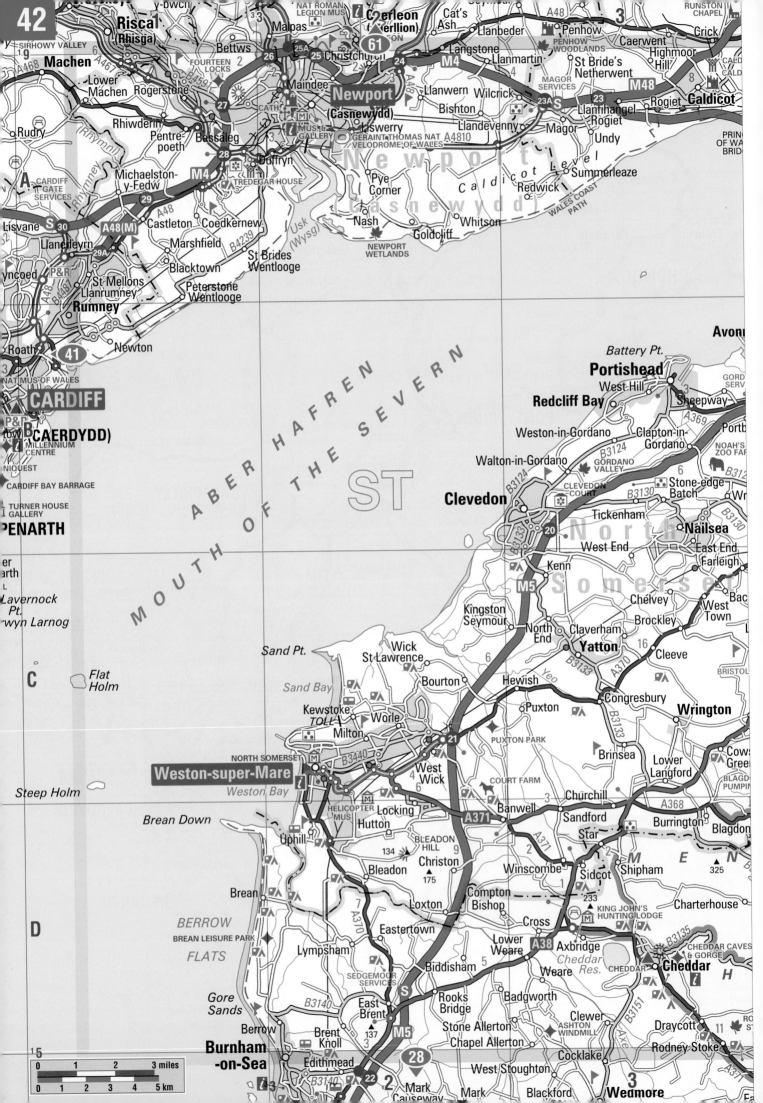

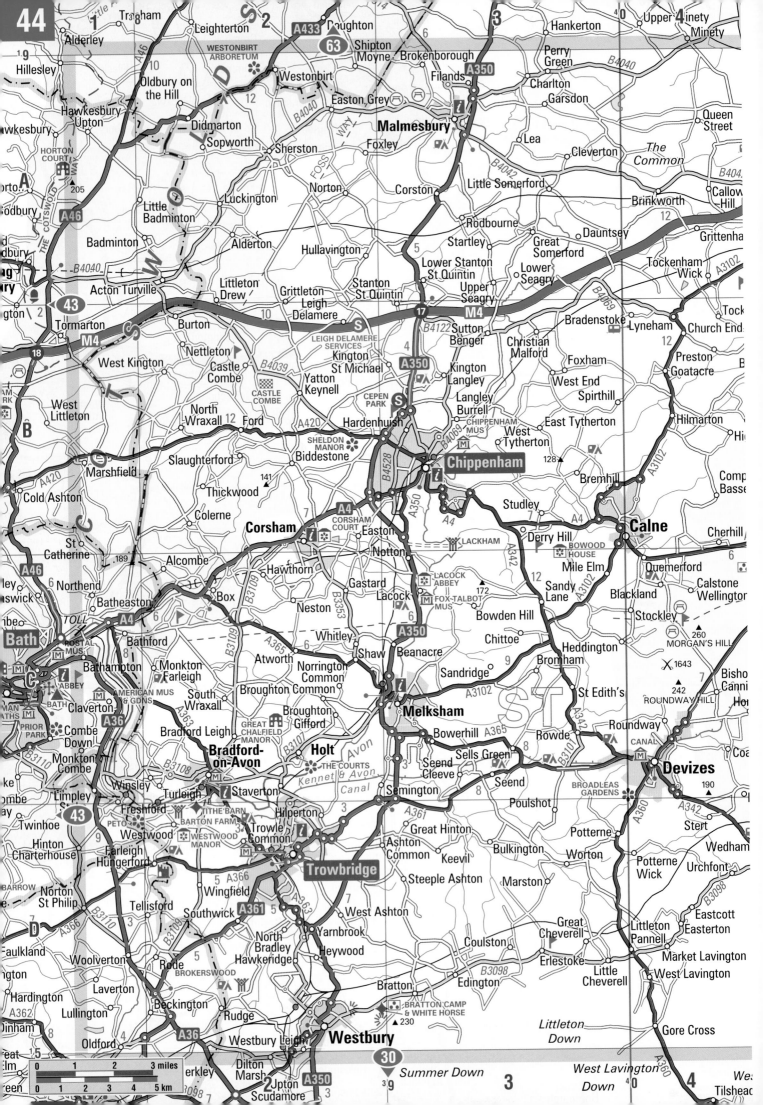

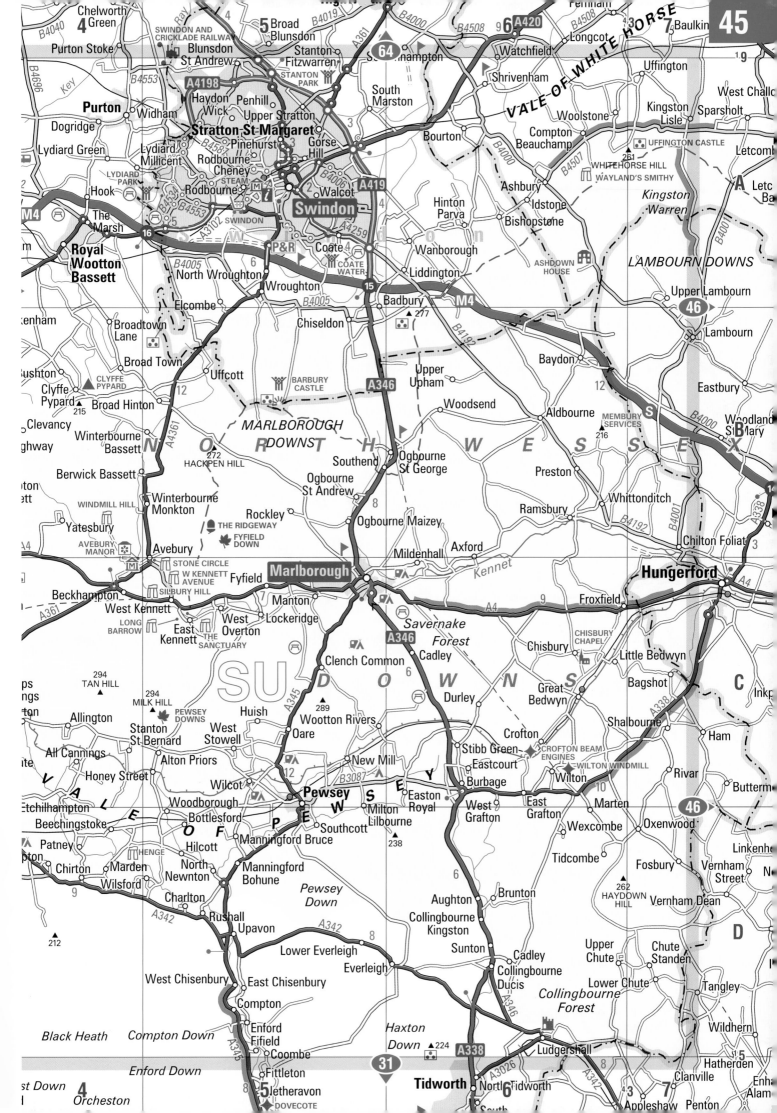

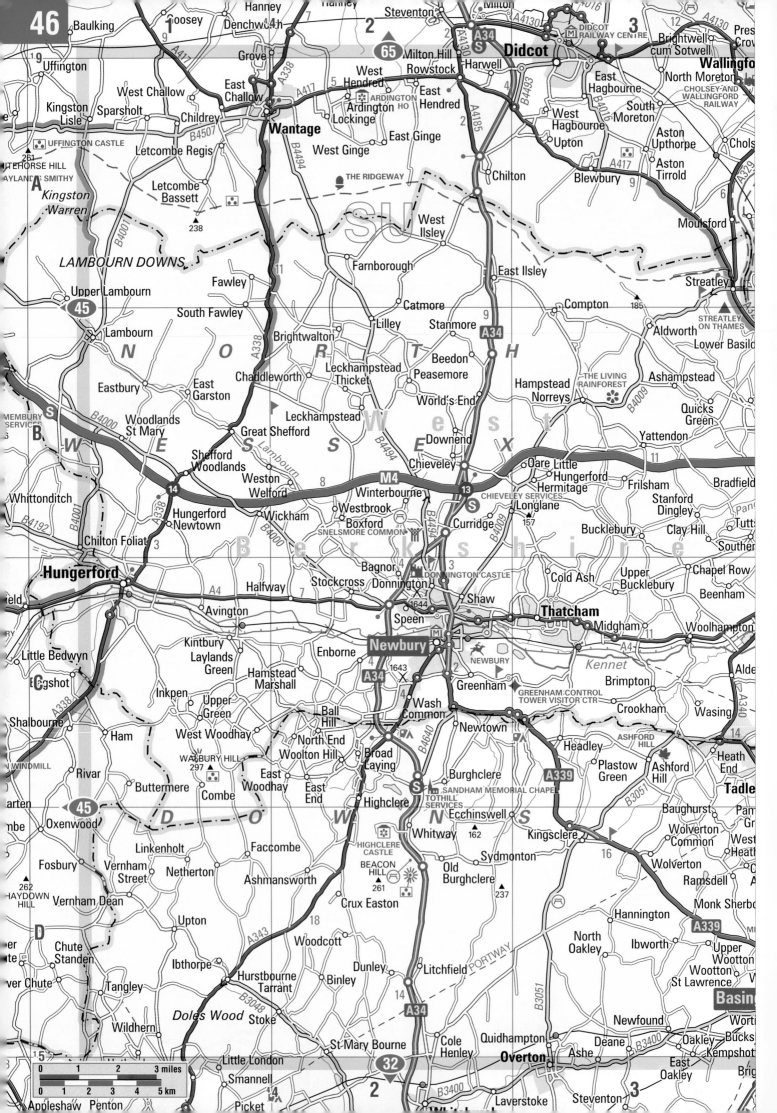

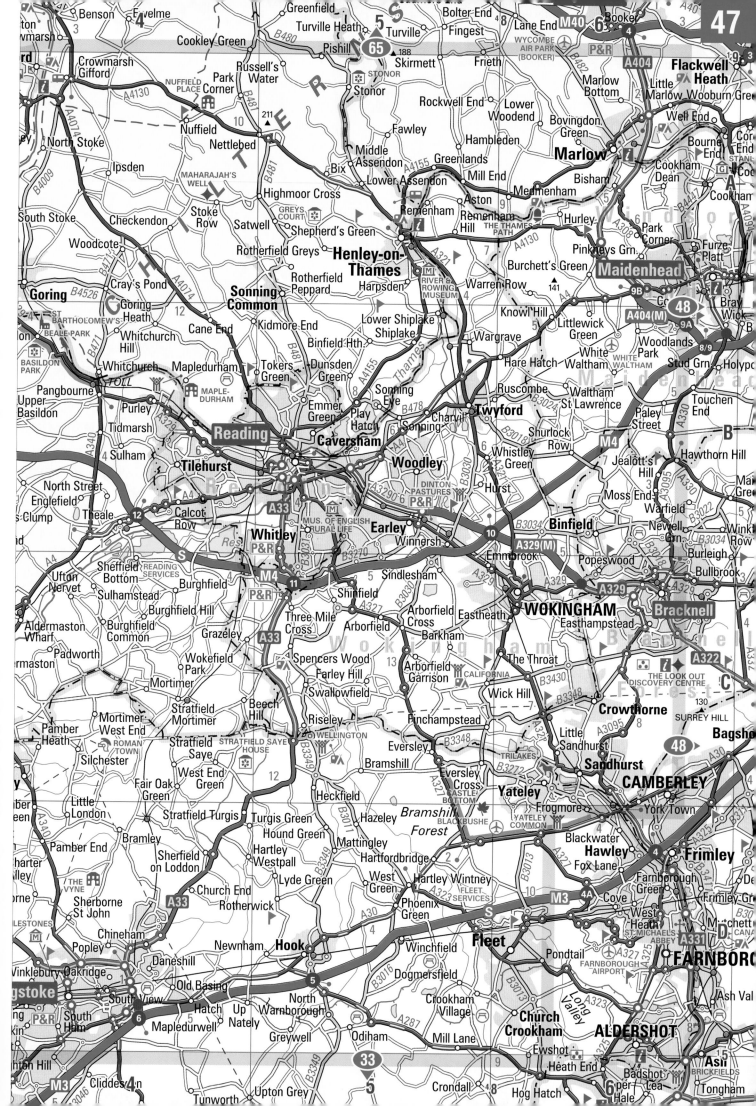

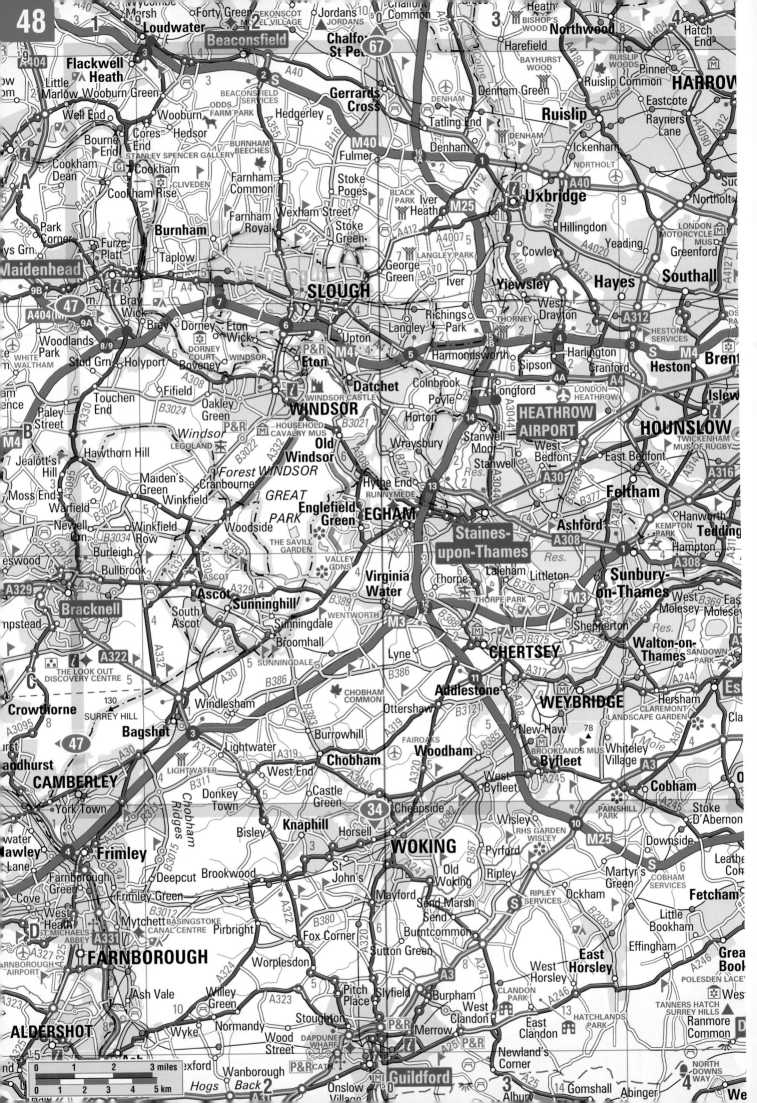

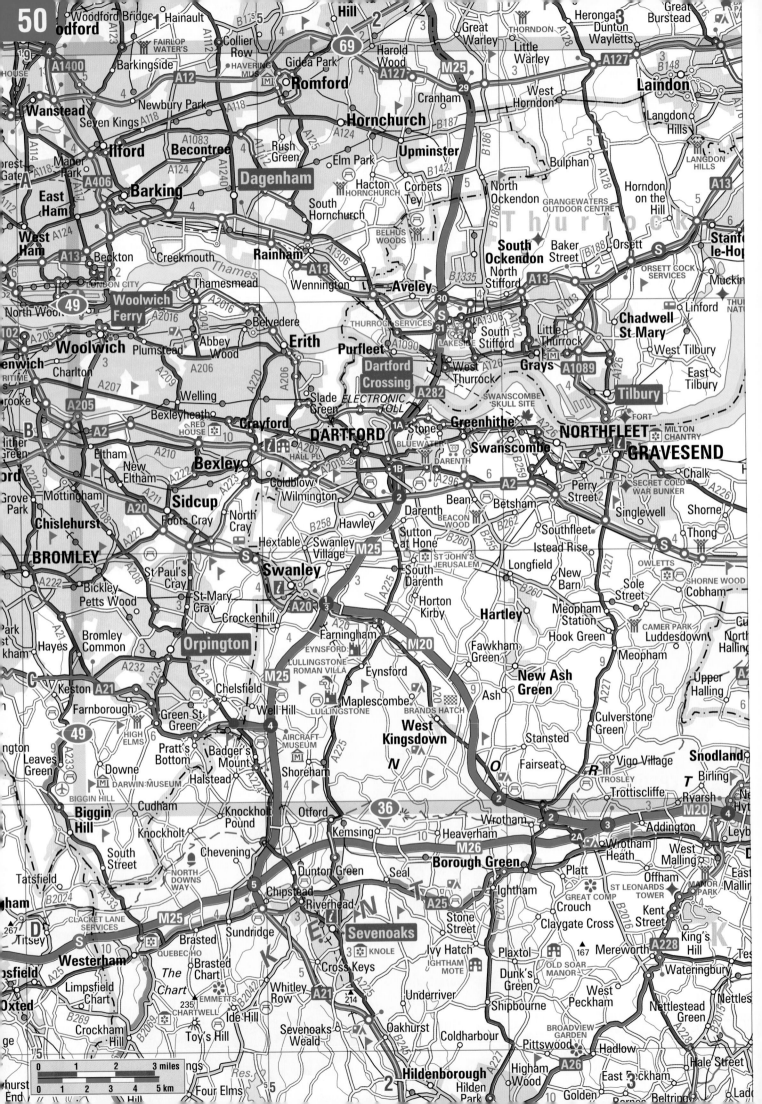

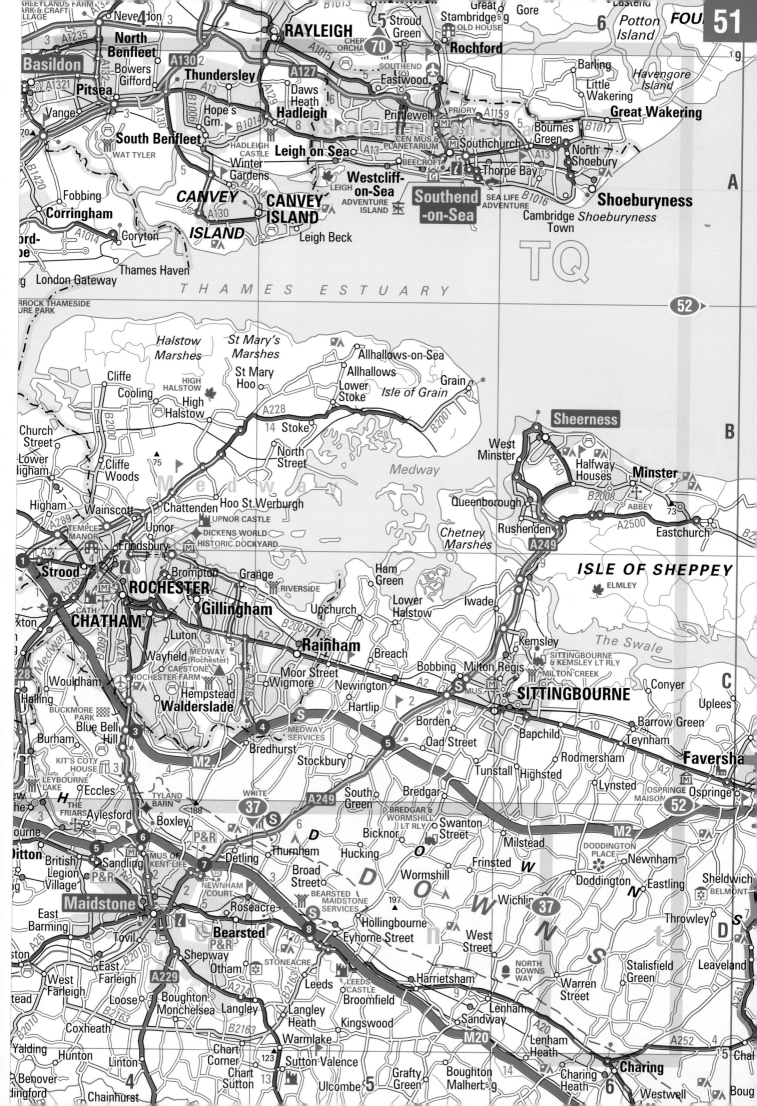

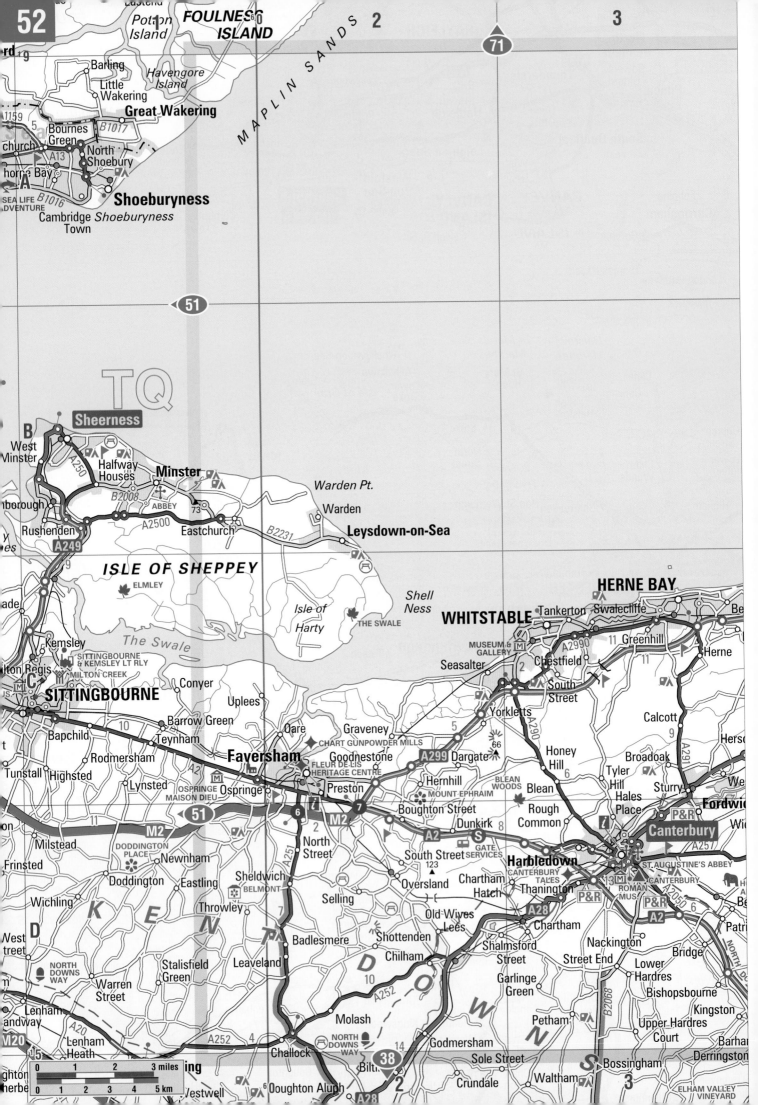

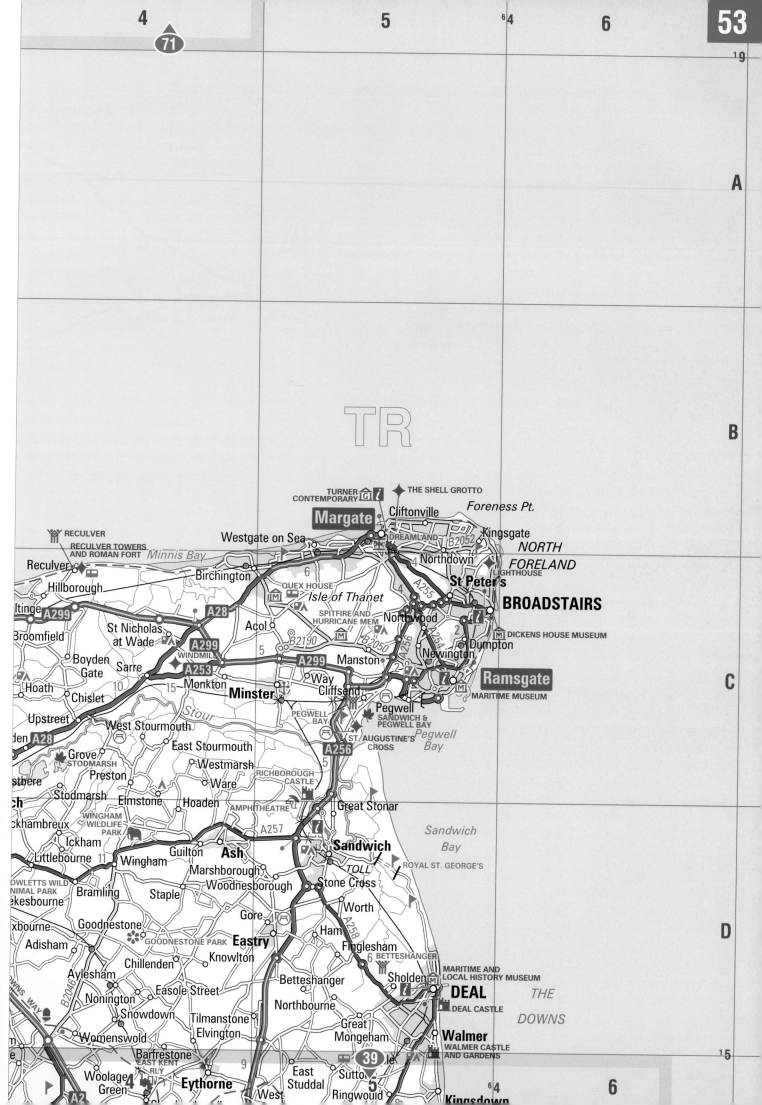

1 ¹6 2 3 4

A

²3

PEMBROKESHIRE COAST
ARFORDIR PENFRO

Ynysduellyn

Penclegyr Porthgain Trefin

Abereiddy Llanrhian

Croes-goch

ST. DAVID'S
HEAD
PENMAEN DEWI

Tretio Treffynnon

Treleddyd-
fawr Carnhedryn Treglemais

Whitesand Bay
Porth-mawr ST DAVID'S Rhodiad

B4583 Caerfarchell

BISHOP'S PALACE

B Rhosson Whitchurch Middle Mill

Ramsey
Island
Ynys Dewi CATHEDRAL St David's
(Tyddewi) Nine
Wells

RAMSEY
ISLAND *i* Solva

A487

Ramsey Sound

C

SM

S T.   B R I D E S

B A Y

BAE SAIN FFRAID

PEMBROKESHIRE
COAST PAT
LLWYBR ARFORD
PENFI

BROAD

Broad H

Broad H

Little Hav

Talbenny

Tower Point
Trwyn Twr St Bride's 82

GRASSHOLM
ISLAND

NATIONAL
NATURE RESERVE 79 *Wooltack Point*
Trwyn Wooltack

Skomer
Island
Ynys Skomer SKOMER
ISLAND Marloes B4327 Hasguard

MARLOES
SANDS

Broad Sound St
Ishmael's Sandy
Haven

Gateholm
Island
Ynys Gateholm Dale

MILFORD
ABERDAUG

D

P
E
M
B
R
O
K
E
S
H
I
R
E

Skokholm
Island
Ynys Skokholm 71

St Ann's Hd.
Pentir St. Ann

ROSSLARE *Sheep
Island
Ynys y Defaid*

²0

E

P
E
N
F

| 0 | 1 | 2 | 3 miles |
| 0 | 1 2 3 | 4 | 5 km |

2 ¹7 3 4

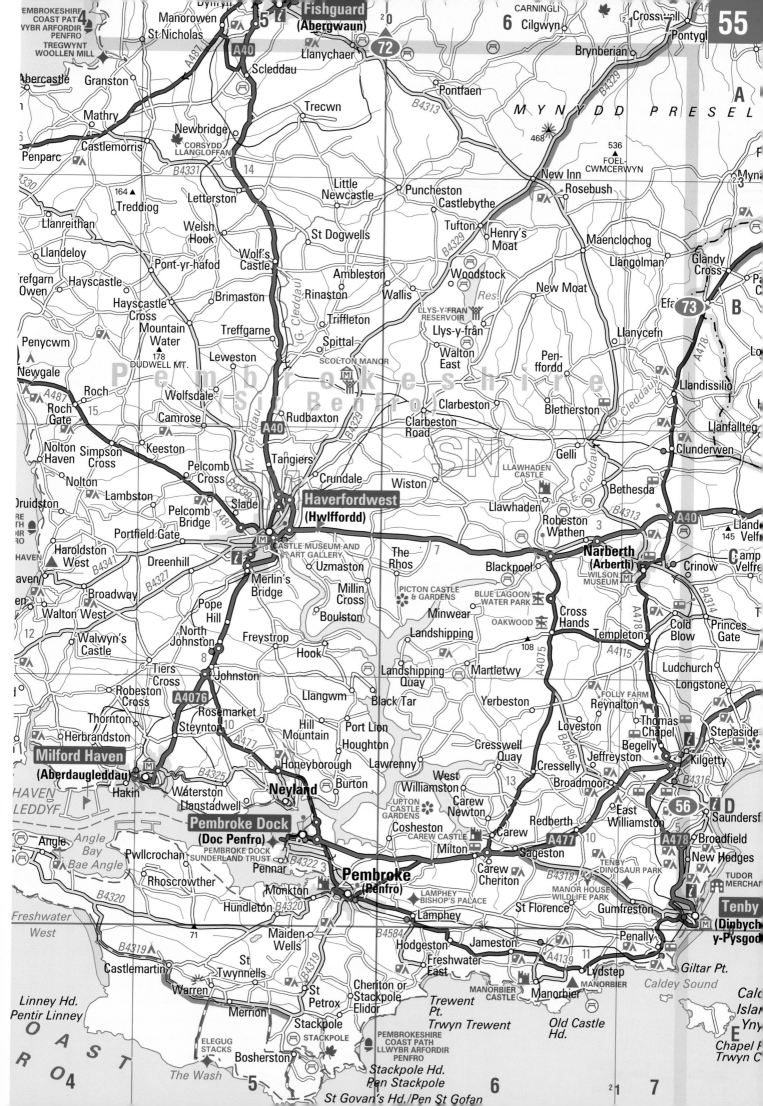

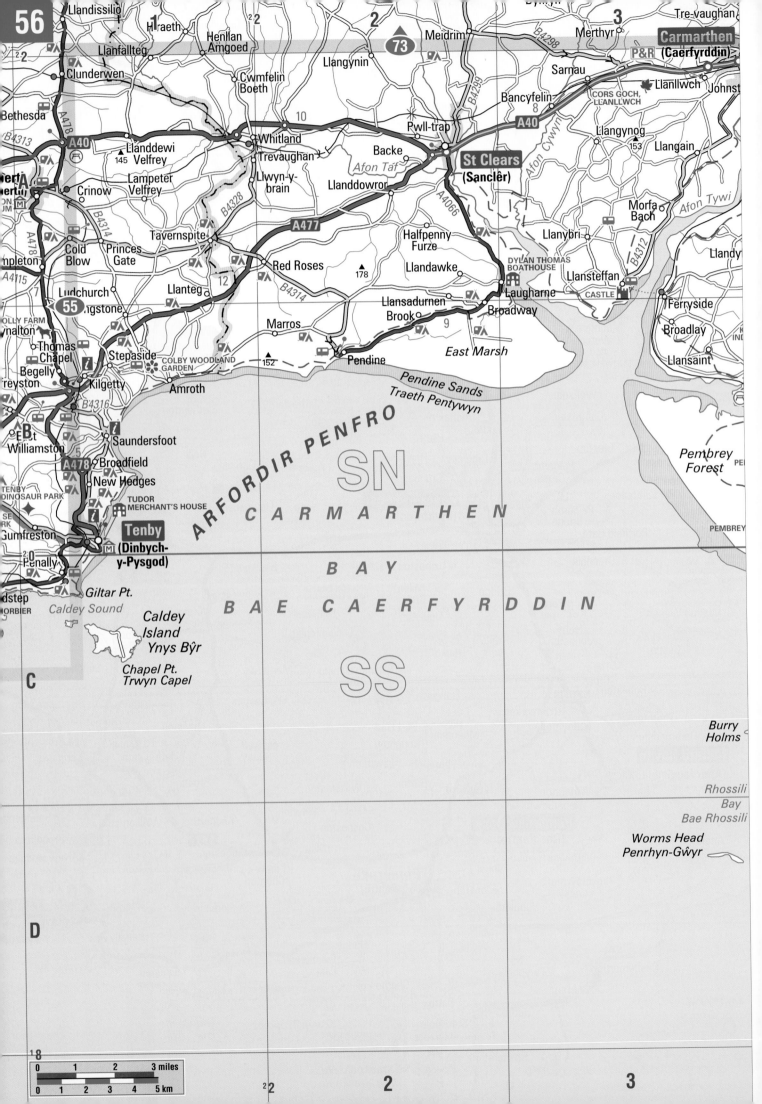

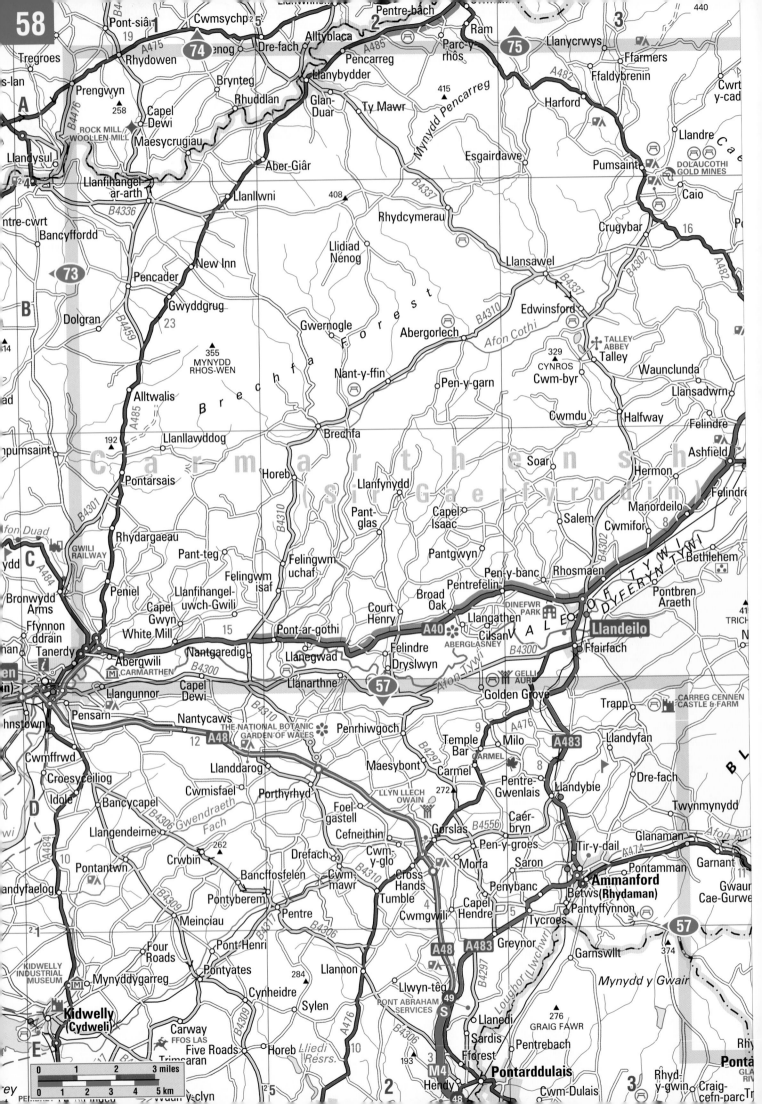

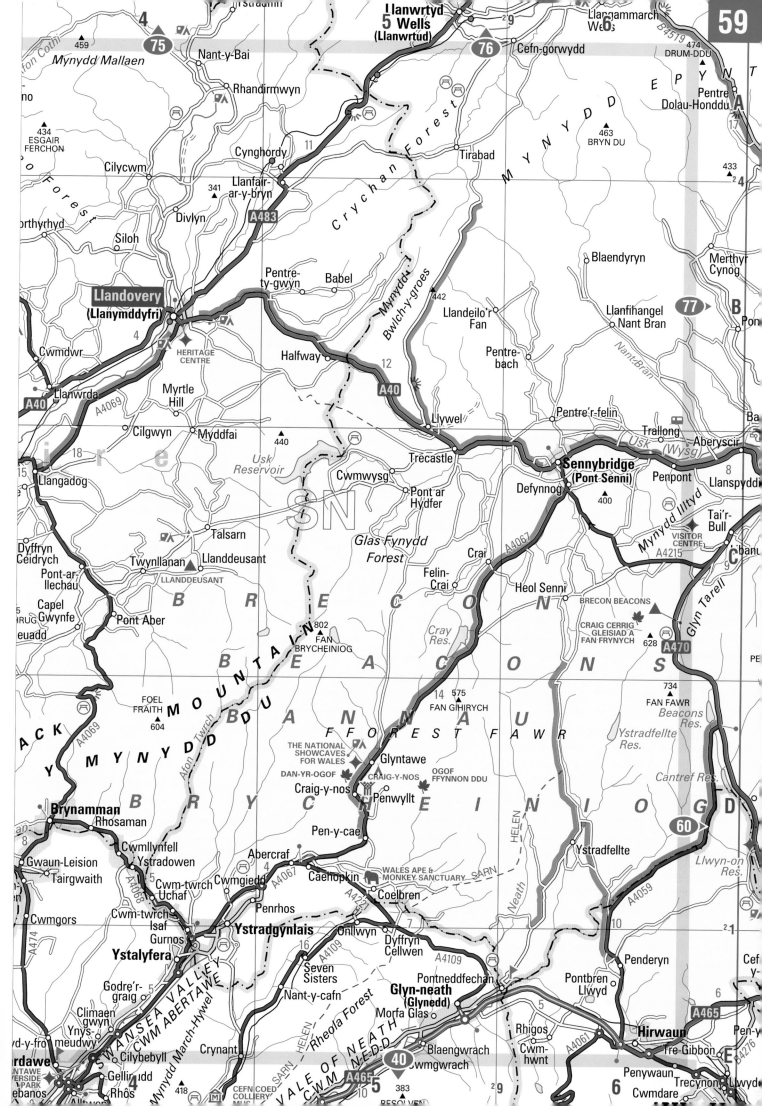

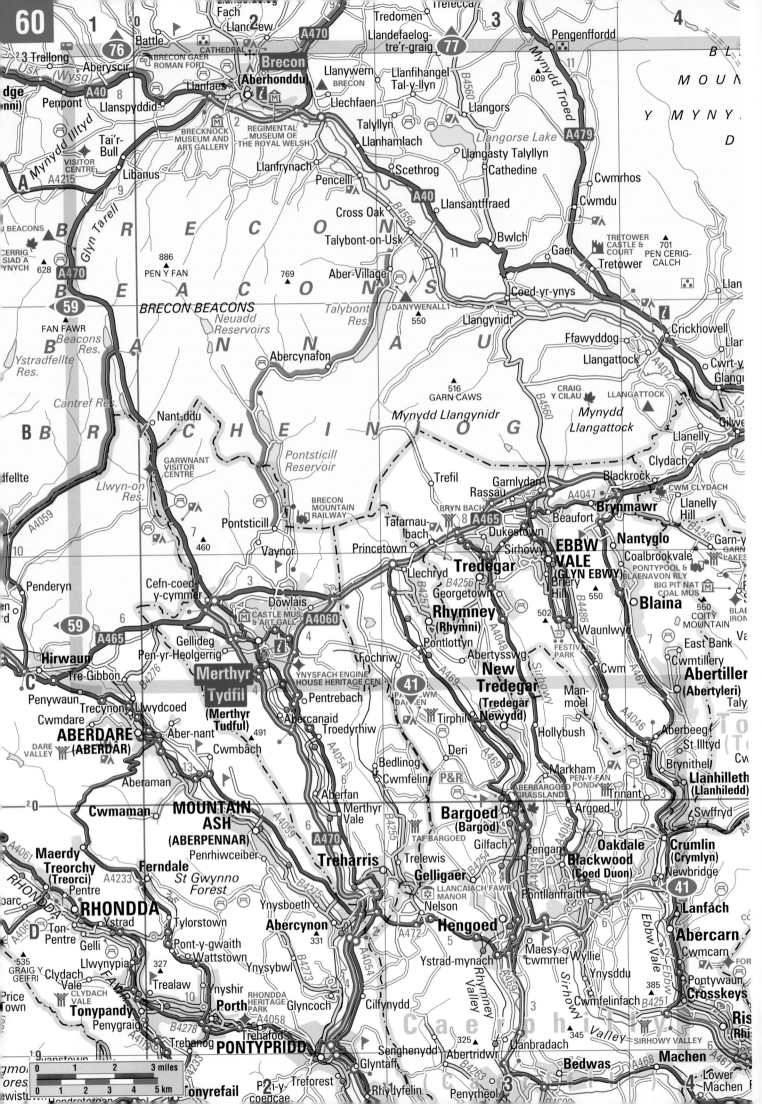

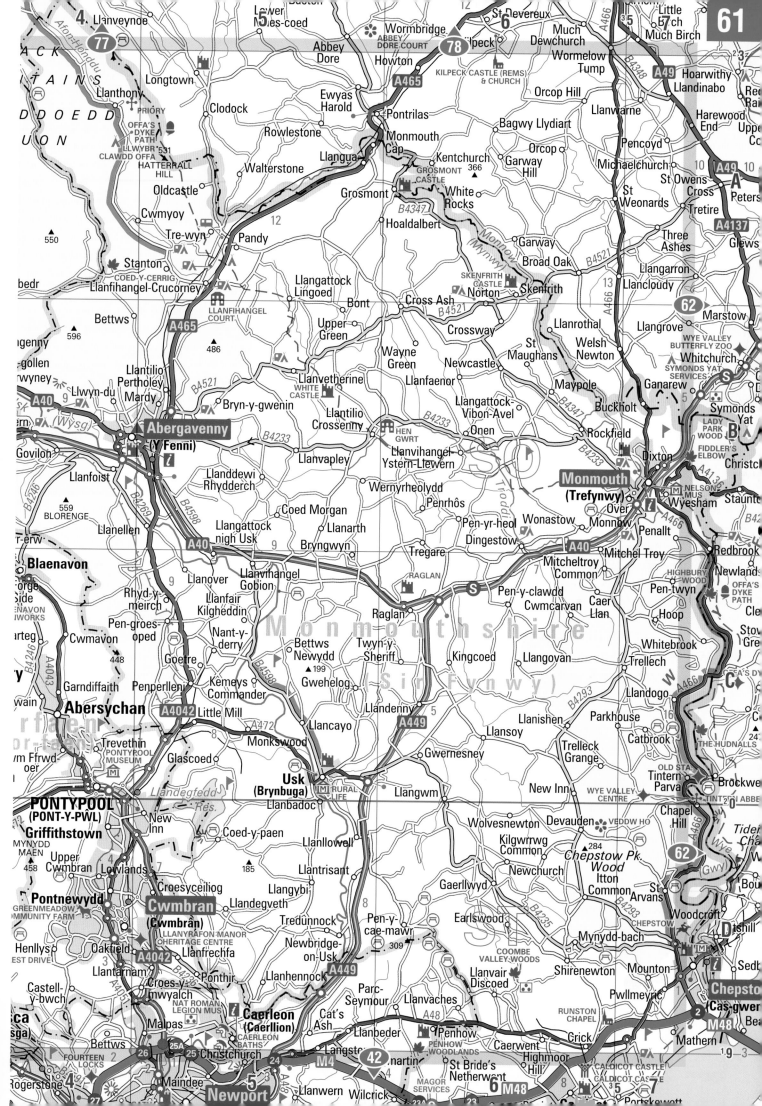

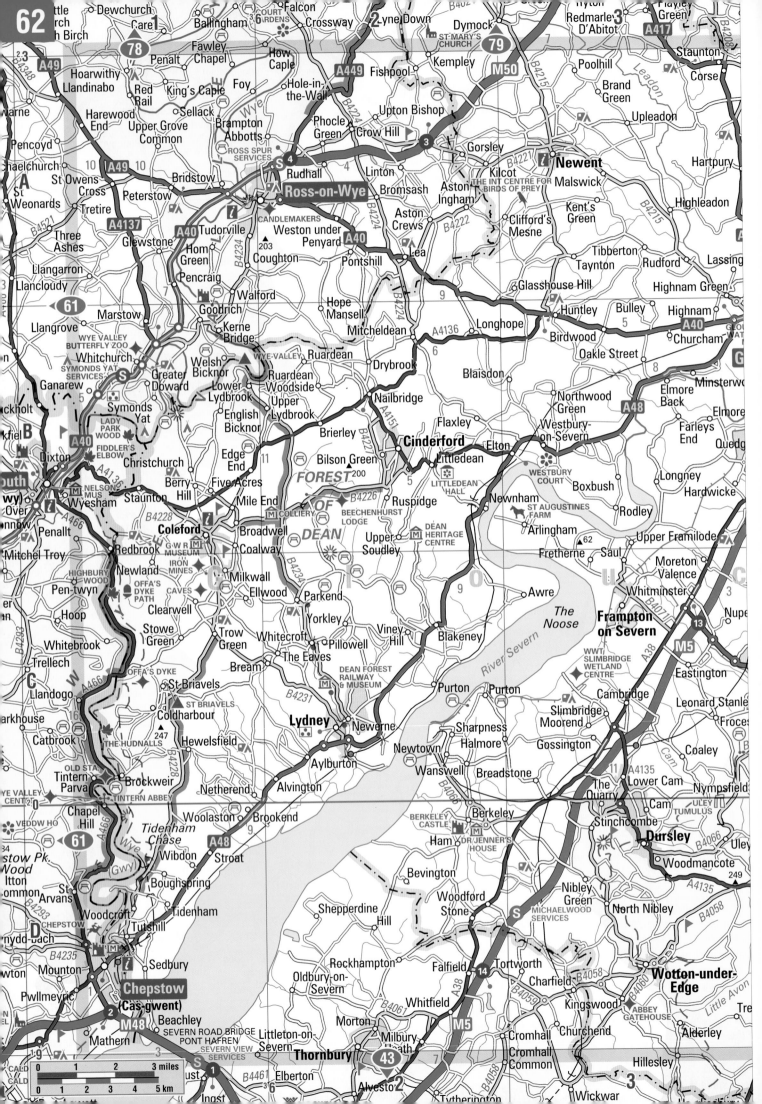

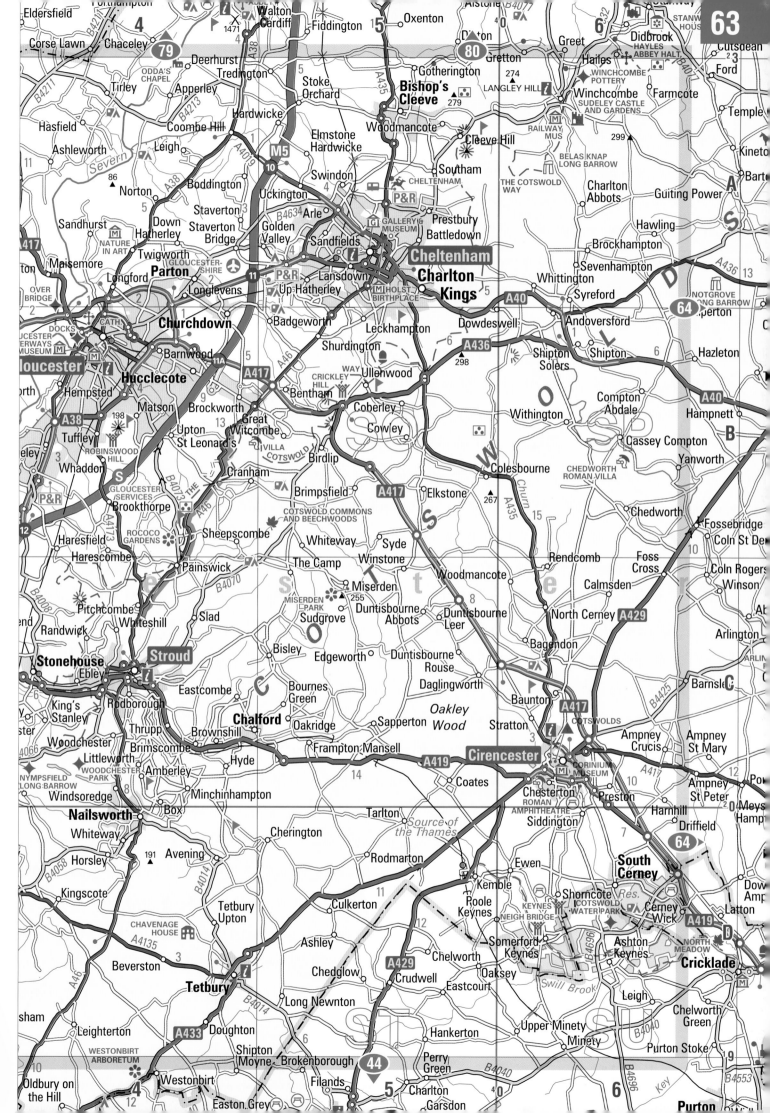

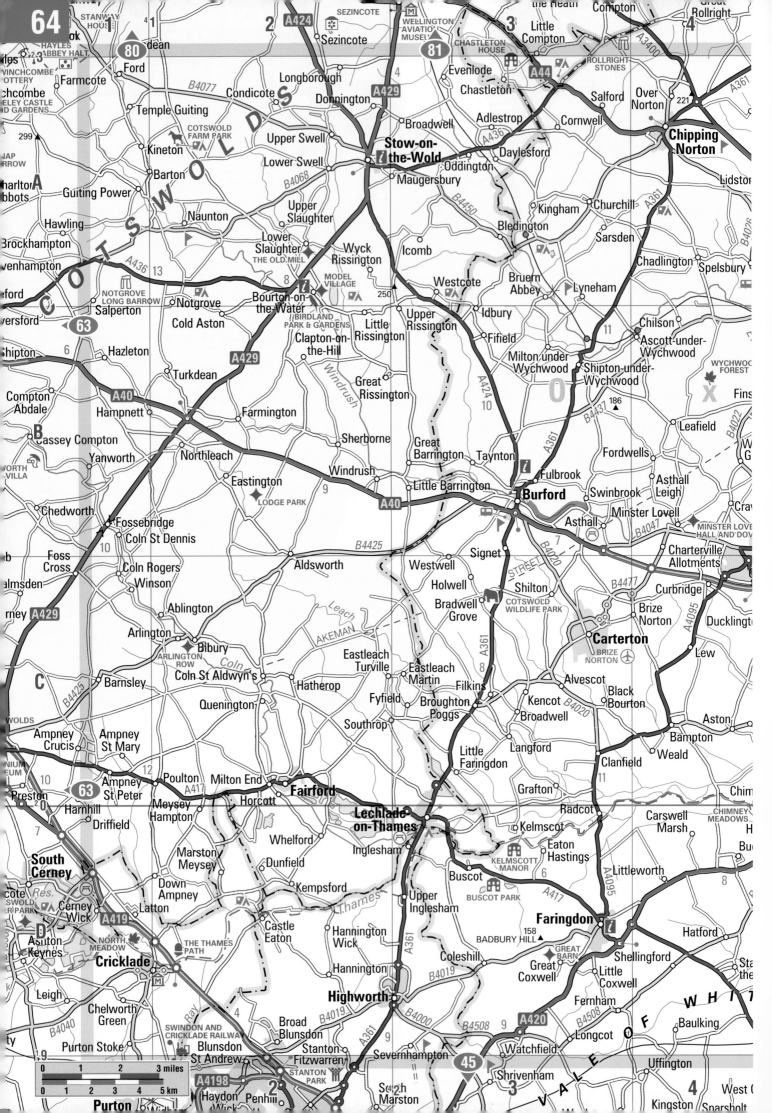

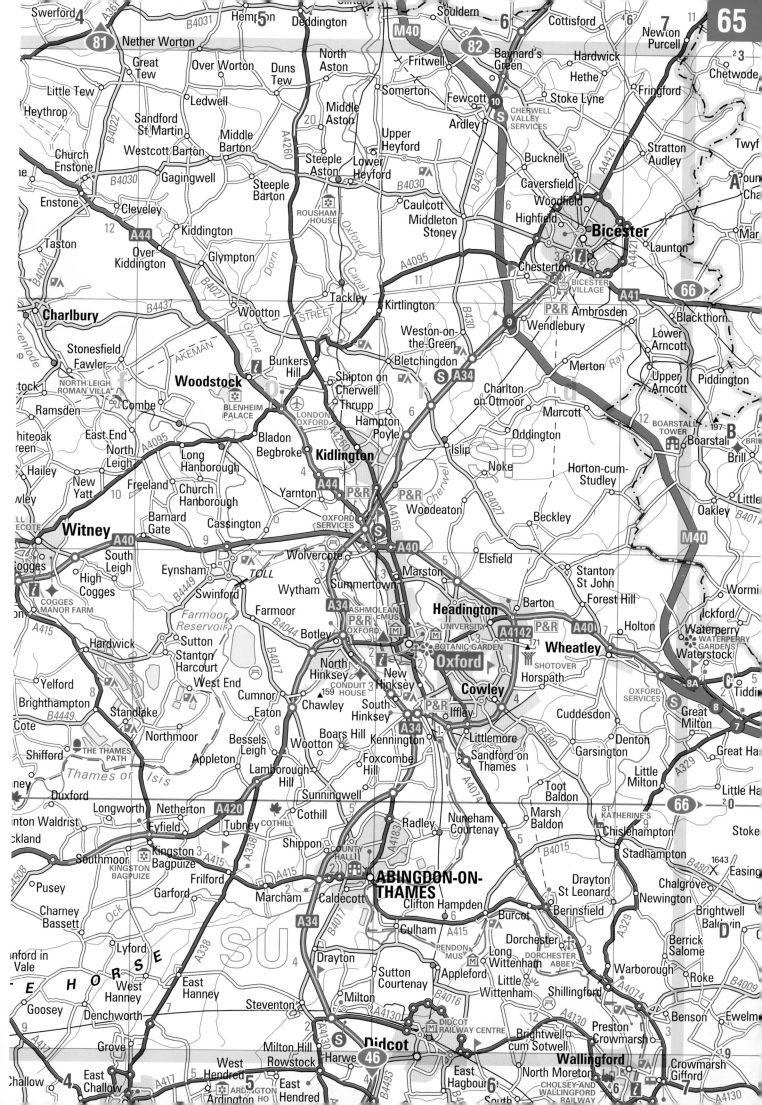

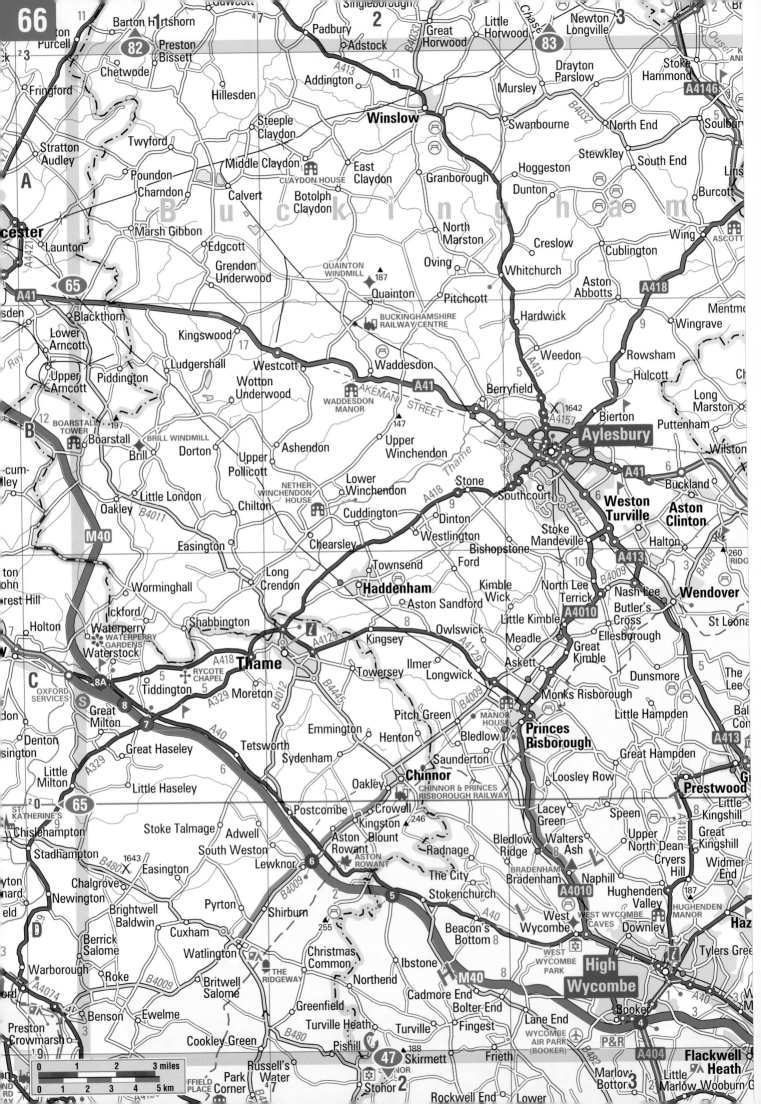

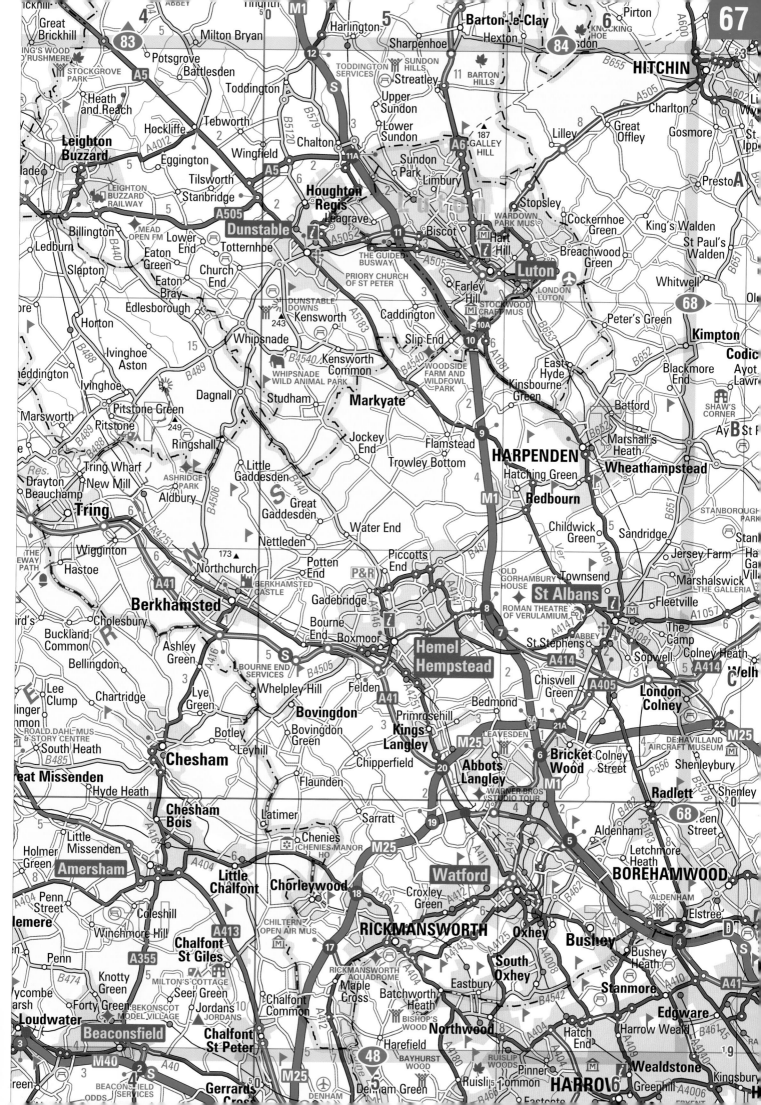

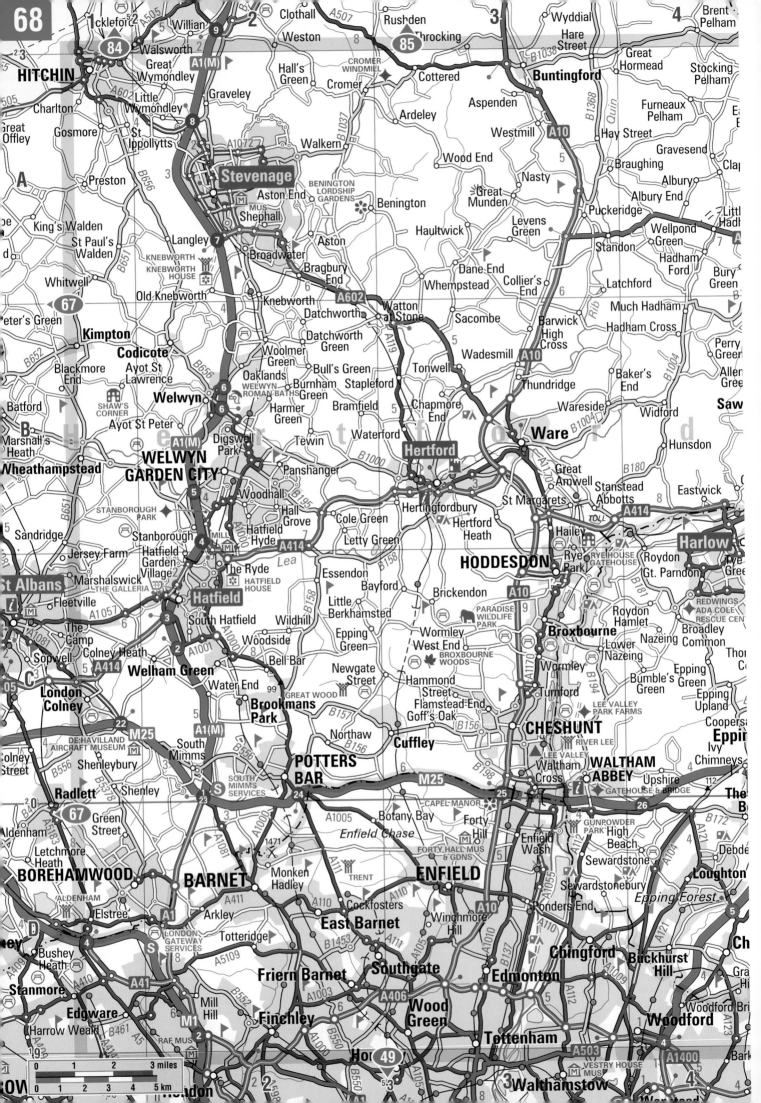

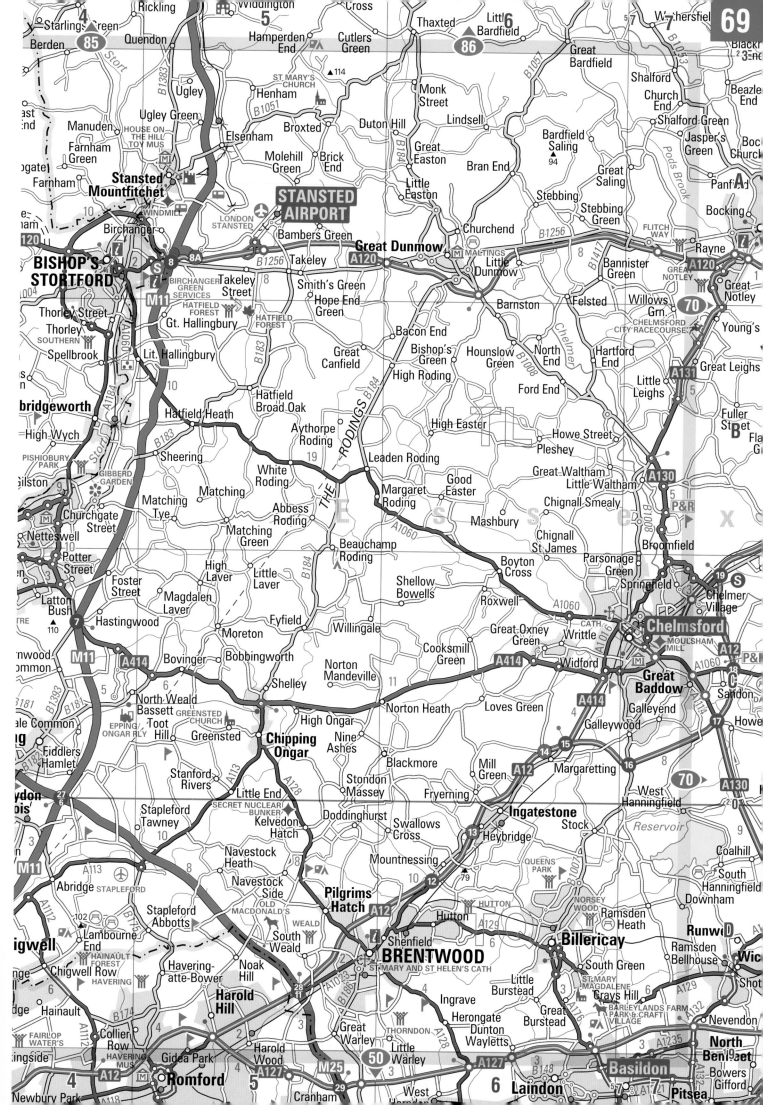

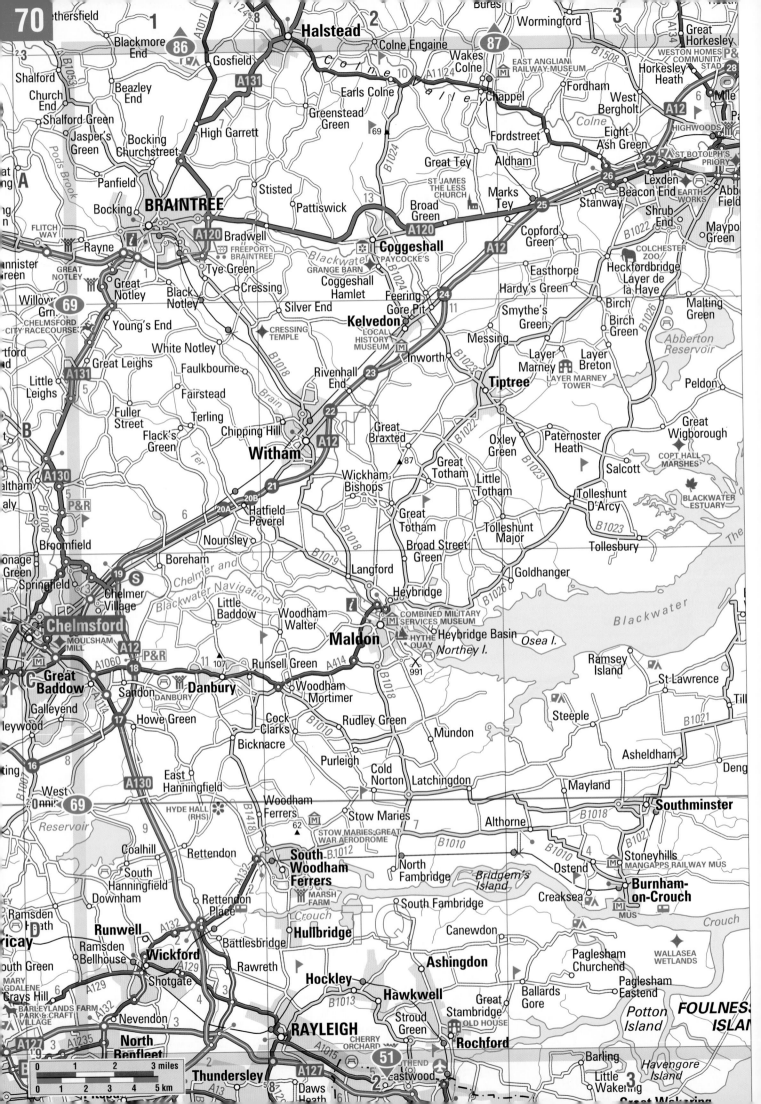

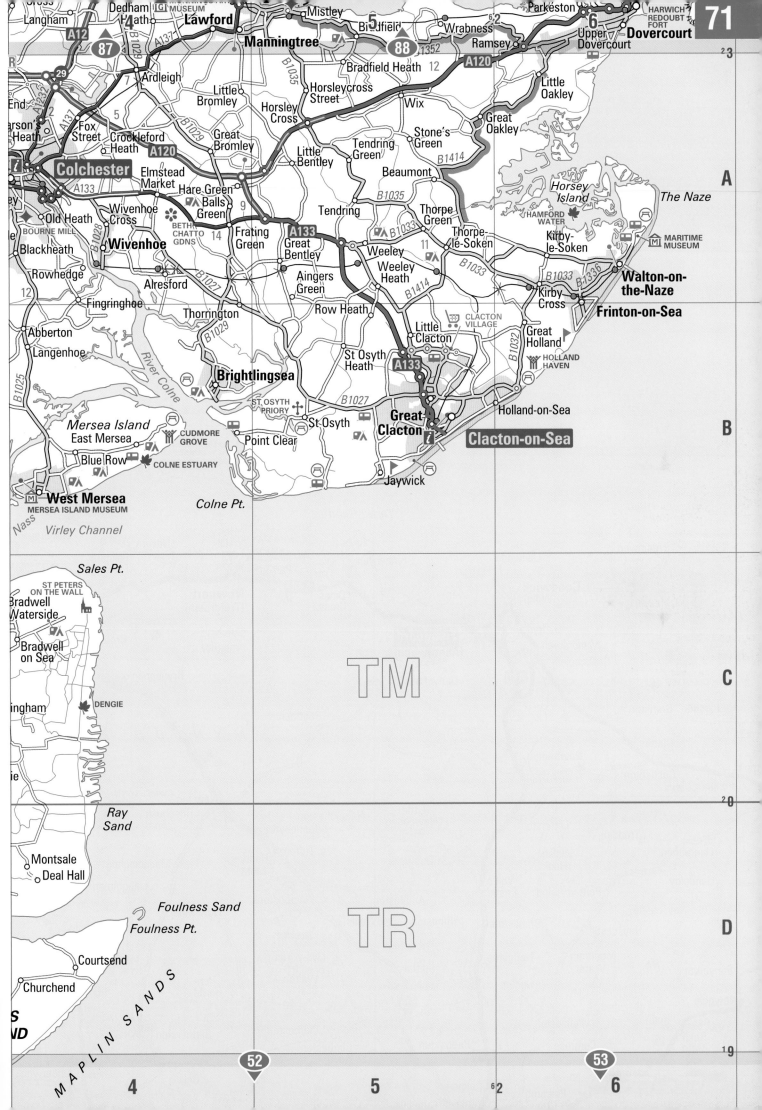

Langham
Dedham **LGI** MUSEUM
Heath **4**
Lawford Mistley **5**dfield Wrabness Parkeston **6** HARWICH REDOUBT FORT
A12 **87** B1029 **Manningtree** Bi dfield Ramsey Upper **Dovercourt**
Dovercourt
A137 Bradfield Heath 12 **A120** Little
Ardleigh B1035 Horsleycross B1352 Wix Oakley
7 Little Street Little
Bromley Horsley Oakley
Fox **B1029** Horsley
Street Cross Stone's Great
Parson's Crockleford Great Cross Green Oakley
Heath Heath Bromley Little Tendring B1414 Horsey
Hea**A120** Bentley Green Island HAMFORD The Naze
End **29** Elmstead Beaumont WATER
A232 Market Hare Green Balls Thorpe MARITIME
Colchester Wivenhoe Green B1035 Tendring Green B1033 Kirby- MUSEUM
A133 Cross BETHE Frating 9 Thorpe- le-Soken
Old Heath CHATTO Green A133 Weeley le-Soken B1033 **Walton-on-**
BOURNE MILL GDNS 14 Great B1033 B1336 **the-Naze**
Blackheath **Wivenhoe** Bentley Weeley 11 Kirby
B1028 Heath B1414 Cross **Frinton-on-Sea**
Rowhedge Alresford Aingers B1033
12 Green Row Heath B1032 Great
Fingringhoe Thorrington Holland HOLLAND
Abberton B1029 Little HAVEN
Langenhoe St Osyth Clacton CLACTON
B1025 Heath VILLAGE
River Colne St Osyth **A133** Holland-on-Sea
Brightlingsea B1027
Mersea Island ST OSYTH **Great**
East Mersea PRIORY St Osyth **Clacton** **Clacton-on-Sea**
CUDMORE Point Clear
Blue Row GROVE
COLNE ESTUARY Jaywick
West Mersea
MERSEA ISLAND MUSEUM Colne Pt.
Nass
Virley Channel

Sales Pt.
ST PETERS
ON THE WALL
Bradwell
Waterside
TM
Bradwell
on Sea
ingham
DENGIE

Ray
Sand

Montsale
Deal Hall

Foulness Sand
Foulness Pt. **TR**

Courtsend

Churchend

52 **53**
4 **5** 62 **6**

A
B
C
D
23
20
19

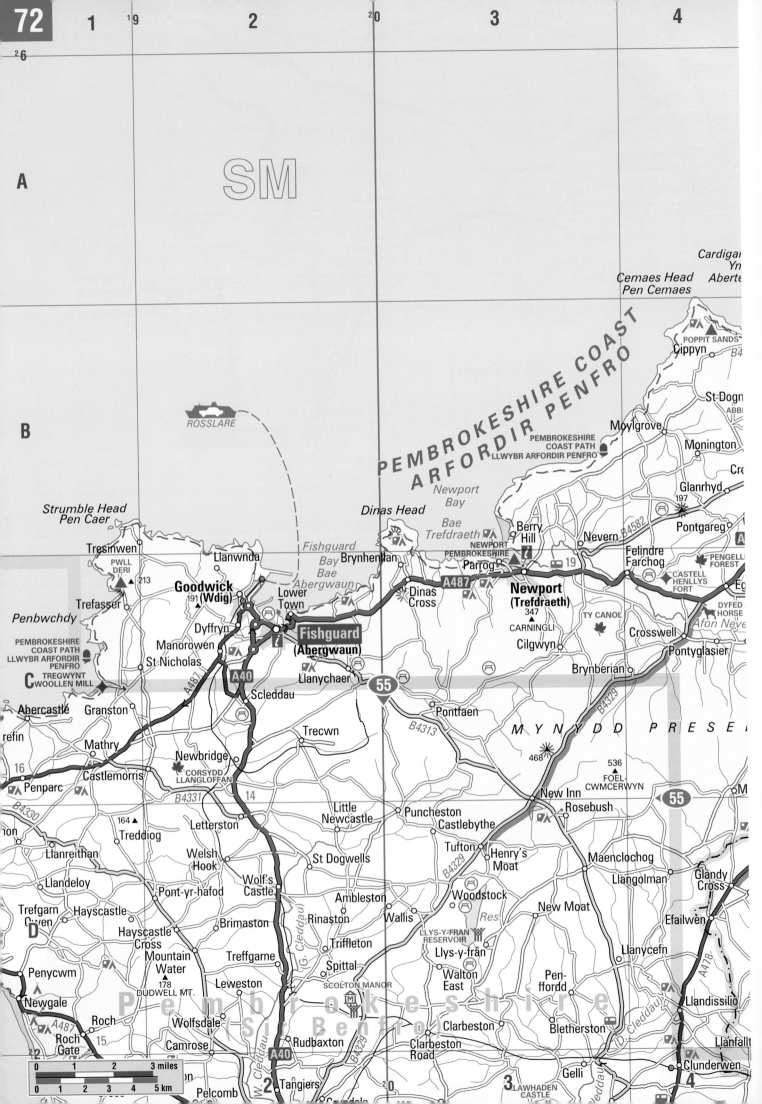

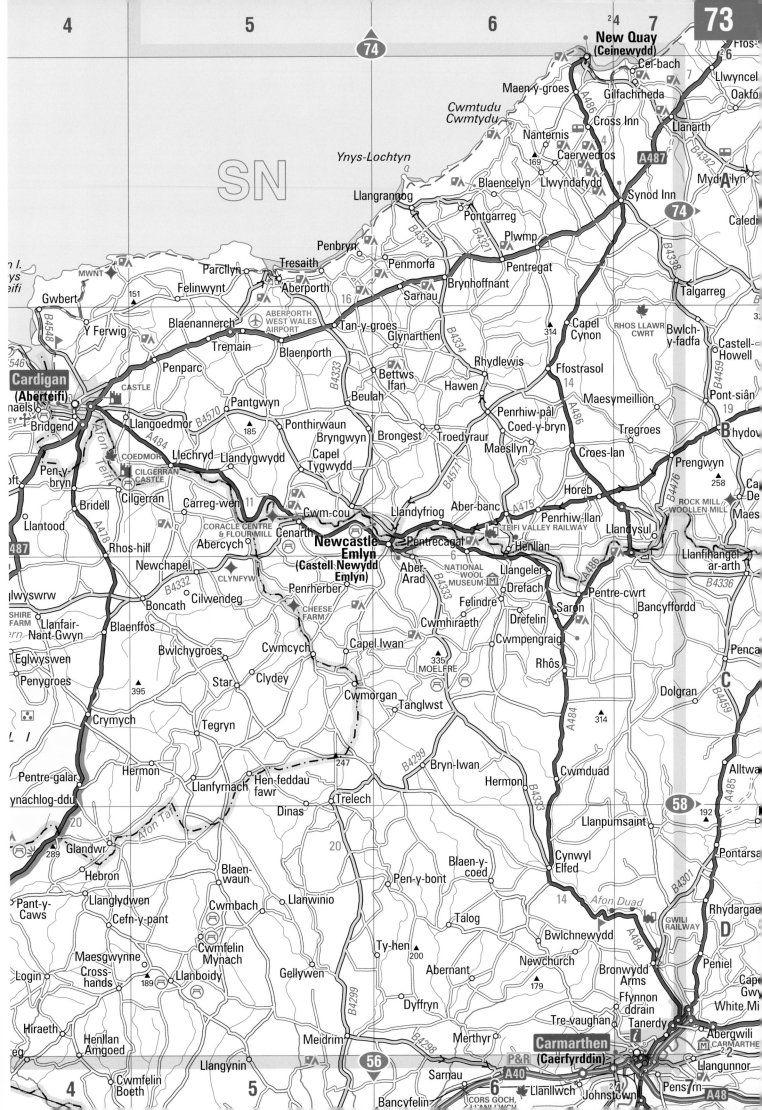

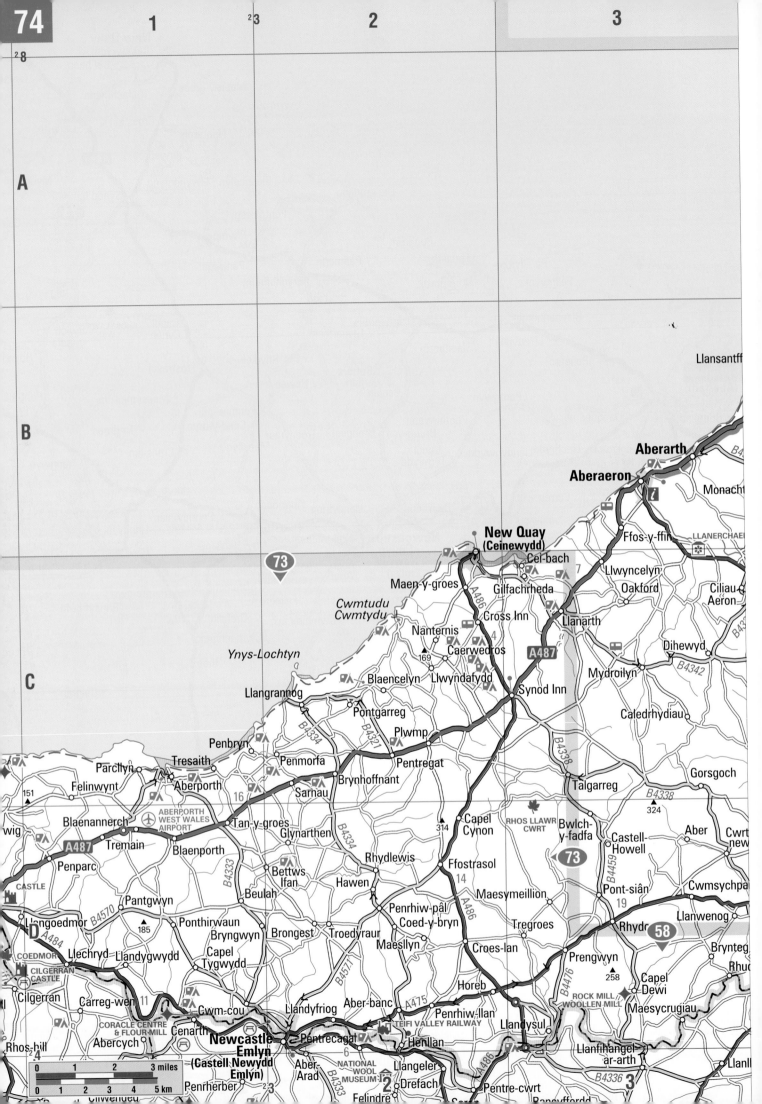

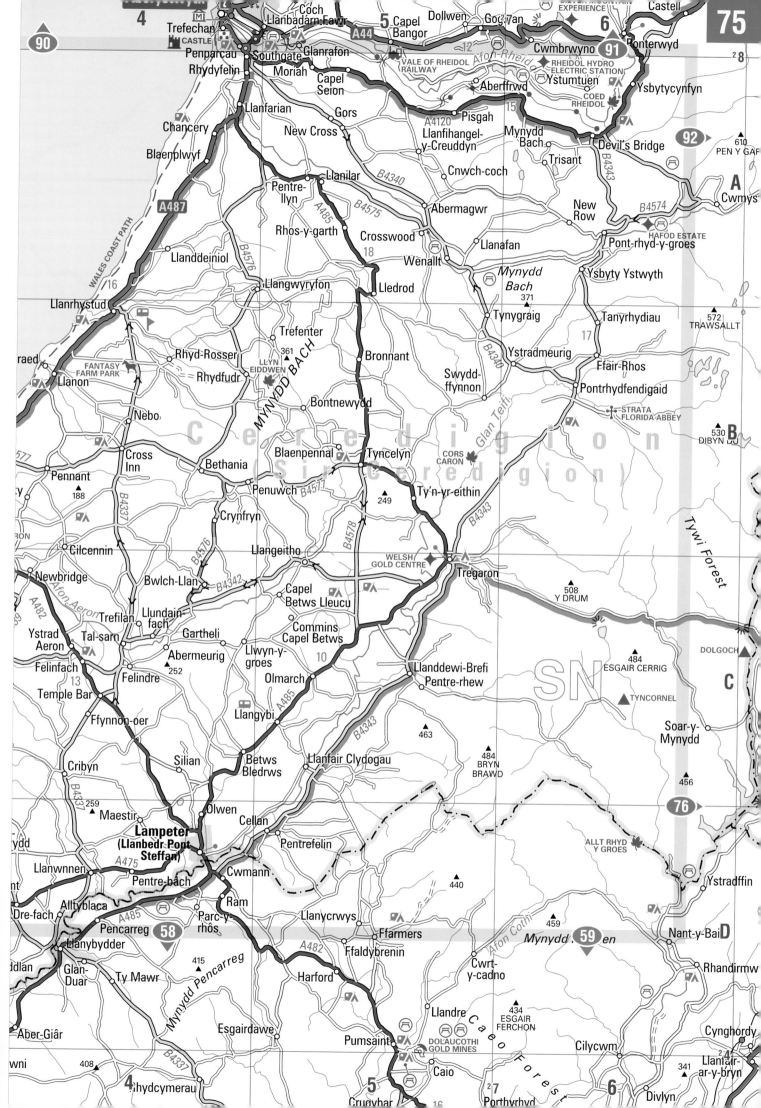

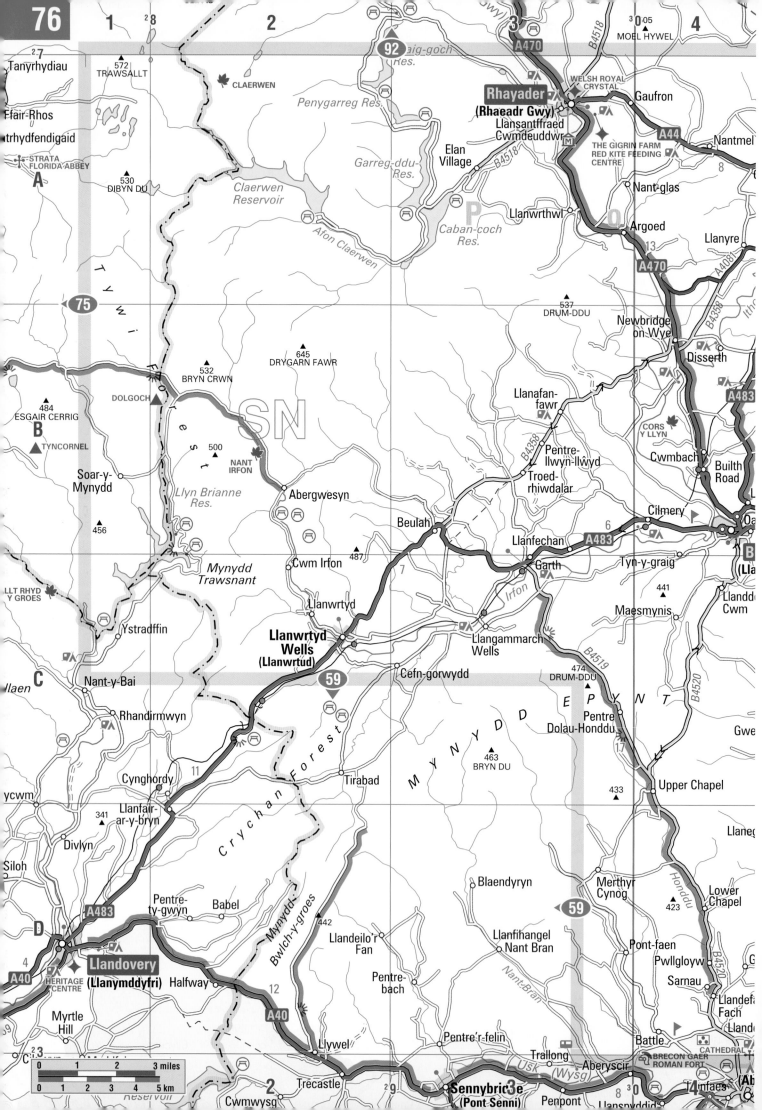

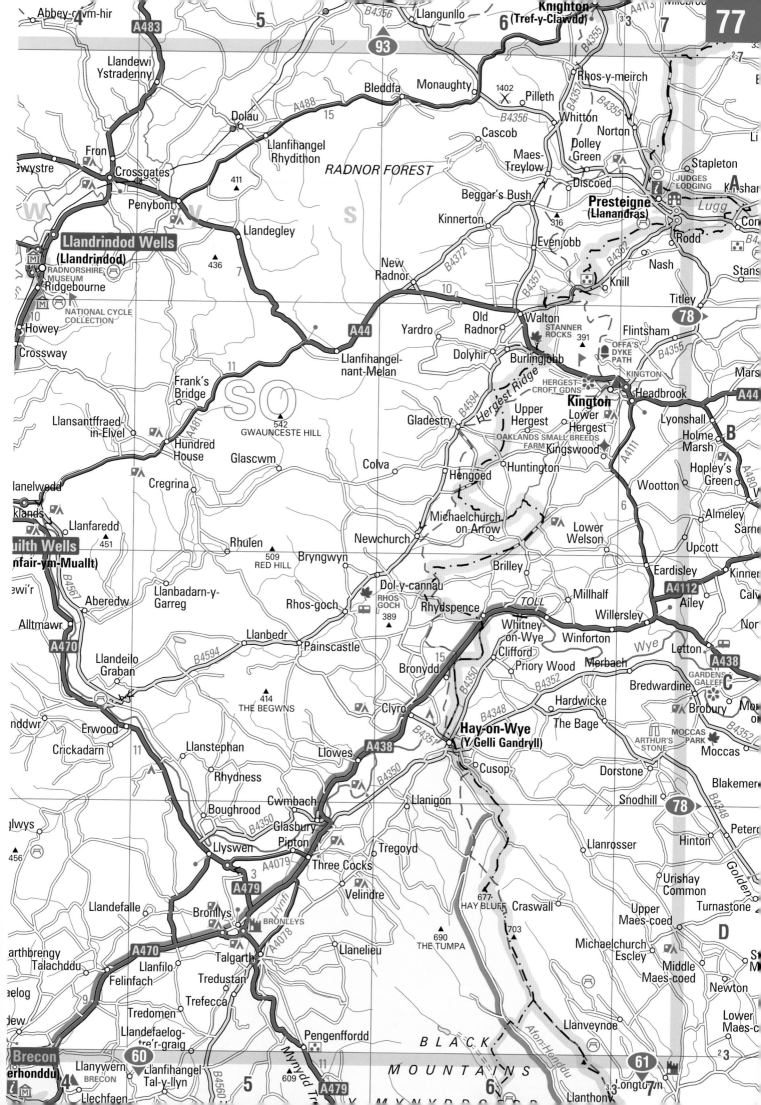

1   **2**   **3**

B4530
▲333
Bryan
Adforton
Elton
Ashford Carbonell
Greete
Letton
B4110
94
Leinthall Starkes
Richards Castle
Middleton
Ashford Bowdler
BURFORD HOUSE & MEADOW GALLERY
Wigmore
Woofferton
Little Hereford
A456
Burford

Birtley
▲338
Brimfield
Gosford
St Michaels
Ongar Street
Lower Lye
Leinthall Earls
Comberton
A49
Call Gra
Lingen
Yatton
Orleton
6
Middleton on the Hill
9
Limebrook
Bircher
Ashton
Leysters Pole

A
Stapleton
Kinsham
CROFT CASTLE
Yarpole
Lucton
Eye
BERRINGTON HALL
The Hundred
JUDGES LODGING
steigne (landras)
Lugg
Combe
Combe Moor
Mortimer's Cross
WATER MILL AND BATTLE CENTRE
Luston
A4112
Rodd
B4362
Ledicot
1461✕
Lugg Green
The Broad
Kimbolton
Whyle
Grafton
Nash
Stansbatch
Shobdon
Kingsland
Cobnash
Stockton
Pudleston

Knill
Staunton on Arrow
Shirl Heath
Lawton
B4360
Cholstrey
LEOMINSTER
Leominster
Steen's Bridge
Titley
77
Eardisland
Monkland
B4529
Barons Cross
A44
Docklow
Grendon Green
Flintsham
B4355
Pembridge
BURTON COURT
Ivington Green
Ivington
Humber
249
OFFA'S DYKE PATH
KINGTON
Marston
Bearwood
Luntley
4
Brierley
Stoke Prior
Risbury
Marston Stannett

B
Headbrook
A44
Haven
Sollers Dilwyn
Aulden
Upper Hill
Marlbrook
Newton
4
Bowley
Hegdon Hill
Lyonshall
Holme Marsh
Broxwood
Dilwyn
Birley
Hope under Dinmore
Pencombe
Hopley's Green
A480
Woonton
Knapton Green
Bush Bank
QUEENSWOOD
Bodenham
A417
Wootton
Almeley
Weobley
Weobley Marsh
HAMPTON COURT
Bodenham Moor
Ullingswick
Upcott
Sarnesfield
Ledgemoor
King's Pyon
Westhope
Urdimarsh
The Vauld
Maund Bryan
Moret Jeffri
Felton

C
Eardisley
Kinnersley
Calver Hill
Wormsley
Canon Pyon
Wellington
Walker's Green
Marden
Preston Wynne
14
Ailey
Norton Canon
Moorhampton
Yarsop
18
Mansel Lacy
12
A49
Moreton on Lugg
Sutton St Nicholas
Ocle Pychard
Willersley
Wye
Letton
A438
Yazor
Mansell Gamage
A480
Brinsop
Tillington Common
Tillington
8
Pipe and Lyde
KENCHESTER WATER GARDENS
Westhide
Withington
Bredwardine
GARDENS & GALLERY
Monnington on Wye
Byford
Bishopstone
Kenchester
Burghill
Credenhill
Stretton Sugwas
Shelwick
A4103
Shucknall
Brobury
B4352
Preston on Wye
13
HEREFORD
Holmer
Wester Beggar

D
MOCCAS PARK
Bridge Sollers
A438
THE WEIR
Swainshill
King's Acre
Hagley
Lugwardine
Bartestree
A438
ARTHUR'S STONE
Moccas
Canon Bridge
Breinton Common
Upper Breinton
CIDER MUSEUM
Hereford
Tupsley
Dormi
Dorstone
Snodhill
Blakemere
Ploughfield
Lulham
Breinton
Ruckhall
Lower Bullingham
ROTHERWAS
Hampton Bishop
77
Tyberton
THE FLITS
Madley
Eaton Bishop
B4352
B4349
Grafton
Dinedor
Mordiford
Llanrosser
Peterchurch
Shenmore
Cublington
Clehonger
Portway
Twyford Common
Holme Lacy
Urishay Common
Vowchurch
Brampton
B4349
Kingstone
Allensmore
A49
B4399
Upper Maes-coed
Turnastone
B4348
Hinton
Thruxton
Callow
Aconbury
Fownhope
B4224
Michaelchurch Escley
St Margaret's
Kerry's Gate
Cockyard
Winnal
A465
Dewshall Court
Kivernoll
King's Thorn
Little Birch
Bolstone
Middle Maes-coed
Newton
Bacton
Didley
Little Dewchurch
Carey
Ballingham
Lower Maes-coed
Wormbridge
St Devereux
12
Much Dewchurch
Much Birch
Fawley Chapel
eynoe
ABBEY DORE COURT
Kilpeck
A466
Wormelow Tump
Hoarwithy
Foy
Abbey Dore
Howton
61
PECK CASTLE (REMS) & CH'CH
2
Orcop Hill
B4348
Llandinabo
62
King's Caple
Ewyas
Ed Rail

Golden Valley
Lugg
Arrow
Wye

0   1   2   3 miles
0   1   2   3   4   5 km

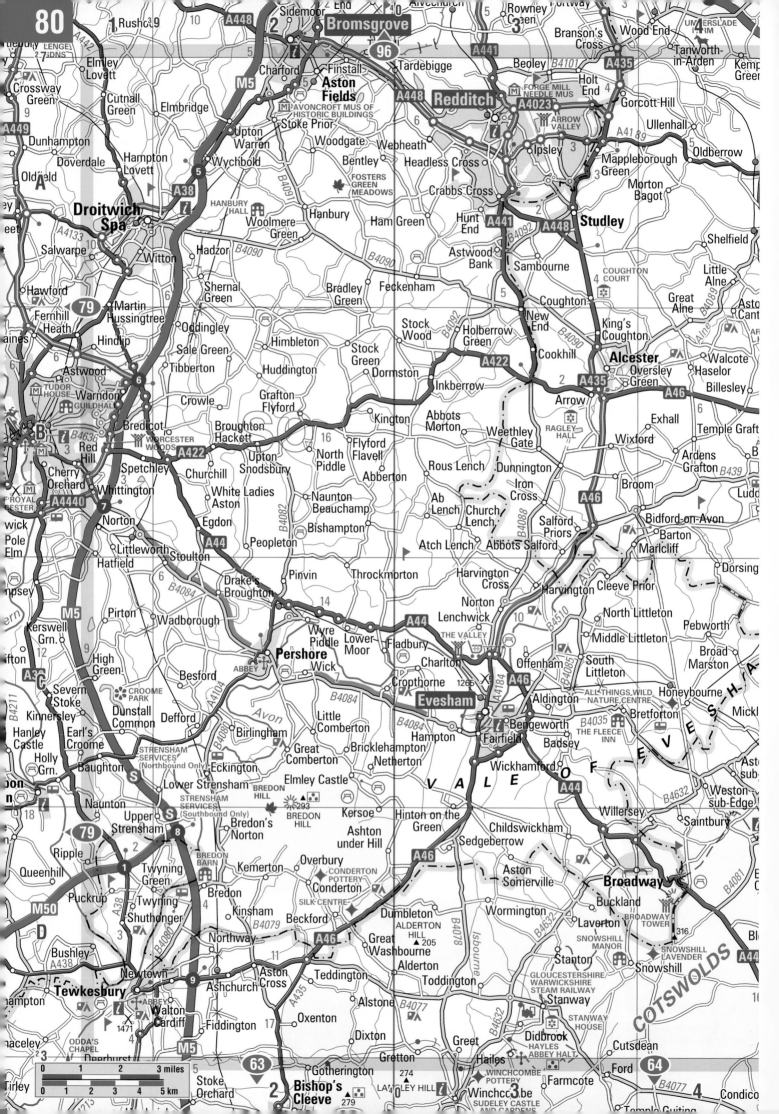

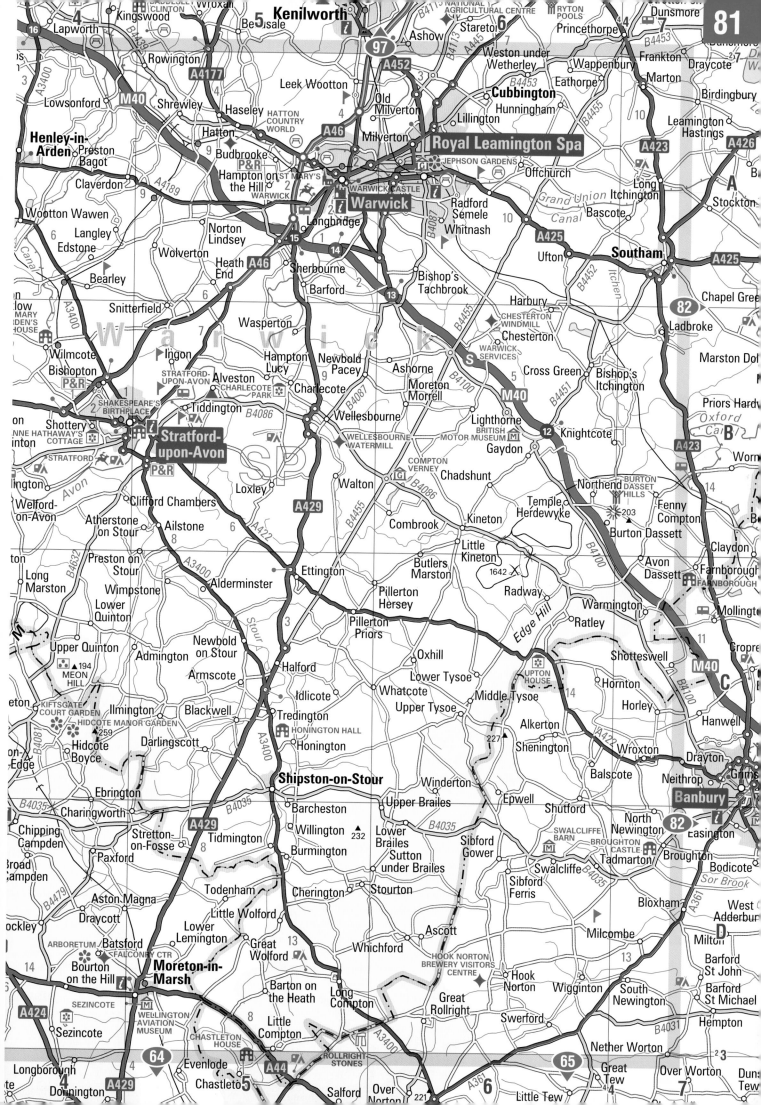

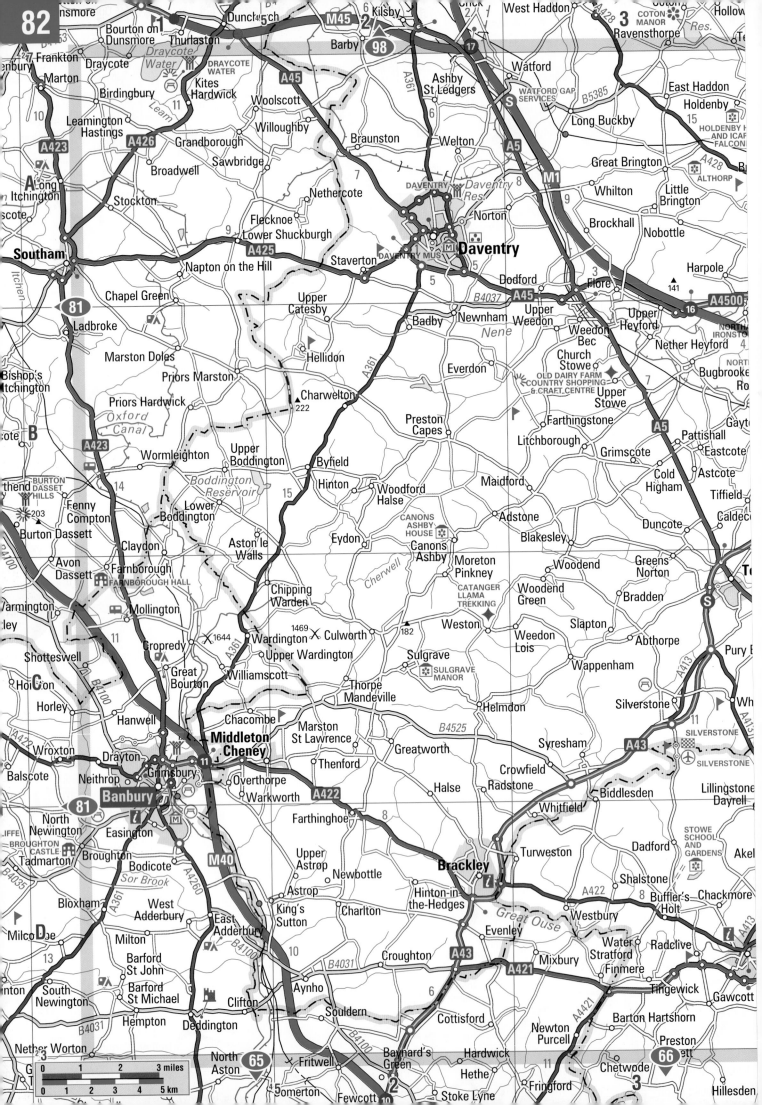

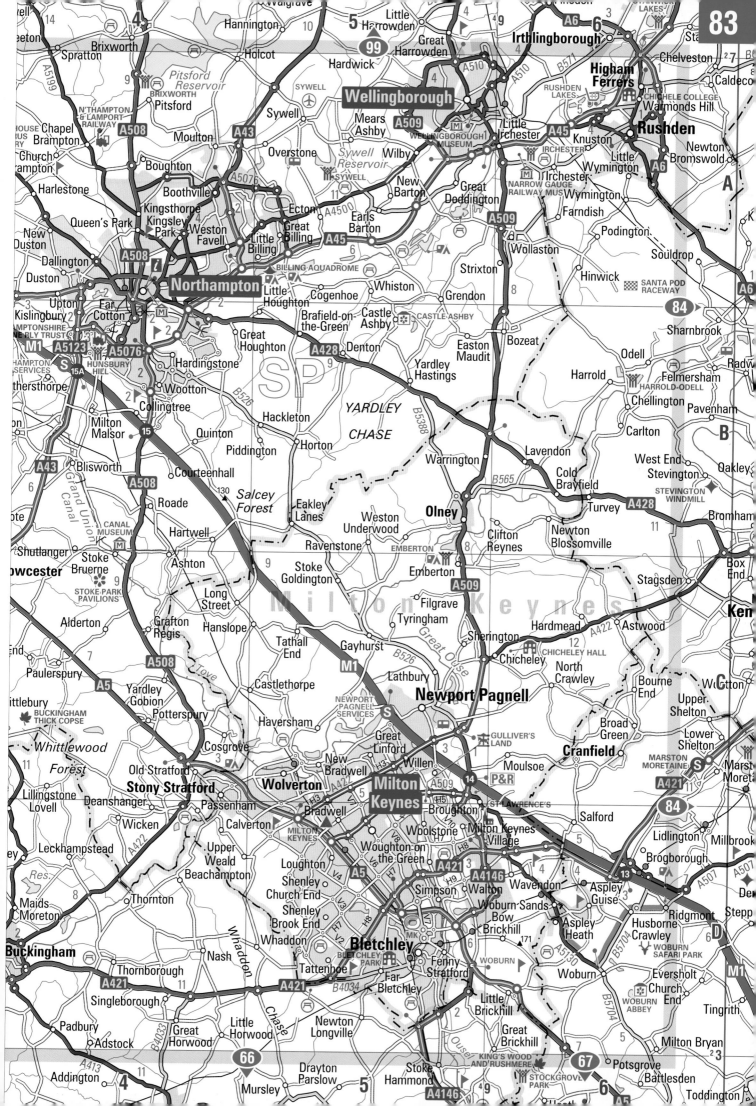

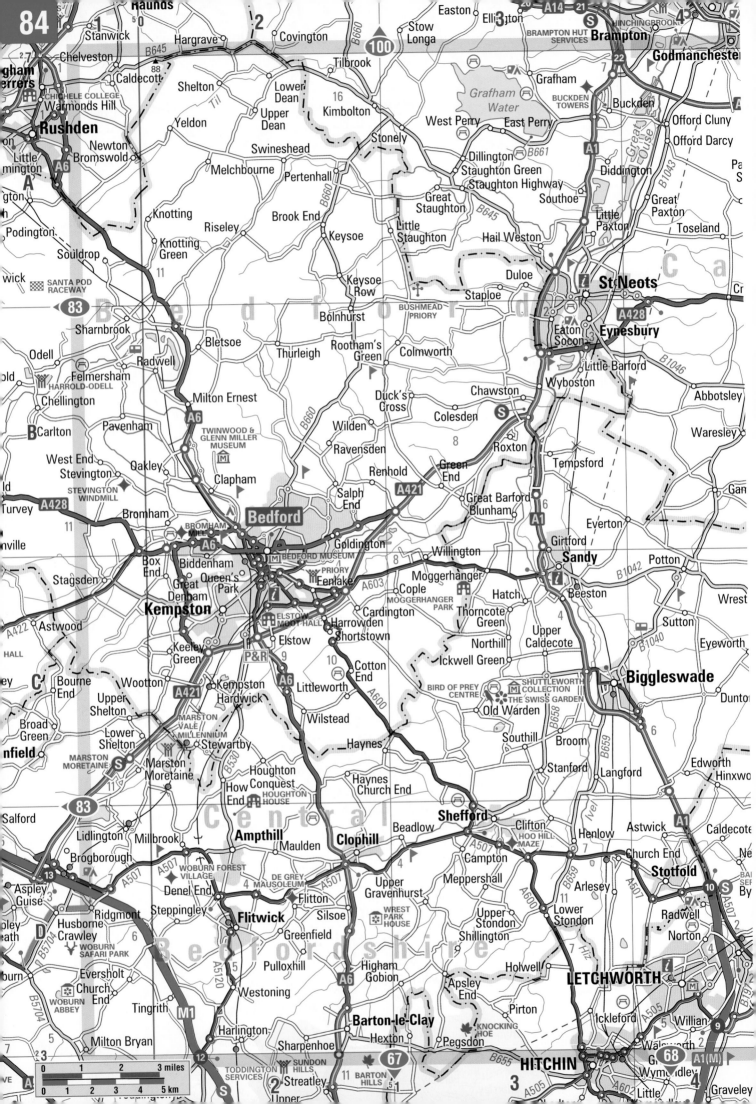

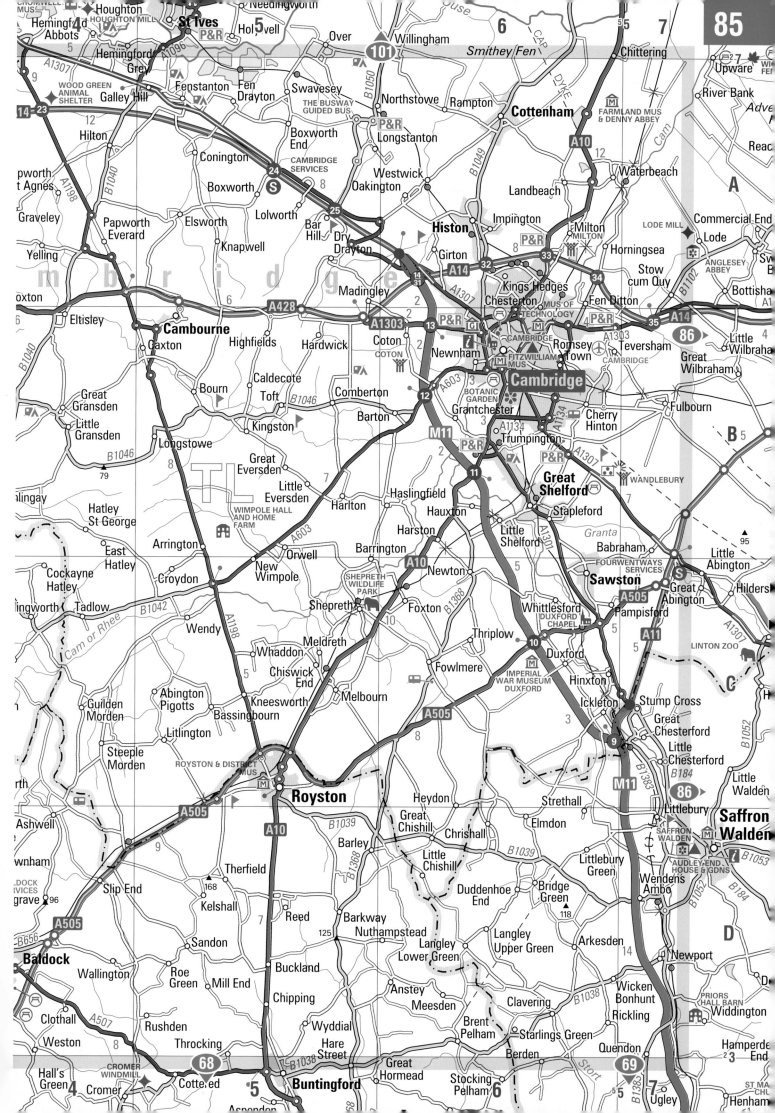

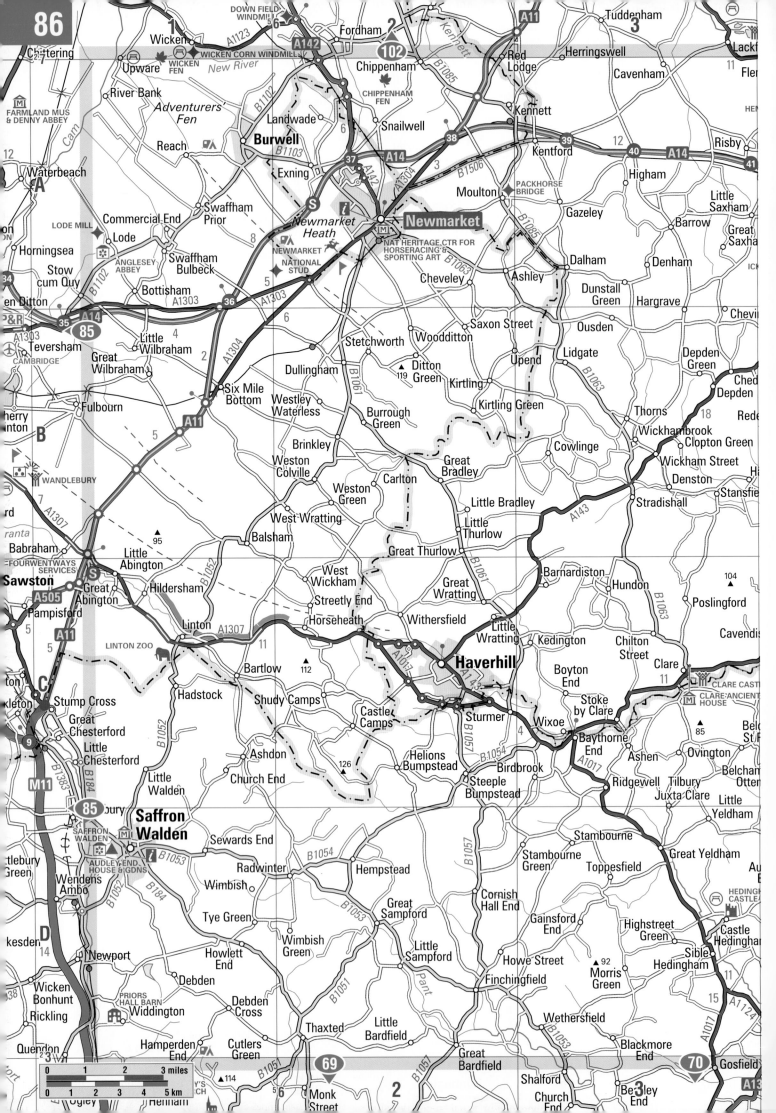

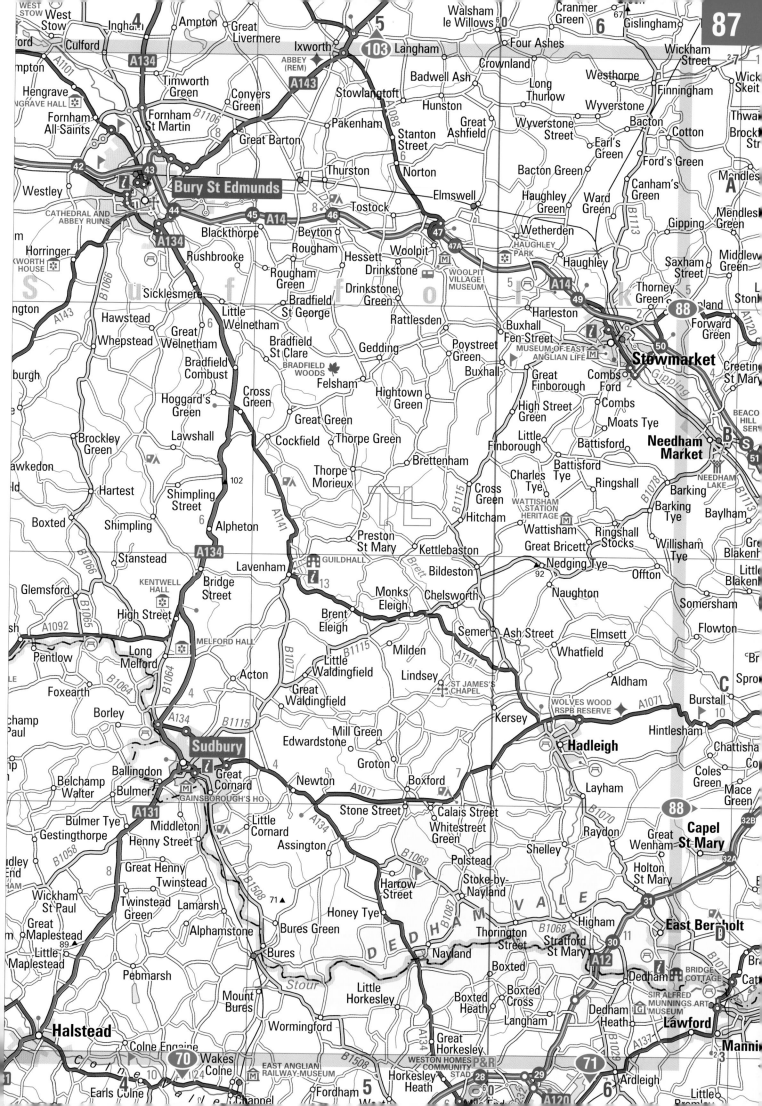

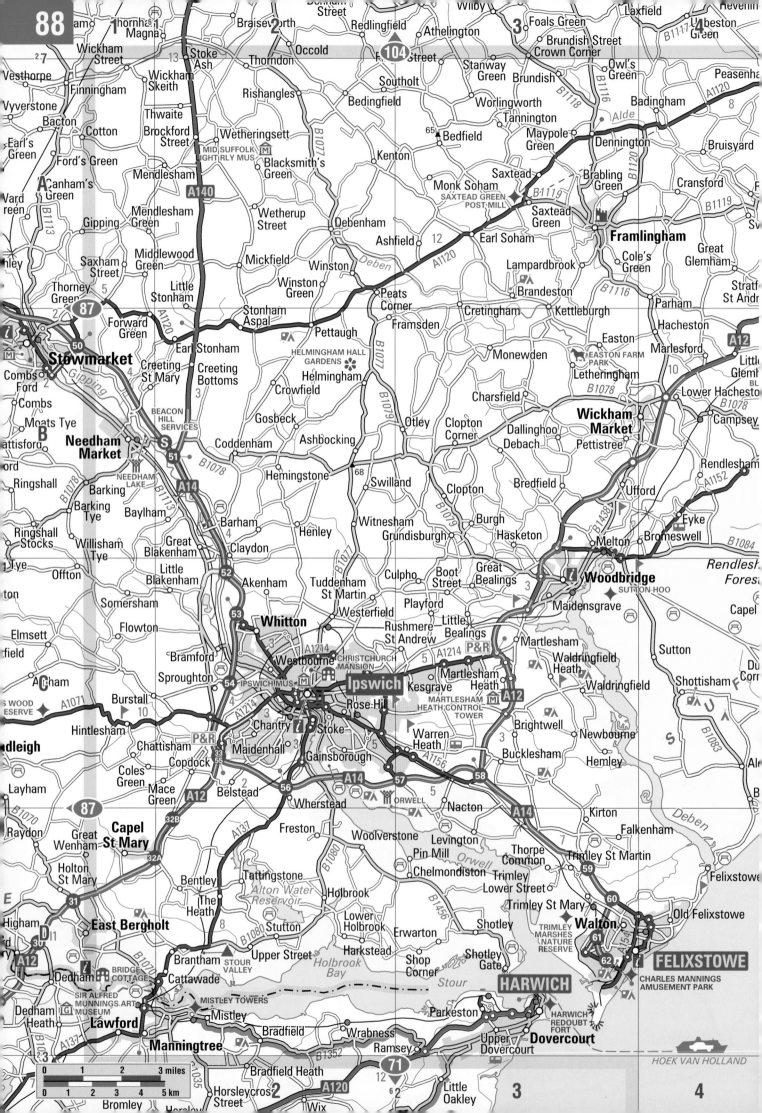

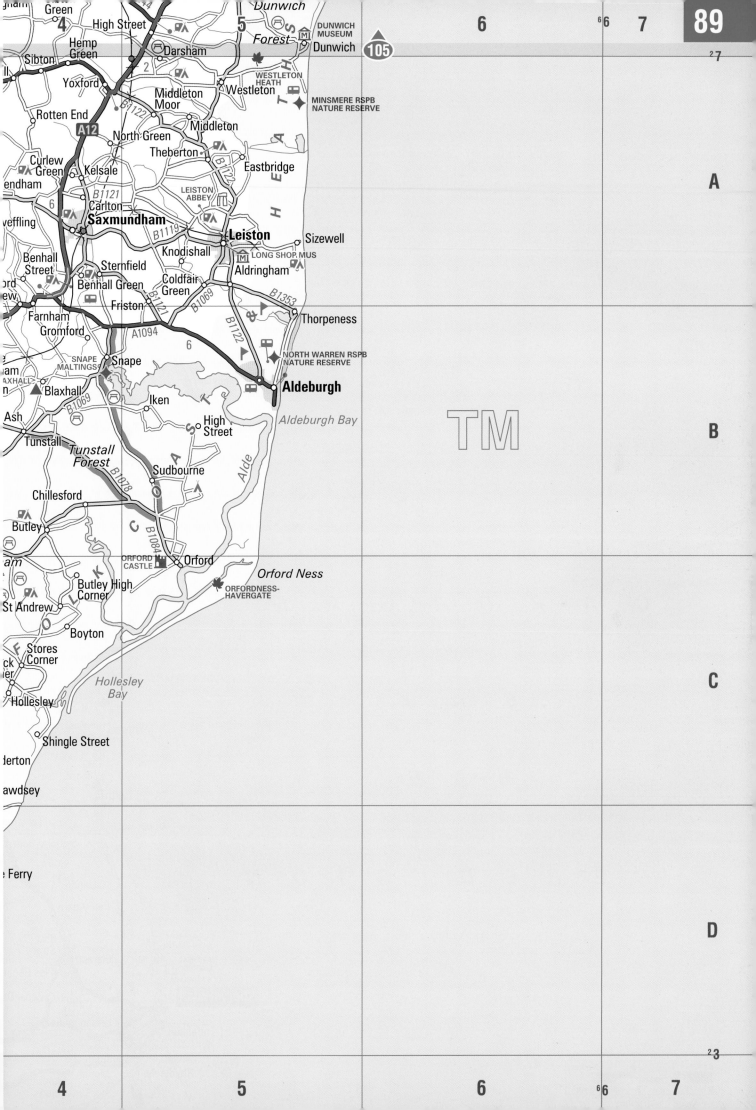

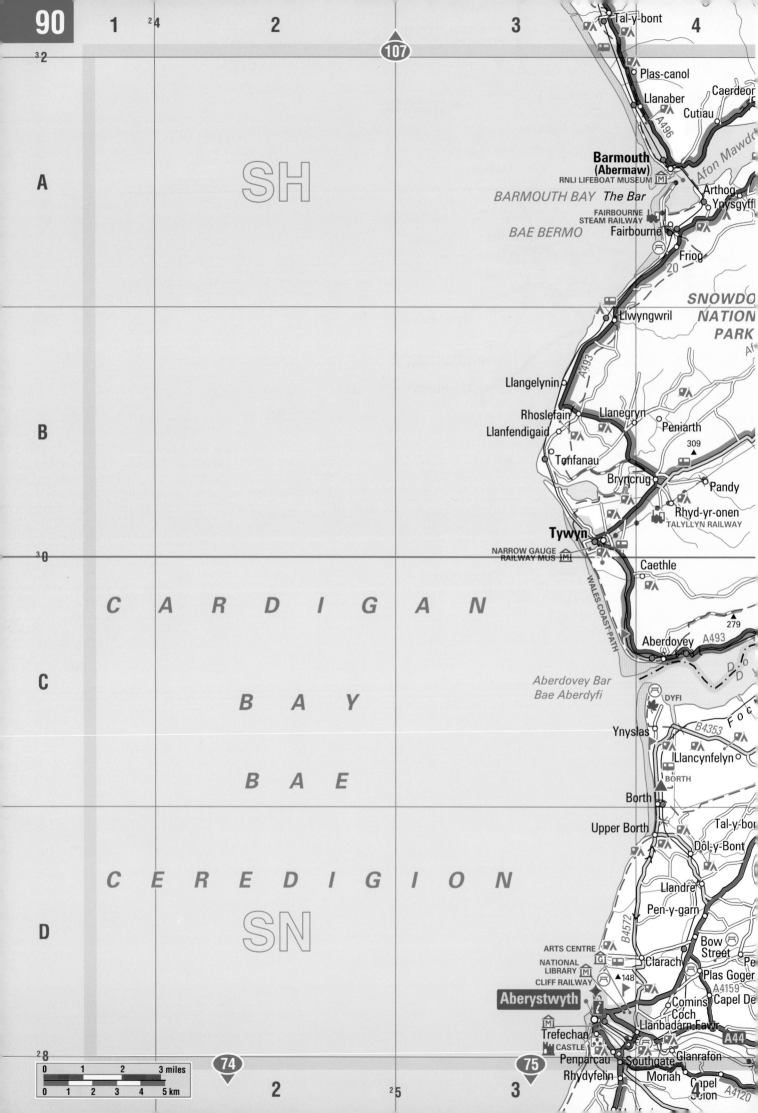

SH

CARDIGAN

BAY

BAE

CEREDIGION

SN

Tal-y-bont
Plas-canol
Llanaber   Caerdeor
           Cutiau
Barmouth
(Abermaw)
RNLI LIFEBOAT MUSEUM
BARMOUTH BAY   The Bar   Arthog
FAIRBOURNE   Ynysgyffl
STEAM RAILWAY
BAE BERMO   Fairbourne
                  Friog
                  20

SNOWDO
NATION
PARK
Llwyngwril

Llangelynin

Rhoslefain   Llanegryn   Peniarth
Llanfendigaid   309

Tonfanau

Bryncrug   Pandy
                Rhyd-yr-onen
Tywyn   TALYLLYN RAILWAY
NARROW GAUGE
RAILWAY MUS
               Caethle

               279
Aberdovey   A493
Aberdovey Bar
Bae Aberdyfi
              DYFI
Ynyslas   B4353

              Llancynfelyn
              BORTH
Borth

Upper Borth   Tal-y-bor
               Dôl-y-Bont

               Llandre
               Pen-y-garn

ARTS CENTRE   Bow
NATIONAL   Clarach   Street
LIBRARY
CLIFF RAILWAY   148   Plas Goger
                       A4159
Aberystwyth
                Comins Capel De
                Coch
                Llanbadarn-Fawr
Trefechan   A44
CASTLE
Penparcau   Southgate Glanrafon
Rhydyfelin   Moriah   Capel
                       A4120

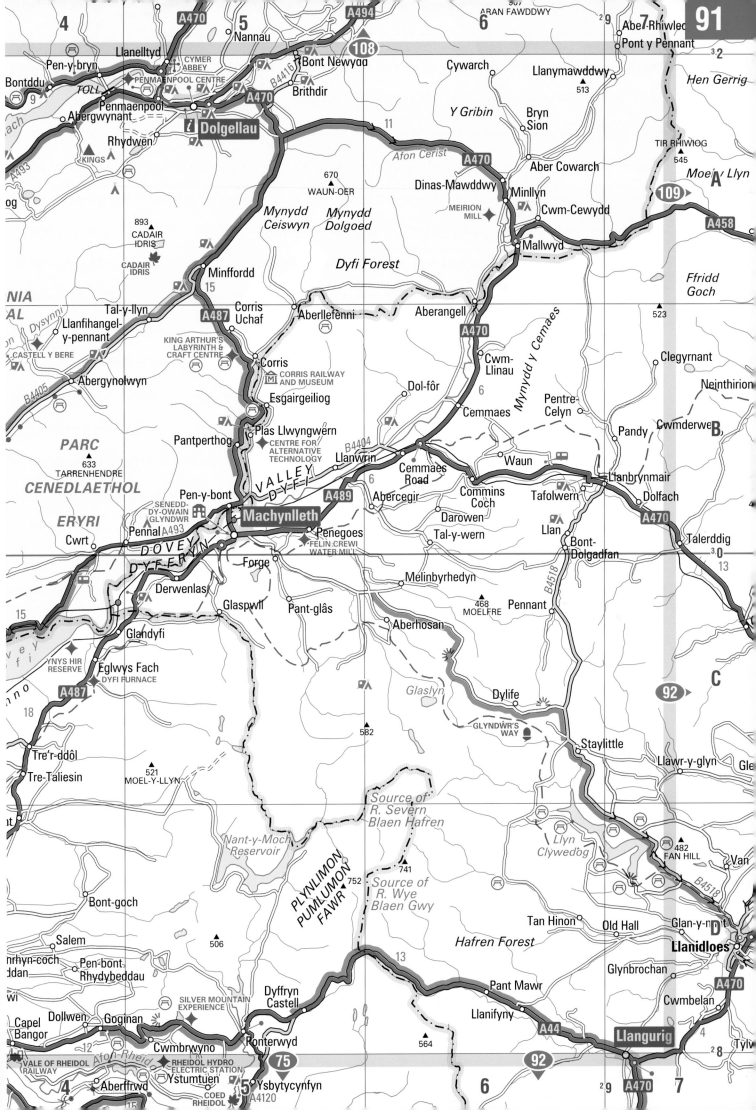

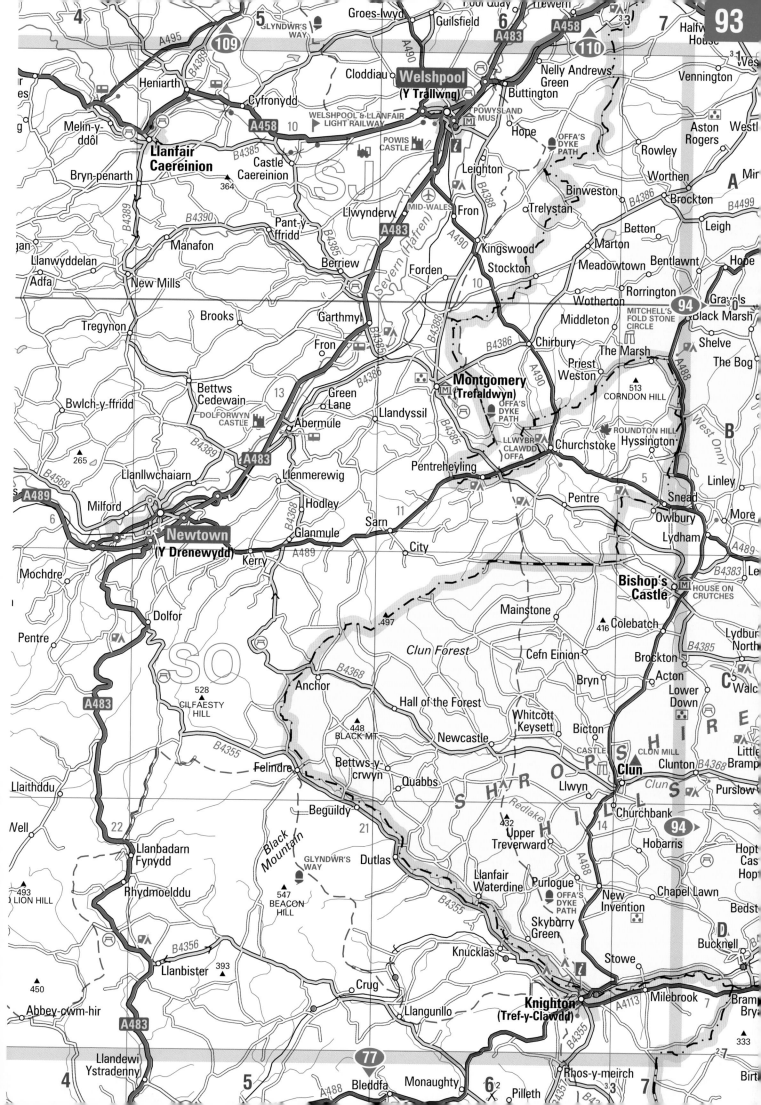

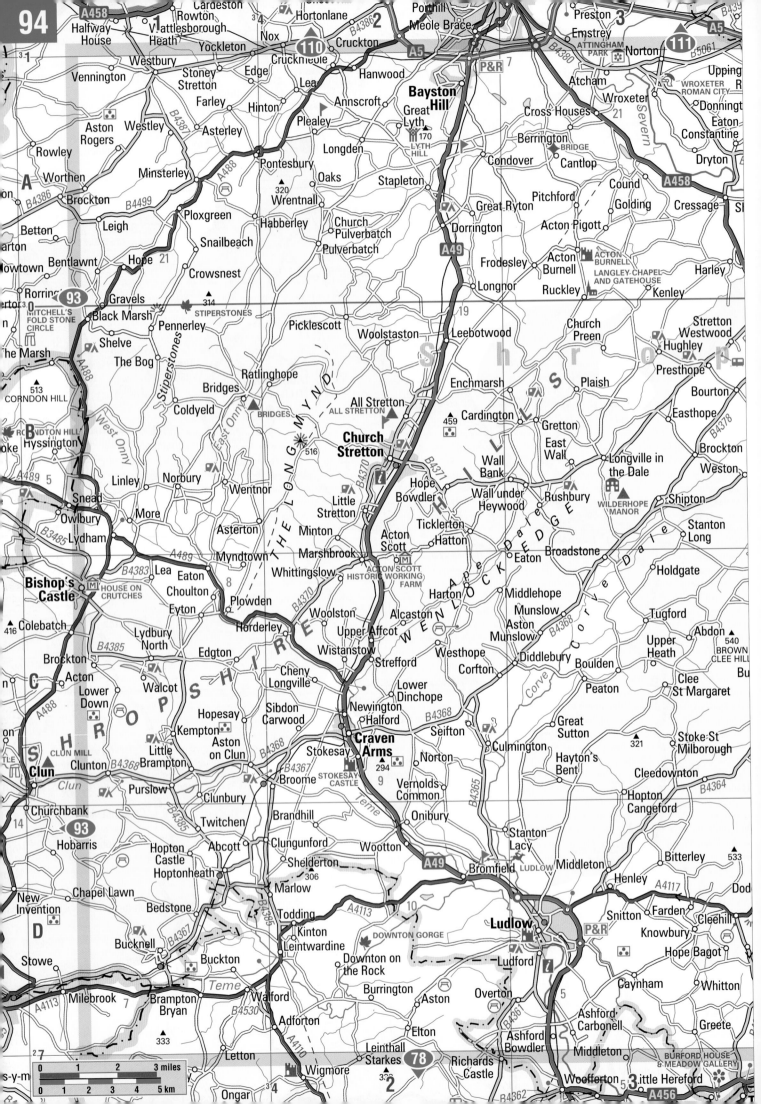

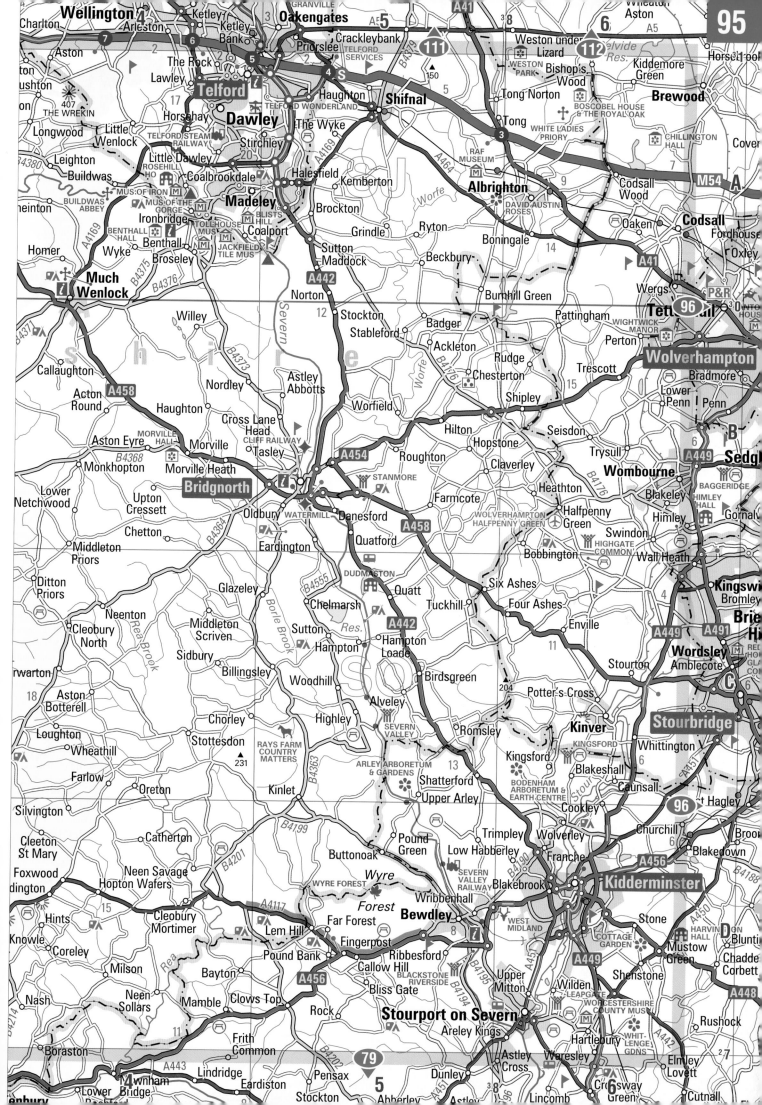

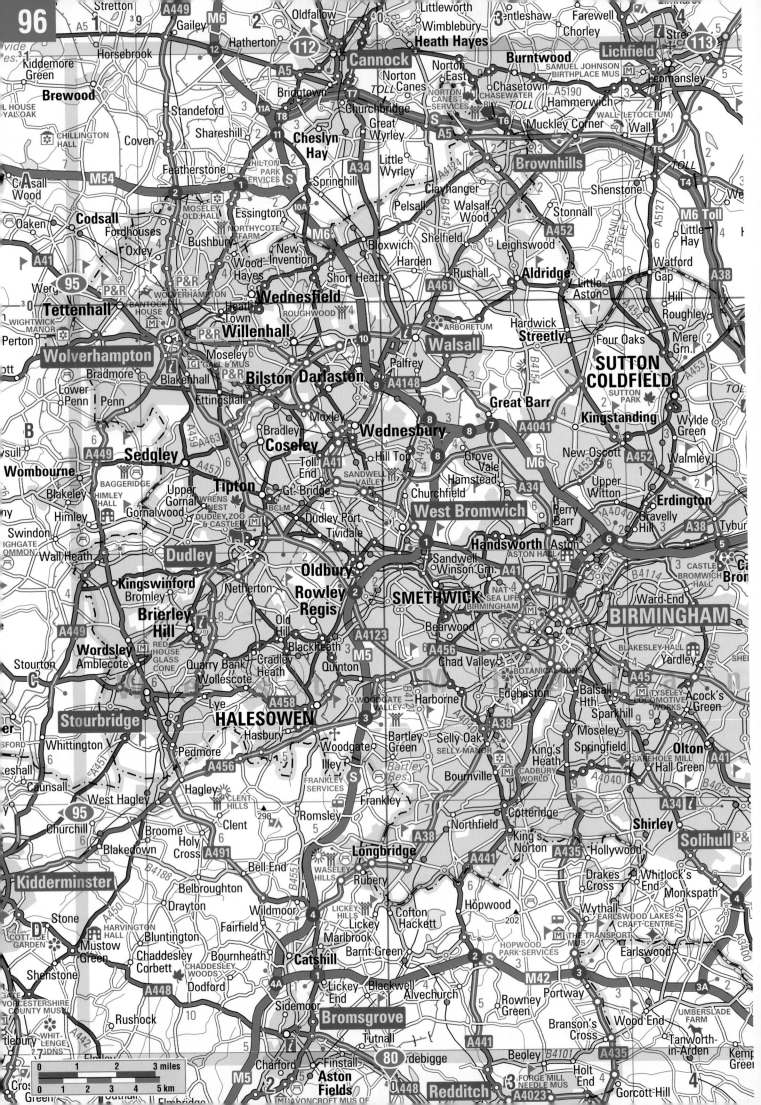

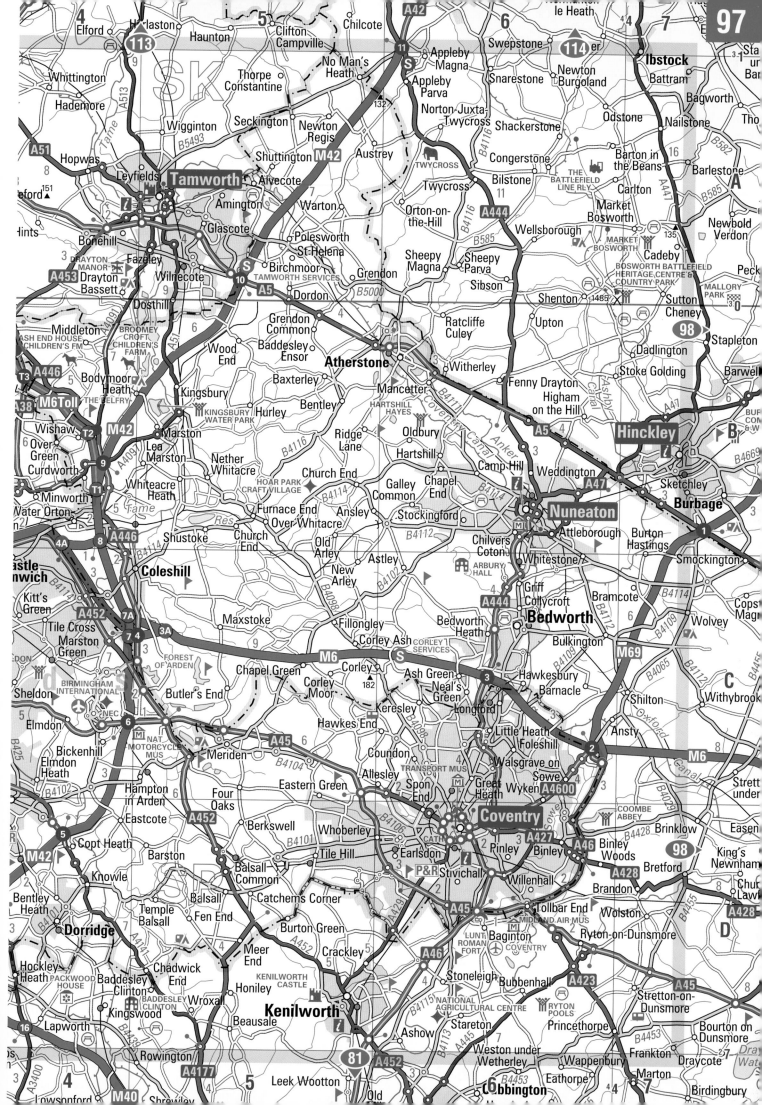

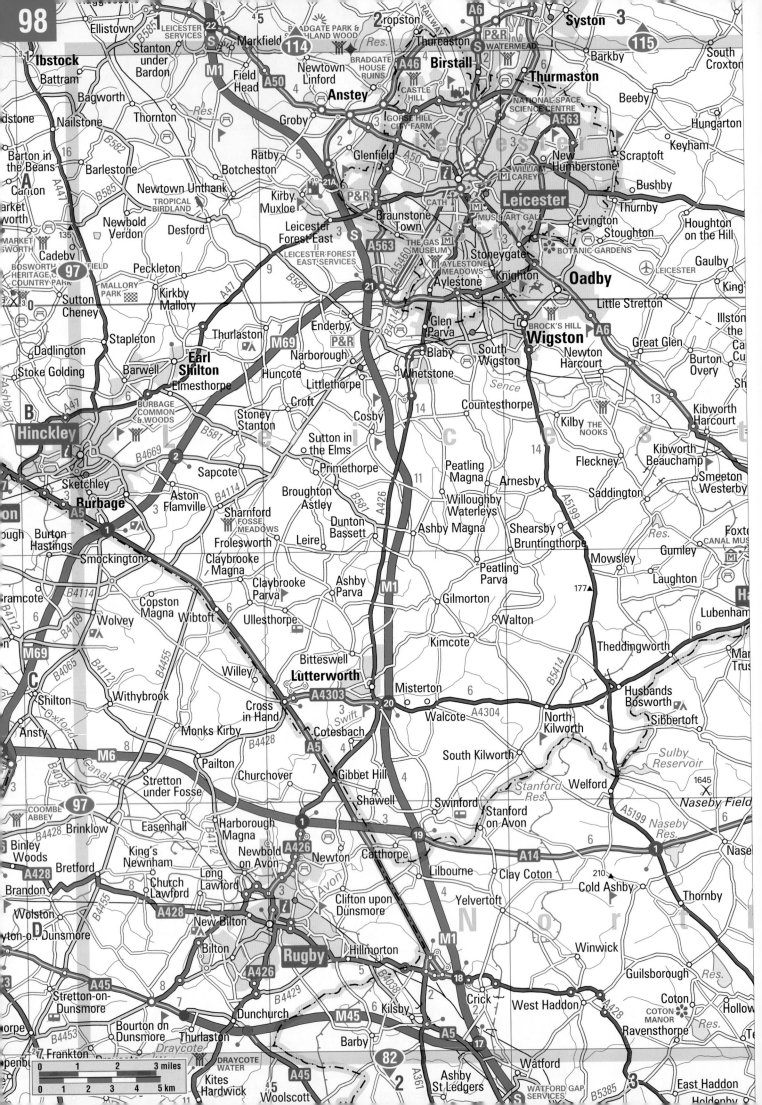

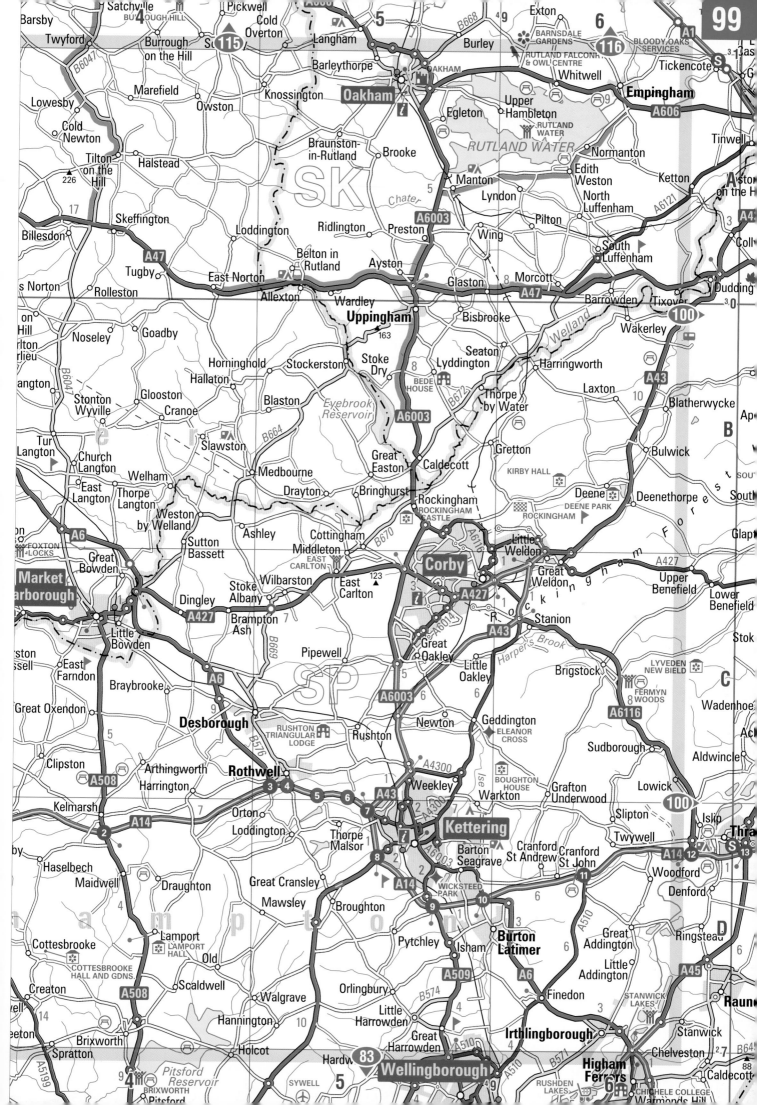

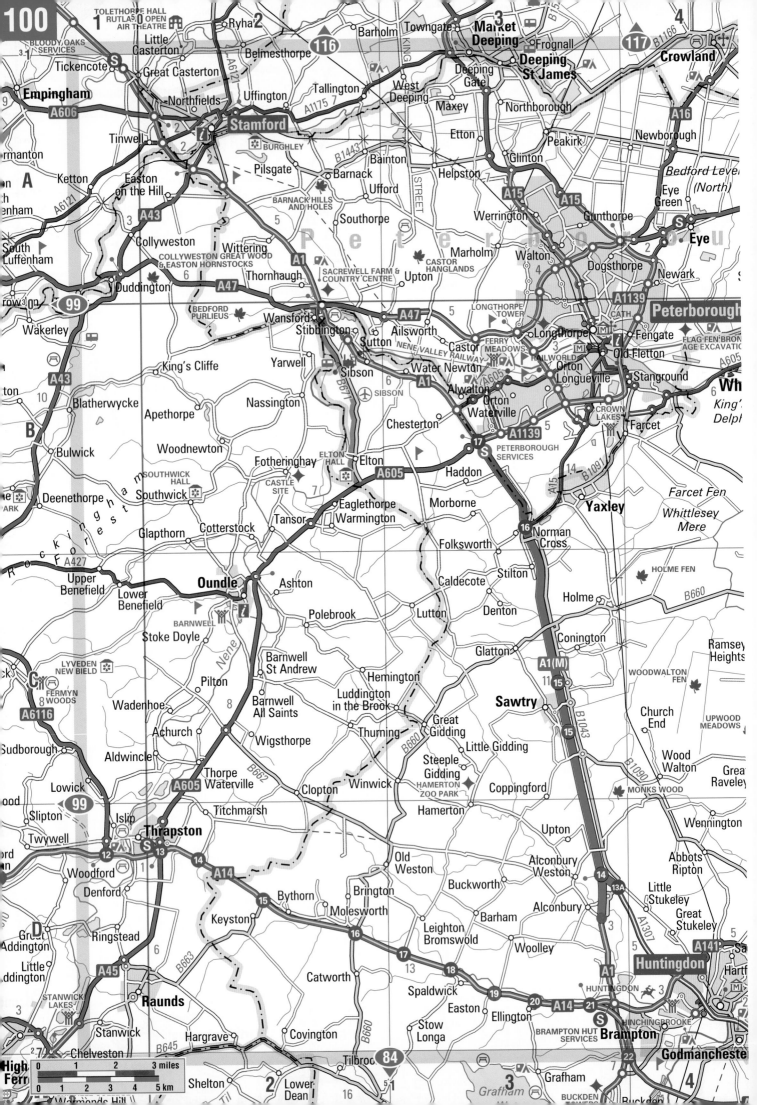

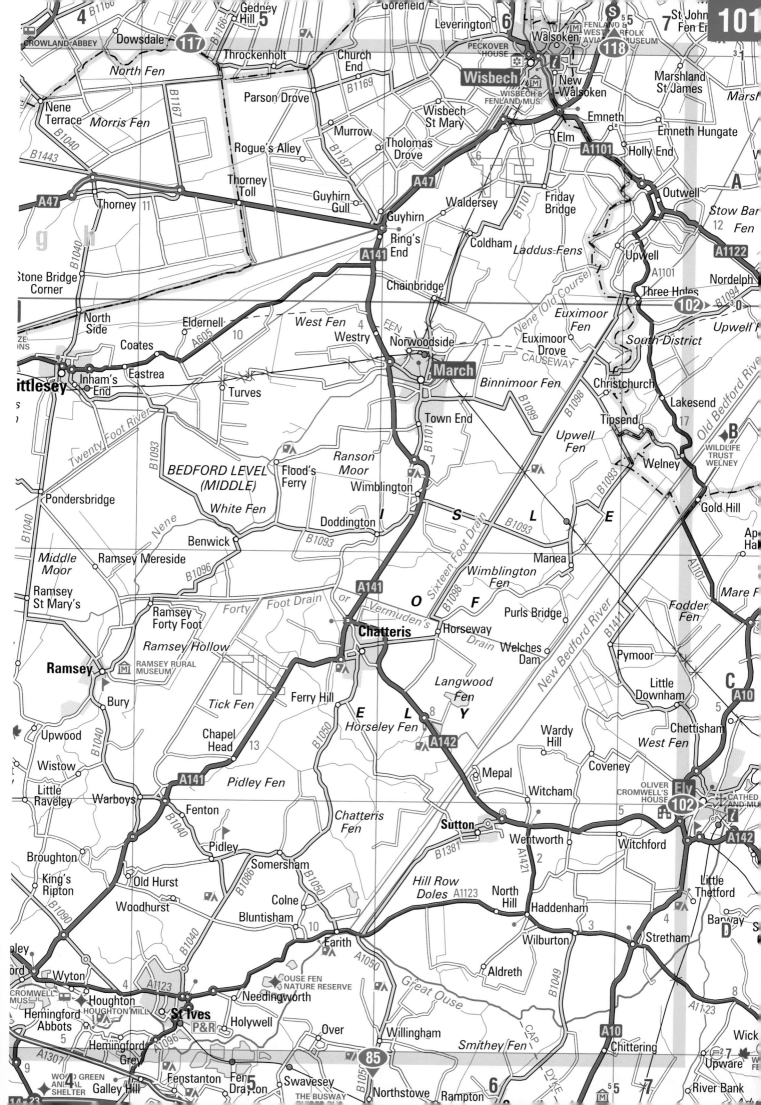

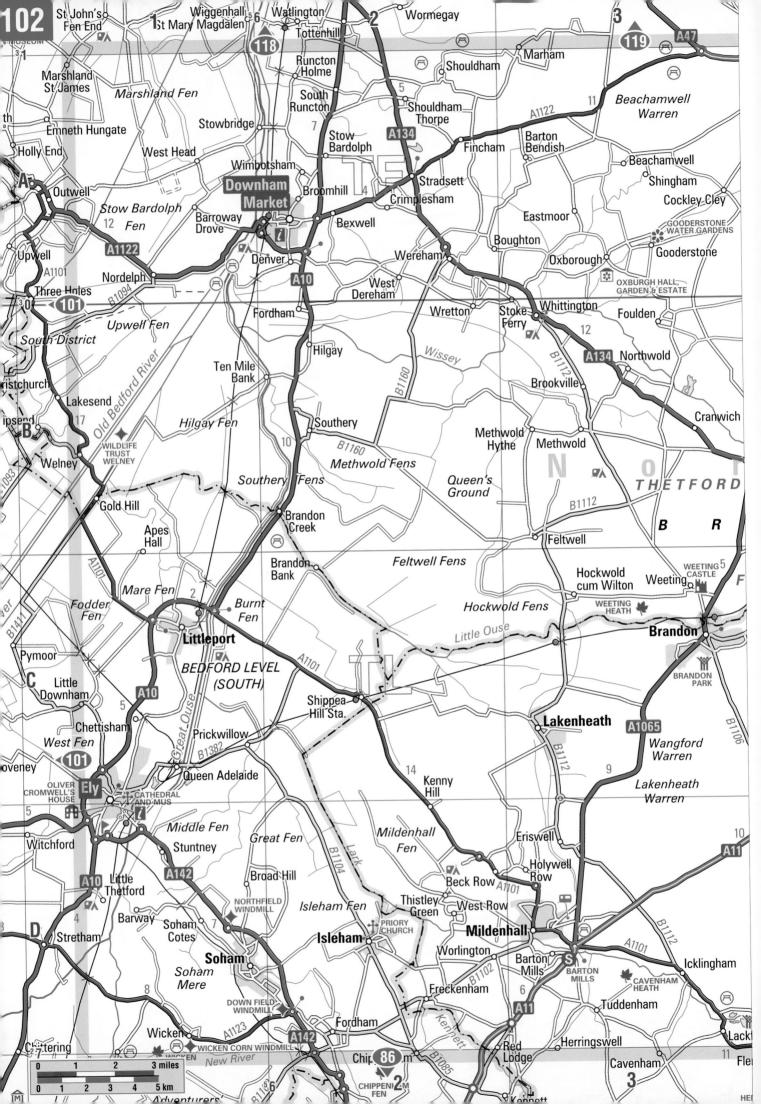

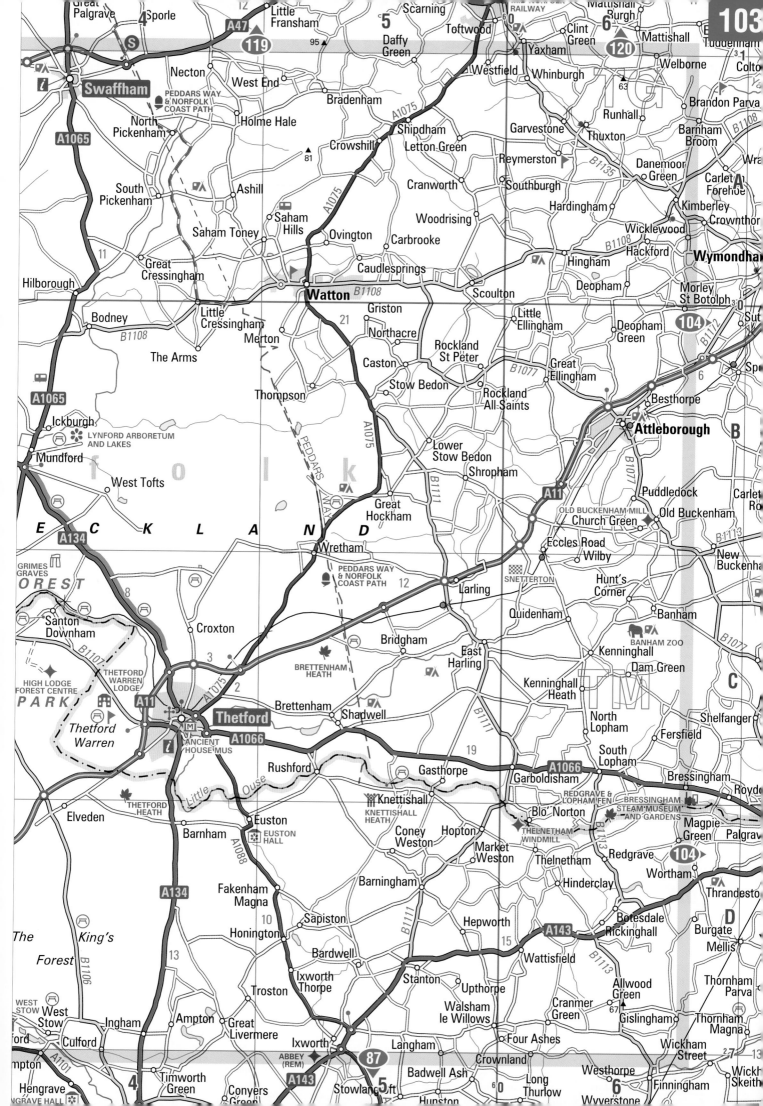

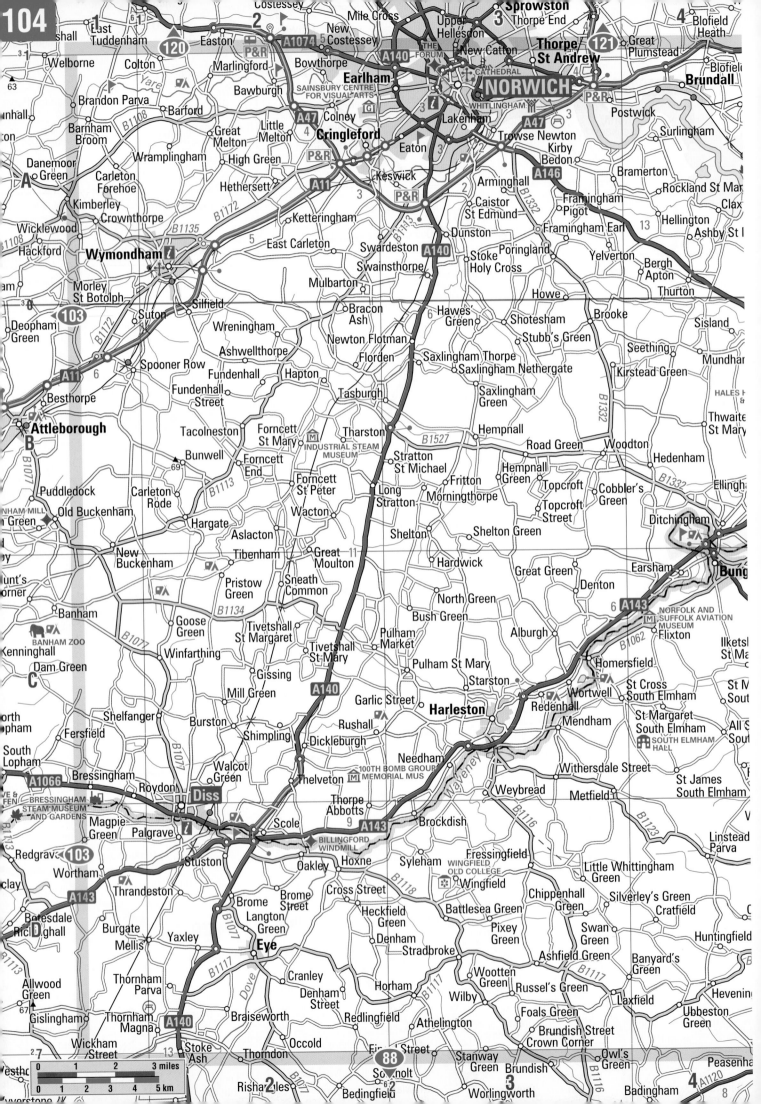

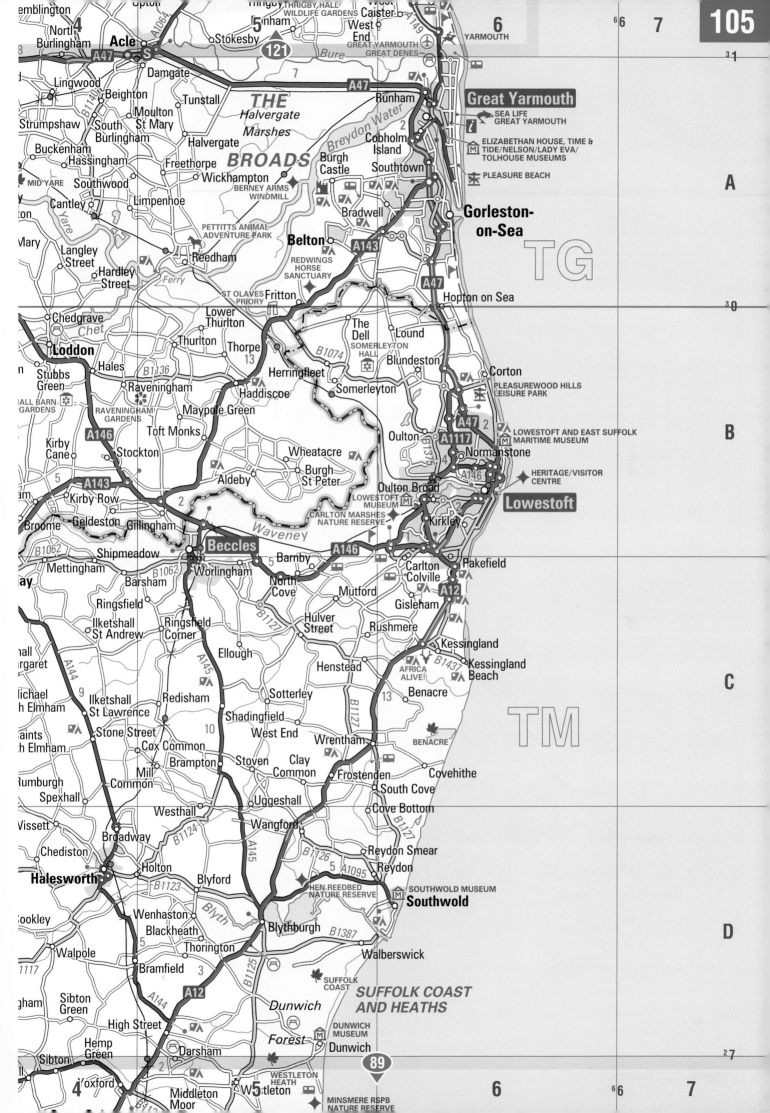

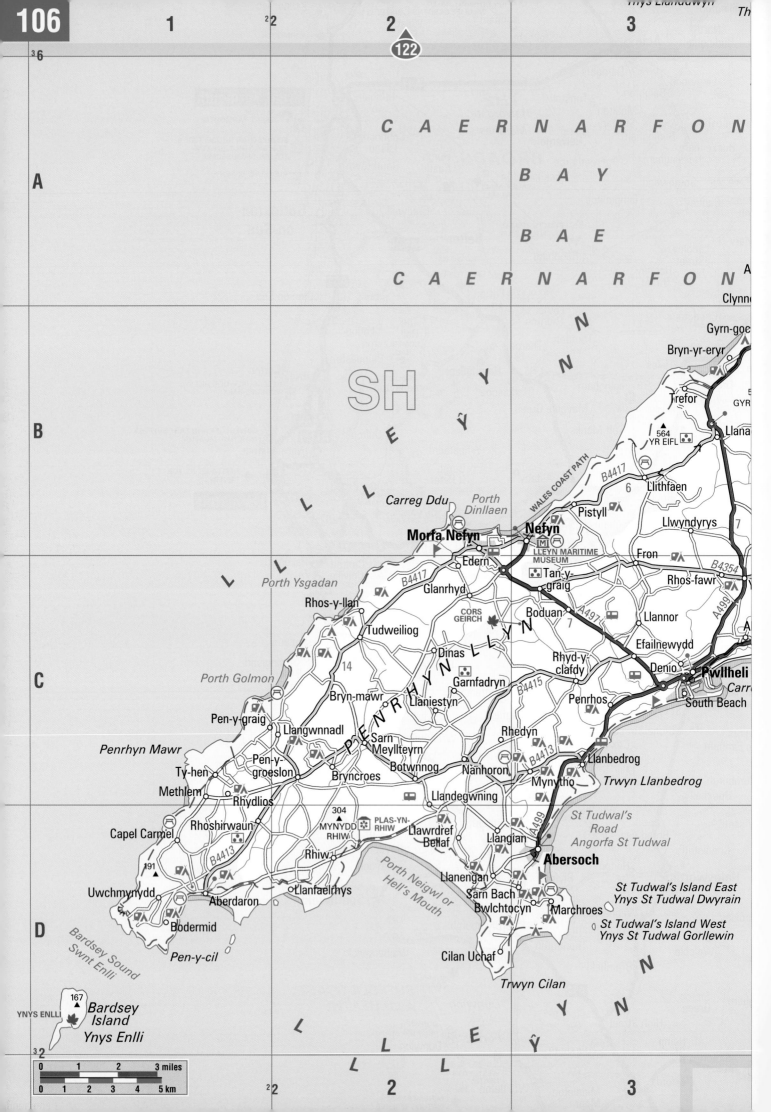

1 **2** **2** **3**

A

CAERNARFON BAY

BAE CAERNARFON

Clynno

Gyrn-goc

Bryn-yr-eryr

SH

Trefor

GYR

B

564 YR EIFL

Llana

Ynys Llanddwyn

Th

122

L L E Ŷ N

B4417

6

Llithfaen

Llwyndyrys

7

Carreg Ddu *Porth Dinllaen* Pistyll

Morfa Nefyn **Nefyn** Fron B4354

LLEYN MARITIME MUSEUM Rhos-fawr

Edern Tan-y-graig

B4417 Glanrhyd A497

Porth Ysgadan Boduan Llannor

Rhos-y-llan CORS GEIRCH Efailnewydd

Tudweiliog Rhyd-y-clafdy Denio **Pwllheli**

Dinas Carr

C *Porth Golmon* Garnfadryn B4415 Penrhos South Beach

14 Bryn-mawr Llaniestyn

Pen-y-graig Rhedyn 7

Llangwnnadl Sarn Llanbedrog

Penrhyn Mawr Meyllteyrn *Trwyn Llanbedrog*

Pen-y-groeslon Botwnnog Nanhoron Mynytho

Ty-hen Bryncroes *St Tudwal's*

Methlem Llandegwning *Road*

Rhydlios *Angorfa St Tudwal*

304 PLAS-YN-RHIW

Rhoshirwaun MYNYDD Llawrdref A499

Capel Carmel RHIW Bellaf Llangian

B4413 Rhiw **Abersoch**

191 *St Tudwal's Island East*

Uwchmynydd Llanengan *Ynys St Tudwal Dwyrain*

Llanfaelrhys Sarn Bach

D Bodermid *Porth Neigwl or* Bwlchtocyn Marchroes *St Tudwal's Island West*

Bardsey Sound *Hell's Mouth* *Ynys St Tudwal Gorllewin*

Swnt Enlli *Pen-y-cil*

Cilan Uchaf

167 *Trwyn Cilan*

YNYS ENLLI **Bardsey Island**

Ynys Enlli L L E Ŷ N

L L Ŷ

2 **2** **2** **3**

PENRHYN LLŶN

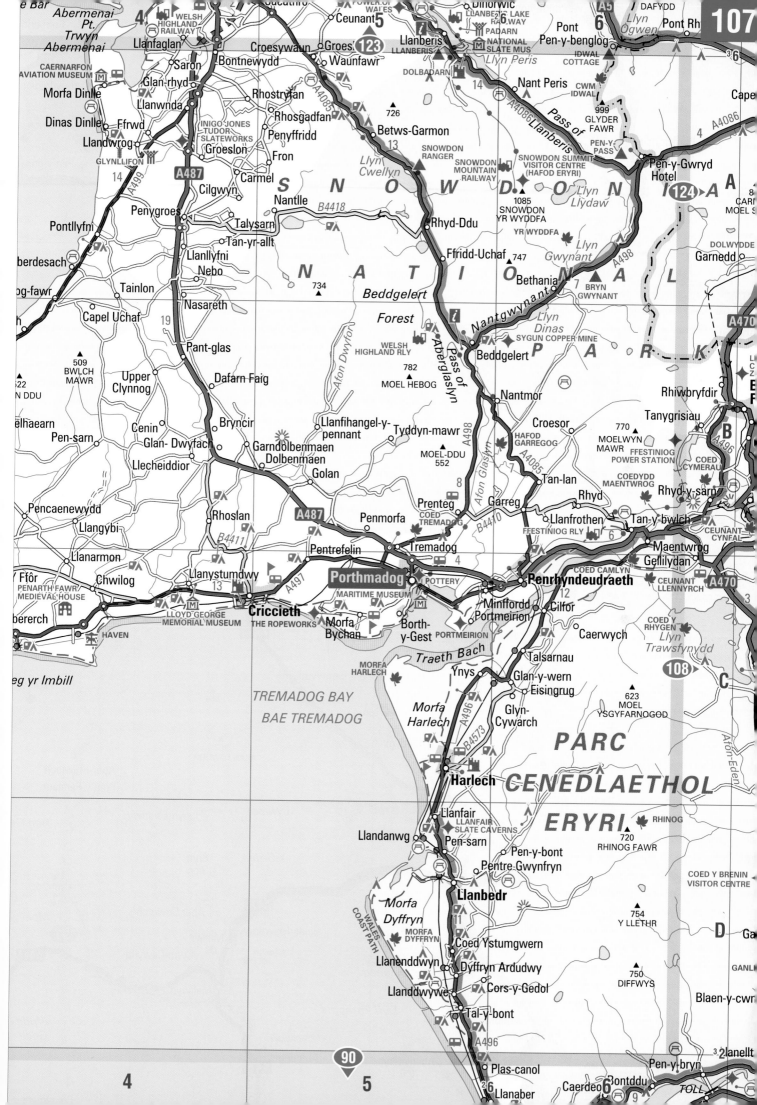

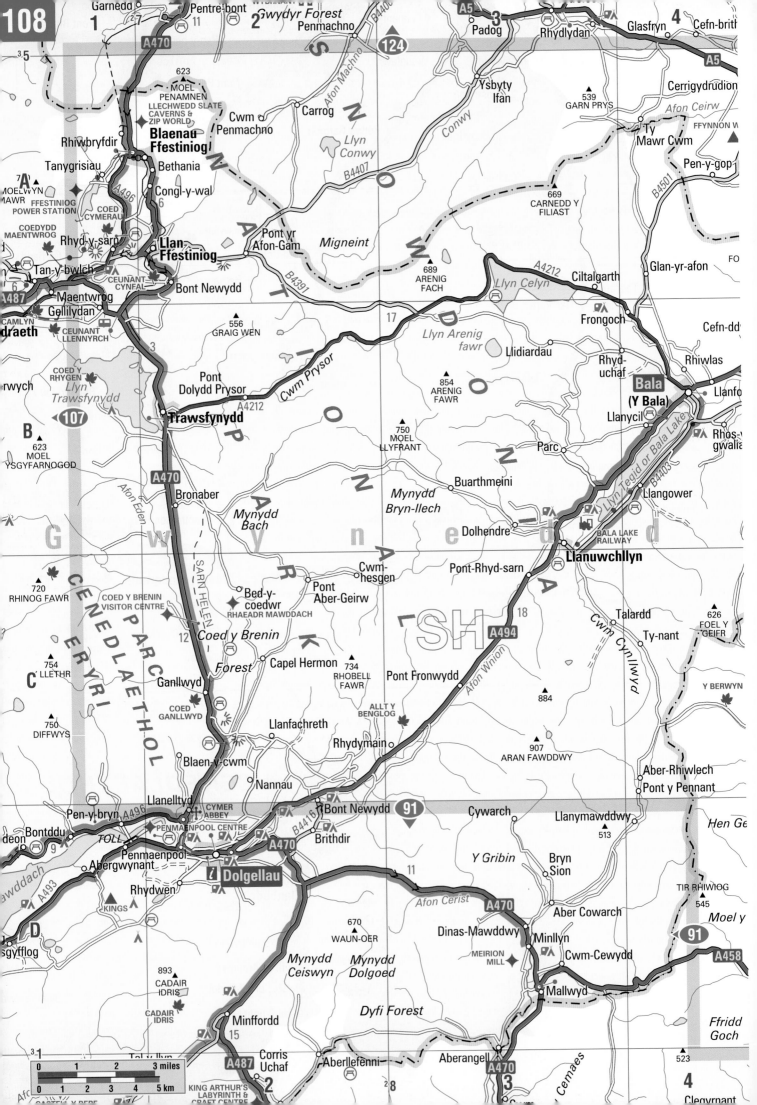

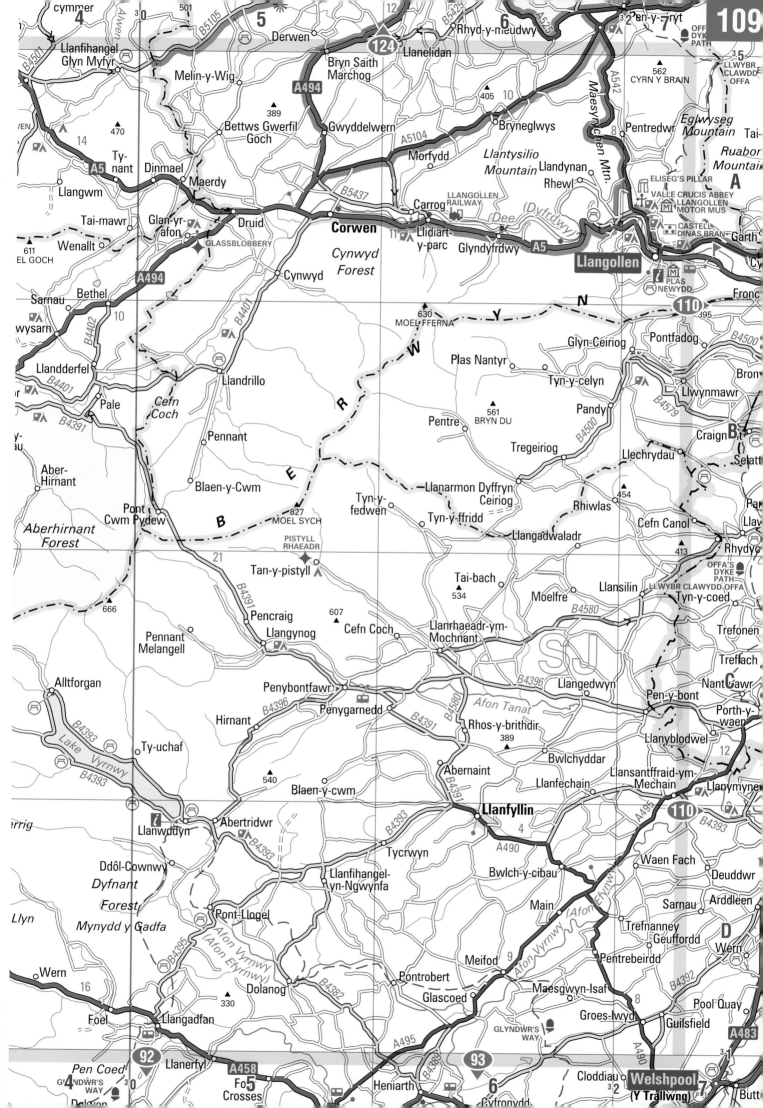

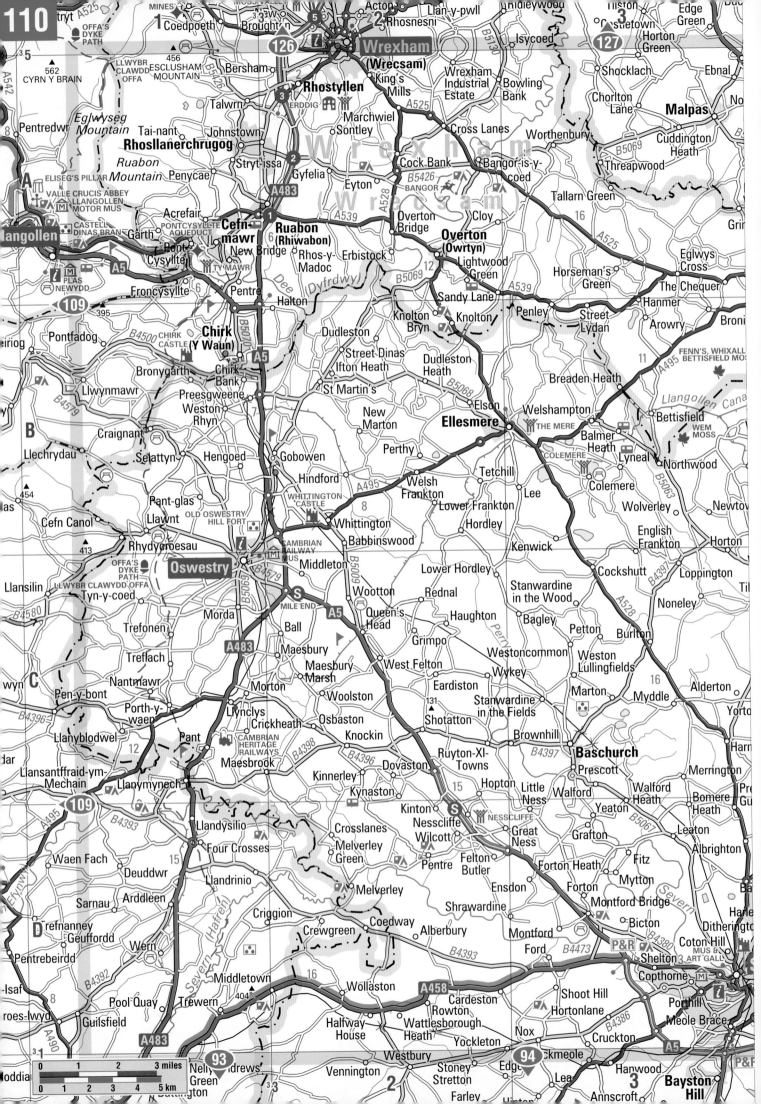

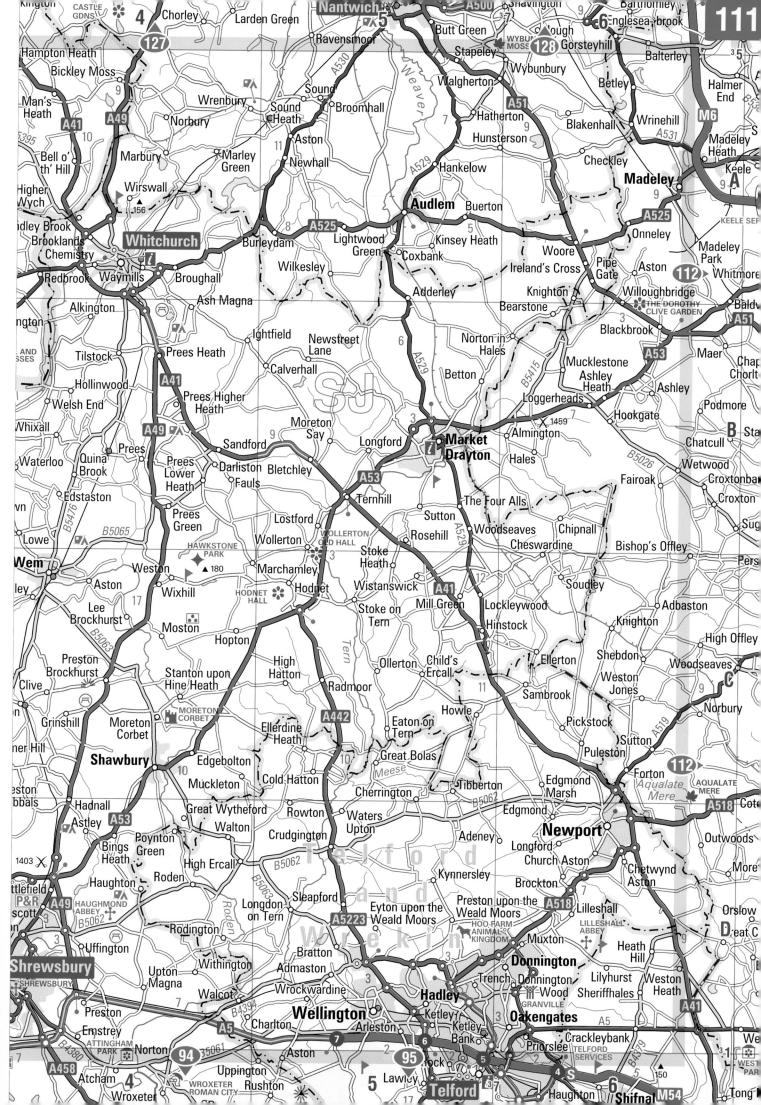

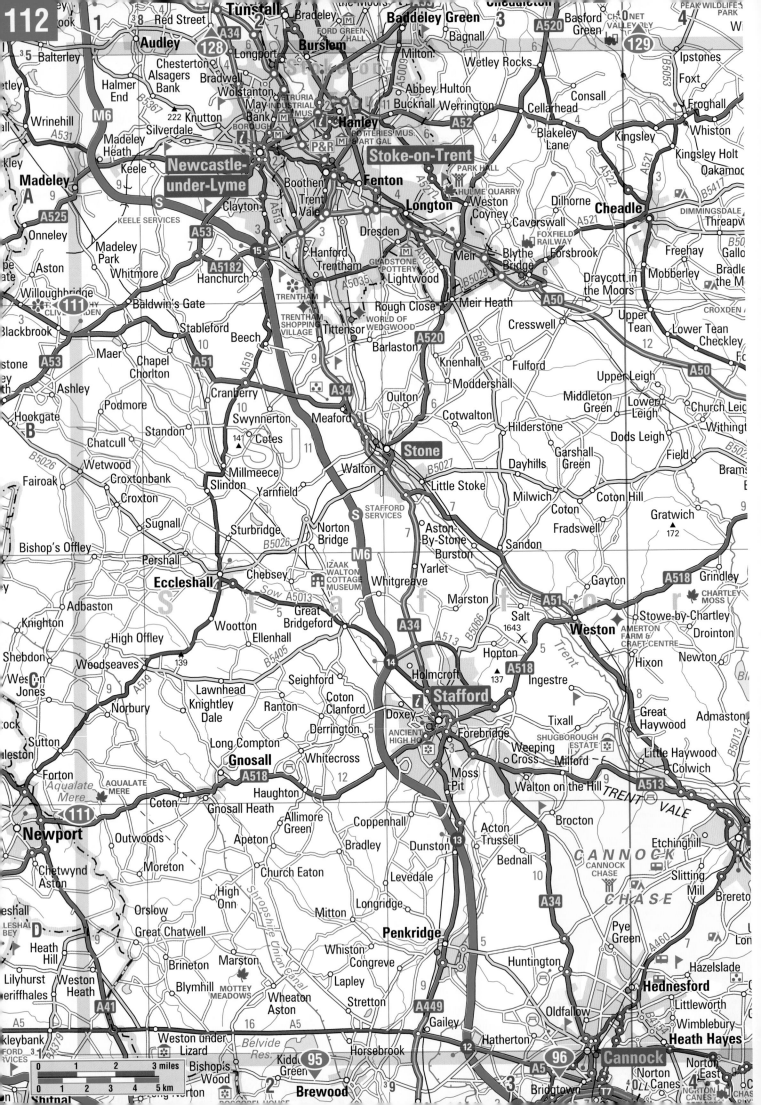

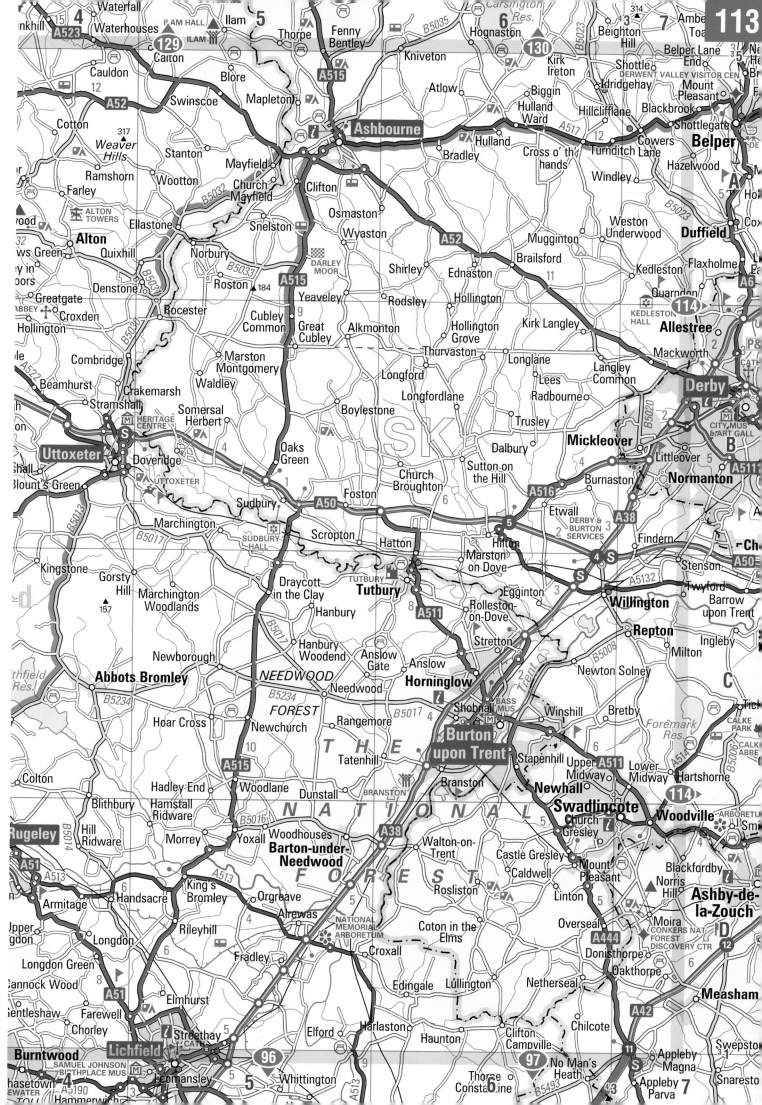

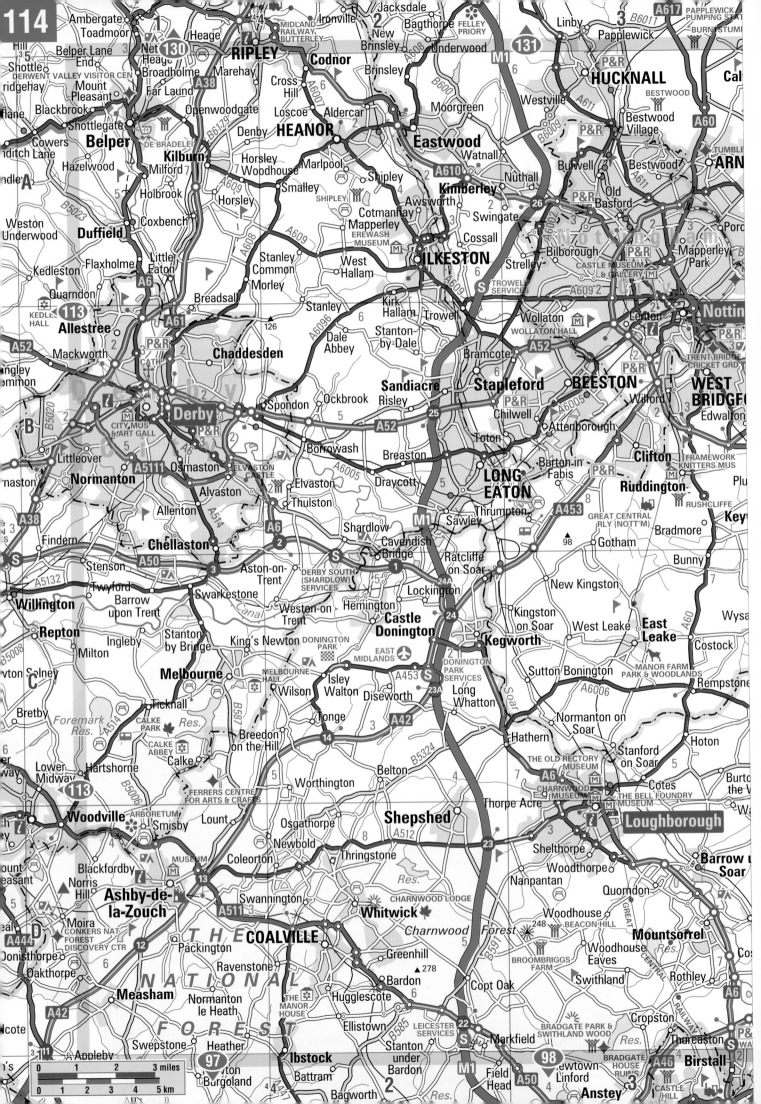

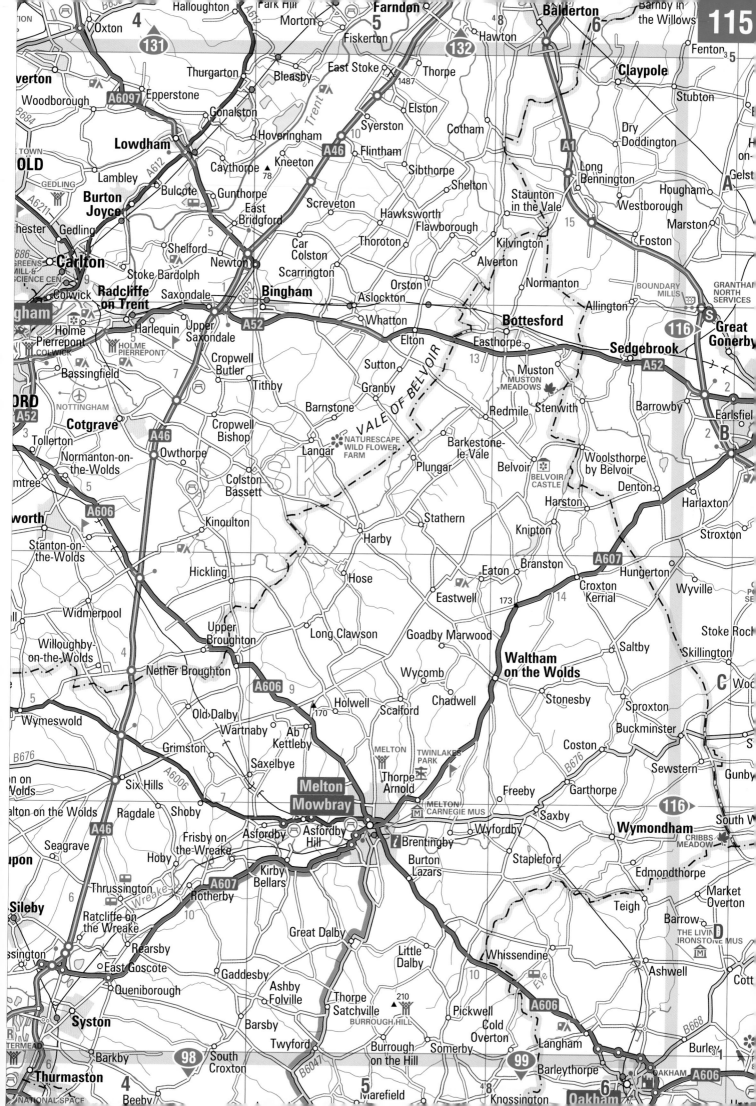

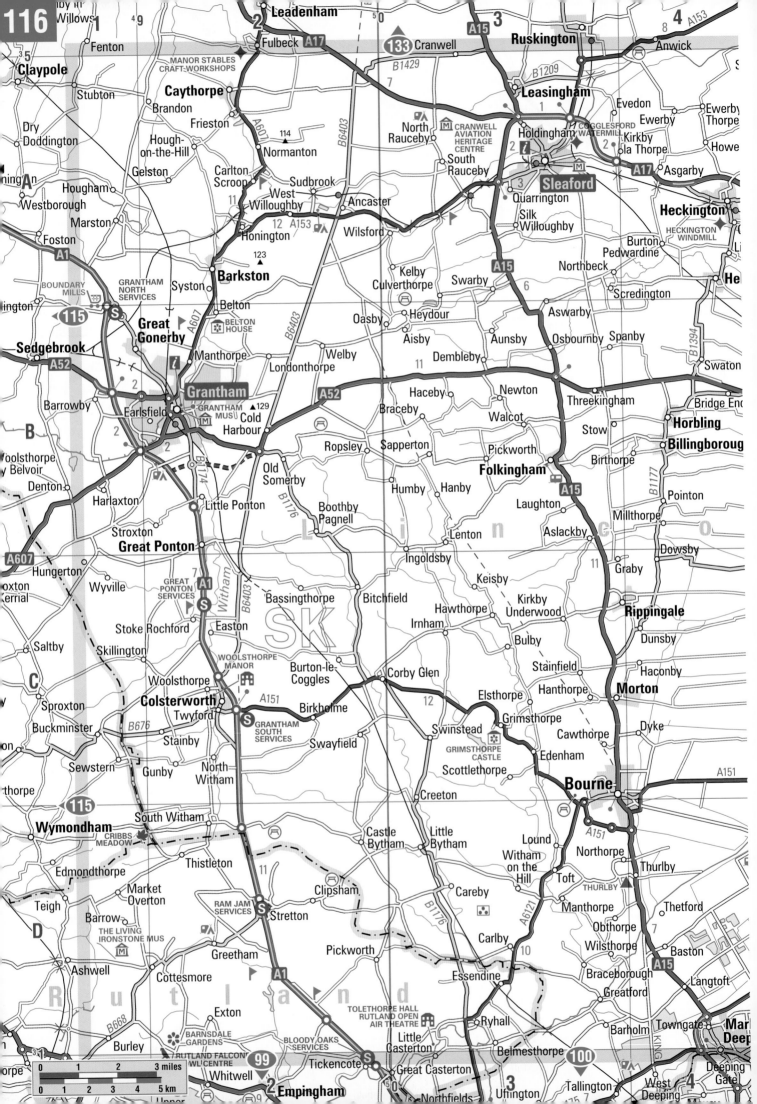

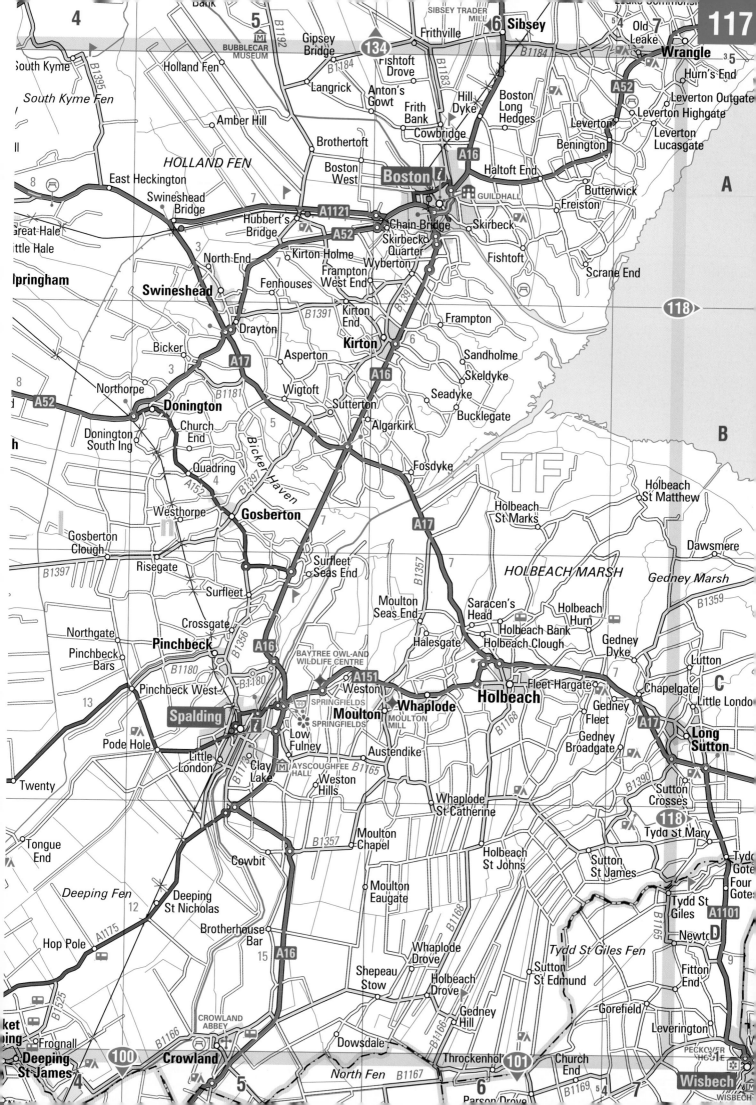

THE WASH

BOSTON DEEPS

LYNN DEEPS

THE WASH

NORFOLK

Wrangle Lowgate
Friskney Flats
135
Wrangle
Hurn's End
A52
Leverton Outgate
Leverton Highgate
Leverton Lucasgate
Butterwick
ton
Scrane End
117

HOLME BIRD OBSERVATORY
Old Hunstanton
Hunstanton
SEA LIFE SANCTUARY
Ringste
HUNSTANTO
Heacham
NOR LAVE
A149
Snettis
SN PAR
Ingol
Shepherd's Port
SNETTISHAM NATURE RESERVE
B1440
10
Ders

B
Holbeach St Matthew
Dawsmere
Gedney Marsh
Gedney Drove End
B1359
DERSINGHAM BOG
Wolferton
SANDRINGHAM
B1439
eachurn
Gedney Dyke
Lutton
Little London
Guy's Head
Terrington Marsh
Ongar Hill
Castle Rising
North Wootton
CASTLE RISING
Roydon
C
Gedney Fleet
Chapelgate
A17
Long Sutton
South Wootton
A1078
A148
A149
ROYDON COMMON
gate
Gedney oadgate
King's Lynn
TRUE'S YARD FISHERFOLK-MUS
Gaywood
Sutton Bridge
Orange Row
Clenchwarton
GUILDHALL
West Lynn
Fairstead
Leziate
Sutton Crosses
A17
Walpole Cross Keys
Terrington St Clement
11
Hardwick
S
2
Fair Green
Tower End
117
Tydd St Mary
Walpole St Andrew
Hay Green
Tilney High End
Tilney All Saints
A10
West Winch
Middleton
Sutton St James
Tydd Gote Four Gotes
Walpole Marsh
Walpole St Peter
A47
Saddle Bow
North Runcton
East Winch
D
Tydd St Giles
A1101
Newton
Ingleborough
St John's Highway
Terrington St John
Tilney St Lawrence
Wiggenhall St Germans
Setchey
Blackborough End
St Giles Fen
Fitton End
West Walton
12
Walpole Highway
Wiggenhall St Mary the Virgin
Tottenhill Row
4
Gorefield
Leverington
West Walton Highway
Marshland
St John's Fen End
Wiggenhall St Mary Magdalen
Watlington
Tottenhill
A134
Wormegay
PECKOVER HOUSE
Walsoken
FENLAND & WEST NORFOLK AVIATION MUSEUM
101
Marshland St James
Runcton Holme
A10
Shouldha
1169
New Walsoken
Marshland Fen
2
102
South
3

0   1   2   3 miles
0 1 2 3 4 5 km

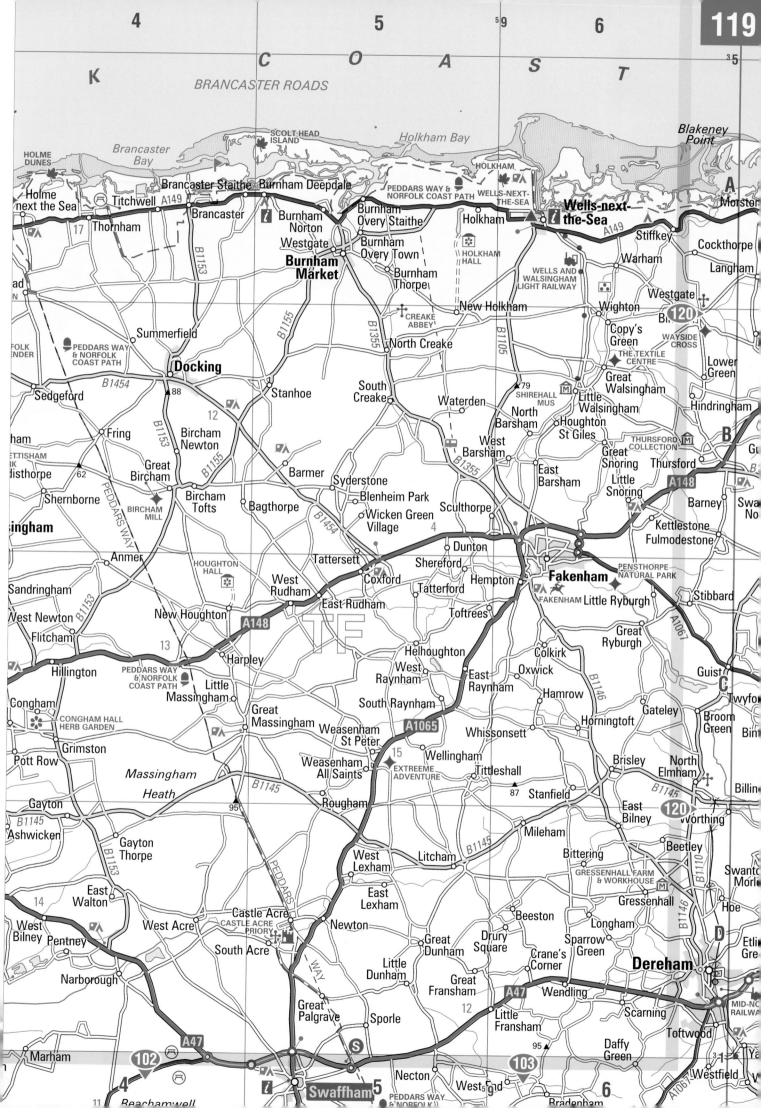

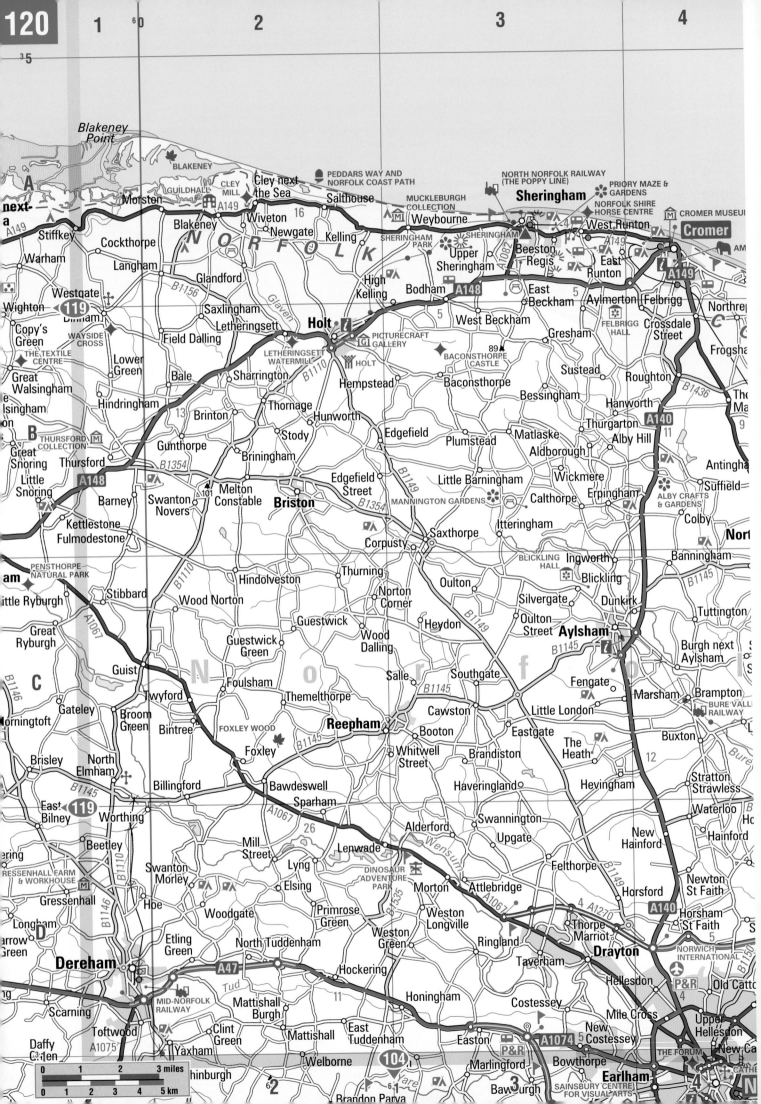

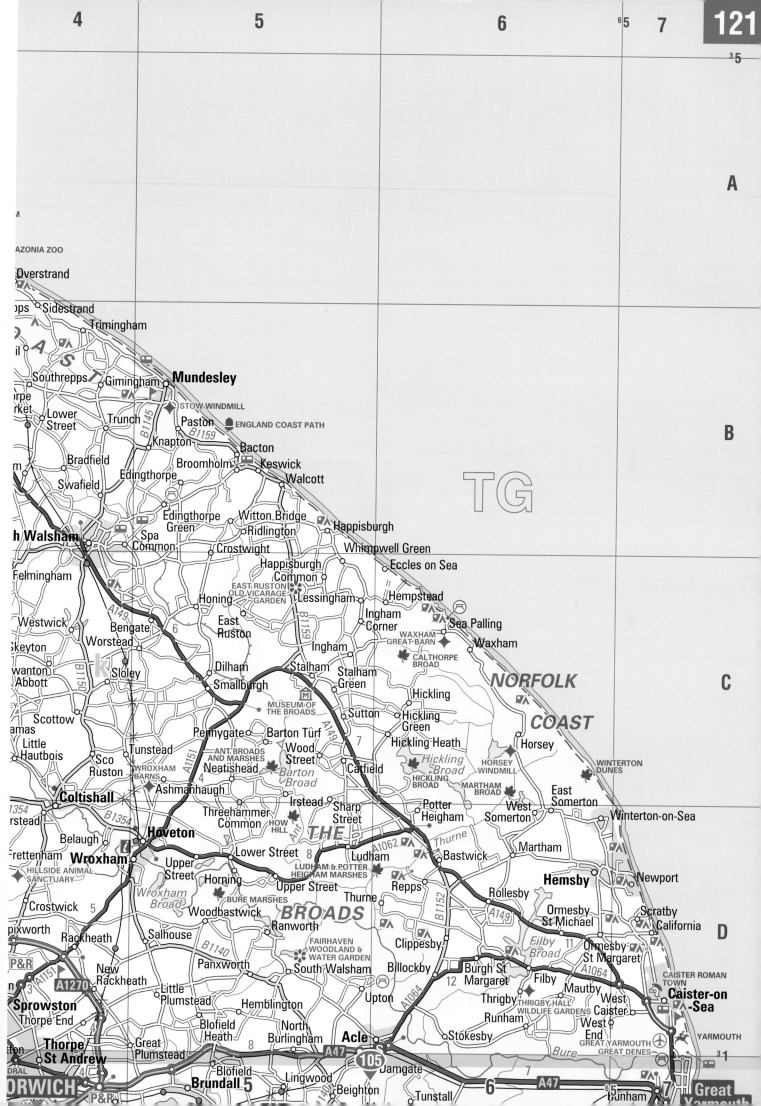

1   2   2   3

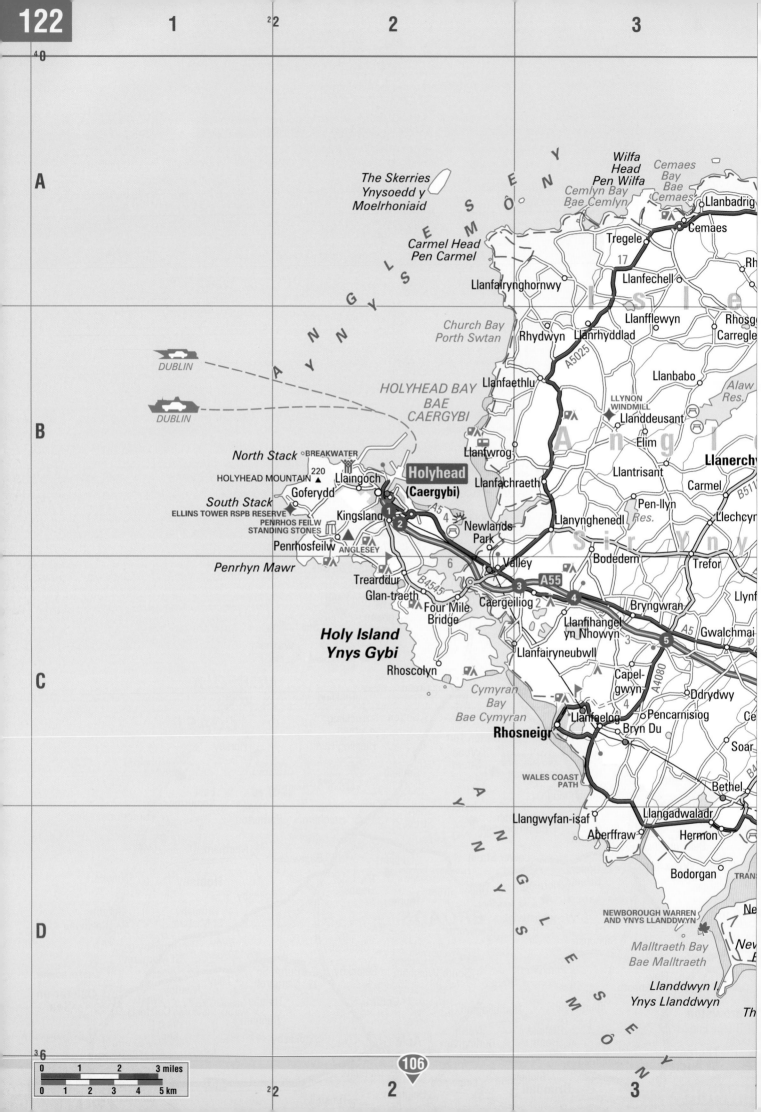

A

The Skerries
Ynysoedd y
Moelrhoniaid

Carmel Head
Pen Carmel

Wilfa
Head
Pen Wilfa

Cemaes
Bay
Bae
Cemaes

Cemlyn Bay
Bae Cemlyn

Llanbadrig

Cemaes

Tregele

Llanfechell

17

Llanfairynghornwy

Llanffflewyn

Rhosg

Carregle

ANGLESEY MÔN

Church Bay
Porth Swtan

Rhydwyn   Llanrhyddlad

Isle

Llanbabo

Alaw
Res.

B

DUBLIN

DUBLIN

North Stack

HOLYHEAD MOUNTAIN 220

South Stack

ELLINS TOWER RSPB RESERVE

PENRHOS FEILW
STANDING STONES

Penrhosfeilw

Penrhyn Mawr

BREAKWATER

Llaingoch

Goferydd

Kingsland

ANGLESEY

HOLYHEAD BAY
BAE
CAERGYBI

Llanfaethlu

A5025

LLYNON
WINDMILL

Llanddeusant

Llanfwrog

Llanfachraeth

Holyhead
(Caergybi)

1

2

A5

4

Newlands
Park

6

Valley

Elim

Llantrisant

Llanynghenedl

Llanghenedl

Bodedern

Anglı

Sir Yny

Llanerch

Carmel

Pen-llyn
Res.

Llechcyn

Trefor

C

Trearddur

Glan-traeth

Four Mile
Bridge

Holy Island
Ynys Gybi

Rhoscolyn

Caergeiliog

B4545

3

A55

2

4

A55

5

Llanfihangel
yn Nhowyn

Bryngwran

A5

Gwalchmai

Llynf

Llanfairyneubwll

Capel-
gwyn

4

Ddrydwy

Cymyran
Bay
Bae Cymyran

WALES COAST
PATH

Llanfaelog

Bryn Du

Pencarnisiog

Soar

Rhosneigr

Llangwyfan-isaf

Aberffraw

Llangadwaladr

Hermon

Bethel

B4

Ce

D

Bodorgan

TRANS

Ne

NEWBOROUGH WARREN
AND YNYS LLANDDWYN

Malltraeth Bay
Bae Malltraeth

Nev
B

Llanddwyn I
Ynys Llanddwyn

Th

0   1   2   3 miles

0   1   2   3   4   5 km

2   2   **106**   2   3

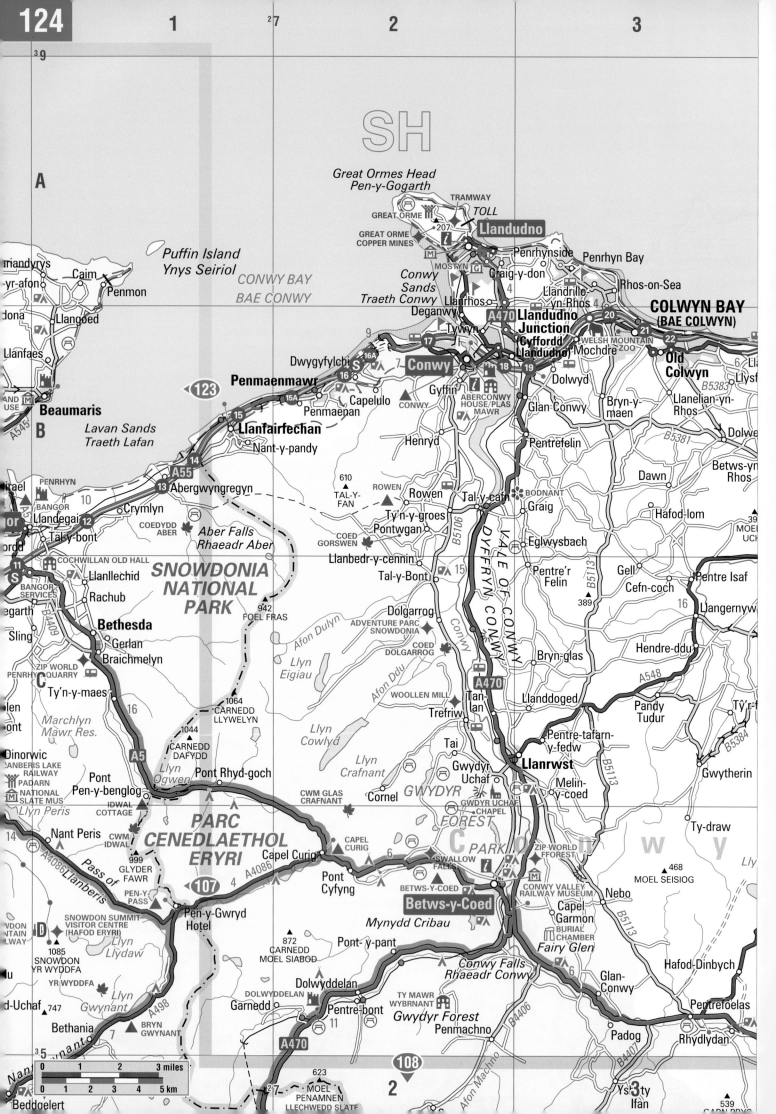

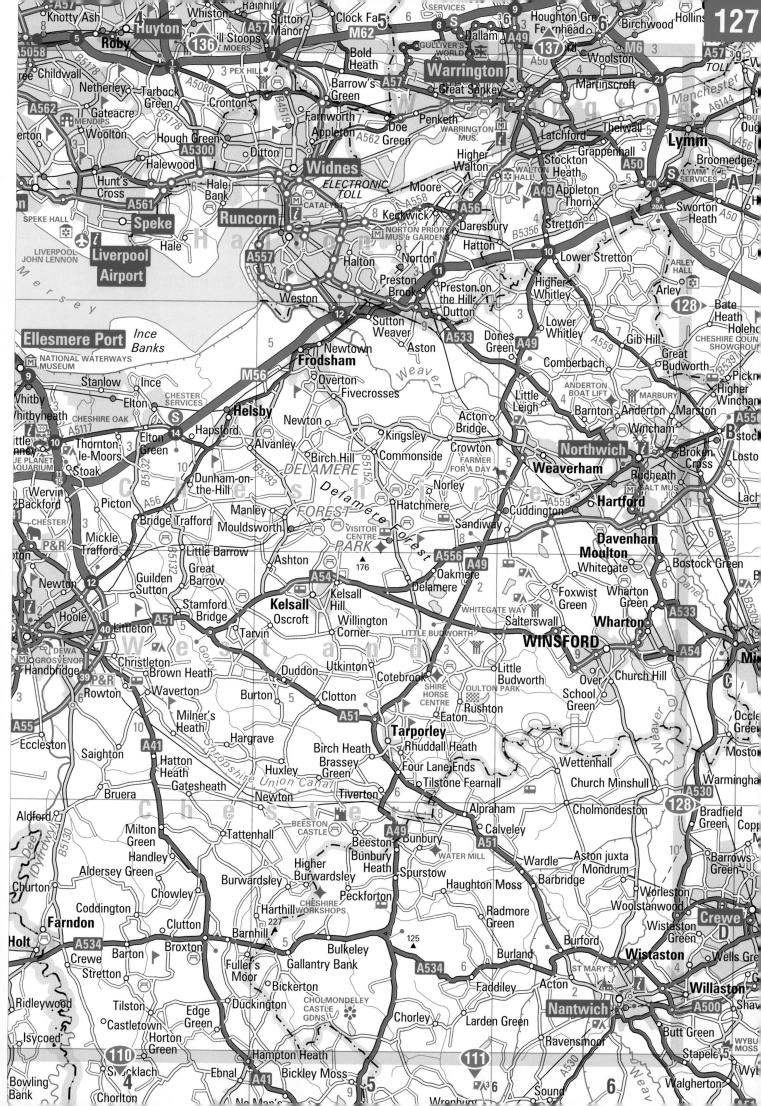

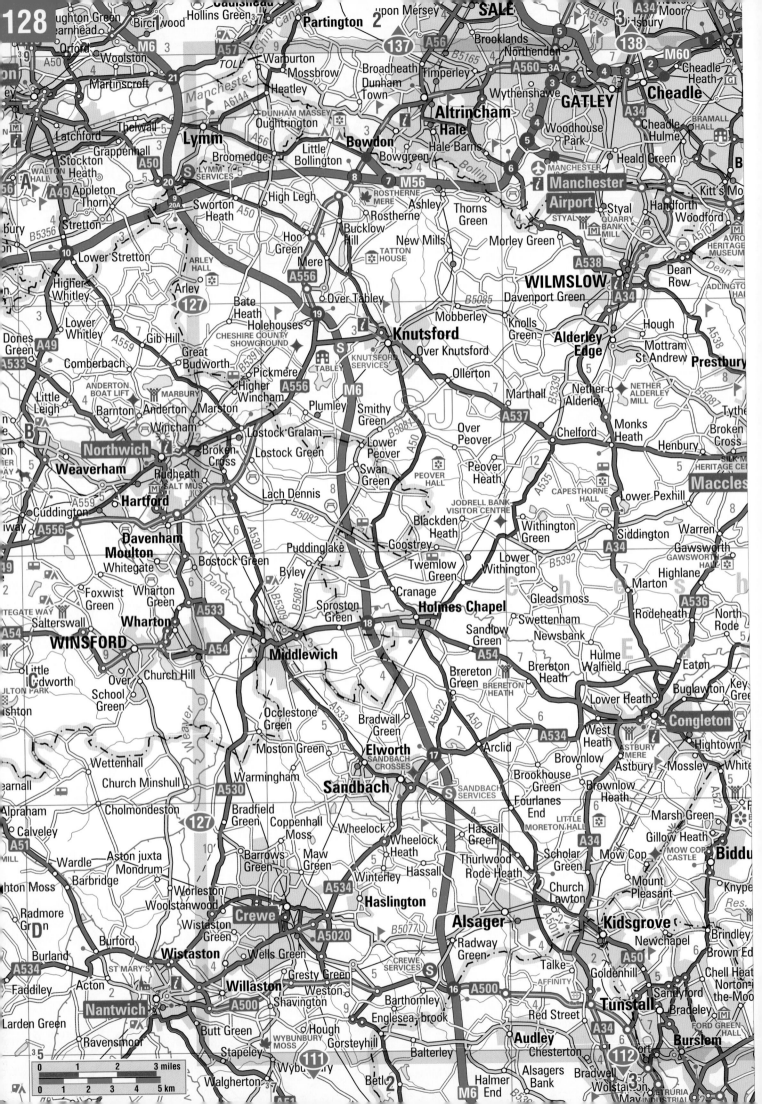

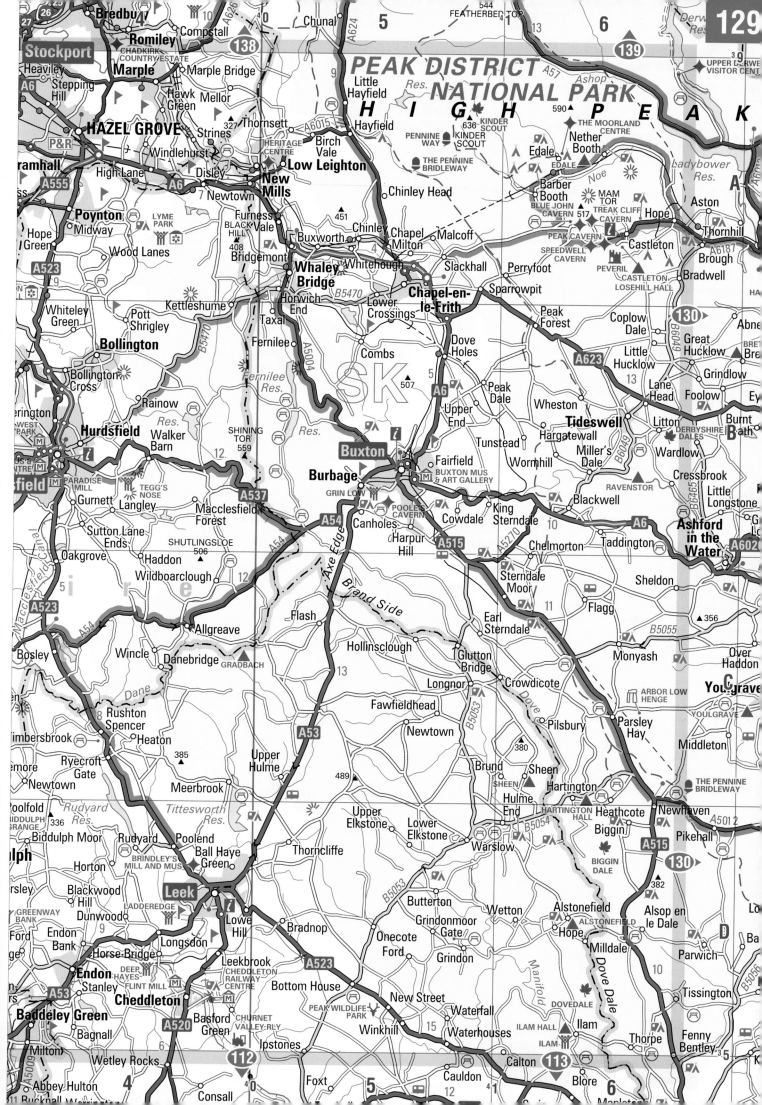

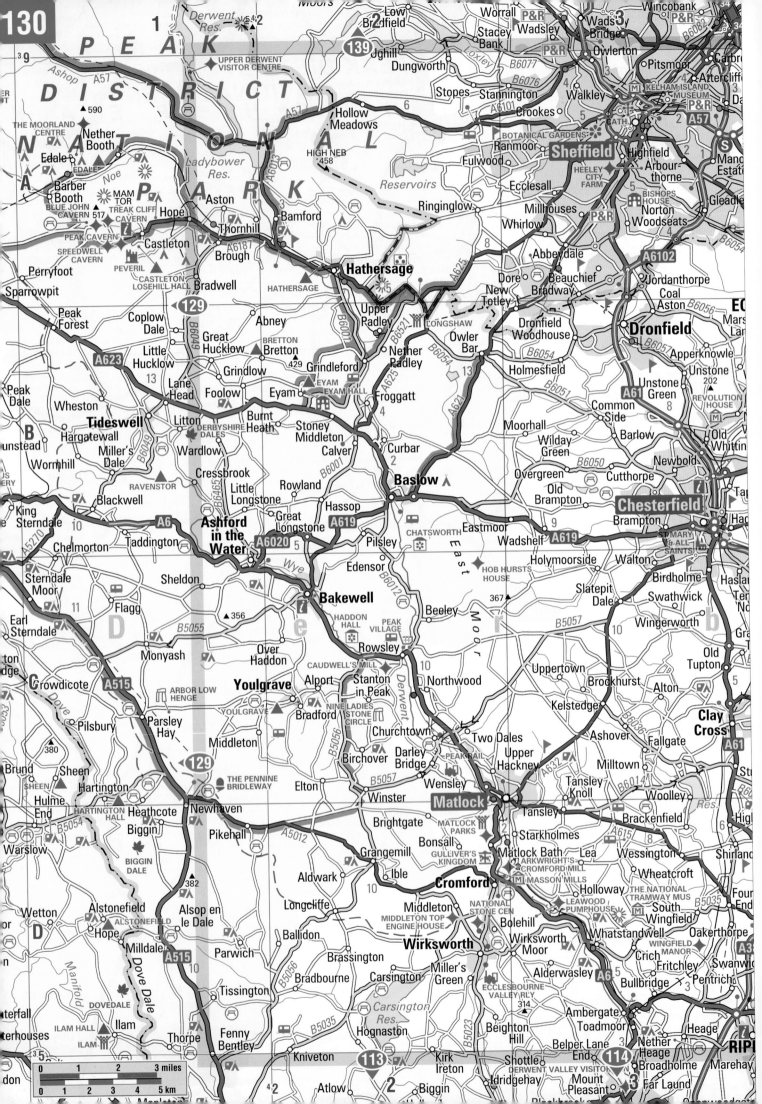

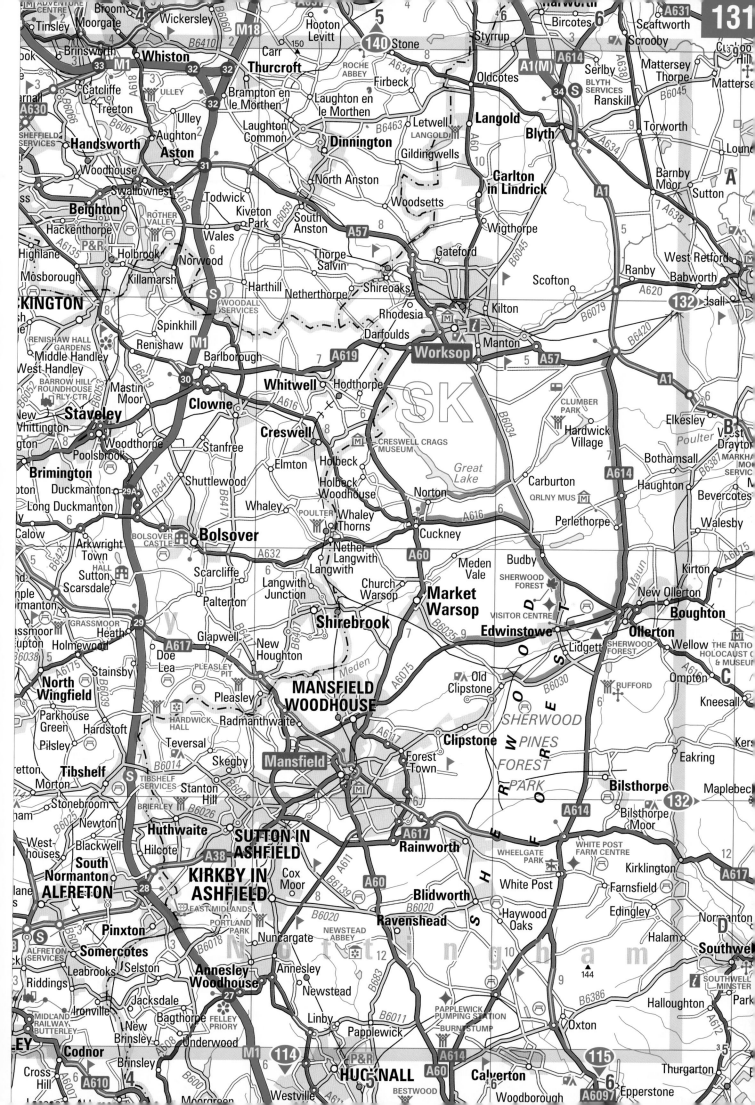

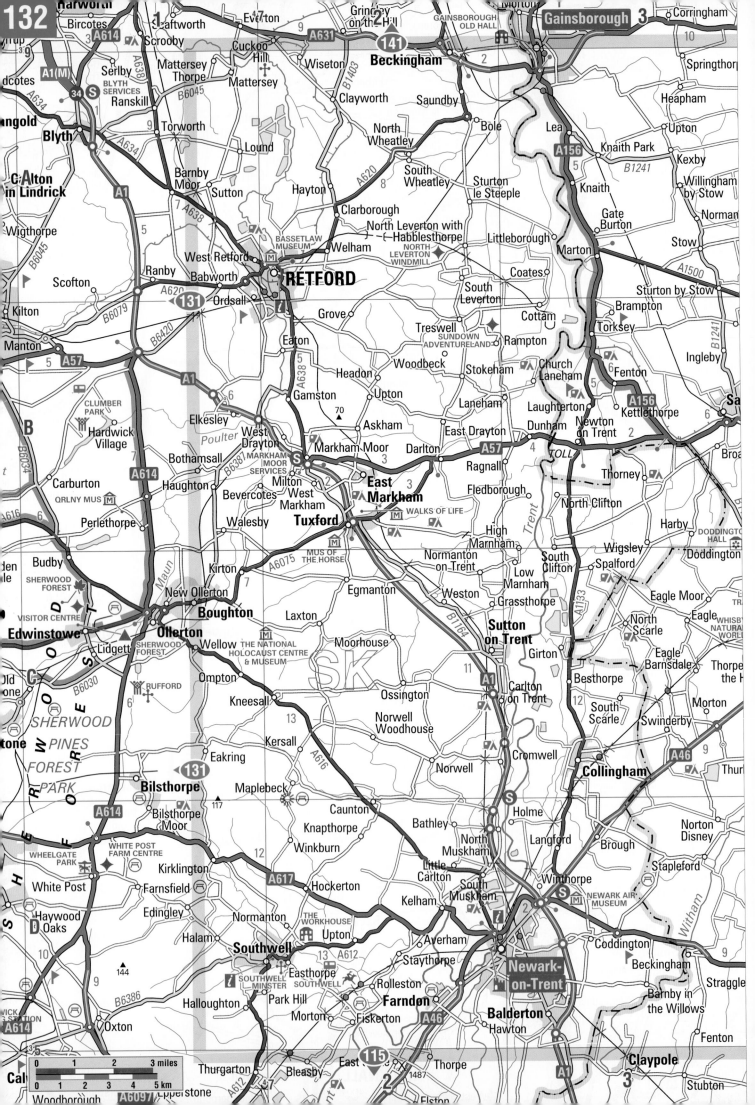

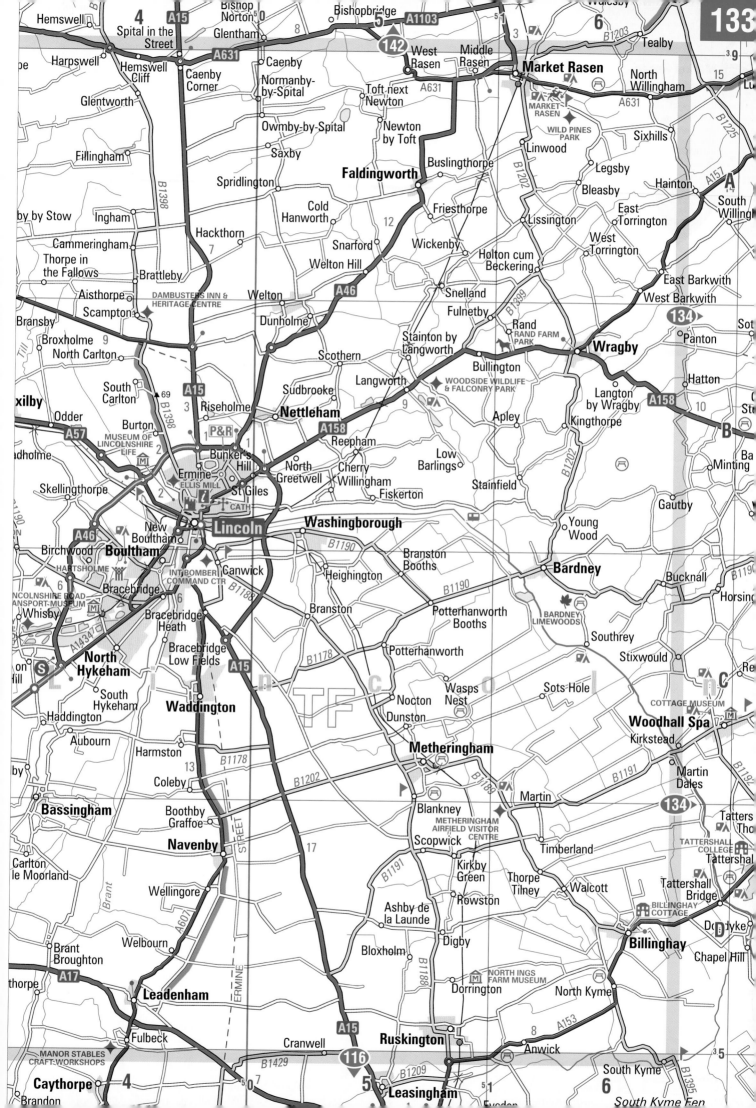

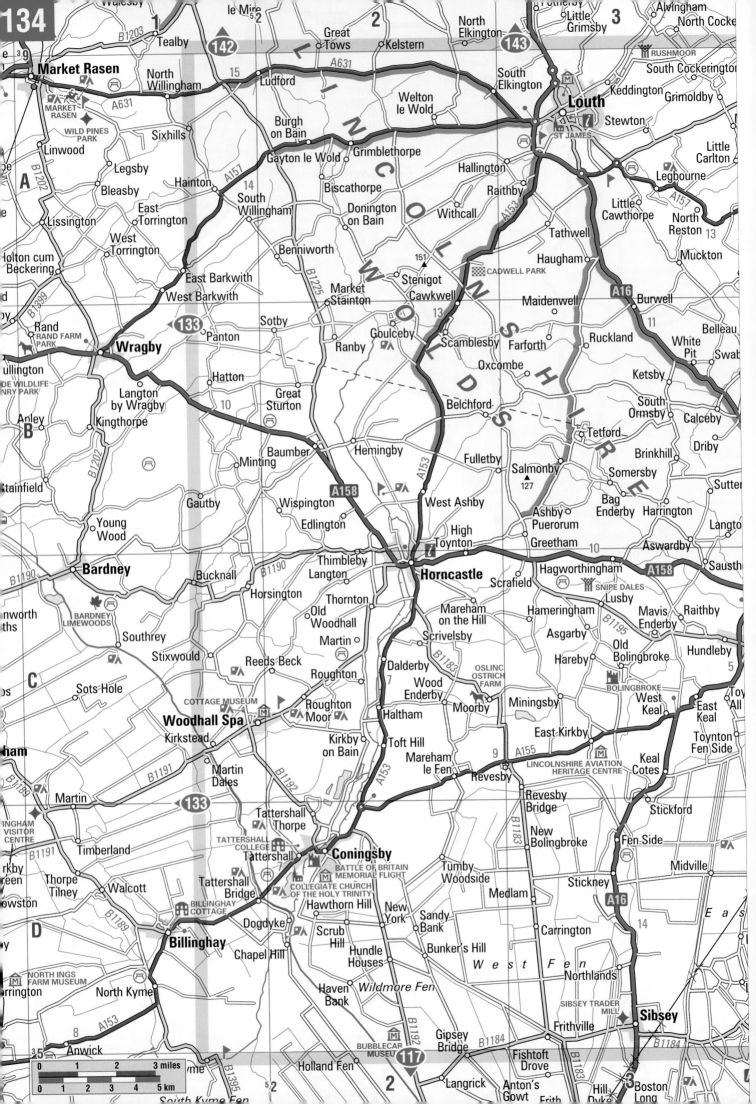

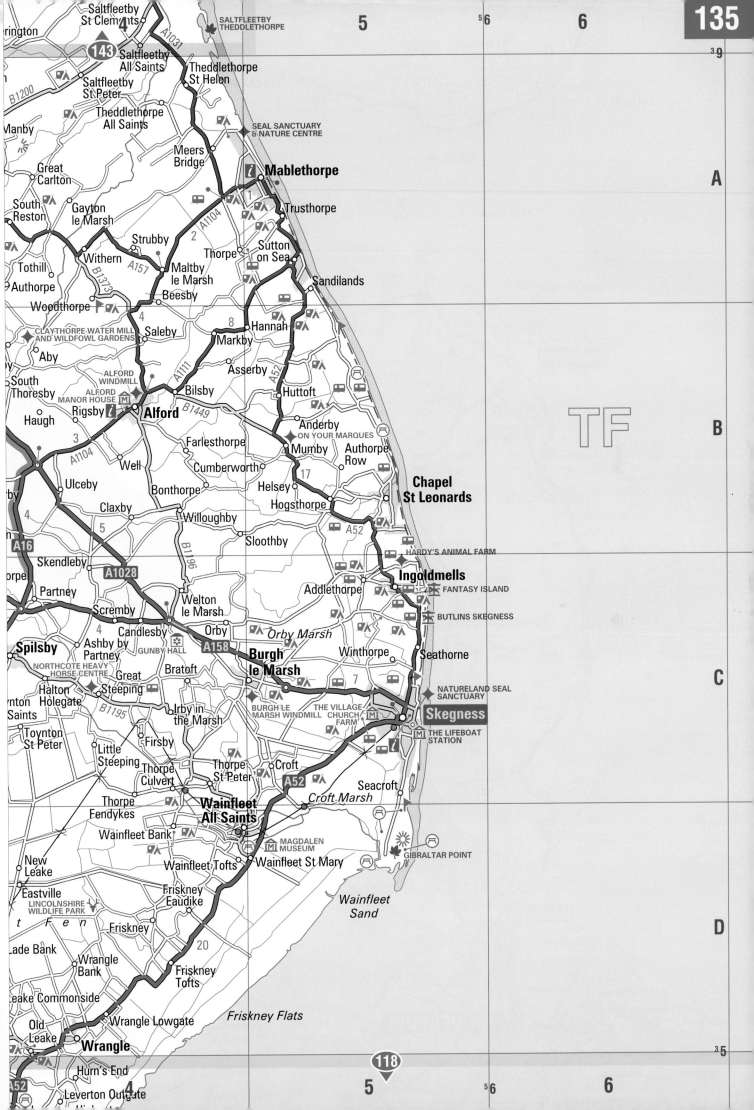

5   5**6**   **6**

3**9**

A

B

TF

C

D

3**5**

Saltfleetby
St Clements
SALTFLEETBY
THEDDLETHORPE
rington
143 Saltfleetby
All Saints
A1031
Saltfleetby
St Peter
Theddlethorpe
St Helen
B1200
Theddlethorpe
All Saints
Manby
SEAL SANCTUARY
& NATURE CENTRE
Meers
Bridge
Great
Carlton
Mablethorpe
South
Reston
Gayton
le Marsh
Trusthorpe
A1104
Strubby
Sutton
on Sea
Withern
A157
Thorpe
Maltby
le Marsh
Sandilands
B1373
Beesby
Tothill
Authorpe
Saleby
Hannah
Woodthorpe
A111
Markby
CLAYTHORPE WATER MILL
AND WILDFOWL GARDENS
Asserby
Aby
A52
Bilsby
Huttoft
ALFORD
WINDMILL
ALFORD
MANOR HOUSE
South
Thoresby
Rigsby
Alford
Anderby
Haugh
B1449
ON YOUR MARQUES
Farlesthorpe
Mumby
Authorpe
Row
A1104
Well
Cumberworth
Chapel
St Leonards
Ulceby
Bonthorpe
Helsey
Claxby
Hogsthorpe
17
Willoughby
A16
Sloothby
HARDY'S ANIMAL FARM
A52
Skendleby
A1028
Addlethorpe
Ingoldmells
orpe
Partney
Welton
le Marsh
FANTASY ISLAND
B1196
Orby
BUTLINS SKEGNESS
Scremby
Orby Marsh
Spilsby
Candlesby
Winthorpe
Seathorne
Ashby by
Partney
GUNBY HALL
A158
**Burgh
le Marsh**
NORTHCOTE HEAVY
HORSE CENTRE
Bratoft
NATURELAND SEAL
SANCTUARY
Halton
Holegate
Great
Steeping
7
ynton
Saints
Irby in
the Marsh
BURGH LE
MARSH WINDMILL
THE VILLAGE
CHURCH
FARM
Skegness
B1195
Toynton
St Peter
Firsby
THE LIFEBOAT
STATION
Little
Steeping
Thorpe
St Peter
Croft
Thorpe
Culvert
Seacroft
A52
Thorpe
Fendykes
**Wainfleet
All Saints**
Croft Marsh
Wainfleet Bank
MAGDALEN
MUSEUM
New
Leake
Wainfleet Tofts
Wainfleet St Mary
GIBRALTAR POINT
Eastville
LINCOLNSHIRE
WILDLIFE PARK
Friskney
Eaudike
Wainfleet
Sand
t   F e n
Friskney
Lade Bank
20
Wrangle
Bank
Friskney
Tofts
eake Commonside
Friskney Flats
Old
Leake
Wrangle Lowgate
A52
Wrangle
Hurn's End
118
Leverton Outgate
4   **5**   5**6**   **6**

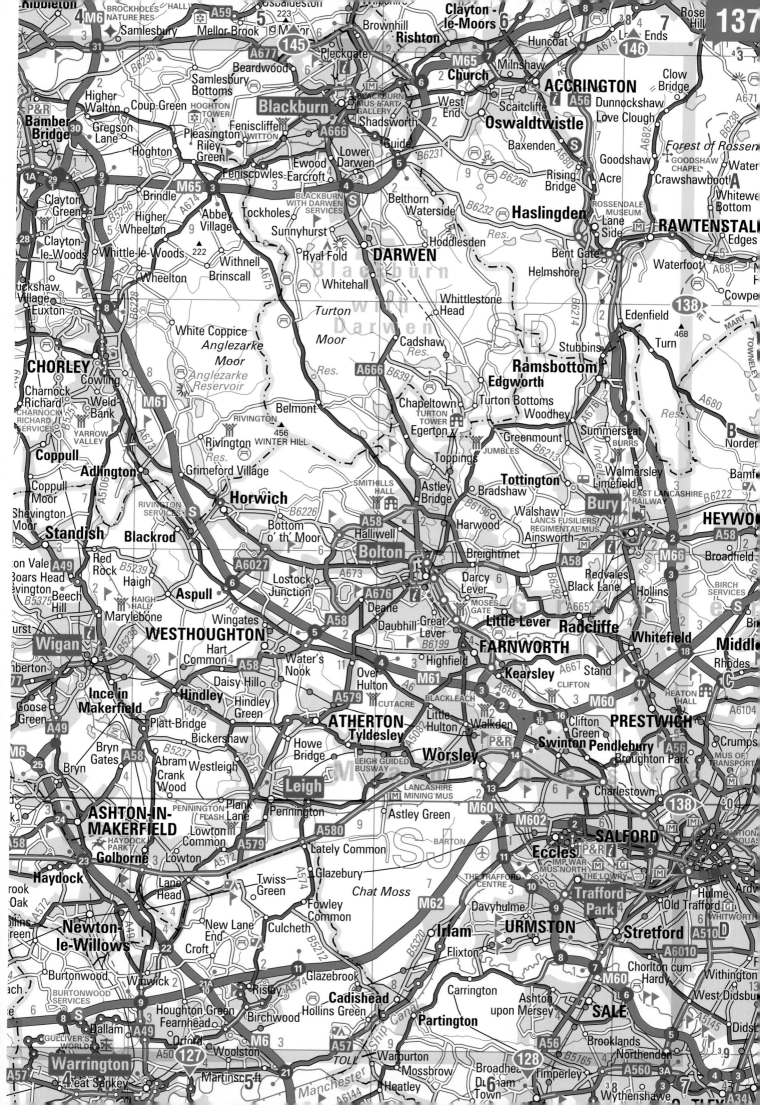

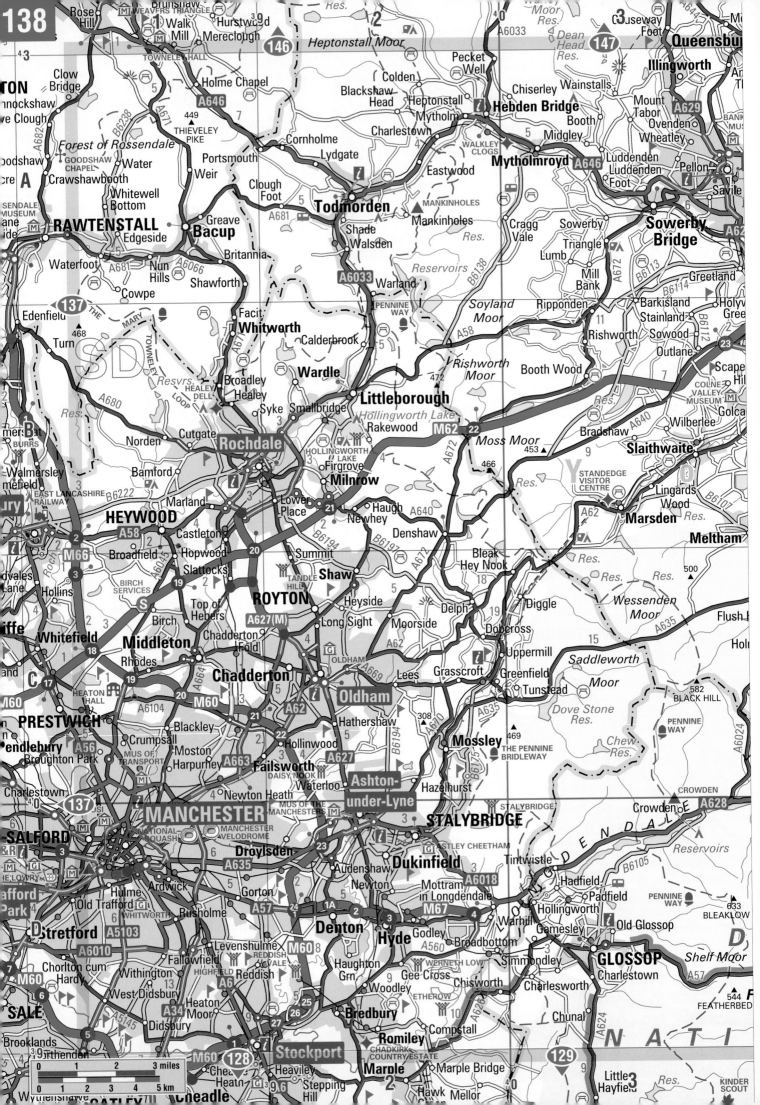

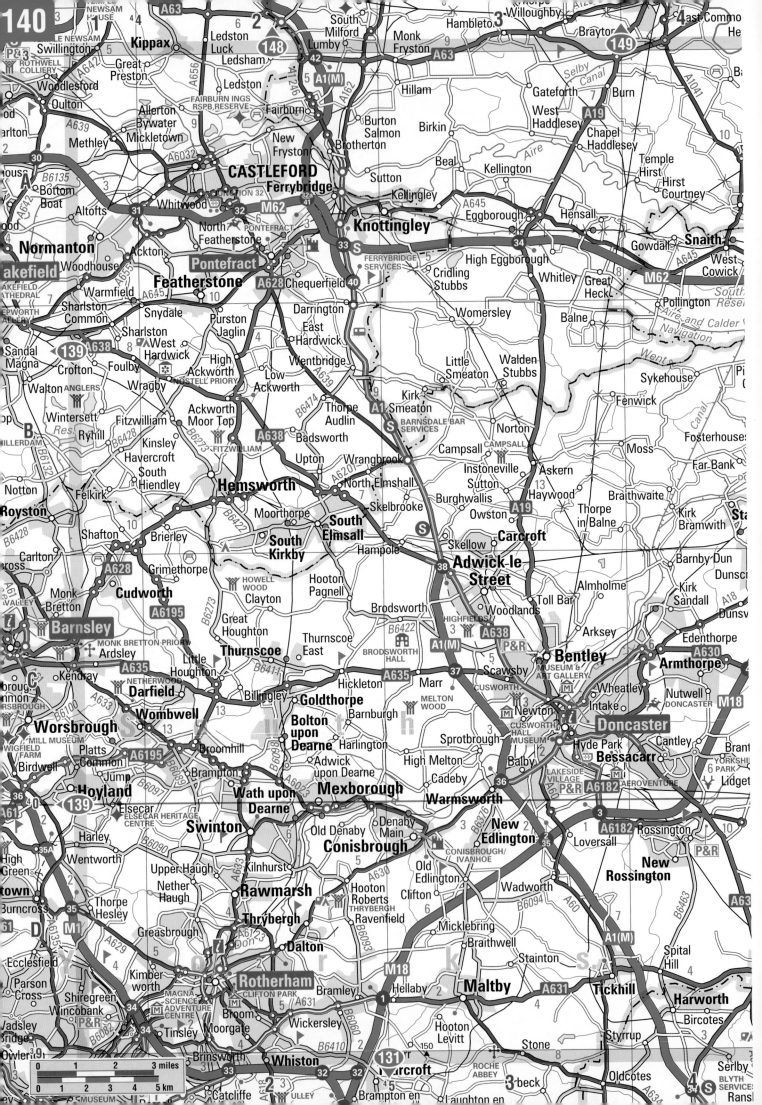

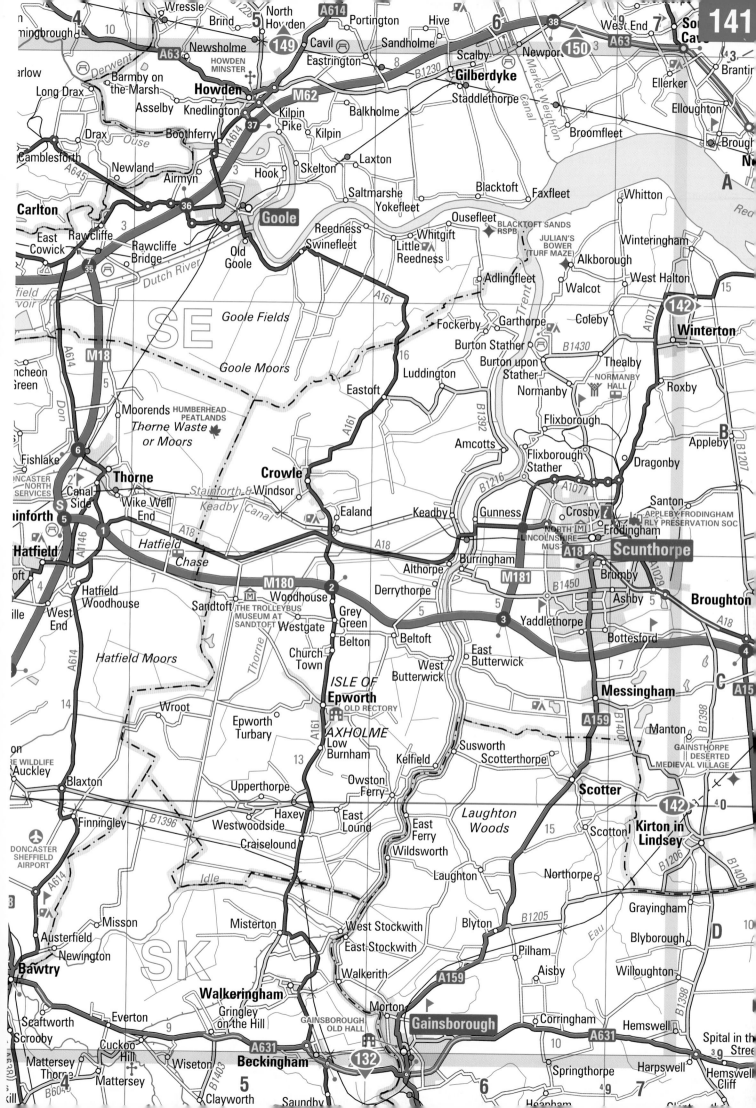

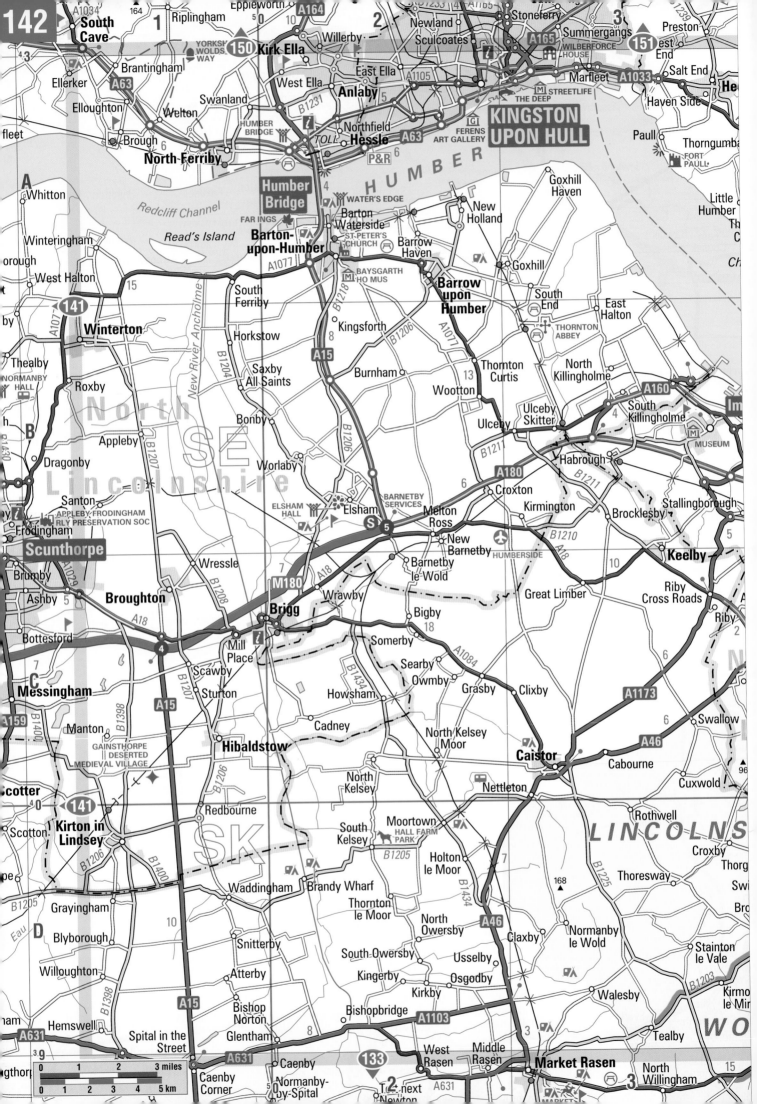

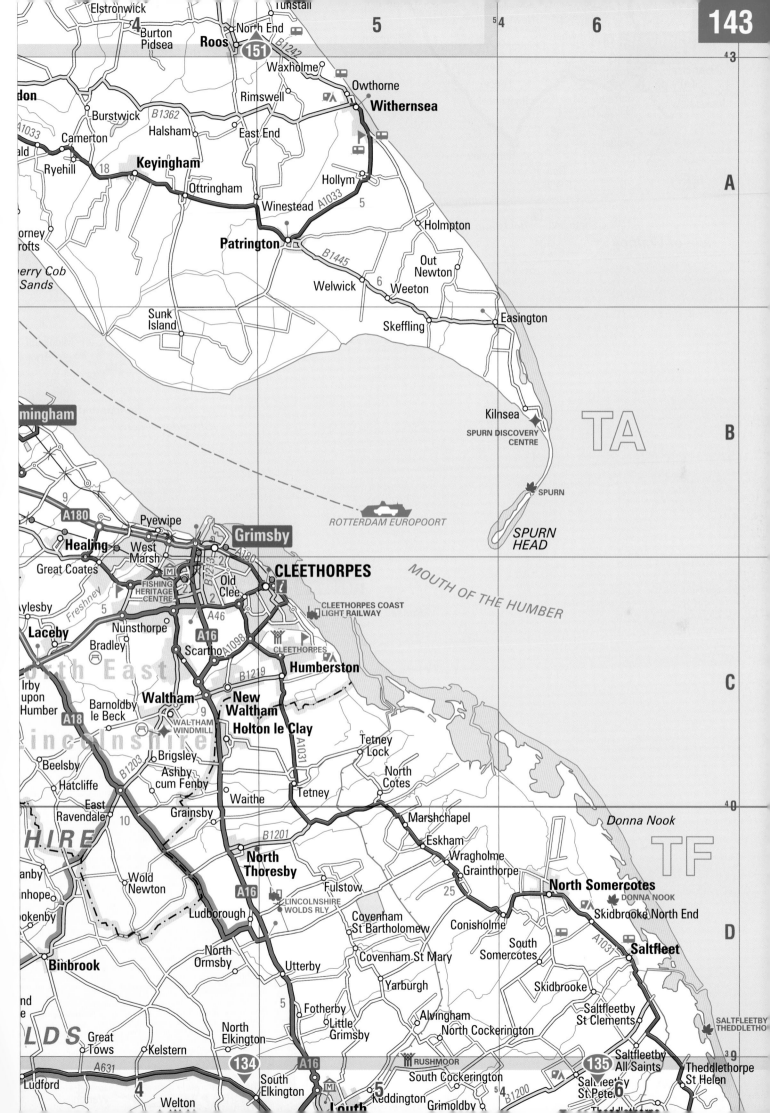

4 5 5**4** **6**

3

Elstronwick
Tunstall
North End
Roos
151
B1242
Waxholme
Burton
Pidsea
Owthorne
Rimswell
Withernsea
Burstwick
East End
B1362
Halsham
A1033
Camerton
Hollym
18
Ryehill
Keyingham
Ottringham
Winestead
A1033
Holmpton
Patrington
B1445
Out
Newton
Welwick
Weeton
Skeffling
Easington
Sunk
Island

A

erry Cob
Sands

Kilnsea
SPURN DISCOVERY
CENTRE

TA

B

mingham

SPURN

ROTTERDAM EUROPOORT

SPURN
HEAD

9
A180
Pyewipe
Healing
West
Marsh
Grimsby
Great Coates
A180
CLEETHORPES
FISHING
HERITAGE
CENTRE
Freshney
B1213
Old
Clee
2
aylesby
5
A46
CLEETHORPES COAST
LIGHT RAILWAY
MOUTH OF THE HUMBER

Nunsthorpe
A16
Laceby
Bradley
Scartho
A1098
CLEETHORPES
Irby
upon
Humber
Barnoldby
le Beck
B1219
Humberston

C

A18
Waltham
New
Waltham
WAL-THAM
WINDMILL
9
Holton le Clay
Tetney
Lock
Beelsby
B1203
Brigsley
A1031
North
Cotes
Hatcliffe
Ashby
cum Fenby
Waithe
Tetney
East
Ravendale
10
Grainsby
Marshchapel
Donna Nook
TF
B1201
Eskham
Wragholme
Grainthorpe
anby
Wold
Newton
North
Thoresby
A16
Fulstow
25
North Somercotes
nhope
DONNA NOOK
okenby
Ludborough
LINCOLNSHIRE
WOLDS RLY
Covenham
St Bartholomew
Conisholme
Skidbrooke North End
A1031
South
Somercotes
Saltfleet

D

Binbrook
North
Ormsby
Utterby
Covenham St Mary
Yarburgh
Skidbrooke
nd
5
Fotherby
Little
Grimsby
Alvingham
North Cockerington
Saltfleetby
St Clements
SALTFLEETBY
THEDDLETHO
e
Great
Tows
Kelstern
North
Elkington
134
A16
135
Saltfleetby
All Saints
Theddlethorpe
St Helen
LDS
A631
RUSHMOOR
South Cockerington
Saltfleetby
St Peter
Ludford
4
South
Elkington
5 **5** 4 **6**
Welton
Keddington
Grimoldby

9

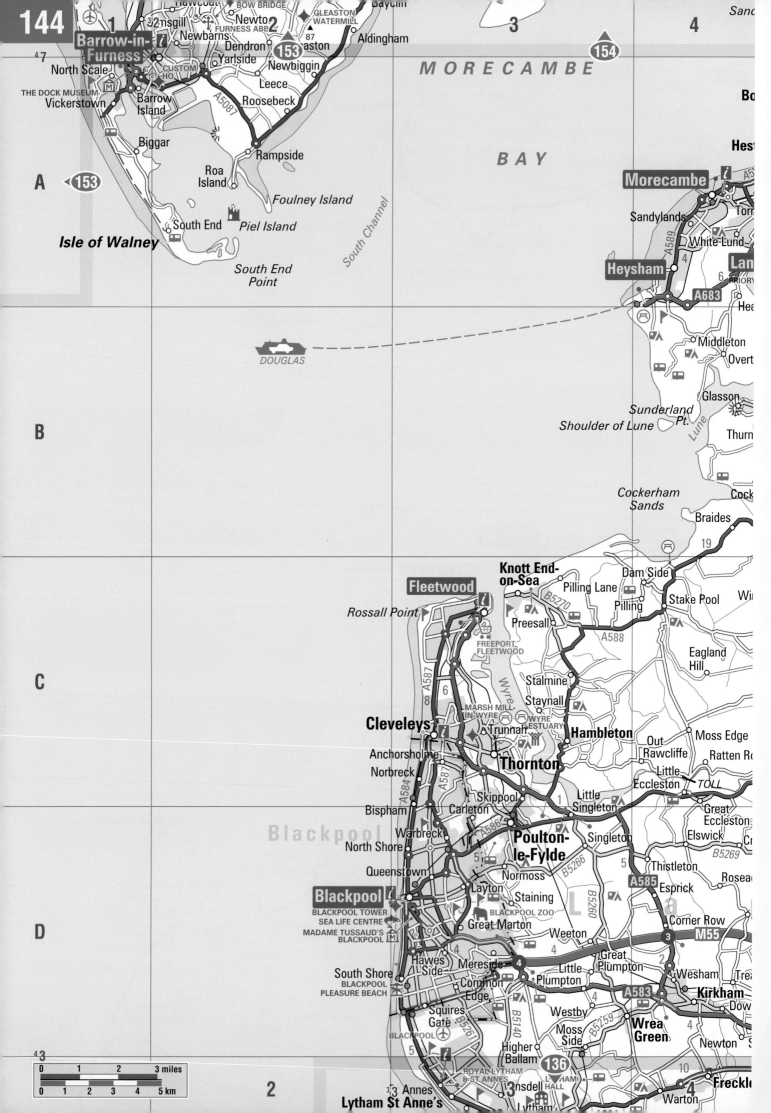

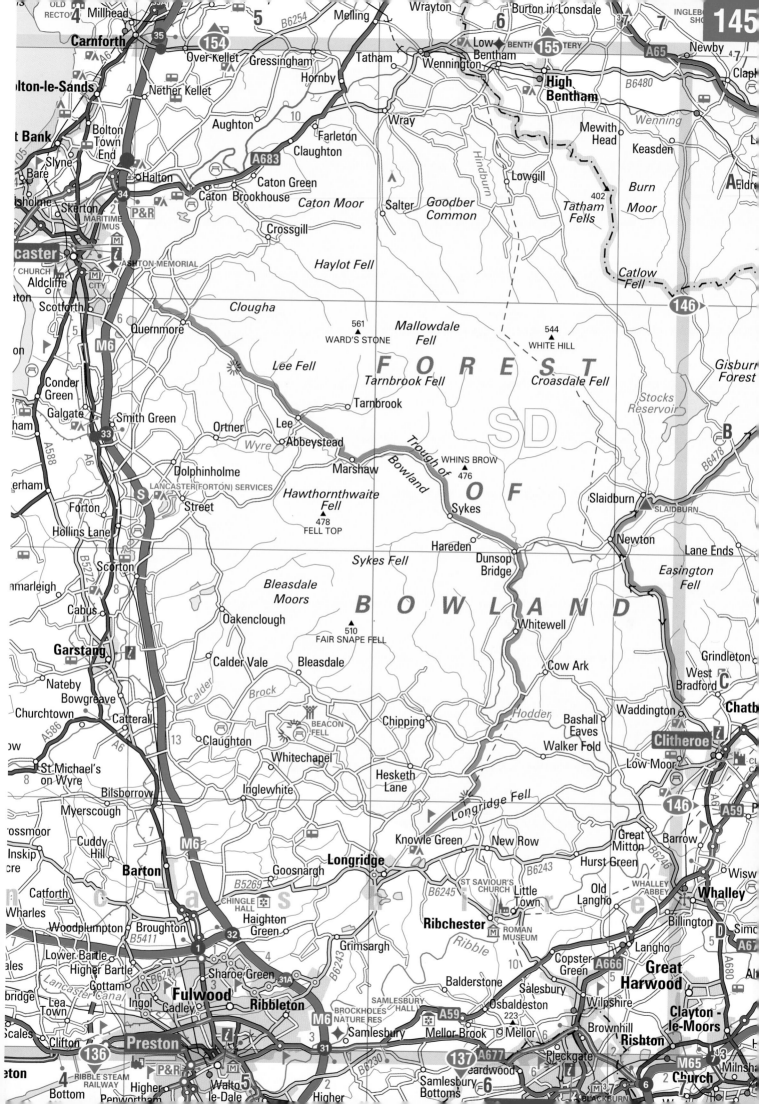

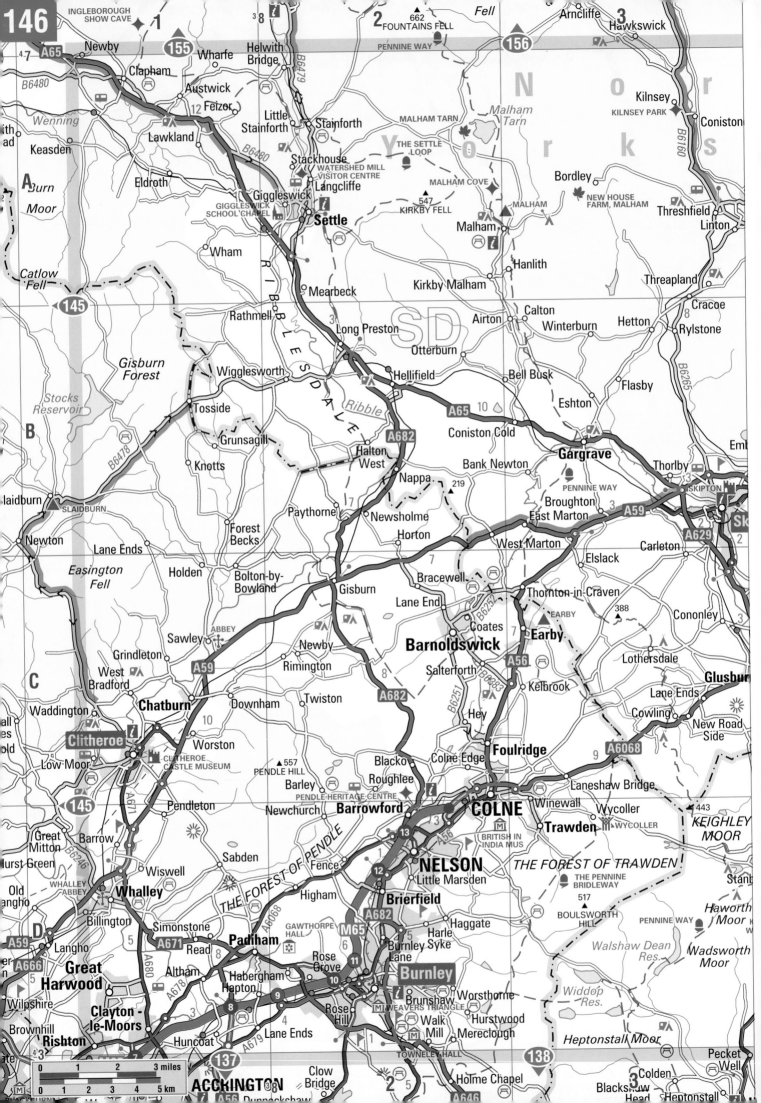

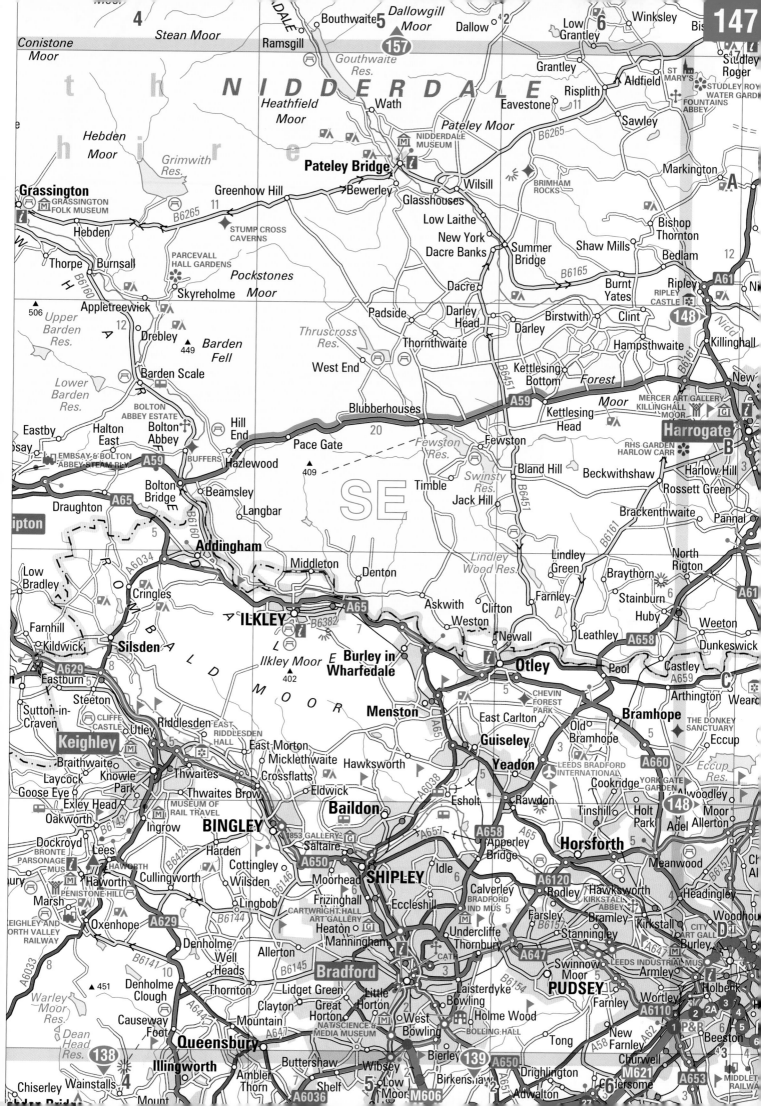

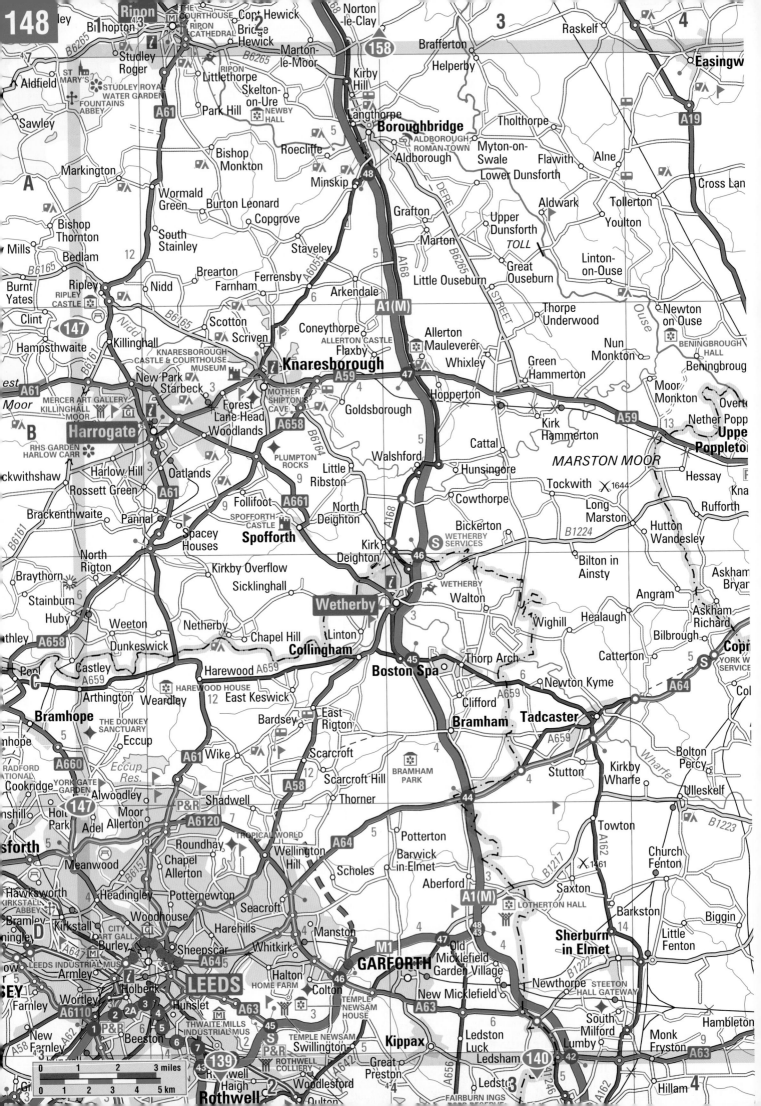

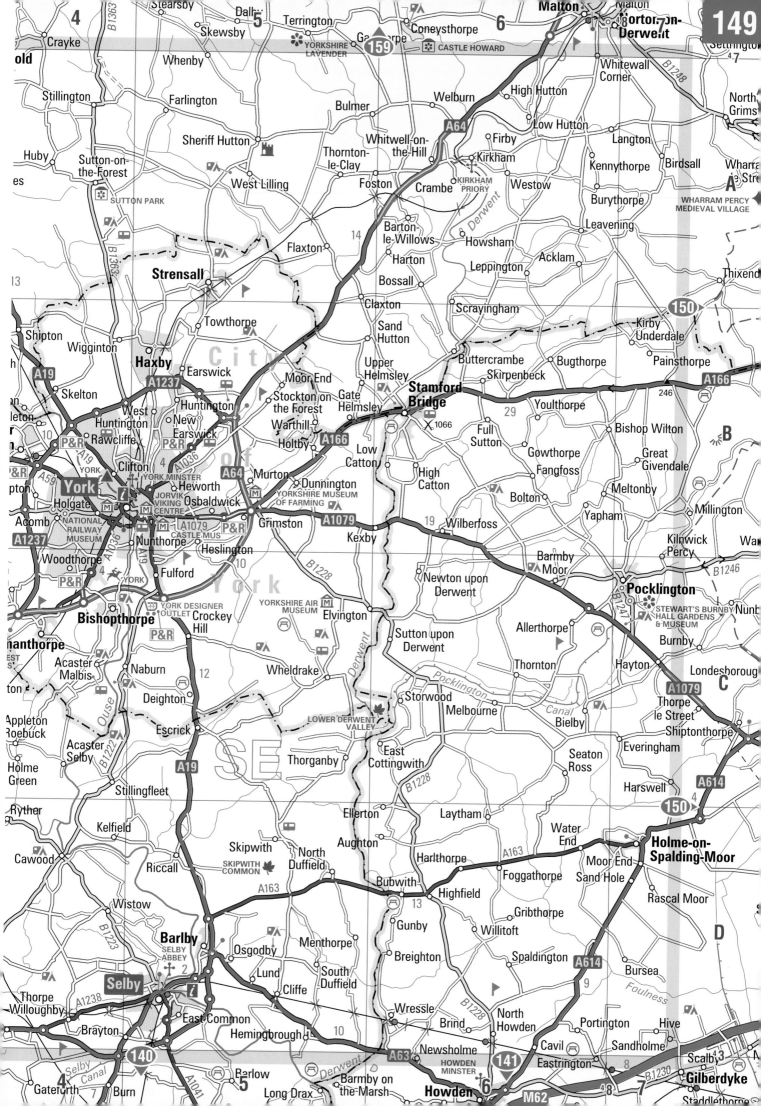

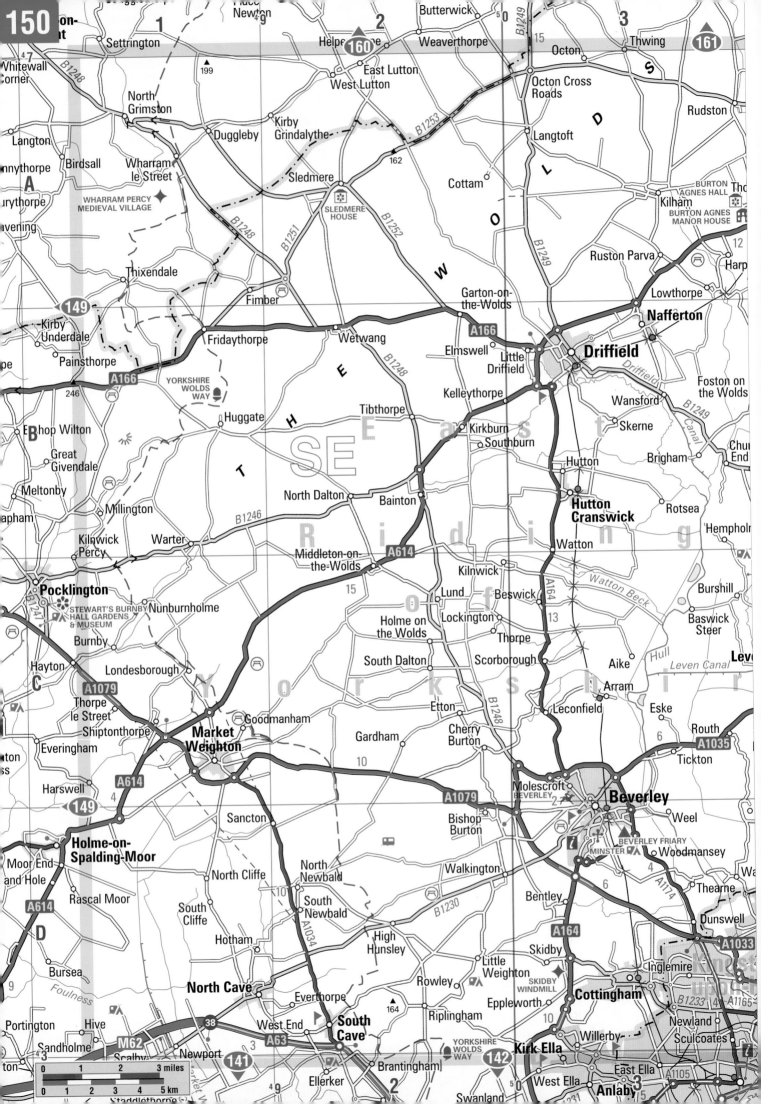

Grindale **A165** 4

Flamborough 5 FLAMBOROUGH HEAD 6

Boynton

PRIORY

BAYLE MUSEUM

Bridlington

SEWERBY HALL AND GARDENS
Sewerby
BONDVILLE MODEL VILLAGE

Bessingby
Carnaby

West Hill
Hilderthorpe
P&R

A614

Haisthorpe
rnholme

OLD PENNY MEMORIES

BRIDLINGTON BIRDS OF PREY & ANIMAL PARK

Burton Agnes

ham

BRIDLINGTON BAY

Fraisthorpe

Gransmoor

Great Kelk
Gembling

Lissett
14

Barmston

A165
16

Ulrome

SKIPSEA CASTLE

B1249

Beeford

Skipsea Brough

Skipsea

ch

North Frodingham

Dunnington

Bewholme

Atwick

North Cliff

Brandesburton

Hornsea Mere

Seaton

Hornsea
HORNSEA MUSEUM

B1244
HORNSEA FREEPORT

Hornsea Bridge

Rolston

Sigglesthorne

Catwick

Goxhill

Mappleton

Little Hatfield

Rise

Great Hatfield

Great Cowden

A165

Long Riston

Arnold

Withernwick

Meaux

New Ellerby

Skirlaugh

Marton

West Newton

Aldbrough

East Newton

17

Old Ellerby
Flinton

BURTON CONSTABLE HALL

Garton

Grimston

awne

Swine

Coniston

Thirtleby

Sproatley

Humbleton

Fitling

Hilston

Bransholme

Sutton on Hull

Ganstead

Bilton

B1238

Lelley

Elstronwick

Owstwick

Tunstall

Sutton Ings

Stoneferry

B1237

B1240

B1239

Preston
West End

Salt nd

Burton Pidsea

North End

A165

Summergangs
WILBERFORCE HOUSE

142

143

Marfleet **A1033** 4

THE DEEP
STREETLIFE

Hedon

5 *B1362*

Rimswell

Roos

Waxholme

Owt orne

Withernsea

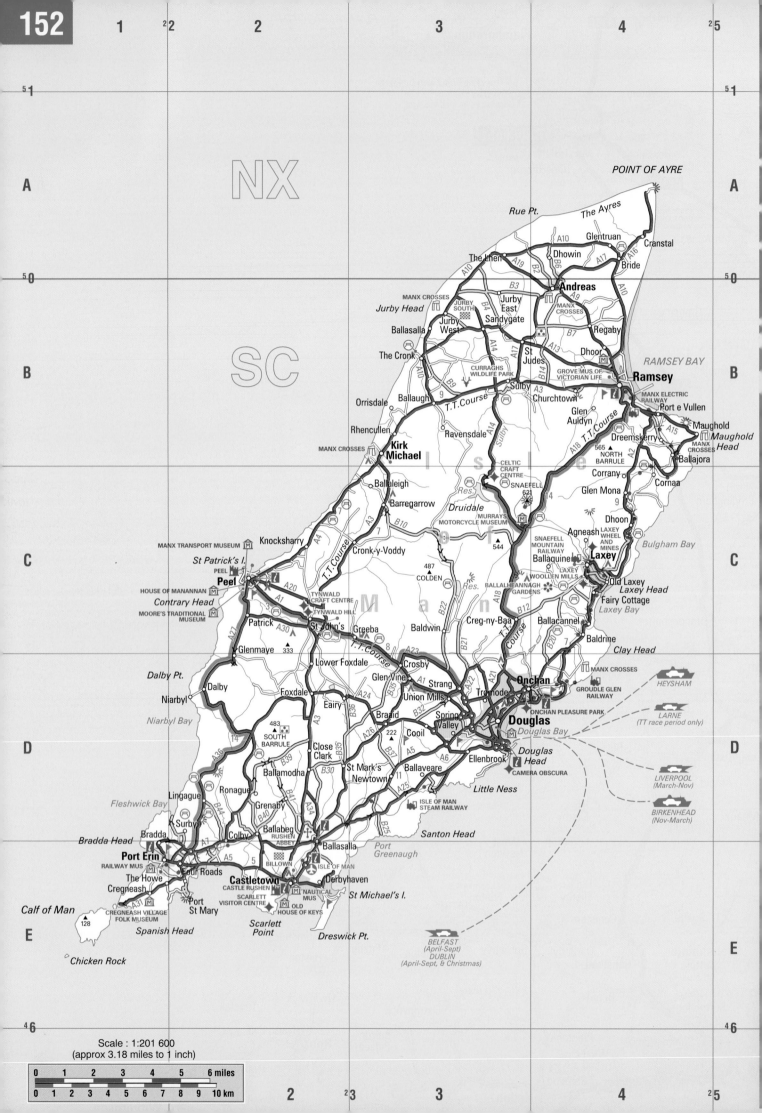

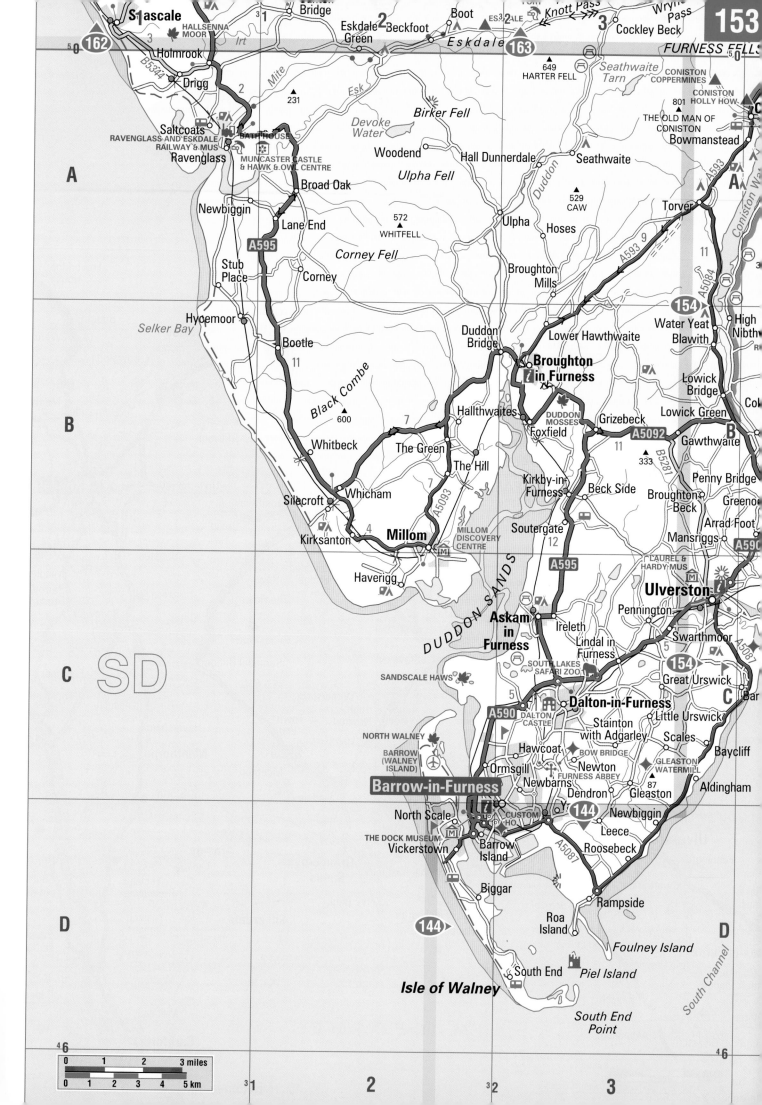

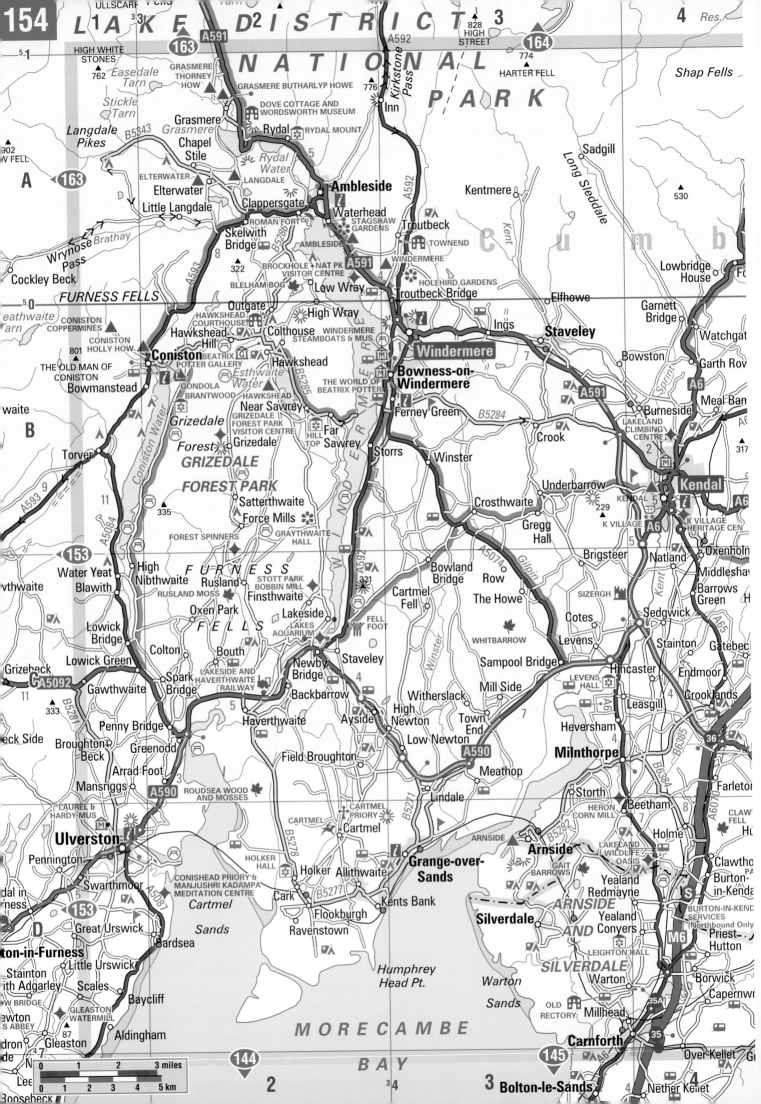

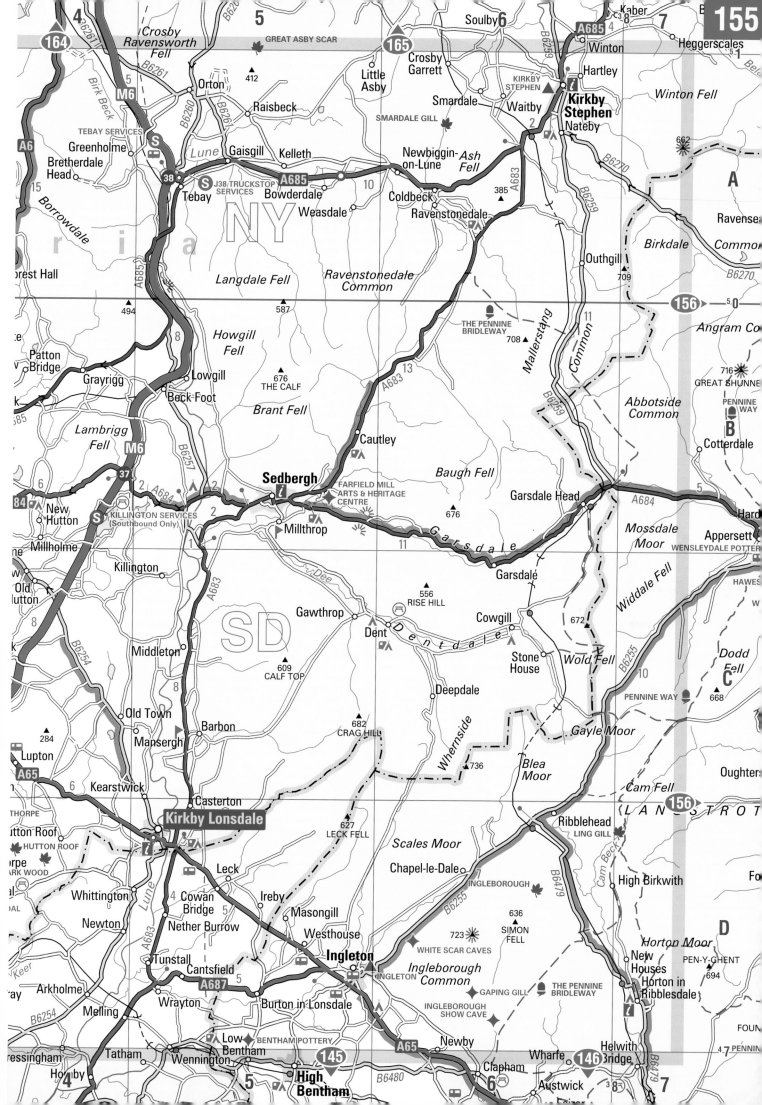

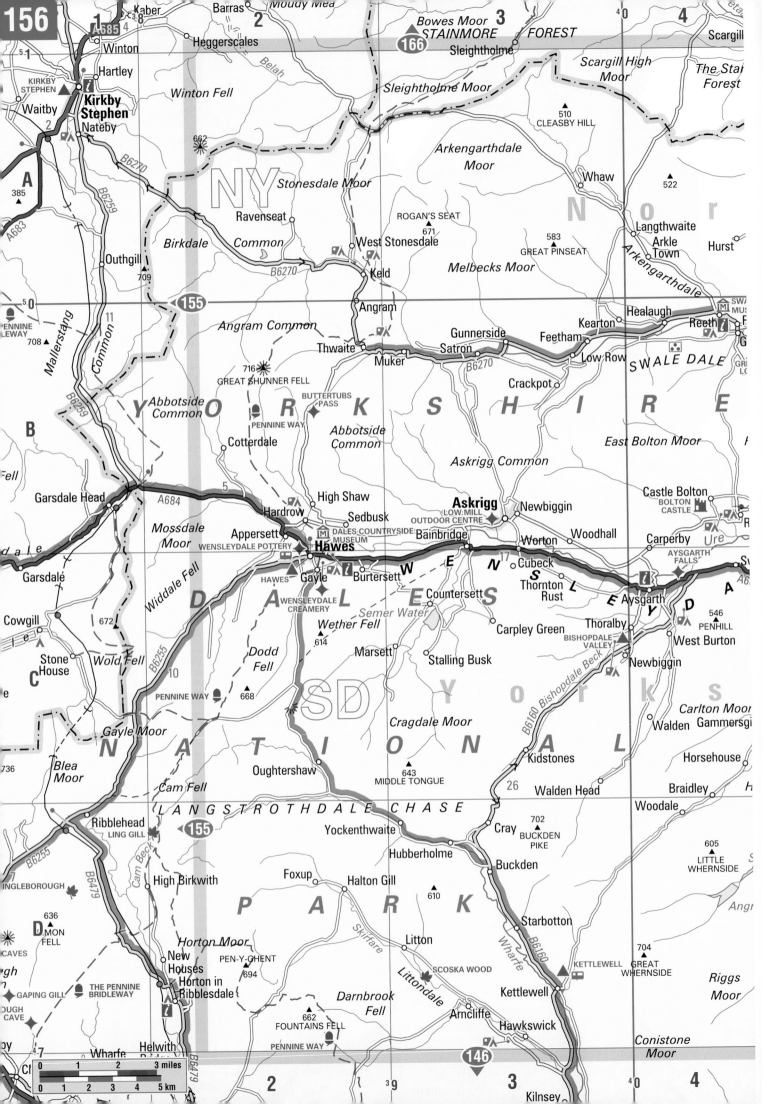

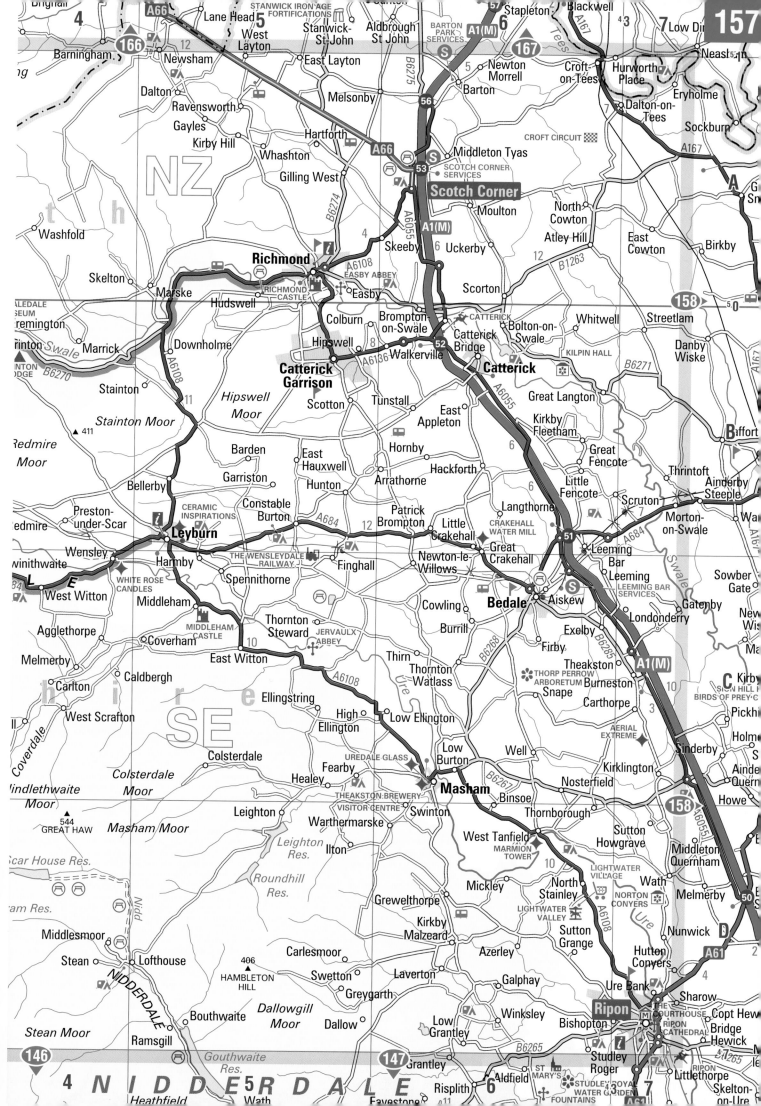

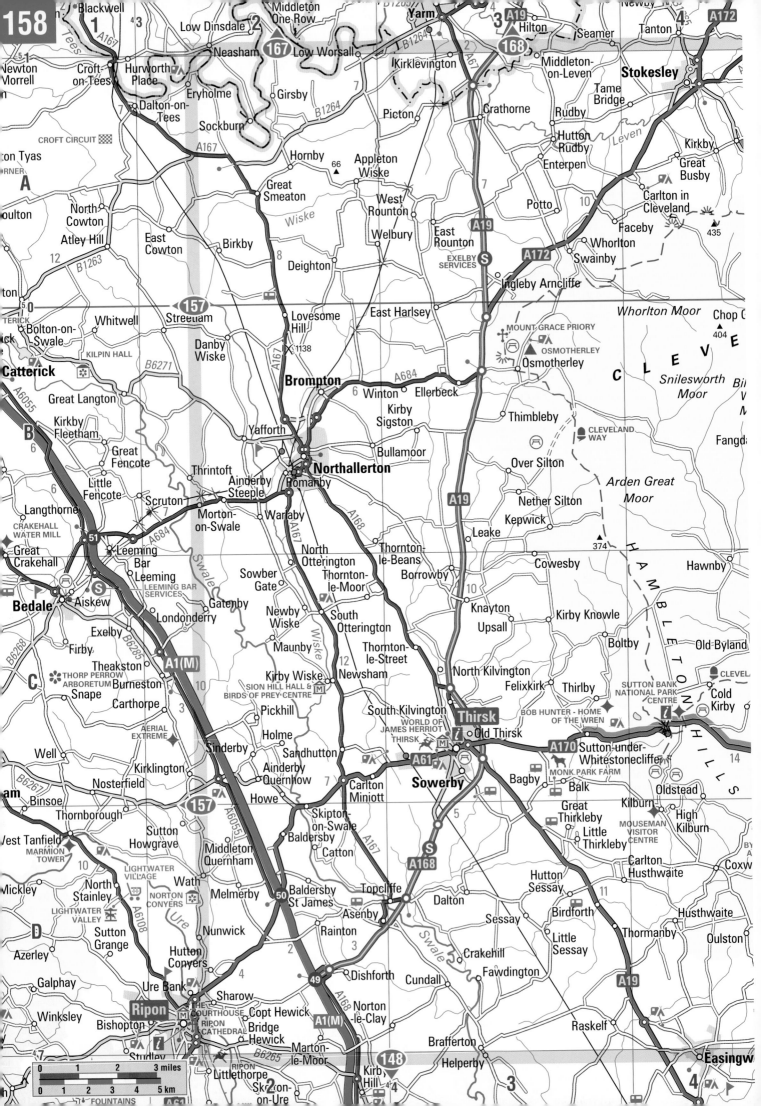

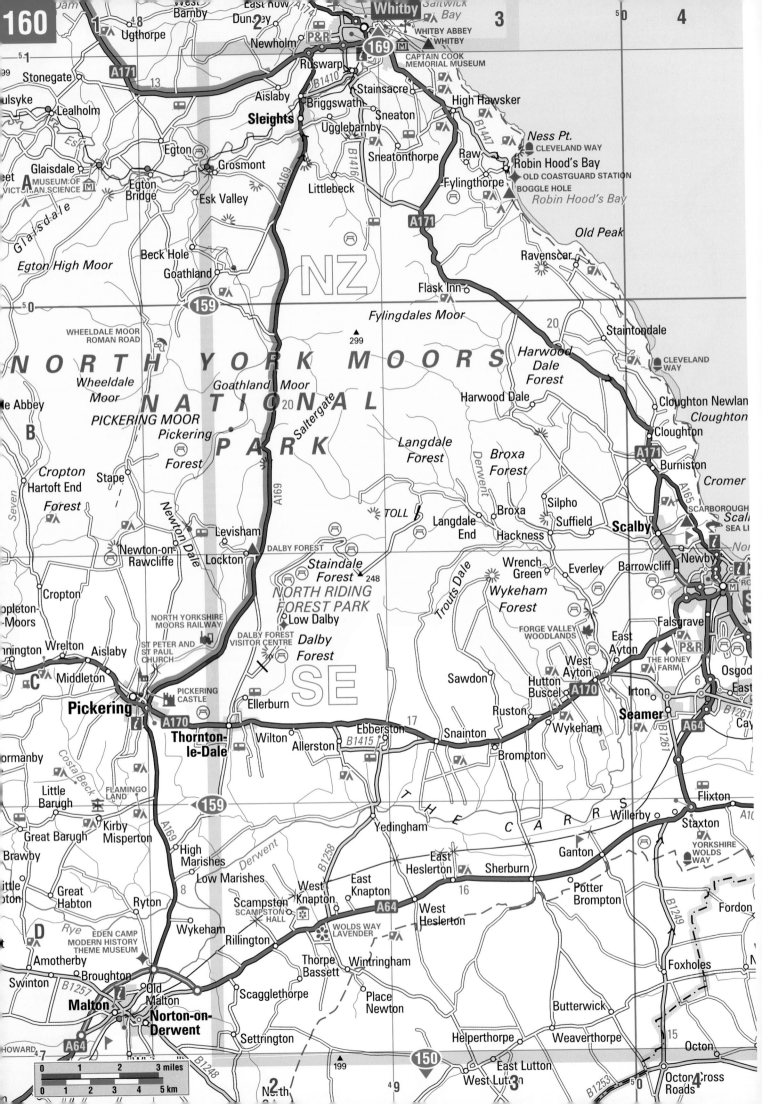

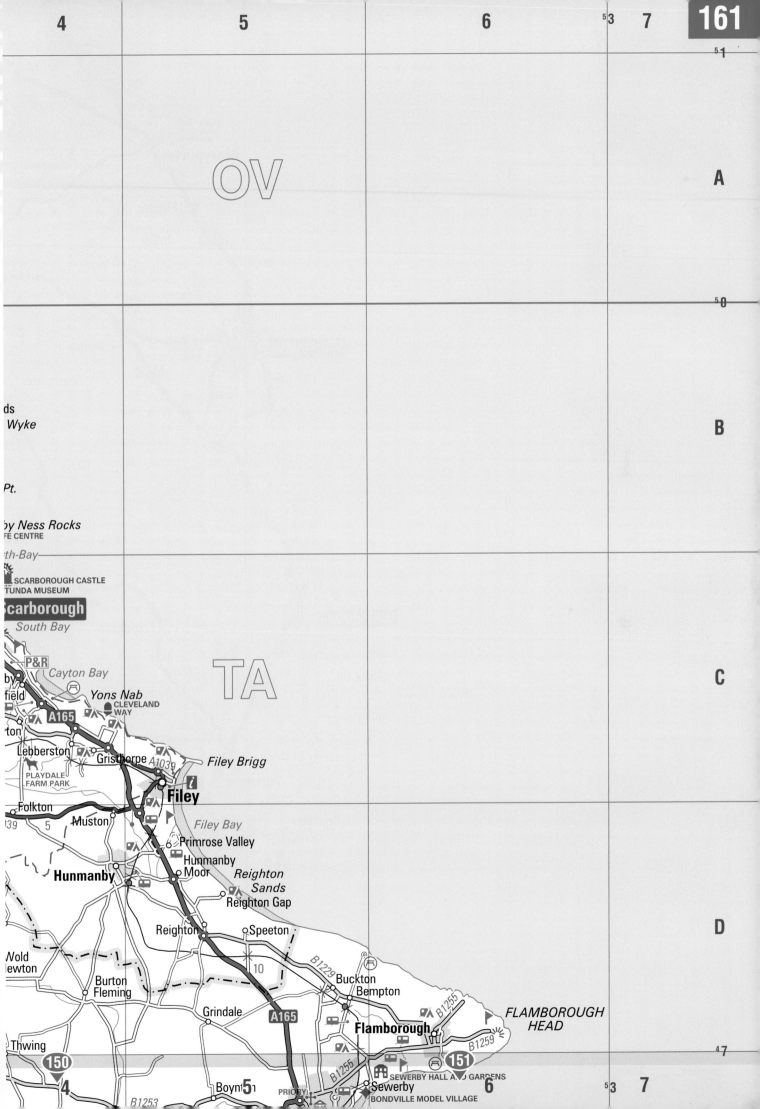

OV

Wyke

by Ness Rocks
FE CENTRE
th-Bay

SCARBOROUGH CASTLE
TUNDA MUSEUM

Scarborough
South Bay

TA

P&R   Cayton Bay

by
field   Yons Nab
CLEVELAND
WAY
A165

Lebberston   Gristhorpe   A1039   Filey Brigg
PLAYDALE
FARM PARK
Filey

Folkton   Filey Bay
039   5   Muston
Primrose Valley
Hunmanby
Moor   Reighton
Sands
Hunmanby   Reighton Gap

Wold   Reighton   Speeton
ewton
B1229
10   Buckton
Burton   Bempton
Fleming
Grindale   A165   B1255
FLAMBOROUGH
HEAD
Thwing   Flamborough
B1259
150   151
B1255   SEWERBY HALL AND GARDENS
Boynton   5   PRIORY   Sewerby
B1253   BONDVILLE MODEL VILLAGE

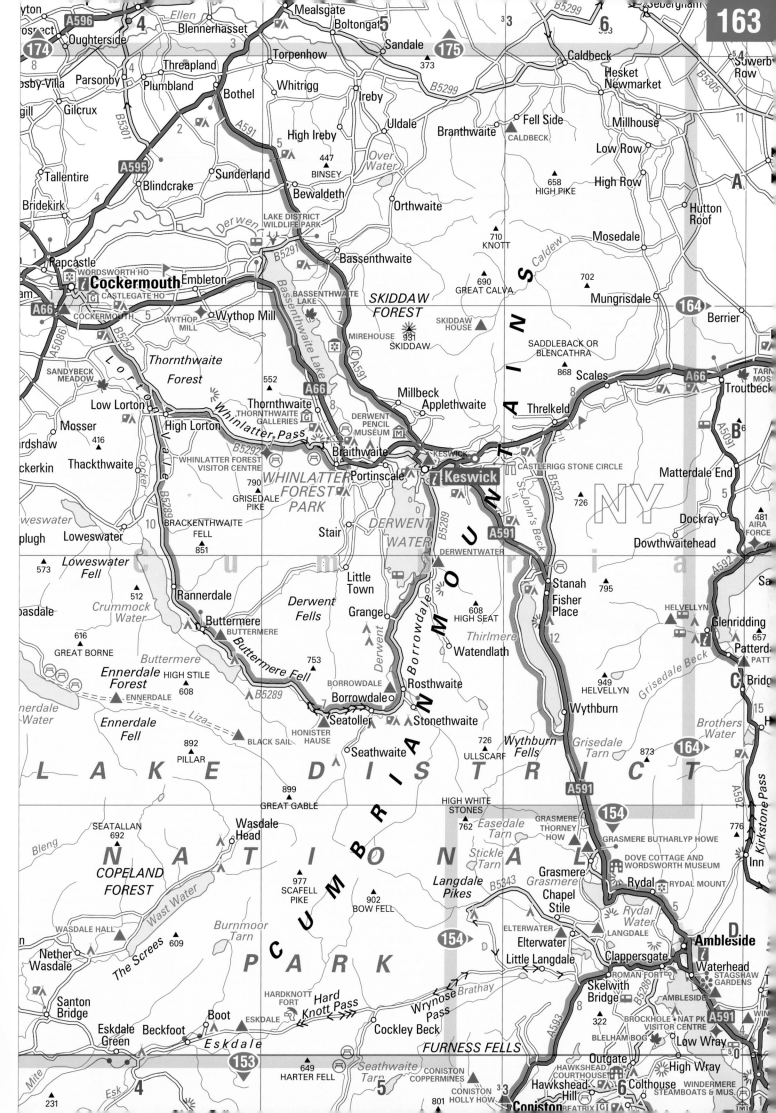

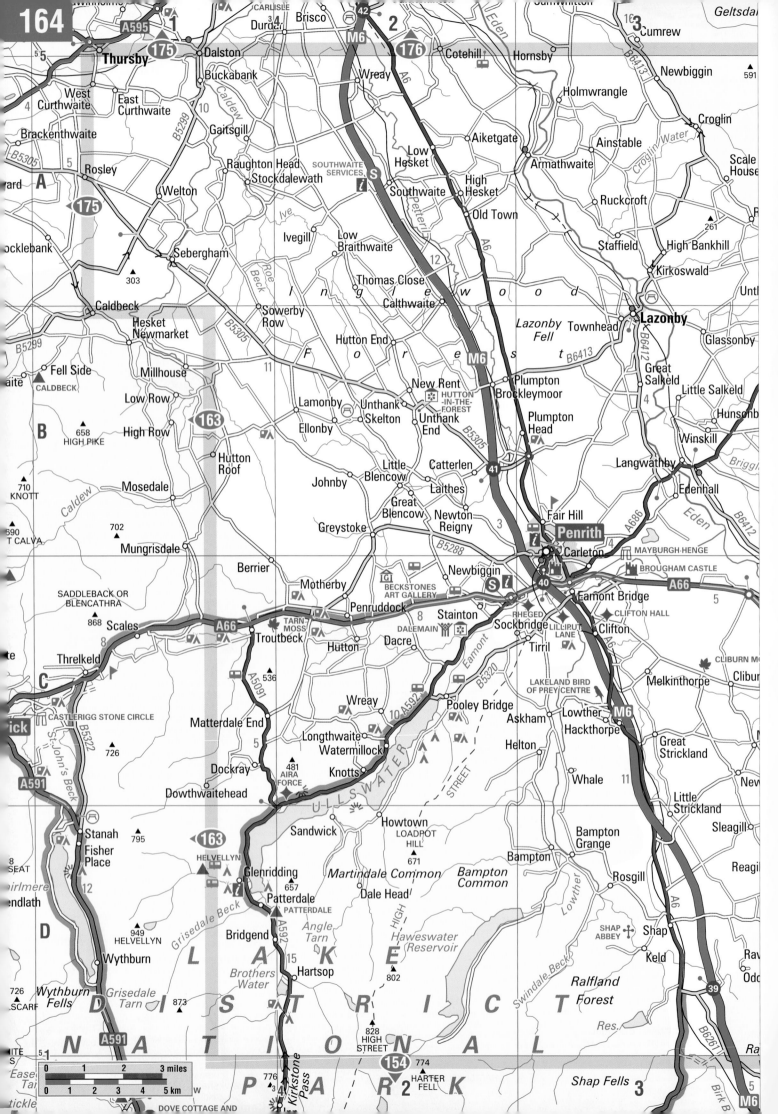

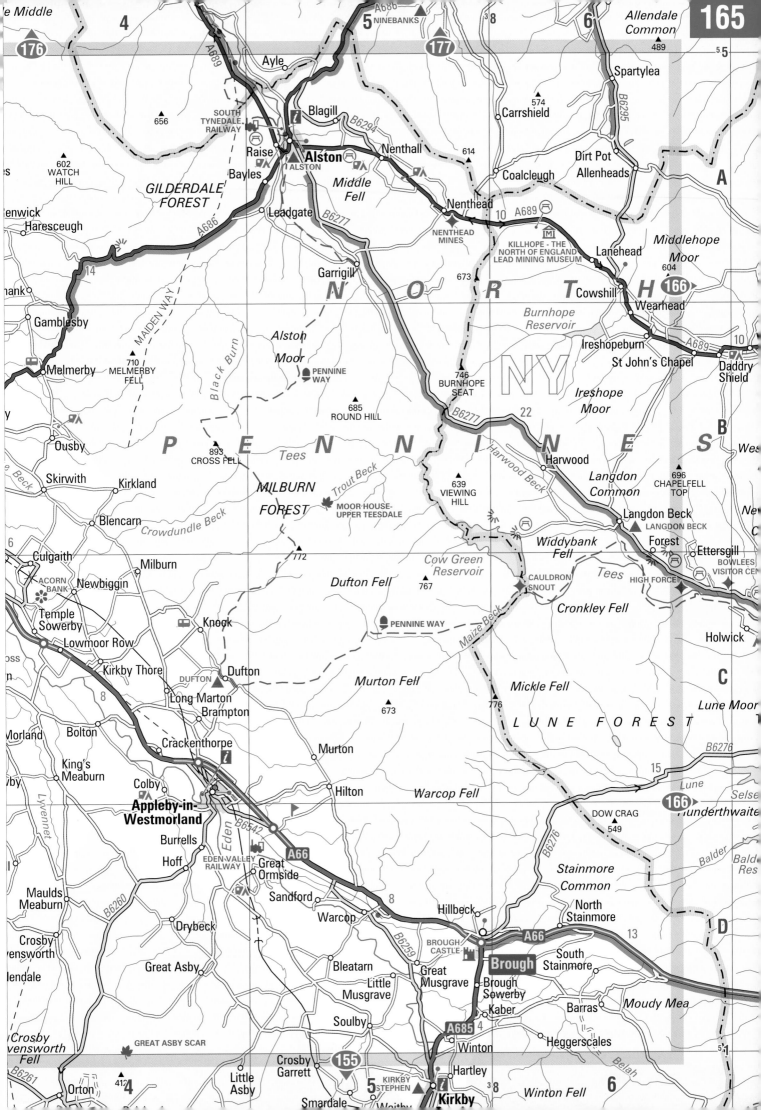

A

B

NZ

C

MINIATURE
RAILWAY

Saltburn-
by-the-Sea

166

SALTBURN
VALLEY

CHRIS BIRKBECK
INTERNATIONAL RALLY
SCHOOL

i

Brotton
Skinningrove

ENGLAND COAST PATH

Carlin
How
Boulby

North
Skelton
Loftus
A174
Staithes

5

Kilton
Thorpe
Easington
Port Mulgrave

sbeck
Lingdale
Hinderwell
Runswick Bay

Margrove
Park
Stanghow
Liverton
Roxby
Runswick
Bay
Kettleness

9

Moorsholm

B1366
Newton
Mulgrave
Goldsborough

D

Res.

A171

Scaling
Ellerby
14

B1266
A174
Lythe
Sandsend

Scaling Dam
Res.
Mickleby
East
Barnby
Sandsend Wyke

ndale
or
West
Barnby
East Row

SUTCLIFFE GALLERY

G

Whitby
Saltwick
Bay

Commondale
Danby Low Moor
Lealholm
Moor
Ugthorpe
Dunsley
Newholm
P&R

WHITBY ABBEY
WHITBY

M

159
Danby
E MOORS
CENTRE
299
Stonegate
160
Ruswarp
i

CAPTAIN COOK
MEMORIAL MUSEUM

51

4
5
6
A171
7

Danby
Houlsyke
ealholm
13
Aislaby
Briggswath
Sta 9 acre
High Hawsker

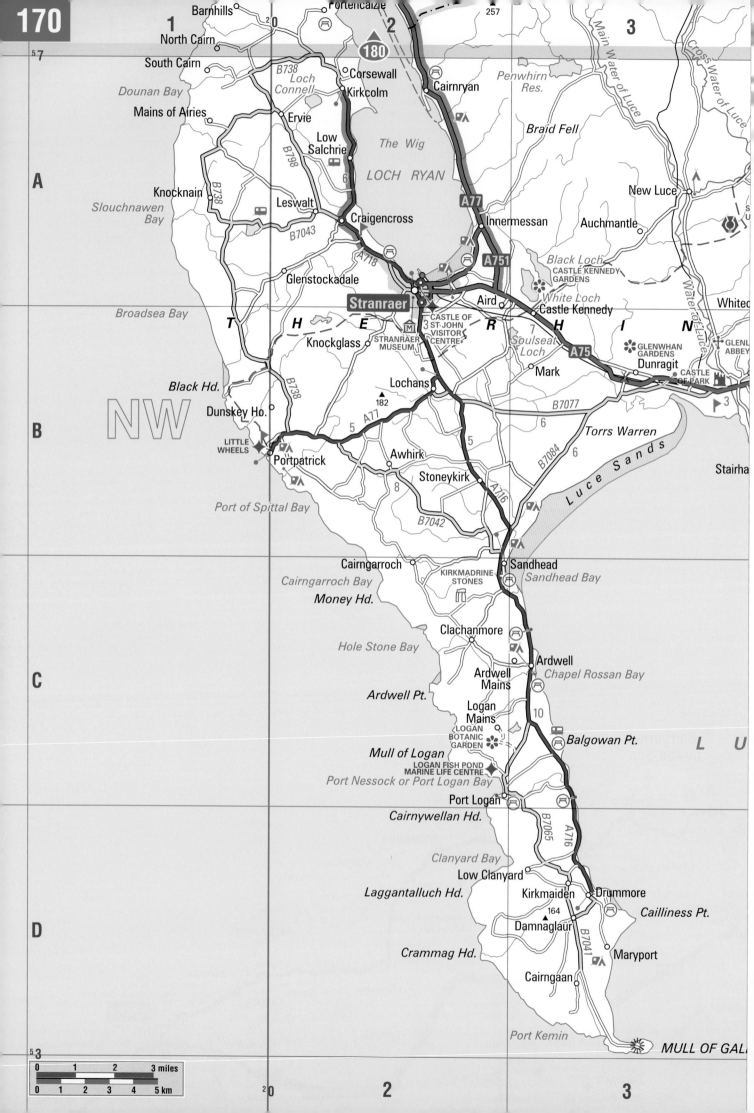

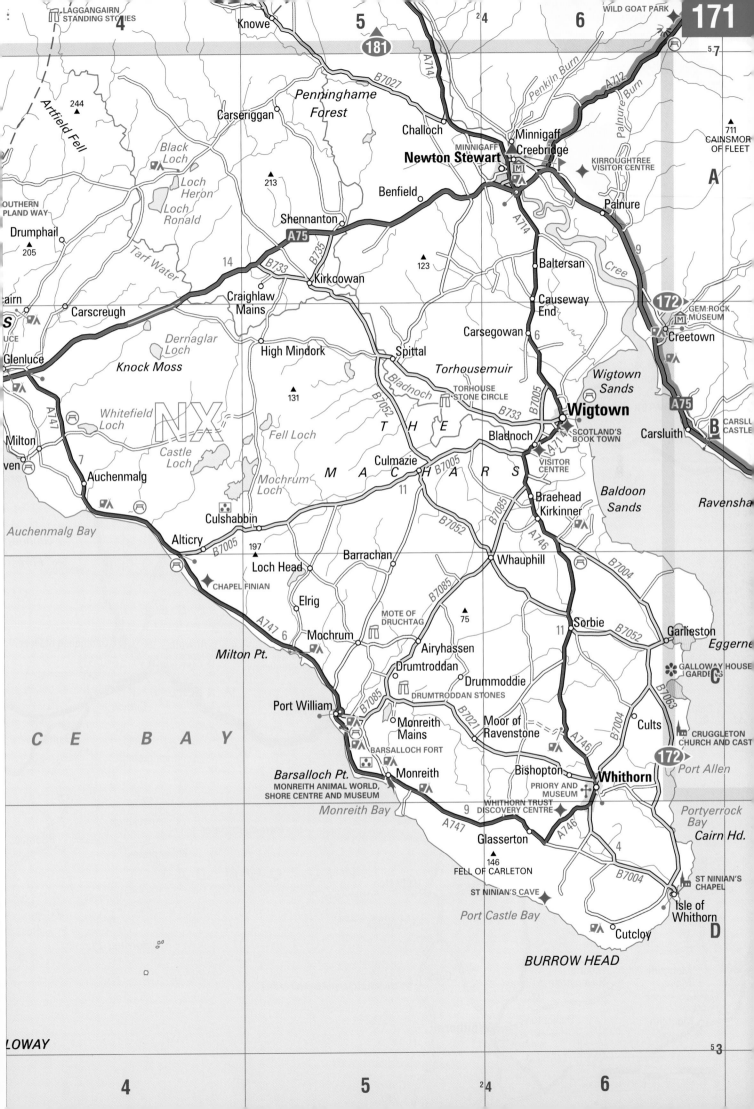

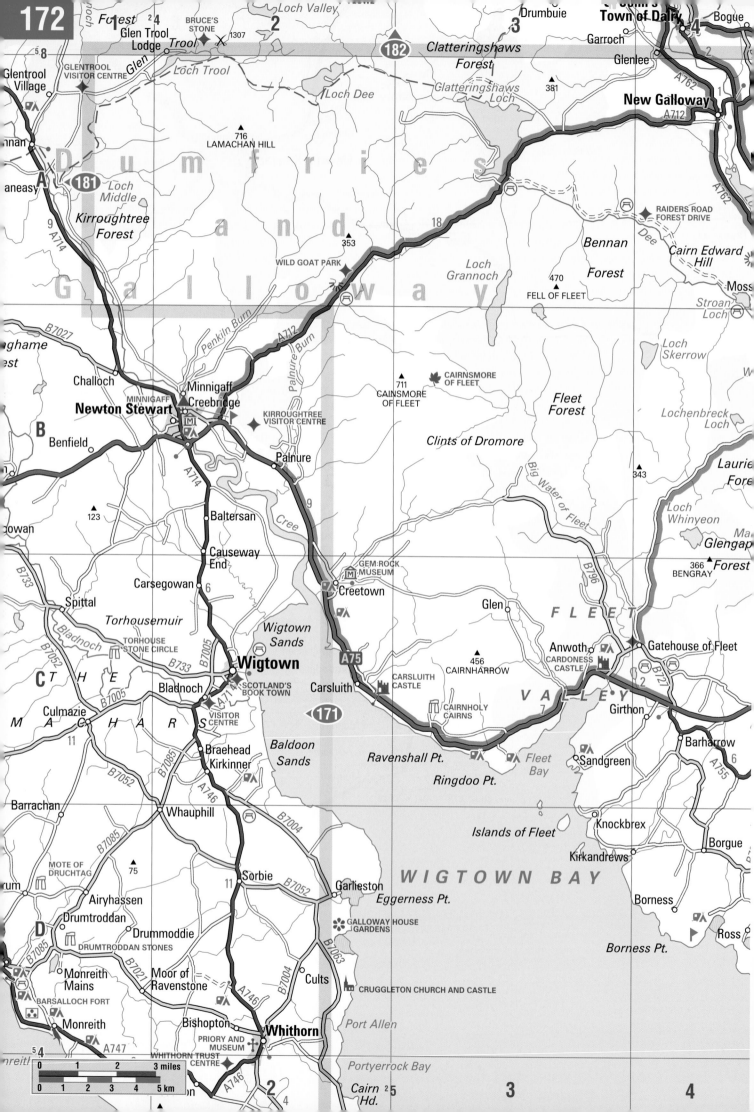

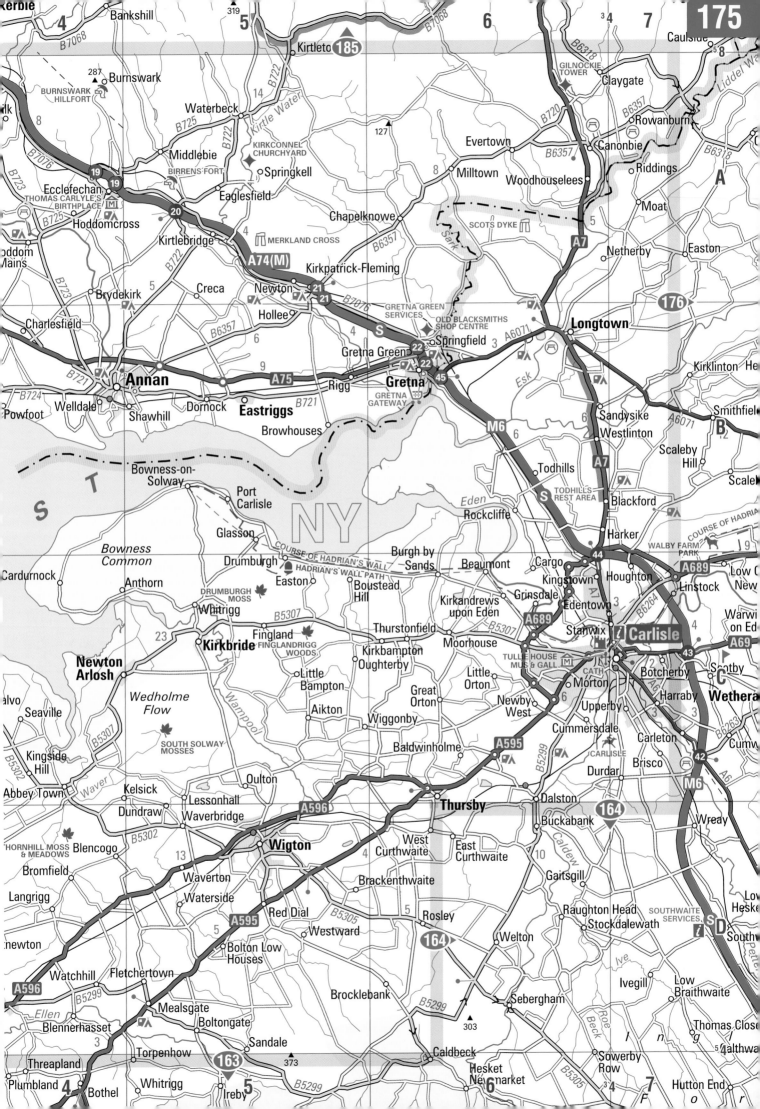

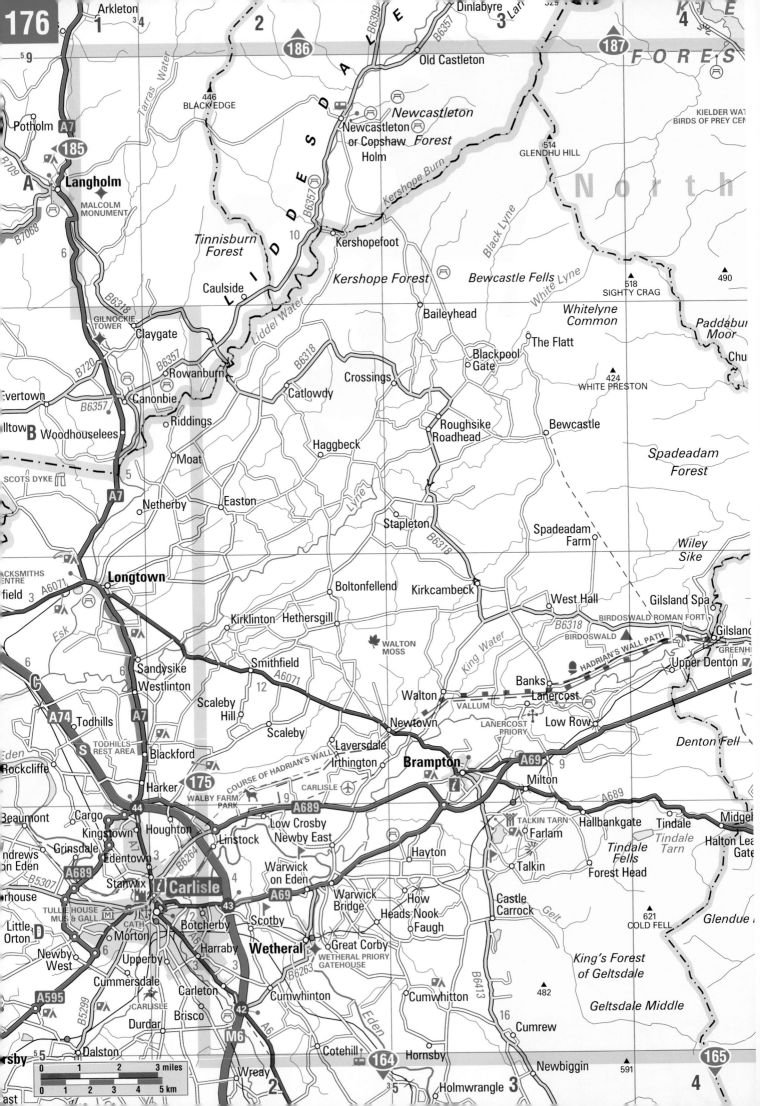

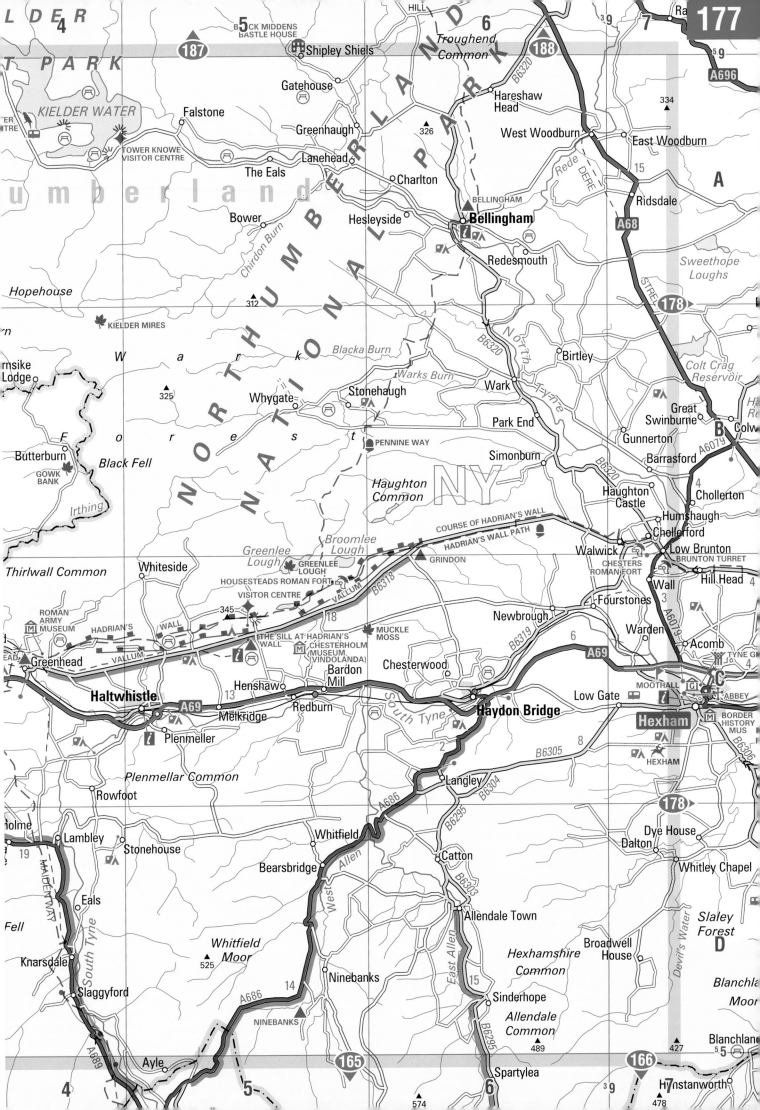

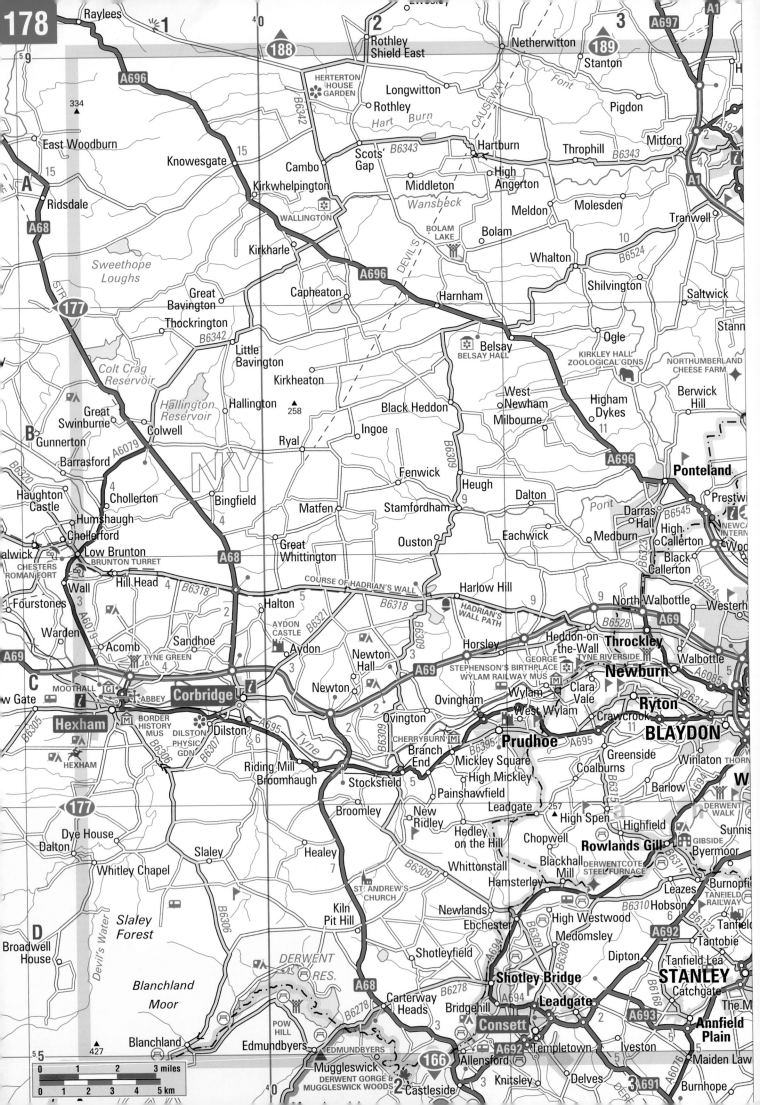

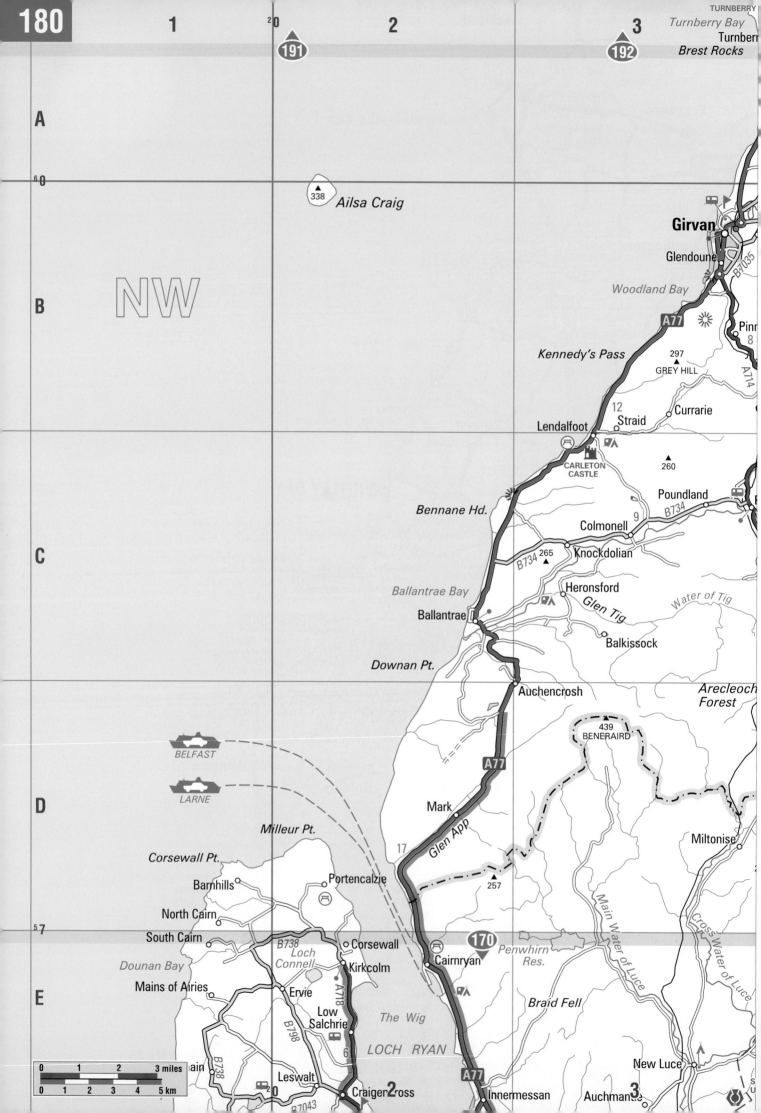

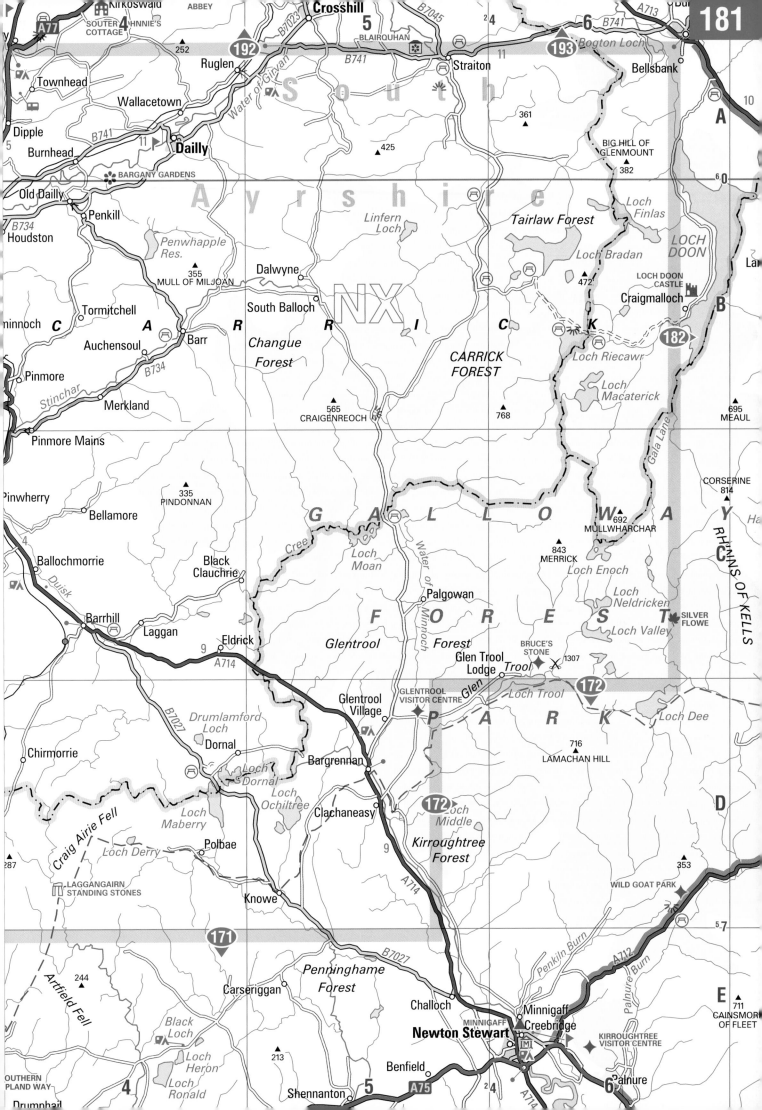

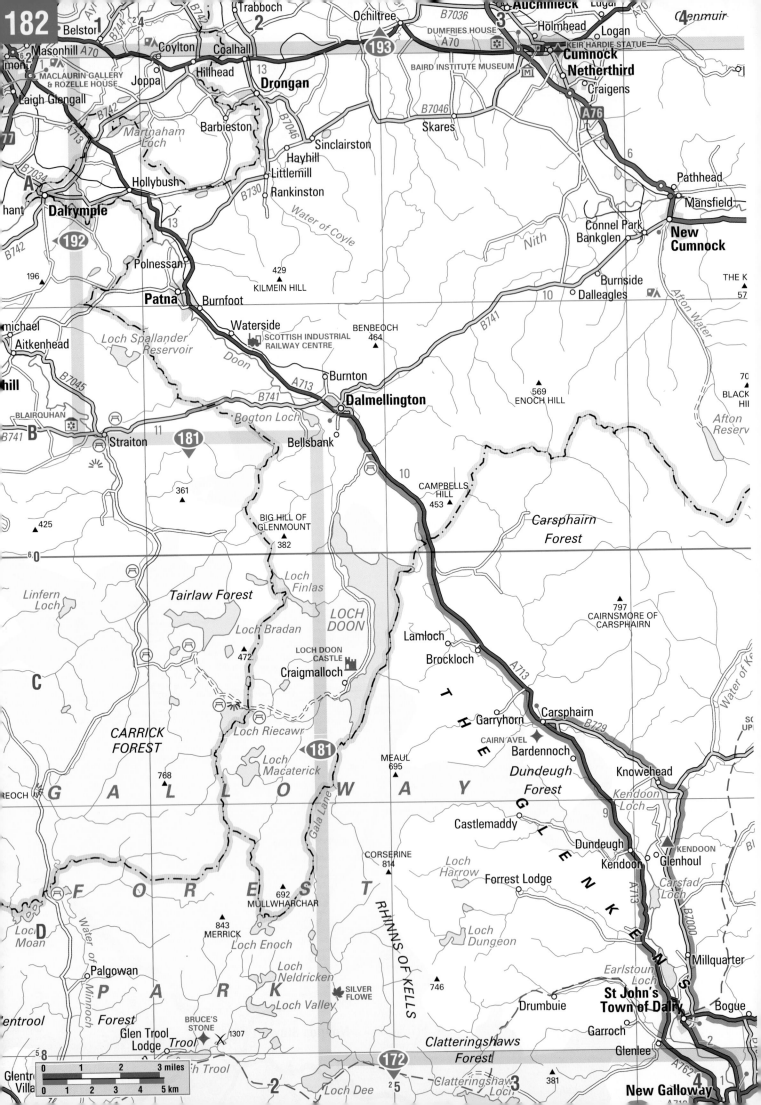

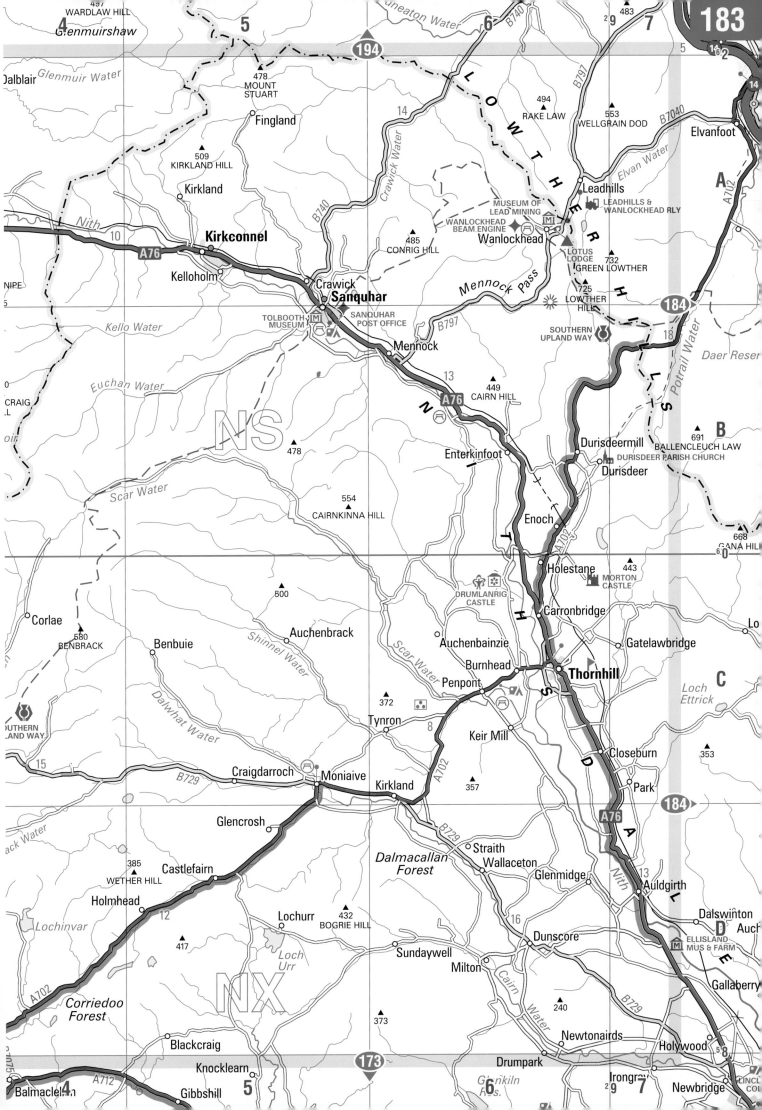

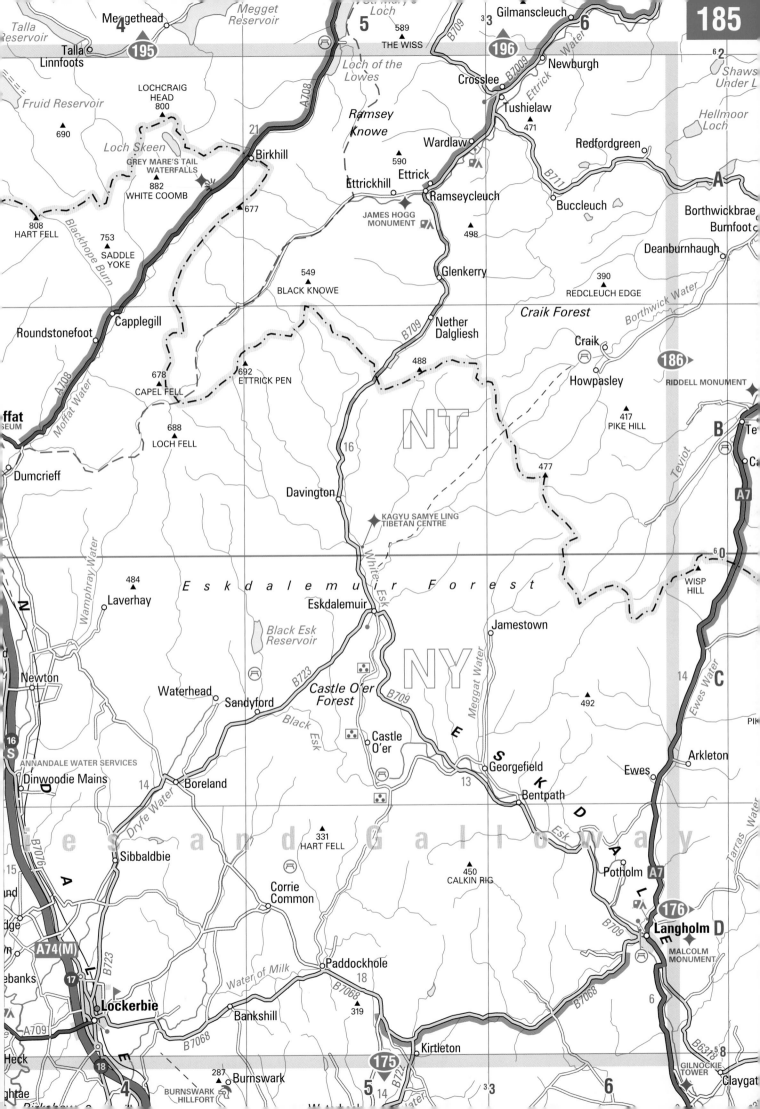

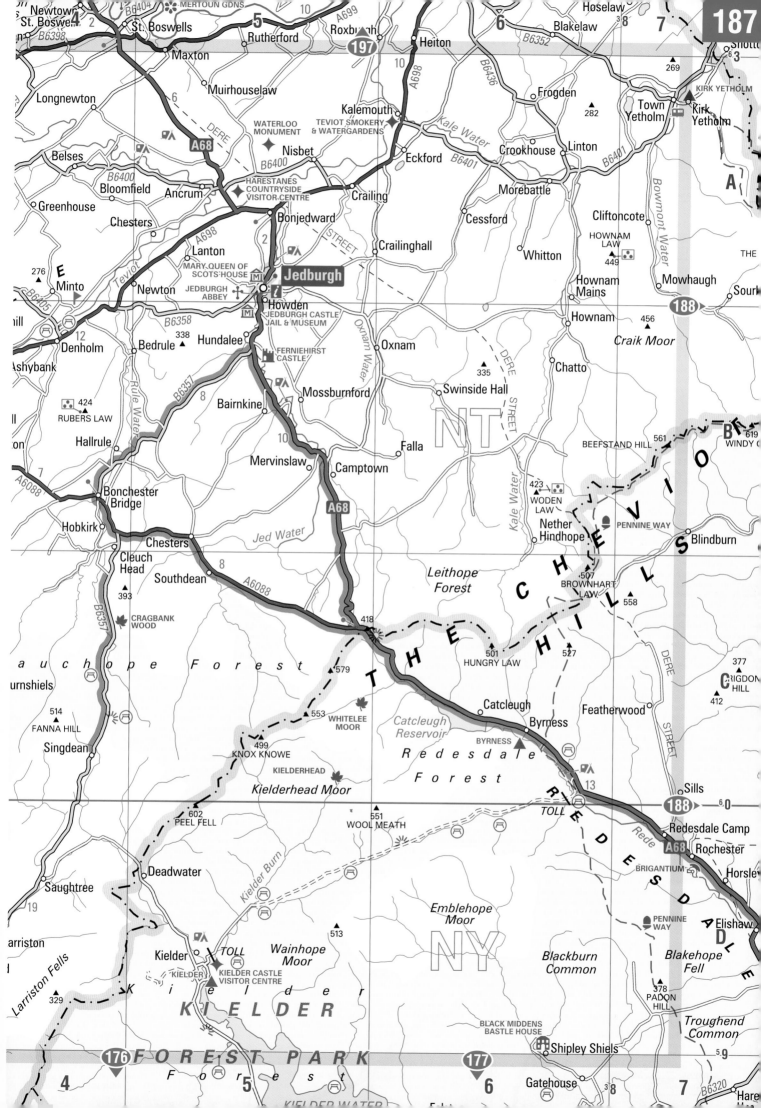

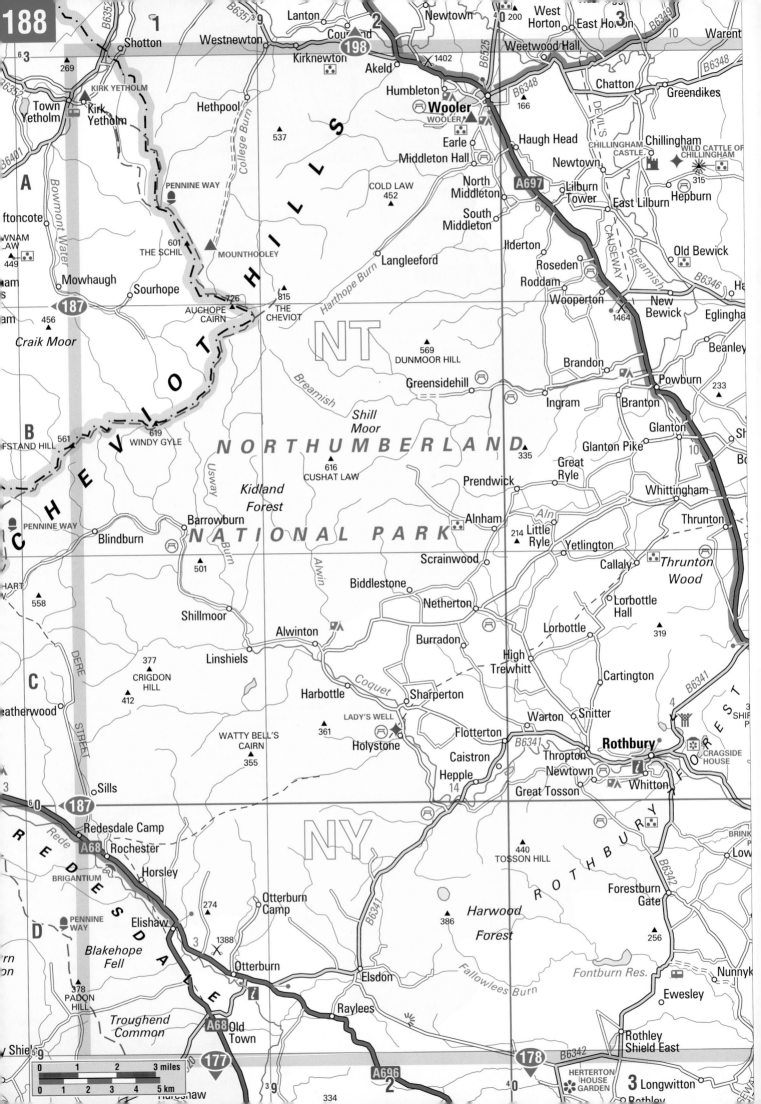

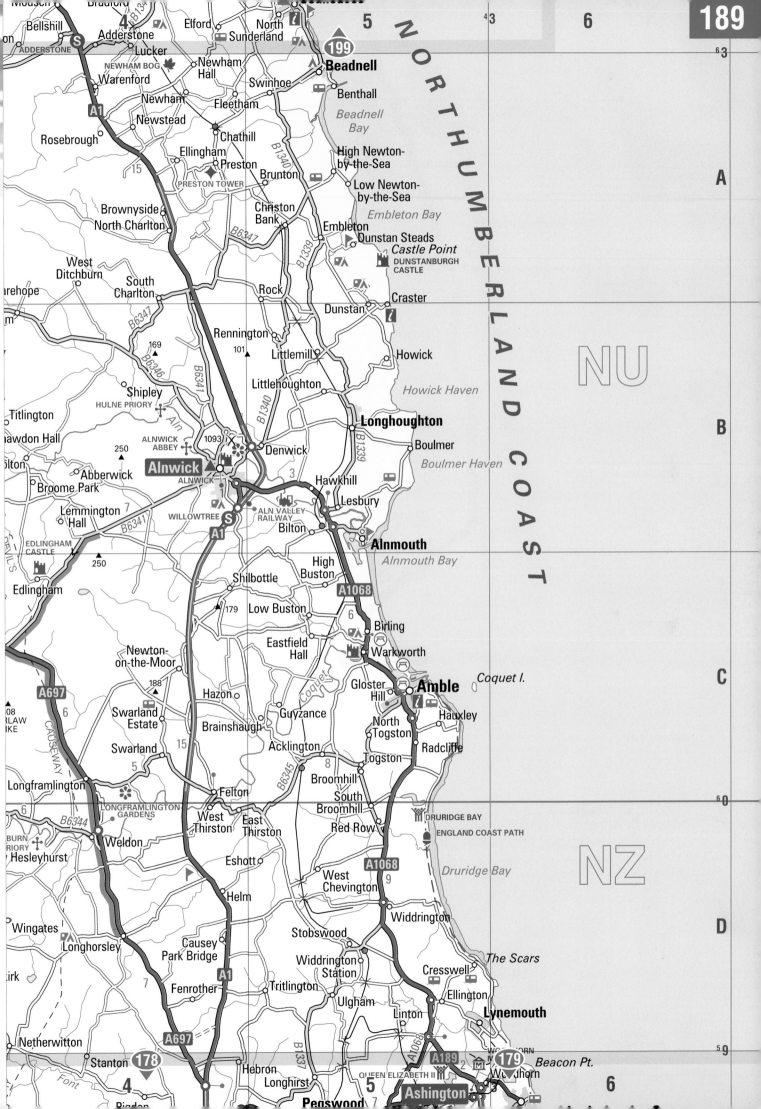

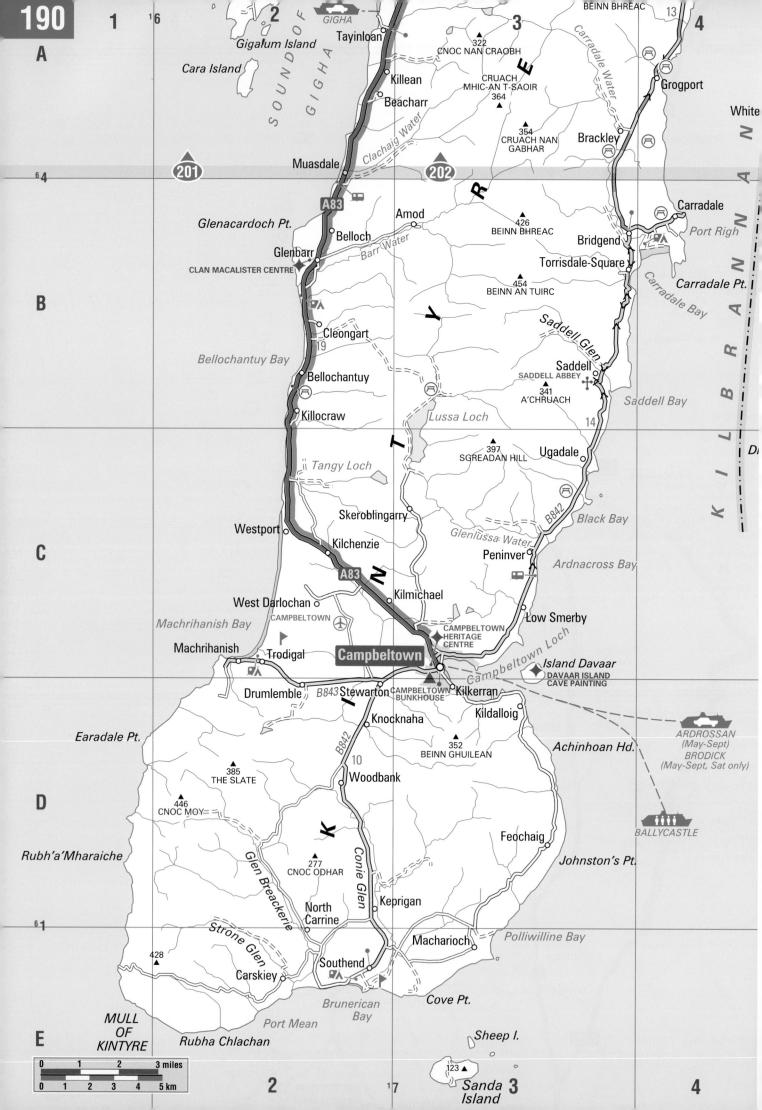

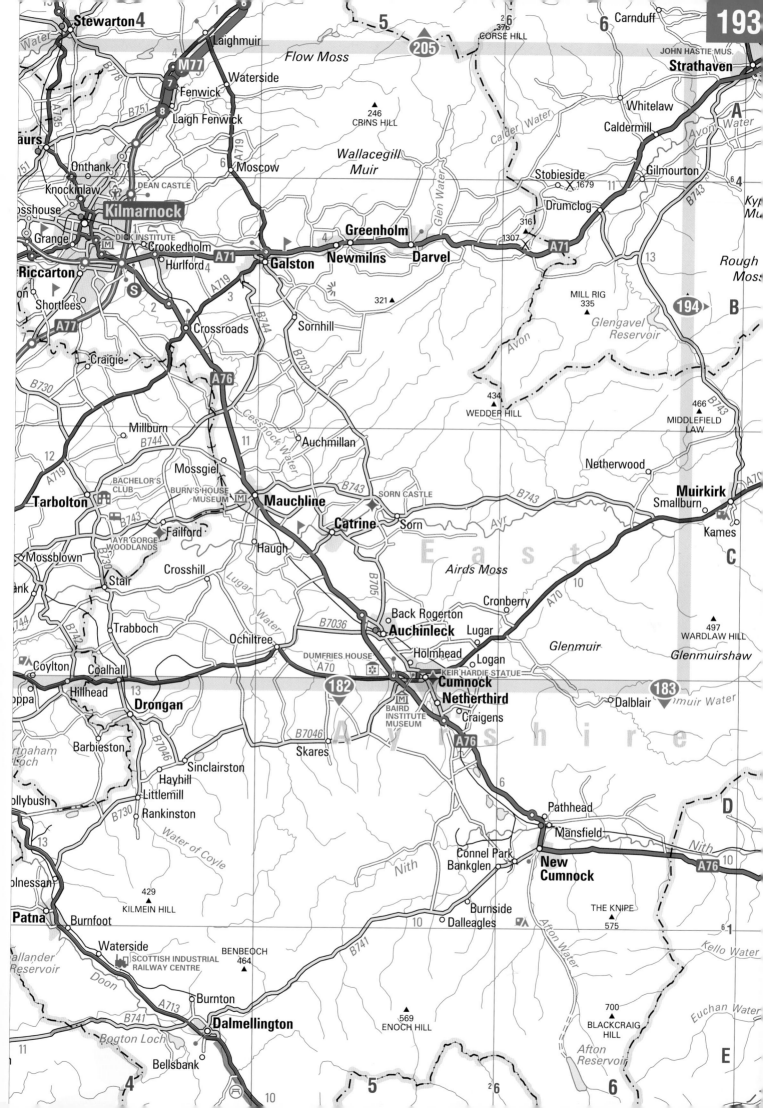

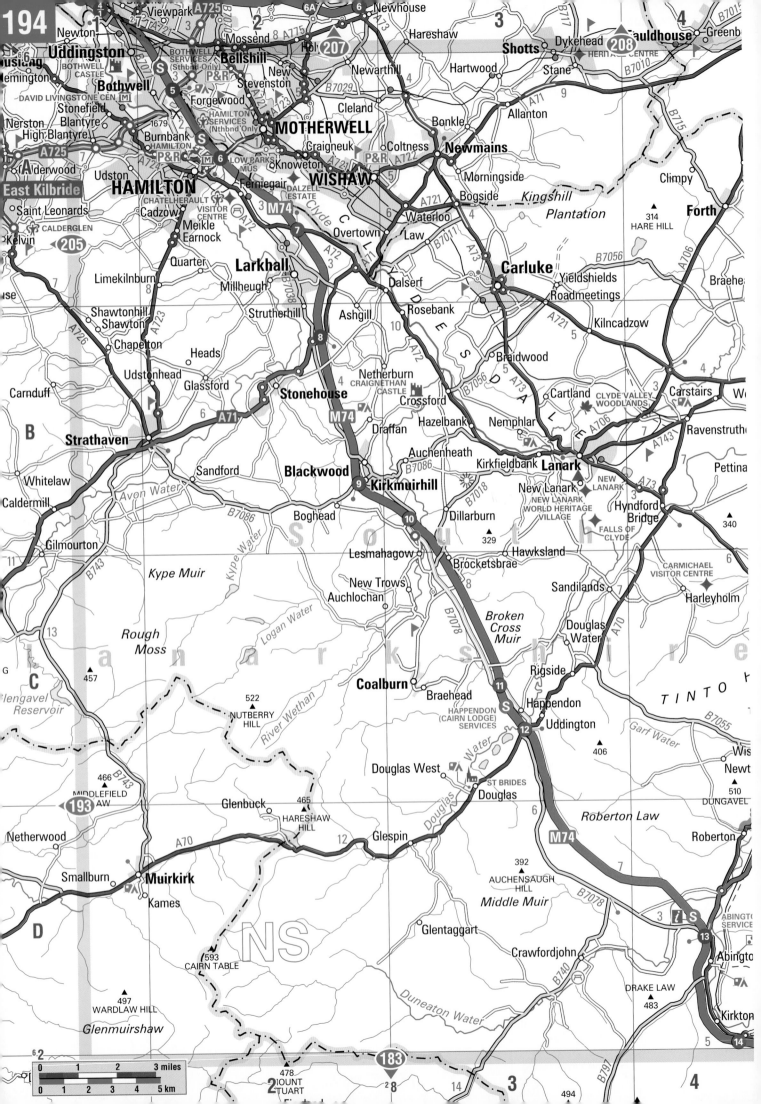

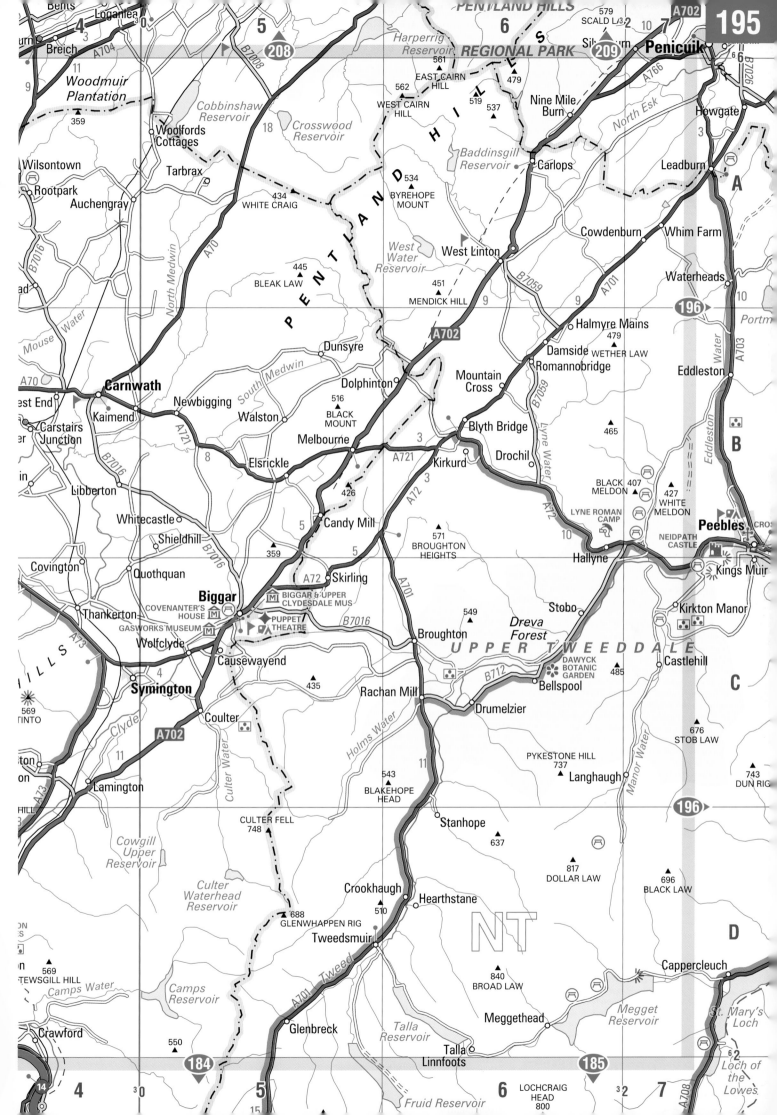

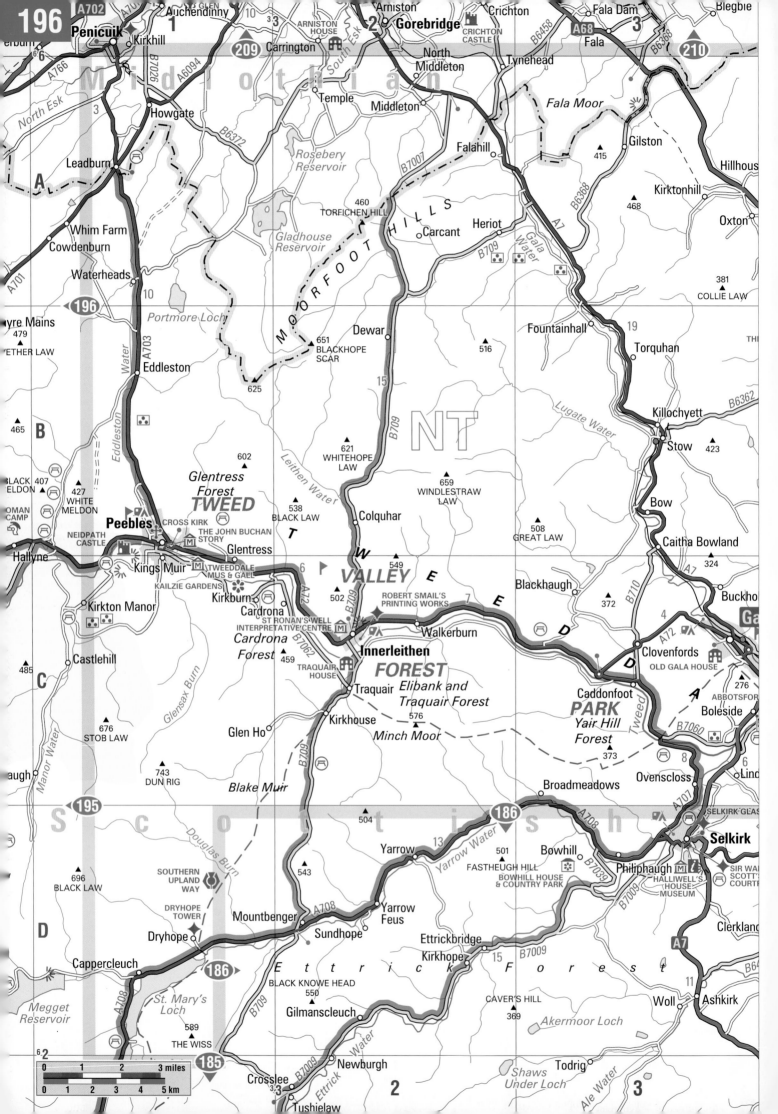

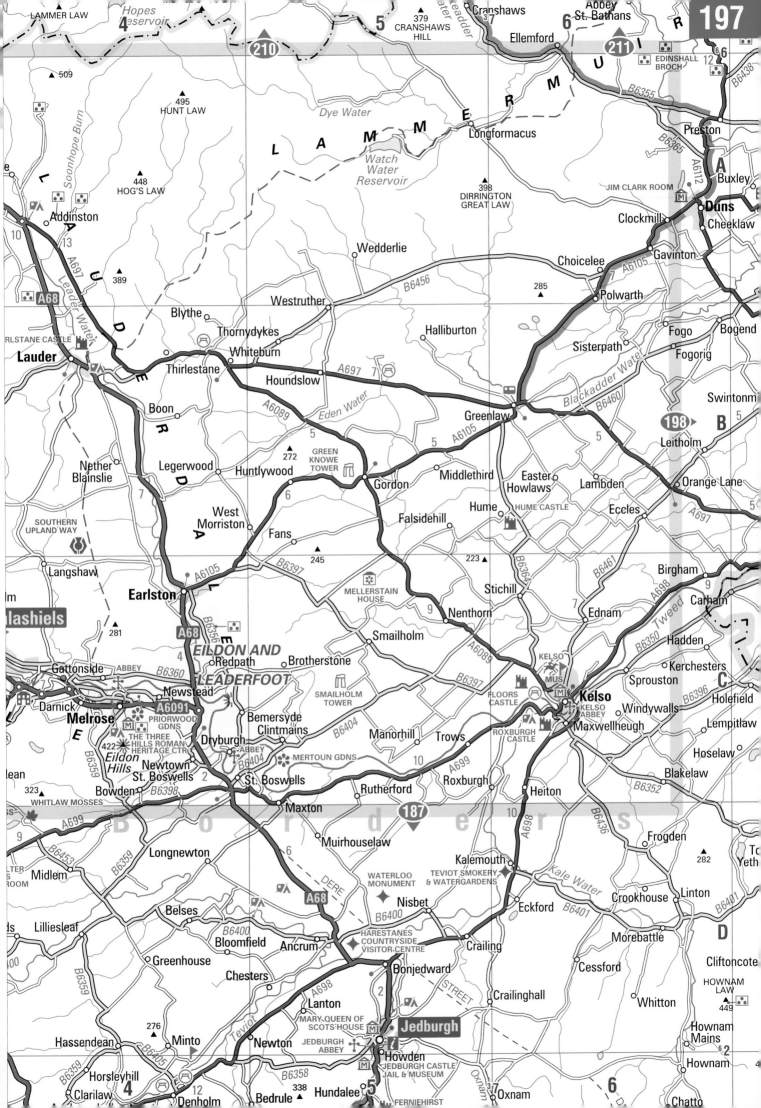

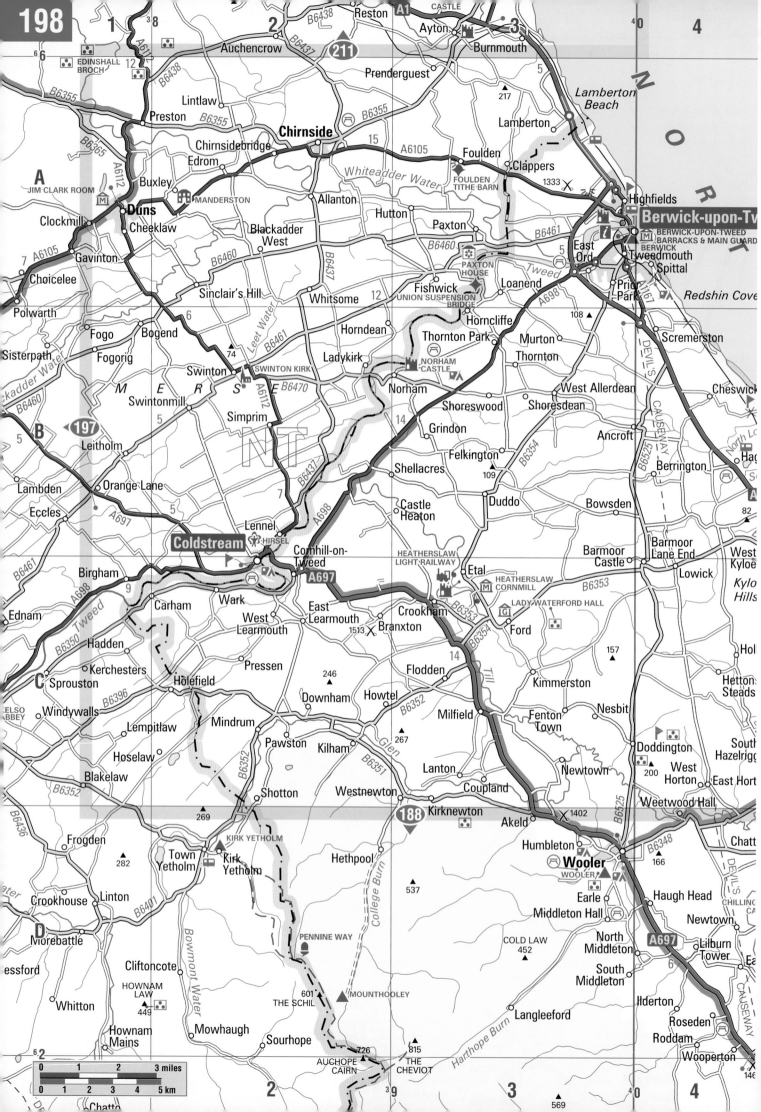

⁶6

A

NU

B

Goswick

ggerston

South Low

Beal

12

96353

Fenwick

East Kyloe

Buckton

burn

Detchant

Middleton

211

North Hazelrigg

Belford

B6349

Mousen

Bellshill

Warenton

10

ADDERSTONE

B6348

on

Greendikes

gham

Chillingham

CASTLE

WILD CATTLE OF CHILLINGHAM

315

Hepburn

ast Lilburn

New Bewick

54

B6346

Harehope

Eglingham

LINDISFARNE

Causeway Holy Island Sands

Fenham

Guile Pt.

Holy Island

HERITAGE CENTRE

Emmanuel Hd.

Holy Island (Lindisfarne)

LINDISFARNE CASTLE

Castle Pt.

LINDISFARNE PRIORY

Elwick

Ross

Budle Bay

Budle

Easington

Waren Mill

5

B1342

Spindlestone

Bradford

B1341

Adderstone

S

Lucker

NEWHAM BOG

Warenford

Newham Hall

Newham

Newstead

Rosebrough

Chathill

Ellingham

Preston

PRESTON TOWER

Brownyside

North Charlton

West Ditchburn

South Charlton

A1

15

B6347

Glororum

Burton

B1340

Elford

North Sunderland

189

Swinhoe

Fleetham

Brunton

Christon Bank

Rock

B6341

169

Rennington

101

Farne Islands

Staple Sound

BAMBURGH CASTLE

Bamburgh

FARNE ISLANDS

Inner Sound

Seahouses

i

Beadnell

Benthall

Beadnell Bay

High Newton-by-the-Sea

Low Newton-by-the-Sea

Embleton Bay

Embleton

Dunstan Steads

Castle Point

DUNSTANBURGH CASTLE

Craster

Dunstan

i

Littlemill

Howick

C

O

A

S

T

C

D

⁶2

⁴3

weed

H U M B E R L A N D

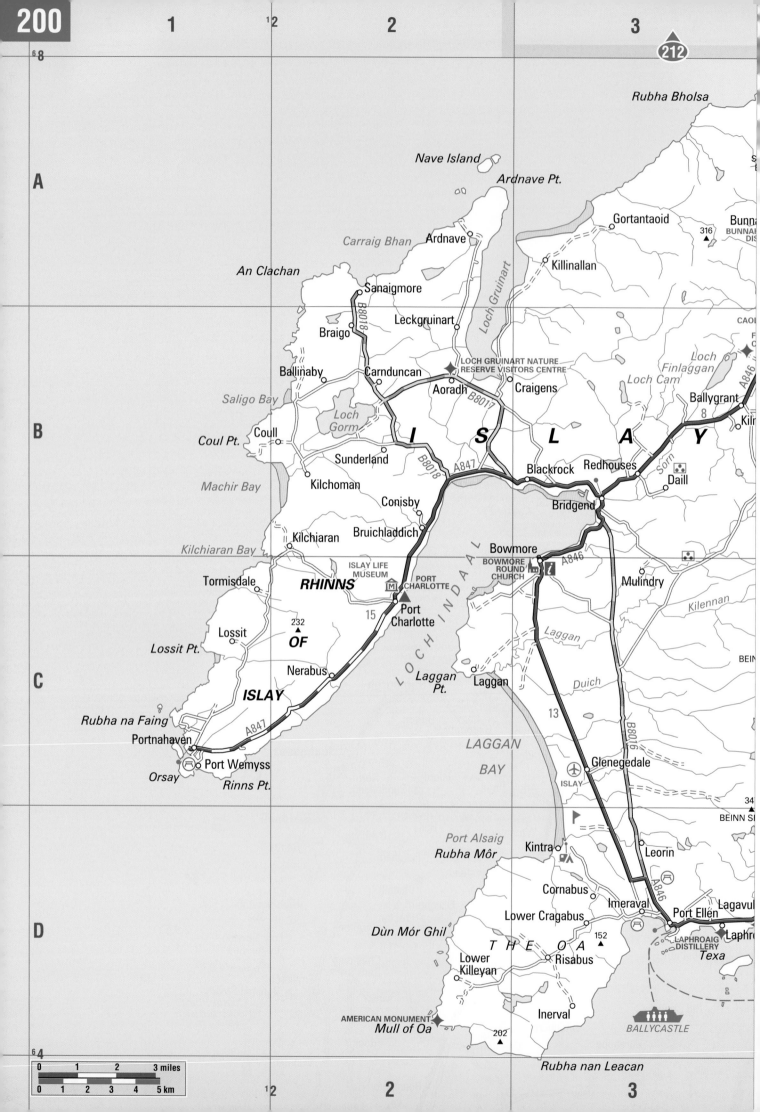

212

6 8

A

Rubha Bholsa

Nave Island

Ardnave Pt.

Gortantaoid

Bunna

316

BUNNA
DIS

Carraig Bhan

Ardnave

Killinallan

CAO

An Clachan

Loch Gruinart

Sanaigmore

Loch
Finlaggan

Loch

Leckgruinart

Braigo

B8018

Loch Gruinart NATURE
RESERVE VISITORS CENTRE

Loch Cam

Ballinaby

Carnduncan

Aoradh

B8017

Craigens

Ballygrant

Saligo Bay

Loch
Gorm

I S L A Y

A846

8

Kil

B

Coul Pt.

Coull

Sunderland

B8018

A847

Blackrock

Redhouses

Sorn

Machir Bay

Kilchoman

Conisby

Bridgend

Daill

Kilchiaran

Bruichladdich

A846

Kilchiaran Bay

ISLAY LIFE
MUSEUM

M

PORT
CHARLOTTE

Bowmore

BOWMORE
ROUND
CHURCH

i

Mulindry

Tormisdale

RHINNS

Port
Charlotte

15

Kilennan

232

OF

Laggan
Pt.

Laggan

Laggan

Duich

13

Lossit

Lossit

Nerabus

C

ISLAY

Rubha na Faing

A847

Portnahaven

Port Wemyss

Orsay

Rinns Pt.

LAGGAN
BAY

ISLAY

Glenegedale

34

BEINN SI

6

Port Alsaig

Rubha Môr

Kintra

Leorin

A846

Cornabus

Imeraval

Port Ellen

Lagavul

Lower Cragabus

D

Dùn Mór Ghil

T H E O A

152

Laphroaig

LAPHROAIG
DISTILLERY

Laphr

Texa

Lower
Killeyan

Risabus

AMERICAN MONUMENT

Mull of Oa

Inerval

BALLYCASTLE

202

6 4

Rubha nan Leacan

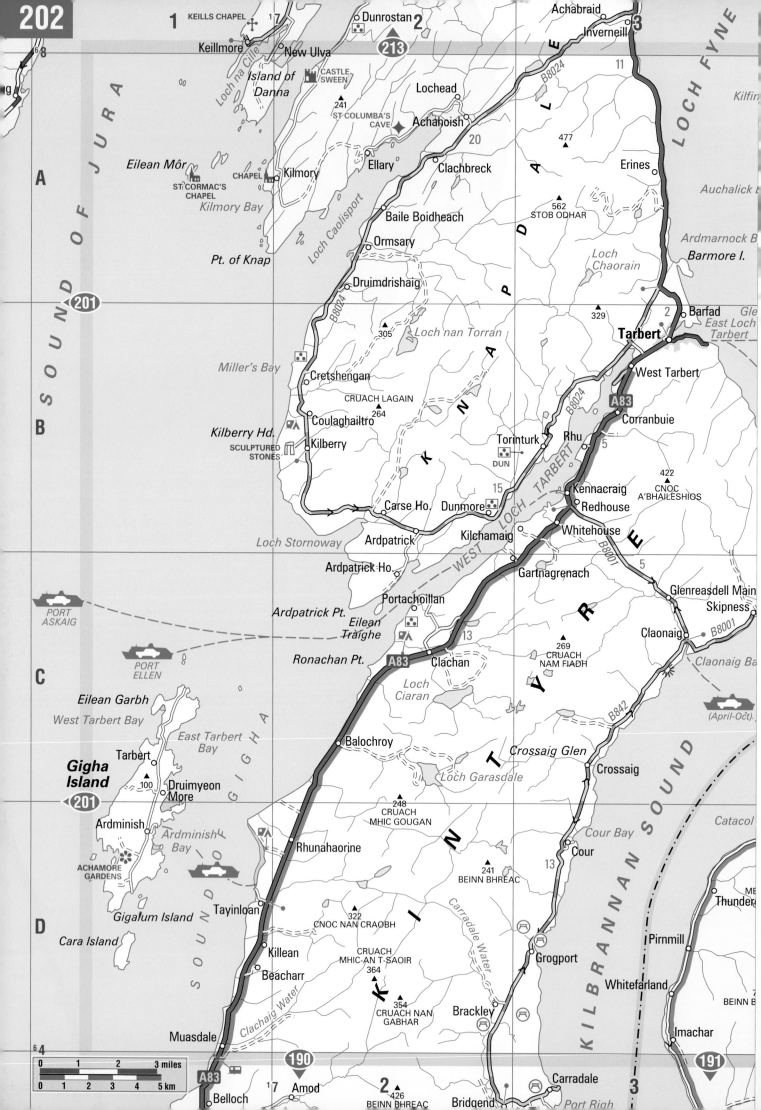

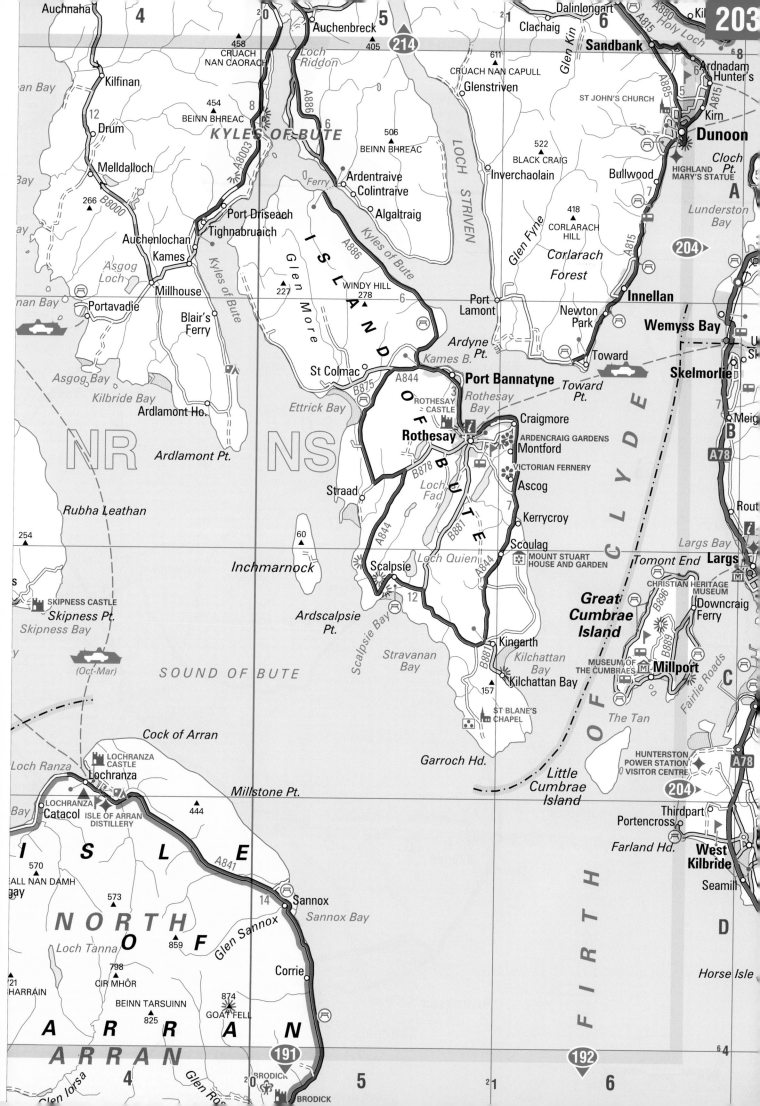

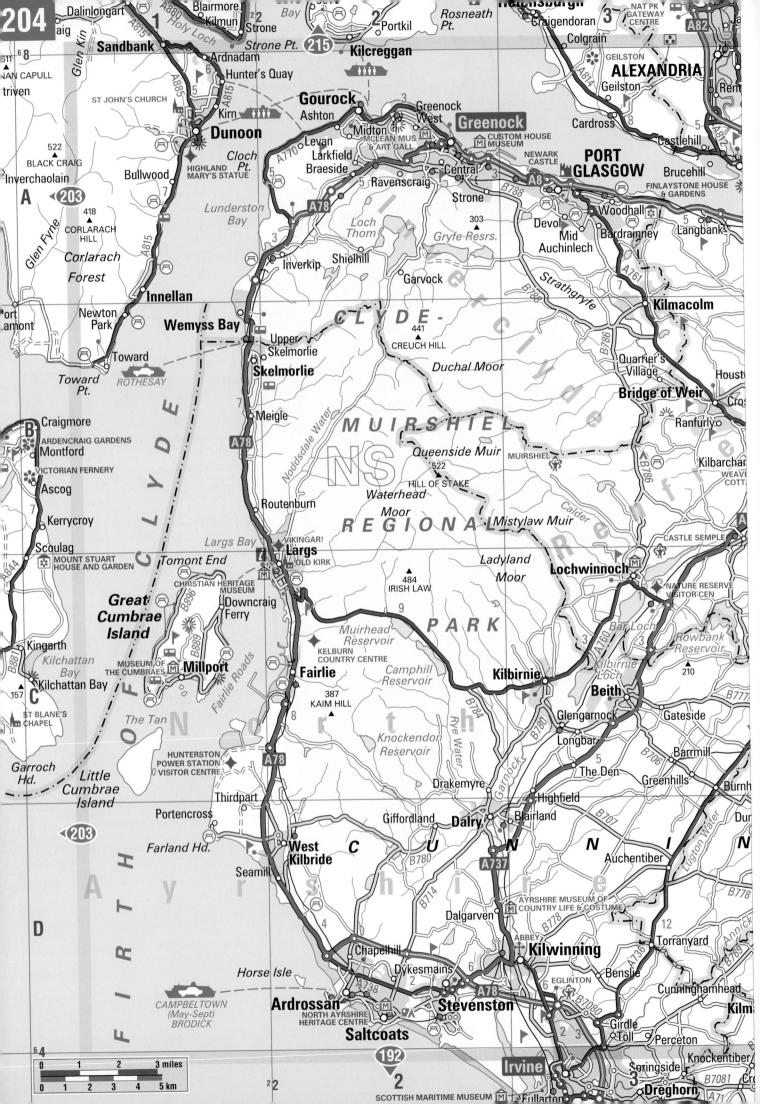

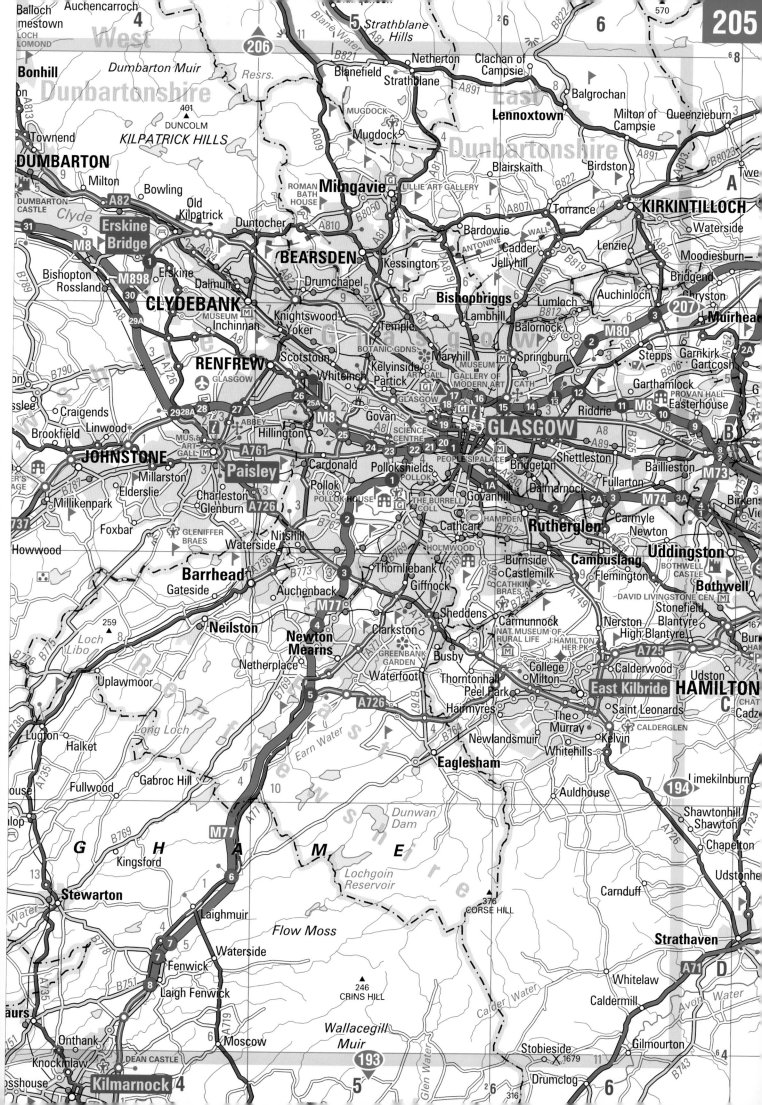

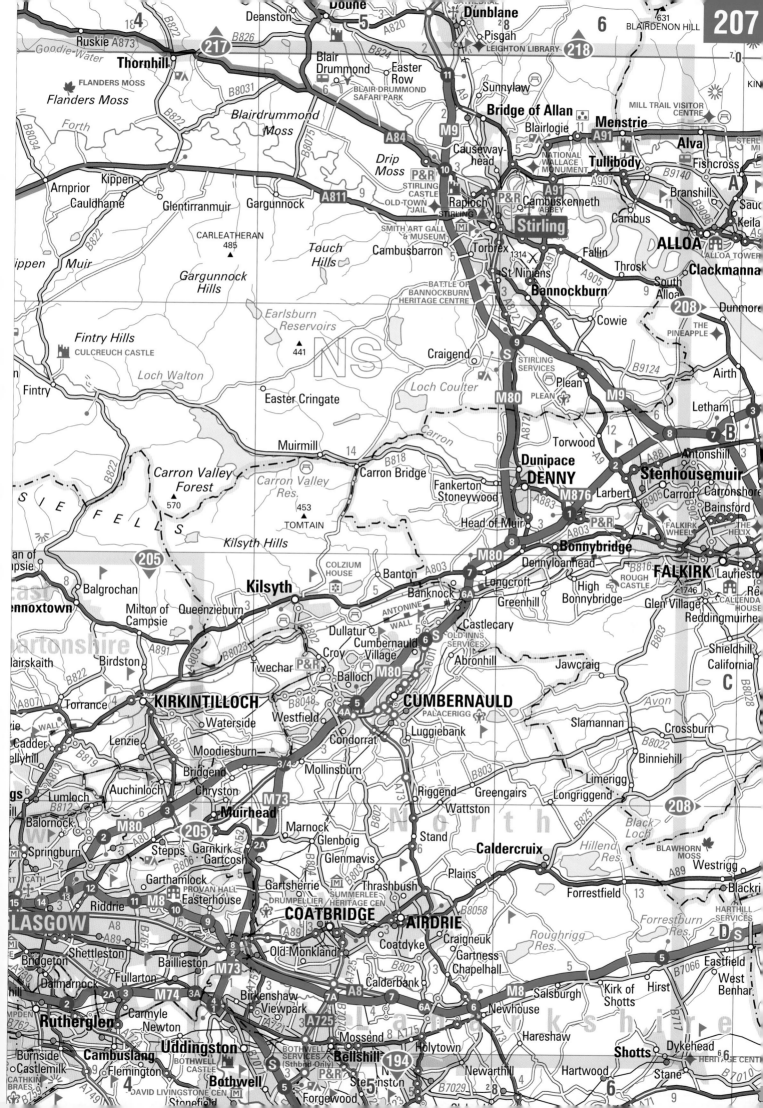

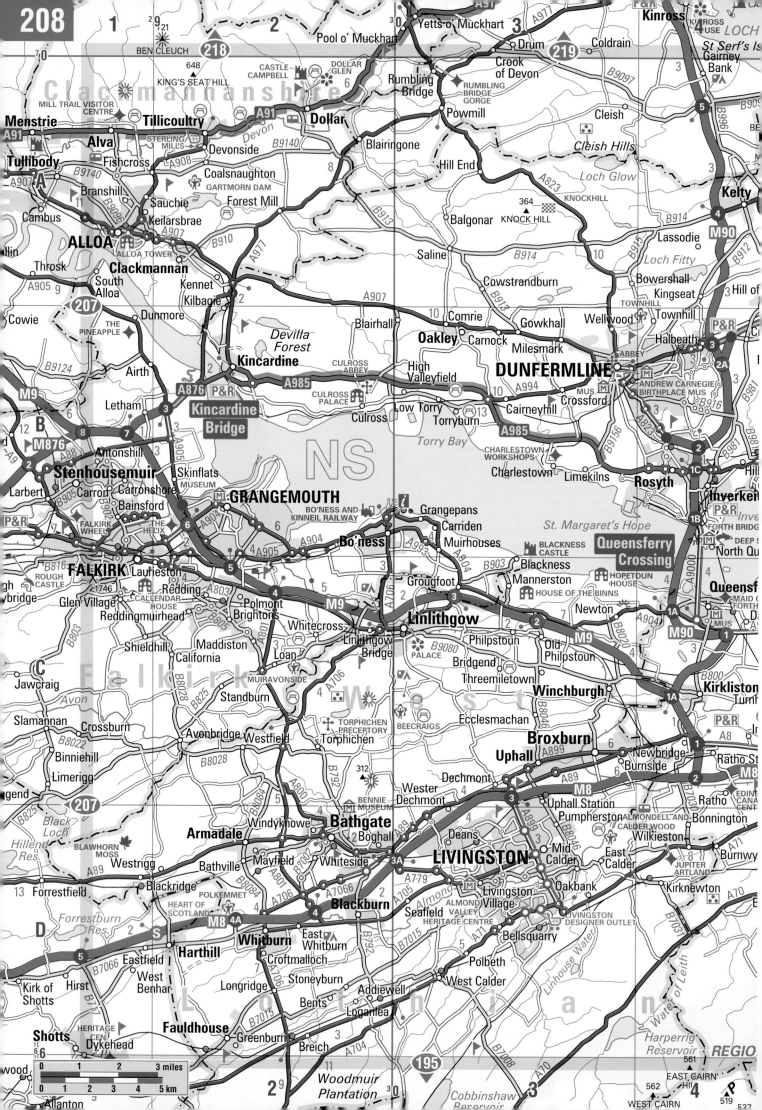

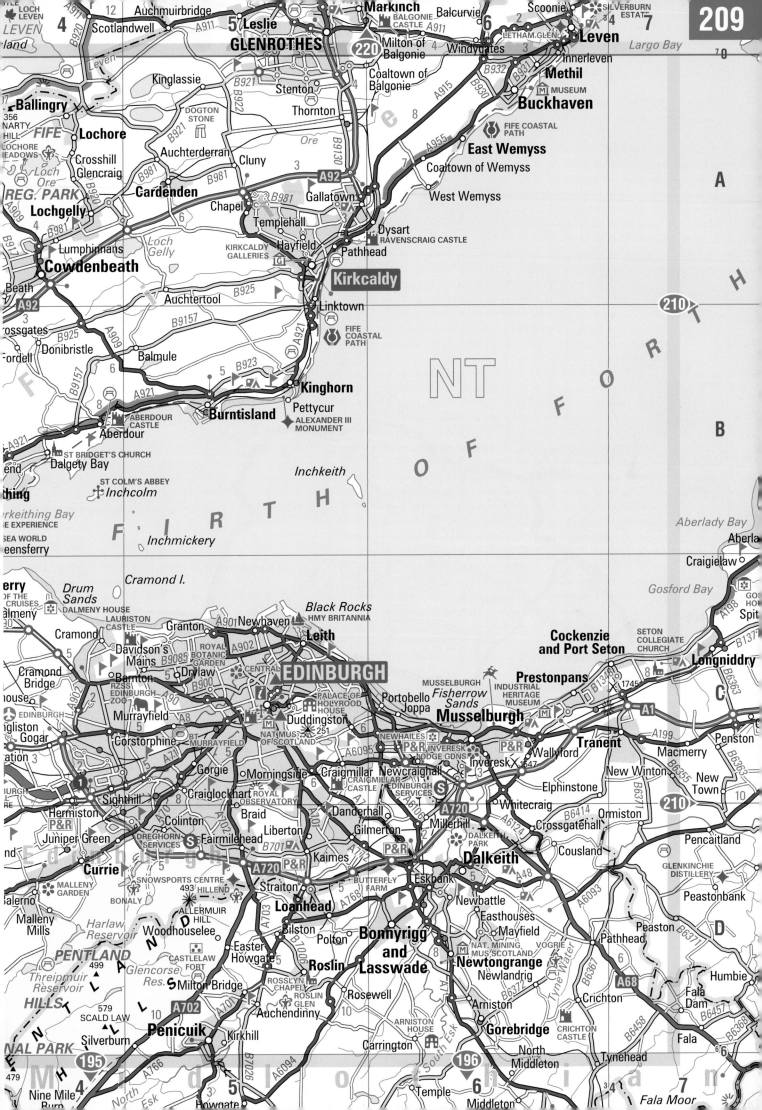

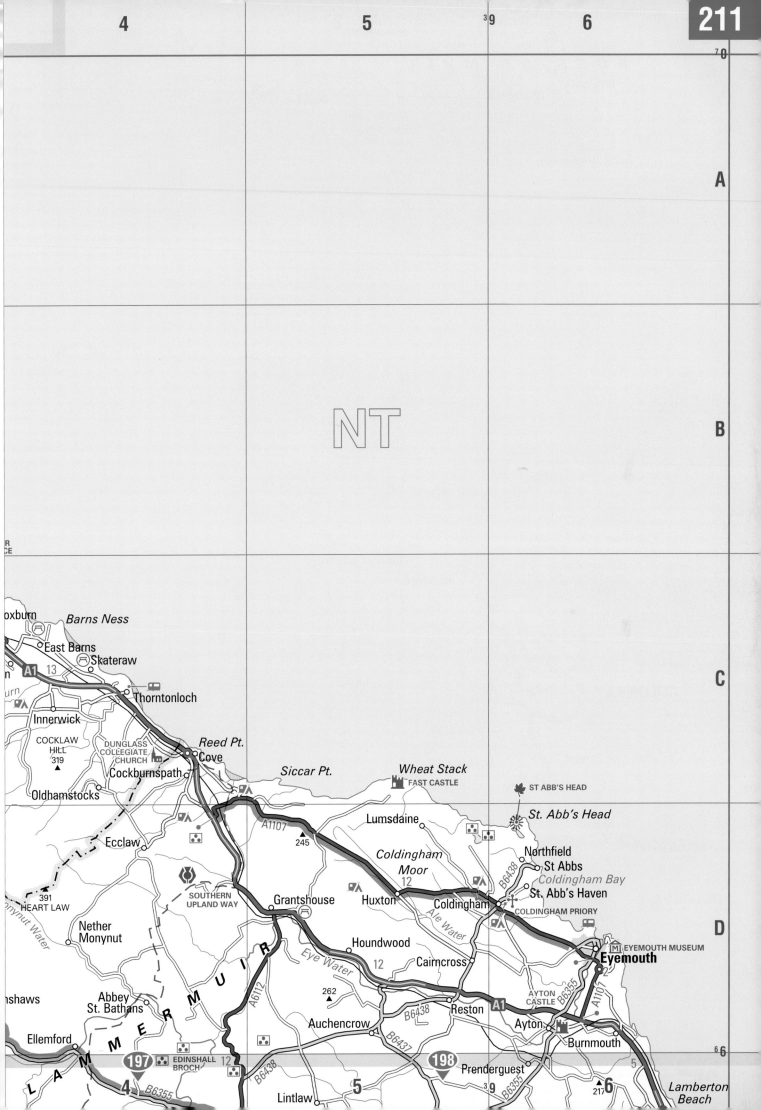

4   5   ³9   6

A

NT

B

oxburn   *Barns Ness*

East Barns   Skateraw

A1 13

Thorntonloch

Innerwick

COCKLAW
HILL
391

DUNGLASS
COLLEGIATE
CHURCH

Reed Pt.

Cove

Cockburnspath

Oldhamstocks

Ecclaw

Siccar Pt.

Wheat Stack

FAST CASTLE

ST ABB'S HEAD

St. Abb's Head

A1107

245

Lumsdaine

Northfield

St Abbs

Coldingham Bay

C

*Coldingham
Moor*

12

SOUTHERN
UPLAND WAY

Grantshouse

Huxton

Coldingham

St. Abb's Haven

COLDINGHAM PRIORY

HEART LAW
391

Nether
Monynut

Monynut Water

Houndwood

Ale Water

EYEMOUTH MUSEUM

Eyemouth

D

Eye Water   12

Cairncross

262

Reston   A1

AYTON
CASTLE

B6355

A1107

shaws   Abbey
St. Bathans

Ellemford

LAMMERMUIR

197

EDINSHALL
BROCH   12

B6355

Auchencrow

B6438

B6437

198

Prenderguest

Ayton

Burnmouth

B6355

217

*Lamberton
Beach*

4   B6355   Lintlaw   5   ³9   6

⁶6

ROSS OF MULL

Tiraghoil
Bunessan
Lee
Carsaig
Rubha
Dubh
A849
376
CRUACHAN MIN
376
Carsaig
Bay
224
Loch
Assapol
225
Ardalanish
Uisken
Scoor
CARSAIG ARCHES
Ardchiavaig
Malcolm's Pt.
125
Rubha nam
Braithrean
Eilean
a'Chalmain
Rubh Ardalanish

A

B

NM

OBAN

Rubh'a'Geadha
Kiloran Bay
Balnahard
KILORAN GARDENS
Kiloran
Kilchattan
B8086
B8087
COLONSAY
136
Scalasaig
NR
Glendeb
Loch Staosnaig
Corpach Bay
Garvard
B8085
Rubha Dubh
BEINN B
467
C

PRIORY
Dubh Eilean
Oronsay
Shian Bay
453
RAINBERG
MOR
Eilean nan Ron
Loch Righ
Mòr
Shian
318
D

Rubh'an t-Sàilein

PORT ASKAIG

0   1   2   3 miles
0 1 2 3 4 5 km

200
Rubha
Bholsa
Rubha Lang-aoinidh
201
Loch Tarbert

Rubha a'Mhail
439
Lagg

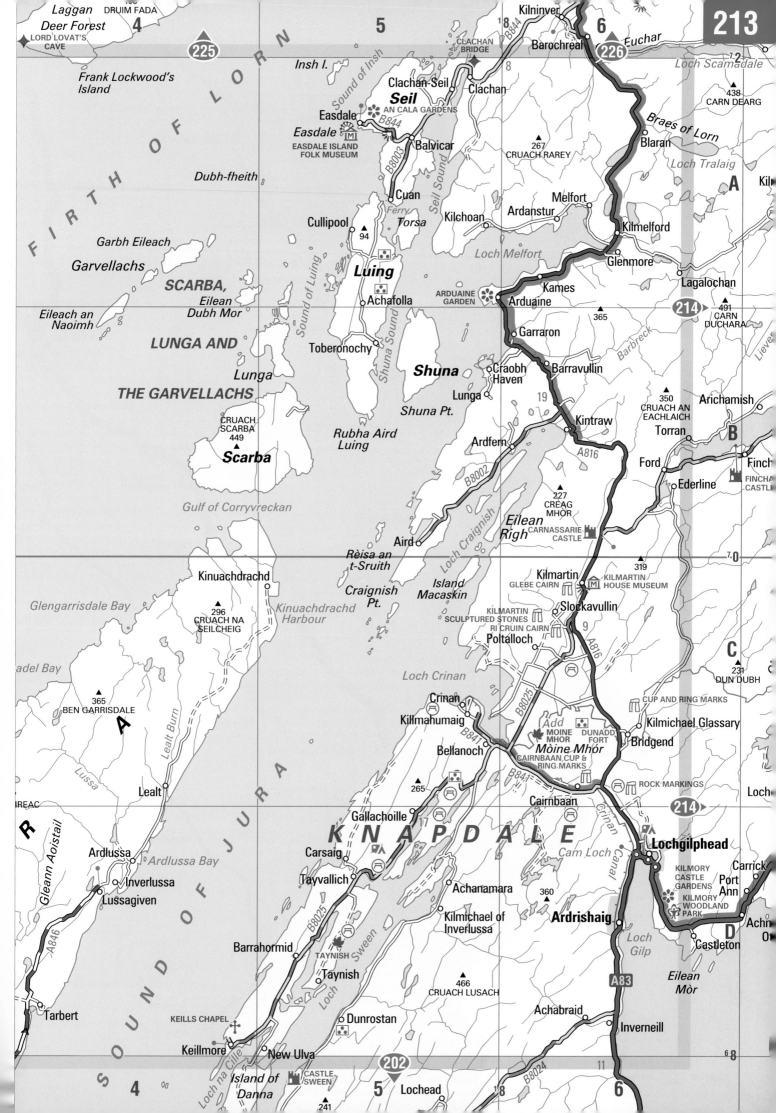

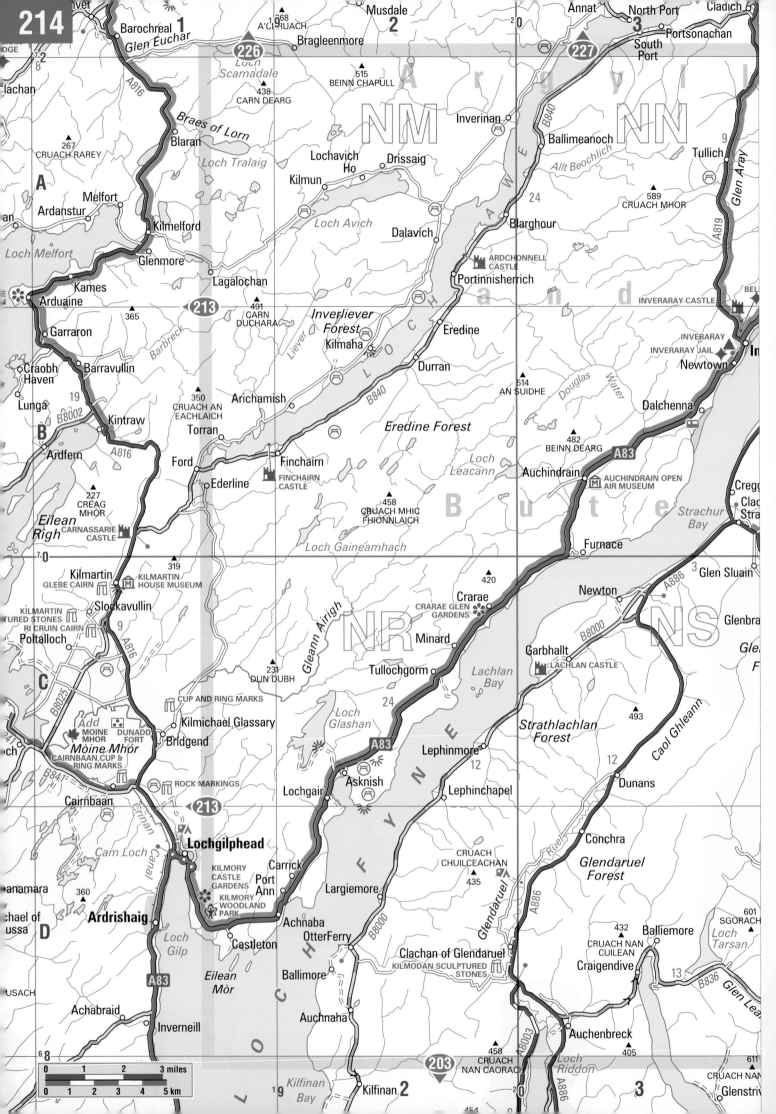

North Port
Annat
Cladich 6
Portsonachan
South Port
3
A'CRUACH
Musdale
2
Barochreal 1
Glen Euchar
Bragleenmore
226
Loch Scamadale
515
BEINN CHAPULL
NM
NN
438
CARN DEARG
Inverinan
Ballimeanoch
227
Braes of Lorn
Allt Beochlich
Blaran
Lochavich Ho
Drissaig
Kilmun
589
CRUACH MHOR
Loch Tralaig
24
Tullich
267
CRUACH RAREY
Loch Avich
Dalavich
9
A
Melfort
Blarghour
Glen Aray
Ardanstur
Kilmelford
ARDCHONNELL CASTLE
A819
Glenmore
Lagalochan
Portinnisherrich
INVERARAY-CASTLE
BEL
Kames
213
491
CARN DUCHARA
Inverliever
Forest
Eredine
INVERARAY
Arduaine
365
INVERARAY JAIL
Garraron
Kilmaha
Newtown
In
Craobh
Haven
Barravullin
Durran
Dalchenna
B840
514
AN SUIDHE
Lunga
19
B8002
Kintraw
Arichamish
Eredine Forest
Douglas Water
350
CRUACH AN
EACHLAICH
B
Ardfern
A816
Torran
Loch
Leacann
482
BEINN DEARG
A83
Ford
Finchairn
Auchindrain
AUCHINDRAIN OPEN
AIR MUSEUM
227
CREAG
MHOR
Ederline
FINCHAIRN
CASTLE
458
CRUACH MHIC
FHIONNLAICH
Cregg
Clad
Stra
Eilean
Righ
CARNASSARIE
CASTLE
Strachur
Bay
Loch Gaineamhach
Bute
Furnace
319
Glen Sluain
Kilmartin
GLEBE CAIRN
KILMARTIN
HOUSE MUSEUM
420
NR
Crarae
CRARAE GLEN
GARDENS
Newton
3
A886
NS
KILMARTIN
TURED STONES
Slockavullin
Minard
Glenbra
RI CRUIN CAIRN
9
A816
Tullochgorm
B8000
Garbhallt
LACHLAN CASTLE
Gle
F
Poltalloch
231
DUN DUBH
Lachlan
Bay
493
C
B8025
CUP AND RING MARKS
24
Strathlachlan
Forest
Caol Ghleann
Add
MOINE
MHOR
DUNADD
FORT
Loch
Glashan
A83
Kilmichael Glassary
Lephinmore
12
Dunans
Bridgend
12
Moine Mhor
CAIRNBAAN,CUP &
RING MARKS
B8000
ch
B841
ROCK MARKINGS
Lochgair
Asknish
Lephinchapel
Cairnbaan
213
Conchra
Crinan Canal
Lochgilphead
CRUACH
CHUILCEACHAN
435
Glendaruel
Forest
Cam Loch
Carrick
KILMORY
CASTLE
GARDENS
Port
Ann
Largiemore
601
SGORACH
anamara
360
KILMORY
WOODLAND
PARK
Achnaba
OtterFerry
Clachan of Glendaruel
432
CRUACH NAN
CUILEAN
Balliemore
Loch
Tarsan
chael of
ussa
Ardrishaig
Castleton
Ballimore
KILMODAN SCULPTURED
STONES
Craigendive
13
B836
USACH
A83
Eilean
Mòr
Loch
Gilp
Glen Lea
Achabraid
Inverneill
Auchnaha
A8003
Auchenbreck
611
CRUACH NAN
6 8
203
458
CRUACH
NAN CAORACH
405
A886
Loch
Riddon
Glenstriv
0 1 2 3 miles
0 1 2 3 4 5 km
9
Kilfinan
Bay
Kilfinan 2
0 3
454

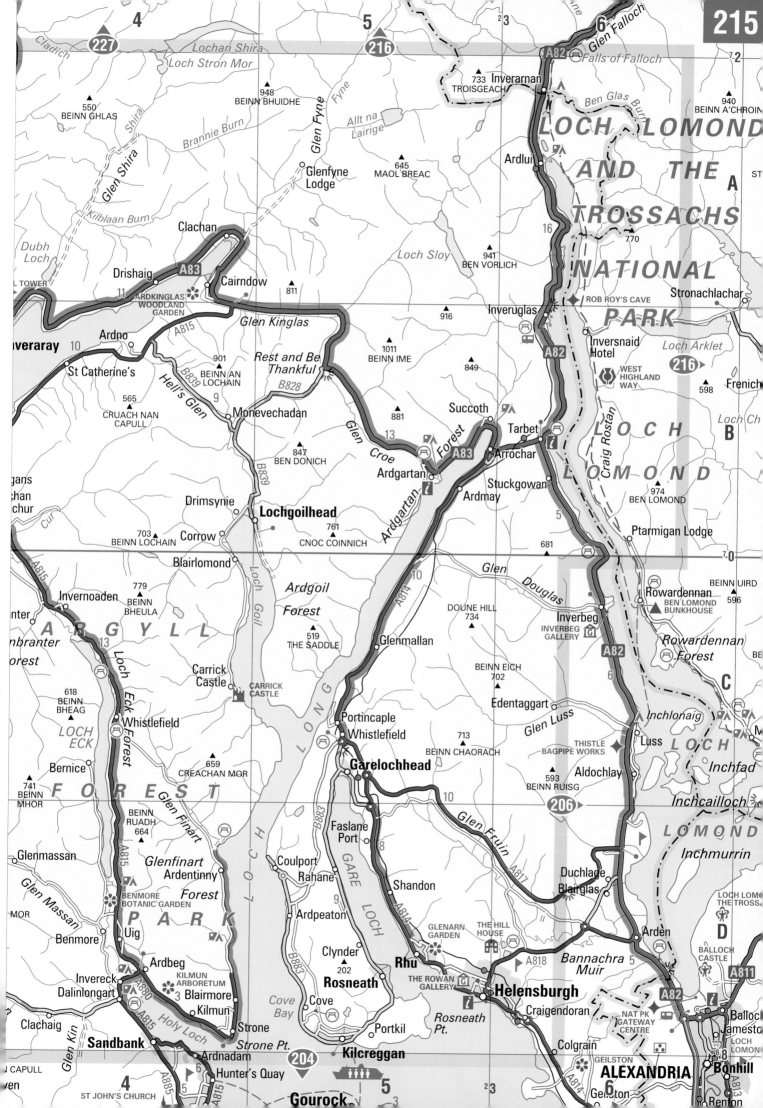

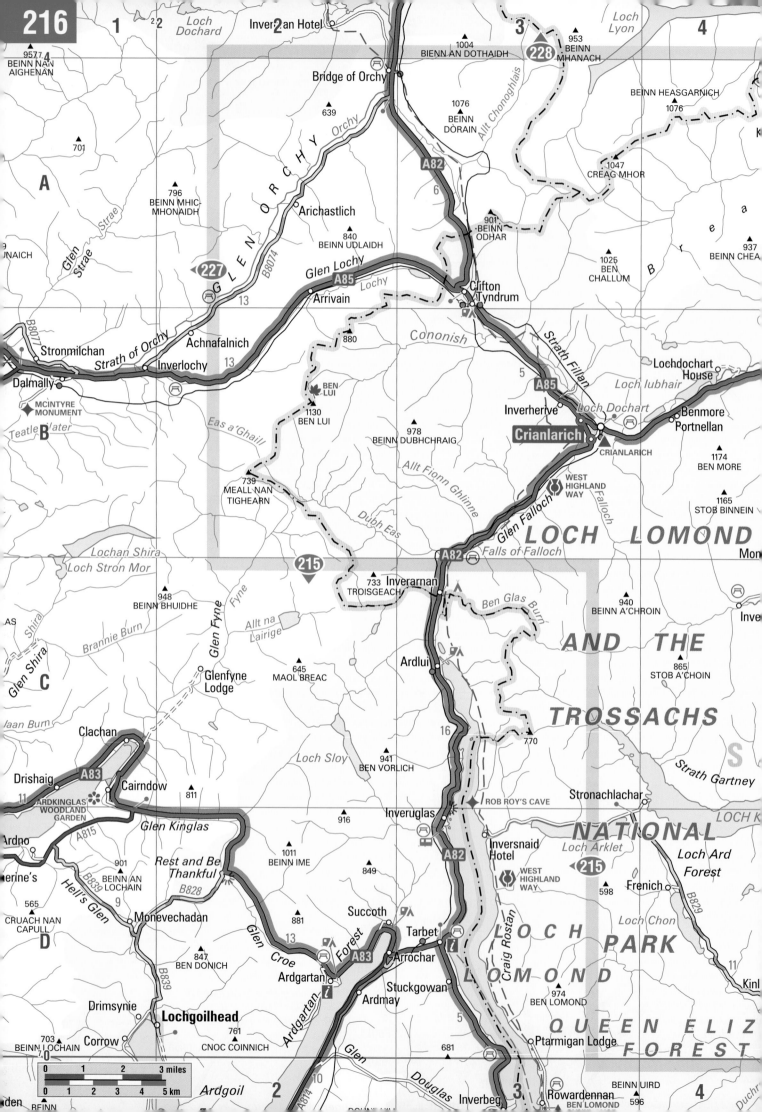

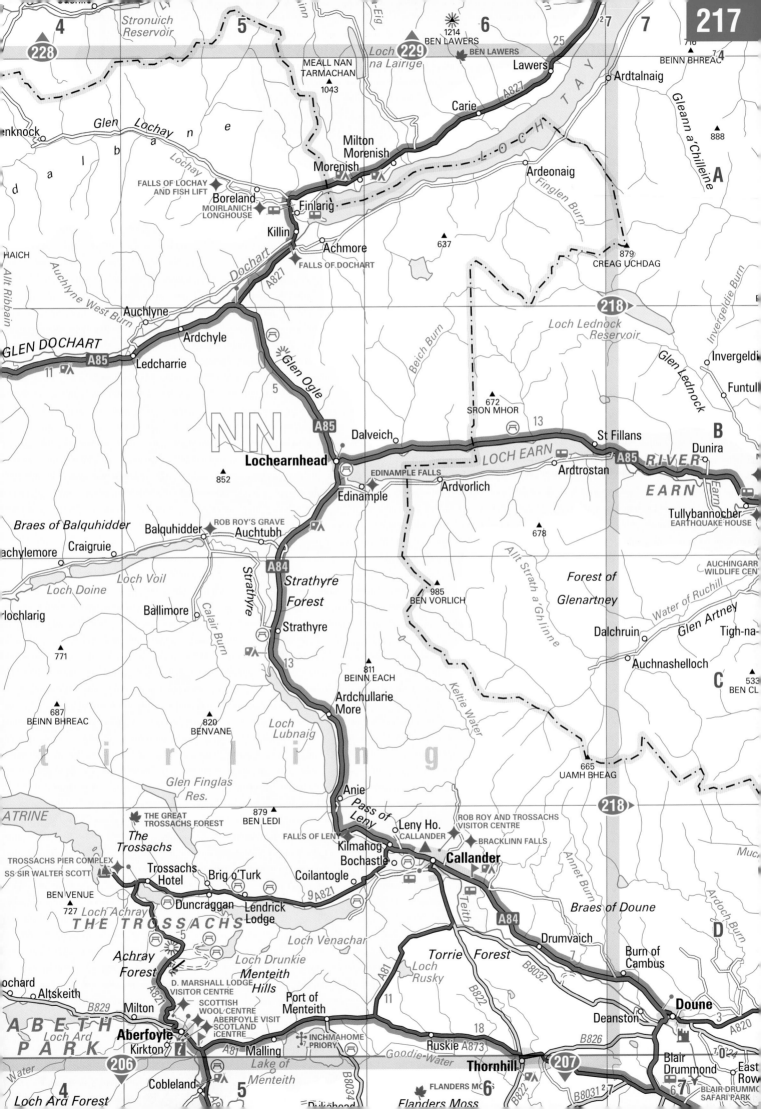

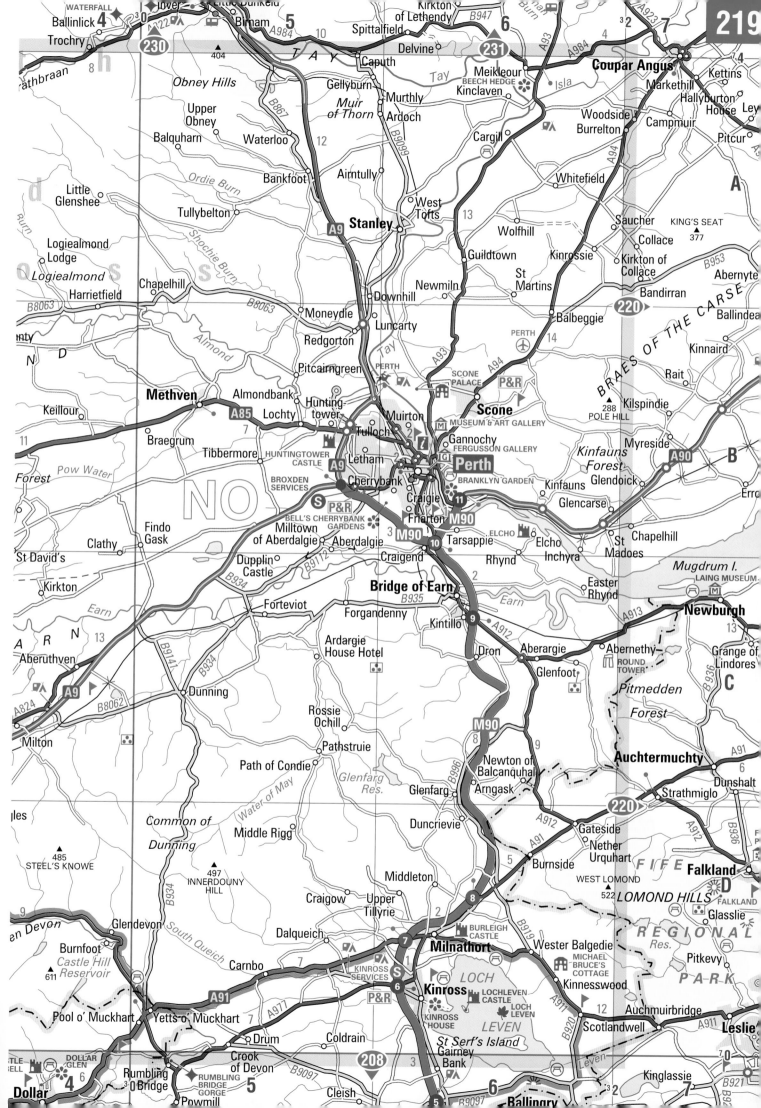

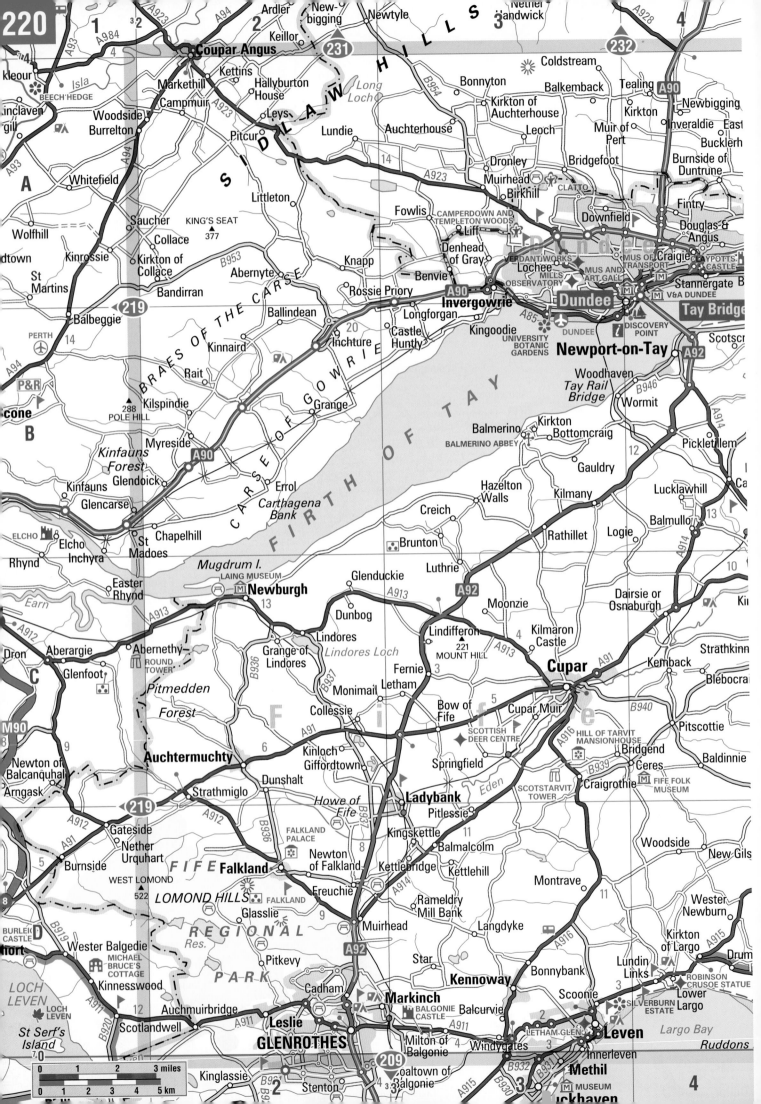

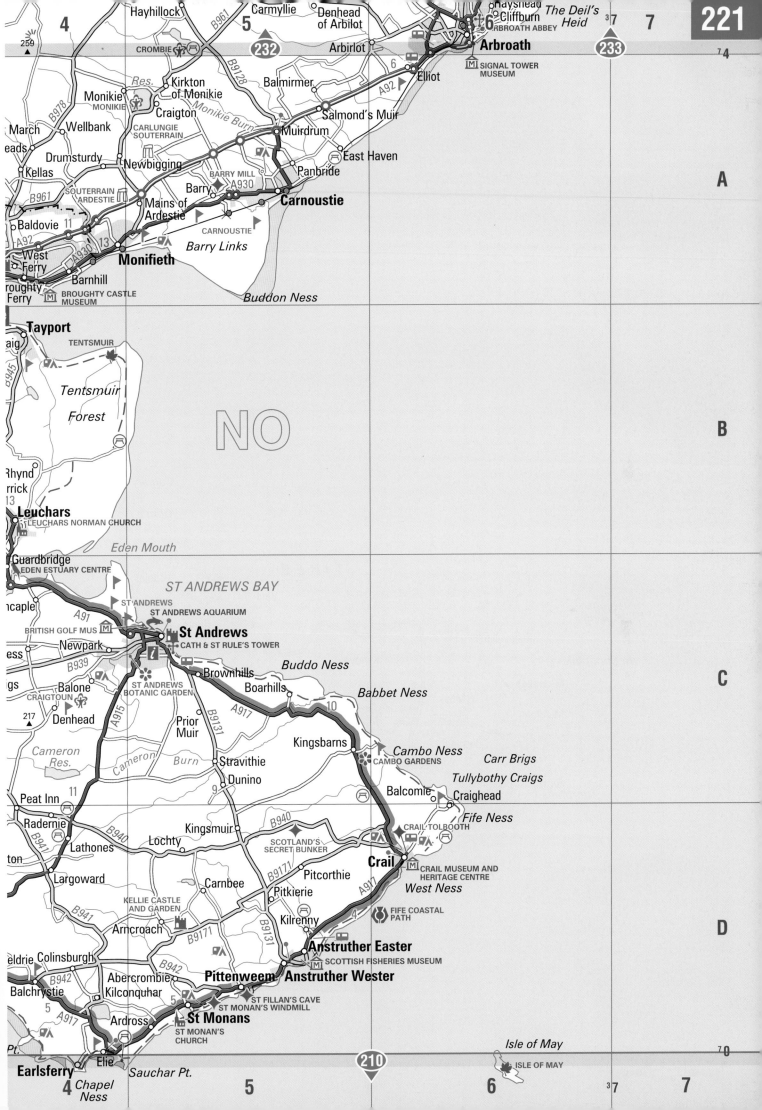

4 5 6 7 7

4

Hayhillock
Carmyllie
Denhead
of Arbilot
Hayshead
Cliffburn
The Deil's
Heid
3 7 7

B961
CROMBIE
259
232
Arbirlot
Arbroath
233
7 4
ARBROATH ABBEY

B9128
Kirkton
of Monikie
Balmirmer
Elliot
SIGNAL TOWER
MUSEUM

Res.
Monikie
MONIKIE
Craigton
A92
6

B978
CARLUNGIE
SOUTERRAIN
Salmond's Muir

March
eads
Wellbank
Muirdrum
Kellas
Drumsturdy
Newbigging
East Haven
A

SOUTERRAIN
ARDESTIE
BARRY MILL
A930
Panbride
B961
Barry

Baldovie
11
Mains of
Ardestie
Carnoustie

A92
13

West
Ferry
CARNOUSTIE
A930
Monifieth
Barry Links

Barnhill
Buddon Ness
roughty
Ferry
BROUGHTY CASTLE
MUSEUM

Tayport
TENTSMUIR

aig
B

Tentsmuir
Forest
NO

Rhynd
rrick
13

Leuchars
LEUCHARS NORMAN CHURCH

Eden Mouth
Guardbridge
EDEN ESTUARY CENTRE

ST ANDREWS BAY
ncaple
A91
ST ANDREWS
ST ANDREWS AQUARIUM
BRITISH GOLF MUS
St Andrews
CATH & ST RULE'S TOWER
C

Newpark
Buddo Ness

B939
Brownhills
Babbet Ness
Balone
Boarhills

CRAIGTOUN
ST ANDREWS
BOTANIC GARDEN
10

gs
217
Denhead
Prior
Muir
B9131
A917
Kingsbarns
Cambo Ness
Carr Brigs

Cameron
Res.
Cameron Burn
Stravithie
CAMBO GARDENS
Tullybothy Craigs

A915
Dunino
9
Balcomie
Craighead

Peat Inn
11
Fife Ness
Radernie
Kingsmuir
B940
CRAIL TOLBOOTH

B941
Lochty
SCOTLAND'S
SECRET BUNKER
Crail
CRAIL MUSEUM AND
HERITAGE CENTRE

Lathones
B940
B9171
Pitcorthie
West Ness

ton
Largoward
Carnbee
Pitkierie
A917
D

KELLIE CASTLE
AND GARDEN
Kilrenny
FIFE COASTAL
PATH

B941
Arncroach
B9171
B9131
Anstruther Easter

eldrie
Colinsburgh
B942
Pittenweem
Anstruther Wester
SCOTTISH FISHERIES MUSEUM

Abercrombie
ST FILLAN'S CAVE
A917
Balchrystie
B942
Kilconquhar
5
ST MONAN'S WINDMILL

Ardross
St Monans
ST MONAN'S
CHURCH

Earlsferry
Elie
Sauchar Pt.
Isle of May
7 0

Pt.
Chapel
Ness
210
ISLE OF MAY

4
5
6
3 7
7

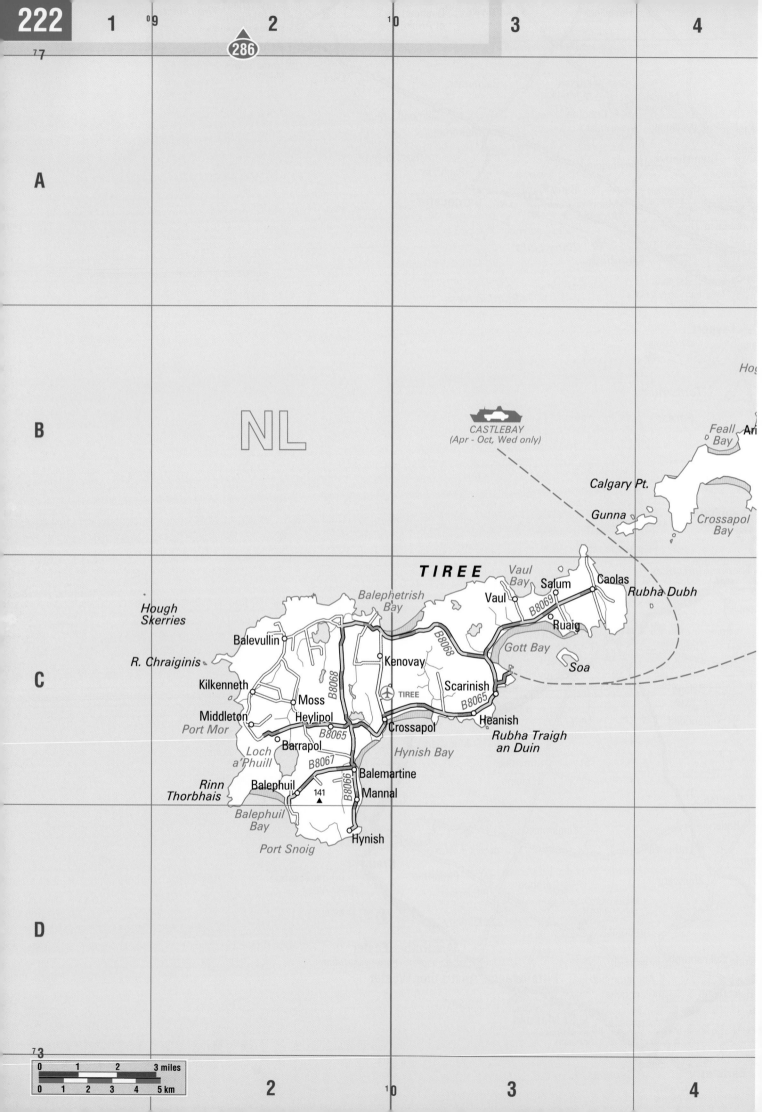

NL

CASTLEBAY
(Apr - Oct, Wed only)

Feall
Bay

Calgary Pt.

Gunna

Crossapol
Bay

TIREE

Balephetrish
Bay

Vaul
Bay

Salum

Caolas

Vaul

Rubha Dubh

B8069

Ruaig

Hough
Skerries

Balevullin

R. Chraiginis

Kenovay

B8068

Gott Bay

Soa

Kilkenneth

Scarinish

Moss

B8068

TIREE

B8065

Middleton

Heylipol

Heanish

Port Mor

Crossapol

*Rubha Traigh
an Duin*

B8065

Barrapol

Loch
a'Phuill

Hynish Bay

B8067

Rinn
Thorbhais

Balemartine

Balephuil

141

Mannal

B8066

Balephuil
Bay

Hynish

Port Snoig

0   1   2   3 miles
0 1 2 3 4 5 km

4 **5** **6** **7**

Sanna Point

Sanna Bay

Sanna

Portuairk

Point of
Ardnamurchan
ARDNAMURCHAN LIGHTHOUSE

Achosni

Ormsai

Ormsaigb

A

An Acairseid

Cairns of Coll

234

Rubha Mor

Eilean Mor

Bousd

Sorisdale

Cliad Bay

Arnabost

Gallanach

B8072

Grishipoll

B8071

▲ 73

COLL

Loch
Cliad

Ardmore
Bay

Glengorm
Castle

Quinish Pt.

M i s h n i s h

Quinish

's

B

Ballyhaugh

B8071

▲
104

Rubha
an Aird

Caliach Pt.

Sunipol

M o r n i s h

MULL
THEATRE

OBAN

Totronald

B8070

Acha

Arinagour

Loch Eatharna

Eilean
Ornsay

Penmore
Mill

Dervaig

Ach

leod

THE OLD BYRE
HERITAGE CENTR

Breachacha
Castle

Friesland

Calgary

Calgary Bay

Soa

Loch Breachacha

Ensay

▲ 342
CARN MOR

Treshnish Pt.

Bellart

Haunn

B8073

Burg

Kilninian

Achnac

Rubh a'Chaoil

224

Achleck

23

Fanmore

▲ 390

C

Treshnish Isles

Fladda

Eilean Dioghlum

L O C H   T U A T H

Ballygown

EAS FORS
WATERFALL

Lunga

Gometra

Bearnus ▲ 313

U l v a

Laggan
Bay

La

Os

Ulva House

Sound of Ulva

Bac Mor

Little
Colonsay

Staffa ⚜ STAFFA

INCH KENNETH
CHAPEL

*Inch
Kenneth*

D

FINGAL'S CAVE

MACKINNON'S CAVE

Ba

Erisgeir

519
▲
BEIN NA SRE
73

224

A R D M E A N A C H

4 **5** **6** **7**

COLL

Arnab 6 Gallanach
B8072
B8071

B8070
Loch
Cliad
73

Arinagour
OBAN

Loch Eatharna

Friesland
Eilean
Ornsay

A

TIREE

Ardmore Bay   Ardmore Pt.

Bloody B

Quinish Pt.
Glengorm
Castle

MULL MUSEUM

Tobermory

Rubha
an Aird
Mornish
Mishnish
'S AIRDE-BEINN

Caliach Pt.
Sunipol
292
7

Penmore
Mill
MULL
THEATRE
Dervaig   Achnadrish

Calgary
SPEINN
44

Calgary Bay
THE OLD BYRE
HERITAGE CENTRE

Loch Frisa

Ensay
Let

Treshnish Pt.
342
CARN MOR
Achnacraig

Haunn
Bellart

Rubh a'Chaoil
Burg   Kilninian

223
Achleck
Cra
23
Fanmore   390

B
Fladda
Ballygown

Treshnish Isles
Eilean Dioghlum
EAS FORS
WATERFALL

Lunga
Gometra
424
BEINN NA DRISE

Bearnus 313
Laggan
Bay
Lagganulva

U l v a
Oskamull

Bac Mor
Ulva House
Killiem

L O C H   N A   K E A L

Little
Colonsay
Eorsa
LOCH

I S L E   O F

Staffa   STAFFA
INCH KENNETH
CHAPEL
Inch
Kenneth
17
Derr

C
FINGAL'S CAVE

Balnahard

MACKINNON'S CAVE
561

Erisgeir
519
Glen Seilisdeir

BEINN NA SREINE
Kil
Ho

A R D M E A N A C H

Eilean
Annraidh
Kilfinich
Bay

MACLEAN'S CROSS
THE BURG

Rubha nan Cearc
L O C H   S C R I D A I N

100
IONA ABBEY AND
CATHEDRAL

Loch na
Lathaich

D
IONA HERITAGE CENTRE

Iona   Baile Mor
Kintra
Torrans

ST COLUMBA EXHIBITION
& WELCOME CENTRE

Stac an
Aoineidh
Aridhglas
Eorabus
18
BRO

Fionnphort
A849

Fidden
Tiraghoil
Lee

Bunessan
376
CRUACHAN MIN

Loch
Assapol

Erraid
212
R O S S   O F   M U L L

0   1   2   3 miles
Ardalanish
Uisken
Scoor

0 1 2 3 4 5 km
Ardchiavaig
Malcolm's Pt.

234

1   1   3   2   3

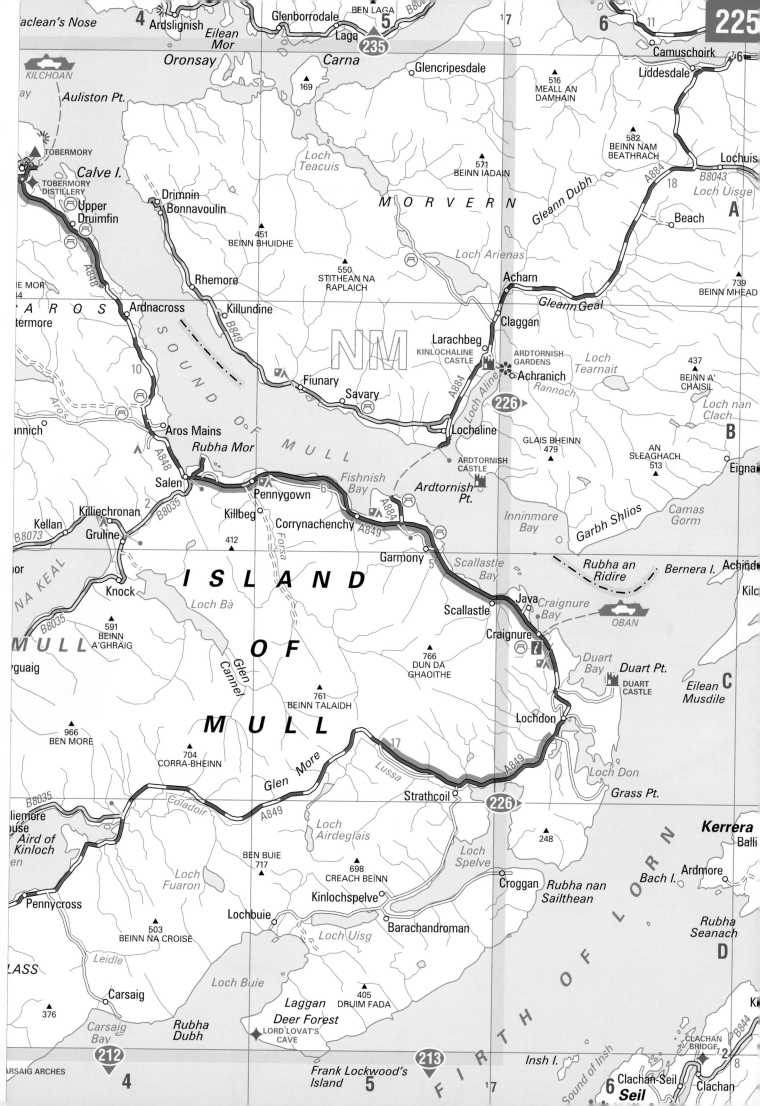

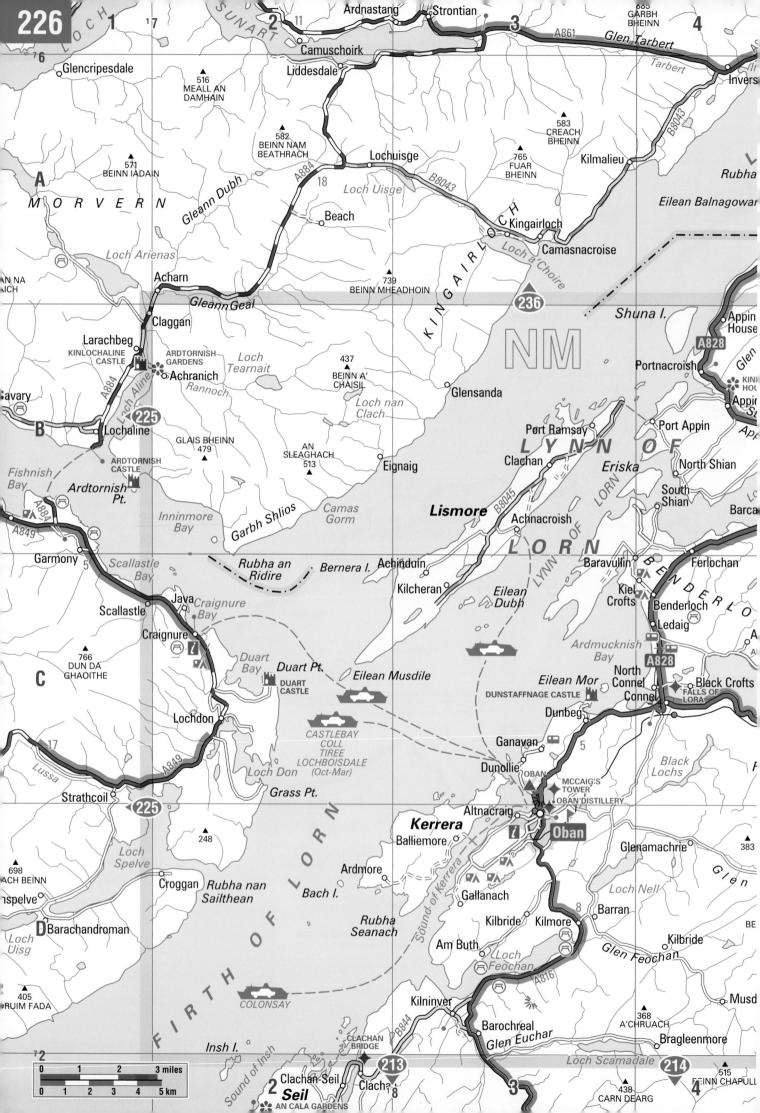

LOCH 1 17 2 11 SUNART 3 A861 Glen Tarbert 4

Ardnastang · Strontian
GARBH BHEINN

Camuschoirk
Liddesdale
Glencripesdale
MEALL AN DAMHAIN 516
Tarbert
Invers
B8043

A
BEINN NAM BEATHRACH 582
BEINN IADAIN 571
Lochuisge
CREACH BHEINN 583
Kilmalieu
Rubha

MORVERN
Gleann Dubh
A884 18
Loch Uisge
B8043
FUAR BHEINN 765
Eilean Balnagowar

Loch Arienas
Beach
Kingairloch
Camasnacroise
Shuna I.

Acharn
Gleann Geal
BEINN MHEADHOIN 739
LOCH a Choire
236
NM

Claggan
Appin House
Larachbeg
KINLOCHALINE CASTLE
ARDTORNISH GARDENS
Loch Tearnait
BEINN A' CHAISIL 437
Glensanda
Portnacroish
A828
Glen

B
Achranich
Rannoch
Loch nan Clach
Port Ramsay
Appin

avary
A884
GLAIS BHEINN 479
AN SLEAGHACH 513
Eignaig
LYNN OF
Clachan
Eriska
North Shian

Lochaline
225
ARDTORNISH CASTLE
Lismore
B8045
South Shian

Fishnish Bay
Ardtornish Pt.
Inninmore Bay
Garbh Shlios
Camas Gorm
Achnacroish
LORN
Barca

Garmony
A849
Scallastle Bay
Rubha an Ridire
Bernera I.
Achinduin
Baravullin
Ferlochan
BENDERLO

5
Java
Craignure Bay
Kilcheran
Eilean Dubh
Kiel Crofts
Benderloch
Ledaig

Scallastle
Craignure
Duart Bay
Eilean Mor
DUNSTAFFNAGE CASTLE
Ardmucknish Bay
A828
North Connel
Black Crofts

C
DUN DA GHAOITHE 766
Duart Pt.
DUART CASTLE
Eilean Musdile
Dunbeg
Connel
FALLS OF LORA

Lochdon
CASTLEBAY COLL TIREE LOCHBOISDALE (Oct-Mar)
Ganavan

Strathcoil
A849
Lussa
17
Grass Pt.
Loch Don
Dunollie
Oban
MCCAIG'S TOWER
OBAN DISTILLERY
Black Lochs

225
248
Kerrera
Altnacraig
Glenamachrie
383

Loch Spelve
Balliemore
Oban

698
ach BEINN
Croggan
Rubha nan Sailthean
Bach I.
Ardmore
Gallanach
Kilbride
Kilmore
Barran
Glen

spelve
Rubha Seanach
Am Buth
8
Kilbride

D
Barachandroman
Loch Uisg
RUIM FADA 405
COLONSAY
Kilninver
Barochreal
Glen Euchar
A'CHRUACH 368
Musd

Insh I.
Sound of Insh
B844
CLACHAN BRIDGE
213
Loch Scamadale
214

0 1 2 3 miles
0 1 2 3 4 5 km
Clachan-Seil
Seil
2
AN CALA GARDENS
Clacha
BEINN CHAPULL 515
CARN DEARG 438
Bragleenmore

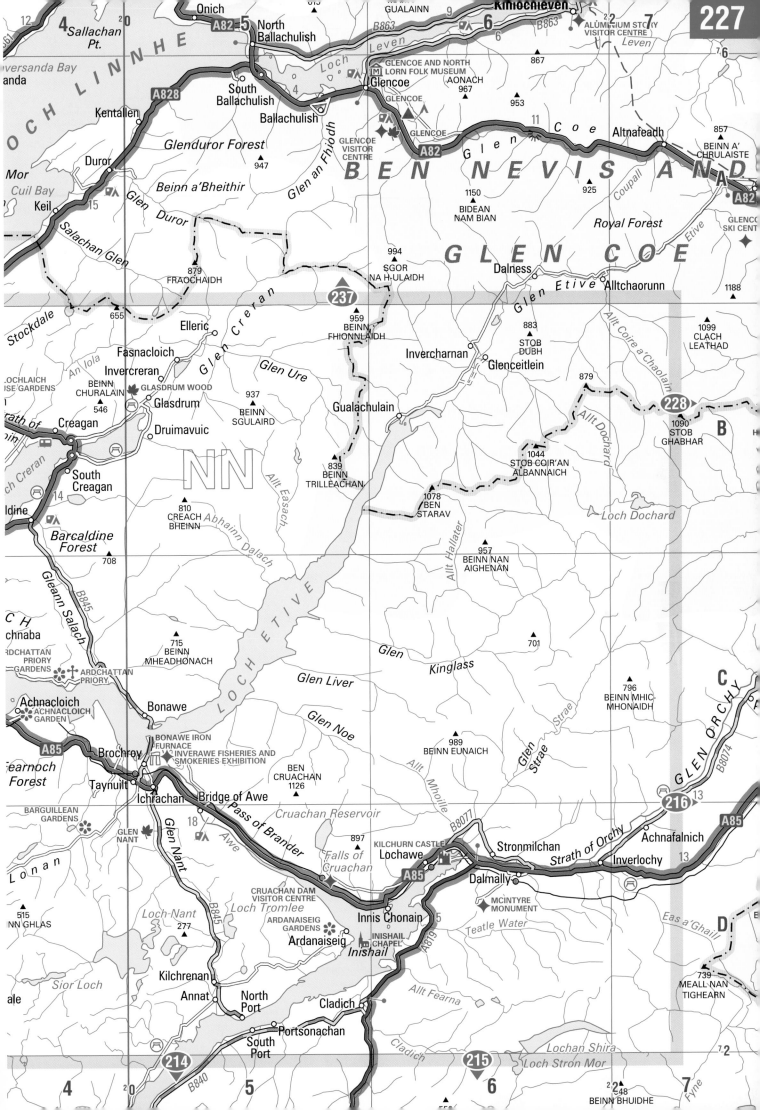

7.8

Killiechonate

Roybridge
Achluachrach Murlaggan Roughburn
Ardverikie Forest

A86
Spean MONESSIE Br 239 Lochaber 2 240 GEA
FALLS

GLEN SPEAN

Leanachan
Forest

Fersit

724
BEINN CHLIANAIG

1087
BEINN A'CHLACHAIR

The Cour

NGE
EXPERIENCE

Allt Lair
Allt Loraich

A

Loch Ghuilbinn

1046
CHNO DEARG

1114
AONACH BEAG

Ossian

1177
STOB CHOIRE
CLAURIGH

1106

Lairig Leacach

1115
STOB
COIRE EASAIN

1148
BEN AL

Uisge Labhair

1234
AONACH
BEAG

1094

Allt na Lairige

LOCH TREIG

Creaguaineach
Lodge

937
BEINN
NA LAP

Corrour Shooting
Lodge

Prince Cha
Cave

Loch Ossian

B

1130
BINNEIN MOR

Amhainn Rath

237

Loch Ossian

Corrour Forest

583

952
SGOR GAIBHRE

MAMORE
FOREST

Loch Eilde Beag

630

Allt na Caim

Rannoch Forest

789

Loch Eilde Mor

906
LEUM
UILLEIM

Ciaran Water

Kinlochmore

ALUMINIUM STORY
VISITOR CENTRE

Black Water

Leven

BLACKWATER RESERVOIR

B E N   N E V I S

Rannoch Station B846

Altnafeadh

857
BEINN A'
CHRULAISTE

Black Corries
Lodge

739
STOB NA CRUAICHE

Loch
Eigheach

Gaur

C

925

Coupall

Kingshouse
Hotel

Loch
Gaineamhach

Loch Laidon

A N D

Etive

GLENCOE
SKI CENTRE A82

R A N N O C H   M O O R

Royal Forest

Alltchaorunn

1188

547

Allt

G L E N   C O E

1099
CLACH
LEATHAD

Ba

Loch na
h-Achlaise 14

Loch Ba

MEALL E

79

B L A C K   M O U N T

Water of Tulla

Loch
an Daimh

Allt Coire a'Chaolain

Eas Daimh

D

1090
STOB
GHABHAR

WEST
HIGHLAND
WAY

Loch
Tulla

907
MEALL
BUIDHE

960
STUCHD AN
LOCHAIN

227

Black
Mount

Achallader

1081
BEINN A'
CHREACHAIN

Pubil Cashlie G

Forest Lodge

Loch
Lyon

Ilt Dochard

Loch Dochard

Inveroran Hotel

7.4

0   1   2   3 miles
0 1 2 3 4 5 km

Bridge
of Orchy

1004
BIENN AN DOTHAIDH

216

953
BEINN
MHANACH

217

1076

BEINN HEASGARNICH

1076

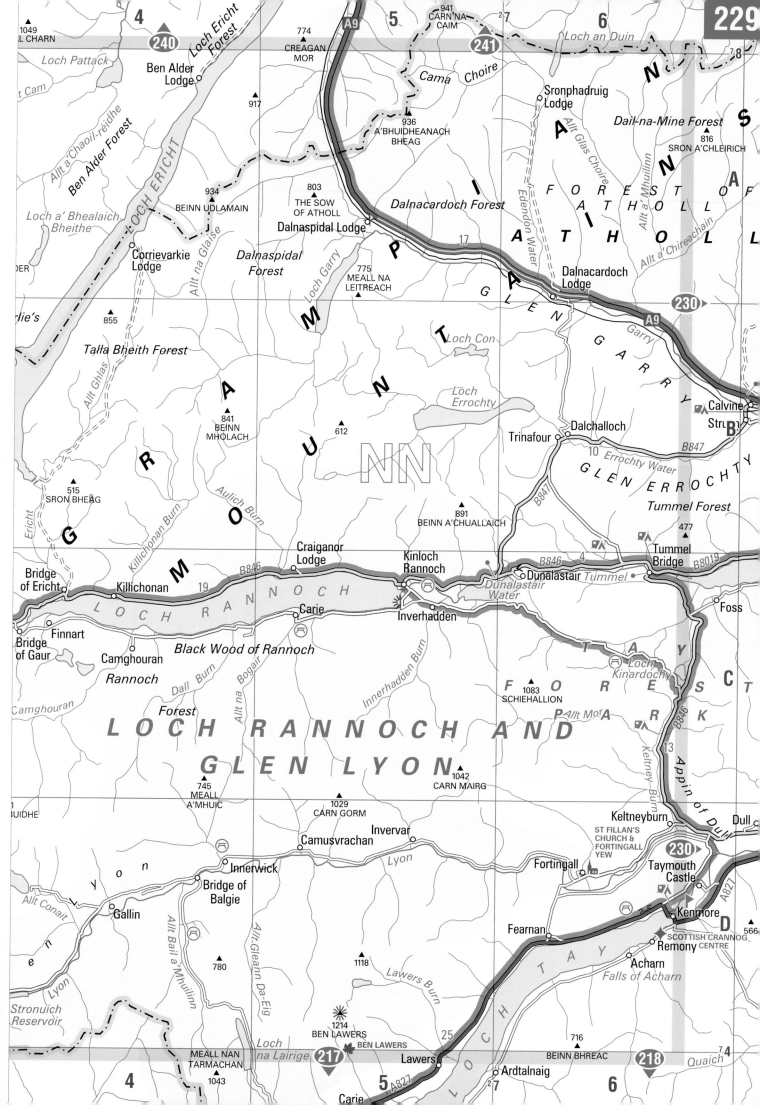

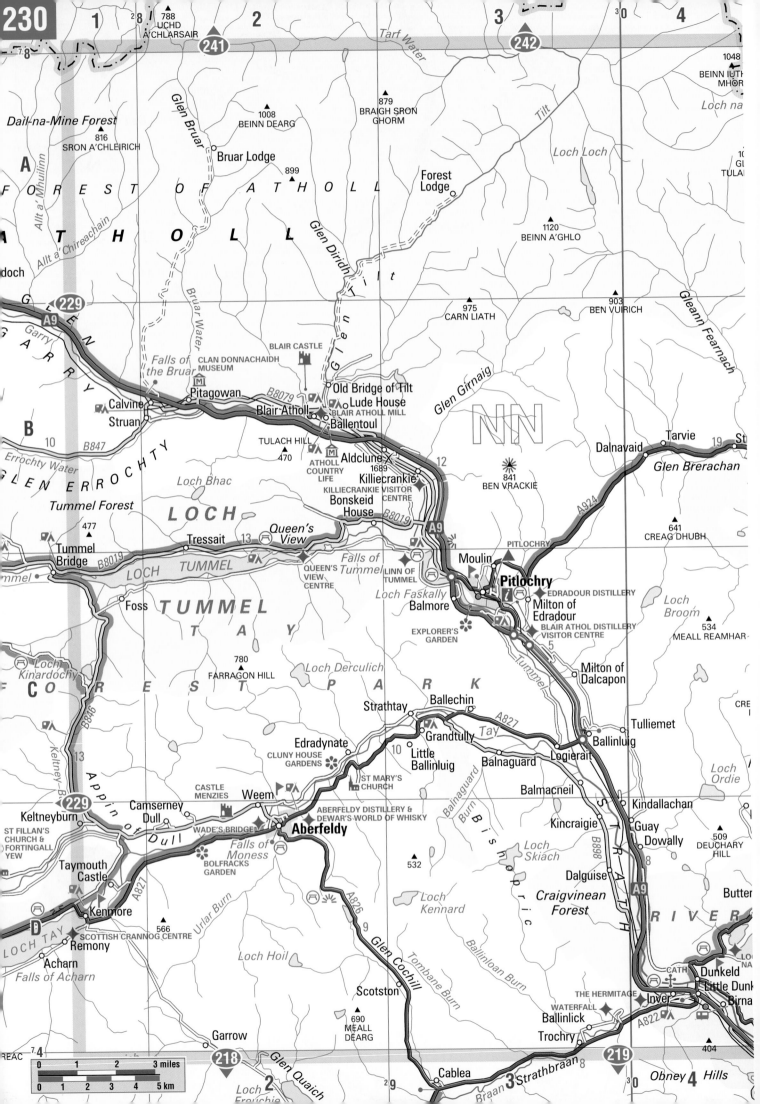

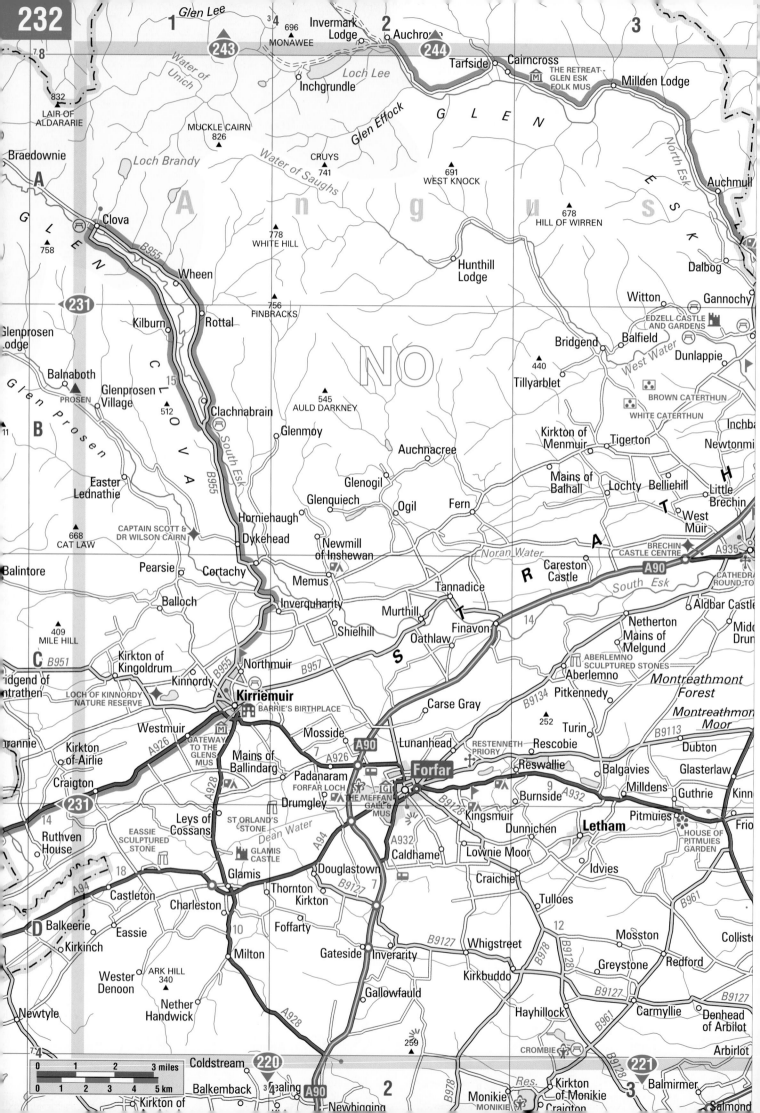

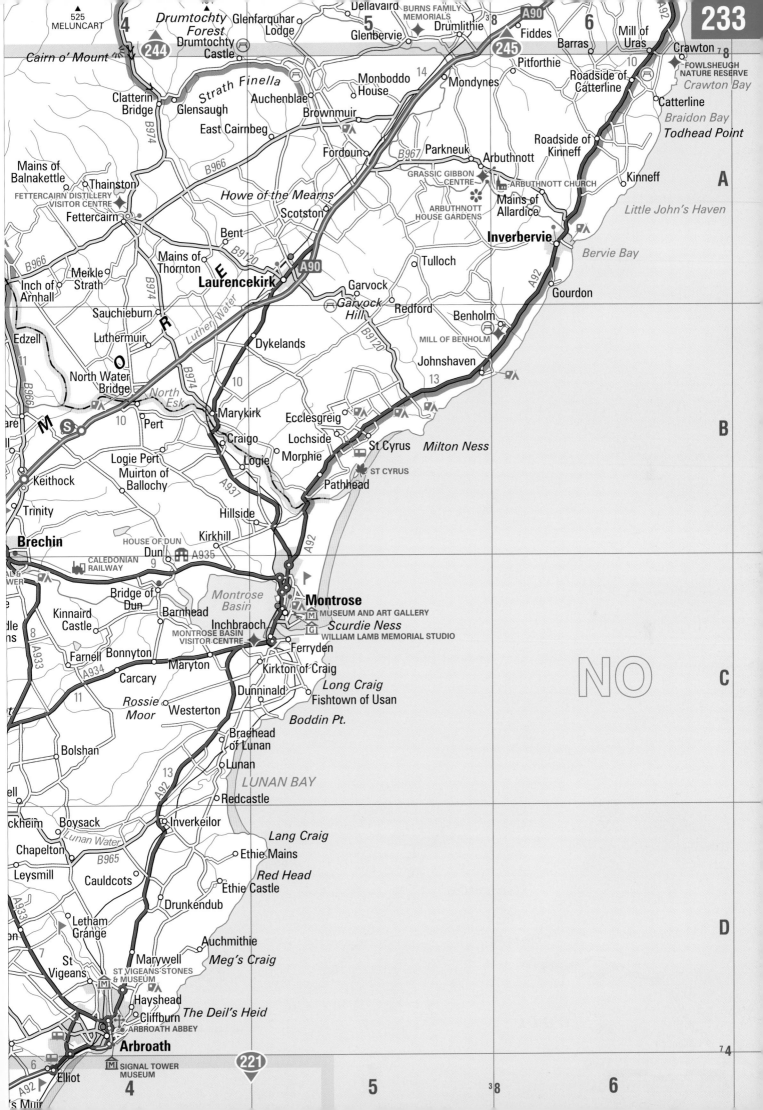

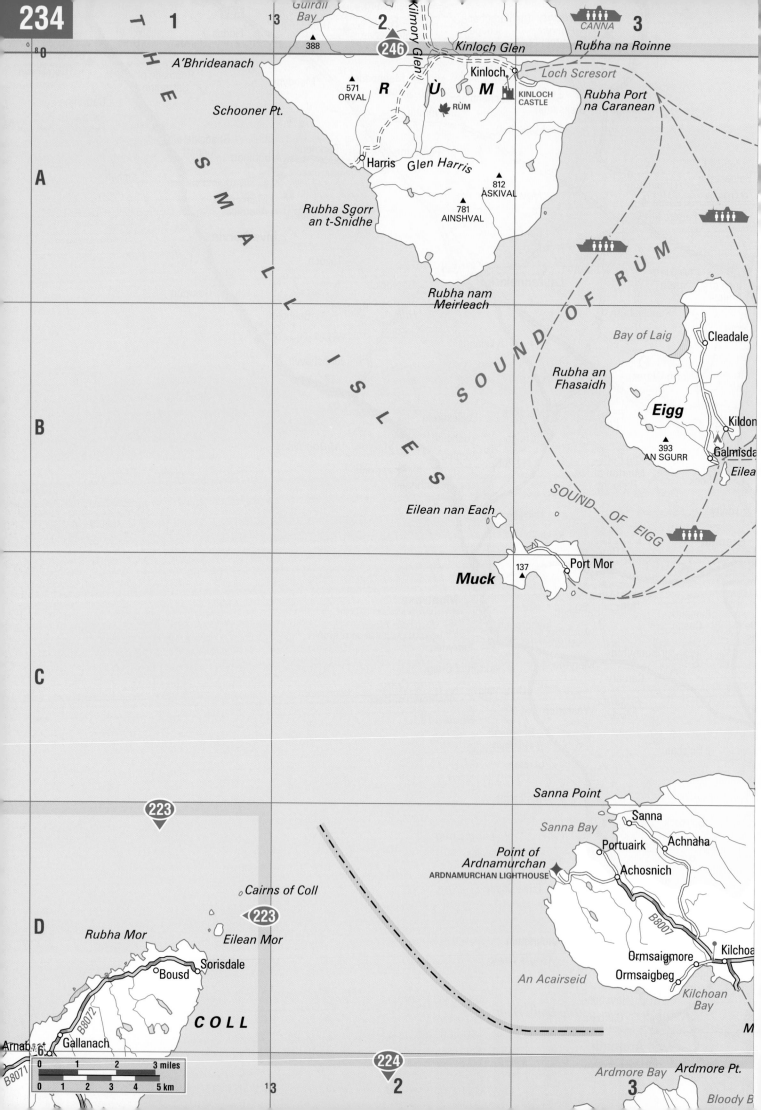

1 **2** **3**

⓪8⓪

A'Bhrideanach

Schooner Pt.

Guirdil Bay

388

Kinloch Glen

246

Kilmory Glen

CANNA

Rubha na Roinne

Kinloch

R Ù M

RÙM

KINLOCH CASTLE

Loch Scresort

Rubha Port na Caranean

571 ORVAL

A

Rubha Sgorr an t-Snidhe

Glen Harris

Harris

812 ASKIVAL

781 AINSHVAL

Rubha nam Meirleach

SOUND OF RÙM

Bay of Laig

Cleadale

Rubha an Fhasaidh

Eigg

Kildon

B

393 AN SGURR

Galmisda

Eilea

SOUND OF EIGG

Eilean nan Each

Muck

137

Port Mor

C

223

Sanna Point

Sanna Bay

Sanna

Achnaha

D

Cairns of Coll

223

Rubha Mor

Eilean Mor

Bousd

Sorisdale

COLL

Arnab

Gallanach

B8071

B8072

Point of Ardnamurchan

ARDNAMURCHAN LIGHTHOUSE

Portuairk

Achosnich

Ormsaigmore

Ormsaigbeg

Kilchoa

B8007

An Acairseid

Kilchoan Bay

0   1   2   3 miles
0   1   2   3   4   5 km

224

2 **3**

Ardmore Bay

Ardmore Pt.

Bloody B

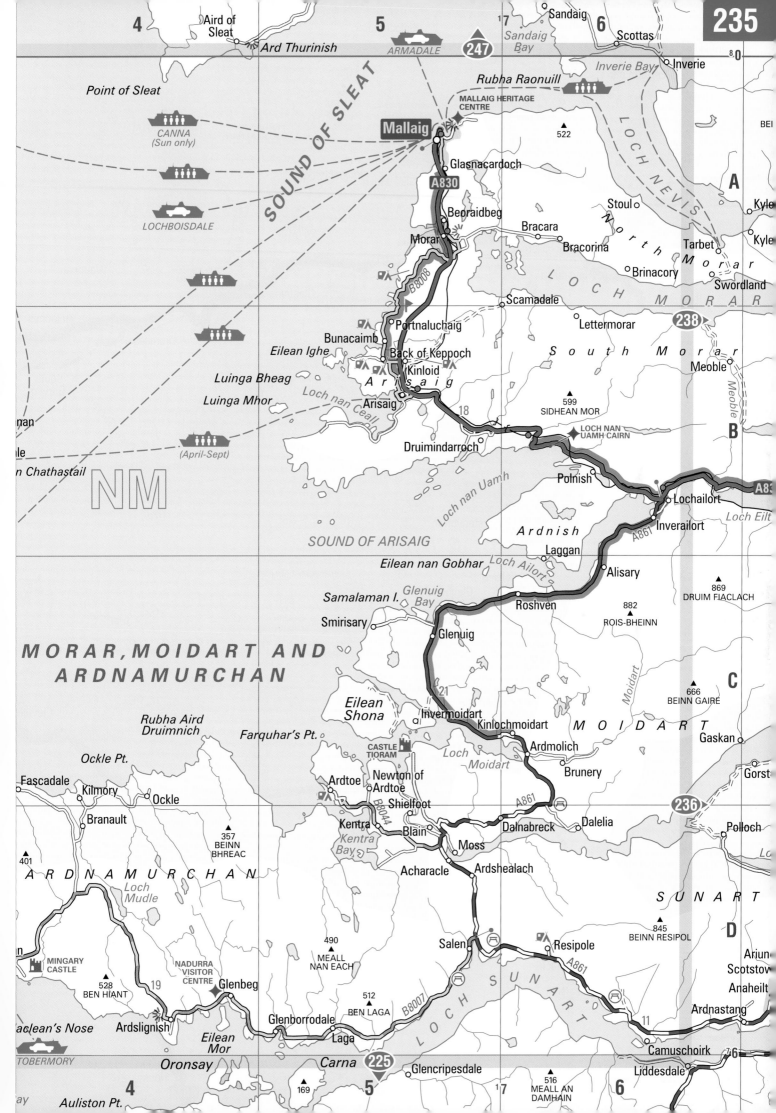

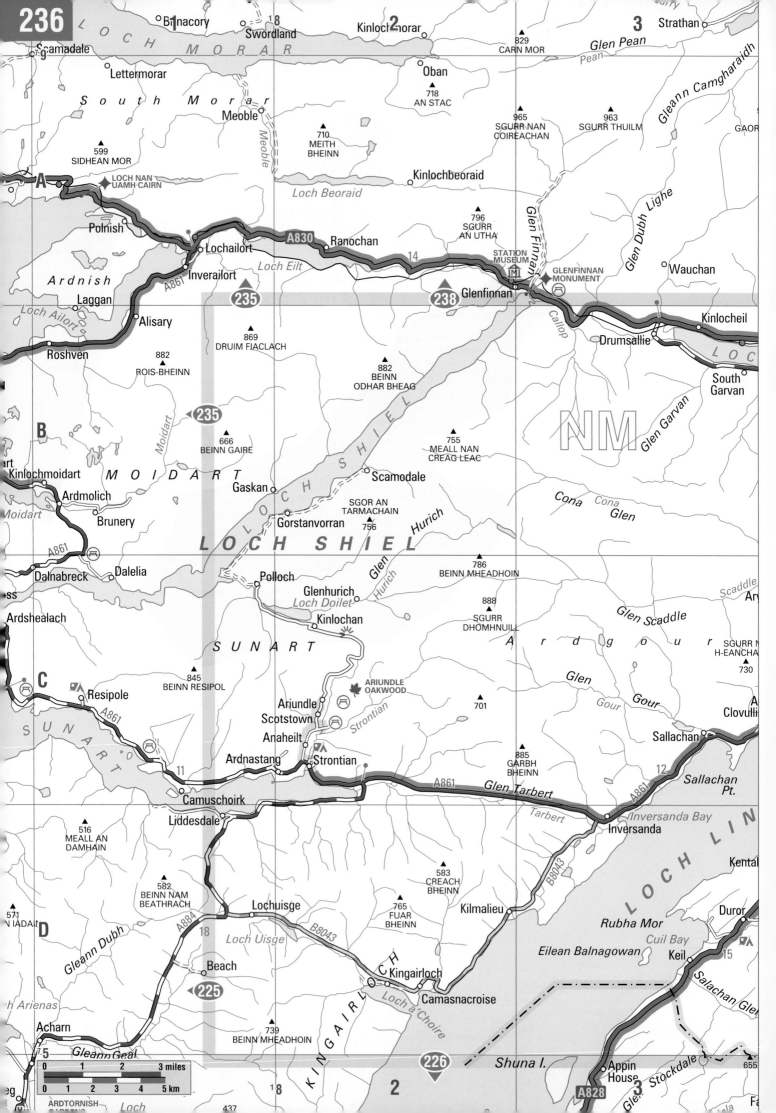

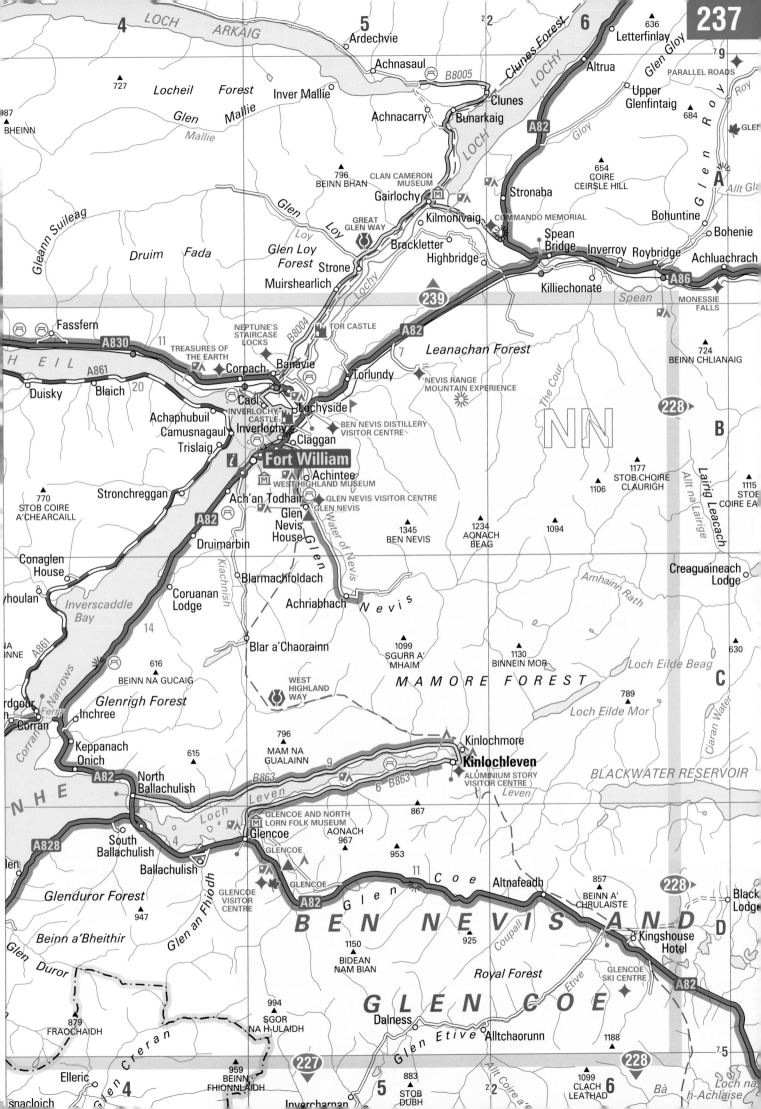

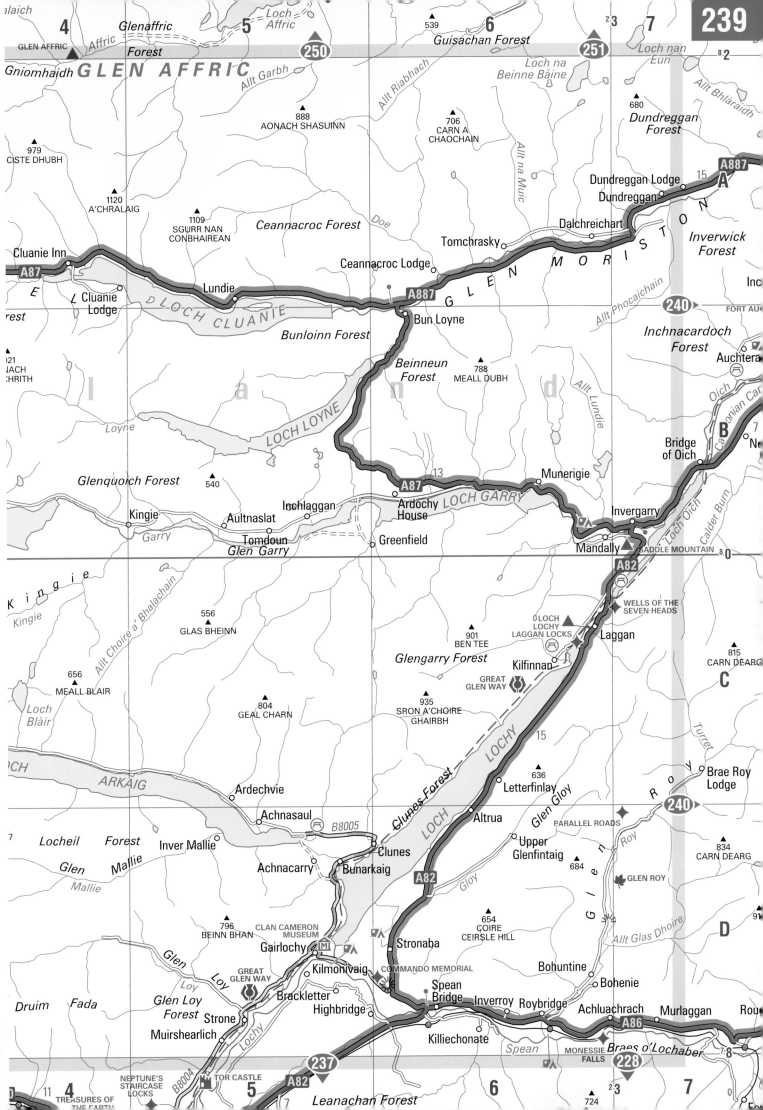

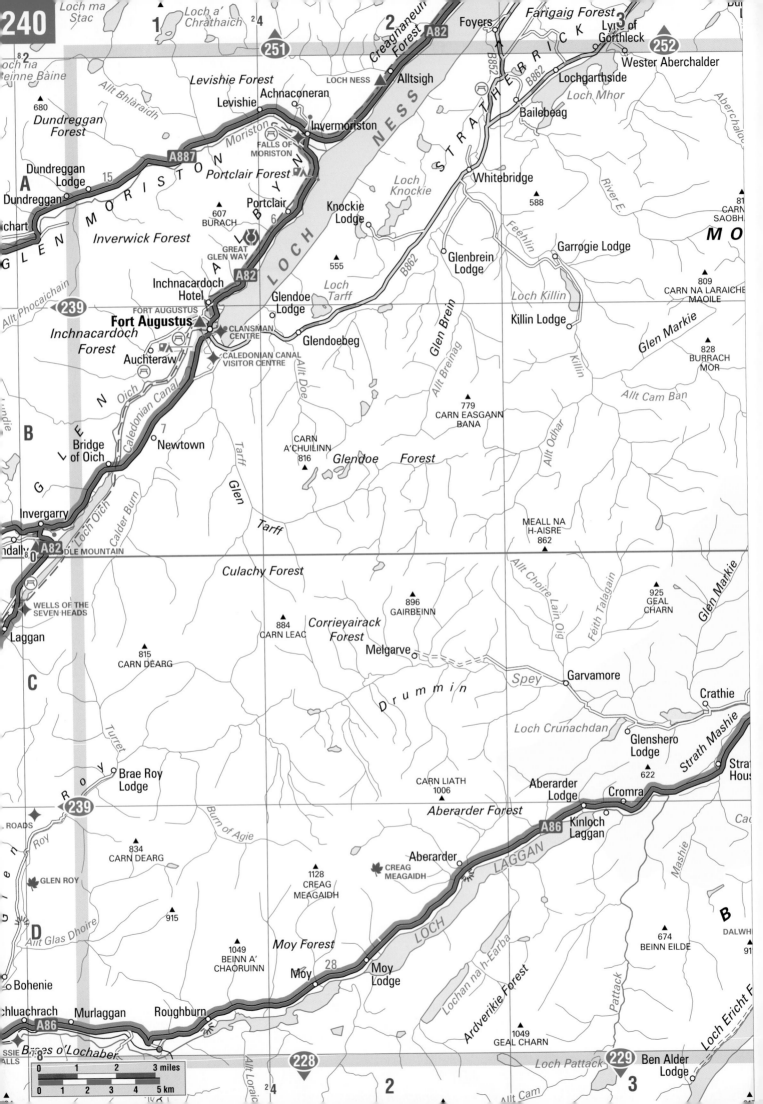

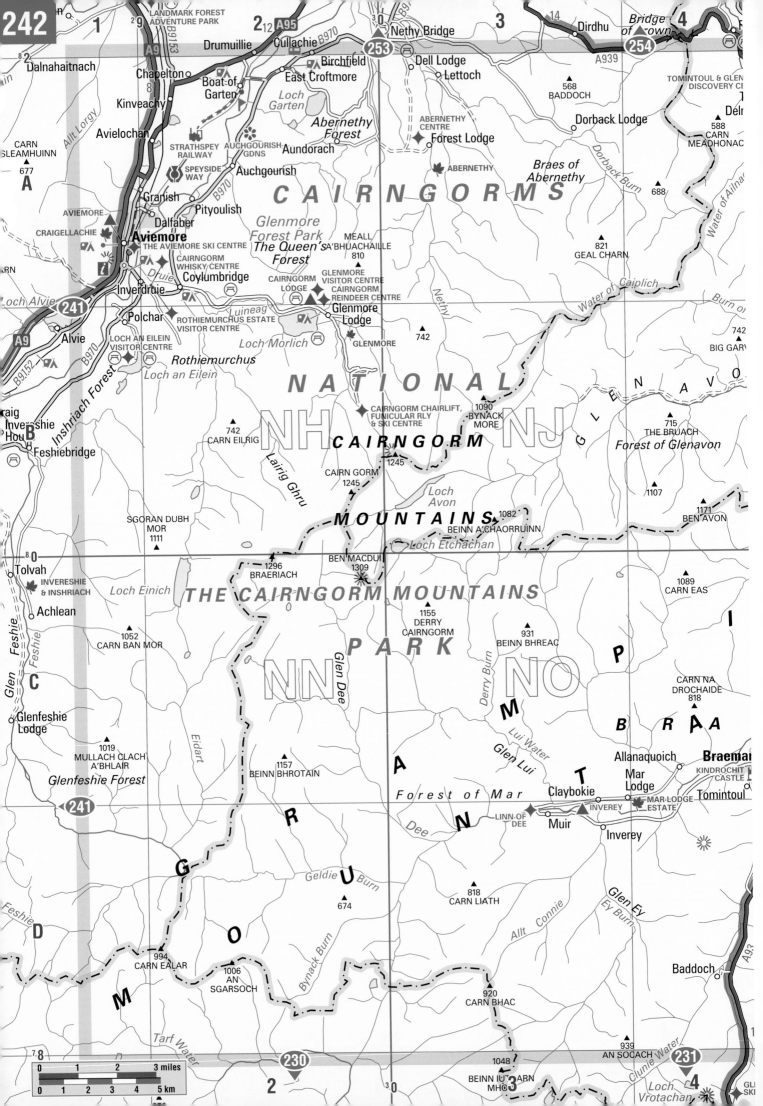

CAIRNGORMS

NATIONAL

CAIRNGORM

MOUNTAINS

THE CAIRNGORM MOUNTAINS

PARK

NH   NJ

NN   NO

GLEN AVON

Forest of Glenavon

Braes of Abernethy

Abernethy Forest

Glenmore Forest Park

The Queen's Forest

Rothiemurchus

Glenfeshie Forest

Forest of Mar

Inshriach Forest

Column headers (top): 1 2 3 4
Row labels (left): A B C D

Places and features:

- Dalnahaitnach
- Chapelton
- Boat of Garten
- Kinveachy
- Avielochan
- CARN SLEAMHUINN 677
- CRAIGELLACHIE
- AVIEMORE
- Aviemore
- THE AVIEMORE SKI CENTRE
- CAIRNGORM WHISKY CENTRE
- Coylumbridge
- Granish
- Pityoulish
- Dalfaber
- Inverdruie
- Polchar
- Alvie
- ROTHIEMURCHUS ESTATE VISITOR CENTRE
- LOCH AN EILEIN VISITOR CENTRE
- Loch an Eilein
- Loch Morlich
- STRATHSPEY RAILWAY
- SPEYSIDE WAY
- AUCHGOURISH GDNS
- Aundorach
- Auchgourish
- MEALL A'BHUACHAILLE 810
- GLENMORE VISITOR CENTRE
- CAIRNGORM LODGE
- CAIRNGORM REINDEER CENTRE
- Glenmore Lodge
- GLENMORE 742
- Drumuillie
- Cullachie
- Nethy Bridge
- Birchfield
- East Croftmore
- Dell Lodge
- Lettoch
- ABERNETHY CENTRE
- Forest Lodge
- ABERNETHY
- 568 BADDOCH
- Dorback Lodge
- 688
- Dirdhu
- Bridge of Brown
- TOMINTOUL & GLEN DISCOVERY CE
- Delr
- 588 CARN MEADHONAC
- 821 GEAL CHARN
- 715 THE BRUACH
- 742 BIG GARV
- 1107
- 1171 BEN AVON
- CAIRNGORM CHAIRLIFT, FUNICULAR RLY & SKI CENTRE
- 1090 BYNACK MORE
- CARN EILRIG 742
- Lairig Ghru
- CAIRN GORM 1245
- 1245
- Loch Avon
- 1082 BEINN A'CHAORRUINN
- Loch Etchachan
- SGORAN DUBH MOR 1111
- Loch Einich
- 1296 BRAERIACH
- BEN MACDUI 1309
- Tolvah
- INVERESHIE & INSHRIACH
- Achlean
- CARN BAN MOR 1052
- 1155 DERRY CAIRNGORM
- 931 BEINN BHREAC
- 1089 CARN EAS
- CARN NA DROCHAIDE 818
- Glenfeshie Lodge
- MULLACH CLACH A'BHLAIR 1019
- Glen Dee
- Derry Burn
- Lui Water
- Glen Lui
- Allanaquoich
- Mar Lodge
- Braemar
- KINDROCHIT CASTLE
- BEINN BHROTAIN 1157
- Eidart
- Claybokie
- INVEREY
- MAR LODGE ESTATE
- Tomintoul
- LINN OF DEE
- Muir
- Inverey
- Geldie Burn
- 674
- CARN LIATH 818
- Allt Connie
- Glen Ey
- Ey Burn
- Baddoch
- CARN EALAR 994
- AN SGARSOCH 1006
- Bynack Burn
- CARN BHAC 920
- Tarf Water
- BEINN IUTHARN MHOR 1048
- AN SOCACH 939
- Clunie Water
- Loch Vrotachan

Roads and refs: A9, A95, B9153, B970, B91, A939, B9152, 253, 254, 241, 230, 231

Scale:
0 1 2 3 miles
0 1 2 3 4 5 km

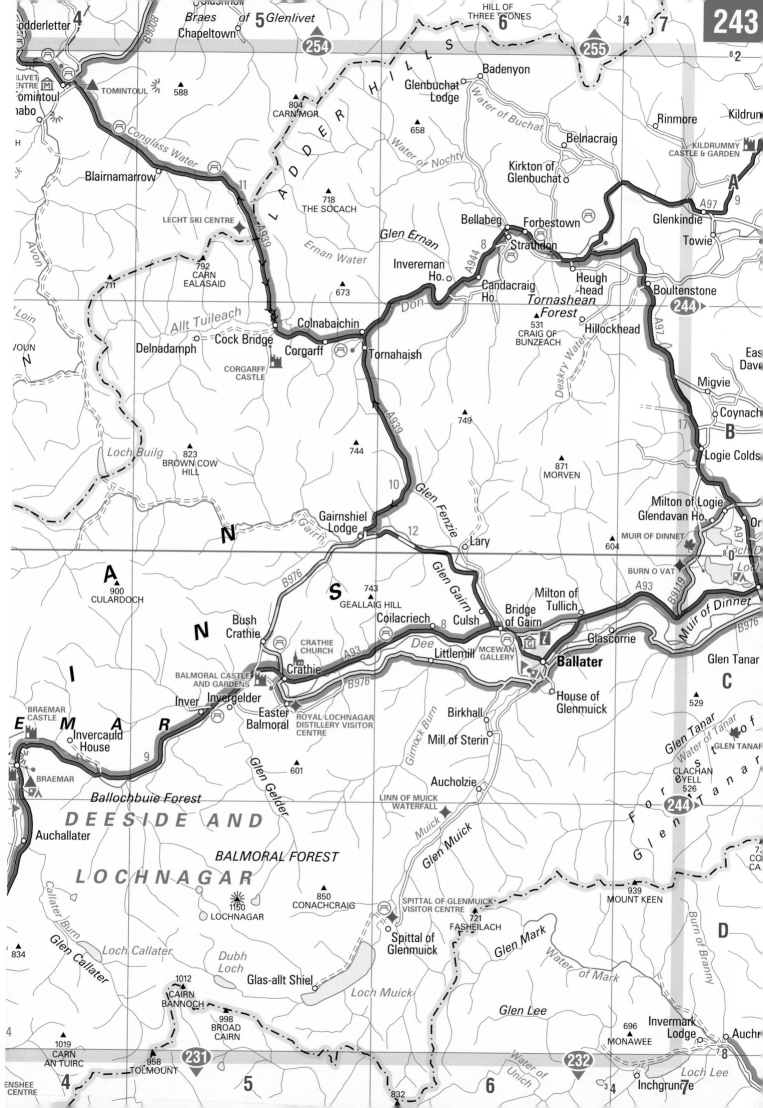

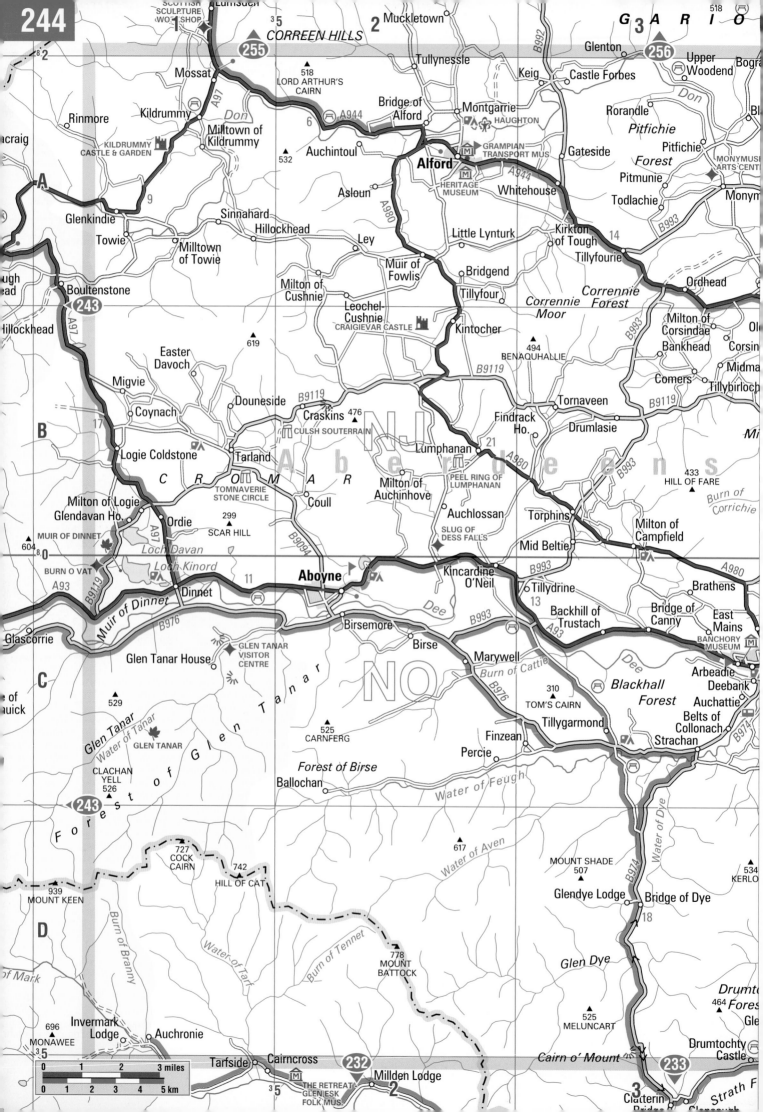

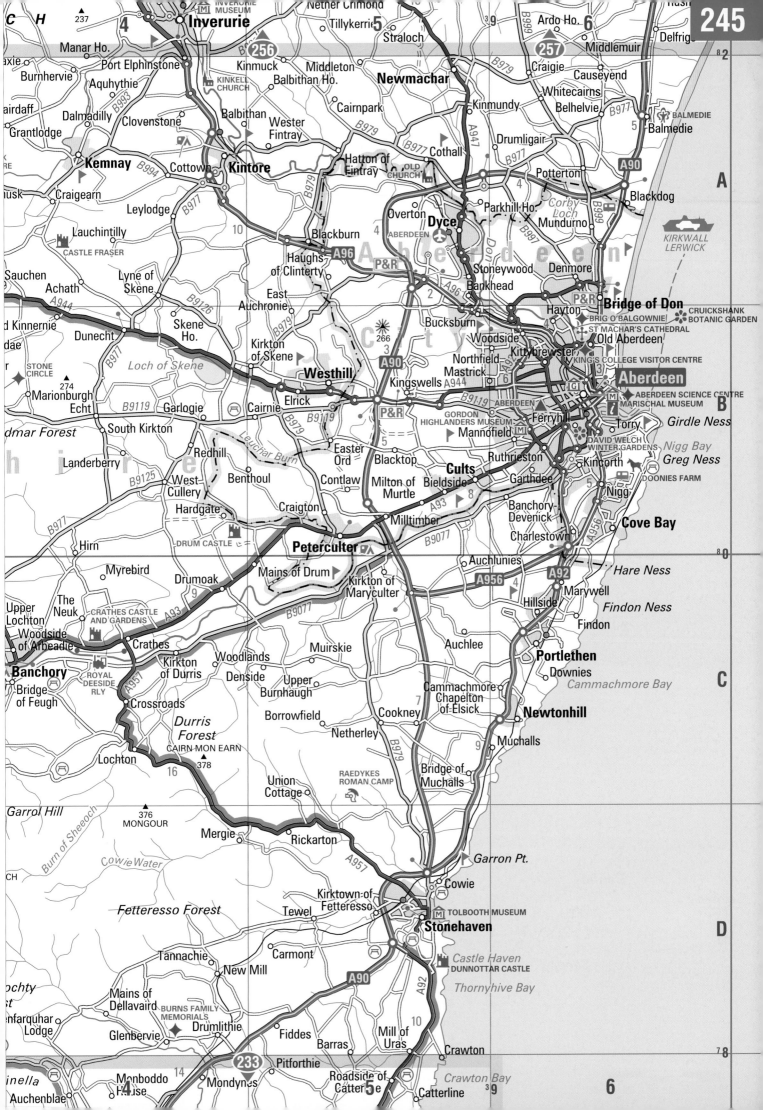

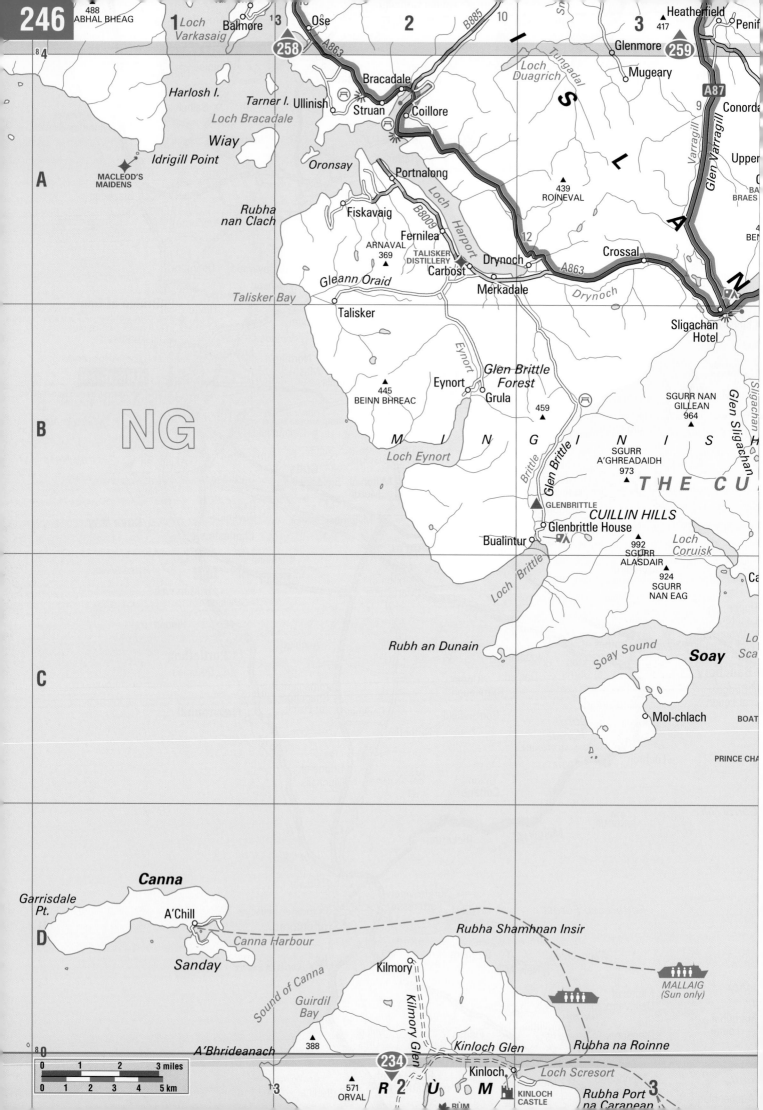

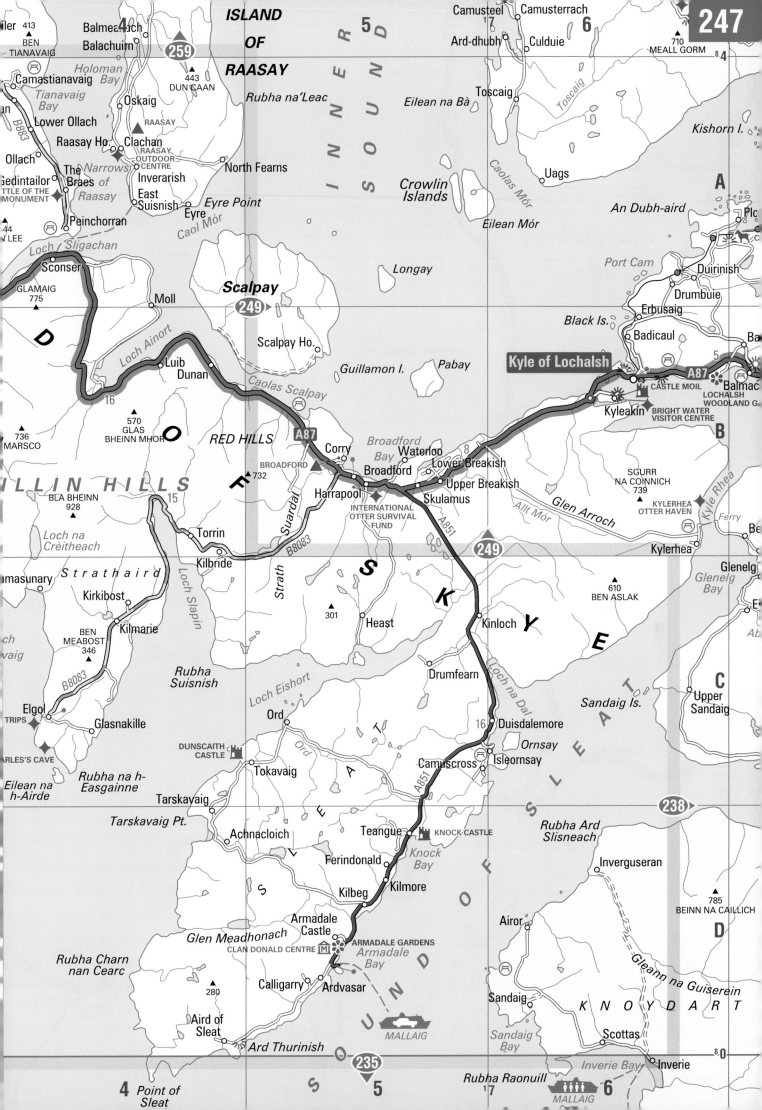

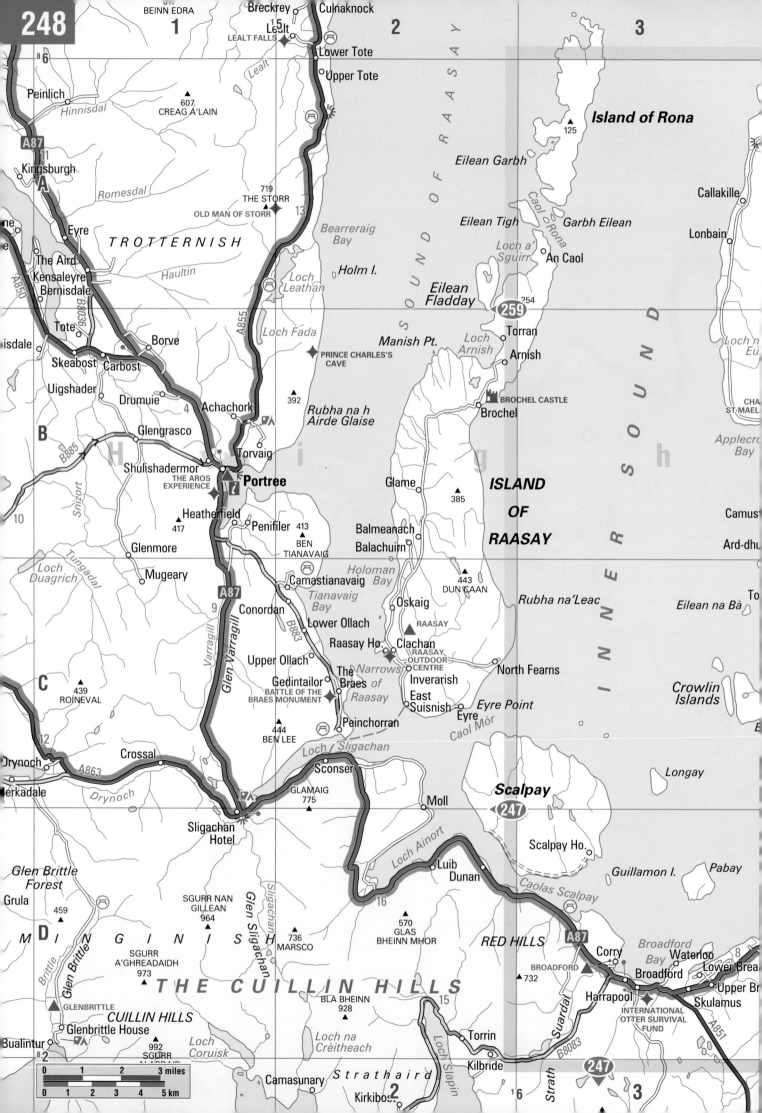

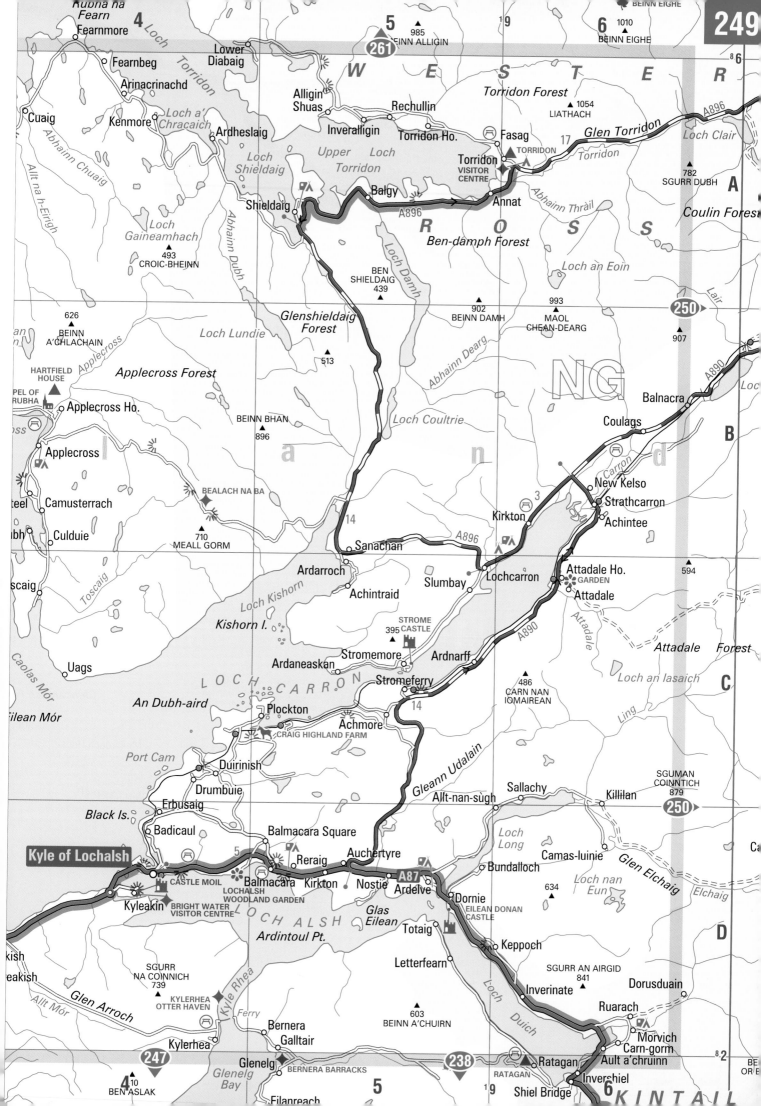

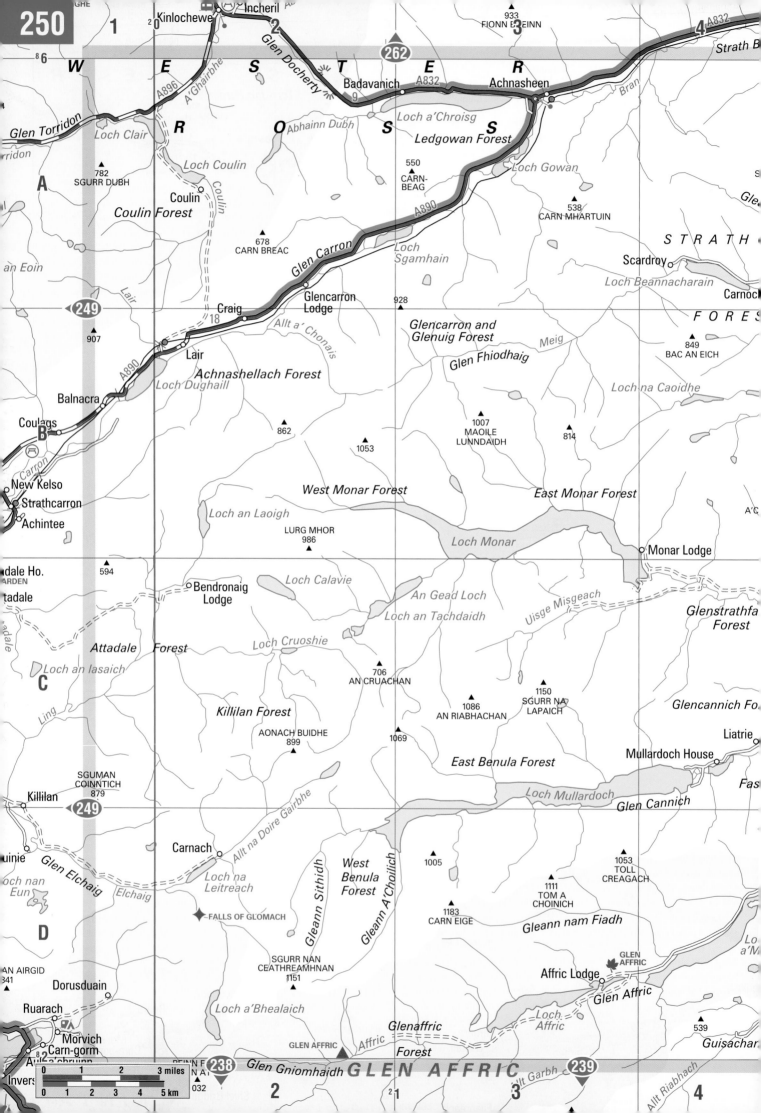

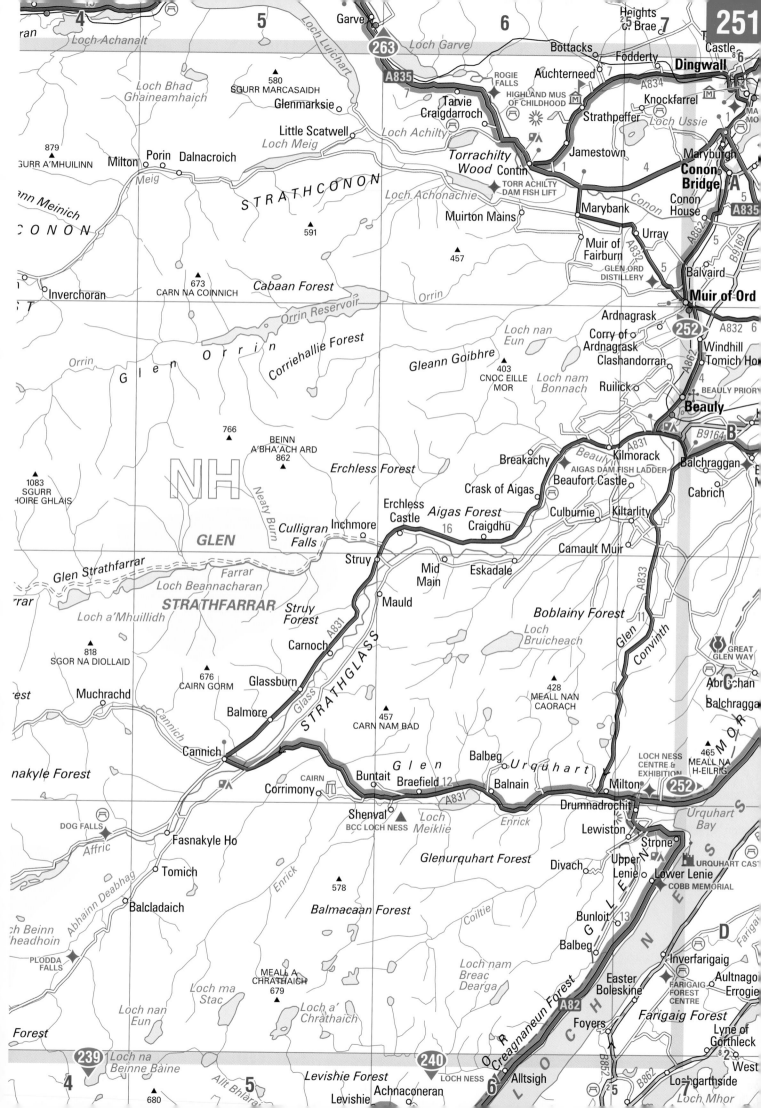

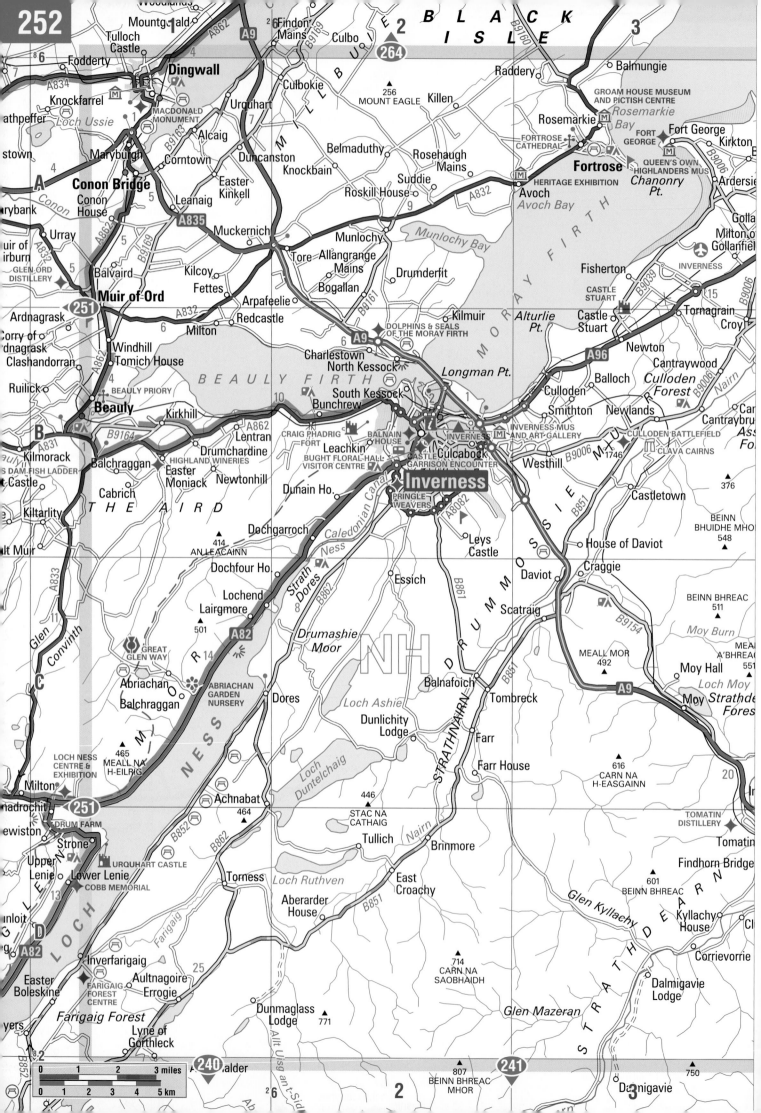

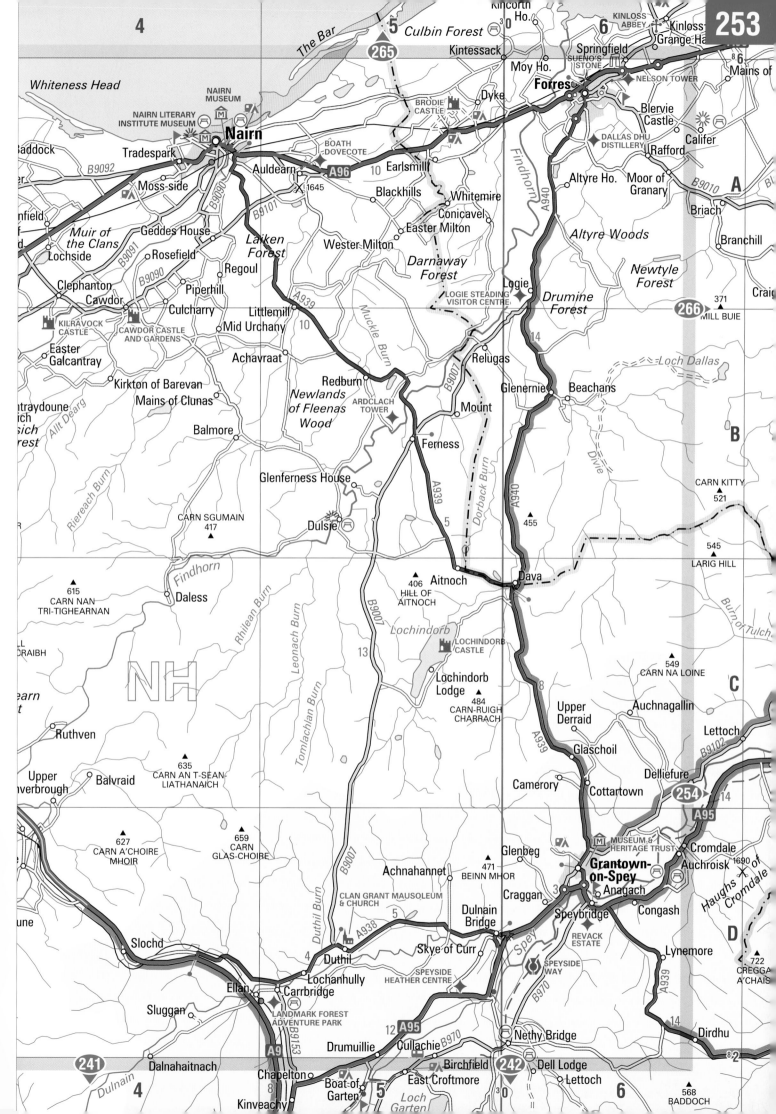

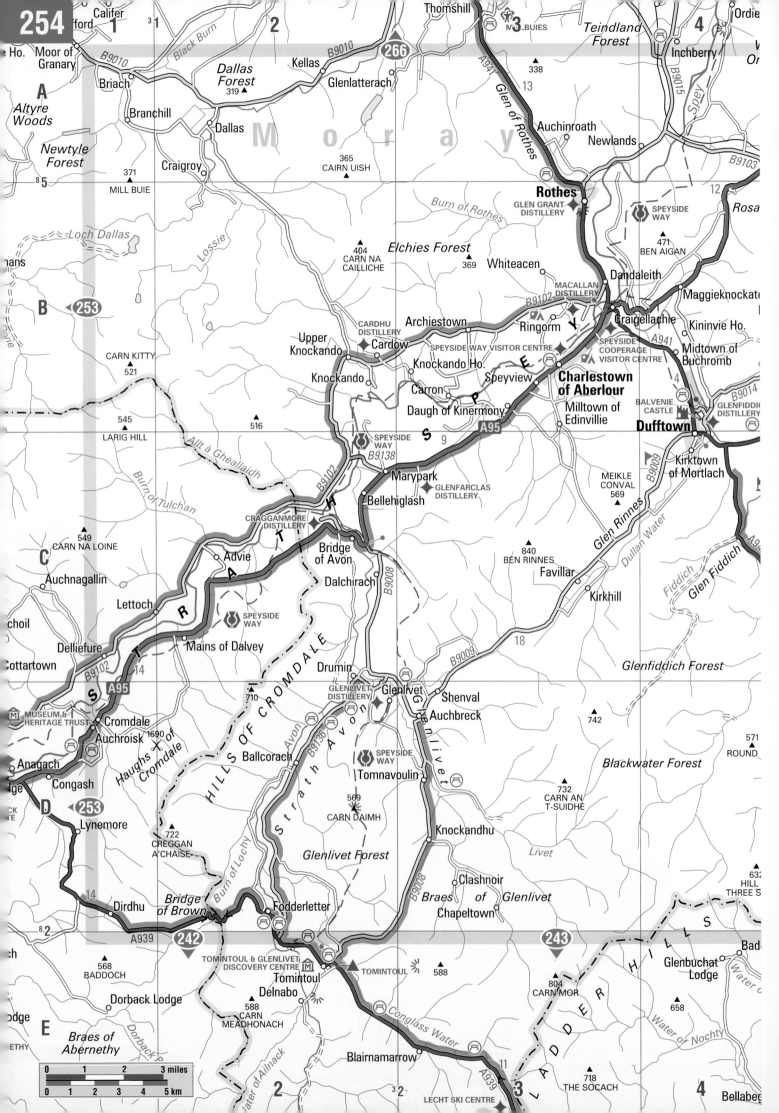

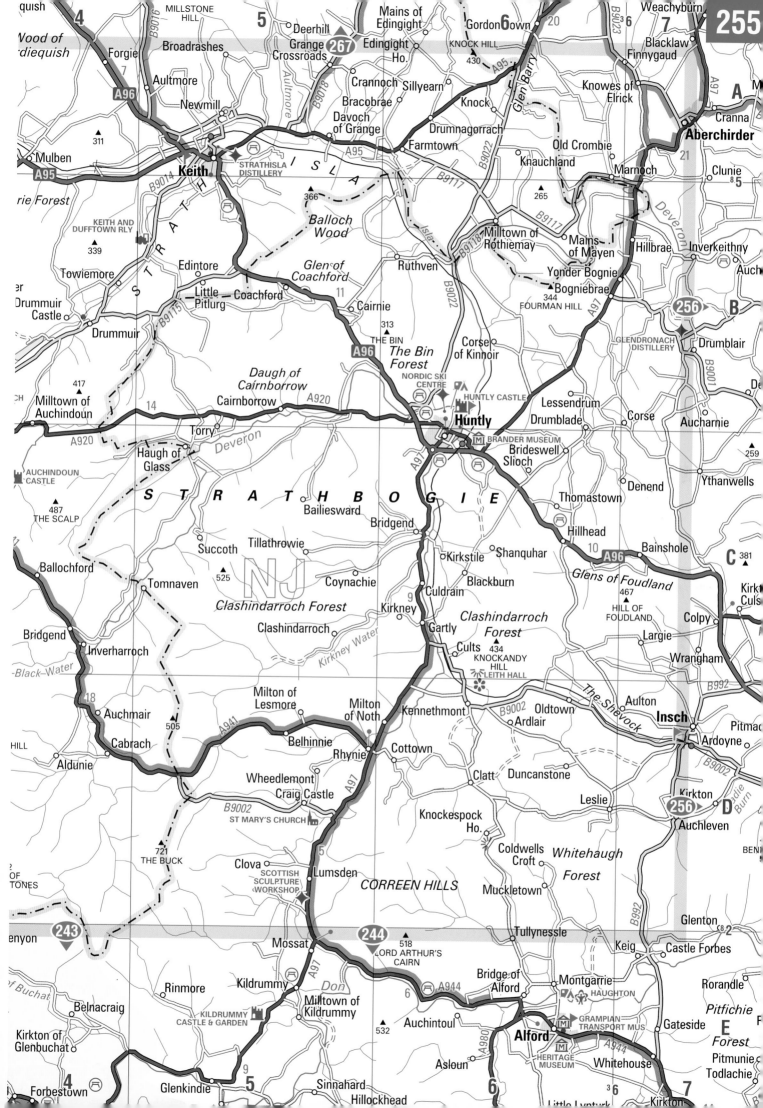

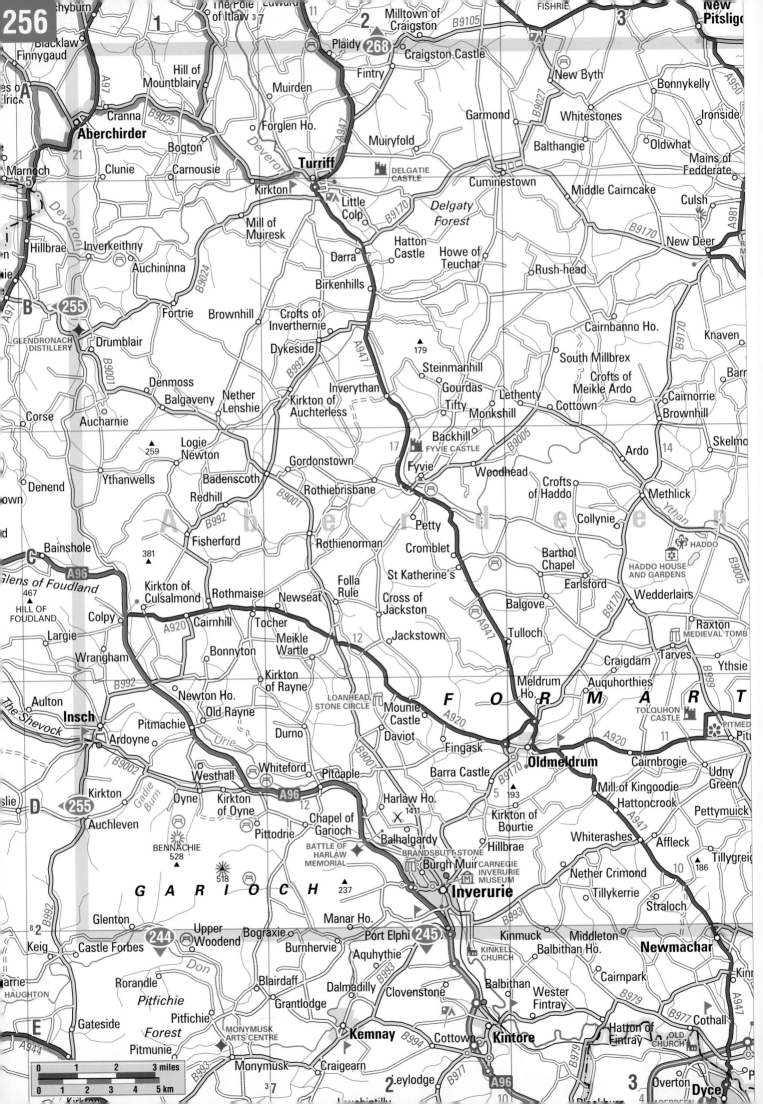

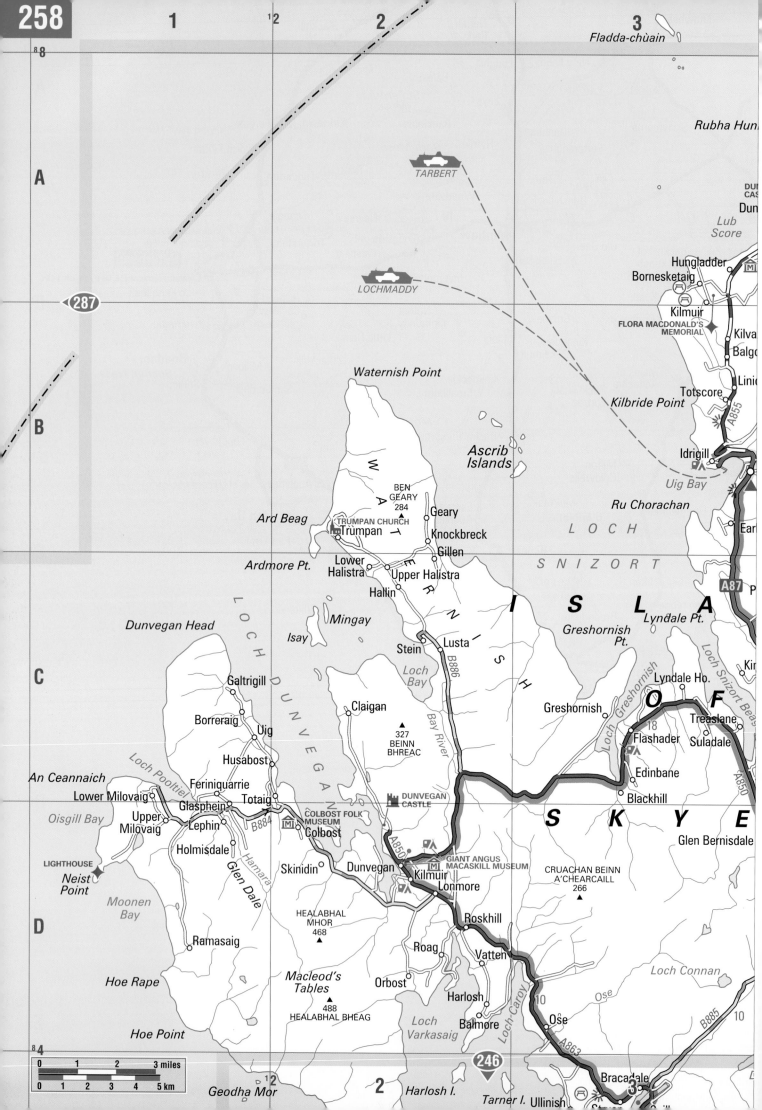

1
5
2
3

Garbh
Eilean

Eilean Mhuire

Eilean an Tighe

Na h-Eileanan Mòra
(Shiant Islands)

A

288

B

NG

288

259

Eilean Trodday

Rubha
Hunish

Rubha na h-Aiseig

C
DUN
CASTLE
Duntulm
Kilmaluag
20
Balmacqueen

MUSEUM OF
ISLAND LIFE

Eilean
Flodigarry

Flodigarry

MEALL NA
SUIRAMACH
543

259

Kilvaxter
Balgown

Digg
Glashvin

THE QUIRAING
Brogaig

Staffin
Bay

Staffin I.

Linicro

Stenscholl
Staffin

TROTTERNISH

Kilt Rock

KILT ROCK & MEALT FALLS

466
BIOD BUIDHE

D
Uig

Maligar

Elishader

Loch Mealt

UIG

Marishader

Valtos

Rubha nam
Brathairean

611
BEINN EDRA

Garros

Balnaknock

Breckrey

Culnaknock

Island of Rona

Earlish

Lealt
LEALT FALLS

8
6

Lower Tote

0   1   2   3 miles
0 1 2 3 4 5 km

Upper Tote

Lealt

5

607
CREAG A'LAIN

Hinnisdal

2

3

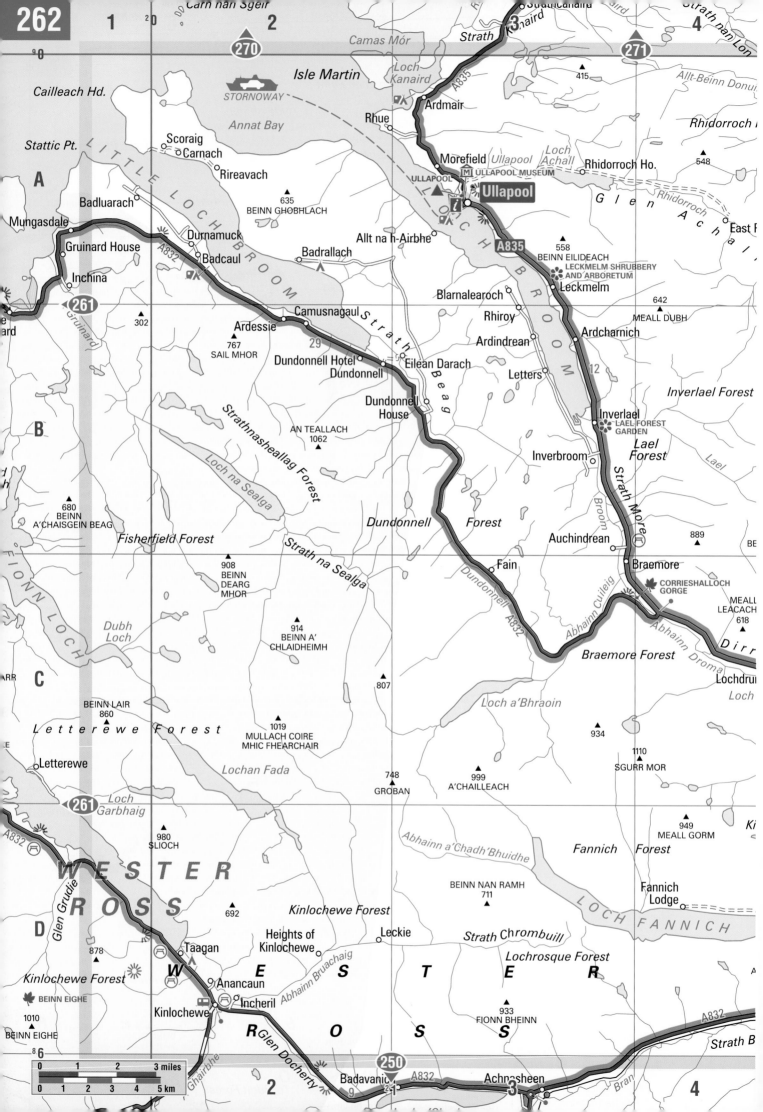

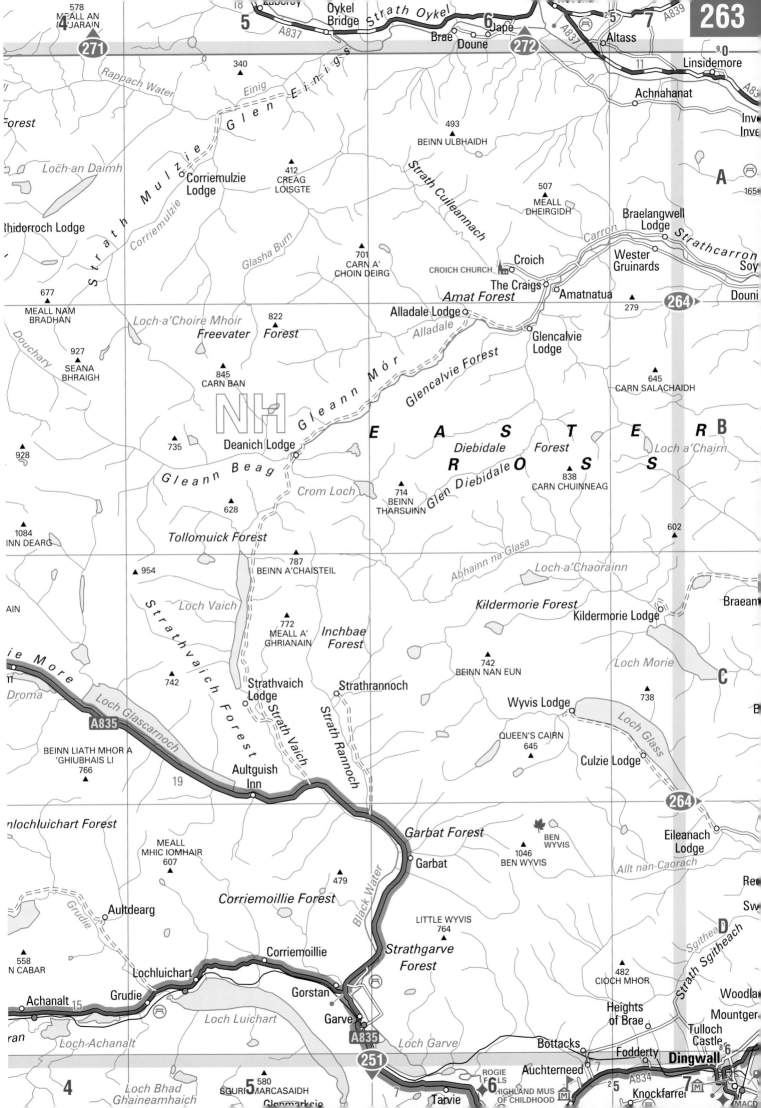

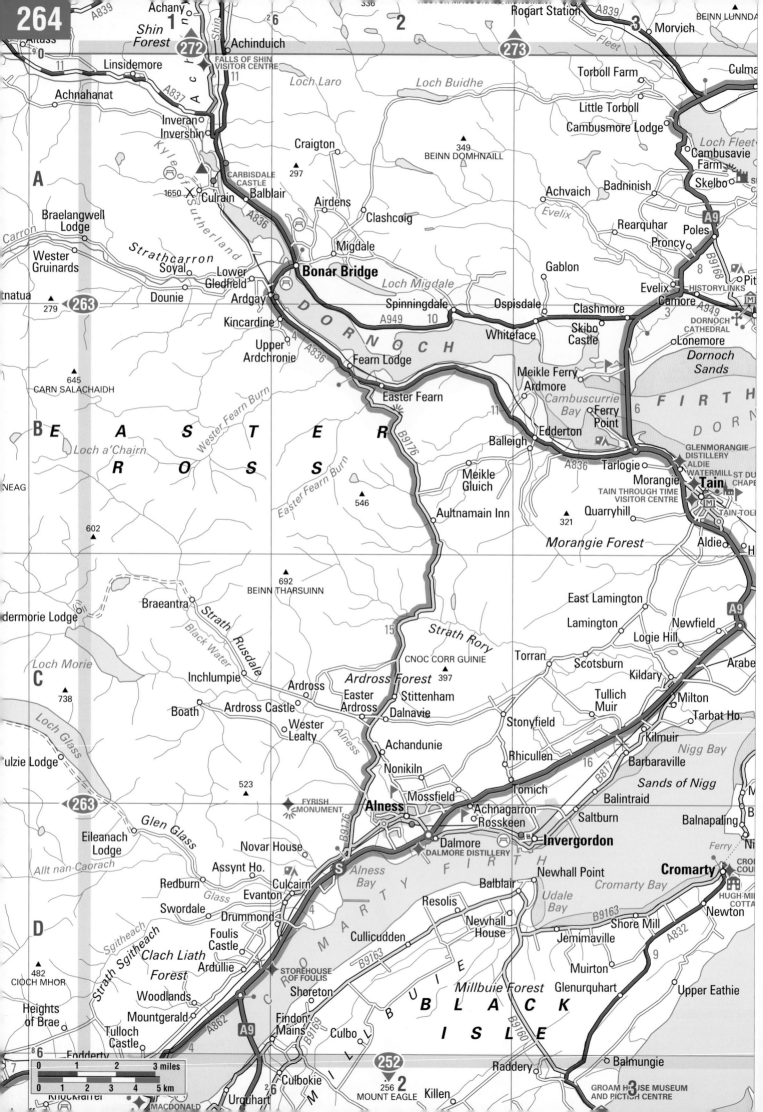

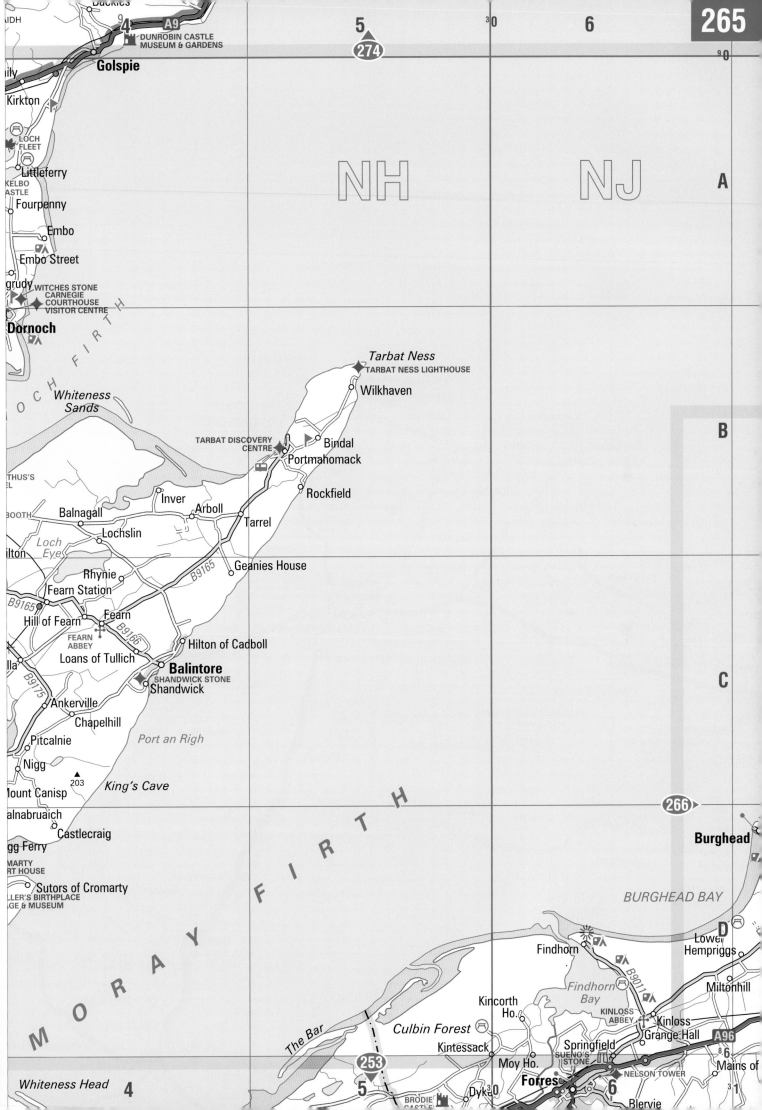

NH **NJ**

4 **A9**
DUNROBIN CASTLE
MUSEUM & GARDENS

Golspie

Kirkton

LOCH
FLEET

Littleferry

Fourpenny

Embo

Embo Street

grudy

WITCHES STONE
CARNEGIE
COURTHOUSE
VISITOR CENTRE

Dornoch

*Whiteness
Sands*

Tarbat Ness
TARBAT NESS LIGHTHOUSE

Wilkhaven

TARBAT DISCOVERY
CENTRE

Bindal

Portmahomack

Rockfield

Inver

Balnagall

Arboll

Lochslin

Tarrel

Geanies House

Rhynie

Fearn Station

B9165

Hill of Fearn

Fearn

FEARN
ABBEY

B9166

Hilton of Cadboll

Loans of Tullich

Balintore
SHANDWICK STONE
Shandwick

Ankerville

Chapelhill

Port an Righ

Pitcalnie

Nigg

203

King's Cave

Mount Canisp

lnabruaich

Castlecraig

gg Ferry

MARTY
RT HOUSE

LER'S BIRTHPLACE
GE & MUSEUM

Sutors of Cromarty

Whiteness Head

Burghead

BURGHEAD BAY

Findhorn

Lower
Hempriggs

Miltonhill

B9011

*Findhorn
Bay*

Kincorth
Ho.

KINLOSS
ABBEY

Kinloss

Grange Hall **A96**

Mains of

Culbin Forest

Springfield

Kintessack

SUENO'S
STONE

Moy Ho.

253

Forres

Dyke

NELSON TOWER

BRODIE
CASTLE

Blervie

266

M O R A Y   F I R T H

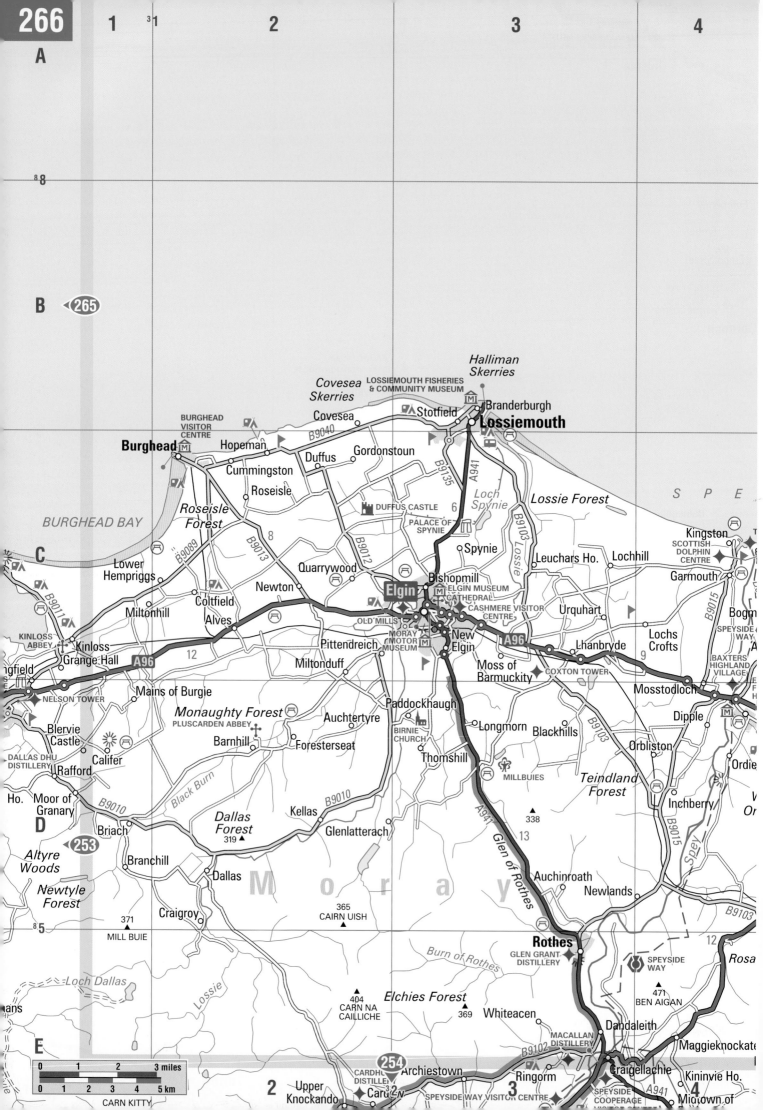

A

B ◄ 265

Burghead
BURGHEAD VISITOR CENTRE
Hopeman
Cummingston
Roseisle

Covesea Skerries
Covesea
B9040
Duffus
Gordonstoun

LOSSIEMOUTH FISHERIES & COMMUNITY MUSEUM
Stotfield
Branderburgh
Lossiemouth
Halliman Skerries

Roseisle Forest
BURGHEAD BAY
B9089
B9013

C
Lower Hempriggs
Miltonhill
Coltfield
Alves
Newton
Quarrywood

DUFFUS CASTLE
PALACE OF SPYNIE
Loch Spynie
Spynie
B9135
A941
B9103
Lossie
Lossie Forest
S P E

Bishopmill
Elgin
ELGIN MUSEUM
CATHEDRAL
CASHMERE VISITOR CENTRE
Urquhart

Leuchars Ho.
Lochhill
Garmouth
Kingston
SCOTTISH DOLPHIN CENTRE
B9015

KINLOSS ABBEY
Kinloss
Grange Hall
A96 12

OLD MILLS
MORAY MOTOR MUSEUM
New Elgin
Pittendreich
Miltonduff

A96
Lhanbryde
Moss of Barmuckity
COXTON TOWER
Lochs Crofts
9
SPEYSIDE WAY
BAXTERS HIGHLAND VILLAGE

gfield
NELSON TOWER

Blervie Castle
Califer
Rafford
DALLAS DHU DISTILLERY

Mains of Burgie
Monaughty Forest
PLUSCARDEN ABBEY
Barnhill
Auchtertyre
Foresterseat
BIRNIE CHURCH
Paddockhaugh

Longmorn
Blackhills
B9103

Mosstodloch
Dipple
Orbliston
Ordie

Ho. Moor of Granary
B9010
Black Burn

Thomshill
MILLBUIES
338
Teindland Forest
Inchberry
B9015
Or

D ◄ 253

Briach
Branchill
Dallas
Kellas
B9010
Glenlatterach

Dallas Forest
319 ▲

A941
Glen of Rothes
13
Auchinroath
Newlands

Altyre Woods

Newtyle Forest

Craigroy
371
MILL BUIE

365
CAIRN UISH ▲

Rothes
GLEN GRANT DISTILLERY
SPEYSIDE WAY
12
B9103
Rosa

8 5

Loch Dallas
Lossie
Burn of Rothes
SPEYSIDE WAY
471
BEN AIGAN ▲

ans

404
CARN NA CAILLICHE ▲
369 ▲
Whiteacen

Elchies Forest
MACALLAN DISTILLERY
Dandaleith
Craigellachie
Maggieknockate

E

CARDHU DISTILLERY
254
Archiestown
B9102
Ringorm
SPEYSIDE WAY VISITOR CENTRE
SPEYSIDE COOPERAGE
Kininvie Ho.
Midtown of
A941

Upper Knockando
Carro n
CARN KITTY

| 0 | 1 | 2 | 3 miles |
| 0 | 1 | 2 | 3 | 4 | 5 km |

1 ³1 2 3 4

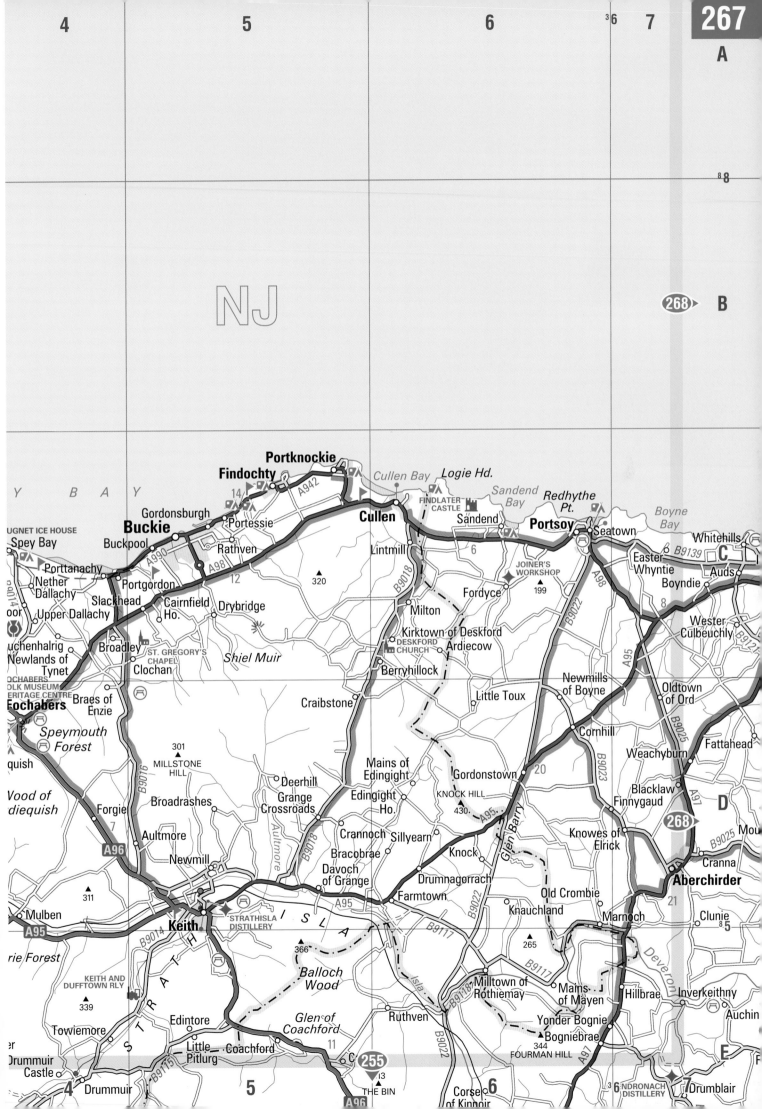

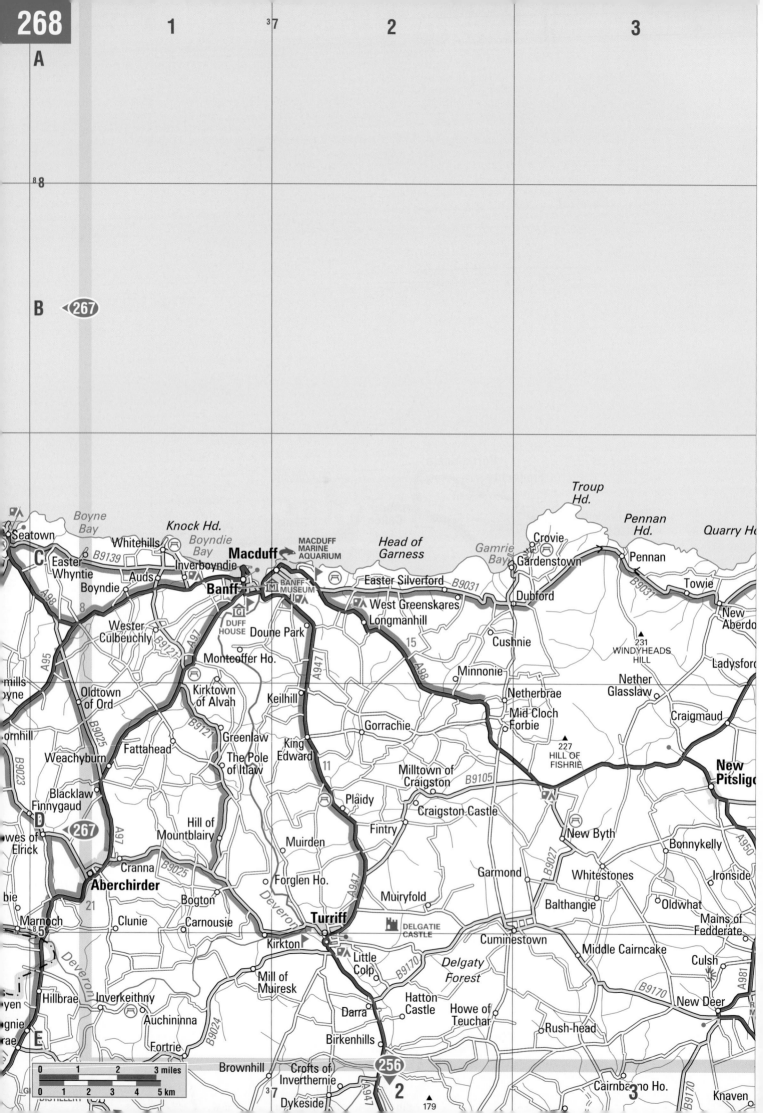

4   **0**   **5**   **1**   **6**

A

B

NJ   NK

SANDHAVEN MEAL MILL
FRASERBURGH HERITAGE CENTRE
Rosehearty   B9031   Pittulie
PITSLIGO CASTLE   Broadsea   **Fraserburgh**
   Sandhaven   *Kinnaird Head*
Peathill   KINNAIRD CASTLE LIGHTHOUSE & SCOTLAND'S LIGHTHOUSE MUSEUM
Percyhorner   Pitblae   *Fraserburgh Bay*   *Cairnbulg Pt.*
Coburty   B9107   **Inverallochy**
Upper Boyndlie   B9032   A981   MAGGIE'S HOOSIE
Mid Ardlaw   A90   B9033   Cairnbulg Castle   St Combs
Tyrie   Memsie   5   Gowanhill   *Inzie Head*
Whitewell   MEMSIE BURIAL CAIRN   Strathellie
A98   10   Rathen   B9033   Cairness   *Loch of Strathbeg*
Hillhead of Auchentumb   Newburgh   Crimonmogate
16   230 MORMOND HILL   Lonmay   *Rattray Head*
Knowhead   Old Rattray
B9093   Strichen   Nether Park   **Crimond**
New Leeds   A952   Longhill   Blackhill
Adziel   B9093   7   Balearn   A90
Little Skillymarno   *North Ugie Water*   Leys   *St Fergus Moss*   12   St Fergus   *Scotstown Hd.*
A981   Denhead   Backfolds   Kirktown   North Kirkton
11   Fetterangus   Hythie   *Rora Moss*   *Kirkton Hd.*
Forest of Deer   Toux   Rora   Lunderton
A950   DEER ABBEY   Dunshillock   Woodside
B U C H A N   *Ugie Water*   Newseat   Inverugie   UGIE SALMON FISH HOUSE
Maud   B9029   ADEN   INVERUGIE CASTLE   Buchanhaven
MAUD RAILWAY MUSEUM   Old Deer   **Mintlaw**   Longside   Torterston   A982   **Peterhead**
B9106   Backhill of Clackriach   ABERDEENSHIRE FARMING MUSEUM   Flushing   ARBUTHNOT MUSEUM & ART GALLERY
Drymuir   Stuartfield   *South Ugie*   Inverquhomery   A950   Keith Inch
Bulwark   Mains of Crichie   Millbreck   Hillhead of Cocklaw
A948   Nethermuir   Crichie   B9030   Neth 257 Kinmundy   *Peterhead Bay*
Kinnadie   Clola   Little Dens   Invernettie
Skelmuir   *Sandford Bay*

4   **0**   **5**   **1**   **6**

C

D

E

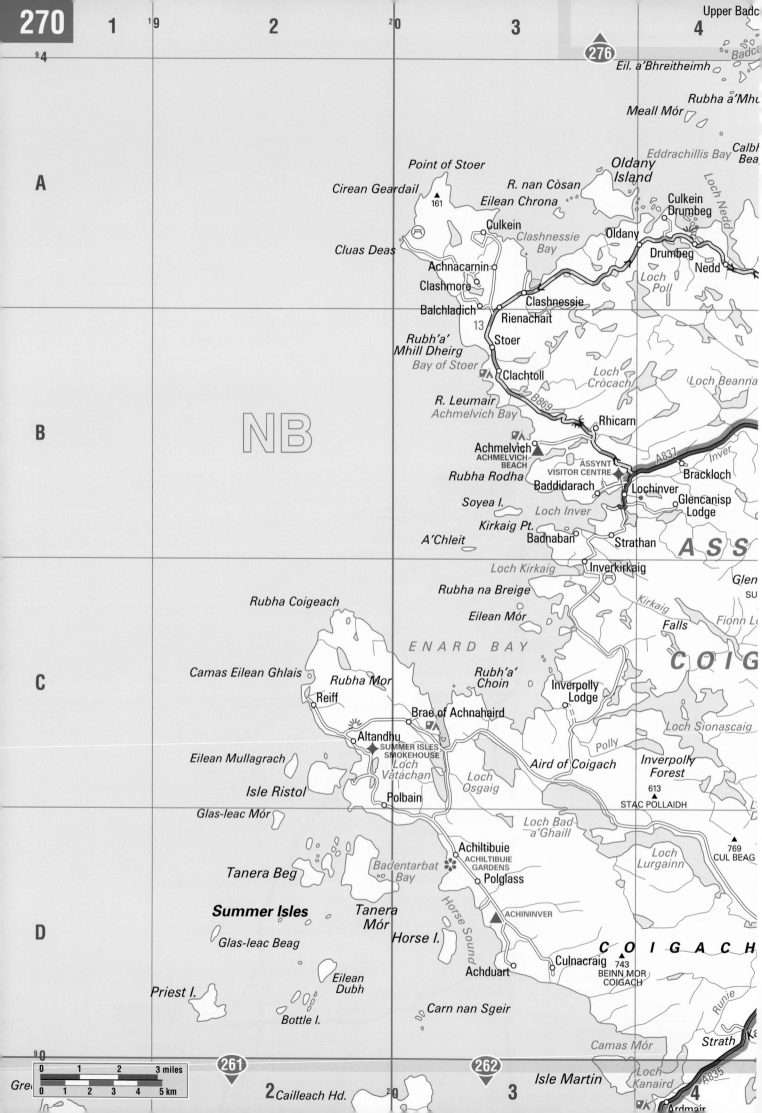

Upper Badc

Eil. a'Bhreitheimh

Rubha a'Mhu

Meall Mór

Eddrachillis Bay Calbh
Bea

Point of Stoer

Cirean Geardail

Oldany
Island

R. nan Còsan

Eilean Chrona

Culkein
Drumbeg

Culkein

Oldany

Clashnessie
Bay

Drumbeg

Loch Nedd

Cluas Deas

Nedd

Achnacarnin

Clashmore

Clashnessie

Loch
Poll

Balchladich

Rienachait

13

Stoer

Rubh 'a'
Mhill Dheirg

Loch
Cròcach

Loch Beanna

Bay of Stoer

Clachtoll

R. Leumair

Achmelvich Bay

B869

Rhicarn

A837

Inver

Achmelvich
ACHMELVICH
BEACH

ASSYNT
VISITOR
CENTRE

Brackloch

Rubha Rodha

Baddidarach

Lochinver

Soyea I.

Loch Inver

Glencanisp
Lodge

Kirkaig Pt.

A'Chleit

Badnaban

Strathan

A S S

Loch Kirkaig

Inverkirkaig

Glen
SU

Rubha na Breige

Rubha Coigeach

Eilean Mór

Kirkaig

Falls

Fionn L

Camas Eilean Ghlais

Rubha Mor

E N A R D B A Y

Rubh 'a'
Choin

Inverpolly
Lodge

C O I G

Reiff

Brae of Achnahaird

Loch Sionascaig

Altandhu

SUMMER ISLES
SMOKEHOUSE

Eilean Mullagrach

Loch
Vatachan

Aird of Coigach

Inverpolly
Forest

Isle Ristol

Loch
Osgaig

613
STAC POLLAIDH

Polbain

Glas-leac Mór

Loch Bad
a'Ghaill

Achiltibuie
ACHILTIBUIE
GARDENS

Loch
Lurgainn

769
CUL BEAG

Tanera Beg

Badentarbat
Bay

Polglass

Summer Isles

Tanera
Mór

Horse I.

ACHININVER

C O I G A C H

Glas-leac Beag

Horse Sound

Culnacraig

743
BEINN MOR
COIGACH

Priest I.

Eilean
Dubh

Achduart

Bottle I.

Carn nan Sgeir

Gre

Camas Mór

Strath

Ka

261

Cailleach Hd.

262

Isle Martin

A835

Loch
Kanaird

Ardmair

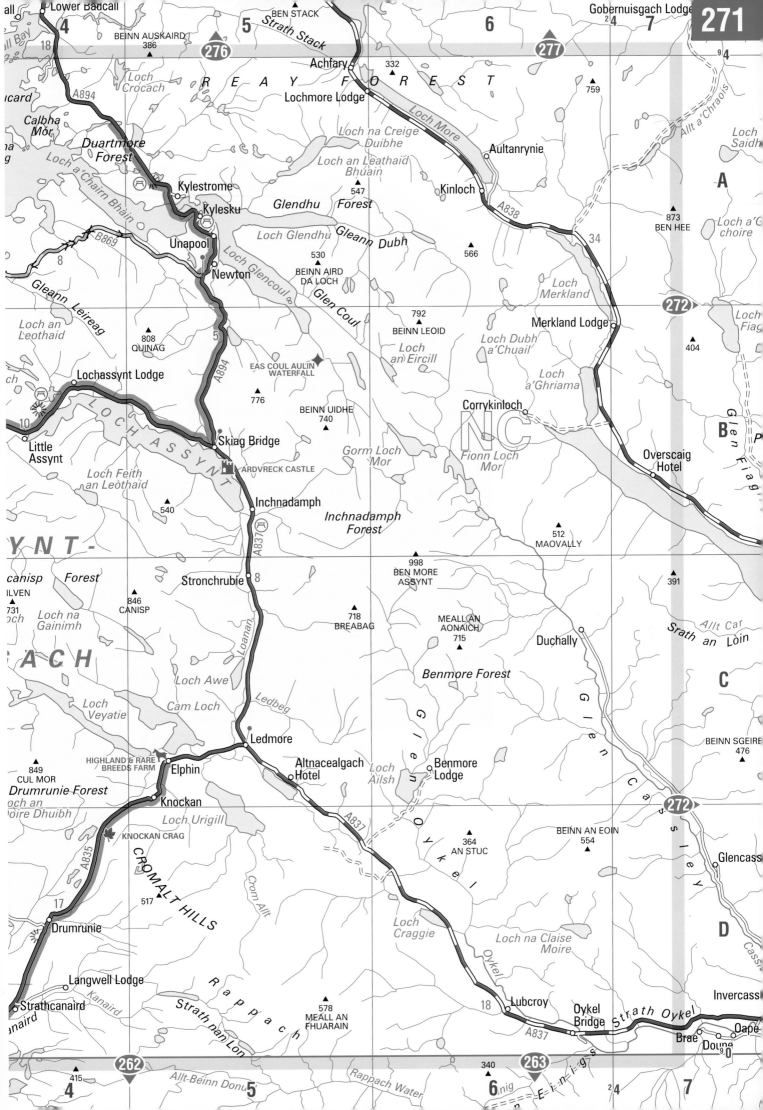

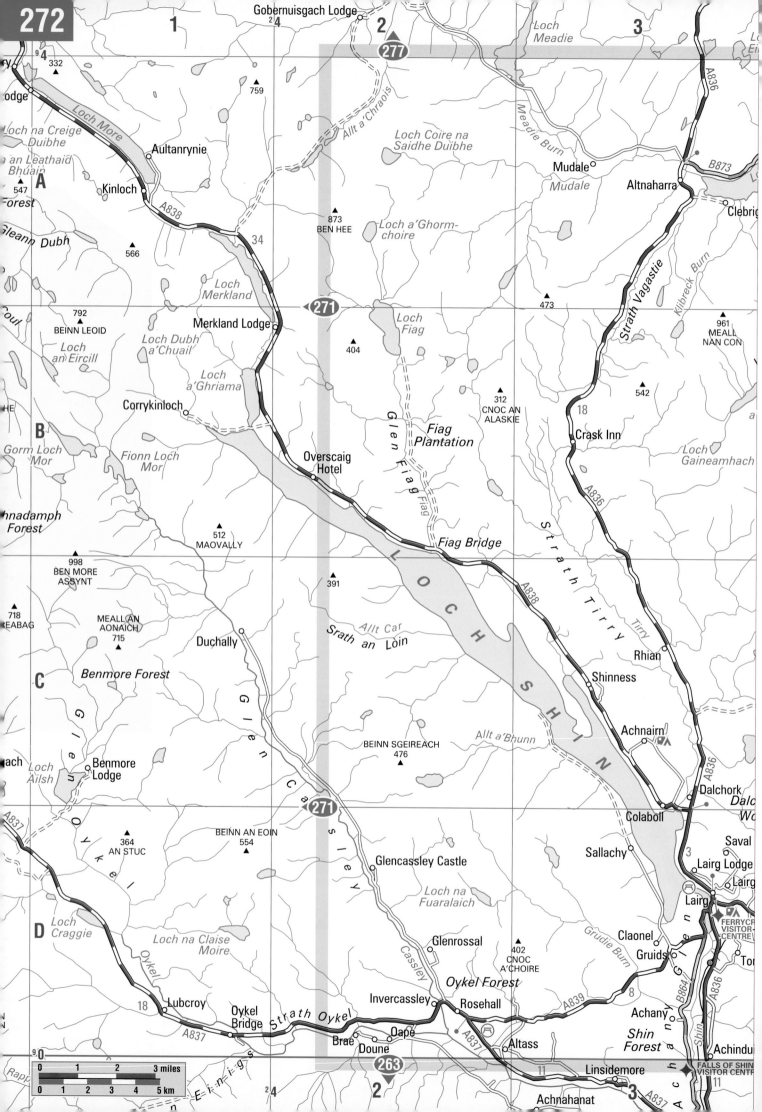

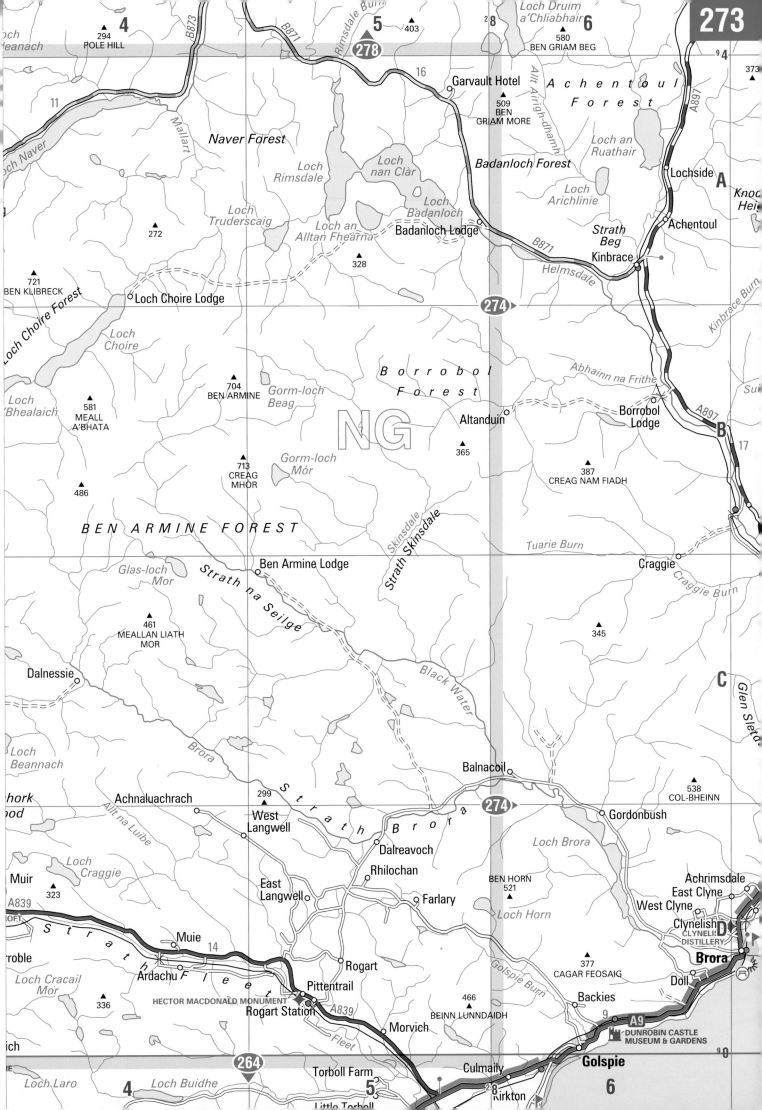

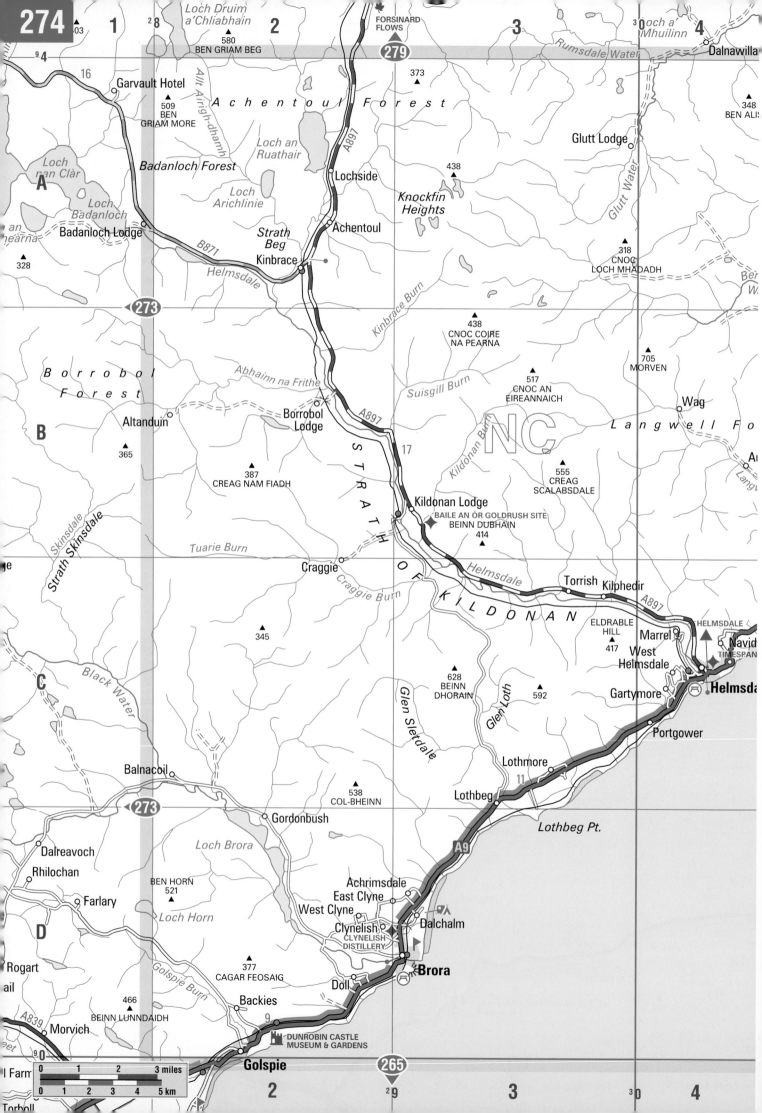

Loch Sand

Loch Thulachán

Loch Rangag

STEMSTER HILL
248

Camster

Ulbster
CAIRN OF GET
Whaligoe

4 **5** **6** **7** 17

9 4

Lodge

280 A9

281

Bruan

Loch Breac

Crofts of Benachielt

Rumster Forest

Roster

HILL O' MANY STANES

SKY

Braehungie

Upper Lybster

Mid Clyth

287

269
CNOCAN CONACHREAG

Houstry

WAG OF FORSE

Forse Ho.

Swiney

West Clyth

Reisgill Burn

Lybster

A99

A

Dunbeath Water

Smerral

Latheron

Forse

CLAN GUNN HERITAGE CENTRE

riedale water

Braemore

Latheronwheel Ho.

Latheronwheel

LAIDHAY CROFT MUSEUM

283

Balnabruich

DUNBEATH HERITAGE CENTRE

Dunbeath

Dunbeath Bay

DUNBEATH CASTLE

Knockally

ND

B

626
SCARABEN

Ramscraigs

rest

Borgue

ultibea

Newport

19

Ceann Leathad nam Bò

Langwell Ho.

Berriedale

422

vell Water

BADBEA CLEARANCE VILLAGE

A9

Ousdale

Ord Point

HERITAGE CENTRE

C

ale

D

9 0

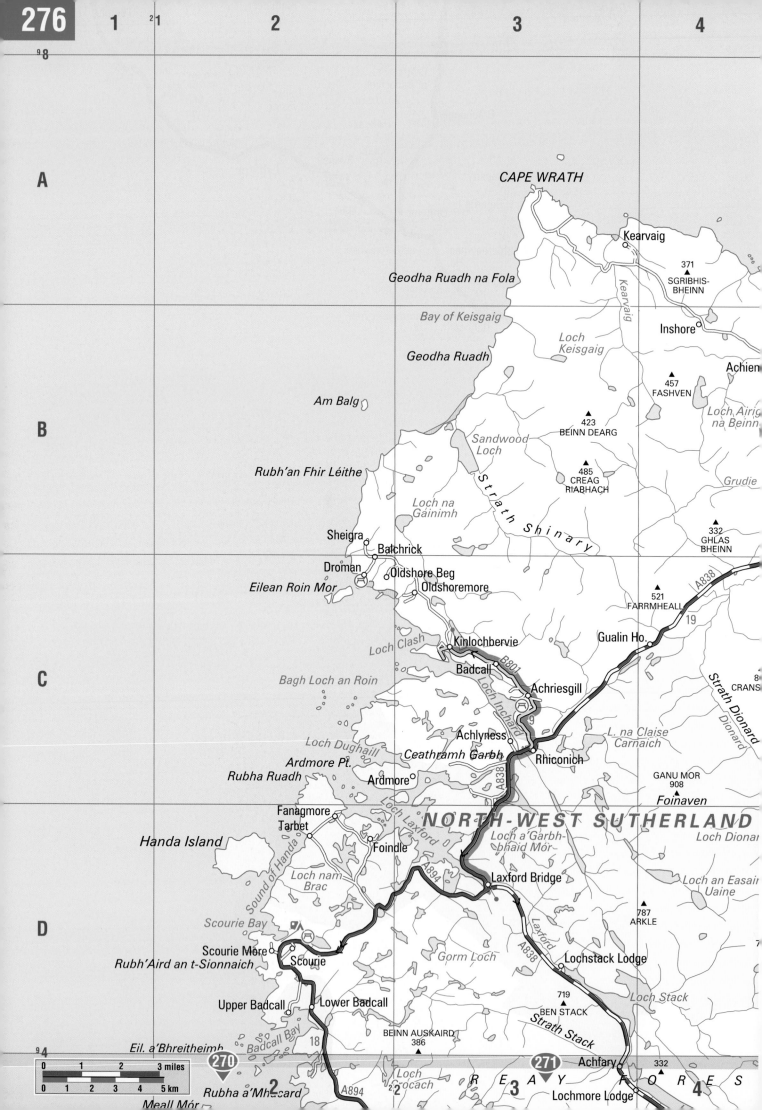

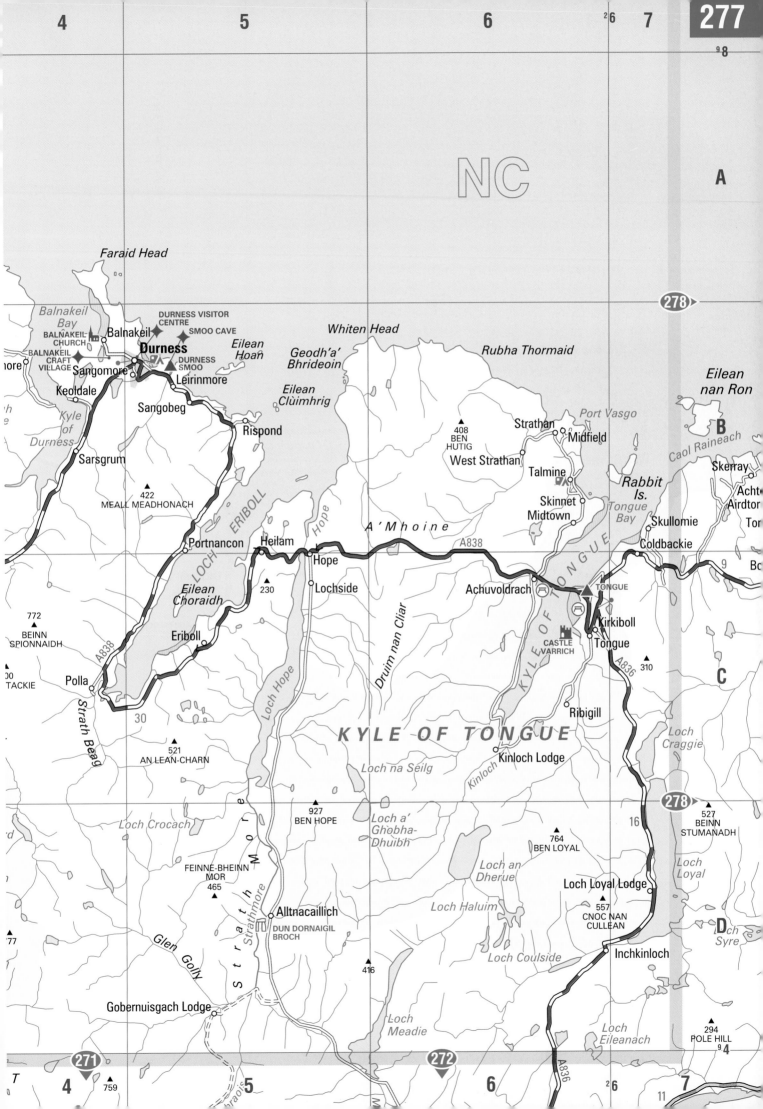

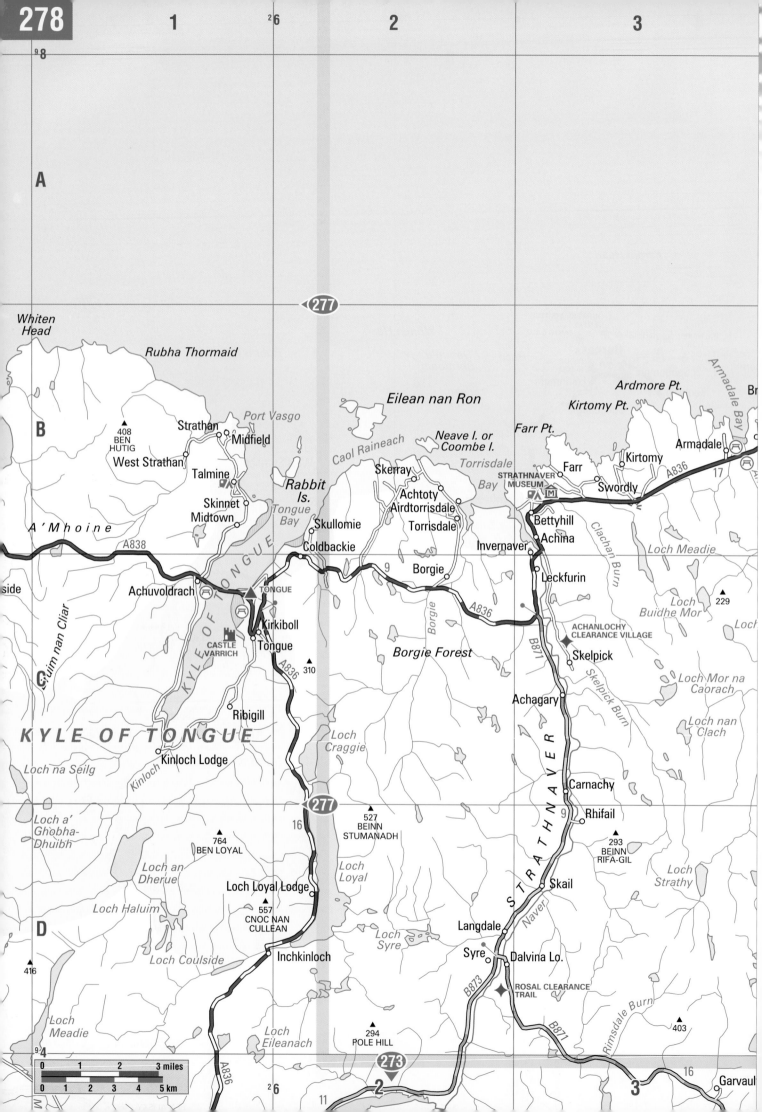

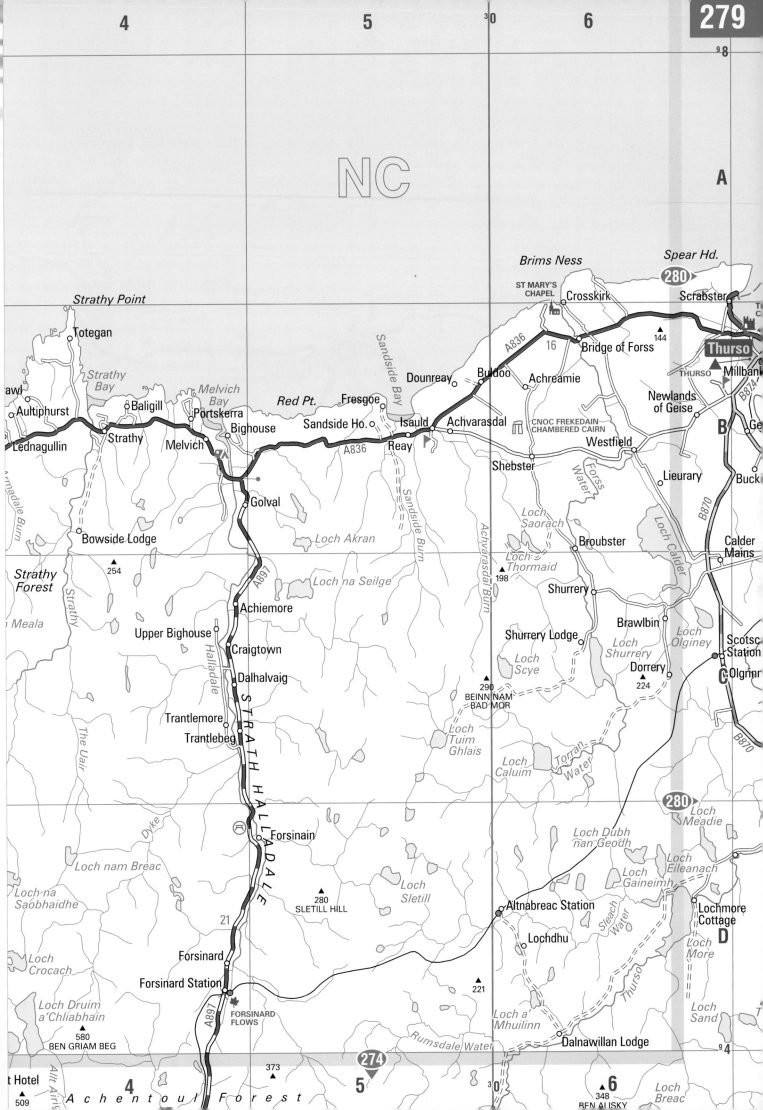

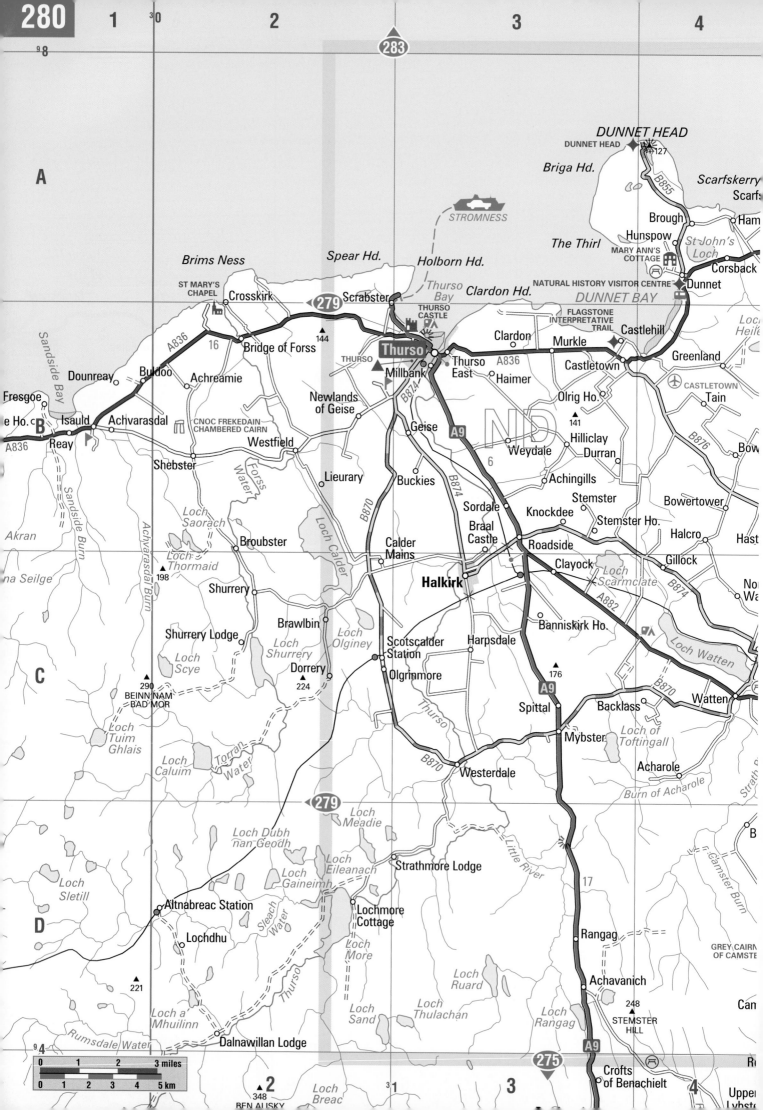

Langaton Point

Nethertown

Red Head

ST. MARGARET'S HOPE

Island of Stroma

53 ▲

Uppertown

BURWICK (May-Sept)

Muckle Skerry

Pentland Skerries

Mell Head

St John's Pt.

Men of Mey

Pt.

...skerry

Boars of Duncansby

Gills Bay

A

East Mey

CASTLE OF MEY

Rattar

Gills

Kirkstyle

Huna

i

DUNCANSBY HEAD

Mey

A836

John o' Groats

Barrock

Canisbay

A99

Stacks of Duncansby

Inkstack

124 ▲

Brabster

Skirza

Gill Burn

Tofts

Skirza Head

Lochend

Freswick

Freswick Bay

Slickly

A99

Ness Head

Reaster

BUCHOLLY CASTLE

Alterwall

CAITHNESS BROCH CENTRE

...ermadden

Lyth

LYTH ARTS CENTRE

Nybster

Auckengill

B

Barrock Ho.

Sortat

Howe

Brough Head

...igrow

Mireland

Keiss

KEISS CASTLE

Kirk

Loch of Wester

Myrelandhorn

B870

SINCLAIR'S

...rth

...atten

BAY

B876

Killimster

Mains of Watten

CASTLE GIRNIGOE

CASTLE SINCLAIR

Noss Head

Reiss

A99

C

15

Winless

60 ▲

B874

Sealky Head

Bilbster

Ackergill

WICK

Staxigoe

Strath

A882

WICK HERITAGE MUS

Papigoe

Wick

Broadhaven

Stirkoke Ho.

Milton

Wick Bay

Old Wick

Newton

South Hd.

Whiterow

CASTLE OF OLD WICK

Gote O'Tram

Tannach

Hempriggs House

Loch Hempriggs

Helman Hd.

141 ▲

HILL OF OLICLETT

A99

Thrumster

D

Gansclet

Sarclet

Loch of Yarrows

Sarclet Hd.

212 ▲

Ulbster

17

CAIRN OF GET

Whaligoe

⁹4

275

HILL O' MANY TANES

Bruan

Mid

ND

283

19

16

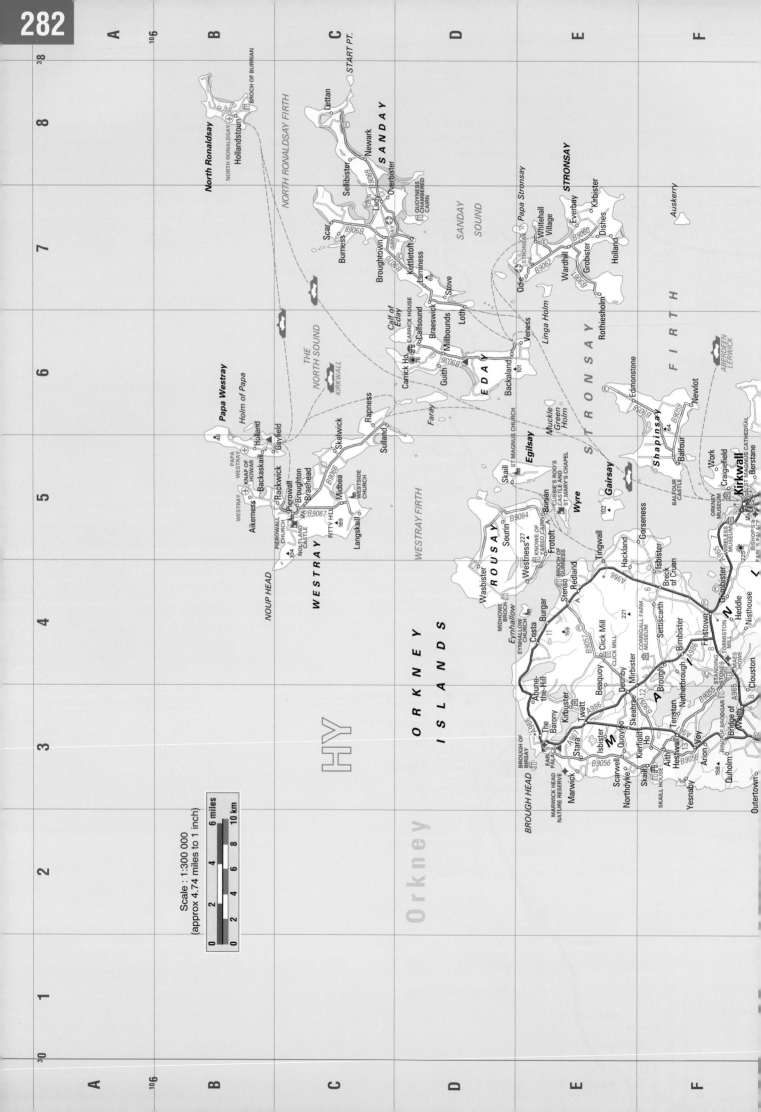

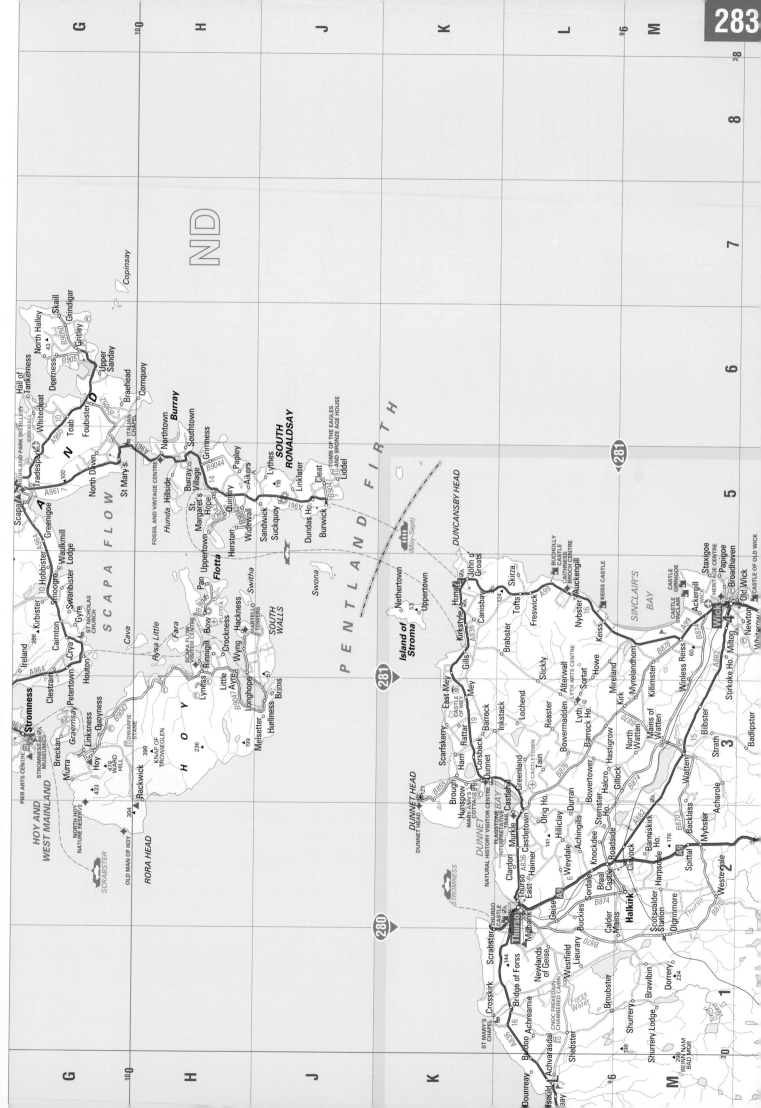

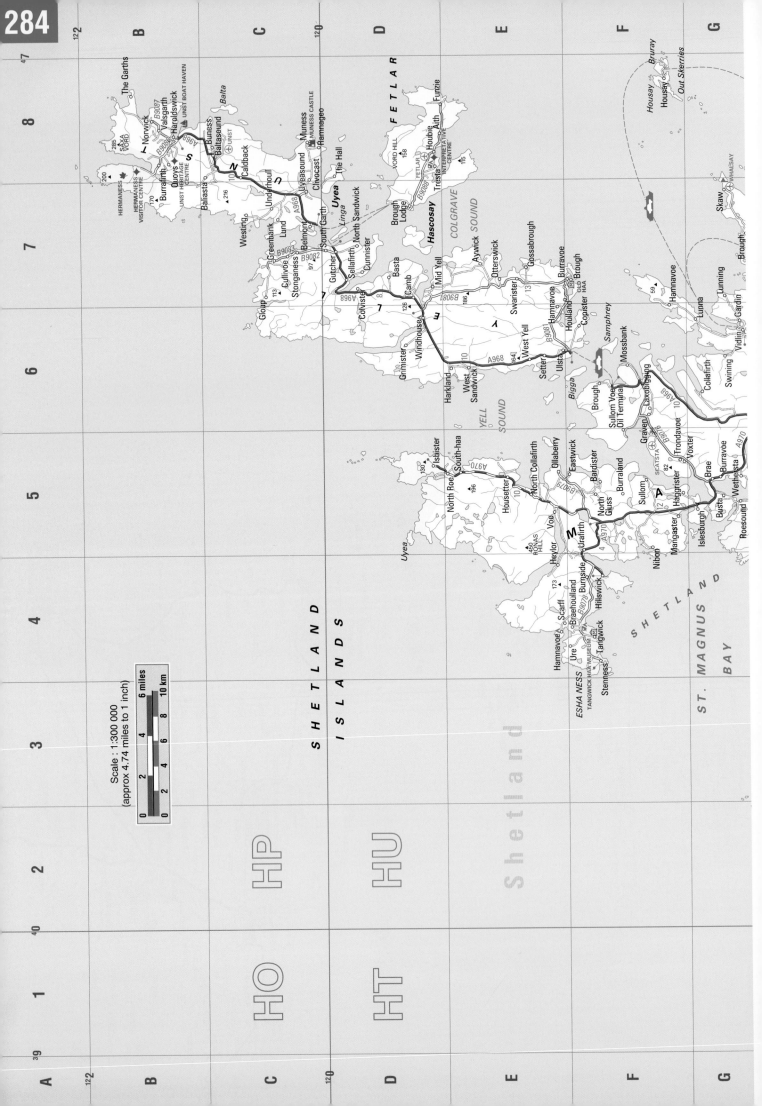

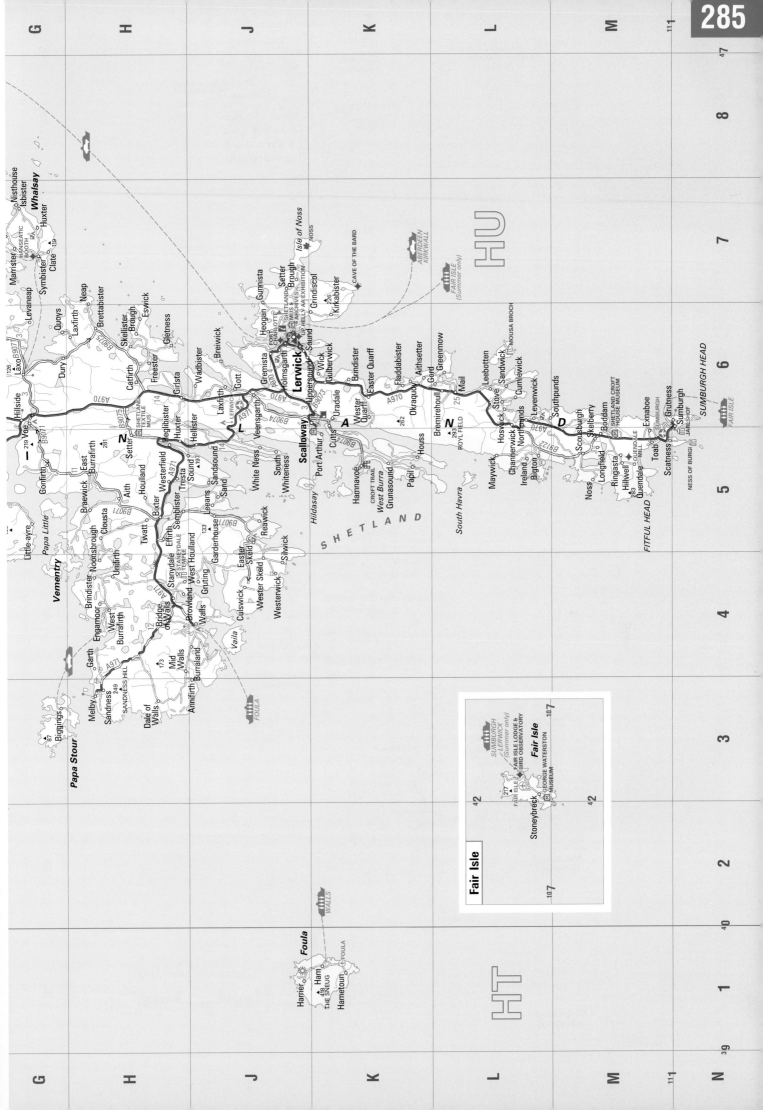

286

05   1   2   3   4   5   10

287

Na h-eileanan Monach
(Heisker or Monach
Islands)

Baile Sear
(Baleshare)

Clachan na Luib
Loch Euphoirt
Teanna Mhachair
Samhla   Corunna   Saighdinis
Bail Uachdraich
TRINITY TEMPLE   Cairinis
Bail Iochdrach
Baile Glas
Uachdar   Baile Glas
Griomasaigh
(Grimsay)
BENBECULA   Scotbheinn
347 EAVAL
Bagh Mor
99 Ronay

A

Baile a Mhanaich
Gramsdal   Flodaigh
Baile nan
Cailleach
BEINN NA
FAOGHLA
(BENBECULA)
Griminis
Torlum   Lionacleit

B

NF

Creag
Ghoraidh
Aird a
Mhachair
Clachan
Iochdar
Loch a
Charnain
Sanndabhaig
Fuidhaigh
(Wiay)
Geirinis
102

OUR LADY OF THE
ISLES STATUE
Stadhlaigearraidh   168
Dreumasdal
Loch Sgioport
Tobha Mor
LOCH DRUIDIBEG
NATURE RESERVE
HECLA
606
527   176
Sniseabhal
Staoinebrig
BEINN MHOR
620
Ormiclate
Castle   12
Bornais   Taobh a Thuath
Loch Aineort

C

OUTER

HEBRIDES

SOUTH UIST MACHAIR

UIBHIST A DEAS
(SOUTH UIST)

Cill
Donnain
KILDONAN
MUSEUM
Unasary
Gearraidh
Bhailteas   Minngearraidh
FLORA MACDONALD'S
BIRTHPLACE
Aisgernis
374
STULAVAL

D

Dalabrog   Taobh a Tuath   357
Crois Dughaill   Loch Baghasdail
Cille Pheadair   Loch Baghasdail
(Lochboisdale)
Baghasdal
Ceann a Deas
Loch Baghasdail
Gearraidh na Monadh
Trosaraidh   MALLAIG
OBAN
(Winter only)
Cille Bhrighde   Smercleit   South
Pol a Charra   Glendale
201
Taobh a   Ludag
Chaolais   Bun a'Mhuillin
Am Baile   Haunn
185
Coilleag   Eiriosgaigh
(Eriskay)

E

Fuideigh
(Fuday)
89

Eolaigearraidh
CILLE BHARRA
EILEAN BHARRAIGH
(BARRA)
BARRA
Cliaid   Aird Mhor
207
Cuidhir   BEN CLIAD   Aird Mhidhinis
Allathasdal   A888   Bagh   Bruairnis
Baile na Creige   Shiarabhagh   Buaile nam Bodach
94
Borgh   383
Tangasdal   HEAVAL
332   Earsairidh
BARRA HERITAGE CENTRE   A888 Breibhig
Bagh a Chaisteil
(Castlebay)   KIESSIMUL (KISIMUL)
CASTLE

F

80

G

Bhatarsaigh
(Vatersay)
190
Uidh
Bhatarsaigh
TIREE
(Apr-Oct, Weds only)
OBAN

Sanndraigh
(Sandray)
207

H

NL

Pabaidh
(Pabbay)
171

Miùgh Laigh
(Mingulay)
273

Bearnaraigh
(Berneray)

Scale : 1:300 000
(approx 4.74 miles to 1 inch)

0   2   4   6 miles
0   2   4   6   8   10 km

78

05   1   2   3   4   5   10

Index to road maps of Britain

Abbreviations used in the index

Aberdeen	Aberdeen City	M Keynes	Milton Keynes	
Aberds	Aberdeenshire	M Tydf	Merthyr Tydfil	
Ald	Alderney	Mbro	Middlesbrough	
Anglesey	Isle of Anglesey	Medway	Medway	
Angus	Angus	Mers	Merseyside	
Argyll	Argyll and Bute	Midloth	Midlothian	
Bath	Bath and North East Somerset	Mon	Monmouthshire	
Bedford	Bedford	Moray	Moray	
Bl Gwent	Blaenau Gwent	N Ayrs	North Ayrshire	
Blackburn	Blackburn with Darwen	N Lincs	North Lincolnshire	
Blackpool	Blackpool	N Lanark	North Lanarkshire	
BCP	Bournemouth, Christchurch and Poole	N Som	North Somerset	
Borders	Scottish Borders	N Yorks	North Yorkshire	
Brack	Bracknell	NE Lincs	North East Lincolnshire	
Bridgend	Bridgend	Neath	Neath Port Talbot	
Brighton	City of Brighton and Hove	Newport	City and County of Newport	
Bristol	City and County of Bristol	Norf	Norfolk	
Bucks	Buckinghamshire	Northants	Northamptonshire	
C Beds	Central Bedfordshire	Northumb	Northumberland	
Caerph	Caerphilly	Nottingham	City of Nottingham	
Cambs	Cambridgeshire	Notts	Nottinghamshire	
Cardiff	Cardiff	Orkney	Orkney	
Carms	Carmarthenshire	Oxon	Oxfordshire	
Ceredig	Ceredigion	Pboro	Peterborough	
Ches E	Cheshire East	Pembs	Pembrokeshire	
Ches W	Cheshire West and Chester	Perth	Perth and Kinross	
Clack	Clackmannanshire	Plym	Plymouth	
Conwy	Conwy	Powys	Powys	
Corn	Cornwall	Ptsmth	Portsmouth	
Cumb	Cumbria	Reading	Reading	
Darl	Darlington	Redcar	Redcar and Cleveland	
Denb	Denbighshire	Renfs	Renfrewshire	
Derby	City of Derby	Rhondda	Rhondda Cynon Taff	
Derbys	Derbyshire	Rutland	Rutland	
Devon	Devon	S Ayrs	South Ayrshire	
Dorset	Dorset	S Glos	South Gloucestershire	
Dumfries	Dumfries and Galloway	S Lanark	South Lanarkshire	
Dundee	Dundee City	S Yorks	South Yorkshire	
Durham	Durham	Scilly	Scilly	
E Ayrs	East Ayrshire	Shetland	Shetland	
E Dunb	East Dunbartonshire	Shrops	Shropshire	
E Loth	East Lothian	Slough	Slough	
E Renf	East Renfrewshire	Som	Somerset	
E Sus	East Sussex	Soton	Southampton	
E Yorks	East Riding of Yorkshire	Staffs	Staffordshire	
Edin	City of Edinburgh	Southend	Southend-on-Sea	
Essex	Essex	Stirling	Stirling	
Falk	Falkirk	Stockton	Stockton-on-Tees	
Fife	Fife	Stoke	Stoke-on-Trent	
Flint	Flintshire	Suff	Suffolk	
Glasgow	City of Glasgow	Sur	Surrey	
Glos	Gloucestershire	Swansea	Swansea	
Gtr Man	Greater Manchester	Swindon	Swindon	
Guern	Guernsey	T&W	Tyne and Wear	
Gwyn	Gwynedd	Telford	Telford and Wrekin	
Halton	Halton	Thurrock	Thurrock	
Hants	Hampshire	Torbay	Torbay	
Hereford	Herefordshire	Torf	Torfaen	
Herts	Hertfordshire	V Glam	The Vale of Glamorgan	
Highld	Highland	W Berks	West Berkshire	
Hrtlpl	Hartlepool	W Dunb	West Dunbartonshire	
Hull	Hull	W Isles	Western Isles	
IoM	Isle of Man	W Loth	West Lothian	
IoW	Isle of Wight	W Mid	West Midlands	
Invclyd	Inverclyde	W Sus	West Sussex	
Jersey	Jersey	W Yorks	West Yorkshire	
Kent	Kent	Warks	Warwickshire	
Lancs	Lancashire	Warr	Warrington	
Leicester	City of Leicester	Wilts	Wiltshire	
Leics	Leicestershire	Windsor	Windsor and Maidenhead	
Lincs	Lincolnshire	Wokingham	Wokingham	
London	Greater London	Worcs	Worcestershire	
Luton	Luton	Wrex	Wrexham	
		York	City of York	

How to use the index

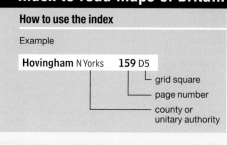

Example

Hovingham N Yorks **159** D5

└ grid square
─ page number
─ county or unitary authority

A

	Abbey Town........**175** C4	Aber..............**74** D3
	Abbey Village......**137** A5	Aberaeron.........**74** B3
	Abbey Wood........**50** B1	Aberaman.........**41** A5
Abbas Combe......**29** C7	Abbots Bickington ..**25** D4	Aberangell........**91** A6
Abberley......**79** A5	Abbots Bromley....**113** C4	Aber-Arad........**73** C6
Abberton	Abbotsbury.........**15** C5	Aberarder.........**240** D2
Essex **71** B4	Abbotsham........**25** C5	Aberarder House..**252** D2
Worcs **80** B2	Abbotskerswell.....**8** A2	Aberarder Lodge..**240** D3
Abberwick......**189** B4	Abbots Langley **67** C5	Aberargie.........**219** C6
Abbess Roding......**69** B5	Abbots Leigh **43** B4	Aberarth **74** B3
Abbey.............**27** D6	Abbotsley **84** B4	Aberavon..........**40** B2
Abbey-cwm-hir ...**93** D4	Abbots Morton.....**80** B3	Aber-banc.........**73** B6
Abbeydale......**130** A3	Abbots Ripton.....**100** D4	Aberbeeg.........**41** A7
Abbey Dore......**78** D1	Abbots Salford.....**80** B3	Abercanaid.......**41** A5
Abbey Field......**70** A3	Abbotswood......**32** C2	Abercarn.........**41** B7
Abbey Hulton.....**112** A3	Abbotts Ann......**32** A2	Abercastle........**55** A4
Abbey St Bathans ..**211** D4	Abcott...........**94** D1	Abercegir.........**91** B6
Abbeystead.......**145** B5	Abdon............**94** C3	Aberchirder.......**268** D1

Aber Cowarch **91** A6	Abereiddy.........**54** A3	
Abercraf.........**59** D5	Abererch..........**106** C3	
Abercrombie **221** D5	Aberfan...........**41** A5	
Abercych.........**73** B5	Aberfeldy.........**230** D2	
Abercynafon.......**60** B2	Aberffraw.........**122** D3	
Abercynon........**41** B5	Aberffrwd.........**75** A5	
Aberdalgie **219** B5	Aberford..........**148** D3	
Aberdare =Aberdâr..**41** A4	Aberfoyle.........**217** D5	
Aberdaron........**106** D1	**Abergavenny =**	
Aberdaugleddau	Y Fenni **61** B4	
=Milford Haven ...**55** D5	Abergele **125** B4	
Aberdeen **245** B6	Aber-Giâr **58** A2	
Aberdesach **107** A4	Abergorlech.......**58** B2	
Aberdour.........**209** B4	**Abergwaun**	
Aberdovey........**90** C4	=Fishguard **72** C2	
Aberdulais **40** A2	Abergwesyn **76** B2	
Aberedw **77** C4	Abergwili **58** C1	

	Abb–Abe
Aber-gwynfi........**40** B3	
Abergwyngregyn...**123** C6	
Abergynolwyn **91** B4	
Aber-Hirnant.....**109** B4	
Aberhonddu	
=Brecon........**60** A2	
Aberhosan.........**91** C6	
Aberkenfig **40** C3	
Aberlady **210** B1	
Aberllemno **232** C3	
Aberllefenni **91** B5	
Abermagwr........**75** A5	
Abermaw	
=Barmouth **90** A4	
Abermeurig.......**75** C4	
Abermule **93** B5	

Abergwynant **91** A4	

Abernaint 109 C6
Abernant 73 D6
Aber-nant 41 A5
Abernethy 219 C6
Abernyte 220 A2
Aberpennar
  = Mountain Ash 41 B5
Aberporth 73 A5
Aber-Rhiwlech 108 C4
Abersoch 106 D3
Abersychan 61 C4
Abertawe
  = Swansea 57 C6
Aberteifi = Cardigan .73 B4
Aberthin 41 D5
Abertillery
  = Abertyleri 41 A7
Abertridwr
  Caerph 41 C6
  Powys 109 D5
Abertyleri
  = Abertillery 41 A7
Abertysswg 60 C3
Aberuthven 219 C4
Aber-Village 60 A3
Aberyscir 60 A1
Aberystwyth 90 D3
Abhainn Suidhe 287 D5
Abingdon-on-
  Thames 65 D5
Abinger Common 35 B4
Abinger Hammer . . . 34 B3
Abington 194 D4
Abington Pigotts 85 C5
Ab Kettleby 115 C5
Ab Lench 80 B3
Ablington
  Glos 64 C2
  Wilts 31 A5
Abney 130 B1
Aboyne 244 C2
Abram 137 C5
Abriachan 252 C1
Abridge 69 D4
Abronhill 207 C5
Abson 43 B6
Abthorpe 82 C3
Abune-the-Hill 282 E3
Aby 135 A4
Acaster Malbis 149 C4
Acaster Selby 149 C4
Accrington 137 A6
Acha 223 B4
Achabraid 213 D6
Achachork 259 D4
Achafolla 213 A5
Achagary 278 C3
Achahoish 202 A2
Achalader 231 D5
Achallader 228 D2
Acha Mor 288 E4
Achanalt 263 D4
Achanamara 213 D5
Achandunie 264 C2
Ach'an Todhair 237 B4
Achany 272 D3
Achaphubuil 237 B4
Acharacle 235 D5
Acharn
  Highld 236 D1
  Perth 229 D6
Acharole 280 C4
Achath 245 A4
Achavanich 280 D3
Achavraat 253 B5
Achddu 57 B4
Achduart 270 D3
Achentoul 274 D2
Achfary 271 A5
Achgarve 261 A5
Achiemore
  Highld 277 B4
  Highld 279 C4
A'Chill 246 D1
Achiltibuie 270 D3
Achina 278 B3
Achinduich 272 D3
Achinduin 226 C3
Achingills 280 B3
Achintee
  Highld 237 B5
  Highld 249 B6
Achintraid 249 C5
Achlean 241 C6
Achleck 224 B3
Achluachrach 239 D6
Achlyness 276 C3
Achmelvich 270 C4

Achmore
  Highld 249 C5
  Stirling 217 A5
Achnaba
  Argyll 214 D2
  Argyll 226 C4
Achnabat 252 C1
Achnacarnin 270 A3
Achnacarry 239 D5
Achnacloich
  Argyll 227 C4
  Highld 247 D4
Achnaconeran 240 A2
Achnacraig 224 B3
Achnacroish 226 B3
Achnadrish 224 A3
Achnafalnich 227 D7
Achnagarron 264 D2
Achnaha 234 D3
Achnahanat 263 A7
Achnahannet 253 D5
Achnairn 272 C3
Achnaluachrach 273 D4
Achnasaul 239 D5
Achnasheen 250 A3
Achosnich 234 D3
Achranich 226 B2
Achreamie 279 B6
Achriabhach 237 C5
Achriesgill 276 C3
Achrimsdale 274 D3
Achtoty 278 B2
Achurch 100 C2
Achuvoldrach 277 C6
Achvaich 264 A3
Achvarasdal 279 B5
Ackergill 281 C5
Acklam
  Mbro 168 D2
  N Yorks 149 A6
Ackleton 95 B5
Acklington 189 C5
Ackton 140 A2
Ackworth Moor
  Top 140 B2
Acle 121 D6
Acock's Green 96 C4
Acol 53 C5
Acomb
  Northumb 178 C1
  York 149 B4
Aconbury 78 D3
Acre 137 A6
Acrefair 110 A1
Acre Street 19 B6
Acton
  Ches E 127 D6
  Dorset 16 D3
  London 49 A5
  Shrops 93 C7
  Suff 87 C4
  Wrex 126 D3
Acton Beauchamp . . 79 B4
Acton Bridge 127 B5
Acton Burnell 94 A3
Acton Green 79 B4
Acton Pigott 94 A3
Acton Round 95 B4
Acton Scott 94 C2
Acton Trussell 112 D3
Acton Turville 44 A2
Adbaston 111 C6
Adber 29 C5
Adderley 111 A5
Adderstone 199 C5
Addiewell 208 D2
Addingham 147 C4
Addington
  Bucks 66 A2
  Kent 37 A4
  London 49 C6
Addinston 197 A4
Addiscombe 49 C6
Addlestone 48 C3
Addlethorpe 135 C5
Adel 148 D1
Adeney 111 D6
Adfa 93 A4
Adforton 94 D2
Adisham 53 D4
Adlestrop 64 A3
Adlingfleet 141 A6
Adlington 137 B5
Admaston
  Staffs 112 C4
  Telford 111 D5
Admington 81 C5
Adstock 83 D4
Adstone 82 B2
Adversane 34 D3

Advie 254 C2
Adwalton 139 A5
Adwell 66 D1
Adwick le Street 140 C3
Adwick upon
  Dearne 140 C2
Adziel 269 D4
Ae Village 184 D2
Affleck 256 D3
Affpuddle 16 B2
Affric Lodge 250 D3
Afon-wen 125 B6
Afton 18 C2
Agglethorpe 157 C4
Agneash 152 C4
Aigburth 126 A3
Aiginis 288 D5
Aike 150 C3
Aikerness 282 B5
Aikers 283 H5
Aiketgate 164 A2
Aikton 175 C5
Ailey 78 C1
Ailstone 81 B5
Ailsworth 100 B3
Ainderby
  Quernhow 158 C2
  Steeple 158 B2
Aingers Green 71 A5
Ainsdale 136 B2
Ainsdale-on-Sea . . .136 B2
Ainstable 164 A3
Ainsworth 137 B6
Ainthorpe 159 A6
Aintree 136 D2
Aird
  Argyll 213 B5
  Dumfries 170 A2
  Highld 261 C4
  W Isles 288 D6
Aird a Mhachair 286 B3
Aird a' Mhulaidh 288 F2
Aird Asaig 288 G2
Aird Dhail 288 A5
Airdens 264 A2
Aird Mhidhinis 286 F3
Aird Mhighe
  W Isles 287 F5
  W Isles 288 H2
Aird Mhor 286 F3
Aird of Sleat 247 D4
Airdrie 207 D5
Aird Thunga 288 D5
Airdtorrisdale 278 B2
Aird Uig 287 A5
Airidh a Bhruaich . . .288 F3
Airieland 173 C5
Airmyn 141 A5
Airntully 219 A5
Airor 247 D6
Airth 208 B1
Airton 146 B3
Airyhassen 171 C5
Aisby
  Lincs 116 B3
  Lincs 141 D6
Aisgernis 286 D3
Aiskew 157 C6
Aislaby
  N Yorks 159 C6
  N Yorks 160 A2
  Stockton 168 D2
Aisthorpe 133 A4
Aith
  Orkney 282 F3
  Shetland 284 D8
  Shetland 285 H5
Aithsetter 285 K6
Aitkenhead 192 E3
Aitnoch 253 C5
Akeld 188 A2
Akeley 83 D4
Akenham 88 C2
Albaston 11 D5
Alberbury 110 D2
Albourne 21 A5
Albrighton
  Shrops 95 A6
  Shrops 110 D3
Alburgh 104 C3
Albury
  Herts 68 A4
  Sur 34 B3
Albury End 68 A4
Alby Hill 120 B3
Alcaig 252 A1
Alcaston 94 C2
Alcester 80 B3
Alciston 22 B3

Alcombe
  Som 27 A4
  Wilts 44 C2
Alconbury 100 D3
Alconbury Weston . .100 D3
Aldbar Castle 232 C3
Aldborough
  Norf 120 B3
  N Yorks 148 A3
Aldbourne 45 B6
Aldbrough 151 D5
Aldbrough St John .167 D5
Aldbury 67 B4
Aldcliffe 145 A4
Aldclune 230 B3
Aldeburgh 89 B5
Aldeby 105 B5
Aldenham 67 D6
Alderbury 31 C5
Aldercar 114 A2
Alderford 120 D3
Alderholt 31 D5
Alderley 62 D3
Alderley Edge 128 B3
Aldermaston 46 C3
Aldermaston Wharf . .47 C4
Alderminster 81 C5
Alder's End 79 C4
Aldersey Green 127 D4
Aldershot 34 A1
Alderton
  Glos 80 D3
  Northants 83 C4
  Shrops 110 C3
  Suff 88 C4
  Wilts 44 A2
Alderwasley 130 D3
Aldfield 147 A6
Aldford 127 D4
Aldham
  Essex 70 A3
  Suff 87 C6
Aldie 264 B3
Aldingbourne 20 B2
Aldingham 154 D1
Aldington
  Kent 38 B2
  Worcs 80 C3
Aldington Frith 38 B2
Aldochlay 206 A1
Aldreth 101 D6
Aldridge 96 A3
Aldringham 89 A5
Aldsworth 64 B2
Aldunie 255 D4
Aldwark
  Derbys 130 D2
  N Yorks 148 A3
Aldwick 20 C2
Aldwincle 100 C2
Aldworth 46 B3
Alexandria 206 C1
Alfardisworthy 24 D3
Alfington 13 B6
Alfold 34 C3
Alfold Bars 34 C3
Alfold Crossways . . .34 C3
Alford
  Aberds 244 A2
  Lincs 135 B4
  Som 29 B6
Alfreton 131 D4
Alfrick 79 B5
Alfrick Pound 79 B5
Alfriston 22 B3
Algaltraig 203 A5
Algarkirk 117 B5
Alhampton 29 B6
Aline Lodge 288 F2
Alisary 235 C6
Alkborough 141 A6
Alkerton 81 C6
Alkham 39 A4
Alkington 111 B4
Alkmonton 113 B5
Alladale Lodge 263 B6
Allaleigh 8 B2
Allanaquoich 242 C4
Allangrange Mains .252 A2
Allanton
  Borders 198 A2
  N Lanark 194 A3
Allathasdal 286 F2
All Cannings 45 C4
Allendale Town 177 D6
Allenheads 165 A6
Allensford 178 D2
Allens Green 69 B4
Allensmore 78 D2
Allenton 114 B1

Aller 28 C4
Allerby 162 A3
Allerford 27 A4
Allerston 160 C2
Allerthorpe 149 C6
Allerton
  Mers 127 A4
  W Yorks 147 D5
Allerton Bywater . . .140 A2
Allerton
  Mauleverer 148 B3
Allesley 97 C6
Allestree 114 B1
Allet 4 C2
Allexton 99 A5
Allgreave 129 C4
Allhallows 51 B5
Allhallows-on-Sea . .51 B5
Alligin Shuas 249 A5
Allimore Green 112 D2
Allington
  Lincs 115 A6
  Wilts 31 B6
  Wilts 45 C4
Allithwaite 154 D2
Alloa 208 A1
Allonby 174 D3
Alloway 192 D3
All Saints South
  Elmham 104 C4
All Stretton 94 B2
Allt 57 B5
Alltchaorunn 237 D5
Alltforgan 109 C4
Alltmawr 77 C4
Alltnacaillich 277 D5
Allt na h-Airbhe 262 A3
Allt-nan-sùgh 249 D6
Alltsigh 240 A2
Alltwalis 58 B1
Alltwen 40 A2
Alltyblaca 75 D4
Allwood Green 103 D6
Almeley 78 B1
Almer 16 B3
Almholme 140 C3
Almington 111 B6
Alminstone Cross . . .24 C4
Almondbank 219 B5
Almondbury 139 B4
Almondsbury 43 A5
Alne 148 A3
Alness 264 D2
Alnham 188 B2
Alnmouth 189 B5
Alnwick 189 B4
Alperton 49 A4
Alphamstone 87 D4
Alpheton 87 B4
Alphington 13 B4
Alport 130 C2
Alpraham 127 D5
Alresford 71 A4
Alrewas 113 D5
Alsager 128 D2
Alsagers Bank 112 A2
Alsop en le Dale 129 D6
Alston
  Cumb 165 A5
  Devon 14 A3
Alstone 80 D2
Alstonefield 129 D6
Alswear 26 C2
Altandhu 270 C2
Altanduin 274 B2
Altarnun 10 C3
Altass 272 D2
Alterwall 281 B4
Altham 146 D1
Althorne 70 D3
Althorpe 141 C6
Alticry 171 B4
Altnabreac Station .279 D6
Altnacealgach
  Hotel 271 C5
Altnacraig 226 D3
Altnafeadh 237 D6
Altnaharra 272 A3
Altofts 139 A6
Alton
  Derbys 130 C3
  Hants 33 B6
  Staffs 113 A4
Alton Pancras 15 A7
Alton Priors 45 C5
Altrincham 128 A2
Altrua 239 D6
Altskeith 217 D4
Altyre House 253 A6
Alva 208 A1

Alvanley 127 B4
Alvaston 114 B1
Alvechurch 96 D3
Alvecote 97 A5
Alvediston 30 C3
Alveley 95 C5
Alverdiscott 25 C4
Alverstoke 19 B5
Alverstone 19 C4
Alverton 115 A5
Alves 266 C2
Alvescot 64 C3
Alveston
  S Glos 43 A5
  Warks 81 A5
Alvie 241 B6
Alvingham 143 D5
Alvington 62 C2
Alwalton 100 B3
Alweston 29 D6
Alwinton 188 C2
Alwoodley 148 C1
Alyth 231 D6
Amatnatua 263 A6
Am Baile 286 E3
Ambergate 130 D3
Amber Hill 117 A5
Amberley
  Glos 63 C4
  W Sus 20 A3
Amble 189 C5
Amblecote 96 C1
Ambler Thorn 138 A3
Ambleside 154 A2
Ambleston 55 B6
Ambrosden 65 B7
Am Buth 226 D3
Amcotts 141 B6
Amersham 67 D4
Amesbury 31 A5
Amington 97 A5
Amisfield 184 D2
Amlwch 123 A4
Amlwch Port 123 A4
Ammanford
  = Rhydaman 57 A6
Amod 190 B3
Amotherby 159 D6
Ampfield 32 C3
Ampleforth 159 D4
Ampney Crucis 63 C6
Ampney St Mary 64 C1
Ampney St Peter 64 C1
Amport 32 A1
Ampthill 84 D2
Ampton 103 D4
Amroth 56 B1
Amulree 218 A3
Anagach 253 D6
Anaheilt 236 C2
Anancaun 262 D2
An Caol 248 B3
Ancaster 116 A2
Anchor 93 C5
Anchorsholme 144 C3
An Cnoc 288 D5
Ancroft 198 B3
Ancrum 187 A5
Anderby 135 B5
Anderson 16 B2
Anderton 127 B6
Andover 32 A2
Andover Down 32 A2
Andoversford 63 B6
Andreas 152 B4
Anfield 136 D2
Angersleigh 28 D2
Angle 55 D4
An Gleann Ur 288 D5
Angmering 20 B3
Angram
  N Yorks 148 C4
  N Yorks 156 B2
Anie 217 D5
Ankerville 265 C4
Anlaby 142 A2
Anmer 119 C4
Annan 175 B4
Annat
  Argyll 227 D5
  Highld 249 A5
Anna Valley 32 A2
Annbank 193 C4
Annesley 131 D5
Annesley
  Woodhouse 131 D4
Annfield Plain 178 D3
Annifirth 285 J3
Annitsford 179 B4
Annscroft 94 A2

Ansdell 136 A2
Ansford 29 B6
Ansley 97 B5
Anslow 113 C6
Anslow Gate 113 C6
Anstey
  Herts. 85 D6
  Leics 98 A2
Anstruther Easter . . 221 D5
Anstruther Wester . . 221 D5
Ansty
  Hants 33 A6
  Warks 97 C6
  Wilts 30 C3
  W Sus 35 D5
Anthill Common 33 D5
Anthorn 175 C4
Antingham 121 B4
An t-Ob
  =Leverburgh 287 F5
Anton's Gowt 117 A5
Antonshill 208 B1
Antony 6 B3
Anwick 133 D6
Anwoth 172 C3
Aoradh 200 B2
Apes Hall 102 B1
Apethorpe 100 B2
Apeton 112 D2
Apley 133 D6
Apperknowle 130 B3
Apperley 63 A4
Apperley Bridge 147 D5
Appersett 156 B2
Appin 226 B4
Appin House 226 B4
Appleby 142 B1
Appleby-in-
  Westmorland 165 C4
Appleby Magna 97 A6
Appleby Parva 97 A6
Applecross 249 B4
Applecross House . . 249 B4
Appledore
  Devon 25 B5
  Devon 27 D5
  Kent 38 C1
Appledore Heath . . . 38 B1
Appleford 65 D6
Applegarthtown . . .185 D4
Appleshaw 32 A2
Applethwaite 163 B5
Appleton
  Halton 127 A5
  Oxon 65 C5
Appleton-le-
  Moors 159 C6
Appleton-le-Street 159 D6
Appleton Roebuck . .149 C4
Appleton Thorn 127 A6
Appleton Wiske 158 A2
Appletreehall 186 B4
Appletreewick 147 A4
Appley 27 C5
Appley Bridge 136 C4
Apse Heath 19 C4
Apsley End 84 D3
Apuldram 20 B1
Aquhythie 245 A4
Arabella 265 C4
Arbeadie 244 C3
Arberth =Narberth . . 55 C7
Arbirlot 233 D4
Arboll 265 B4
Arborfield 47 C5
Arborfield Cross 47 C5
Arborfield Garrison . 47 C5
Arbourthorne 130 A3
Arbroath 233 D4
Arbuthnott 233 A5
Archiestown 254 B3
Arclid 128 C2
Ardachu 273 D4
Ardalanish 224 E2
Ardanaiseig 227 D5
Ardaneaskan 249 C5
Ardanstur 213 A6
Ardargie House
  Hotel 219 C5
Ardarroch 249 C5
Ardbeg
  Argyll 201 D4
  Argyll 215 D4
Ardcharnich 262 B3
Ardchiavaig 224 E2
Ardchullarie More . 217 C5
Ardchyle 217 B5
Ard-dhubh 249 B4
Arddleen 110 D1
Ardechvie 239 C5

Ardeley 68 A3
Ardelve 249 D5
Arden 206 B1
Ardens Grafton 80 B4
Ardentinny 215 D4
Ardentraive 203 A5
Ardeonaig 217 A6
Ardersier 252 A2
Ardessie 262 B2
Ardfern 213 B6
Ardgartan 215 B5
Ardgay 264 A1
Ardgour 237 C4
Ardheslaig 249 A4
Ardiecow 267 C6
Ardindrean 262 B3
Ardingly 35 D6
Ardington 46 A2
Ardlair 255 D6
Ardleigh 71 A4
Ardler 231 D6
Ardley 65 A6
Ardlui 215 A6
Ardlussa 213 D4
Ardmair 262 A3
Ardmay 215 B5
Ardminish 202 D1
Ardmolich 235 C6
Ardmore
  Argyll 226 D2
  Highld 264 B3
  Highld 276 C2
Ardnacross 225 B4
Ardnadam 203 A6
Ardnagrask 251 B7
Ardnarff 249 C5
Ardnastang 236 C2
Ardnave 200 A2
Ardno 215 B4
Ardo 256 C3
Ardoch 219 A5
Ardochy House 239 B6
Ardo House 257 C4
Ardoyne 256 D1
Ardpatrick 202 B2
Ardpatrick House . . 202 C2
Ardpeaton 215 D5
Ardrishaig 213 D6
Ardross
  Fife 221 D5
  Highld 264 C2
Ardrossan 204 D2
Ardross Castle 264 C2
Ardshealach 235 D5
Ardsley 140 C1
Ardslignish 235 D4
Ardtalla 201 C4
Ardtalnaig 218 A2
Ardtoe 235 C5
Ardtrostan 217 B6
Arduaine 213 A5
Ardullie 264 D1
Ardvasar 247 D5
Ardvorlich 217 B6
Ardwell 170 C3
Ardwell Mains 170 C3
Ardwick 138 D1
Areley Kings 95 D6
Arford 34 C1
Argoed
  Caerph 41 B6
  Powys 76 A3
Arichamish 214 B2
Arichastlich 216 A2
Aridhglas 224 D2
Arileod 223 B4
Arinacrinachd 249 A4
Arinagour 223 B5
Arion 282 F3
Arisaig 235 B5
Ariundle 236 C2
Arkendale 148 A2
Arkesden 85 D6
Arkholme 155 D4
Arkleton 186 D2
Arkle Town 156 A4
Arkley 68 D2
Arksey 140 C3
Arkwright Town 131 B4
Arle 63 A5
Arlecdon 162 C3
Arlesey 84 D3
Arleston 111 D5
Arley 128 A1
Arlingham 62 B3
Arlington
  Devon 25 A7
  E Sus. 22 B3
  Glos 64 C2

Armadale
  Highld 278 B3
  W Loth 208 D2
Armadale Castle . . . 247 D5
Armathwaite 164 A3
Arminghall 104 A3
Armitage 113 D4
Armley 148 D1
Armscote 81 C5
Armthorpe 140 C4
Arnabost 223 B5
Arncliffe 156 D3
Arncroach 221 D5
Arne 16 C3
Arnesby 98 B3
Arngask 219 C6
Arnisdale 238 A2
Arnish 248 B2
Arniston Engine . . . 209 D6
Arnol 288 C4
Arnold
  E Yorks 151 C4
  Notts 114 A3
Arnprior 207 A4
Arnside 154 D3
Aros Mains 225 B4
Arowry 110 B3
Arpafeelie 252 A2
Arrad Foot 154 C2
Arram 150 C3
Arrathorne 157 B6
Arreton 18 C4
Arrington 85 B5
Arrivain 216 A2
Arrochar 215 B5
Arrow 80 B3
Arthington 147 C6
Arthingworth 99 C4
Arthog 90 A4
Arthrath 257 C4
Arthurstone 231 D6
Artrochie 257 C5
Arundel 20 B3
Aryhoulan 237 C4
Asby 162 B3
Ascog 203 B6
Ascot 48 C2
Ascott 81 D6
Ascott-under-
  Wychwood 64 B4
Asenby 158 D2
Asfordby 115 D5
Asfordby Hill 115 D5
Asgarby
  Lincs 116 A4
  Lincs 134 C3
Ash
  Kent 50 C2
  Kent 53 D4
  Som 29 C4
  Sur 34 A1
Ashampstead 46 B3
Ashbocking 88 B2
Ashbourne 113 A5
Ashbrittle 27 C5
Ash Bullayne 12 A2
Ashburton 7 A6
Ashbury
  Devon 11 B6
  Oxon 45 A6
Ashby 141 C7
Ashby by Partney . . 135 C4
Ashby cum Fenby . . 143 C4
Ashby de la
  Launde 133 D5
Ashby-de-la-
  Zouch 114 D1
Ashby Folville 115 D5
Ashby Magna 98 B2
Ashby Parva 98 C2
Ashby Puerorum . . . 134 B3
Ashby St Ledgers . . 82 A2
Ashby St Mary 104 A4
Ashchurch 80 D2
Ashcombe 13 D4
Ashcott 28 B4
Ashdon 86 C1
Ashe 32 A4
Asheldham 70 C3
Ashen 86 C3
Ashendon 66 B2
Ashfield
  Carms 58 C3
  Stirling 218 D2
  Suff. 88 A3
Ashfield Green 104 D3
Ashfold Crossways . 35 D5
Ashford
  Devon 25 B6
  Hants 31 D5

Ashford continued
  Kent 38 A2
  Sur 48 B3
Ashford Bowdler . . . 94 D3
Ashford Carbonell . . 94 D3
Ashford Hill 46 C3
Ashford in the
  Water 130 C1
Ashgill 194 B2
Ash Green 97 C6
Ashill
  Devon 27 D5
  Norf 103 A4
  Som. 28 D3
Ashingdon 70 D2
Ashington
  Northumb 179 A4
  Som. 29 C5
  W Sus 21 A4
Ashintully Castle . . .231 B5
Ashkirk 186 A3
Ashlett 18 A3
Ashleworth 63 A4
Ashley
  Cambs. 86 A2
  Ches E. 128 A2
  Devon 26 D1
  Dorset. 17 A5
  Glos 63 D5
  Hants 17 B6
  Hants 32 B2
  Northants 99 B4
  Staffs 111 B6
Ashley Green 67 C4
Ashley Heath
  Dorset. 17 A5
  Staffs 111 B6
Ash Magna 111 B4
Ashmanhaugh 121 C5
Ashmansworth 46 D2
Ashmansworthy . . . 24 D4
Ash Mill 26 C2
Ashmore 30 D3
Ashorne 81 B6
Ashover 130 C3
Ashow 97 D6
Ashprington 8 B2
Ash Priors 27 C6
Ashreigney 26 D1
Ash Street 87 C6
Ashtead 35 A4
Ash Thomas 27 D5
Ashton
  Ches W 127 C5
  Corn 3 C4
  Hants 33 D4
  Hereford 78 A3
  Invclyd 204 A2
  Northants 83 C4
  Northants 100 C2
Ashton Common . . . 44 D2
Ashton-In-
  Makerfield 137 D4
Ashton Keynes 63 D6
Ashton under Hill . . 80 D2
Ashton-under-
  Lyne 138 D2
Ashton upon
  Mersey 137 D6
Ashurst
  Hants 32 D2
  Kent 36 C3
  W Sus 21 A4
Ashurstwood 36 C2
Ash Vale 34 A1
Ashwater 11 B4
Ashwell
  Herts 85 D4
  Rutland 115 D6
  Som. 28 D3
Ashwellthorpe 104 B2
Ashwick 29 A6
Ashwicken 119 D4
Ashybank 186 B4
Askam in Furness . . 153 C2
Askern 140 B3
Askerswell 15 B5
Askett 66 C3
Askham
  Cumb 164 C3
  Notts 132 B2
Askham Bryan 149 C4
Askham Richard . . . 148 C4
Asknish 214 C2
Askrigg 156 B3
Askwith 147 C5
Aslackby 116 B3
Aslacton 104 B2
Aslockton 115 B3
Asloun 244 A2

Aspatria 174 D4
Aspenden 68 A3
Asperton 117 B5
Aspley Guise. 83 D6
Aspley Heath 83 D6
Aspull 137 C5
Asselby 141 A5
Asserby 135 B4
Assington 87 D5
Assynt House 264 D1
Astbury 128 C3
Astcote 82 B3
Asterley 94 A1
Asterton 94 B1
Asthall 64 B3
Asthall Leigh 64 B4
Astley
  Shrops 111 D4
  Warks 97 C6
  Worcs 79 A5
Astley Abbotts 95 B5
Astley Bridge 137 B6
Astley Cross 79 A6
Astley Green 137 D6
Aston
  Ches E. 111 A5
  Ches W 127 B5
  Derbys 130 A1
  Hereford 94 D2
  Herts 68 A2
  Oxon 64 C4
  Shrops 111 C4
  Staffs 111 A6
  Telford 95 A4
  W Mid 96 C3
  Wokingham 47 A5
Aston Abbotts 66 A3
Aston Botterell 95 C4
Aston-By-Stone . . . 112 B3
Aston Cantlow 80 B4
Aston Clinton 66 B3
Aston Crews 62 A2
Aston Cross 80 D2
Aston End 68 A2
Aston Eyre 95 B4
Aston Fields 80 A2
Aston Flamville 98 B1
Aston juxta
  Mondrum 127 D6
Aston le Walls 82 B1
Aston Magna 81 D4
Aston Munslow 94 C3
Aston on Clun 94 C1
Aston-on-Trent 114 C2
Aston Rogers 94 A1
Aston Rowant 66 D2
Aston Sandford 66 C2
Aston Somerville . . . 80 D3
Aston Subedge 80 C4
Aston Tirrold 46 A3
Aston Upthorpe 46 A3
Astrop 82 D2
Astwick 84 D4
Astwood
  M Keynes 83 C6
  Worcs 79 B6
Astwood Bank 80 A3
Aswarby 116 B3
Aswardby 134 B3
Atcham 94 A3
Atch Lench 80 B3
Athelhampton 16 B1
Athelington 104 D3
Athelney 28 C3
Athelstaneford 210 C2
Atherington 25 C6
Atherstone 97 B6
Atherstone on Stour . 81 B5
Atherton 137 C5
Atley Hill 157 A6
Atlow 113 A6
Attadale 249 C6
Attadale House 249 C6
Attenborough 114 B3
Atterby 142 D1
Attercliffe 130 A3
Attleborough
  Norf 103 B6
  Warks 97 B6
Attlebridge 120 D3
Atwick 151 B4
Atworth 44 C2
Aubourn 133 C4
Auchagallon 191 B4
Auchallater 243 D4
Aucharnie 256 B1
Auchattie 244 C3
Auchavan 231 B5

Auchbreck 254 D3
Auchenback 205 C5
Auchenbainzie 183 C6
Auchenblae 233 A5
Auchenbrack 183 C5
Auchenbreck 214 D3
Auchencairn
  Dumfries 173 C5
  Dumfries. 184 D2
  N Ayrs 191 C6
Auchencrosh 180 C3
Auchencrow 211 D5
Auchendinny 209 D5
Auchengray 195 A4
Auchenhalrig 267 C4
Auchenheath 194 B3
Auchenlochan 203 A4
Auchenmalg 171 B4
Auchensoul 181 B4
Auchentiber 204 D3
Auchertyre 249 C5
Auchgourish 242 A2
Auchincarroch 206 B2
Auchindrain 214 B3
Auchindrean 262 B3
Auchininna 256 B2
Auchinleck 193 C5
Auchinloch 205 A6
Auchinroath 266 D3
Auchintoul 244 A2
Auchiries. 257 C5
Auchlee 245 C5
Auchleven 256 D1
Auchlochan 194 C3
Auchlossan 244 B2
Auchlunies 245 C5
Auchlyne 217 B5
Auchmacoy 257 C5
Auchmair 255 D4
Auchmantle 170 A3
Auchmillan 193 C5
Auchmithie 233 D4
Auchmuirbridge . . . 220 D2
Auchmull 232 A3
Auchnacree 232 B2
Auchnagallin 253 C6
Auchnagatt 257 B4
Auchnaha 214 D2
Auchnashelloch . . . 218 C2
Aucholzie 243 C6
Auchrannie 231 C6
Auchroisk 253 D6
Auchronie 244 D1
Auchterarder 218 C4
Auchteraw 240 B1
Auchterderran 209 A5
Auchterhouse 220 A3
Auchtermuchty 220 C2
Auchterneed 251 A6
Auchtertool 209 A5
Auchtertyre 266 D2
Auchtubh 217 B5
Auckengill 281 B5
Auckley 140 C4
Audenshaw 138 D2
Audlem 111 A5
Audley 128 D2
Audley End 87 D4
Auds 268 C1
Aughton
  E Yorks 149 D6
  Lancs 136 C2
  Lancs 145 A5
  S Yorks 131 A4
  Wilts 45 D6
Aughton Park 136 C3
Auldearn 253 A5
Aulden 78 B2
Auldgirth 183 D7
Auldhame 210 B2
Auldhouse 205 C6
Ault a'chruinn 249 D6
Aultanrynie 271 A6
Aultbea 261 B5
Aultdearg 263 D4
Aultgrishan 261 B4
Aultguish Inn 263 C5
Aultibea 274 B4
Aultiphurst 279 B4
Aultmore 267 D5
Aultnagoire 252 D1
Aultnamain Inn 264 B2
Aultnaslat 239 B5
Aulton 255 D7
Aundorach 242 A2
Aunsby 116 B3
Auquhorthies 256 D3
Aust 43 A4

Austendike 117 C5
Austerfield 141 D4
Austrey 97 A5
Austwick 146 A1
Authorpe 135 A4
Authorpe Row 135 B5
Avebury 45 C5
Aveley 50 A2
Avening 63 D4
Averham 132 D2
Aveton Gifford 7 C5
Avielochan 242 A2
Aviemore 242 A1
Avington
    Hants 32 B4
    W Berks 46 C1
Avoch 252 A3
Avon 17 B5
Avonbridge 208 C2
Avon Dassett 81 C7
Avonmouth 43 B4
Avonwick 7 B6
Awbridge 32 C2
Awhirk 170 B2
Awkley 43 A4
Awliscombe 13 A6
Awre 62 C3
Awsworth 114 A2
Axbridge 42 D3
Axford
    Hants 33 A5
    Wilts 45 C4
Axminster 14 B2
Axmouth 14 B2
Axton 125 A6
Aycliff 39 A5
Aycliffe 167 C5
Aydon 178 C2
Aylburton 62 C2
Ayle 165 A5
Aylesbeare 13 B5
Aylesbury 66 B3
Aylesby 143 C4
Aylesford 37 A5
Aylesham 53 D4
Aylestone 98 A2
Aylmerton 120 B3
Aylsham 120 C3
Aylton 79 D4
Aymestrey 78 A2
Aynho 82 D2
Ayot St Lawrence . . . 68 B1
Ayot St Peter 68 B2
Ayr 192 C5
Aysgarth 156 C4
Ayside 154 C2
Ayston 99 A5
Aythorpe Roding 69 B5
Ayton 211 D6
Aywick 284 E7
Azerley 157 D6

B

Babbacombe 8 A3
Babbinswood 110 B2
Babcary 29 C5
Babel 59 B5
Babell 125 B6
Babraham 85 B7
Babworth 132 A1
Bac 288 C5
Bachau 123 B4
Backaland 282 D6
Backaskaill 282 B5
Backbarrow 154 C2
Backe 56 A2
Backfolds 269 D5
Backford 127 B4
Backford Cross 126 B3
Backhill
    Aberds 256 C2
    Aberds 257 C5
Backhill of
    Clackriach 257 B4
Backhill of
    Fortree 257 B4
Backhill of
    Trustach 244 C3
Backies 274 D2
Backlass 280 C4
Back of Keppoch . . . 235 B5
Back Rogerton 193 C5
Backwell 42 C3
Backworth 179 B5
Bacon End 69 B6
Baconsthorpe 120 B3

Bacton
    Hereford 78 D1
    Norf 121 B5
    Suff 87 A6
Bacton Green 87 A6
Bacup 138 A1
Badachro 261 C4
Badanloch Lodge . . 273 A5
Badavanich 250 A3
Badbury 45 A5
Badby 82 B2
Badcall 276 C3
Badcaul 262 A2
Baddeley Green . . . 129 D4
Baddesley Clinton . . 97 D5
Baddesley Ensor . . . 97 B5
Baddidarach 270 B3
Baddoch 242 D4
Baddock 252 A3
Badenscoth 256 C2
Badenyon 243 A6
Badger 95 B5
Badger's Mount 50 C1
Badgeworth 63 B5
Badgworth 42 D2
Badicaul 249 D4
Badingham 88 A4
Badlesmere 52 D2
Badlipster 280 D4
Badluarach 262 A1
Badminton 44 A2
Badnaban 270 B3
Badninish 264 A3
Badrallach 262 A2
Badsey 80 C3
Badshot Lea 34 B1
Badsworth 140 B2
Badwell Ash 87 A5
Bae Colwyn
    = Colwyn Bay 124 B3
Bagby 158 C3
Bag Enderby 134 B3
Bagendon 63 C6
Bagh a Chaisteil
    = Castlebay 286 G2
Baghasdal 286 E3
Bagh Mor 286 A4
Bagh Shiarabhagh . 286 F3
Bagillt 126 B2
Baginton 97 D6
Baglan 40 B2
Bagley 110 C3
Bagnall 129 D4
Bagnor 46 C2
Bagshot
    Sur 48 C2
    Wilts 45 C7
Bagthorpe
    Norf 119 B4
    Notts 131 D4
Bagworth 98 A1
Bagwy Llydiart 61 A6
Bail Àrd Bhuirgh . . 288 B5
Baildon 147 D5
Baile 287 F4
Baile Ailein 288 E3
Baile a Mhanaich . . 286 A3
Baile an Truiseil . . . 288 B4
Bailebeag 240 A3
Baile Boidheach . . . 202 A2
Baile Glas 286 A4
Baile Mhartainn . . . 287 G2
Baile Mhic Phail . . . 287 G3
Baile Mor
    Argyll 224 D1
    W Isles 287 H2
Baile na Creige 286 F2
Baile nan
    Cailleach 286 A3
Baile Raghaill 287 G2
Baileyhead 176 B3
Bailiesward 255 C5
Baillieston 205 B6
Bail' Iochdrach 286 A4
Bail Uachdraich . . . 287 H3
Bail' Ur
    Tholastaidh 288 C6
Bainbridge 156 B3
Bainsford 208 B1
Bainshole 255 C7
Bainton
    E Yorks 150 B2
    Pboro 100 A2
Bairnkine 187 B5
Baker's End 68 B3
Baker Street 50 A3
Bakewell 130 C2
Bala = Y Bala 108 B4
Balachuirn 248 B2
Balavil 241 B5

Balbeg
    Highld 251 C6
    Highld 251 D6
Balbeggie 219 B6
Balbithan 245 A4
Balbithan House . . . 245 A5
Balblair
    Highld 264 A1
    Highld 264 D3
Balby 140 C3
Balchladich 270 A3
Balchraggan
    Highld 252 B1
    Highld 252 C1
Balchrick 276 C2
Balchrystie 221 D4
Balcladaich 251 D4
Balcombe 35 C6
Balcombe Lane 35 C6
Balcomie 221 C6
Balcurvie 220 D3
Baldersby 158 D2
Baldersby
    St James 158 D2
Balderstone 145 D6
Balderton
    Ches W 126 C3
    Notts 132 D3
Baldhu 4 C2
Baldinnie 220 C4
Baldock 84 D4
Baldovie 221 A4
Baldrine 152 C4
Baldslow 23 A5
Baldwin 152 C3
Baldwinholme 175 C6
Baldwin's Gate 112 A1
Bale 120 B2
Balearn 269 D5
Balemartine 222 C2
Balephuil 222 C2
Balerno 209 D4
Balevullin 222 C2
Balfield 232 B3
Balfour 282 F5
Balfron 206 B3
Balfron Station 206 B3
Balgaveny 256 B1
Balgavies 232 C3
Balgonar 208 A3
Balgove 256 C3
Balgowan 241 C4
Balgown 258 B3
Balgrochan 205 A6
Balgy 249 A5
Balhaldie 218 D3
Balhalgardy 256 D2
Balham 49 B5
Balhary 231 D6
Baliasta 284 C8
Baligill 279 B4
Balintore
    Angus 231 C6
    Highld 265 C4
Balintraid 264 C3
Balk 158 C3
Balkeerie 232 D1
Balkemback 220 A4
Balkholme 141 A5
Balkissock 180 C3
Ball 110 C2
Ballabeg 152 D2
Ballacannel 152 C4
Ballachulish 237 D4
Ballajora 152 B4
Ballaleigh 152 C3
Ballamodha 152 D2
Ballantrae 180 C2
Ballaquine 152 C4
Ballards Gore 70 D3
Ballasalla
    IoM 152 B3
    IoM 152 D2
Ballater 243 C6
Ballaugh 152 B3
Ballaveare 152 D3
Ballcorach 254 D2
Ballechin 230 C3
Balleigh 264 B3
Ballencrieff 210 C1
Ballentoul 230 B2
Ball Haye
    Green 129 D4
Ball Hill 46 C2
Ballidon 130 D2
Balliemore
    Argyll 214 D3
    Argyll 226 D3
Ballikinrain 206 B3
Ballimeanoch 214 A3

Ballimore
    Argyll 214 D2
    Stirling 217 C5
Ballinaby 200 B2
Ballindean 220 B2
Ballingdon 87 C4
Ballinger Common . . 67 C4
Ballingham 78 D3
Ballingry 209 A4
Ballinlick 230 D3
Ballinluig 230 C3
Ballintuim 231 C5
Balloch
    Angus 232 C1
    Highld 252 B3
    N Lanark 207 C5
    W Dunb 206 B1
Ballochan 244 C2
Ballochford 255 C4
Ballochmorrie 181 C4
Balls Cross 34 D2
Balls Green 71 A4
Ballygown 224 B3
Ballygrant 200 B3
Ballyhaugh 223 B4
Balmacara 249 D5
Balmacara Square . . 249 D5
Balmaclellan 173 A4
Balmacneil 230 C3
Balmacqueen 259 A4
Balmae 173 D4
Balmaha 206 A2
Balmalcolm 220 D3
Balmeanach 248 B2
Balmedie 245 A6
Balmer Heath 110 B3
Balmerino 220 B3
Balmerlawn 18 A2
Balmichael 191 B5
Balmirmer 221 A5
Balmore
    Highld 251 C5
    Highld 253 B4
    Highld 258 D2
    Perth 230 C3
Balmule 209 B5
Balmullo 220 B4
Balmungie 252 A3
Balnaboth 231 B7
Balnabruaich 264 D3
Balnabruich 275 B5
Balnacoil 274 C2
Balnacra 250 B1
Balnafoich 252 C2
Balnagall 265 B4
Balnaguard 230 C3
Balnahard
    Argyll 212 C2
    Argyll 224 C3
Balnain 251 C6
Balnakeil 277 B4
Balnaknock 259 B4
Balnapaling 264 D3
Balne 140 B3
Balochroy 202 C2
Balone 221 C4
Balornock 205 B6
Balquharn 219 A5
Balquhidder 217 B5
Balsall 97 D5
Balsall Common . . . 97 D5
Balsall Heath 96 C3
Balscott 81 C6
Balsham 86 B1
Baltasound 284 C8
Balterley 128 D2
Baltersan 171 A6
Balthangie 268 D3
Baltonsborough 29 B5
Balvaird 252 A1
Balvicar 213 A5
Balvraid
    Highld 238 A2
    Highld 253 C4
Bamber Bridge 137 A4
Bambers Green 69 A5
Bamburgh 199 C5
Bamff 231 C6
Bamford
    Derbys 130 A2
    Gtr Man 138 B1
Bampton
    Cumb 164 D3
    Devon 27 C4
    Oxon 64 C4
Bampton Grange . . . 164 D3
Banavie 237 B5
Banbury 82 C1
Bancffosfelen 57 A4
Banchory 244 C3

Banchory-
    Devenick 245 B6
Bancycapel 57 A4
Bancyfelin 56 A3
Bancyffordd 73 C7
Bandirran 220 A2
Banff 268 C1
Bangor 123 C5
Bangor-is-y-coed
    = Bangor-on-Dee . 110 A2
Bangor-on-Dee
    = Bangor-is-y-coed 110 A2
Banham 103 C6
Bank 18 A1
Bankend 174 B3
Bankfoot 219 A5
Bankglen 182 A4
Bankhead
    Aberdeen 245 A5
    Aberds 244 B3
Bank Newton 146 B3
Banknock 207 C5
Banks
    Cumb 176 C3
    Lancs 136 A2
Bankshill 185 D4
Bank Street 79 A4
Banningham 120 C4
Banniskirk House . . 280 C3
Bannister Green 69 A6
Bannockburn 207 A6
Banstead 35 A5
Bantham 7 C5
Banton 207 C5
Banwell 42 D2
Banyard's Green . . . 104 D3
Bapchild 51 C6
Barabhas 288 C4
Barabhas Iarach . . . 288 C4
Barabhas Uarach . . 288 B4
Barachandroman . . 225 D5
Barassie 192 B3
Baravaille 226 C3
Barbaraville 264 C3
Barber Booth 129 A6
Barbieston 182 A2
Barbon 155 C5
Barbridge 127 D6
Barbrook 26 A2
Barby 98 D2
Barcaldine 227 B4
Barcheston 81 D5
Barcombe 22 A2
Barcombe Cross 22 A2
Barden 157 B5
Bardennoch 182 C3
Barden Scale 147 B4
Bardfield Saling 69 A6
Bardister 284 F5
Bardney 133 C6
Bardon 114 D2
Bardon Mill 177 C5
Bardowie 205 A5
Bardrainney 204 A3
Bardsea 154 D2
Bardsey 148 C2
Bardwell 103 D5
Bare 145 A4
Barfad 202 B3
Barford
    Norf 104 A2
    Warks 81 A5
Barford St John 82 D1
Barford St Martin . . . 31 B4
Barford
    St Michael 82 D1
Barfrestone 53 D4
Bargod = Bargoed . . 41 B6
Bargoed = Bargod . . 41 B6
Bargrennan 181 D5
Barham
    Cambs 100 D3
    Kent 53 D4
    Suff 88 B2
Barharrow 172 C4
Barhill 173 B6
Bar Hill 85 A5
Barholm 116 D3
Barkby 98 A3
Barkestone-
    le-Vale 115 B5
Barkham 47 C5
Barking
    London 50 A1
    Suff 87 B6
Barkingside 50 A1
Barking Tye 87 B6
Barkisland 138 B3
Barkston
    Lincs 116 A2

Barkston *continued*
    N Yorks 148 A5
Barkway 85 D5
Barlaston 112 B2
Barlavington 20 A2
Barlborough 131 B4
Barlby 149 D5
Barlestone 98 A1
Barley
    Herts 85 D5
    Lancs 146 C2
Barley Mow 179 D4
Barleythorpe 99 A5
Barling 51 A6
Barlow
    Derbys 130 B3
    N Yorks 140 A4
    T&W 178 C3
Barmby Moor 149 C6
Barmby on the
    Marsh 141 A4
Barmer 119 B5
Barmoor Castle . . . 198 C3
Barmoor Lane End . 198 C4
Barmouth
    = Abermaw 90 A4
Barmpton 167 D6
Barmston 151 B4
Barnack 100 A3
Barnacle 97 C6
Barnard Castle 166 D3
Barnard Gate 65 B5
Barnardiston 86 C3
Barnbarroch 173 C6
Barnburgh 140 C2
Barnby 105 C5
Barnby Dun 140 C4
Barnby in the
    Willows 132 D3
Barnby Moor 131 A6
Barnes Street 36 B4
Barnet 68 D2
Barnetby le Wold . . 142 C2
Barney 120 B1
Barnham
    Suff 103 D4
    W Sus 20 B3
Barnham Broom . . . 104 A1
Barnhead 233 C4
Barnhill
    Ches W 127 D4
    Dundee 221 A4
    Moray 266 D2
Barnhills 180 C1
Barningham
    Durham 166 D3
    Suff 103 D5
Barnoldby le Beck . 143 C4
Barnoldswick 146 C2
Barns Green 35 D4
Barnsley
    Glos 64 C1
    S Yorks 139 C6
Barnstaple 25 B6
Barnston
    Essex 69 B6
    Mers 126 A2
Barnstone 115 B5
Barnt Green 96 D3
Barnton
    Ches W 127 B6
    Edin 209 C4
Barnwell All Saints . 100 C2
Barnwell
    St Andrew 100 C2
Barnwood 63 B4
Barochreal 226 D3
Barons Cross 78 B2
Barr 181 B4
Barra Castle 256 D2
Barrachan 171 C5
Barrack 256 B3
Barraglom 288 D2
Barrahormid 213 D5
Barran 226 D3
Barrapol 222 C2
Barras
    Aberds 245 D5
    Cumb 165 D6
Barrasford 177 B7
Barravullin 213 B6
Barregarrow 152 C3
Barrhead 205 C4
Barrhill 181 C4
Barrington
    Cambs 85 C5
    Som 28 D3
Barripper 3 B4
Barrmill 204 C3
Barrock 281 A4

Barrock House.....281 B4
Barrow
  Lancs.........146 D1
  Rutland.......116 D1
  Suff..........86 A3
Barroway Drove...102 A1
Barrowburn......188 B1
Barrowby........116 B1
Barrowcliff.....160 C4
Barrowden.......99 A6
Barrowford......146 D2
Barrow Green......51 C6
Barrow Gurney......43 C4
Barrow Haven....142 A2
Barrow-in-Furness 153 D3
Barrow Island....153 D2
Barrow Nook.....136 C3
Barrows Green
  Ches E........128 D1
  Cumb..........154 C4
Barrow's Green...127 A5
Barrow Street.......30 B2
Barrow upon
  Humber.......142 A2
Barrow upon Soar..114 D3
Barrow uponTrent.114 C1
Barry...........221 A5
Barry = Y Barri.......41 E6
Barry Island.......41 E6
Barsby..........115 D4
Barsham.........105 C4
Barston.........97 D5
Bartestree.......78 C3
Barthol Chapel...256 C3
Barthomley......128 D2
Bartley.........32 D2
Bartley Green......96 C3
Bartlow.........86 C1
Barton
  Cambs.........85 B6
  Ches W........127 D4
  Glos..........64 A2
  Lancs.........136 C4
  Lancs.........145 D5
  N Yorks.......157 A6
  Oxon..........65 C6
  Torbay.........8 A3
  Warks.........80 B4
Barton Bendish...102 A3
Barton Hartshorn...82 D3
Barton in Fabis....114 B3
Barton in the Beans.97 A6
Barton-le-Clay....84 D2
Barton-le-Street..159 D6
Barton-le-Willows.149 A6
Barton Mills.....102 D3
Barton on Sea......17 B6
Barton on the Heath.81 D5
Barton St David....29 B5
Barton Seagrave....99 D5
Barton Stacey......32 A3
BartonTurf.......121 C5
Barton-under-
  Needwood.......113 D5
Barton-upon-
  Humber.........142 A2
Barton Waterside.142 A2
Barugh..........139 C6
Barway..........102 D1
Barwell..........98 B1
Barwick
  Herts.........68 B3
  Som...........29 D5
Barwick in Elmet..148 D2
Baschurch......110 C3
Bascote.........81 A7
Basford Green...129 D4
Bashall Eaves...145 C6
Bashley.........17 B6
Basildon.........51 A4
Basingstoke........47 D4
Baslow.........130 B2
Bason Bridge.......28 A3
Bassaleg.........42 A1
Bassenthwaite...163 A5
Bassett.........32 D3
Bassingbourn....85 C5
Bassingfield.....115 B4
Bassingham.....133 C4
Bassingthorpe...116 C2
Basta..........284 D7
Baston.........116 D4
Bastwick.......121 D6
Baswick Steer...150 C3
Batchworth Heath..67 D5
Batcombe
  Dorset.........15 A6
  Som...........29 B6
Bate Heath.....128 B1
Batford.........67 B6

Bath.........43 C6
Bathampton......44 C1
Bathealton......27 C5
Batheaston......44 C1
Bathford........44 C1
Bathgate........208 D2
Bathpool
  Corn..........10 D3
  Som...........28 C2
Bathley.........132 D2
Bathville.......208 D2
Batley.........139 A5
Batsford.........81 D4
Battersby.......159 A4
Battersea.......49 B5
Battisborough Cross.7 C4
Battisford......87 B6
BattisfordTye...87 B6
Battle
  E Sus.........23 A5
  Powys.........76 D4
Battledown......63 A5
Battlefield....111 A4
Battlesbridge...70 D1
Battlesden......67 A4
Battlesea Green..104 D3
Battleton........27 C4
Battram.........98 A1
Battramsley......18 B2
Baughton........80 C1
Baughurst........46 D3
Baulking........64 D4
Baumber.......134 B2
Baunton.........63 C6
Baverstock......31 B4
Bawburgh......104 A2
Bawdeswell.....120 C2
Bawdrip.........28 B3
Bawdsey.........88 C4
Bawtry.........141 D4
Baxenden.......137 A6
Baxterley........97 B5
Baybridge........32 C4
Baycliff.......154 D1
Baydon..........45 B6
Bayford
  Herts.........68 C3
  Som...........30 C1
Bayles.........165 A5
Baylham.........88 B2
Baynard's Green...65 A6
Bayston Hill......94 A2
Baythorn End......86 C3
Bayton.........95 D4
Beach.........236 D1
Beachampton......83 D4
Beachamwell...102 A3
Beachans......253 B6
Beacharr.......202 D1
Beachborough....38 B3
Beachley........62 D1
Beacon..........14 A1
Beacon End.......70 A3
Beacon Hill.......34 C1
Beacon's Bottom...66 D2
Beaconsfield......67 E4
Beacrabhaic.....288 H2
Beadlam........159 C5
Beadlow.........84 D3
Beadnell.......189 A5
Beaford.........25 D6
Beal
  Northumb.......199 B4
  N Yorks.......140 A3
Beamhurst.......113 B4
Beaminster.......15 A4
Beamish........179 D4
Beamsley.......147 B4
Bean..........50 B2
Beanacre.......44 C3
Beanley.........188 B3
Beaquoy........282 E4
Bear Cross.......17 B4
Beardwood......137 A5
Beare Green......35 B4
Bearley.........81 A4
Bearnus........224 B2
Bearpark.......167 A5
Bearsbridge....177 D5
Bearsden.......205 A5
Bearsted........37 A5
Bearstone......111 B6
Bearwood
  BCP...........17 B4
  Hereford.......78 B1
  W Mid.........96 C3
Beattock.......184 B3
Beauchamp Roding.69 B5
Beauchief......130 A3
Beaufort........60 B3

Beaufort Castle....251 B7
Beaulieu........18 A2
Beauly.........252 B1
Beaumaris......123 C6
Beaumont
  Cumb..........175 C6
  Essex.........71 A5
Beaumont Hill....167 D5
Beausale........97 D5
Beauworth........33 C4
Beaworthy.......11 B5
Beazley End......70 A1
Bebington......126 A3
Bebside........179 A4
Beccles........105 B5
Becconsall.....136 A3
Beckbury........95 A5
Beckenham......49 C6
Beckermet......162 D3
Beckfoot
  Cumb..........163 D4
  Cumb..........174 D3
Beck Foot......155 B5
Beckford........80 D2
Beckhampton......45 C4
Beck Hole......159 A7
Beckingham
  Lincs.........132 D3
  Notts.........141 E5
Beckington......44 D2
Beckley
  E Sus.........37 D6
  Hants.........17 B6
  Oxon..........65 B6
Beck Row......102 D2
Beck Side......153 B3
Beckton.........50 A1
Beckwithshaw...147 B6
Becontree.......50 A1
Bedale.........157 C6
Bedburn........166 B4
Bedchester......30 D2
Beddau.........41 C5
Beddgelert......107 B5
Beddingham......22 B2
Beddington......49 C6
Bedfield........88 A3
Bedford.........84 B2
Bedham.........34 D3
Bedhampton......19 A6
Bedingfield......88 A2
Bedlam.........147 A6
Bedlington.....179 A4
Bedlington Station.179 A4
Bedlinog........41 A5
Bedminster......43 B4
Bedmond.........67 C5
Bednall........112 D3
Bedrule........187 B5
Bedstone.......94 D1
Bedwas.........41 C6
Bedworth........97 C6
Bedworth Heath...97 C6
Bed-y-coedwr...108 C2
Beeby..........98 A3
Beech
  Hants.........33 B5
  Staffs.........112 B2
Beech Hill
  Gtr Man.......137 C4
  W Berks........47 C4
Beechingstoke...45 D4
Beedon.........46 B2
Beeford........151 B4
Beeley.........130 C2
Beelsby.........143 C4
Beenham........46 C3
Beeny..........10 B2
Beer..........14 C2
Beercrocombe....28 C3
Beer Hackett......29 D6
Beesands........8 C2
Beesby.........135 A4
Beeson.........8 C2
Beeston
  C Beds........84 C3
  Ches W........127 D5
  Norf..........119 D6
  Notts.........114 B3
  W Yorks.......148 D1
Beeston Regis...120 A3
Beeswing.......173 B6
Beetham........154 D3
Beetley........119 D6
Begbroke........65 B5
Begelly........55 D7
Beggar's Bush....77 A6
Beguildy.......93 D5
Beighton
  Norf..........105 A4

Beighton *continued*
  S Yorks.......131 A4
Beighton Hill....130 D2
Beith.........204 C3
Bekesbourne......52 D3
Belaugh........121 D4
Belbroughton.....96 D2
Belchamp Otten...87 C4
Belchamp St Paul..86 C3
Belchamp Walter...87 C4
Belchford......134 B2
Belford........199 C5
Belhaven.......210 C3
Belhelvie......245 A6
Belhinnie......255 D5
Bellabeg.......243 A6
Bellamore......181 C4
Bellanoch......213 C5
Bellaty........231 C6
Bell Bar........68 C2
Bell Busk......146 B3
Belleau........135 B4
Bellehiglash....254 C2
Bell End........96 D2
Bellerby.......157 B5
Bellever........12 D1
Belliehill......232 B3
Bellingdon......67 C4
Bellingham.....177 A6
Belloch........190 B2
Bellochantuy....190 B2
Bell o' th' Hill...111 A4
Bellsbank......182 B2
Bellshill
  N Lanark......207 D5
  Northumb......199 C5
Bellspool......195 C6
Bellsquarry....208 D3
Bells Yew Green...36 C4
Belmaduthy.....252 A2
Belmesthorpe...116 D3
Belmont
  Blackburn.......137 B5
  London........49 C5
  S Ayrs........192 C3
  Shetland.......284 C7
Belnacraig......243 A6
Belowda.........5 A4
Belper.........114 A1
Belper Lane End..114 A1
Belsay.........178 B3
Belses.........187 A4
Belsford........7 B6
Belstead........88 C2
Belston........192 C3
Belstone........11 B7
Belthorn.......137 A6
Beltinge........52 C3
Beltoft........141 C6
Belton
  Leics.........114 C2
  Lincs.........116 B2
  N Lincs.......141 C5
  Norf..........105 A5
Belton in Rutland...99 A5
Beltring........37 B4
Belts of Collonach.244 C3
Belvedere......50 B1
Belvoir........115 B6
Bembridge.......19 C5
Bemersyde......197 C4
Bemerton.......31 B5
Bempton.......161 D5
Benacre........105 C6
Ben Alder Lodge...229 A4
Ben Armine Lodge.273 C5
Benbuie........183 C5
Ben Casgro......288 C5
Benderloch.....226 C4
Bendronaig Lodge.250 C2
Benenden.......37 C6
Benfield.......171 A5
Bengate........121 C5
Bengeworth......80 C3
Benhall Green....89 A4
Benhall Street....89 A4
Benholm........233 B6
Beningbrough...148 B4
Benington
  Herts.........68 A2
  Lincs.........117 A6
Benllech.......123 B5
Benmore
  Argyll........215 D4
  Stirling.......216 B4
Benmore Lodge...271 C6
Bennacott.......10 B3
Bennan........191 C5
Benniworth.....134 A2
Benover........37 B4

Bensham.......179 C4
Benslie........204 D3
Benson.........65 D7
Bent.........233 A4
Bent Gate......137 A6
Benthall
  Northumb.......189 A5
  Shrops.......95 A4
Bentham.........63 B5
Benthoul......245 B5
Bentlawnt......94 A1
Bentley
  E Yorks.......150 D3
  Hants.........33 A6
  Suff..........88 C2
  S Yorks.......140 C5
  Warks.........97 B5
  Worcs.........80 A2
Bentley Heath....97 C4
Benton.........26 B1
Bentpath.......185 C6
Bents.........208 D2
Benvie.........220 A3
Benwick.......101 B5
Beoley.........80 A3
Beoraidbeg.....235 A5
Bepton.........20 A1
Berden.........69 A4
Bere Alston......6 A3
Bere Ferrers......6 A3
Berepper........3 C4
Bere Regis.......16 B2
Bergh Apton....104 A4
Berinsfield......65 D6
Berkeley........62 D2
Berkhamsted......67 C4
Berkley........30 A2
Berkswell.......97 D5
Bermondsey......49 B6
Bernera........249 D5
Bernice........215 C4
Bernisdale.....259 C4
Berrick Salome...65 D7
Berriedale.....275 B5
Berrier........164 C1
Berriew........93 A5
Berrington
  Northumb......198 B4
  Shrops........94 A3
Berrow.........42 D2
Berrow Green.....79 B5
Berry Down Cross..25 A6
Berry Hill
  Glos..........62 B1
  Pembs........72 B3
Berryhillock...267 C6
Berrynarbor.....25 A6
Berry Pomeroy....8 A2
Bersham.......110 A2
Berstane......282 F5
Berwick........22 B3
Berwick Bassett...45 B4
Berwick Hill....178 B3
Berwick St James..31 B4
Berwick St John...30 C3
Berwick St Leonard.30 B3
Berwick-upon-
  Tweed.........198 A3
Bescar.........136 B2
Besford........80 C2
Bessacarr.......140 C4
Bessels Leigh....65 C5
Bessingby......151 A4
Bessingham.....120 B3
Bestbeech Hill...36 C4
Besthorpe
  Norf..........103 B6
  Notts.........132 C3
Bestwood.......114 A3
Bestwood Village..114 A3
Beswick........150 C3
Betchworth......35 B5
Bethania
  Ceredig........75 B4
  Gwyn.........107 A6
  Gwyn.........108 A2
Bethel
  Anglesey.......122 C3
  Gwyn.........109 B4
  Gwyn.........123 D5
Bethersden......38 A1
Bethesda
  Gwyn.........123 D6
  Pembs.........55 C6
Bethlehem......58 C3
Bethnal Green....49 A6
Betley.........111 A6
Betsham........50 B3
Betteshanger....53 D5

Bettiscombe.......14 B3
Bettisfield......110 B3
Betton
  Shrops.........93 A7
  Shrops.........111 B5
Bettws
  Bridgend.......40 C4
  Mon...........61 B4
  Newport.......61 D4
Bettws Cedewain...93 B5
Bettws Gwerfil
  Goch.........109 A5
Bettws Ifan......73 B6
Bettws Newydd...61 C5
Bettws-y-crwyn...93 C6
Bettyhill......278 B3
Betws.........57 A6
Betws Bledrws....75 C4
Betws-Garmon...107 A5
Betws-y-Coed...124 D2
Betws-yn-Rhos...125 B4
Beulah
  Ceredig........73 B5
  Powys.........76 B3
Bevendean.......21 B6
Bevercotes.....132 B1
Beverley.......150 D3
Beverston.......63 D4
Bevington.......62 D2
Bewaldeth......163 A5
Bewcastle......176 B3
Bewdley.........95 D5
Bewerley.......147 A5
Bewholme.......151 B4
Bexhill.........23 B5
Bexley.........50 B1
Bexleyheath......50 B1
Bexwell.........102 A2
Beyton.........87 A5
Bhaltos........287 A5
Bhatarsaigh....286 G2
Bibury.........64 C2
Bicester........65 A6
Bickenhall......28 D2
Bickenhill......97 C4
Bicker.........117 B5
Bickershaw.....137 C5
Bickerstaffe...136 C3
Bickerton
  Ches E.........127 D5
  N Yorks.......148 B3
Bickington
  Devon.........12 D2
  Devon.........25 B6
Bickleigh
  Devon..........7 A4
  Devon.........13 A4
Bickleton.......25 B6
Bickley.........49 C7
Bickley Moss....111 A4
Bicknacre.......70 C1
Bicknoller......27 B6
Bicknor.........37 A6
Bickton.........31 D5
Bicton
  Shrops.........93 C6
  Shrops.........110 D3
Bidborough......36 B3
Biddenden.......37 C6
Biddenham......84 C2
Biddestone......44 B2
Biddisham.......42 D2
Biddlesden......82 C3
Biddlestone....188 C2
Biddulph......128 D3
Biddulph Moor...129 D4
Bideford........25 C5
Bidford-on-Avon...80 B4
Bidston.......136 D1
Bielby.........149 C6
Bieldside......245 B5
Bierley
  IoW..........18 D4
  W Yorks.......147 D5
Bierton.........66 B3
Bigbury........7 C5
Bigbury on Sea....7 C5
Bigby.........142 C2
Biggar
  Cumb.........153 D2
  S Lanark......195 C5
Biggin
  Derbys.......113 A6
  Derbys.......129 D6
  N Yorks.......148 D4
Biggings......285 G3
Biggin Hill......36 A2
Biggleswade......84 C3

Bighouse 279 B4
Bighton 33 B5
Bignor 20 A2
Big Sand 261 C4
Bigton 285 L5
Bilberry 5 A5
Bilborough 114 A3
Bilbrook 27 A5
Bilbrough 148 C4
Bilbster 281 C4
Bildershaw 167 C5
Bildeston 87 C5
Billericay 69 D6
Billesdon 99 A4
Billesley 80 B4
Billingborough 116 B4
Billinge 136 C4
Billingford 120 C2
Billingham 168 C2
Billinghay 133 D6
Billingley 140 C2
Billingshurst 34 D3
Billingsley 95 C5
Billington
 C Beds 67 A4
 Lancs 145 D7
Billockby 121 D6
Billy Row 167 B4
Bilsborrow 145 D5
Bilsby 135 B4
Bilsham 20 B2
Bilsington 38 B2
Bilson Green 62 B2
Bilsthorpe 131 C6
Bilsthorpe Moor . . . 131 D6
Bilston
 Midloth 209 D5
 W Mid 96 B2
Bilstone 97 A6
Bilting 38 A2
Bilton
 E Yorks 151 D4
 Northumb 189 B5
 Warks 98 D1
Bilton in Ainsty 148 C3
Bimbister 282 F4
Binbrook 143 D4
Binchester Blocks . . 167 B5
Bincombe 15 C6
Bindal 265 B5
Binegar 29 A6
Binfield 47 B6
Binfield Heath 47 B5
Bingfield 178 B1
Bingham 115 B5
Bingley 147 D5
Bings Heath 111 D4
Binham 120 B1
Binley
 Hants 46 D2
 W Mid 97 D6
Binley Woods 97 D6
Binniehill 207 C6
Binsoe 157 D6
Binstead 19 B4
Binsted 33 A6
Binton 80 B4
Bintree 120 C2
Binweston 93 A7
Birch
 Essex 70 B3
 Gtr Man 138 C1
Bircham Newton . . . 119 B4
Bircham Tofts 119 B4
Birchanger 69 A5
Birchencliffe 139 B4
Bircher 78 A2
Birch Green 70 B3
Birchgrove
 Cardiff 41 D6
 Swansea 40 B2
Birch Heath 127 C5
Birch Hill 127 B5
Birchington 53 C4
Birchmoor 97 A5
Birchover 130 C2
Birch Vale 129 A5
Birchwood
 Lincs 133 C4
 Warr 137 D5
Bircotes 140 D4
Birdbrook 86 C3
Birdforth 158 D3
Birdham 20 C1
Birdholme 130 C2
Birdingbury 82 A1
Birdlip 63 B5
Birdsall 149 A7

Birds Edge 139 C5
Birdsgreen 95 C5
Birdsmoor Gate 14 A3
Birdston 205 A6
Birdwell 139 C6
Birdwood 62 B3
Birgham 198 C1
Birkby 158 A2
Birkdale 136 B2
Birkenhead 126 A3
Birkenhills 256 B2
Birkenshaw
 N Lanark 207 D4
 W Yorks 139 A5
Birkhall 243 C6
Birkhill
 Angus 220 A3
 Borders 185 A5
Birkholme 116 C2
Birkin 140 A3
Birley 78 B2
Birling
 Kent 50 C3
 Northumb 189 C5
Birling Gap 22 C3
Birlingham 80 C2
Birmingham 96 C3
Birnam 230 D4
Birse 244 C2
Birsemore 244 C2
Birstall
 Leics 98 A2
 W Yorks 139 A5
Birstwith 147 B6
Birthorpe 116 B4
Birtley
 Hereford 78 A1
 Northumb 177 B6
 T&W 179 D4
Birts Street 79 D5
Bisbrooke 99 B5
Biscathorpe 134 A2
Biscot 67 A5
Bisham 47 A6
Bishampton 80 B2
Bish Mill 26 C2
Bishop Auckland . . . 167 C5
Bishopbridge 142 D2
Bishopbriggs 205 B6
Bishop Burton 150 D2
Bishop Middleham . 167 B6
Bishopmill 266 C3
Bishop Monkton . . . 148 A2
Bishop Norton 142 D1
Bishopsbourne 52 D3
Bishops Cannings . . . 44 C4
Bishop's Castle 93 C7
Bishop's Caundle . . . 29 D6
Bishop's Cleeve 63 A5
Bishops Frome 79 C4
Bishop's Green 69 B6
Bishop's Hull 28 C2
Bishop's Itchington . . 81 B6
Bishops Lydeard 27 C6
Bishops Nympton . . . 26 C2
Bishop's Offley 112 C1
Bishop'S Stortford . . . 69 A4
Bishop's Sutton 33 B5
Bishop's Tachbrook . . 81 A6
Bishops Tawton 25 B6
Bishopsteignton 13 D4
Bishopstoke 32 D3
Bishopston 57 D5
Bishopstone
 Bucks 66 B3
 E Sus 22 B2
 Hereford 78 C2
 Swindon 45 A6
 Wilts 31 C4
Bishopstrow 30 A2
Bishop Sutton 43 D4
Bishop's Waltham . . . 33 D4
Bishopswood 28 D2
Bishop's Wood 95 A6
Bishopsworth 43 C4
Bishop Thornton . . . 147 A6
Bishopthorpe 149 C4
Bishopton
 Darl 167 C6
 Dumfries 171 D4
 N Yorks 157 D7
 Renfs 205 A4
 Warks 81 A4
Bishop Wilton 149 B6
Bishton 42 A2
Bisley
 Glos 63 C5
 Sur 34 A2
Bispham 144 C3
Bispham Green 136 B3

Bissoe 4 C2
Bisterne Close 17 A6
Bitchfield 116 C2
Bittadon 25 A6
Bittaford 7 B5
Bittering 119 D6
Bitterley 94 D3
Bitterne 32 D3
Bitteswell 98 C2
Bitton 43 C5
Bix 47 A5
Bixter 285 H5
Blaby 98 B2
Blackacre 184 C3
Blackadder West . . . 198 A2
Blackawton 8 B2
Blackborough 13 A5
Blackborough End . . 118 D3
Black Bourton 64 C3
Blackboys 36 D3
Blackbrook
 Derbys 114 A1
 Mers 136 D4
 Staffs 111 B6
Blackburn
 Aberds 245 A5
 Aberds 255 C6
 Blackburn 137 A5
 W Loth 208 D2
Black Callerton 178 C3
Black Clauchrie 181 C4
Black Corries
 Lodge 228 C1
Blackcraig 183 D5
Black Crofts 226 C4
Blackden Heath 128 B2
Blackdog 245 A6
Black Dog 12 A3
Blackfell 179 D4
Blackfield 18 A3
Blackford
 Cumb 175 B6
 Perth 218 D2
 Som 28 A4
 Som 29 C6
Blackfordby 114 D1
Blackgang 18 D3
Blackhall Colliery . . . 168 B2
Blackhall Mill 178 D3
Blackhall Rocks 168 B2
Blackham 36 C2
Blackhaugh 196 C3
Blackheath
 Essex 71 A4
 Suff 105 D5
 Sur 34 B3
 W Mid 96 C2
Black Heddon 178 B2
Blackhill
 Aberds 257 B5
 Aberds 269 D5
 Highld 258 C3
Blackhills
 Highld 253 A5
 Moray 266 D3
Blackhorse 43 B5
Blackland 44 C4
Black Lane 137 C6
Blacklaw 268 D1
Blackley 138 C1
Blacklunans 231 B5
Black Marsh 94 B1
Blackmill 40 C4
Blackmoor 33 B6
Blackmoor Gate 26 A1
Blackmore 69 C6
Blackmore End
 Essex 86 D3
 Herts 67 B6
Black Mount 228 D1
Blackness 208 C3
Blacknest 33 A6
Black Notley 70 A1
Blacko 146 C2
Black Pill 57 C6
Blackpool
 Blackpool 144 D3
 Devon 8 C2
 Pembs 55 C6
Blackpool Gate 176 B3
Blackridge 208 D1
Blackrock
 Argyll 200 B3
 Mon 60 B4
Blackrod 137 B5
Blackshaw 174 B3
Blackshaw Head 138 A2
Blacksmith's Green . . 88 A2
Blackstone 21 A5
Black Tar 55 D5

Blackthorn 65 B7
Blackthorpe 87 A5
Blacktoft 141 A6
Blacktop 245 B5
Black Torrington 11 A5
Blacktown 42 A1
Blackwall Tunnel . . . 49 A6
Blackwater
 Corn 4 C2
 Hants 34 A1
 IoW 18 C4
Blackwaterfoot 191 C4
Blackwell
 Darl 167 D5
 Derbys 129 B6
 Derbys 131 D4
 Warks 81 C5
 Worcs 96 D2
 W Sus 36 C1
Blackwood 194 B2
Blackwood
 = Coed Duon 41 B6
Blackwood Hill 129 D4
Blacon 126 C3
Bladnoch 171 B6
Bladon 65 B5
Blaenannerch 73 B5
Blaenau Ffestiniog . . 108 A2
Blaenavon 61 C4
Blaencelyn 73 A6
Blaendyryn 59 B6
Blaenffos 73 C4
Blaengarw 40 B4
Blaengwrach 59 E5
Blaen-gwynfi 40 B3
Blaenpennal 75 B5
Blaenplwyf 75 A4
Blaenporth 73 B5
Blaenrhondda 40 A4
Blaen-waun 73 D5
Blaen-y-coed 73 D6
Blaenycwm 92 D2
Blaen-y-Cwm
 Denb 109 B5
 Gwyn 108 C4
 Powys 109 C5
Blagdon
 N Som 43 D4
 Torbay 8 A2
Blagdon Hill 28 D2
Blagill 165 A5
Blaguegate 136 C3
Blaich 237 B4
Blain 235 D5
Blaina 60 C4
Blair Atholl 230 B2
Blairbeg 191 B6
Blairdaff 244 A3
Blair Drummond . . . 207 A5
Blairglas 206 B1
Blairgowrie 231 D5
Blairhall 208 B3
Blairingone 208 A2
Blairland 204 D3
Blairlogie 207 A6
Blairlomond 215 C4
Blairmore 215 D4
Blairnamarrow 243 A5
Blairquhosh 206 B3
Blair's Ferry 203 B4
Blairskaith 205 A5
Blaisdon 62 B3
Blakebrook 95 D6
Blakedown 96 D1
Blakelaw 197 C5
Blakeley 95 B6
Blakeley Lane 112 A3
Blakemere 78 C1
Blakeney
 Glos 62 C2
 Norf 120 A2
Blakenhall
 Ches E 111 A6
 W Mid 96 B2
Blakeshall 95 C6
Blakesley 82 B3
Blanchland 178 D1
Blandford Forum 16 A2
Blandford St Mary . . . 16 A2
Bland Hill 147 B6
Blanefield 205 A5
Blankney 133 C5
Blantyre 194 A1
Blar a'Chaorainn . . . 237 C5
Blaran 214 A1
Blarghour 214 A2
Blarmachfoldach . . . 237 C4
Blarnalearoch 262 A3
Blashford 17 A5
Blaston 99 B5

Blatherwycke 99 B6
Blawith 154 C1
Blaxhall 89 B4
Blaxton 141 C4
Blaydon 178 C3
Bleadon 42 D2
Bleak Hey Nook . . . 138 C3
Blean 52 C3
Bleasby
 Lincs 133 A6
 Notts 115 A3
Bleasdale 145 C5
Bleatarn 165 D5
Blebocraigs 220 C4
Bleddfa 77 A6
Bledington 64 A3
Bledlow 66 C2
Bledlow Ridge 66 D2
Blegbie 210 D1
Blencarn 165 B4
Blencogo 175 D4
Blendworth 33 D6
Blenheim Park 119 B5
Blennerhasset 175 D4
Blervie Castle 253 A6
Bletchingdon 65 B6
Bletchingley 35 A6
Bletchley
 M Keynes 83 D5
 Shrops 111 B5
Bletherston 55 B6
Bletsoe 84 B2
Blewbury 46 A3
Blickling 120 C3
Blidworth 131 D5
Blindburn 188 B1
Blindcrake 163 A4
Blindley Heath 35 B6
Blisland 10 D2
Blissford 31 D5
Bliss Gate 95 D5
Blisworth 83 B4
Blithbury 113 C4
Blitterlees 174 C4
Blockley 81 D4
Blofield 104 A4
Blofield Heath 121 D5
Blo' Norton 103 D6
Bloomfield 187 A4
Blore 113 A5
Blount's Green 113 B4
Blowick 136 B2
Bloxham 82 D1
Bloxholm 133 D5
Bloxwich 96 A2
Bloxworth 16 B2
Blubberhouses 147 B5
Blue Anchor
 Som 27 A5
 Swansea 57 C5
Blue Row 71 B4
Blundeston 105 B6
Blunham 84 B3
Blunsdon St Andrew . 45 A5
Bluntington 96 D1
Bluntisham 101 D5
Blunts 6 A2
Blyborough 142 D1
Blyford 105 D5
Blymhill 112 D2
Blyth
 Northumb 179 A5
 Notts 131 A6
Blyth Bridge 195 B6
Blythburgh 105 D5
Blythe 197 B4
Blythe Bridge 112 A3
Blyton 141 D6
Boarhills 221 C5
Boarhunt 19 A5
Boars Head 137 C4
Boars Hill 65 C5
Boarstall 66 B1
Boasley Cross 11 B5
Boath 264 C1
Boat of Garten 242 A2
Bobbing 51 C5
Bobbington 95 B6
Bobbingworth 69 C5
Bocaddon 5 B6
Bochastle 217 D6
Bocking 70 A1
Bocking
 Churchstreet 70 A1
Boddam
 Aberds 257 B6
 Shetland 285 M5
Boddington 63 A4
Bodedern 122 B3

Bodelwyddan 125 B5
Bodenham
 Hereford 78 B3
 Wilts 31 C5
Bodenham Moor 78 B3
Bodermid 106 D1
Bodewryd 122 A3
Bodfari 125 B5
Bodffordd 123 C4
Bodham 120 A3
Bodiam 37 D5
Bodicote 82 D1
Bodieve 9 D5
Bodinnick 5 B6
Bodle Street Green . . 23 A4
Bodmin 5 A5
Bodney 103 B4
Bodorgan 122 D3
Bodsham 38 A3
Boduan 106 C3
Bodymoor Heath 97 B4
Bogallan 252 A2
Bogbrae 257 C5
Bogend
 Borders 198 B1
 S Ayrs 192 B3
Boghall 208 D2
Boghead 194 B3
Bogmoor 267 C4
Bogniebrae 255 B6
Bognor Regis 20 C2
Bograxie 256 E2
Bogside 194 A3
Bogton 268 C2
Bogue 182 D4
Bohenie 239 D6
Bohortha 4 D3
Bohuntine 239 D6
Boirseam 287 F5
Bojewyan 2 B1
Bolam
 Durham 167 C4
 Northumb 178 A2
Bolberry 7 D5
Bold Heath 127 A5
Boldon 179 C5
Boldon Colliery 179 C5
Boldre 18 B2
Boldron 166 D3
Bole 132 A2
Bolehill 130 D2
Boleside 196 C3
Bolham 27 D4
Bolham Water 27 D6
Bolingey 4 B2
Bollington 129 B4
Bollington Cross . . . 129 B4
Bolney 35 D5
Bolnhurst 84 B2
Bolshan 233 C4
Bolsover 131 B4
Bolsterstone 139 D5
Bolstone 78 D3
Boltby 158 C3
Bolter End 66 D2
Bolton
 Cumb 165 C4
 E Loth 210 C2
 E Yorks 149 B6
 Gtr Man 137 C6
 Northumb 189 B4
Bolton Abbey 147 B4
Bolton Bridge 147 B4
Bolton-by-
 Bowland 146 C1
Boltonfellend 176 C3
Boltongate 175 D5
Bolton-le-Sands . . . 145 A4
Bolton Low Houses . 175 D5
Bolton-on-Swale . . . 157 B6
Bolton Percy 148 C4
Bolton Town End . . . 145 A4
Bolton upon
 Dearne 140 C2
Bolventor 10 D2
Bomere Heath 110 D3
Bonar Bridge 264 A2
Bonawe 227 C5
Bonby 142 B2
Boncath 73 C5
Bonchester Bridge . . 187 A4
Bonchurch 19 D4
Bondleigh 12 A1
Bonehill
 Devon 12 D2
 Staffs 97 A4
Bo'ness 208 B2
Bonhill 206 C1
Boningale 95 A6
Bonjedward 187 A5

Bonkle 194 A3
Bonnavoulin 225 A4
Bonnington
  Edin 208 D4
  Kent 38 B2
Bonnybank 220 D3
Bonnybridge 207 B6
Bonnykelly 268 D3
Bonnyrigg and Lasswade 209 D6
Bonnyton
  Aberds 256 C1
  Angus 220 A3
  Angus 233 C4
Bonsall 130 D2
Bonskeid House 230 B2
Bont 61 B5
Bontddu 91 A4
Bont-Dolgadfan 91 B6
Bont-goch 91 D4
Bonthorpe 135 B4
Bontnewydd
  Ceredig 75 B5
  Gwyn 107 A4
Bont-newydd 125 B5
Bont Newydd
  Gwyn 108 A2
  Gwyn 108 C2
Bontuchel 125 D5
Bonvilston 41 D5
Bon-y-maen 57 C6
Booker 66 D3
Boon 197 B4
Boosbeck 169 D4
Boot 163 D4
Booth 138 A3
Boothby Graffoe 133 D4
Boothby Pagnell 116 B2
Boothen 112 A2
Boothferry 141 A5
Boothville 83 A4
Booth Wood 138 B3
Bootle
  Cumb 153 B2
  Mers 136 D2
Booton 120 C3
Boot Street 88 C3
Boquhan 206 B3
Boraston 95 D4
Borden
  Kent 51 C5
  W Sus 34 D1
Bordley 146 A3
Bordon 33 B7
Bordon Camp 33 B6
Boreham
  Essex 70 C1
  Wilts 30 A2
Boreham Street 23 A4
Borehamwood 68 D1
Boreland
  Dumfries 185 C4
  Stirling 217 A5
Borgh
  W Isles 286 F2
  W Isles 287 F4
Borghastan 288 C3
Borgie 278 C2
Borgue
  Dumfries 172 D4
  Highld 275 B5
Borley 87 C4
Bornais 286 D3
Bornesketaig 258 A3
Borness 172 D4
Boroughbridge 148 A2
Borough Green 36 A4
Borras Head 126 D3
Borreraig 258 C1
Borrobol Lodge 274 B2
Borrowash 114 B2
Borrowby 158 C3
Borrowdale 163 C5
Borrowfield 245 C5
Borth 90 C4
Borthwickbrae 186 B3
Borthwickshiels 186 B3
Borth-y-Gest 107 C5
Borve 259 D4
Borve Lodge 287 E5
Borwick 154 D4
Bosavern 2 B1
Bosbury 79 C4
Boscastle 10 B2
Boscombe
  BCP 17 B5
  Wilts 31 B6
Boscoppa 5 B5
Bosham 19 A7
Bosherston 55 E5
Boskenna 2 C2
Bosley 129 C4
Bossall 149 A6
Bossiney 9 C6
Bossingham 38 A3
Bossington 26 A3
Bostock Green 127 C6
Boston 117 A6
Boston Long Hedges 117 A6
Boston Spa 148 C3
Boston West 117 A5
Boswinger 5 C4
Botallack 2 B1
Botany Bay 68 D2
Botcherby 175 C7
Botcheston 98 A1
Botesdale 103 D6
Bothal 179 A4
Bothamsall 131 B6
Bothel 163 A4
Bothenhampton 15 B4
Bothwell 194 A2
Botley
  Bucks 67 C4
  Hants 32 D4
  Oxon 65 C5
Botolph Claydon 66 A2
Botolphs 21 B4
Bottacks 263 D6
Bottesford
  Leics 115 B6
  N Lincs 141 C6
Bottisham 86 A1
Bottlesford 45 D5
Bottom Boat 139 A6
Bottomcraig 220 B3
Bottom House 129 D5
Bottom of Hutton 136 A3
Bottom o' th' Moor 137 B5
Botusfleming 6 A3
Botwnnog 106 C2
Bough Beech 36 B2
Boughrood 77 D5
Boughspring 62 D1
Boughton
  Norf 102 A2
  Northants 83 A4
  Notts 131 C6
Boughton Aluph 38 A2
Boughton Lees 38 A2
Boughton Malherbe 37 B6
Boughton Monchelsea 37 A5
Boughton Street 52 D2
Boulby 169 D5
Boulden 94 C3
Boulmer 189 B5
Boulston 55 C5
Boultenstone 243 A7
Boultham 133 C4
Bourn 85 B5
Bourne 116 C3
Bourne End
  Bucks 48 A1
  C Beds 83 C6
  Herts 67 C5
Bournemouth 17 B4
Bournes Green
  Glos 63 C5
  Southend 51 A6
Bournheath 96 D2
Bournmoor 179 D5
Bournville 96 C3
Bourton
  Dorset 30 B1
  N Som 42 C2
  Oxon 45 A6
  Shrops 94 B3
Bourton on Dunsmore 98 D1
Bourton on the Hill 81 D4
Bourton-on-the-Water 64 A2
Bousd 223 A5
Boustead Hill 175 C5
Bouth 154 C2
Bouthwaite 157 D5
Boveney 48 B2
Boverton 41 E4
Bovey Tracey 12 D3
Bovingdon 67 C5
Bovingdon Green
  Bucks 47 A6
  Herts 67 C5
Bovinger 69 C5
Bovington Camp 16 C2
Bow
  Borders 196 B3
  Devon 12 A2
Bow *continued*
  Orkney 283 H4
Bowbank 166 C2
Bow Brickhill 83 D6
Bowburn 167 B6
Bowcombe 18 C3
Bowd 13 B6
Bowden
  Borders 197 C4
  Devon 8 C2
Bowden Hill 44 C3
Bowderdale 155 A5
Bowdon 128 A2
Bower 177 A5
Bowerchalke 31 C4
Bowerhill 44 C3
Bower Hinton 29 D4
Bowermadden 280 B4
Bowers Gifford 51 A4
Bowershall 208 A3
Bowertower 280 B4
Bowes 166 D2
Bowgreave 145 C4
Bowgreen 128 A2
Bowhill 186 A3
Bowhouse 174 B3
Bowland Bridge 154 C3
Bowley 78 B3
Bowlhead Green 34 C2
Bowling
  W Dunb 205 A4
  W Yorks 147 D5
Bowling Bank 110 A2
Bowling Green 79 B6
Bowmanstead 154 B2
Bowmore 200 C3
Bowness-on-Solway 175 B5
Bowness-on-Windermere 154 B3
Bow of Fife 220 C3
Bowsden 198 B3
Bowside Lodge 279 B4
Bowston 154 B3
Bow Street 90 D4
Bowthorpe 104 A2
Box
  Glos 63 C4
  Wilts 44 C2
Boxbush 62 B3
Box End 84 C2
Boxford
  Suff 87 C5
  W Berks 46 B2
Boxgrove 20 B2
Boxley 37 A5
Boxmoor 67 C5
Boxted
  Essex 87 D6
  Suff 87 B4
Boxted Cross 87 D6
Boxted Heath 87 D6
Boxworth 85 A5
Boxworth End 85 A5
Boyden Gate 53 C4
Boylestone 113 B5
Boyndie 268 C1
Boynton 151 A4
Boysack 233 D4
Boyton
  Corn 10 B4
  Suff 89 C4
  Wilts 30 B3
Boyton Cross 69 C6
Boyton End 86 C3
Bozeat 83 B6
Braaid 152 D3
Braal Castle 280 B3
Brabling Green 88 A3
Brabourne 38 A2
Brabourne Lees 38 A2
Brabster 281 B5
Bracadale 246 A2
Bracara 235 A6
Braceborough 116 D3
Bracebridge 133 C4
Bracebridge Heath 133 C4
Bracebridge Low Fields 133 C4
Braceby 116 B3
Bracewell 146 C2
Brackenfield 130 D3
Brackenthwaite
  Cumb 175 D5
  N Yorks 148 B1
Bracklesham 19 B7
Brackletter 239 D5
Brackley
  Argyll 202 D2
  Northants 82 D2
Brackloch 270 B4
Bracknell 47 C6
Braco 218 D3
Bracobrae 267 D6
Bracon Ash 104 B2
Bracorina 235 A6
Bradbourne 130 D2
Bradbury 167 C6
Bradda 152 E1
Bradden 82 C3
Braddock 5 A6
Bradeley 128 D3
Bradenham
  Bucks 66 D3
  Norf 103 A5
Bradenstoke 44 B4
Bradfield
  Essex 88 D2
  Norf 121 B4
  W Berks 47 B4
Bradfield Combust 87 B4
Bradfield Green 128 D1
Bradfield Heath 71 A5
Bradfield St Clare 87 B5
Bradfield St George 87 A5
Bradford
  Corn 10 D2
  Derbys 130 C2
  Devon 11 A5
  Northumb 199 C5
  W Yorks 147 D5
Bradford Abbas 29 D5
Bradford Leigh 44 C2
Bradford-on-Avon 44 C2
Bradford-on-Tone 28 C1
Bradford Peverell 15 B6
Brading 19 C5
Bradley
  Derbys 113 A6
  Hants 33 A5
  NE Lincs 143 C4
  Staffs 112 D2
  W Mid 96 B2
  W Yorks 139 A4
Bradley Green 80 A2
Bradley in the Moors 113 A4
Bradley Stoke 43 A5
Bradlow 79 D5
Bradmore
  Notts 114 B3
  W Mid 96 B1
Bradninch 13 A5
Bradnop 129 D5
Bradpole 15 B4
Bradshaw
  Gtr Man 137 B6
  W Yorks 138 B3
Bradstone 11 C4
Bradwall Green 128 C2
Bradway 130 A3
Bradwell
  Derbys 129 A6
  Essex 70 A2
  M Keynes 83 D5
  Norf 105 A6
  Staffs 112 A2
Bradwell Grove 64 C3
Bradwell on Sea 71 C4
Bradwell Waterside 70 C3
Bradworthy 24 D4
Bradworthy Cross 24 D4
Brae
  Dumfries 173 A6
  Highld 261 B5
  Highld 272 D2
  Shetland 284 G5
Braeantra 264 C1
Braedownie 231 A6
Braefield 251 C6
Braegrum 219 B5
Braehead
  Dumfries 171 B6
  Orkney 282 C5
  Orkney 283 G6
  S Lanark 194 C3
  S Lanark 195 A4
Braehead of Lunan 233 C4
Braehoulland 284 F4
Braehungie 275 A5
Braelangwell Lodge 263 A7
Braemar 243 C4
Braemore
  Highld 262 C3
  Highld 275 A4
Brae of Achnahaird 270 C3
Brae Roy Lodge 240 C1
Braeside 204 A2
Braes of Enzie 267 D4
Braeswick 282 D7
Braewick 285 H5
Brafferton
  Darl 167 C5
  N Yorks 158 D3
Brafield-on-the-Green 83 B5
Bragar 288 C3
Bragbury End 68 A2
Bragleenmore 226 D4
Braichmelyn 123 D6
Braid 209 D5
Braides 144 B4
Braidley 156 C4
Braidwood 194 B3
Braigo 200 B2
Brailsford 113 A6
Brainshaugh 189 C5
Braintree 70 A1
Braiseworth 104 D2
Braishfield 32 C2
Braithwaite
  Cumb 163 B5
  S Yorks 140 B4
  W Yorks 147 C4
Braithwell 140 D3
Bramber 21 A4
Bramcote
  Notts 114 B3
  Warks 97 C7
Bramdean 33 C5
Bramerton 104 A3
Bramfield
  Herts 68 B2
  Suff 105 D4
Bramford 88 C2
Bramhall 128 A3
Bramham 148 C3
Bramhope 147 C6
Bramley
  Hants 47 D4
  Sur 34 B3
  S Yorks 140 D2
  W Yorks 147 D6
Bramling 53 D4
Brampford Speke 13 B4
Brampton
  Cambs 100 D4
  Cumb 165 C4
  Cumb 176 C3
  Derbys 130 B3
  Hereford 78 D2
  Lincs 132 B3
  Norf 120 C4
  Suff 105 C5
  S Yorks 140 C2
Brampton Abbotts 62 A2
Brampton Ash 99 C4
Brampton Bryan 94 D1
Brampton en le Morthen 131 A4
Bramshall 113 B4
Bramshaw 31 D6
Bramshill 47 C5
Bramshott 34 C1
Branault 235 D4
Brancaster 119 A4
Brancaster Staithe 119 A4
Brancepeth 167 B5
Branch End 178 C2
Branchill 266 D1
Branderburgh 266 B3
Brandesburton 151 C4
Brandeston 88 A3
Brand Green 62 A3
Brandhill 94 D2
Brandis Corner 11 A5
Brandiston 120 C3
Brandon
  Durham 167 B5
  Lincs 116 A2
  Northumb 188 B3
  Suff 102 C3
  Warks 97 D7
Brandon Bank 102 C2
Brandon Creek 102 B2
Brandon Parva 104 A1
Brandsby 159 D4
Brandy Wharf 142 D2
Brane 2 C2
Bran End 69 A6
Branksome 17 B4
Branksome Park 17 B4
Bransby 132 B3
Branscombe 14 C1
Bransford 79 B5
Bransgore 17 B5
Branshill 208 A1
Bransholme 151 D4
Branson's Cross 96 D3
Branston
  Leics 115 C6
  Lincs 133 C5
  Staffs 113 C6
Branston Booths 133 C5
Branstone 19 C4
Bransty 162 C2
Brant Broughton 133 D4
Brantham 88 D2
Branthwaite
  Cumb 162 B3
  Cumb 163 A5
Brantingham 142 A1
Branton
  Northumb 188 B3
  S Yorks 140 C4
Branxholme 186 B3
Branxholm Park 186 B3
Branxton 198 C2
Brassey Green 127 C5
Brassington 130 D2
Brasted 36 A2
Brasted Chart 36 A2
Brathens 244 C3
Bratoft 135 C4
Brattleby 133 A4
Bratton
  Telford 111 D5
  Wilts 44 D3
Bratton Clovelly 11 B5
Bratton Fleming 26 B1
Bratton Seymour 29 C6
Braughing 68 A3
Braunston 82 A2
Braunstone Town 98 A2
Braunston-in-Rutland 99 A5
Braunton 25 B5
Brawby 159 D6
Brawl 279 B4
Brawlbin 279 C6
Bray 48 B2
Braybrooke 99 C4
Braye 7
Brayford 26 B1
Bray Shop 10 D4
Braystones 162 D3
Braythorn 147 C6
Brayton 149 D5
Bray Wick 48 B1
Brazacott 10 B3
Breach 51 C5
Breachacha Castle 223 B4
Breachwood Green 67 A6
Breacleit 288 D2
Breaden Heath 110 B3
Breadsall 114 B1
Breadstone 62 C3
Breage 3 C4
Breakachy 251 B6
Bream 62 C2
Breamore 31 D5
Brean 42 D1
Breanais 287 B4
Brearton 148 A2
Breascleit 288 D3
Breaston 114 B2
Brechfa 58 B2
Brechin 232 B3
Breckan 283 G3
Breck of Cruan 282 F4
Breckrey 259 B5
Brecon
  =*Aberhonddu* 60 A2
Bredbury 138 D2
Brede 23 A6
Bredenbury 79 B4
Bredfield 88 B3
Bredgar 51 C5
Bredhurst 51 C4
Bredicot 80 B2
Bredon 80 D2
Bredon's Norton 80 D2
Bredwardine 78 C1
Breedon on the Hill 114 C2
Breibhig
  W Isles 286 G2
  W Isles 288 D5
Breich 208 D2
Breightmet 137 C6
Breighton 149 D6
Breinton 78 D2
Breinton Common 78 C2
Breiwick 285 J6
Bremhill 44 B3
Bremirehoull 285 L6
Brenchley 37 B4

Brendon 26 A2
Brenkley 179 B4
Brent Eleigh 87 C5
Brentford 49 B4
Brentingby 115 D5
Brent Knoll 42 D2
Brent Pelham 85 D6
Brentwood 69 D5
Brenzett 38 C2
Brereton 113 D4
Brereton Green 128 C2
Brereton Heath 128 C3
Bressingham 104 C1
Bretby 113 D6
Bretford 98 D1
Bretforton 80 C3
Bretherdale Head . .155 A4
Bretherton 136 A3
Brettabister 285 H6
Brettenham
  Norf 103 C5
  Suff 87 B5
Bretton
  Derbys 130 B2
  Flint 126 C3
Brewer Street. 35 A6
Brewlands Bridge . .231 B5
Brewood 96 A1
Briach 266 D1
Briants Puddle 16 B2
Brick End 69 A5
Brickendon 68 C3
Bricket Wood 67 C6
Bricklehampton 80 C2
Bride 152 A4
Bridekirk 163 A4
Bridell 73 B4
Bridestowe 11 C6
Brideswell 255 C6
Bridford 12 C3
Bridfordmills 12 C3
Bridge 52 D3
Bridge End 116 B4
Bridgefoot
  Angus 220 A3
  Cumb 162 B3
Bridge Green 85 D6
Bridgehampton 29 C5
Bridge Hewick 158 D2
Bridgehill 178 D2
Bridgemary 19 A4
Bridgemont 129 A5
Bridgend
  Aberds 244 A4
  Aberds 255 C6
  Angus 232 B3
  Argyll 190 B3
  Argyll 200 B3
  Argyll 214 C1
  Cumb 164 D1
  Fife 220 C3
  Moray 255 C4
  N Lanark 207 C4
  Pembs 73 B4
  W Loth 208 C3
Bridgend =Pen-y-bont
  ar Ogwr 40 D4
Bridgend of
  Lintrathen 231 C6
Bridge of Alford . . .244 A2
Bridge of Allan 207 A5
Bridge of Avon 254 C2
Bridge of Awe 227 D5
Bridge of Balgie . . .229 D4
Bridge of Cally 231 C5
Bridge of Canny . . .244 C3
Bridge of Craigisla .231 C6
Bridge of Dee 173 C5
Bridge of Don 245 A6
Bridge of Dun 233 C4
Bridge of Dye 244 D3
Bridge of Earn 219 C6
Bridge of Ericht 229 C4
Bridge of Feugh 245 C4
Bridge of Forss 279 B6
Bridge of Gairn 243 C6
Bridge of Gaur 229 C4
Bridge of Muchalls .245 C5
Bridge of Oich 240 B1
Bridge of Orchy 216 A2
Bridge of Waith 282 F3
Bridge of Walls 285 H4
Bridge of Weir 204 B3
Bridgerule 10 A3
Bridges 94 B1
Bridge Sollers 78 C2
Bridge Street 87 C4
Bridgeton 205 B6

Bridgetown
  Corn 10 C4
  Som 27 B4
Bridge Trafford 127 B4
Bridge Yate 43 B5
Bridgham 103 C5
Bridgnorth 95 B5
Bridgtown 96 A2
Bridgwater 28 B2
Bridlington 151 A4
Bridport 15 B4
Bridstow 62 A1
Brierfield 146 D2
Brierley
  Glos 62 B2
  Hereford 78 B2
  S Yorks 140 B2
Brierley Hill 96 C2
Briery Hill 60 C3
Brigg 142 C2
Briggswath 160 A2
Brigham
  Cumb 162 A3
  E Yorks 150 B3
Brighouse 139 A4
Brighstone 18 C3
Brightgate 130 D2
Brighthampton 65 C4
Brightling 37 D4
Brightlingsea 71 B4
Brighton
  Brighton 21 B6
  Corn 4 B4
Brighton Hill 33 A5
Brightons 208 C2
Brightwalton 46 B2
Brightwell 88 C3
Brightwell Baldwin . .66 D1
Brightwell cum
  Sotwell 65 D6
Brignall 166 D3
Brig o'Turk 217 D6
Brigsley 143 C4
Brigsteer 154 C3
Brigstock 99 C6
Brill 66 B1
Brilley 77 C6
Brimaston 55 B5
Brimfield 78 A3
Brimington 131 B4
Brimley 12 D2
Brimpsfield 63 B5
Brimpton 46 C3
Brims 283 J3
Brimscombe 63 C4
Brinacory 235 A6
Brind 149 D6
Brindister
  Shetland 285 H4
  Shetland 285 K6
Brindle 137 A5
Brindley Ford 128 D3
Brineton 112 D2
Bringhurst 99 B5
Brington 100 D2
Brinian 282 E5
Briningham 120 B2
Brinkhill 134 B3
Brinkley 86 B2
Brinklow 98 D1
Brinkworth 44 A4
Brinmore 252 D2
Brinscall 137 A5
Brinsea 42 C3
Brinsley 114 A2
Brinsop 78 C2
Brinsworth 131 A4
Brinton 120 B2
Brisco 175 C7
Brisley 119 C6
Brislington 43 B5
Bristol 43 B4
Briston 120 B2
Britannia 138 A1
Britford 31 C5
Brithdir 91 A5
British Legion
  Village 37 A5
Briton Ferry 40 B2
Britwell Salome 66 D1
Brixham 8 B3
Brixton
  Devon 7 B4
  London 49 B6
Brixton Deverill 30 B2
Brixworth 99 D4
Brize Norton 64 C4
Broad Blunsdon 64 D2
Broadbottom 138 D2

Broadbridge 19 A7
Broadbridge Heath. . .35 C4
Broad Campden 81 D4
Broad Chalke 31 C4
Broadclyst 13 B4
Broadfield
  Gtr Man 138 B1
  Lancs 136 A4
  Pembs 56 B1
  W Sus 35 C5
Broadford 247 B5
Broadford Bridge 34 D3
Broad Green
  C Beds 83 C6
  Essex 70 A2
  Worcs 79 B5
Broadhaugh 186 C3
Broadhaven 281 C5
Broad Haven 55 C4
Broadheath 128 A2
Broad Heath 79 A4
Broadhembury. 13 A6
Broadhempston. 8 A2
Broad Hill 102 D1
Broad Hinton 45 B5
Broadholme
  Derbys 114 A1
  Lincs 132 B3
Broadland Row 23 A6
Broadlay 56 B3
Broad Laying 46 C2
Broadley
  Lancs 138 B1
  Moray 267 C4
Broadley Common . . .68 C4
Broad Marston 80 C4
Broadmayne 16 C1
Broadmeadows 196 C3
Broadmere 33 A5
Broadmoor 55 D6
Broadoak 52 C3
Broad Oak
  Carms 58 C2
  Cumb 153 A2
  Dorset 14 B4
  Dorset 30 D1
  E Sus 23 A6
  E Sus 36 D4
  Hereford 61 A6
  Mers 136 D4
Broadrashes 267 D5
Broadsea 269 C4
Broadstairs 53 C5
Broadstone
  BCP 17 B4
  Shrops 94 C3
Broad Street 37 A6
Broad Street Green. . .70 C2
Broad Town 45 B4
Broadtown Lane 45 B4
Broadwas 79 B5
Broadwater
  Herts 68 A2
  W Sus 21 B4
Broadway
  Carms 56 B2
  Pembs 55 C4
  Som 28 D3
  Suff 105 D4
  Worcs 80 D3
Broadwell
  Glos 62 B1
  Glos 64 A3
  Oxon 64 C3
  Warks 82 A1
Broadwell House . . .177 D7
Broadwey 15 C6
Broadwindsor 14 A4
Broadwood Kelly 11 A7
Broadwoodwidger . .11 C5
Brobury 78 C1
Brochel 248 B2
Brochloch 182 C3
Brochroy 227 C5
Brockamin 79 B5
Brockbridge 33 D5
Brockdam 189 A4
Brockdish 104 D3
Brockenhurst 18 A2
Brocketsbrae 194 C3
Brockford Street 88 A2
Brockhall 82 A3
Brockham 35 B4
Brockhampton
  Glos 63 A6
  Hereford 78 D3
Brockholes 139 B4
Brockhurst
  Derbys 130 C3
  Hants 19 A5

Brocklebank 175 D6
Brocklesby 142 B3
Brockley 42 C3
Brockley Green 87 B4
Brockleymoor 164 B2
Brockton
  Shrops 93 A7
  Shrops 94 B3
  Shrops 94 C1
  Shrops 95 A5
  Telford 111 D6
Brockweir 62 C1
Brockwood 33 C5
Brockworth 63 B4
Brocton 112 D3
Brodick 191 B6
Brodsworth 140 C3
Brogaig 259 B4
Brogborough 83 D6
Brokenborough 44 A3
Broken Cross
  Ches E. 128 B3
  Ches W 128 B1
Bromborough 126 A3
Brome 104 D2
Brome Street 104 D2
Bromeswell 88 B4
Bromfield
  Cumb 175 D4
  Shrops 94 D2
Bromham
  Bedford 84 B2
  Wilts 44 C3
Bromley
  London 49 C7
  W Mid 96 C2
Bromley Common . . .49 C7
Bromley Green 38 B1
Brompton
  Medway 51 C4
  N Yorks 158 B2
  N Yorks 160 C3
Brompton-on-
  Swale 157 B6
Brompton Ralph 27 B5
Brompton Regis 27 B4
Bromsash 62 A2
Bromsberrow Heath. .79 D5
Bromsgrove 96 D2
Bromyard 79 B4
Bromyard Downs 79 B4
Bronaber 108 B2
Bronant 75 B5
Bronbydd Arms 73 D7
Bronnant 75 B5
Bronllys 77 D5
Bronnant 75 B5
Bronwydd Arms 73 D7
Bronydd 77 C6
Brongarth 110 B1
Brook
  Carms 56 B2
  Hants 32 C2
  Hants 32 D1
  IoW 18 C2
  Kent 38 A2
  Sur 34 B3
  Sur 34 C2
Brooke
  Norf 104 B3
  Rutland 99 A5
Brookenby 143 D4
Brookend 62 D1
Brook End 84 A2
Brookfield 205 B4
Brook Hill 31 D6
Brookhouse 145 A4
Brookhouse Green . .128 C3
Brookland 38 C1
Brooklands
  Dumfries 173 A6
  Gtr Man 137 D6
  Shrops 111 A4
Brookmans Park 68 C2
Brooks 93 B5
Brooks Green 35 D4
Brook Street
  Kent 36 B3
  Kent 38 B1
  W Sus 35 D6
Brookthorpe 63 B4
Brookville 102 B3
Brookwood 34 A2
Broom
  C Beds 84 C3
  S Yorks 140 D2
  Warks 80 B3
  Worcs 96 D2
Broome
  Norf 105 B4
  Shrops 94 C2

Broomedge 128 A2
Broome Park 189 B4
Broomer's Corner. . . .35 D4
Broomfield
  Aberds 257 C4
  Essex 69 B7
  Kent 37 A6
  Kent 52 C3
  Som 28 B2
Broomfleet 141 A6
Broom Green 120 C1
Broomhall
  Ches E. 111 A5
  Windsor 48 C2
Broomhaugh 178 C2
Broomhill
  Norf 102 A2
  Northumb 189 C5
  S Yorks 140 C2
Broom Hill 17 A4
Broomholm 121 B5
Broomley 178 C2
Broompark 167 A5
Broom's Green 79 D5
Broomy Lodge 31 D6
Brora 274 D3
Broseley 95 A4
Brotherhouse Bar . . .117 D5
Brotherstone 197 C5
Brothertoft 117 A5
Brotherton 140 A2
Brotton 169 D4
Broubster 279 B6
Brough
  Cumb 165 D5
  Derbys 130 A1
  E Yorks 142 A1
  Highld 280 A4
  Notts 132 D3
  Orkney 282 F4
  Shetland 284 F6
  Shetland 284 F7
  Shetland 284 G7
  Shetland 285 H6
  Shetland 285 J7
Broughall 111 A4
Brough Lodge 284 D7
Brough Sowerby 165 D5
Broughton
  Borders 195 C6
  Cambs 101 D4
  Flint 126 C3
  Hants 32 B2
  Lancs 145 D5
  M Keynes 83 D5
  N Lincs 142 C1
  Northants 99 D5
  N Yorks 146 B3
  N Yorks 159 D6
  Orkney 282 C5
  Oxon 81 D7
  V Glam 40 D4
Broughton Astley 98 B2
Broughton Beck 154 C1
Broughton
  Common 44 C2
Broughton Gifford . . .44 C2
Broughton Hackett. . .80 B2
Broughton in
  Furness 153 B3
Broughton Mills. . . .153 A3
Broughton Moor 162 A3
Broughton Park 138 C1
Broughton Poggs 64 C3
Broughtown 282 C7
Broughty Ferry 221 A4
Browhouses 175 B5
Browland 285 H4
Brown Candover 33 B4
Brown Edge
  Lancs 136 B2
  Staffs 129 D4
Brown Heath 127 C4
Brownhill
  Aberds 256 B1
  Aberds 256 B3
  Blackburn 145 D6
  Shrops 110 C3
Brownhills
  Fife 221 C5
  W Mid 96 A3
Brownlow 128 C3
Brownlow Heath 128 C3
Brownmuir 233 A5
Brown's End 79 D5
Brownshill 63 C4
Brownston 7 B6
Brownyside 189 A4
Broxa 160 B3
Broxbourne 68 C3

Broxburn
  E Loth 210 C2
  W Loth 208 C3
Broxholme 133 B4
Broxted 69 A5
Broxton 127 D4
Broxwood 78 B1
Broyle Side 22 A2
Brù 288 C4
Bruairnis 286 F3
Bruan 275 A6
Bruar Lodge 230 A2
Brucehill 206 C1
Bruera 127 C4
Bruern Abbey 64 A3
Bruichladdich 200 B2
Bruisyard 88 A4
Brumby 141 C6
Brund 129 C6
Brundall 104 A4
Brundish 88 A3
Brundish Street 104 D3
Brunery 235 C6
Brunshaw 146 D2
Brunswick Village . . .179 B4
Bruntcliffe 139 A5
Bruntingthorpe 98 B3
Brunton
  Fife 220 B3
  Northumb 189 A5
  Wilts 45 D6
Brushford
  Devon 12 A1
  Som 27 C4
Bruton 29 B6
Bryanston 16 A2
Brydekirk 175 A4
Bryher Scilly 2 E3
Brymbo 126 D2
Brympton 29 D5
Bryn
  Carms 57 B5
  Gtr Man 137 C4
  Neath 40 B3
  Shrops 93 C6
Brynamman 59 D4
Brynberian 72 C4
Brynbryddan 40 B2
Brynbuga =Usk 61 C5
Bryncae 41 C4
Bryncethin 40 C4
Bryncir 107 B4
Bryn-coch 40 B2
Bryncroes 106 C2
Bryncrug 90 B4
Bryn Du 122 C3
Bryneglwys 109 A6
Brynford 126 B1
Bryn Gates 137 C4
Bryn-glas 124 C3
Bryn Golau 41 C4
Bryngwran 122 C3
Bryngwyn
  Ceredig 73 B5
  Mon 61 C5
  Powys 77 C5
Brynhenllan 72 C3
Brynhoffnant 73 A6
Brynithel 41 A7
Bryn-Iwan 73 C6
Brynmawr 60 B3
Bryn-mawr 106 C2
Brynmenyn 40 C4
Brynmill 57 C6
Brynna 41 C4
Bryn-nantllech 125 C4
Bryn-penarth 93 A5
Brynrefail
  Anglesey 123 B4
  Gwyn 123 D5
Bryn Rhyd-yr-
  Arian 125 C4
Brynsadler 41 C5
Bryn Saith
  Marchog 125 D5
Brynsiencyn 123 D4
Bryn Sion 91 A5
Brynteg
  Anglesey 123 B4
  Ceredig 58 A1
Bryn-y-gwenin 61 B5
Bryn-y-maen 124 B3
Bryn-yr-eryr 106 B3
Buaile nam Bodach 286 F3
Bualintur 246 B3
Buarthmeini 108 B3
Bubbenhall 97 D6
Bubwith 149 D6
Buccleuch 185 A6
Buchanhaven 257 B6

Buchanty 218 B4
Buchlyvie 206 A3
Buckabank 164 A1
Buckden
  Cambs 84 B5
  N Yorks 156 D3
Buckenham 105 A4
Buckerell 13 A6
Buckfast 7 A6
Buckfastleigh 7 A6
Buckhaven 209 A6
Buckholm 196 C3
Buckholt 61 B7
Buckhorn Weston . . 30 C1
Buckhurst Hill 68 D4
Buckie 267 C5
Buckies 280 B5
Buckingham 82 D3
Buckland
  Bucks 66 B3
  Devon 7 C5
  Glos 80 D3
  Hants 18 B2
  Herts 85 D5
  Kent 39 A5
  Oxon 64 D4
  Sur 35 A5
Buckland Brewer . . . 25 C5
Buckland Common . . 67 C4
Buckland Dinham . . . 43 D6
Buckland Filleigh . . . 11 A5
Buckland in the
  Moor 12 D2
Buckland
  Monachorum 6 A3
Buckland Newton . . 15 A6
Buckland St Mary . . 28 D2
Bucklebury 46 B3
Bucklegate 117 B6
Bucklerheads 221 A4
Bucklers Hard 18 B3
Bucklesham 88 C3
Buckley =Bwcle . . 126 C2
Bucklow Hill 128 A2
Buckminster 116 C1
Bucknall
  Lincs 133 C6
  Stoke 112 A3
Bucknell
  Oxon 65 A6
  Shrops 94 D1
Buckpool 267 C5
Bucksburn 245 B5
Buck's Cross 24 C4
Bucks Green 34 C3
Buckshaw Village . . 137 A4
Bucks Horn Oak . . . 33 A7
Buckskin 47 D4
Buck's Mills 25 C4
Buckton
  E Yorks 161 D5
  Hereford 94 D1
  Northumb 199 C4
Buckworth 100 D3
Budbrooke 81 A5
Budby 131 C6
Budd's Titson 10 A3
Bude 10 A3
Budlake 13 B4
Budle 199 C5
Budleigh Salterton . . 13 C5
Budock Water 4 D2
Buerton 111 A5
Buffler's Holt 82 D3
Bugbrooke 82 B3
Buglawton 128 C3
Bugle 5 B5
Bugley 30 A2
Bugthorpe 149 B6
Buildwas 95 A4
Builth Road 76 B4
Builth Wells
  =Llanfair-ym-Muallt . 76 B4
Buirgh 287 E5
Bulby 116 C3
Bulcote 115 A4
Buldoo 279 B5
Bulford 31 A5
Bulford Camp 31 A5
Bulkeley 127 D5
Bulkington
  Warks 97 C6
  Wilts 44 D3
Bulkworthy 25 D4
Bullamoor 158 B2
Bullbridge 130 D3
Bullbrook 48 C1
Bulley 62 B3
Bullgill 162 A3
Bull Hill 18 B2

Bullington
  Hants 32 A3
  Lincs 133 B5
Bull's Green 68 B2
Bullwood 203 A6
Bulmer
  Essex 87 C4
  N Yorks 149 A5
Bulmer Tye 87 D4
Bulphan 50 A3
Bulverhythe 23 B5
Bulwark 257 B4
Bulwell 114 A3
Bulwick 99 B6
Bumble's Green 68 C4
Bun Abhainn
  Eadarra 288 G2
Bunacaimb 235 B5
Bun a'Mhuillin . . . 286 E3
Bunarkaig 239 D5
Bunbury 127 D5
Bunbury Heath . . . 127 D5
Bunchrew 252 B2
Bundalloch 249 D5
Buness 284 C8
Bunessan 224 D2
Bungay 104 C4
Bunkers Hill 65 B5
Bunker's Hill
  Lincs 133 B4
  Lincs 134 D2
Bunloit 251 D7
Bun Loyne 239 B6
Bunnahabhain . . . 201 A4
Bunny 114 C3
Buntait 251 C5
Buntingford 68 A3
Bunwell 104 B2
Burbage
  Derbys 129 B5
  Leics 98 B1
  Wilts 45 C6
Burchett's Green . . . 47 A6
Burcombe 31 B4
Burcot 65 D6
Burcott 66 A3
Burdon 179 D5
Bures 87 D5
Bures Green 87 D5
Burford
  Ches E 127 D6
  Oxon 64 B3
  Shrops 78 A3
Burg 224 B2
Burgar 282 E4
Burgate
  Hants 31 D5
  Suff 104 D1
Burgess Hill 21 A6
Burgh 88 B3
Burgh by Sands . . . 175 C6
Burgh Castle 105 A5
Burghclere 46 C2
Burghead 266 C2
Burghfield 47 C4
Burghfield Common . 47 C4
Burghfield Hill 47 C4
Burgh Heath 35 A5
Burghill 78 C2
Burgh le Marsh . . . 135 C5
Burgh Muir 256 D2
Burgh next
  Aylsham 120 C4
Burgh on Bain . . . 134 A2
Burgh St Margaret . . 121 D6
Burgh St Peter . . . 105 B5
Burghwallis 140 B3
Burham 51 C4
Buriton 33 C6
Burland 127 D6
Burlawn 9 D5
Burleigh 48 C1
Burlescombe 27 C5
Burleston 16 B1
Burley
  Hants 17 A6
  Rutland 116 D1
  W Yorks 148 D1
Burleydam 111 A5
Burley Gate 78 C3
Burley in
  Wharfedale 147 C5
Burley Lodge 17 A6
Burley Street 17 A6
Burlingjobb 77 B6
Burlow 22 A3
Burlton 110 C3
Burmarsh 38 B2
Burmington 81 D5
Burn 140 A3

Burnaston 113 B6
Burnbank 194 A2
Burnby 150 C1
Burncross 139 D6
Burneside 154 B4
Burness 282 C7
Burneston 157 C7
Burnett 43 C5
Burnfoot
  Borders 186 B3
  Borders 186 B4
  E Ayrs 182 B2
  Perth 219 D4
Burnham
  Bucks 48 A2
  N Lincs 142 B2
Burnham Deepdale 119 A5
Burnham Green 68 B2
Burnham Market . . . 119 A5
Burnham Norton . . . 119 A5
Burnham-on-
  Crouch 70 D3
Burnham-on-Sea . . 28 A3
Burnham Overy
  Staithe 119 A5
Burnham Overy
  Town 119 A5
Burnham Thorpe . . 119 A5
Burnhead
  Dumfries 183 C6
  S Ayrs 181 A4
Burnhervie 245 A4
Burnhill Green 95 A5
Burnhope 167 A4
Burnhouse 204 C3
Burniston 160 B4
Burnlee 139 C4
Burnley 146 D2
Burnley Lane . . . 146 D2
Burnmouth 211 D6
Burn of Cambus . . 218 D2
Burnopfield 178 D3
Burnsall 147 A4
Burnside
  Angus 232 C3
  E Ayrs 182 A3
  Fife 219 D6
  Shetland 284 F4
  S Lanark 205 B6
  W Loth 208 C3
Burnside of
  Duntrune 220 A4
Burnswark 175 A4
Burntcommon 34 A3
Burnt Heath 130 B2
Burnthouse 4 D2
Burnt Houses . . . 166 C4
Burntisland 209 B5
Burnton 182 B2
Burntwood 96 A3
Burnt Yates 147 A6
Burnwynd 208 D4
Burpham
  Sur 34 A3
  W Sus 20 B3
Burradon
  Northumb 188 C2
  T&W 179 B4
Burrafirth 284 B8
Burraland
  Shetland 284 F5
  Shetland 285 J4
Burras 3 B4
Burravoe
  Shetland 284 F7
  Shetland 284 G5
Burray Village 283 H5
Burrells 165 D4
Burrelton 220 A2
Burridge
  Devon 25 B6
  Hants 32 D4
Burrill 157 C6
Burringham 141 C6
Burrington
  Devon 26 D1
  Hereford 94 D2
  N Som 42 D3
Burrough Green . . . 86 B2
Burrough on the
  Hill 115 D5
Burrow-bridge . . . 28 C3
Burrowhill 48 C2
Burry 57 C4
Burry Green 57 C4
Burry Port
  =Porth Tywyn . . . 57 B4
Burscough 136 B3
Burscough Bridge . . 136 B3
Bursea 149 D7

Burshill 150 C3
Bursledon 18 A3
Burslem 112 A2
Burstall 88 C1
Burstock 14 A4
Burston
  Norf 104 C2
  Staffs 112 B3
Burstow 35 B6
Burstwick 143 A4
Burtersett 156 C2
Burtle 28 A3
Burton
  BCP 17 B5
  Ches W 126 B3
  Ches W 127 C5
  Lincs 133 B4
  Northumb 199 C5
  Pembs 55 D5
  Som 28 A1
  Wilts 44 B2
Burton Agnes . . . 151 A4
Burton Bradstock . . 15 C4
Burton Dassett . . . 81 B6
Burton Fleming . . . 161 D4
Burton Green
  W Mid 97 D5
  Wrex 126 D3
Burton Hastings 97 B7
Burton-in-Kendal . . 154 D4
Burton in Lonsdale . 155 D5
Burton Joyce . . . 115 A4
Burton Latimer . . . 99 D6
Burton Lazars . . . 115 D5
Burton-le-Coggles . 116 C2
Burton Leonard . . . 148 A2
Burton on the
  Wolds 114 C3
Burton Overy 98 B3
Burton Pedwardine 116 A4
Burton Pidsea . . . 151 D5
Burton Salmon . . 140 A2
Burton Stather . . . 141 B6
Burton upon
  Stather 141 B6
Burton upon Trent . 113 D4
Burtonwood 137 D4
Burwardsley . . . 127 D5
Burwarton 95 C4
Burwash 37 D4
Burwash Common . . 36 D4
Burwash Weald . . . 36 D4
Burwell
  Cambs 86 A1
  Lincs 134 B3
Burwen 123 A4
Burwick 283 J5
Bury
  Cambs 101 C4
  Gtr Man 137 B7
  Som 27 C4
  W Sus 20 A3
Bury Green 68 A4
Bury St Edmunds . . 87 A4
Burythorpe 149 A6
Busby 205 C5
Buscot 64 D3
Bush Bank 78 B2
Bushbury 96 A2
Bushby 98 A3
Bush Crathie . . . 243 C5
Bushey 67 D6
Bushey Heath 67 D6
Bush Green 104 C3
Bushley 80 D1
Bushton 45 B4
Buslingthorpe . . 133 A5
Busta 284 G5
Butcher's Cross . . . 36 D3
Butcombe 43 C4
Butetown 41 D6
Butleigh 29 B5
Butleigh Wootton . . 29 B5
Butler's Cross . . . 66 C3
Butler's End 97 C5
Butlers Marston . . . 81 C6
Butley 89 B4
Butley High Corner . 89 C4
Butterburn 177 B4
Buttercrambe . . . 149 B6
Butterknowle . . . 166 C4
Butterleigh 13 A4
Buttermere
  Cumb 163 C4
  Wilts 46 C1
Buttershaw 139 A4
Butterstone 231 D4
Butterton 129 D5
Butterwick
  Durham 167 C6

Butterwick *continued*
  Lincs 117 A6
  N Yorks 159 D6
  N Yorks 160 D3
Butt Green 127 D6
Buttington 93 A6
Buttonoak 95 D5
Butt's Green 32 C2
Buxhall 87 B6
Buxhall Fen Street . . 87 B6
Buxley 198 A2
Buxted 36 D2
Buxton
  Derbys 129 B5
  Norf 120 C4
Buxworth 129 A5
Bwcle =Buckley . . 126 C2
Bwlch 60 A3
Bwlchgwyn 126 D2
Bwlch-Llan 75 C4
Bwlchnewydd 73 D6
Bwlchtocyn 106 D3
Bwlch-y-cibau . . 109 D6
Bwlchyddar 109 C6
Bwlch-y-fadfa 74 D3
Bwlch-y-ffridd . . . 93 B4
Bwlchygroes 73 C5
Bwlch-y-sarnau . . . 92 D4
Byermoor 178 D3
Byers Green 167 B5
Byfield 82 B2
Byfleet 48 C3
Byford 78 C1
Bygrave 85 D4
Byker 179 C4
Bylchau 125 C4
Byley 128 C2
Bynea 57 C5
Byrness 187 C6
Bythorn 100 D2
Byton 78 A1
Byworth 34 D2

C

Cabharstadh 288 E4
Cablea 218 A4
Cabourne 142 C3
Cabrach
  Argyll 201 B4
  Moray 255 D4
Cabrich 252 B1
Cabus 145 C4
Cackle Street 36 D2
Cadbury 13 A4
Cadbury Barton . . . 26 D1
Cadder 205 A6
Caddington 67 B5
Caddonfoot 196 C3
Cadeby
  Leics 97 A7
  S Yorks 140 C3
Cadeleigh 13 A4
Cade Street 36 D4
Cadgwith 3 D5
Cadham 220 D2
Cadishead 137 D6
Cadle 57 C6
Cadley
  Lancs 145 D5
  Wilts 45 C6
  Wilts 45 D6
Cadmore End 66 D2
Cadnam 32 D1
Cadney 142 C2
Cadole 126 C2
Cadoxton 41 E6
Cadoxton-Juxta-
  Neath 40 B2
Cadshaw 137 B6
Cadzow 194 A2
Caeathro 123 D4
Caehopkin 59 D5
Caenby 133 A5
Caenby Corner . . . 133 A4
Caerau
  Bridgend 40 B3
  Cardiff 41 D6
Caér-bryn 57 A5
Caerdeon 90 A4
Caerdydd =Cardiff . . 41 D6
Caerfarchell 54 B3
Caerffili
  =Caerphilly 41 C6
Caerfyrddin
  =Carmarthen . . . 73 D7
Caergeiliog 122 C3
Caergwrle 126 D3

Caergybi
  =Holyhead 122 B2
Caerleon
  =Caerllion 61 D5
Caer Llan 61 C6
Caerllion
  =Caerleon 61 D5
Caernarfon 123 D4
Caerphilly
  =Caerffili 41 C6
Caersws 92 B4
Caerwedros 73 A6
Caerwent 61 D6
Caerwych 107 C6
Caerwys 125 B6
Caethle 90 C4
Caim 123 B6
Caio 58 B3
Cairinis 287 H3
Cairisiadar 287 F5
Cairminis 287 F5
Cairnbaan 213 C6
Cairnbanno House 256 B3
Cairnborrow . . . 255 B5
Cairnbrogie . . . 256 D3
Cairnbulg Castle . . 269 C5
Cairncross
  Angus 232 A2
  Borders 211 D5
Cairndow 215 A4
Cairness 269 C5
Cairneyhill 208 B3
Cairnfield House . . 267 C5
Cairngaan 170 D3
Cairngarroch . . . 170 C2
Cairnhill 256 C1
Cairnie
  Aberds 245 B5
  Aberds 255 B5
Cairnorrie 256 B3
Cairnpark 245 A5
Cairnryan 170 A2
Cairnton 283 G4
Caister-on-Sea . . . 121 D7
Caistor 142 C3
Caistor St Edmund . 104 A3
Caistron 188 C2
Caitha Bowland . . . 196 B3
Calais Street 87 D5
Calanais 288 D3
Calbost 288 F5
Calbourne 18 C3
Calceby 134 B3
Calcot Row 47 B4
Calcott 52 C3
Caldback 284 C8
Caldbeck 163 A6
Caldbergh 157 C4
Caldecote
  Cambs 85 B5
  Cambs 100 C3
  Herts 84 D4
  Northants 82 B3
Caldecott
  Northants 84 A1
  Oxon 65 D5
  Rutland 99 B5
Calderbank 207 D5
Calder Bridge . . . 162 D3
Calderbrook . . . 138 B2
Caldercruix . . . 207 D6
Calder Hall . . . 162 D3
Calder Mains . . . 280 C2
Caldermill 205 D6
Calder Vale . . . 145 C5
Calderwood . . . 205 C6
Caldhame 232 D2
Caldicot 42 A3
Caldwell
  Derbys 113 D6
  N Yorks 167 D4
Caldy 126 A2
Caledrhydiau 74 C3
Calfsound 282 D6
Calgary 224 A2
Califer 266 D1
California
  Falk 208 C2
  Norf 121 D7
Calke 114 C1
Callakille 248 A3
Callaly 188 C3
Callander 217 D6
Callaughton 95 B4
Callestick 4 B2
Calligarry 247 D5
Callington 6 A2
Callow 78 D2

Callow End 79 C6
Callow Hill
  Wilts 44 A4
  Worcs 95 D5
Callows Grave 78 A3
Calmore 32 D2
Calmsden 63 C6
Calne 44 A4
Calow 131 B4
Calshot 18 A3
Calstock 6 A3
Calstone Wellington . 44 C4
Calthorpe 120 B3
Calthwaite 164 A2
Calton
  N Yorks 146 B3
  Staffs 129 D6
Calveley 127 D5
Calver 130 B2
Calverhall 111 B5
Calver Hill 78 C1
Calverleigh 27 A4
Calverley 147 D6
Calvert 66 A1
Calverton
  M Keynes 83 D4
  Notts 115 A4
Calvine 230 B2
Calvo 174 C4
Cam 62 D3
Camas-luinie 249 D6
Camasnacroise 236 D2
Camastianavaig 247 A4
Camasunary 247 C4
Camault Muir 251 B7
Camb 284 D7
Camber 38 D1
Camberley 47 C6
Camberwell 49 B6
Camblesforth 141 A4
Cambo 178 A2
Cambois 179 A5
Camborne 3 A4
Cambourne 85 B5
Cambridge
  Cambs 85 B6
  Glos 62 C3
Cambridge Town 51 A6
Cambus 207 A6
Cambusavie Farm . . 264 A3
Cambusbarron 207 A6
Cambuskenneth . . . 207 A6
Cambuslang 205 B6
Cambusmore
  Lodge 264 A3
Camden 49 A5
Camelford 10 C2
Camelsdale 34 C1
Camerory 253 C6
Camer's Green 79 D5
Camerton
  Bath 43 D5
  Cumb 162 A3
  E Yorks 143 A4
Camghouran 229 C4
Cammachmore 245 C6
Cammeringham . . . 133 A4
Camore 264 A3
Campbeltown 190 C3
Camperdown 179 B4
Camp Hill 97 B6
Campmuir 220 A2
Campsall 140 B3
Campsey Ash 88 B4
Campton 84 D3
Camptown 187 B5
Camrose 55 B5
Camserney 230 D2
Camster 281 D4
Camuschoirk 235 D6
Camuscross 247 C5
Camusnagaul
  Highld 237 B4
  Highld 262 B2
Camusrory 238 C2
Camusteel 249 B4
Camusterrach 249 B4
Camusvrachan 229 D5
Canada 32 D1
Canadia 23 A5
Canal Side 141 B4
Candacraig House . . 243 A6
Candlesby 135 C4
Candy Mill 195 B5
Cane End 47 B4
Canewdon 70 D2
Canford Bottom 17 A4
Canford Cliffs 17 C4

Canford Magna 17 B4
Canham's Green 87 A6
Canholes 129 B5
Canisbay 281 A5
Cann 30 C2
Cannard's Grave 29 A6
Cann Common 30 C2
Cannich 251 C5
Cannington 28 B2
Cannock 96 A2
Cannock Wood 112 D4
Canonbie 175 A6
Canon Bridge 78 C2
Canon Frome 79 C4
Canon Pyon 78 C2
Canons Ashby 82 B2
Canonstown 2 B3
Canterbury 52 D3
Cantley
  Norf 105 A4
  S Yorks 140 C4
Cantlop 94 A3
Canton 41 D6
Cantraybruich 252 B3
Cantraydoune 252 B3
Cantraywood 252 B3
Cantsfield 155 D5
Canvey Island 51 A4
Canwick 133 C4
Canworthy Water . . . 10 B3
Caol 237 B5
Caolas 222 C3
Caolas Scalpaigh . . 288 H3
Caolas Stocinis . . . 288 H2
Caol Ila 201 A4
Capel 35 B4
Capel Bangor 91 D4
Capel Betws Lleucu . 75 C5
Capel Carmel 106 D1
Capel Coch 123 B4
Capel Curig 124 D2
Capel Cynon 73 B6
Capel Dewi
  Carms 58 C1
  Ceredig 58 A1
  Ceredig 90 D4
Capel Garmon 124 D3
Capel-gwyn 122 C3
Capel Gwyn 58 C1
Capel Gwynfe 59 C4
Capel Hendre 57 A5
Capel Hermon 108 C2
Capel Isaac 58 C2
Capel Iwan 73 C5
Capel le Ferne 39 B4
Capel Llanilltern . . . 41 C5
Capel Mawr 123 C4
Capel St Andrew 89 C4
Capel St Mary 88 D1
Capel Seion 75 A5
Capel Tygwydd 73 B5
Capel Uchaf 107 B4
Capelulo 124 B2
Capel-y-graig 123 D5
Capenhurst 126 B3
Capernwray 154 D4
Capheaton 178 A2
Cappercleuch 196 D1
Capplegill 185 B4
Capton 8 B2
Caputh 219 A5
Carbis Bay 2 B3
Carbost
  Highld 246 A2
  Highld 259 D4
Carbrook 130 A3
Carbrooke 103 A5
Carburton 131 B6
Carcant 196 A2
Carcary 233 C4
Carclaze 5 B5
Car Colston 115 A5
Carcroft 140 B3
Cardenden 209 A5
Cardeston 110 D2
Cardiff = Caerdydd . . 41 D6
Cardigan = Aberteifi . 73 B4
Cardington
  Bedford 84 C2
  Shrops 94 B3
Cardinham 5 A6
Cardonald 205 B5
Cardow 254 B2
Cardrona 196 C2
Cardross 206 C1
Cardurnock 175 C4
Careby 116 D3
Careston Castle . . . 232 C3
Carew 55 D6
Carew Cheriton 55 D6

Carew Newton 55 D6
Carey 78 D3
Carfrae 210 D2
Cargenbridge 174 A2
Cargill 219 A6
Cargo 175 C6
Cargreen 6 A3
Carham 198 C2
Carhampton 27 A5
Carharrack 4 C2
Carie
  Perth 217 A6
  Perth 229 C5
Carines 4 B2
Carisbrooke 18 C3
Cark 154 D2
Carlabhagh 288 C3
Carland Cross 4 B3
Carlby 116 D3
Carlecotes 139 C4
Carlesmoor 157 D5
Carleton
  Cumb 164 C3
  Cumb 176 D3
  Lancs 144 D3
  N Yorks 146 C3
Carleton Forehoe . . 104 A1
Carleton Rode 104 B2
Carlingcott 43 D5
Carlin How 169 D5
Carlisle 175 C7
Carlops 195 A6
Carlton
  Bedford 83 B6
  Cambs 86 B2
  Leics 97 A6
  Notts 115 A4
  N Yorks 140 A4
  N Yorks 157 C4
  N Yorks 159 C5
  N Yorks 167 D4
  Stockton 167 C6
  Suff 89 A4
  S Yorks 139 B6
  W Yorks 139 A6
Carlton Colville . . . 105 C6
Carlton Curlieu 98 B3
Carlton Husthwaite 158 D3
Carlton in
  Cleveland 158 A4
Carlton in Lindrick . 131 A5
Carlton le
  Moorland 133 D4
Carlton Miniott . . . 158 C4
Carlton on Trent . . . 132 C2
Carlton Scroop 116 A2
Carluke 194 A3
Carmarthen
  = Caerfyrddin 73 D7
Carmel
  Anglesey 122 B3
  Carms 57 A5
  Flint 125 B6
  Guern 6
  Gwyn 107 A4
Carmont 245 D5
Carmunnock 205 C6
Carmyle 205 B6
Carmyllie 232 D3
Carnaby 151 A4
Carnach
  Highld 250 D2
  Highld 262 A2
  W Isles 288 H3
Carnachy 278 C2
Càrnais 287 A5
Carnbee 221 D5
Carnbo 219 D5
Carnbrea 3 A4
Carnduff 205 D6
Carnduncan 200 B2
Carne 4 D4
Carnforth 154 D4
Carn-gorm 249 D6
Carnhedryn 54 B4
Carnhell Green 3 B4
Carnkie
  Corn 3 B4
  Corn 4 D2
Carno 92 B3
Carnoch
  Highld 251 A4
  Highld 251 C5
Carnock 208 B3
Carnon Downs 4 C2
Carnousie 268 D1
Carnoustie 221 A5
Carnwath 195 B4
Carnyorth 2 B1
Carperby 156 C4

Carpley Green 156 C3
Carr 140 D3
Carradale 190 B4
Carragraich 288 H2
Carrbridge 253 D5
Carrefour Selous 6
Carreglefn 122 B3
Carreg-wen 73 B5
Carr Hill 179 C4
Carrick
  Argyll 214 D2
  Fife 220 B4
Carrick Castle 215 C4
Carrick House 282 D6
Carriden 208 B3
Carrington
  Gtr Man 137 D6
  Lincs 134 D3
  Midloth 209 D6
Carrog
  Conwy 108 A2
  Denb 109 A6
Carron
  Falk 208 B1
  Moray 254 B3
Carronbridge 183 C6
Carron Bridge 207 B5
Carronshore 208 B1
Carrshield 165 A6
Carrutherstown . . . 174 A4
Carrville 167 A4
Carsaig
  Argyll 213 D5
  Argyll 225 D4
Carscreugh 171 B4
Carsegowan 171 B6
Carse Gray 232 C2
Carse House 202 B2
Carseriggan 171 A5
Carsethorn 174 C2
Carshalton 49 C5
Carsington 130 D2
Carskiey 190 E2
Carsluith 171 B6
Carsphairn 182 C3
Carstairs 194 B4
Carstairs Junction . 195 B4
Carswell Marsh 64 D4
Carter's Clay 32 C2
Carterton 64 C3
Carterway Heads . . 178 D2
Carthew 5 B5
Carthorpe 157 C7
Cartington 188 C3
Cartland 194 B3
Cartmel 154 D2
Cartmel Fell 154 C3
Carway 57 B4
Cary Fitzpaine 29 C5
Cascob 77 A6
Cas-gwent
  = Chepstow 62 D1
Cashlie 228 D3
Cashmoor 30 D3
Casnewydd
  = Newport 42 A2
Cassey Compton . . . 63 B6
Cassington 65 B5
Cassop 167 B6
Castell 125 C6
Castellau 41 C5
Castell-Howell 74 D3
Castell-Nedd
  = Neath 40 B2
Castell Newydd Emlyn
  = Newcastle Emlyn . 73 B6
Castell-y-bwch 61 D4
Casterton 155 D5
Castle Acre 119 D5
Castle Ashby 83 B5
Castlebay
  = Bagh a Chaisteil . 286 G2
Castle Bolton 156 B4
Castle Bromwich . . . 96 C4
Castle Bytham 116 D2
Castlebythe 55 B6
Castle Caereinion . . 93 A5
Castle Camps 86 C2
Castle Carrock 176 D3
Castlecary 207 C5
Castle Cary 29 B6
Castle Combe 44 B2
Castlecraig 265 D4
Castle Donington . . 114 C2
Castle Douglas 173 B5
Castle Eaton 64 D2
Castle Eden 168 B2
Castlefairn 183 D5
Castle Forbes 244 A3
Castleford 140 A2

Castle Frome 79 C4
Castle Green 48 C2
Castle Gresley 113 D6
Castle Heaton 198 B3
Castle Hedingham . . 86 D3
Castlehill
  Borders 195 C7
  Highld 280 B3
  W Dunb 206 C1
Castle Hill 37 B4
Castle Huntly 220 B3
Castle Kennedy . . . 170 B2
Castlemaddy 182 D3
Castlemartin 55 E5
Castlemilk
  Dumfries 174 A4
  Glasgow 205 C6
Castlemorris 55 A5
Castlemorton 79 D5
Castle O'er 185 C5
Castle Pulverbatch . 94 A2
Castle Rising 118 C3
Castleside 166 A3
Castle Stuart 252 B3
Castlethorpe 83 C5
Castleton
  Angus 232 D1
  Argyll 214 D1
  Derbys 129 A6
  Gtr Man 138 B1
  Newport 42 A1
  N Yorks 159 A5
Castletown
  Ches W 127 D4
  Highld 252 B3
  Highld 280 B3
  IoM 152 E2
  T&W 179 D5
Castleweary 186 C3
Castley 147 C6
Caston 103 B5
Castor 100 B3
Catacol 203 D4
Catbrain 43 A4
Catbrook 61 C7
Catchall 2 C2
Catchems Corner . . . 97 D5
Catchgate 178 D3
Catcleugh 187 C6
Catcliffe 131 A4
Catcott 28 B3
Caterham 35 A6
Catfield 121 C5
Catfirth 285 H6
Catford 49 B6
Catforth 145 D4
Cathays 41 D6
Cathcart 205 B5
Cathedine 60 A3
Catherington 33 D5
Catherton 95 D4
Catlodge 241 C4
Catlowdy 176 B2
Catmore 46 A2
Caton 145 A5
Caton Green 145 A5
Catrine 193 C5
Cat's Ash 61 D5
Catsfield 23 A5
Catshill 96 D2
Cattal 148 B3
Cattawade 88 D2
Catterall 145 C4
Catterick 157 B6
Catterick Bridge . . 157 B6
Catterick Garrison . 157 B5
Catterlen 164 B2
Catterline 233 A6
Catterton 148 C4
Catthorpe 98 D2
Cattistock 15 B5
Catton
  Northumb 177 D6
  N Yorks 158 D2
Catwick 151 C4
Catworth 100 D2
Caudlesprings 103 A5
Caulcott 65 A6
Cauldcots 233 D4
Cauldhame 207 A4
Cauldmill 186 B4
Cauldon 113 A4
Caulkerbush 174 C2
Caulside 176 A2
Caunsall 95 C6
Caunton 132 D2
Causewayend 195 C5
Causeway End 171 A6
Causeway Foot 147 D4
Causewayhead 174 C4

Causeway-head . . . 207 A5
Causeyend 245 A6
Causey Park
  Bridge 189 D4
Cautley 155 B5
Cavendish 87 C4
Cavendish Bridge . . 114 C2
Cavenham 86 A3
Caversfield 65 A6
Caversham 47 B5
Caverswall 112 A3
Cavil 149 D6
Cawdor 253 B4
Cawkwell 134 B2
Cawood 149 D4
Cawsand 6 B3
Cawston 120 C3
Cawthorne 139 C5
Cawthorpe 116 C3
Cawton 159 D5
Caxton 85 B5
Caynham 94 D3
Caythorpe
  Lincs 116 A2
  Notts 115 A4
Cayton 161 C4
Ceann a Bhaigh . . . 287 H2
Ceannacroc Lodge . 239 A6
Ceann a Deas Loch Bag-
  hasdail 286 E3
Ceann Shiphoirt . . . 288 F3
Ceann Tarabhaigh . . 288 F3
Cearsiadair 288 E4
Cefn Berain 125 C4
Cefn-brith 125 D4
Cefn Canol 110 B1
Cefn-coch 124 C3
Cefn Coch 109 C6
Cefn-coed-y-
  cymmer 60 C2
Cefn Cribbwr 40 C3
Cefn Cross 40 C3
Cefn-ddwysarn . . . 109 B4
Cefn Einion 93 C6
Cefneithin 57 A5
Cefn-gorwydd 76 C3
Cefn-mawr 110 A1
Cefn-y-bedd 126 D3
Cefn-y-pant 73 D4
Cei-bach 73 A7
Ceinewydd
  = New Quay 73 A6
Ceint 123 C4
Cellan 75 D5
Cellarhead 112 A3
Cemaes 122 A3
Cemmaes 91 B6
Cemmaes Road 91 B6
Cenarth 73 B5
Cenin 107 B4
Central 204 A2
Ceos 288 E4
Ceres 220 C4
Cerne Abbas 15 A6
Cerney Wick 63 D6
Cerrigceinwen 123 C4
Cerrigydrudion . . . 109 A4
Cessford 187 A6
Ceunant 123 D5
Chaceley 79 D6
Chacewater 4 C2
Chackmore 82 D3
Chacombe 82 C1
Chadderton 138 C2
Chadderton Fold . . 138 C1
Chaddesden 114 B1
Chaddesley Corbett . 96 D1
Chaddleworth 46 B2
Chadlington 64 A4
Chadshunt 81 B6
Chad Valley 96 C3
Chadwell 115 C5
Chadwell St Mary . . 50 B3
Chadwick End 97 D5
Chadwick Green . . 136 D4
Chaffcombe 28 D3
Chagford 12 C2
Chailey 22 A1
Chainbridge 101 A6
Chain Bridge 117 A6
Chainhurst 37 B5
Chalbury 17 A4
Chalbury Common . 17 A4
Chaldon 35 A6
Chaldon Herring or . 16 C1
Chale 18 D3
Chale Green 18 D3
Chalfont Common . . 67 D5
Chalfont St Giles . . . 67 D4
Chalfont St Peter . . 67 D5

Chalford 63 C4
Chalgrove 66 D1
Chalk 50 B3
Challacombe 26 A1
Challoch 171 A5
Challock 52 D2
Chalton
  C Beds 67 A5
  Hants 33 D6
Chalvington 22 B3
Chancery 75 A4
Chandler's Ford 32 C3
ChannelTunnel 38 B3
Channerwick 285 L6
Chantry
  Som 29 A7
  Suff 88 C2
Chapel 209 A5
Chapel Allerton
  Som 42 D3
  W Yorks 148 D2
Chapel Amble 9 D5
Chapel Brampton . . 83 A4
Chapel Chorlton . . . 112 B2
Chapel End 97 B6
Chapel-en-le-Frith 129 A5
Chapelgate 117 C7
Chapel Green
  Warks 82 A1
  Warks 97 C5
Chapel Haddlesey . 140 A3
Chapelhall 207 D5
Chapel Head 101 C5
Chapelhill
  Dumfries 184 C3
  Highld 265 C4
  N Ayrs 204 D2
  Perth 219 A5
  Perth 220 B2
Chapel Hill
  Aberds 257 C5
  Lincs 134 D2
  Mon 62 D1
  N Yorks 148 C2
Chapelknowe 175 A6
Chapel Lawn 93 D7
Chapel-le-Dale 155 D6
Chapel Milton 129 A5
Chapel of Garioch . 256 D2
Chapel Row 46 C3
Chapel St Leonards 135 B5
Chapel Stile 154 A2
Chapelton
  Angus 233 D4
  Devon 25 C6
  Highld 242 A4
  S Lanark 194 B1
Chapeltown
  Blackburn 137 B6
  Moray 254 D3
  S Yorks 139 D6
Chapmanslade 30 A2
Chapmans Well 11 B4
Chapmore End 68 B3
Chappel 70 A2
Chard 14 A3
Chardstock 14 A3
Charfield 62 D3
Charford 80 A2
Charing 38 A1
Charing Cross 31 D5
Charing Heath 38 A1
Charingworth 81 D5
Charlbury 65 B4
Charlcombe 43 C6
Charlecote 81 B5
Charles 26 B1
Charlesfield 175 B4
Charleston
  Angus 232 D1
  Renfs 205 B4
Charlestown
  Aberdeen 245 B6
  Corn 5 B5
  Derbys 138 D3
  Dorset 15 D6
  Fife 208 B3
  Gtr Man 137 C7
  Highld 252 B2
  Highld 261 C5
  W Yorks 138 A2
Charlestown of
  Aberlour 254 B3
Charles Tye 87 B6
Charlesworth 138 D3
Charleton 7 C6
Charlton
  Hants 32 A2
  Herts 68 A1
  London 49 B7

Charlton continued
  Northants 82 D2
  Northumb 177 A6
  Som 43 D5
  Telford 111 D4
  Wilts 30 C3
  Wilts 44 A3
  Wilts 45 D5
  Worcs 80 C3
  W Sus 20 A1
Charlton Abbots . . . 63 A6
Charlton Adam 29 C5
Charlton-All-Saints . 31 C5
Charlton Down 15 B6
Charlton
  Horethorne 29 C6
Charlton Kings 63 A5
Charlton Mackerell . 29 C5
Charlton Marshall . . 16 A2
Charlton Musgrove . 29 C7
Charlton on Otmoor 65 B6
Charltons 168 D4
Charlwood 35 B5
Charlynch 28 B2
Charndon 66 A1
Charney Bassett . . . 65 D4
Charnock Richard . 137 B4
Charsfield 88 B3
Chart Corner 37 A5
Charter Alley 46 D3
Charterhouse 42 D3
Charterville
  Allotments 64 B4
Chartham 52 D3
Chartham Hatch . . . 52 D3
Chartridge 67 C4
Chart Sutton 37 B6
Charvil 47 B5
Charwelton 82 B2
Chasetown 96 A3
Chastleton 64 A3
Chasty 10 A4
Chatburn 146 C1
Chatcull 112 B1
Chatham 51 C4
Chathill 189 A4
Chatteris 101 C5
Chattisham 88 C1
Chatto 187 B6
Chatton 188 A3
Chawleigh 26 D2
Chawley 65 C5
Chawston 84 B3
Chawton 33 B6
Cheadle
  Gtr Man 128 A3
  Staffs 112 A4
Cheadle Heath 128 A3
Cheadle Hulme 128 A3
Cheam 49 C5
Cheapside 34 C3
Chearsley 66 B2
Chebsey 112 C2
Checkendon 47 A4
Checkley
  Ches E 111 A6
  Hereford 78 D3
  Staffs 112 B4
Chedburgh 86 B3
Cheddar 42 D3
Cheddington 67 B4
Cheddleton 129 D4
Cheddon Fitzpaine . 28 C2
Chedglow 63 D5
Chedgrave 105 B4
Chedington 15 A4
Chediston 105 D4
Chedworth 63 B6
Chedzoy 28 B3
Cheeklaw 198 A1
Cheeseman's Green 38 B2
Cheglinch 25 A6
Cheldon 26 D2
Chelford 128 B3
Chellaston 114 B1
Chell Heath 128 D3
Chellington 83 B6
Chelmarsh 95 C5
Chelmer Village . . . 70 C1
Chelmondiston 88 D3
Chelmorton 129 C6
Chelmsford 69 C7
Chelsea 49 B5
Chelsfield 50 C1
Chelsworth 87 C5
Cheltenham 63 A5
Chelveston 84 A1

Chelvey 42 C3
Chelwood 43 C5
Chelwood Common . 36 D2
Chelwood Gate 36 D2
Chelworth 63 D5
Chelworth Green . . . 64 D1
Chemistry 111 A4
Chenies 67 D5
Cheny Longville . . . 94 C2
Chepstow
  = Cas-gwent 62 D1
Chequerfield 140 A2
Cherhill 44 B4
Cherington
  Glos 63 D5
  Warks 81 D5
Cheriton
  Devon 26 A2
  Hants 33 C4
  Kent 38 B3
  Swansea 57 C4
Cheriton Bishop . . . 12 B2
Cheriton Fitzpaine . 12 A3
Cheriton or Stackpole
  Elidor 55 E5
Cherrington 111 C5
Cherrybank 219 B6
Cherry Burton 150 C2
Cherry Hinton 85 B6
Cherry Orchard . . . 79 B6
Cherry Willingham . 133 B5
Chertsey 48 C3
Cheselbourne 16 B1
Chesham 67 C4
Chesham Bois 67 D4
Cheshunt 68 C3
Cheslyn Hay 96 A2
Chessington 49 C4
Chester 127 C4
Chesterblade 29 A6
Chesterfield 130 B3
Chester-le-Street . . 179 D4
Chester Moor 167 A5
Chesters
  Borders 187 A5
  Borders 187 B5
Chesterton
  Cambs 85 A6
  Cambs 100 B3
  Glos 63 C6
  Oxon 65 A6
  Shrops 95 B5
  Staffs 112 A2
  Warks 81 B6
Chesterwood 177 C6
Cheswick 198 B4
Chestfield 52 C3
Cheston 7 B5
Cheswardine 111 C6
Chetnole 15 A6
Chettiscombe 27 D4
Chettisham 102 C1
Chettle 30 D3
Chetton 95 B4
Chetwode 66 A1
Chetwynd Aston . . . 111 D6
Cheveley 86 A2
Chevening 36 A2
Chevington 86 B3
Chevithorne 27 D4
Chew Magna 43 C4
Chew Stoke 43 C4
Chewton Keynsham . 43 C5
Chewton Mendip . . . 43 D4
Chicheley 83 C6
Chichester 20 B1
Chickerell 15 C6
Chicklade 30 B3
Chicksgrove 30 B3
Chidden 33 D5
Chiddingfold 34 C2
Chiddingly 22 A3
Chiddingstone 36 B2
Chiddingstone
  Causeway 36 B3
Chiddingstone
  Hoath 36 B2
Chideock 14 B4
Chidham 19 A6
Chidswell 139 A5
Chieveley 46 B2
Chignall St James . . 69 C6
Chignall Smealy . . . 69 B6
Chigwell 68 D4
Chigwell Row 69 D4
Chilbolton 32 B2
Chilcomb 32 C4
Chilcombe 15 B5
Chilcompton 43 D5
Chilcote 113 D6

Childer Thornton . . . 126 B3
Child Okeford 30 D2
Childrey 46 A1
Child's Ercall 111 C5
Childswickham 80 D3
Childwall 127 A4
Childwick Green . . . 67 B6
Chilfrome 15 B5
Chilgrove 20 A1
Chilham 52 D2
Chilhampton 31 B4
Chilla 11 A5
Chillaton 11 C5
Chillenden 53 D4
Chillerton 18 C3
Chillesford 89 B4
Chillingham 188 A3
Chillington
  Devon 8 C1
  Som 28 D3
Chilmark 30 B3
Chilson 64 B4
Chilsworthy
  Corn 11 D5
  Devon 10 A4
Chilthorne Domer . . 29 D5
Chiltington 22 A1
Chilton
  Bucks 66 B1
  Durham 167 C5
  Oxon 46 A2
Chilton Cantelo . . . 29 C5
Chilton Foliat 45 B7
Chilton Lane 167 B6
Chilton Polden 28 B3
Chilton Street 86 C3
Chilton Trinity 28 B2
Chilvers Coton 97 B6
Chilwell 114 B3
Chilworth
  Hants 32 D3
  Sur 34 B3
Chimney 65 C4
Chineham 47 D4
Chingford 68 D3
Chinley 129 A5
Chinley Head 129 A5
Chinnor 66 C2
Chipnall 111 B6
Chippenhall Green . 104 D3
Chippenham
  Cambs 86 A2
  Wilts 44 B3
Chipperfield 67 C5
Chipping
  Herts 85 D5
  Lancs 145 C6
Chipping Campden . 81 D4
Chipping Hill 70 B2
Chipping Norton . . . 64 A4
Chipping Ongar . . . 69 C5
Chipping Sodbury . . 43 A6
Chipping Warden . . 82 C1
Chipstable 27 C5
Chipstead
  Kent 36 A2
  Sur 35 A5
Chirbury 93 B6
Chirk = Y Waun . . . 110 B1
Chirk Bank 110 B1
Chirmorrie 181 D4
Chirnside 198 A2
Chirnsidebridge . . . 198 A2
Chirton 45 D4
Chisbury 45 C6
Chiselborough 29 D4
Chiseldon 45 A5
Chiserley 138 A3
Chislehampton 65 D6
Chislehurst 50 B1
Chislet 53 C4
Chiswell Green 67 C6
Chiswick 49 B5
Chiswick End 85 C5
Chisworth 138 D2
Chithurst 34 D1
Chittering 101 D6
Chitterne 30 A3
Chittlehamholt 26 C1
Chittlehampton 26 C1
Chittoe 44 C3
Chivenor 25 B6
Chobham 48 C2
Choicelee 197 A6
Cholderton 31 A6
Cholesbury 67 C4
Chollerford 177 B7
Chollerton 178 B1
Cholmondeston . . . 127 C6
Cholsey 46 A3

Cholstrey 78 B2
Chop Gate 159 B4
Choppington 179 A4
Chopwell 178 D3
Chorley
  Ches E 127 D5
  Lancs 137 B4
  Shrops 95 C4
  Staffs 113 D4
Chorleywood 67 D5
Chorlton cum
  Hardy 137 D7
Chorlton Lane 110 A3
Choulton 94 C1
Chowdene 179 D4
Chowley 127 C4
Chrishall 85 D6
Christchurch
  BCP 17 B5
  Cambs 101 B6
  Glos 62 B1
  Newport 42 A2
Christian Malford . . 44 B3
Christleton 127 C4
Christmas Common . 66 D2
Christon 42 D2
Christon Bank 189 A5
Christow 12 C3
Chryston 207 C4
Chudleigh 12 D3
Chudleigh Knighton . 12 D3
Chulmleigh 26 D1
Chunal 138 D3
Church 137 A6
Churcham 62 B3
Church Aston 111 D6
Churchbank 93 D7
Church Brampton . . 83 A4
Churchbridge 96 A2
Church Broughton . 113 B6
Church Crookham . . 47 D6
Churchdown 63 B4
Church Eaton 112 D2
Churchend
  Essex 69 A6
  Essex 71 D4
  S Glos 62 D3
Church End
  Cambs 100 C4
  Cambs 101 A5
  C Beds 67 A4
  C Beds 84 D1
  C Beds 84 D3
  Essex 69 A7
  Essex 86 C1
  E Yorks 150 B3
  Hants 47 D4
  Lincs 117 B5
  Warks 97 B5
  Warks 97 B5
  Wilts 44 B4
Church Enstone . . . 65 A4
Church Fenton 148 C4
Churchfield 96 B3
Churchgate Street . . 69 B4
Church Green
  Devon 14 B1
  Norf 103 B6
Church Gresley . . . 113 D6
Church Hanborough . 65 B5
Church Hill 127 C6
Church Houses . . . 159 B5
Churchill
  Devon 14 A3
  Devon 25 A6
  N Som 42 D3
  Oxon 64 A3
  Worcs 80 B2
  Worcs 96 D1
Churchinford 28 D2
Church Knowle 16 C3
Church Laneham . . . 132 B3
Church Langton . . . 99 B4
Church Lawford . . . 98 D1
Church Lawton 128 D3
Church Leigh 112 B4
Church Lench 80 B3
Church Mayfield . . . 113 A5
Church Minshull . . . 127 C6
Church Norton 20 C1
Church
  Pulverbatch 94 A2
Churchstanton 28 D1
Church Stoke 93 B6
Churchstow 7 C6
Church Stowe 82 B3
Church Street 51 B4
Church Stretton . . . 94 B2

Churchtown
  Derbys 130 C2
  IoM 152 B4
  Lancs 145 C4
  Mers 136 B2
Church Town
  N Lincs 141 C5
  Sur 35 A6
Church Village 41 C5
Church Warsop . . . 131 C5
Churnsike Lodge . . 177 B4
Churston Ferrers . . . 8 B3
Churt 34 C1
Churton 127 C4
Churwell 139 A5
Chute Standen 45 D7
Chwilog 107 C4
Chyandour 2 B2
Cilan Uchaf 106 D2
Cilcain 126 C1
Cilcennin 75 B4
Cilfor 107 C6
Cilfrew 40 A2
Cilfynydd 41 B5
Cilgerran 73 B4
Cilgwyn
  Carms 59 C4
  Gwyn 107 A4
  Pembs 72 C3
Ciliau Aeron 74 C3
Cill Donnain 286 D3
Cille Bhrighde 286 E3
Cille Pheadair 286 E3
Cilmery 76 B4
Cilsan 58 C2
Ciltalgarth 108 A3
Cilwendeg 73 C5
Cilybebyll 40 A2
Cilycwm 59 B4
Cimla 40 B2
Cinderford 62 B2
Cippyn 72 B4
Circebost 288 D2
Cirencester 63 C6
Ciribhig 288 C2
City
  London 49 A6
  Powys 93 C6
City Dulas 123 B4
Clachaig 215 D4
Clachan
  Argyll 202 C2
  Argyll 213 A5
  Argyll 215 A4
  Argyll 226 B3
  Highld 248 C2
  W Isles 286 B3
Clachaneasy 181 D5
Clachanmore 170 C2
Clachan na Luib . . . 287 H3
Clachan of
  Campsie 205 A6
Clachan of
  Glendaruel 214 D2
Clachan-Seil 213 A5
Clachan Strachur . . 214 B3
Clachbreck 202 A2
Clachnabrain 232 B1
Clachtoll 270 B3
Clackmannan 208 A2
Clacton-on-Sea . . . 71 B5
Cladach Chireboist . 287 H2
Claddach-
  knockline 287 H2
Cladich 227 D5
Claggan
  Highld 225 B5
  Highld 237 D5
Claigan 258 C2
Claines 79 B6
Clandown 43 D5
Clanfield
  Hants 33 D5
  Oxon 64 C3
Clanville 32 A2
Claonaig 202 C3
Claonel 272 D3
Clapgate
  Dorset 17 A4
  Herts 68 A4
Clapham
  Bedford 84 B2
  London 49 B5
  N Yorks 146 A1
  W Sus 20 B3
Clap Hill 38 B2
Clappers 198 A3
Clappersgate 154 A2

Clapton 14 A4
Clapton-in-Gordano 42 B3
Clapton-on-the-Hill 64 B2
Clapworthy 26 C1
Clarach 90 D4
Clara Vale 178 C3
Clarbeston 55 B6
Clarbeston Road 55 B6
Clarborough 132 A2
Clardon 280 B3
Clare 86 C3
Clarebrand 173 B5
Clarencefield 174 B3
Clarilaw 186 B4
Clark's Green 35 C4
Clarkston 205 C5
Clashandorran 251 B7
Clashcoig 264 A2
Clashindarroch 255 C5
Clashmore
  Highld 264 B3
  Highld 270 A3
Clashnessie 270 A3
Clashnoir 254 D3
Clate 285 G7
Clathy 219 C4
Clatt 255 D6
Clatter 92 B3
Clatterford 18 C3
Clatterin Bridge 233 A4
Clatworthy 27 B5
Claughton
  Lancs 145 A5
  Lancs 145 C5
  Mers 126 A3
Claverdon 81 A4
Claverham 42 C3
Clavering 85 D6
Claverley 95 B5
Claverton 44 C1
Clawdd-newydd 125 D5
Clawthorpe 154 D4
Clawton 11 B4
Claxby
  Lincs 135 B4
  Lincs 142 D3
Claxton
  Norf 104 A4
  N Yorks 149 A5
Claybokie 242 D3
Claybrooke Magna . . .98 C1
Claybrooke Parva . . .98 C1
Clay Common 105 C5
Clay Coton 98 D2
Clay Cross 130 C3
Claydon
  Oxon 82 B1
  Suff 88 B2
Claygate
  Dumfries 175 A6
  Kent 37 B5
  Sur 49 C4
Claygate Cross 36 A4
Clayhanger
  Devon 27 C5
  W Mid 96 A3
Clayhidon 27 D6
Clayhill
  E Sus 37 D6
  Hants 18 A2
Clay Hill 46 B3
Clay Lake 117 C5
Clayock 280 C3
Claypole 115 A6
Clayton
  Staffs 112 A2
  S Yorks 140 C2
  W Sus 21 A5
  W Yorks 147 D5
Clayton Green 137 A4
Clayton-le-Moors .146 D1
Clayton-le-Woods .137 A4
Clayton West 139 B5
Clayworth 132 A2
Cleadale 234 B3
Cleadon 179 C5
Clearbrook 7 A4
Clearwell 62 C1
Cleasby 167 D5
Cleat 283 J5
Cleatlam 166 D4
Cleator 162 C3
Cleator Moor 162 C3
Clebrig 272 A3
Cleckheaton 139 A4
Cleedownton 94 C3
Cleehill 94 D3
Clee St Margaret 94 C3

Cleethorpes 143 C5
Cleeton St Mary 95 D4
Cleeve 42 C3
Cleeve Hill 63 A5
Cleeve Prior 80 C3
Clegyrnant 91 B7
Clehonger 78 D2
Cleish 208 A3
Cleland 194 A3
Clench Common 45 C5
Clenchwarton 118 C2
Clent 96 D2
Cleobury Mortimer . . .95 D4
Cleobury North 95 C4
Cleongart 190 B2
Clephanton 253 A4
Clerklands 186 A4
Clestrain 283 G4
Cleuch Head 187 B4
Cleughbrae 174 A3
Clevancy 45 B4
Clevedon 42 B3
Cleveley 65 A4
Cleveleys 144 C3
Cleverton 44 A3
Clevis 40 D3
Clewer 42 D3
Cley next the Sea . . .120 A2
Cliaid 286 F2
Cliasmol 287 D5
Cliburn 164 C3
Click Mill 282 E4
Cliddesden 33 A5
Cliffburn 233 D4
Cliffe
  Medway 51 B4
  N Yorks 149 D5
Cliff End 23 A6
Cliffe Woods 51 B4
Clifford
  Hereford 77 C6
  W Yorks 148 C3
Clifford Chambers . .81 B4
Clifford's Mesne 62 A3
Cliffsend 53 C5
Clifton
  Bristol 43 B4
  C Beds 84 D3
  Cumb 164 C3
  Derbys 113 A5
  Lancs 145 D4
  Northumb 179 A4
  Nottingham 114 B3
  N Yorks 147 C5
  Oxon 82 D1
  Stirling 216 A3
  S Yorks 140 D3
  Worcs 79 C6
  York 149 B4
Clifton Campville . . .113 D6
Cliftoncote 187 A7
Clifton Green 137 C6
Clifton Hampden 65 D6
Clifton Reynes 83 B6
Clifton upon
  Dunsmore 98 D2
Clifton upon Teme . . .79 A5
Cliftonville 53 B5
Climaen gwyn 59 E4
Climping 20 B3
Climpy 194 A4
Clink 30 A1
Clint 147 B6
Clint Green 120 D2
Clintmains 197 C5
Cliobh 287 A5
Clippesby 121 D6
Clipsham 116 D2
Clipston 99 C4
Clipstone 131 C5
Clitheroe 146 C1
Cliuthar 288 H2
Clive 111 C4
Clivocast 284 C8
Clixby 142 C3
Clocaenog 125 D5
Clochan 267 C5
Clock Face 136 D4
Clockmill 197 A6
Cloddiau 93 A6
Clodock 61 A5
Clola 257 B5
Clophill 84 D2
Clopton
  Northants 100 C2
  Suff 88 B3
Clopton Corner 88 B3
Clopton Green 86 B3
Closeburn 183 C6
Close Clark 152 D2

Closworth 29 D5
Clothall 85 D4
Clotton 127 C5
Clough Foot 138 A2
Cloughton 160 B4
Cloughton
  Newlands 160 B4
Clousta 285 H5
Clouston 282 F3
Clova
  Aberds 255 D5
  Angus 232 A1
Clovelly 24 C4
Clove Lodge 166 D2
Clovenfords 196 C3
Clovenstone 245 A4
Clovullin 237 C4
Clow Bridge 137 A7
Clowne 131 B4
Clows Top 95 D5
Cloy 110 A2
Cluanie Inn 239 A4
Cluanie Lodge 239 A4
Clun 93 C7
Clunbury 94 C1
Clunderwen 55 C7
Clune 252 D3
Clunes 239 C4
Clungunford 94 D1
Clunie
  Aberds 268 D1
  Perth 231 D5
Clunton 94 C1
Cluny 209 A5
Cluny Castle 241 C4
Clutton
  Bath 43 D5
  Ches W 127 D4
Clwt-grugoer 125 C5
Clwt-y-bont 123 D5
Clydach
  Mon 60 B4
  Swansea 40 A1
Clydach Vale 41 B4
Clydebank 205 A4
Clydey 73 C5
Clyffe Pypard 45 B4
Clynder 215 D5
Clyne 40 A3
Clynelish 274 D2
Clynnog-fawr 107 A4
Clyro 77 C6
Clyst Honiton 13 B4
Clyst Hydon 13 A5
Clyst St George 13 C4
Clyst St Lawrence . .13 A5
Clyst St Mary 13 B4
Cnoc Amhlaigh 288 D6
Cnwch-coch 75 A5
Coachford 255 B5
Coad's Green 10 D3
Coal Aston 130 B3
Coalbrookdale 95 A4
Coalbrookvale 60 C3
Coalburn 194 C3
Coalburns 178 C3
Coalcleugh 165 A6
Coaley 62 C3
Coalhall 182 A2
Coalhill 70 D1
Coalpit Heath 43 A5
Coalport 95 A4
Coalsnaughton 208 A2
Coaltown of
  Balgonie 209 A5
Coaltown of
  Wemyss 209 A6
Coalville 114 D2
Coalway 62 B1
Coat 29 C4
Coatbridge 207 D5
Coatdyke 207 D5
Coate
  Swindon 45 A5
  Wilts 44 C4
Coates
  Cambs 101 B5
  Glos 63 C5
  Lancs 146 C2
  Notts 132 A3
  W Sus 20 A2
Coatham 168 C3
Coatham
  Mundeville 167 C5
Coatsgate 184 B3
Cobbaton 25 C7
Cobbler's Green 104 B3
Coberley 63 B5
Cobham
  Kent 50 C3

Cobham continued
  Sur 48 C4
Cobholm Island 105 A6
Cobleland 206 A3
Cobnash 78 A2
Coburty 269 C4
Cockayne 159 B5
Cockayne Hatley . . .85 C4
Cock Bank 110 A2
Cock Bridge 243 B5
Cockburnspath 211 C4
Cock Clarks 70 C2
Cockenzie and Port
  Seton 209 C7
Cockerham 145 B4
Cockermouth 163 A4
Cockernhoe Green . .67 A6
Cockfield
  Durham 166 C4
  Suff 87 B5
Cockfosters 68 D2
Cocking 20 A1
Cockington 8 A2
Cocklake 28 A4
Cockley Beck 163 D5
Cockley Cley 102 A3
Cockshutt 110 C3
Cockthorpe 120 A1
Cockwood 13 C4
Cockyard 78 D2
Codda 10 D2
Coddenham 88 B2
Coddington
  Ches W 127 D4
  Hereford 79 C5
  Notts 132 D3
Codford St Mary 30 B3
Codford St Peter 30 B3
Codicote 68 B2
Codmore Hill 34 D3
Codnor 114 A2
Codrington 43 B6
Codsall 95 A6
Codsall Wood 95 A6
Coed Duon
  = Blackwood 41 B6
Coedely 41 C5
Coedkernew 42 A1
Coed Mawr 123 C5
Coed Morgan 61 B5
Coedpoeth 126 D2
Coed-Talon 126 D2
Coedway 110 D2
Coed-y-bryn 73 B6
Coed-y-paen 61 D5
Coed-yr-ynys 60 A3
Coed Ystumgwern . .107 D5
Coelbren 59 D5
Coffinswell 8 A2
Cofton Hackett 96 D3
Cogan 41 D6
Cogenhoe 83 A5
Cogges 65 C4
Coggeshall 70 A2
Coggeshall Hamlet . .70 A2
Coggins Mill 36 D3
Coignafearn Lodge . .241 A4
Coig Peighinnean . . .288 A6
Coig Peighinnean
  Bhuirgh 288 B5
Coilacriech 243 C6
Coilantogle 217 D5
Coilleag 286 E3
Coillore 246 A2
Coity 40 C4
Col 288 C5
Colaboll 272 C3
Colan 4 A3
Colaton Raleigh 13 C5
Colbost 258 D2
Colburn 157 B5
Colby
  Cumb 165 C4
  IoM 152 D2
  Norf 120 B4
Colchester 71 A4
Colcot 41 E6
Cold Ash 46 C3
Cold Ashby 98 D3
Cold Ashton 43 B6
Cold Aston 64 B2
Coldbackie 277 C7
Coldbeck 155 A6
Coldblow 50 B2
Cold Blow 55 C7
Cold Brayfield 83 B6
Coldean 21 B6
Coldeast 12 D3
Colden 138 A2
Colden Common 32 C3

Coldfair Green 89 A5
Coldham 101 A6
Cold Hanworth 133 A5
Coldharbour
  Glos 62 C1
  Kent 36 A3
  Sur 35 B4
Cold Harbour 116 B2
Cold Hatton 111 C5
Cold Hesledon 168 A2
Cold Higham 82 B3
Coldingham 211 D6
Cold Kirby 158 C5
Cold Newton 99 A4
Cold Northcott 10 C3
Cold Norton 70 C2
Cold Overton 115 D6
Coldrain 219 D5
Coldred 39 A4
Coldridge 12 A1
Coldstream
  Angus 220 A3
  Borders 198 C2
Coldwaltham 20 A3
Coldwells 257 B6
Coldwells Croft 255 D6
Coldyeld 94 B1
Cole 29 B6
Colebatch 93 C7
Colebrook 13 A5
Colebrooke 12 B2
Coleby
  Lincs 133 C4
  N Lincs 141 B6
Coleford
  Devon 12 A2
  Glos 62 B1
  Som 29 A6
Cole Green 68 B2
Cole Henley 46 D2
Colehill 17 A4
Coleman's Hatch . . .36 C2
Colemere 110 B3
Colemore 33 B6
Coleorton 114 D2
Colerne 44 B2
Colesbourne 63 B5
Colesden 84 B3
Coles Green 88 C1
Cole's Green 88 A3
Coleshill
  Bucks 67 D4
  Oxon 64 D3
  Warks 97 C5
Colestocks 13 A5
Colgate 35 C5
Colgrain 206 B1
Colinsburgh 221 D4
Colinton 209 D5
Colintraive 203 A5
Colkirk 119 C6
Collace 220 A2
Collafirth 284 G6
Collaton St Mary 8 B2
College Milton 205 C6
Collessie 220 C2
Collier Row 69 D5
Collier's End 68 A3
Collier's Green 37 C5
Collier Street 37 B5
Colliery Row 167 A6
Collieston 257 D5
Collin 174 A3
Collingbourne Ducis 45 D6
Collingbourne
  Kingston 45 D6
Collingham
  Notts 132 C3
  W Yorks 148 C3
Collington 79 A4
Collingtree 83 B4
Collins Green 137 A4
Colliston 233 D4
Collycroft 97 C6
Collynie 256 C3
Collyweston 100 A1
Colmonell 180 C3
Colmworth 84 B3
Colnabaichin 243 B5
Colnbrook 48 B3
Colne
  Cambs 101 D5
  Lancs 146 C2
Colne Edge 146 C2
Colne Engaine 87 D4
Colney 104 A2
Colney Heath 68 C2
Colney Street 67 C6
Coln Rogers 64 C1
Coln St Aldwyn's . . .64 C2

Coln St Dennis 64 B1
Colpy 256 C1
Colquhar 196 B2
Colsterdale 157 C5
Colsterworth 116 C2
Colston Bassett 115 B4
Coltfield 266 C2
Colthouse 154 B2
Coltishall 121 D4
Coltness 194 A3
Colton
  Cumb 154 C2
  Norf 104 A2
  N Yorks 148 C5
  Staffs 113 C4
  W Yorks 148 D2
Col Uarach 288 D5
Colva 77 B6
Colvend 173 C6
Colvister 284 D7
Colwall Green 79 C5
Colwall Stone 79 C5
Colwell 178 B1
Colwich 112 C4
Colwick 115 A4
Colwinston 40 D4
Colworth 20 B2
Colwyn Bay
  = Bae Colwyn 124 B3
Colyford 14 B2
Colyton 14 B2
Combe
  Hereford 78 A1
  Oxon 65 B5
  W Berks 46 C1
Combe Common 34 C2
Combe Down 43 C6
Combe Florey 27 B6
Combe Hay 43 D6
Combeinteignhead . .13 D4
Combe Martin 25 A6
Combe Moor 78 A1
Combe Raleigh 13 A6
Comberbach 127 B6
Comberton
  Cambs 85 B5
  Hereford 78 A2
Combe St Nicholas . .28 D3
Combpyne 14 B2
Combridge 113 B4
Combrook 81 B6
Combs
  Derbys 129 B5
  Suff 87 B6
Combs Ford 87 B6
Combwich 28 A2
Comers 244 B3
Comins Coch 90 D4
Commercial End 86 A1
Commins Capel
  Betws 75 C5
Commins Coch 91 B6
Commondale 169 D4
Common Edge 144 D3
Commonmoor 6 A1
Commonside 127 B5
Common Side 130 B3
Compstall 138 D2
Compton
  Devon 8 A2
  Hants 32 C3
  Sur 34 B1
  Sur 34 B2
  W Berks 46 B3
  Wilts 45 D5
  W Sus 33 D6
Compton Abbas 30 D2
Compton Abdale 63 B6
Compton Bassett . . .44 B4
Compton
  Beauchamp 45 A6
Compton Bishop 42 D2
Compton
  Chamberlayne 31 C4
Compton Dando 43 C5
Compton Dundon . . .29 B4
Compton Martin 43 D4
Compton
  Pauncefoot 29 C6
Compton Valence . . .15 C3
Comrie
  Fife 208 B3
  Perth 218 B2
Conaglen House 237 C4
Conchra 214 D3
Concraigie 231 D5
Conder Green 145 B4
Conderton 80 D2
Condicote 64 A2
Condorrat 207 C5

Condover 94 A2
Coneyhurst 35 D4
Coneysthorpe 159 D6
Coneythorpe 148 B2
Coney Weston 103 D5
Conford 33 B7
Congash 253 D6
Congdon's Shop 10 D3
Congerstone 97 A6
Congham 119 C4
Congleton 128 C3
Congl-y-wal 108 A2
Congresbury 42 C3
Congreve 112 D3
Conicavel 253 A5
Coningsby 134 D2
Conington
  Cambs 85 A5
  Cambs 100 C3
Conisbrough 140 D3
Conisby 200 B2
Conisholme 143 D6
Coniston
  Cumb 154 B2
  E Yorks 151 D4
Coniston Cold 146 B3
Conistone 146 A3
Connah's Quay 126 C2
Connel 226 C4
Connel Park 182 A4
Connor Downs 2 B3
Conon Bridge 252 A1
Conon House 252 A1
Cononley 146 C3
Conordan 247 A4
Consall 112 A3
Consett 178 D3
Constable Burton . . 157 B5
Constantine 3 C5
Constantine Bay 9 D4
Contin 251 A6
Contlaw 245 B5
Conwy 124 B2
Conyer 51 C6
Conyers Green 87 A4
Cooden 23 B5
Cooil 152 D3
Cookbury 11 A5
Cookham 48 A1
Cookham Dean 47 A6
Cookham Rise 48 A1
Cookhill 80 B3
Cookley
  Suff 104 D4
  Worcs 95 C6
Cookley Green 66 D1
Cookney 245 C5
Cookridge 147 C6
Cooksbridge 22 A2
Cooksmill Green 69 C6
Coolham 35 D4
Cooling 51 B4
Coombe
  Corn 4 B4
  Corn 24 D3
  Hants 33 C5
  Wilts 45 D5
Coombe Bissett 31 C5
Coombe Hill 63 A4
Coombe Keynes 16 C2
Coombes 21 B4
Coopersale
  Common 69 C4
Cootham 20 A3
Copdock 88 C2
Copford Green 70 A3
Copgrove 148 A2
Copister 284 F6
Cople 84 C3
Copley 166 C3
Coplow Dale 129 B6
Copmanthorpe 149 C4
Coppathorne 10 A3
Coppenhall 112 B3
Coppenhall Moss . . 128 D2
Copperhouse 2 B3
Coppingford 100 C3
Copplestone 12 A2
Coppull 137 B4
Coppull Moor 137 B4
Copsale 35 D4
Copster Green 145 D6
Copston Magna 98 C1
Copt Heath 97 D4
Copt Hewick 158 D2
Copthorne
  Shrops 110 D3
  Sur 35 C6
Copt Oak 114 D2
Copy's Green 119 B6

Copythorne 32 D2
Corbets Tey 50 A2
Corbridge 178 C1
Corby 99 C5
Corby Glen 116 C2
Cordon 191 B6
Coreley 95 D4
Cores End 48 A2
Corfe 28 D2
Corfe Castle 16 C3
Corfe Mullen 16 B3
Corfton 94 C2
Corgarff 243 B5
Corhampton 33 C5
Corlae 183 C4
Corley 97 C6
Corley Ash 97 C5
Corley Moor 97 C5
Cornaa 152 C4
Cornabus 200 D3
Cornel 124 C2
Corner Row 144 D4
Corney 153 C2
Cornforth 167 B6
Cornhill 267 D6
Cornhill-on-Tweed 198 C2
Cornholme 138 A2
Cornish Hall End . . . 86 D2
Cornquoy 283 H6
Cornsay 166 A4
Cornsay Colliery . . 167 A4
Corntown
  Highld 252 A1
  V Glam 40 D4
Cornwell 64 A3
Cornwood 7 B5
Cornworthy 8 B2
Corpach 237 B4
Corpusty 120 B3
Corran
  Highld 237 C4
  Highld 238 B2
Corranbuie 202 B3
Corrany 152 C4
Corrie 203 D5
Corrie Common . . . 185 D5
Corriecravie 191 C5
Corriemoillie 263 D6
Corriemulzie
  Lodge 263 A5
Corrievarkie Lodge 229 A4
Corrievorrie 252 D3
Corrimony 251 C5
Corringham
  Lincs 141 D6
  Thurrock 51 A4
Corris 91 B5
Corris Uchaf 91 B5
Corrour Shooting
  Lodge 228 B3
Corrow 215 B4
Corry 247 B5
Corrykinloch 271 B6
Corrymuckloch . . . 218 A3
Corrynachenchy . . 225 B5
Corry of
  Ardnagrask . . . 251 B7
Corsback 280 A4
Corscombe 15 A5
Corse
  Aberds 255 B7
  Glos 62 A3
Corse Lawn 79 D6
Corse of Kinnoir . . 255 B6
Corsewall 170 A2
Corsham 44 B2
Corsindae 244 B3
Corsley 30 A2
Corsley Heath 30 A2
Corsock 173 A5
Corston
  Bath 43 C5
  Wilts 44 A3
Corstorphine 209 C4
Cors-y-Gedol 107 D5
Cortachy 232 C1
Corton
  Suff 105 B6
  Wilts 30 A3
Corton Denham . . . 29 C6
Coruanan Lodge . . 237 C4
Corunna 287 H3
Corwen 109 A5
Coryton
  Devon 11 C5
  Thurrock 51 A4
Cosby 98 B2
Coseley 96 B2
Cosgrove 83 C4
Cosham 19 A5

Cosheston 55 D6
Cossall 114 A2
Cossington
  Leics 115 D4
  Som 28 A3
Costa 282 E4
Costessey 120 D3
Costock 114 C3
Coston 115 C6
Cote 64 C4
Cotebrook 127 C5
Cotehill 176 D2
Cotes
  Cumb 154 C3
  Leics 114 C3
  Staffs 112 B2
Cotesbach 98 C2
Cotgrave 115 B4
Cothall 245 A5
Cotham 115 A5
Cothelstone 28 B1
Cotherstone 166 D3
Cothill 65 D5
Cotleigh 14 A2
Cotmanhay 114 A2
Cotmaton 13 C6
Coton
  Cambs 85 B6
  Northants 98 D3
  Staffs 112 B3
  Staffs 112 C3
Coton Clanford . . . 112 C2
Coton Hill
  Shrops 110 D3
  Staffs 112 B3
Coton in the Elms . 113 D6
Cott 8 A1
Cottam
  E Yorks 150 A2
  Lancs 145 D5
  Notts 132 B3
Cottartown 253 C6
Cottenham 85 A6
Cotterdale 156 B2
Cottered 68 A3
Cotteridge 96 D3
Cotterstock 100 B2
Cottesbrooke 99 D4
Cottesmore 116 C2
Cotteylands 27 D4
Cottingham
  E Yorks 150 D3
  Northants 99 B5
Cottingley 147 D5
Cottisford 82 D2
Cotton
  Staffs 113 A4
  Suff 87 A6
Cotton End 84 C2
Cottown
  Aberds 245 A4
  Aberds 255 D6
  Aberds 256 B3
Cotwalton 112 B3
Couch's Mill 5 B6
Coughton
  Hereford 62 A1
  Warks 80 A3
Coulaghailtro 202 B2
Coulags 249 B6
Coulby Newham . . 168 D3
Coulderton 162 D2
Coulin 250 A2
Coull
  Aberds 244 B2
  Argyll 200 B2
Coulport 215 D5
Coulsdon 35 A5
Coulston 44 D3
Coulter 195 C5
Coulton 159 D5
Cound 94 A3
Coundon
  Durham 167 C5
  W Mid 97 C6
Coundon Grange . . 167 C5
Countersett 156 C3
Countess 31 A5
Countess Wear . . . 13 C4
Countesthorpe 98 B2
Countisbury 26 A2
County Oak 35 C5
Coupar Angus . . . 231 D6
Coup Green 137 A4
Coupland 198 C3
Cour 202 D3
Courance 184 C3
Court-at-Street . . . 38 B2
Courteenhall 83 B4
Court Henry 58 C2

Courtsend 71 D4
Courtway 28 B2
Cousland 209 D6
Cousley Wood 37 C4
Cove
  Argyll 215 D5
  Borders 211 C4
  Devon 27 D4
  Hants 34 A1
  Highld 261 A5
Cove Bay 245 B6
Cove Bottom 105 D5
Covehithe 105 C6
Coven 96 A2
Coveney 101 C6
Covenham
  St Bartholomew . . 143 D5
Covenham
  St Mary 143 D5
Coventry 97 D6
Coverack 3 D5
Coverham 157 C5
Covesea 266 B2
Covington
  Cambs 100 D2
  S Lanark 195 C4
Cowan Bridge . . . 155 D5
Cow Ark 145 C6
Cowbeech 22 A4
Cowbit 117 D5
Cowbridge
  Lincs 117 A6
  Som 27 A4
Cowbridge
  = Y Bont-Faen . . 41 D4
Cowdale 129 B5
Cowden 36 B2
Cowdenbeath 209 A4
Cowdenburn 195 A7
Cowers Lane 113 A7
Cowes 18 B3
Cowesby 158 C3
Cowfold 35 D5
Cowgill 155 C6
Cowie
  Aberds 245 D5
  Stirling 207 B6
Cowley
  Devon 13 B4
  Glos 63 B5
  London 48 A3
  Oxon 65 C6
Cowleymoor 27 D4
Cowling
  Lancs 137 B4
  N Yorks 146 C3
  N Yorks 157 C6
Cowlinge 86 B3
Cowpe 138 A1
Cowpen 179 A4
Cowpen Bewley . . 168 C2
Cowplain 33 D5
Cowshill 165 A6
Cowslip Green . . . 42 C3
Cowstrandburn . . 208 A3
Cowthorpe 148 B3
Coxbank 111 A5
Coxbench 114 A1
Cox Common 105 C4
Coxford
  Norf 119 C5
  Soton 32 D2
Cox Green 48 B1
Coxheath 37 A5
Coxhill 39 A4
Coxhoe 167 B6
Coxley 29 A5
Cox Moor 131 D5
Coxwold 158 D4
Coychurch 40 D4
Coylton 193 C4
Coylumbridge . . . 242 A2
Coynach 244 B1
Coynachie 255 C5
Coytrahen 40 C3
Crabadon 7 B6
Crabbs Cross 80 A3
Crabtree 35 D5
Crackenthorpe . . . 165 C4
Crackington Haven . 10 B2
Crackley 97 D5
Cracklybank 111 D6
Crackpot 156 B3
Cracoe 146 A3
Craddock 27 D5
Cradhlastadh 287 A5
Cradley 79 C5
Cradley Heath . . . 96 C2
Crafthole 6 B2
Craggan 253 D6

Craggie
  Highld 252 C3
  Highld 274 C2
Cragg Vale 138 A3
Craghead 179 D4
Crai 59 C5
Craibstone 267 D5
Craichie 232 D3
Craig
  Dumfries 173 A4
  Dumfries 173 B4
  Highld 250 B2
Craiganor Lodge . 229 C5
Craig Castle 255 D5
Craig-cefn-parc . . 40 A1
Craigdam 256 C3
Craigdarroch
  Dumfries 183 C5
  Highld 251 A5
Craigdhu 251 B6
Craigearn 245 A4
Craigellachie 254 B3
Craigencross 170 A2
Craigend
  Perth 219 B6
  Stirling 207 B5
Craigendive 214 D3
Craigendoran . . . 215 D6
Craigends 205 B4
Craigens
  Argyll 200 B2
  E Ayrs 182 A3
Craighat 206 B2
Craighead 221 D6
Craighlaw Mains . 171 A5
Craighouse 201 B5
Craigie
  Aberds 245 A6
  Dundee 220 A4
  Perth 219 B6
  Perth 231 D5
  S Ayrs 193 B4
Craigiefield 282 F5
Craigielaw 210 C1
Craiglockhart . . . 209 C5
Craigmalloch . . . 182 C2
Craigmaud 268 D3
Craigmillar 209 C5
Craigmore 203 B6
Craignant 110 B1
Craigneuk
  N Lanark 194 A2
  N Lanark 207 D5
Craignure 225 C6
Craigo 233 B4
Craigow 219 D5
Craig Penllyn 41 D4
Craigrothie 220 C3
Craigroy 266 D2
Craigruie 217 B4
Craigston Castle . 268 D2
Craigton
  Aberdeen 245 B5
  Angus 221 A5
  Angus 232 C1
  Highld 264 A2
Craigtown 279 C4
Craig-y-don 124 A2
Craig-y-nos 59 D5
Craik 185 B6
Crail 221 D6
Crailing 187 A5
Crailinghall 187 A5
Craiselound 141 D5
Crakehill 158 D3
Crakemarsh 113 B4
Crambe 149 A6
Cramlington 179 B4
Cramond 209 C4
Cramond Bridge . 209 C4
Cranage 128 C2
Cranberry 112 B2
Cranborne 31 D4
Cranbourne 48 B2
Cranbrook
  Devon 13 B5
  Kent 37 C5
Cranbrook Common. 37 C5
Crane Moor 139 C6
Crane's Corner . . 119 D6
Cranfield 83 C6
Cranford 48 B4
Cranford St Andrew . 99 D6
Cranford St John . 99 D6
Cranham
  Glos 63 B4
  London 50 A2
Crank 136 D4
Crank Wood 137 C5
Cranleigh 34 C3

Con–Cri 301

Cranley 104 D2
Cranmer Green . . 103 D6
Cranmore 18 C2
Cranna 268 D1
Crannich 225 B4
Crannoch 267 D5
Cranoe 99 B5
Cransford 88 A4
Cranshaws 210 D3
Cranstal 152 A4
Crantock 4 A2
Cranwell 116 A3
Cranwich 102 B3
Cranworth 103 A5
Craobh Haven . . 213 B5
Crapstone 7 A4
Crarae 214 C2
Crask Inn 272 B3
Craskins 244 B2
Crask of Aigas . . 251 B6
Craster 189 B5
Craswall 77 D6
Cratfield 104 D4
Crathes 245 C4
Crathie
  Aberds 243 C5
  Highld 240 C3
Crathorne 158 A3
Craven Arms 94 C2
Crawcrook 178 C3
Crawford
  Lancs 136 C3
  S Lanark 195 D4
Crawfordjohn . . . 194 D3
Crawick 183 A5
Crawley
  Hants 32 B3
  Oxon 64 B4
  W Sus 35 C5
Crawley Down . . . 35 C6
Crawleyside 166 A2
Crawshawbooth . 137 A7
Crawton 233 A6
Cray
  N Yorks 156 D3
  Perth 231 B5
Crayford 50 B2
Crayke 159 D4
Crays Hill 69 D7
Cray's Pond 47 A4
Creacombe 26 D3
Creagan 227 B4
Creag Ghoraidh . . 286 B3
Creaguaineach
  Lodge 228 B2
Creaksea 70 D3
Creaton 99 D4
Creca 175 A5
Credenhill 78 C2
Crediton 12 A3
Creebridge 171 A6
Creech Heathfield . 28 C2
Creech St Michael . 28 C2
Creed 4 C4
Creekmouth 50 A1
Creeting Bottoms . 88 B2
Creeting St Mary . 88 B1
Creeton 116 C3
Creetown 171 B6
Creggans 214 B3
Cregneash 152 E1
Creg-ny-Baa . . . 152 C3
Cregrina 77 B5
Creich 220 B3
Creigiau 41 C5
Cremyll 6 B3
Cressage 94 A3
Cressbrook 129 B6
Cresselly 55 D6
Cressing 70 A1
Cresswell
  Northumb 189 D5
  Staffs 112 B3
Cresswell Quay . . 55 D6
Creswell 131 B5
Cretingham 88 A3
Cretshengan . . . 202 B2
Crewe
  Ches E 128 D2
  Ches W 127 D4
Crewgreen 110 D2
Crewkerne 14 A4
Crianlarich 216 B3
Cribyn 75 C4
Criccieth 107 C4
Crich 130 D3
Crichie 257 B4

Crichton 209 D6
Crick
  Mon. 61 D6
  Northants 98 D2
Crickadarn 77 C4
Cricket Malherbie . . 28 C3
Cricket St Thomas . . 14 A3
Crickheath 110 C1
Crickhowell 60 B4
Cricklade 64 D2
Cricklewood 49 A5
Cridling Stubbs 140 A3
Crieff 218 B3
Criggion 110 D1
Crigglestone 139 D6
Crimond 269 D5
Crimonmogate 269 D5
Crimplesham 102 A2
Crinan 213 C5
Cringleford 104 A2
Cringles 147 C4
Crinow 56 A1
Cripplesease 2 B3
Cripplestyle 31 D4
Cripp's Corner 37 D5
Croasdale 162 C3
Crockenhill 50 C2
Crockernwell 12 B2
Crockerton 30 A2
Crocketford or Ninemile
  Bar 173 A6
Crockey Hill 149 C5
Crockham Hill 36 A2
Crockleford Heath . . 71 A4
Crockness 283 H4
Crock Street 28 D3
Croeserw 40 B3
Croes-goch 54 A4
Croes-lan 73 B6
Croesor 107 B6
Croesyceiliog
  Carms 57 A4
  Torf 61 D5
Croes-y-mwyalch . . 61 D5
Croesywaun 107 A5
Croft
  Leics 98 B2
  Lincs 135 C5
  Pembs 73 B4
  Warr 137 D5
Croftamie 206 B2
Croftmalloch 208 D2
Crofton
  Wilts 45 C6
  W Yorks 140 B1
Croft-on-Tees 157 A6
Crofts of
  Benachielt 275 A5
Crofts of Haddo . . 256 C3
Crofts of
  Inverthernie 256 B2
Crofts of Meikle
  Ardo 256 B3
Crofty 57 C5
Croggan 225 D6
Croglin 164 A3
Croich 263 A6
Crois Dughaill 286 D3
Cromarty 264 D3
Cromblet 256 C2
Cromdale 253 D6
Cromer
  Herts 68 A2
  Norf 120 A4
Cromford 130 D2
Cromhall 62 D2
Cromhall Common . . 43 A5
Cromor 288 E5
Cromra 240 C3
Cromwell 132 C2
Cronberry 193 C6
Crondall 33 A6
Cronk-y-Voddy 152 C3
Cronton 127 A4
Crook
  Cumb 154 B3
  Durham 167 B4
Crookedholm 193 B4
Crookes 130 A3
Crookham
  Northumb 198 C3
  W Berks 46 C3
Crookham Village . . 47 D5
Crookhaugh 195 D6
Crookhouse 187 A6
Crooklands 154 C4
Crook of Devon . . . 219 D5
Cropredy 82 C1

Cropston 114 D3
Cropthorne 80 C2
Cropton 159 C6
Cropwell Bishop . . . 115 B4
Cropwell Butler . . . 115 B4
Cros 288 A6
Crosbost 288 E4
Crosby
  Cumb 162 A3
  IoM 152 D3
  N Lincs 141 B6
Crosby Garrett 155 A6
Crosby
  Ravensworth 165 D4
Crosby Villa 162 A3
Croscombe 29 A5
Cross 42 D3
Crossaig 202 C3
Crossal 246 A3
Crossapol 222 C2
Cross Ash 61 B6
Cross-at-Hand 37 B5
Crossburn 207 C6
Crossbush 20 B3
Crosscanonby 162 A3
Crossdale Street . . . 120 B4
Crossens 136 B2
Crossflatts 147 C5
Crossford
  Fife 208 B3
  S Lanark 194 B3
Crossgate 117 C5
Crossgatehall 209 D6
Crossgates
  Fife 208 B4
  Powys 77 A4
Crossgill 145 A5
Cross Green
  Devon 11 C4
  Suff 87 B4
  Suff 87 B5
  Warks 81 B6
Cross Hands 57 A5
Cross-hands 73 D4
Cross Hands 55 C6
Crosshill
  E Ayrs 193 C4
  Fife 209 A4
  S Ayrs 192 E3
Cross Hill 114 A2
Crosshouse 192 B3
Cross Houses 94 A3
Crossings 176 B3
Cross in Hand
  E Sus 36 D3
  Leics 98 C2
Cross Inn
  Ceredig 73 A6
  Ceredig 75 B4
  Rhondda 41 C5
Crosskeys 41 B7
Cross Keys 36 A3
Crosskirk 279 A6
Cross Lane Head . . . 95 B5
Crosslanes 110 D2
Cross Lanes
  Corn 3 C4
  N Yorks 148 A4
  Wrex 110 A2
Crosslee
  Borders 185 A6
  Renfs 205 B4
Crossmichael 173 B5
Crossmoor 144 D4
Cross Oak 60 A3
Cross of Jackston . . 256 C2
Cross o' th' hands . . 113 A6
Crossroads
  Aberds 245 C4
  E Ayrs 193 B4
Cross Street 104 D2
Cross Trickett's 17 A4
Crossway
  Hereford 79 D4
  Mon 61 B6
  Powys 77 B4
Crossway Green . . . 79 A6
Crossways 16 C1
Crosswell 72 C4
Crosswood 75 A5
Crosthwaite 154 B3
Croston 136 B3
Crostwick 121 D4
Crostwight 121 C5
Crothair 288 D2
Crouch 36 A4
Croucheston 31 C4
Crouch Hill 29 D7
Crouch House Green 36 B2
Croughton 82 D2

Crovie 268 C3
Crowan 3 B4
Crowborough 36 C3
Crowcombe 27 B6
Crowdecote 129 C6
Crowden 138 D3
Crow Edge 139 C4
Crowell 66 D2
Crowfield
  Northants 82 C3
  Suff 88 B2
Crow Hill 62 A2
Crowhurst
  E Sus 23 A5
  Sur 36 B1
Crowhurst Lane End . 36 B1
Crowland 117 D5
Crowlas 2 B3
Crowle
  N Lincs 141 B5
  Worcs 80 B2
Crowmarsh Gifford . . 47 A4
Crown Corner 104 D3
Crownhill 6 B3
Crownland 103 E6
Crownthorpe 104 A1
Crowntown 3 B4
Crows-an-wra 2 C1
Crowshill 103 A5
Crowsnest 94 A1
Crowthorne 47 C6
Crowton 127 B5
Croxall 113 D5
Croxby 142 D3
Croxdale 167 B5
Croxden 113 A4
Croxley Green 67 D5
Croxton
  Cambs 84 A4
  N Lincs 142 B2
  Norf 103 C4
  Staffs 112 B1
Croxtonbank 112 B1
Croxton Kerrial . . . 115 C6
Croy
  Highld 252 B3
  N Lanark 207 C5
Croyde 25 B5
Croydon
  Cambs 85 C5
  London 49 C6
Crubenmore Lodge 241 C4
Cruckmeole 94 A2
Cruckton 110 D3
Cruden Bay 257 C5
Crudgington 111 D5
Crudwell 63 D5
Crug 93 D5
Crugmeer 9 D5
Crugybar 58 B3
Crulabhig 288 D2
Crumlin = Crymlyn . . 41 B7
Crumpsall 138 C1
Crundale
  Kent 38 A2
  Pembs 55 C5
Cruwys Morchard . . 26 D3
Crux Easton 46 D2
Crwbin 57 A4
Crya 283 G4
Cryers Hill 66 D3
Crymlyn 123 C6
Crymlyn = Crumlin . . 41 B7
Crymych 73 C4
Crynant 40 A2
Crynfryn 75 B4
Cuaig 249 A4
Cuan 213 A5
Cubbington 81 A6
Cubeck 156 C3
Cubert 4 B2
Cubley 139 C5
Cubley Common . . . 113 B5
Cublington
  Bucks 66 A3
  Hereford 78 D2
Cuckfield 35 D6
Cucklington 30 C1
Cuckney 131 B5
Cuckoo Hill 141 D5
Cuddesdon 65 C7
Cuddington
  Bucks 66 B2
  Ches W 127 B6
Cuddington Heath . 110 A3
Cuddy Hill 145 D4
Cudham 36 A2
Cudliptown 11 D6
Cudworth
  Som 28 D3

Cudworth continued
  S Yorks 140 C1
Cuffley 68 C3
Cuiashader 288 B6
Cuidhir 286 F2
Cuidhtinis 287 F5
Culbo 264 D2
Culbokie 252 A2
Culburnie 251 B6
Culcabock 252 B2
Culcairn 264 D2
Culcharry 253 A4
Culcheth 137 D5
Culdrain 255 C6
Culduie 249 B4
Culford 103 D4
Culgaith 165 C4
Culham 65 D6
Culkein 270 A3
Culkein Drumbeg . . 270 A4
Culkerton 63 D5
Cullachie 253 D5
Cullen 267 C6
Cullercoats 179 B5
Cullicudden 264 D2
Cullingworth 147 D4
Cullipool 213 A5
Cullivoe 284 C7
Culloch 218 C2
Culloden 252 B3
Cullompton 13 A5
Culmaily 265 A4
Culmazie 171 B5
Culmington 94 C2
Culmstock 27 D6
Culnacraig 270 D3
Culnaknock 259 B5
Culpho 88 C3
Culrain 264 A1
Culross 208 B2
Culroy 192 D3
Culsh
  Aberds 243 C6
  Aberds 256 B3
Culshabbin 171 B5
Culswick 285 J4
Cultercullen 257 D4
Cults
  Aberdeen 245 B5
  Aberds 255 C6
  Dumfries 171 C6
Culverstone Green . . 50 C3
Culverthorpe 116 A3
Culworth 82 C2
Culzie Lodge 263 C7
Cumbernauld 207 C5
Cumbernauld
  Village 207 C5
Cumberworth 135 B5
Cuminestown 268 D3
Cumlewick 285 L6
Cummersdale 175 C6
Cummertrees 174 B4
Cummingston 266 C2
Cumnock 193 C5
Cumnor 65 C5
Cumrew 176 D3
Cumwhinton 176 D2
Cumwhitton 176 D3
Cundall 158 D3
Cunninghamhead . . 204 D3
Cunnister 284 D7
Cupar 220 C3
Cupar Muir 220 C3
Cupernham 32 C2
Curbar 130 B2
Curbridge
  Hants 32 D4
  Oxon 64 C4
Curdridge 32 D4
Curdworth 97 B4
Curland 28 D2
Curlew Green 89 A4
Currarie 180 B3
Curridge 46 B2
Currie 209 D4
Curry Mallet 28 C3
Curry Rivel 28 C3
Curtisden Green . . . 37 B5
Curtisknowle 7 B6
Cury 3 C4
Cushnie 268 C2
Cushuish 28 B1
Cusop 77 C6
Cutcloy 171 D6
Cutcombe 27 B4
Cutgate 138 B1
Cutiau 90 A4
Cutlers Green 86 D1
Cutnall Green 80 A1

Cutsdean 80 D3
Cutthorpe 130 B3
Cutts 285 K6
Cuxham 66 D1
Cuxton 51 C4
Cuxwold 142 C3
Cwm
  Bl Gwent 60 C3
  Denb 125 B5
  Swansea 40 B1
Cwmafan 40 B2
Cwmaman 41 B5
Cwmann 75 D4
Cwmavon 61 C4
Cwmbach
  Carms 57 B4
  Carms 73 D5
  Powys 76 B4
  Powys 77 D5
Cwmbâch 41 A5
Cwmbelan 92 C3
Cwmbran
  = Cwmbrân 61 D4
Cwmbrân
  = Cwmbran 61 D4
Cwmbrwyno 91 D5
Cwm-byr 58 B3
Cwmcarn 41 B7
Cwmcarvan 61 C6
Cwm-Cewydd 91 A6
Cwm-cou 73 B5
Cwmcych 73 C5
Cwmdare 41 A4
Cwmderwen 92 A3
Cwmdu
  Carms 58 B3
  Powys 60 A3
  Swansea 57 C6
Cwmduad 73 C6
Cwm-Dulais 57 B6
Cwmdwr 59 B4
Cwmfelin
  Bridgend 40 C3
  M Tydf 41 A5
Cwmfelin Boeth . . . 56 A1
Cwm-felin-fach . . . 41 B6
Cwmfelin Mynach . . 73 D5
Cwmffrwd 57 A4
Cwm Ffrwd-oer . . . 61 C4
Cwmgiedd 59 D4
Cwmgors 59 D4
Cwmgwili 57 A5
Cwmgwrach 40 A3
Cwm-hesgen 108 C2
Cwmhiraeth 73 C6
Cwm-hwnt 59 E6
Cwmifor 58 C3
Cwm Irfon 76 C2
Cwmisfael 57 A4
Cwm-Llinau 91 B6
Cwmllynfell 59 D4
Cwm-mawr 57 A5
Cwmorgan 73 C5
Cwm-parc 40 B4
Cwmpengraig 73 C6
Cwm Penmachno . . 108 A2
Cwmrhos 60 A3
Cwmsychpant 74 D3
Cwmtillery 60 C4
Cwm-twrch Isaf . . . 59 D4
Cwm-twrch Uchaf . 59 D4
Cwmwysg 59 C5
Cwm-y-glo
  Carms 57 A5
  Gwyn 123 D5
Cwmyoy 61 A4
Cwmystwyth 92 D1
Cwrt 91 B4
Cwrt-newydd 74 D3
Cwrt-y-cadno 58 A3
Cwrt-y-gollen 60 B4
Cydweli = Kidwelly . . 57 B4
Cyffordd Llandudno
  = Llandudno
  Junction 124 B2
Cyffylliog 125 D5
Cyfronydd 93 A5
Cymer 40 B3
Cyncoed 41 C6
Cynghordy 59 A5
Cynheidre 57 B4
Cynwyd 109 A5
Cynwyl Elfed 73 D6
Cywarch 91 A6

Dacre
  Cumb 164 C2
  N Yorks 147 A5
Dacre Banks 147 A5
Daddry Shield 166 B1
Dadford 82 D3
Dadlington 97 B7
Dafarn Faig 107 A5
Dafen 57 B5
Daffy Green 103 A5
Dagenham 50 A1
Daglingworth 63 C5
Dagnall 67 B4
Dail Beag 288 C3
Dail bho Dheas . . . 288 A5
Dail bho Thuath . . . 288 A5
Daill 200 B3
Dailly 181 A4
Dail Mor 288 C3
Dairsie or
  Osnaburgh 220 C4
Daisy Hill 137 C5
Dalabrog 286 D3
Dalavich 214 A2
Dalbeattie 173 B6
Dalblair 182 A4
Dalbog 232 A3
Dalbury 113 B6
Dalby
  IoM 152 D2
  N Yorks 159 D5
Dalchalloch 229 B6
Dalchalm 274 C2
Dalchenna 214 B3
Dalchirach 254 C2
Dalchork 272 C3
Dalchreichart 239 A6
Dalchruin 218 C2
Dalderby 134 C2
Dale 54 D4
Dale Abbey 114 B2
Dale Head 164 D2
Dalelia 235 D6
Dale of Walls 285 H3
Daless 253 C4
Dalfaber 242 A2
Dalgarven 204 D2
Dalgety Bay 209 B4
Dalginross 218 B2
Dalguise 230 D3
Dalhalvaig 279 C4
Dalham 86 A3
Dalinlongart 215 D4
Dalkeith 209 D6
Dallam 137 D4
Dallas 266 D2
Dalleagles 182 A3
Dallinghoo 88 B3
Dallington
  E Sus 23 A4
  Northants 83 A4
Dallow 157 D5
Dalmadilly 245 A4
Dalmally 227 D6
Dalmarnock 205 B6
Dalmary 206 A3
Dalmellington 182 B2
Dalmeny 208 C4
Dalmigavie 241 A5
Dalmigavie Lodge . 252 A2
Dalmore 264 D2
Dalmuir 205 A4
Dalnabreck 235 D5
Dalnacardoch
  Lodge 229 A6
Dalnacroich 251 A5
Dalnaglar Castle . . 231 B5
Dalnahaitnach 253 D4
Dalnaspidal Lodge . 229 A5
Dalnavaid 230 B4
Dalnavie 264 C2
Dalnawillan Lodge . 279 D6
Dalness 237 D5
Dalnessie 273 C4
Dalqueich 219 D5
Dalreavoch 273 D5
Dalry 204 D2
Dalrymple 192 D3
Dalserf 194 A3
Dalston 175 C6
Dalswinton 184 D2
Dalton
  Dumfries 174 A4
  Lancs 136 C3
  Northumb 177 D7
  Northumb 178 B3
  N Yorks 157 A5

Dalton continued
N Yorks **158** D3
S Yorks **140** D2
Dalton-in-Furness . **153** C3
Dalton-le-Dale **168** A2
Dalton-on-Tees . . . **157** A6
Dalton Piercy **168** B2
Dalveich **217** B6
Dalwhinnie **241** D4
Dalwood **14** A2
Dalwyne **181** B5
Damerham **31** D5
Damgate **105** A5
Dam Green **103** C6
Damnaglaur **170** D3
Damside **195** B6
Dam Side **144** C4
Danbury **70** C1
Danby **159** A6
Danby Wiske **158** B2
Dandaleith **254** B3
Danderhall **209** D6
Danebridge **129** C4
Dane End **68** A3
Danehill **36** D2
Danemoor Green . . **103** A6
Danesford **95** B5
Daneshill **47** D4
Dangerous Corner . **136** B4
Danskine **210** D2
Darcy Lever **137** C6
Darenth **50** B2
Daresbury **127** A5
Darfield **140** C2
Darfoulds **131** B5
Dargate **52** C2
Darite **6** A1
Darlaston **96** B2
Darley **147** B6
Darley Bridge **130** C2
Darley Head **147** B5
Darlingscott **81** C5
Darlington **167** D5
Darliston **111** B4
Darlton **132** B2
Darnall **130** A3
Darnick **197** C4
Darowen **91** B6
Darra **256** B2
Darracott **25** B5
Darras Hall **178** B3
Darrington **140** A2
Darsham **89** A5
Dartford **50** B2
Dartford Crossing . . . **50** B2
Dartington **8** A1
Dartmeet **12** D1
Dartmouth **8** B2
Darton **139** C6
Darvel **193** B5
Darwell Hole **23** A4
Darwen **137** A5
Datchet **48** B2
Datchworth **68** B2
Datchworth Green . . **68** B2
Daubhill **137** C6
Daugh of
Kinermony **254** B3
Dauntsey **44** A3
Dava **253** C6
Davenham **127** B6
Davenport Green . . **128** B3
Daventry **82** A2
Davidson's Mains . **209** C5
Davidstow **10** C2
David's Well **93** D4
Davington **185** B5
Daviot
Aberds **256** D2
Highld **252** C3
Davoch of Grange . **267** D5
Davyhulme **137** D6
Dawley **95** A4
Dawlish **13** D4
Dawlish Warren **13** D4
Dawn **124** B3
Daws Heath **51** A4
Daw's House **10** C4
Dawsmere **118** B1
Dayhills **112** B3
Daylesford **64** A3
Ddôl-Cownwy **109** D5
Ddrydwy **122** C3
Deadwater **187** D5
Deaf Hill **167** B6
Deal **53** D5
Deal Hall **71** D4
Dean
Cumb **162** B3

Dean continued
Devon **7** A6
Devon **25** A6
Dorset **30** D3
Hants **33** D4
Som **29** A6
Deanburnhaugh . . **186** B2
Deane
Gtr Man **137** C5
Hants **46** D3
Deanich Lodge . . . **263** B5
Deanland **30** D3
Dean Prior **7** A6
Dean Row **128** A3
Deans **208** D3
Deanscales **162** B3
Deanshanger **83** D4
Deanston **218** D2
Dearham **162** A3
Debach **88** B3
Debden
Essex **68** D3
Essex **86** D1
Debden Cross **86** D1
Debenham **88** A2
Dechmont **208** C3
Deddington **82** D1
Dedham **87** D6
Dedham Heath **87** D6
Deebank **244** C3
Deene **99** B6
Deenethorpe **99** B6
Deepcar **139** D5
Deepcut **34** A2
Deepdale **155** C6
Deeping Gate **100** A3
Deeping St James . **100** A3
Deeping
St Nicholas **117** D5
Deerhill **267** D5
Deerhurst **63** A4
Deerness **283** G6
Defford **80** C2
Defynnog **59** C6
Deganwy **124** B2
Deighton
N Yorks **158** A2
W Yorks **139** B4
York **149** C5
Deiniolen **123** D5
Delabole **9** C6
Delamere **127** C5
Delfrigs **257** D4
Delliefure **254** C1
Dell Lodge **242** A3
Delnabo **243** A4
Delnadamph **243** B5
Delph **138** C2
Delves **166** A4
Delvine **231** D5
Dembleby **116** B3
Denaby Main **140** D2
Denbigh = Dinbych . **125** C5
Denbury **8** A2
Denby **114** A1
Denby Dale **139** C5
Denchworth **65** D4
Dendron **153** C3
Denel End **84** D2
Denend **255** C7
Denford **100** D1
Dengie **70** C3
Denham
Bucks **48** A3
Suff **86** A3
Suff **104** D2
Denham Street **104** D2
Denhead
Aberds **269** D4
Fife **221** C4
Denhead of
Arbilot **232** D3
Denhead of Gray . . **220** A3
Denholm **187** B4
Denholme **147** D4
Denholme Clough . **147** D4
Denio **106** C3
Denmead **33** D5
Denmore **245** A6
Denmoss **256** B1
Dennington **88** A3
Denny **207** B6
Dennyloanhead . . . **207** B6
Denny Lodge **18** A2
Denshaw **138** B2
Denside **245** C5
Densole **39** A4
Denston **86** B3
Denstone **113** A5
Dent **155** C6

Denton
Cambs **100** C3
Darl **167** D5
E Sus **22** B2
Gtr Man **138** D2
Kent **39** A4
Lincs **115** B6
Norf **104** C3
Northants **83** B5
N Yorks **147** C5
Oxon **65** C6
Denton's Green . . . **136** D3
Denver **102** A2
Denwick **189** B5
Deopham **103** A6
Deopham Green . . . **103** B6
Depden **86** B3
Depden Green **86** B3
Deptford
London **49** B6
Wilts **31** B4
Derby **114** B1
Derbyhaven **152** E2
Dereham **120** D1
Deri **41** A6
Derril **10** A4
Derringstone **39** A4
Derrington **112** C2
Derriton **10** A4
Derryguaig **224** C3
Derry Hill **44** B3
Derrythorpe **141** C6
Dersingham **118** B3
Dervaig **224** A3
Derwen **125** D5
Derwenlas **91** C5
Desborough **99** C5
Desford **98** A1
Detchant **199** C4
Detling **37** A5
Deuddwr **110** D1
Devauden **61** D6
Devil's Bridge **75** A6
Devizes **44** C4
Devol **204** A3
Devonport **6** B3
Devonside **208** A2
Devoran **4** D2
Dewar **196** B2
Dewlish **16** B1
Dewsbury **139** A5
Dewsbury Moor . . . **139** A5
Dewshall Court **78** D2
Dhoon **152** C4
Dhoor **152** B4
Dhowin **152** A4
Dial Post **21** A4
Dibden **18** A3
Dibden Purlieu **18** A3
Dickleburgh **104** C2
Didbrook **80** D3
Didcot **46** A3
Diddington **84** A3
Diddlebury **94** C3
Didley **78** D2
Didling **20** A1
Didmarton **44** A2
Didsbury **138** D1
Didworthy **7** A5
Digby **133** D5
Digg **259** B4
Diggle **138** C3
Digmoor **136** C3
Digswell Park **68** B2
Dihewyd **74** C3
Dilham **121** C5
Dilhorne **112** A3
Dillarburn **194** B3
Dillington **84** A3
Dilston **178** C1
Dilton Marsh **30** A2
Dilwyn **78** B2
Dinas
Carms **73** C5
Gwyn **106** C2
Dinas Cross **72** C3
Dinas Dinlle **107** A4
Dinas-Mawddwy . . . **91** A6
Dinas Powys **41** D6
Dinbych = Denbigh . **125** C5
Dinbych-y-Pysgod
= Tenby **56** B1
Dinder **29** A5
Dinedor **78** D3
Dingestow **61** B6
Dingle **126** A3
Dingleden **37** C6
Dingley **99** C4
Dingwall **252** A1
Dinlabyre **186** D4

Dinmael **109** A5
Dinnet **244** C1
Dinnington
Som **28** D4
S Yorks **131** A5
T&W **179** B4
Dinorwic **123** D5
Dinton
Bucks **66** B2
Wilts **31** B4
Dinwoodie Mains . . **185** C4
Dinworthy **24** D4
Dippen **191** C6
Dippenhall **33** A7
Dipple
Moray **266** D4
S Ayrs **181** A4
Diptford **7** B6
Dipton **178** D3
Dirdhu **254** D1
Dirleton **210** B1
Dirt Pot **165** A6
Discoed **77** A6
Diseworth **114** C2
Dishes **282** E7
Dishforth **158** D2
Disley **129** A4
Diss **104** D2
Disserth **76** B4
Distington **162** B3
Ditchampton **31** B4
Ditcheat **29** B6
Ditchingham **104** B4
Ditchling **21** A6
Ditherington **111** D4
Dittisham **8** B2
Ditton
Halton **127** A4
Kent **37** A5
Ditton Green **86** B2
Ditton Priors **95** C4
Divach **251** D6
Divlyn **59** B4
Dixton
Glos **80** D2
Mon **61** B7
Dobcross **138** C2
Dobwalls **5** A7
Doccombe **12** C2
Dochfour House . . . **252** C2
Dochgarroch **252** B2
Docking **119** B4
Docklow **78** B3
Dockray **164** C1
Dockroyd **147** D4
Doc Penfro
= Pembroke Dock . . . **55** D5
Dodburn **186** C3
Doddinghurst **69** D5
Doddington
Cambs **101** B5
Kent **51** D6
Lincs **133** B4
Northumb **198** C3
Shrops **95** D4
Doddiscombsleigh . . **12** C3
Dodford
Northants **82** A3
Worcs **96** D2
Dodington **43** A6
Dodleston **126** C3
Dods Leigh **112** B4
Dodworth **139** C6
Doe Green **127** A5
Doe Lea **131** C4
Dogdyke **134** D2
Dogmersfield **47** D5
Dogridge **45** A4
Dogsthorpe **100** A3
Dog Village **13** B4
Dolanog **109** D5
Dolau
Powys **77** A5
Rhondda **41** C4
Dolbenmaen **107** B5
Dolfach **91** B7
Dolfor **93** C5
Dol-fôr **91** B6
Dolgarrog **124** C2
Dolgellau **91** A5
Dolgran **58** B1
Dolhendre **108** B3
Doll **274** D2
Dollar **208** A2
Dolley Green **77** A6
Dollwen **91** D4
Dolphin **126** B1
Dolphinholme **145** B5
Dolphinton **195** B6
Dolton **25** D6

Dolwen
Conwy **124** B3
Powys **92** A3
Dolwyd **124** B3
Dolwyddelan **124** D2
Dôl-y-Bont **90** D4
Dol-y-cannau **77** C6
Dolyhir **77** B6
Doncaster **140** C3
Dones Green **127** B6
Donhead St Andrew . **30** C3
Donhead St Mary . . **30** C3
Donibristle **209** B4
Donington **117** B5
Donington on Bain . **134** A2
Donington South
Ing. **117** B5
Donisthorpe **113** D7
Donkey Town **48** C2
Donnington
Glos **64** A2
Hereford **79** D5
Shrops **94** A3
Telford **111** D6
W Berks **46** C2
W Sus **20** B1
Donnington Wood . **111** D6
Donyatt **28** D3
Doonfoot **192** D3
Dorback Lodge . . . **242** A3
Dorchester
Dorset **15** B6
Oxon **65** D6
Dordon **97** A5
Dore **130** A3
Dores **252** C1
Dorking **35** B4
Dormansland **36** B2
Dormanstown **168** C3
Dormington **78** C3
Dormston **80** B2
Dornal **181** D4
Dorney **48** B2
Dornie **249** D5
Dornoch **264** B3
Dornock **175** B5
Dorrery **279** C6
Dorridge **97** D4
Dorrington
Lincs **133** D5
Shrops **94** A2
Dorsington **80** C4
Dorstone **77** C7
Dorton **66** B1
Dorusduain **250** D1
Dosthill **97** B5
Dottery **15** B4
Doublebois **5** A6
Dougarie **191** B4
Doughton **63** D4
Douglas
IoM **152** D3
S Lanark **194** C3
Douglas & Angus . . **220** A4
Douglastown **232** D2
Douglas Water **194** C3
Douglas West **194** C3
Doulting **29** A6
Dounby **282** E3
Doune
Highld **272** D2
Stirling **218** D2
Doune Park **268** C2
Douneside **244** B1
Dounie **264** A1
Dounreay **279** B5
Dousland **7** A4
Dovaston **110** C2
Dove Holes **129** B5
Dovenby **162** A3
Dover **39** A5
Dovercourt **88** D3
Doverdale **79** A6
Doveridge **113** B5
Doversgreen **35** B5
Dowally **230** D4
Dowbridge **144** D4
Dowdeswell **63** B5
Dowlais **60** C2
Dowland **25** D6
Dowlish Wake **28** D3
Down Ampney **64** D2
Downcraig Ferry . . . **204** C1
Downderry **6** B2
Downe **50** C1
Downend
IoW **18** C4
S Glos **43** B5
W Berks **46** B2
Downfield **220** A3

Dal–Dro 303

Downgate **11** D4
Downham
Essex **70** D1
Lancs **146** C1
Northumb **198** C2
Downham Market . **102** A2
Down Hatherley **63** A4
Downhead **29** A6
Downhill
Perth **219** A5
T&W **179** D5
Downholland Cross **136** C2
Downholme **157** B5
Downies **245** C6
Downley **66** D3
Down St Mary **12** A2
Downside
Som **29** A6
Sur **35** A4
Down Thomas **7** B4
Downton
Hants **17** B6
Wilts **31** C5
Downton on the
Rock **94** D2
Dowsby **116** C4
Dowsdale **117** D5
Dowthwaitehead . . **163** B6
Doxey **112** C3
Doxford **189** A4
Doxford Park **179** D5
Doynton **43** B6
Draffan **194** B2
Dragonby **141** B7
Drakeland Corner **7** B4
Drakemyre **204** C2
Drake's Broughton . . **80** C2
Drakes Cross **96** D3
Drakewalls **11** D5
Draughton
Northants **99** D4
N Yorks **147** B4
Drax **141** A4
Draycote **98** D1
Draycott
Derbys **114** B2
Glos **81** D4
Som **42** D3
Draycott in the
Clay. **113** C5
Draycott in the
Moors **112** A3
Drayford **26** D2
Drayton
Leics **99** B5
Lincs **117** B5
Norf **120** D3
Oxon **65** D5
Oxon **82** C1
Ptsmth **19** A5
Som **28** C4
Worcs **96** D2
Drayton Bassett **97** A4
Drayton Beauchamp **67** B4
Drayton Parslow **66** A3
Drayton St Leonard . **65** D6
Drebley **147** B4
Dreemskerry **152** B4
Dreenhill **55** C5
Drefach
Carms **57** A5
Carms **73** C6
Dre-fach
Carms **57** A6
Ceredig **75** D4
Drefelin **73** C6
Dreghorn **192** B3
Drellingore **39** A4
Drem **210** C2
Dresden **112** A3
Dreumasdal **286** C3
Drewsteignton **12** B2
Driby **134** B3
Driffield
E Yorks **150** B3
Glos **63** D6
Drigg **153** A1
Drighlington **139** A5
Drimnin **225** A4
Drimpton **14** A4
Drimsynie **215** B4
Drinisiadar **288** H2
Drinkstone **87** A5
Drinkstone Green . . . **87** A5
Drishaig **215** A4
Drissaig **214** A2
Drochil **195** B6
Droitwich **79** A6
Droman **276** C2
Dron **219** C6
Dronfield **130** B3
Dronfield
Woodhouse **130** B3
Drongan **182** A2
Dronley **220** A3
Droxford **33** D5
Droylsden **138** D2
Drointon **112** C4

Droitwich Spa 80 A1
Droman 276 C2
Dron 219 C6
Dronfield 130 B3
Dronfield
  Woodhouse 130 B3
Drongan 182 A2
Dronley 220 A3
Droxford 33 D5
Droylsden 138 D2
Druid 109 A5
Druidston 55 C4
Druimarbin 237 B4
Druimavuic 227 B5
Druimdrishaig 202 A2
Druimindarroch ... 235 B5
Druimyeon More .. 202 C1
Drum
  Argyll 203 A4
  Perth 219 D5
Drumbeg 270 A4
Drumblade 255 B6
Drumblair 256 B1
Drumbuie
  Dumfries 182 D3
  Highld 249 C4
Drumburgh 175 C5
Drumburn 174 B2
Drumchapel 205 A5
Drumchardine ... 252 B1
Drumchork 261 B5
Drumclog 193 B6
Drumderfit 252 A2
Drumeldrie 220 D4
Drumelzier 195 C6
Drumfearn 247 C5
Drumgask 241 C4
Drumgley 232 C2
Drumguish 241 C5
Drumin 254 C2
Drumlasie 244 B3
Drumlemble 190 D2
Drumligair 245 A6
Drumlithie 245 D4
Drummoddie 171 C5
Drummond 264 D2
Drummore 170 D2
Drummuir 255 B4
Drummuir Castle .. 255 B4
Drumnadrochit ... 251 D7
Drumnagorrach ... 267 D6
Drumoak 245 C4
Drumpark 183 D6
Drumphail 171 A4
Drumrash 173 A4
Drumrunie 271 D4
Drums 257 D4
Drumsallie 236 B3
Drumstinchall ... 173 C6
Drumsturdy 221 A4
Drumtochty Castle .244 E3
Drumtroddan 171 C5
Drumuie 259 D4
Drumuillie 253 D5
Drumvaich 217 D6
Drumwhindle ... 257 C4
Drunkendub 233 D4
Drury 126 C2
Drury Square 119 D6
Drybeck 165 D4
Drybridge
  Moray 267 C5
  N Ayrs 192 B3
Drybrook 62 B2
Dryburgh 197 C4
Dry Doddington ...115 A6
Dry Drayton 85 A5
Dryhope 196 D1
Drylaw 209 C5
Drym 3 B4
Drymen 206 B2
Drymuir 257 B4
Drynoch 246 A3
Dryslwyn 58 C2
Dryton 94 A3
Dubford 268 C3
Dubton 232 C3
Duchally 271 C6
Duchlage 206 B1
Duck Corner 89 C4
Duckington 127 C6
Ducklington 65 C4
Duckmanton 131 B4
Duck's Cross 84 B3
Duddenhoe End.. 85 D6
Duddingston 209 C5
Duddington 100 A1
Duddleswell 36 D2

Duddo 198 B3
Duddon 127 C5
Duddon Bridge ... 153 B3
Dudleston 110 B2
Dudleston Heath .. 110 B2
Dudley
  T&W 179 B4
  W Mid 96 B2
Dudley Port 96 B2
Duffield 114 A1
Duffryn
  Neath 40 B3
  Newport 42 A1
Dufftown 254 C4
Duffus 266 C2
Dufton 165 C4
Duggleby 150 A1
Duirinish 249 C4
Duisdalemore 247 C6
Duisky 237 B4
Dukestown 60 B3
Dukinfield 138 D2
Dulas 123 B4
Dulcote 29 A5
Dulford 13 A5
Dull 230 D2
Dullatur 207 C5
Dullingham 86 B2
Dulnain Bridge ... 253 D5
Duloe
  Bedford 84 A3
  Corn 6 B1
Dulsie 253 B5
Dulverton 27 C4
Dulwich 49 B6
Dumbarton 205 A3
Dumbleton 80 D3
Dumcrieff 185 B4
Dumfries 174 A2
Dumgoyne 206 B3
Dummer 33 A4
Dumpford 34 D1
Dumpton 53 C5
Dun 233 C4
Dunain House 252 B2
Dunalastair 229 C6
Dunan 247 B4
Dunans 214 C3
Dunball 28 A3
Dunbar 210 C3
Dunbeath 275 B5
Dunbeg 226 C3
Dunblane 218 D2
Dunbog 220 C2
Duncanston 252 A1
Duncanstone 255 D6
Dun Charlabhaigh .288 C2
Dunchurch 98 D1
Duncote 82 B3
Duncow 184 D2
Duncraggan 217 D5
Duncrievie 219 D6
Duncton 20 A2
Dundas House 283 J5
Dundee 220 A4
Dundeugh 182 D3
Dundon 29 B4
Dundonald 192 B3
Dundonnell 262 B2
Dundonnell Hotel .262 B2
Dundonnell House .262 B3
Dundraw 175 D5
Dundreggan 239 A7
Dundreggan
  Lodge 240 A1
Dundrennan 173 D5
Dundry 43 C4
Dunecht 245 B4
Dunfermline 208 B3
Dunfield 64 D2
Dunford Bridge 139 C4
Dungworth 130 A2
Dunham 132 B3
Dunham-on-
  the-Hill 127 B4
Dunhampton 79 A6
Dunham Town 128 A2
Dunholme 133 B5
Dunino 221 C5
Dunipace 207 B6
Dunira 218 B2
Dunkeld 230 D4
Dunkerton 43 D6
Dunkeswell 13 A6
Dunkeswick 148 C2
Dunkirk
  Kent 52 D2
  Norf 120 C4
Dunk's Green 36 A4
Dunlappie 232 B3

Dunley
  Hants 46 D2
  Worcs 79 A5
Dunlichity Lodge.. 252 C2
Dunlop 205 D4
Dunmaglass Lodge.252 D1
Dunmore
  Argyll 202 B2
  Falk 208 B1
Dunnet 280 A4
Dunnichen 232 D3
Dunninald 233 C5
Dunning 219 C5
Dunnington
  E Yorks 151 B4
  Warks 80 B3
  York 149 B5
Dunnockshaw 137 A7
Dunollie 226 C3
Dunoon 203 A6
Dunragit 170 B3
Dunrostan 213 D5
Duns 198 A1
Dunsby 116 C4
Dunscore 183 D6
Dunscroft 141 C4
Dunsdale 168 D4
Dunsden Green ... 47 B5
Dunsfold 34 C3
Dunsford 12 C3
Dunshalt 220 C2
Dunshillock 257 B4
Dunskey House ... 170 B2
Dunsley 169 D6
Dunsmore 66 C3
Dunsop Bridge ... 145 B6
Dunstable 67 A5
Dunstall 113 C5
Dunstall Common .. 80 C1
Dunstall Green ... 86 A3
Dunstan 189 B5
Dunstan Steads ... 189 A5
Dunster 27 A4
Duns Tew 65 A5
Dunston
  Lincs 133 C5
  Norf 104 A3
  Staffs 112 D3
  T&W 179 C4
Dunsville 140 C4
Dunswell 150 D3
Dunsyre 195 B5
Dunterton 11 D4
Duntisbourne
  Abbots 63 C5
Duntisbourne Leer .. 63 C5
Duntisbourne Rouse 63 C5
Duntish 15 A6
Duntocher 205 A4
Dunton
  Bucks 66 A3
  C Beds 84 C4
  Norf 119 B5
Dunton Bassett ... 98 B2
Dunton Green ... 36 A3
Dunton Wayletts ... 69 D6
Duntulm 259 A4
Dunure 192 D2
Dunvant 57 C5
Dunvegan 258 D2
Dunwich 105 D5
Dunwood 129 D4
Dupplin Castle ... 219 C5
Durdar 175 C7
Durgates 36 C4
Durham 167 A5
Durisdeer 183 B6
Durisdeermill 183 B6
Durkar 139 B6
Durleigh 28 B2
Durley
  Hants 32 D4
  Wilts 45 C6
Durnamuck 262 A2
Durness 277 B5
Durno 256 D2
Duror 236 D3
Durran
  Argyll 214 B2
  Highld 280 B3
Durrington
  Wilts 31 A5
  W Sus 21 B4
Dursley 62 D3
Durston 28 C2
Durweston 16 A2
Dury 285 G6
Duston 83 A4
Duthil 253 D5
Dutlas 93 D6

Duton Hill 69 A6
Dutson 10 C4
Dutton 127 B5
Duxford
  Cambs 85 C6
  Oxon 65 D4
Dwygyfylchi 124 B2
Dwyran 123 D4
Dyce 245 A5
Dye House 178 D1
Dyffryn
  Bridgend 40 B3
  Carms 73 D6
  Pembs 72 C2
Dyffryn Ardudwy ...107 D5
Dyffryn Castell 91 D5
Dyffryn Ceidrych ... 59 C4
Dyffryn Cellwen ... 59 E5
Dyke
  Lincs 116 C4
  Moray 253 A5
Dykehead
  Angus 232 B1
  N Lanark 207 E6
  Stirling 206 A3
Dykelands 233 B5
Dykends 231 C6
Dykeside 256 B2
Dykesmains 204 D2
Dylife 91 C6
Dymchurch 38 C2
Dymock 79 D5
Dyrham 43 B6
Dysart 209 A6
Dyserth 125 B5

E

Eachwick 178 B3
Eadar Dha
  Fhadhail 287 A5
Eagland Hill 144 C4
Eagle 132 C3
Eagle
  Barnsdale 132 C3
Eagle Moor 132 C3
Eaglescliffe 168 D2
Eaglesfield
  Cumb 162 B3
  Dumfries 175 A5
Eaglesham 205 C5
Eaglethorpe 100 B2
Eairy 152 D2
Eakley Lanes 83 B5
Eakring 132 C1
Ealand 141 B5
Ealing 49 A4
Eals 177 D4
Eamont Bridge 164 C3
Earby 146 C3
Earcroft 137 A5
Eardington 95 B5
Eardisland 78 B2
Eardisley 77 C7
Eardiston
  Shrops 110 C2
  Worcs 79 A4
Earith 101 D5
Earle 188 A2
Earley 47 B5
Earlham 104 A3
Earlish 258 B3
Earls Barton 83 A5
Earls Colne 70 A2
Earl's Croome 79 C6
Earlsdon 97 D6
Earlsferry 221 E4
Earlsfield 116 B2
Earlsford 256 C3
Earl's Green 87 A6
Earlsheaton 139 A5
Earl Shilton 98 B1
Earlsmill 253 A5
Earl Soham 88 A3
Earl Sterndale 129 C5
Earlston
  Borders 197 C4
  E Ayrs 193 B4
Earl Stonham 88 B2
Earlswood
  Mon 61 D6
  Sur 35 B5
  Warks 96 D4
Earnley 19 B7
Earsairidh 286 G3
Earsdon 179 B5
Earsham 104 C4
Earswick 149 B5
Eartham 20 B2

Easby
  N Yorks 157 A5
  N Yorks 159 A4
Easdale 213 A5
Easebourne 34 D1
Easenhall 98 D1
Eashing 34 B2
Easington
  Bucks 66 B1
  Durham 168 A2
  E Yorks 143 B5
  Northumb 199 C5
  Oxon 66 D1
  Oxon 82 D1
  Redcar 169 D5
Easington Colliery .168 A2
Easington Lane 167 A6
Easingwold 148 A4
Easole Street 53 D4
Eassie 232 D1
East Aberthaw 41 E5
East Adderbury 82 D1
East Allington 7 C6
East Anstey 26 C3
East Appleton 157 B6
East Ardsley 139 A6
East Ashling 19 A7
East Auchronie ... 245 B5
East Ayton 160 C3
East Bank 60 C4
East Barkwith 133 A6
East Barming 37 A5
East Barnby 169 D6
East Barnet 68 D2
East Barns 211 C4
East Barsham 119 B6
East Beckham 120 B3
East Bedfont 48 B3
East Bergholt 87 D6
East Bilney 119 D6
East Blatchington .. 22 B2
East Boldre 18 A2
Eastbourne 22 C4
East Brent 42 D2
Eastbridge 89 A5
East Bridgford 115 A4
East Buckland 26 B1
East Budleigh 13 C5
Eastburn 147 C4
East Burrafirth 285 H5
East Burton 16 C2
Eastbury
  London 67 D5
  W Berks 46 B1
East Butsfield 166 A4
East Butterwick ... 141 C6
Eastby 147 B4
East Cairnbeg 233 A5
East Calder 208 D3
East Carleton 104 A2
East Carlton
  Northants 99 C5
  W Yorks 147 C6
East Chaldon 16 C1
East Challow 46 A1
East Chiltington ... 21 A6
East Chinnock 29 D4
East Chisenbury ... 45 D5
Eastchurch 52 B1
East Clandon 34 A3
East Claydon 66 A2
East Clyne 274 D2
East Coker 29 D5
Eastcombe 63 C4
East Combe 27 B6
East Common 149 D5
East Compton 29 A6
Eastcote
  London 48 A4
  Northants 82 B3
  W Mid 97 D4
Eastcott
  Corn 24 D3
  Wilts 44 D4
East Cottingwith .. 149 C6
Eastcourt
  Wilts 45 C6
  Wilts 63 D5
East Cowes 18 B4
East Cowick 141 A4
East Cowton 157 A7
East Cramlington .. 179 B4
East Cranmore 29 A6
East Creech 16 C3
East Croachy 252 D2
East Croftmore ... 242 A2
East Curthwaite ...164 A1
East Dean
  E Sus 22 C3
  Hants 31 C6

East Dean continued
  W Sus 20 A1
East Down 25 A7
East Drayton 132 B2
East Ella 142 A2
East End
  Dorset 16 B3
  E Yorks 143 A4
  Hants 18 B2
  Hants 33 C5
  Hants 46 C2
  Herts 69 A4
  Kent 37 C6
  N Som 42 B3
  Oxon 65 B4
Easter Ardross 264 C2
Easter Balmoral ...243 C5
Easter Boleskine .. 251 D7
Easter Compton ... 43 A4
Easter Cringate ... 207 B5
Easter Davoch 244 B1
Easter Earshaig ...184 B3
Easter Fearn 264 B2
Easter Galcantray .253 B4
Eastergate 20 B2
Easterhouse 207 D4
Easter Howgate ...209 D5
Easter Howlaws ...197 B6
Easter Kinkell 252 B1
Easter Lednathie ..232 B1
Easter Milton 253 A5
Easter Moniack ... 252 B1
Eastern Green 97 C5
Easter Ord 245 B5
Easter Quarff 285 K6
Easter Rhynd 219 C6
Easter Row 207 A5
Easter Silverford ..268 C2
Easter Skeld 285 J5
Easterton 44 D4
Eastertown 42 D2
Eastertown of
  Auchleuchries ...257 C5
Easter Whyntie ... 267 C7
East Farleigh 37 A5
East Farndon 99 C4
East Ferry 141 D6
Eastfield
  N Lanark 208 D1
  N Yorks 160 C4
Eastfield Hall 189 C5
East Fortune 210 C2
East Garston 46 B1
Eastgate
  Durham 166 B2
  Norf 120 C3
East Ginge 46 A2
East Goscote 115 D4
East Grafton 45 C6
East Grimstead ... 31 C6
East Grinstead 36 C1
East Guldeford 38 C1
East Haddon 82 A3
East Hagbourne .. 46 A3
East Halton 142 B3
Eastham 126 A3
East Ham 50 A1
Eastham Ferry 126 A3
Easthampstead ... 47 C6
East Hanney 65 D5
East Hanningfield .. 70 C1
East Hardwick 140 B2
East Harling 103 C5
East Harlsey 158 B3
East Harnham 31 C5
East Harptree 43 D4
East Hartford 179 B4
East Harting 33 D6
East Hatley 85 B4
East Hauxwell 157 B5
East Haven 221 A5
Eastheath 47 C6
East Heckington .. 117 A4
East Hedleyhope ..167 A4
East Hendred 46 A2
East Herrington ...179 D5
East Heslerton ... 160 D3
East Hoathly 22 A3
Easthope 94 B3
Easthorpe
  Essex 70 A3
  Leics 115 B6
  Notts 132 D2
East Horrington ... 29 A5
East Horsley 34 A3
East Horton 198 C4
Easthouses 209 D6
East Huntspill 28 A3
East Hyde 67 B6
East Ilkerton 26 A2

East Ilsley . . . 46 A2
Eastington
  Devon . . . 12 A2
  Glos . . . 62 C3
  Glos . . . 64 B2
East Keal . . . 134 C3
East Kennett . . . 45 C5
East Keswick . . . 148 C2
East Kilbride . . . 205 C6
East Kirkby . . . 134 C3
East Knapton . . . 160 D2
East Knighton . . . 16 C2
East Knoyle . . . 30 B2
East Kyloe . . . 199 C4
East Lambrook . . . 28 D4
East Lamington . . . 264 C2
East Langdon . . . 39 A5
East Langton . . . 99 B4
East Langwell . . . 273 D5
East Lavant . . . 20 B1
East Lavington . . . 20 A2
East Layton . . . 157 A5
Eastleach Martin . . . 64 C2
Eastleach Turville . . . 64 C2
East Leake . . . 114 C3
East Learmouth . . . 198 C2
Eastleigh
  Devon . . . 25 C5
  Hants . . . 32 D3
East Leigh . . . 12 A1
East Lexham . . . 119 D5
East Lilburn . . . 188 A3
Eastling . . . 51 D6
East Linton . . . 210 C2
East Liss . . . 33 C6
East Looe . . . 6 B1
East Lound . . . 141 D5
East Lulworth . . . 16 C2
East Lutton . . . 150 A2
East Lydford . . . 29 B5
East Mains . . . 244 C3
East Malling . . . 37 A5
East March . . . 220 A4
East Marden . . . 33 D7
East Markham . . . 132 B2
East Marton . . . 146 B3
East Meon . . . 33 C5
East Mere . . . 27 D4
East Mersea . . . 71 B4
East Mey . . . 281 A5
East Molesey . . . 49 C4
Eastmoor
  Derbys . . . 130 B3
  Norf . . . 102 A3
East Morden . . . 16 B3
East Morton . . . 147 C4
East Ness . . . 159 D5
East Newton . . . 151 D5
Eastney . . . 19 B5
Eastnor . . . 79 D5
East Norton . . . 99 A4
East Nynehead . . . 27 C6
East Oakley . . . 46 D3
Eastoft . . . 141 B6
East Ogwell . . . 12 D3
Eastoke . . . 19 B6
Easton
  Cambs . . . 100 D3
  Cumb . . . 175 C5
  Cumb . . . 176 B2
  Devon . . . 12 C2
  Dorset . . . 15 D6
  Hants . . . 32 B4
  Lincs . . . 116 C2
  Norf . . . 120 D3
  Som . . . 29 A5
  Suff . . . 88 B3
  Wilts . . . 44 B2
Easton Grey . . . 44 A2
Easton-in-
  Gordano . . . 43 B4
Easton Maudit . . . 83 B5
Easton on the Hill . . 100 A4
Easton Royal . . . 45 C6
East Orchard . . . 30 D2
East Ord . . . 198 A3
East Panson . . . 11 B4
Eastpark . . . 174 B3
East Peckham . . . 37 B4
East Pennard . . . 29 B5
East Perry . . . 84 A3
East Portlemouth . . . 7 D6
East Prawle . . . 8 D1
East Preston . . . 20 B3
East Putford . . . 25 D4
East Quantoxhead . . 27 A6
East Rainton . . . 167 A6
East Ravendale . . . 143 D4
East Raynham . . . 119 C5
Eastrea . . . 101 B4

East Rhidorroch
  Lodge . . . 262 A4
Eastriggs . . . 175 B5
East Rigton . . . 148 C2
Eastrington . . . 141 A5
East Rounton . . . 158 A3
East Row . . . 169 D6
East Rudham . . . 119 C5
East Runton . . . 120 A3
East Ruston . . . 121 C5
Eastry . . . 53 D5
East Saltoun . . . 210 D1
East Sleekburn . . . 179 A4
East Somerton . . . 121 D6
East Stockwith . . . 141 D5
East Stoke
  Dorset . . . 16 C2
  Notts . . . 115 A5
East Stour . . . 30 C2
East Stourmouth . . . 53 C4
East Stowford . . . 26 C1
East Stratton . . . 32 B4
East Studdal . . . 39 A5
East Suisnish . . . 248 C2
East Taphouse . . . 5 A6
East-the-Water . . . 25 C5
East Thirston . . . 189 D4
East Tilbury . . . 50 B3
East Tisted . . . 33 B6
East Torrington . . . 133 A6
East Tuddenham . . . 120 D2
East Tytherley . . . 32 C1
East Tytherton . . . 44 B3
East Village . . . 12 A3
Eastville
  Bristol . . . 43 B5
  Lincs . . . 135 D4
East Wall . . . 94 B3
East Walton . . . 119 D4
Eastwell . . . 115 C5
East Wellow . . . 32 C2
East Wemyss . . . 209 A6
East Whitburn . . . 208 D2
Eastwick
  Herts . . . 68 B4
  Shetland . . . 284 F5
East Williamston . . . 55 D6
East Winch . . . 118 D3
East Winterslow . . . 31 B6
East Wittering . . . 19 B6
East Witton . . . 157 C5
Eastwood
  Notts . . . 114 A2
  Southend . . . 51 A5
  W Yorks . . . 138 A2
East Woodburn . . . 177 A7
East Woodhay . . . 46 C2
East Worldham . . . 33 B6
East Worlington . . . 26 D2
East Worthing . . . 21 B4
Eathorpe . . . 81 A6
Eaton
  Ches E . . . 128 C3
  Ches W . . . 127 C4
  Leics . . . 115 C5
  Norf . . . 104 A3
  Notts . . . 132 B2
  Oxon . . . 65 C5
  Shrops . . . 94 C1
  Shrops . . . 94 C3
Eaton Bishop . . . 78 D2
Eaton Bray . . . 67 A4
Eaton Constantine . . 94 A3
Eaton Green . . . 67 A4
Eaton Hastings . . . 64 D3
Eaton on Tern . . . 111 C5
Eaton Socon . . . 84 B3
Eavestone . . . 147 A6
Ebberston . . . 160 C2
Ebbesbourne Wake . . 30 C3
Ebbw Vale
  = Glyn Ebwy . . . 60 C3
Ebchester . . . 178 D3
Ebford . . . 13 C4
Ebley . . . 63 C4
Ebnal . . . 110 A3
Ebrington . . . 81 D4
Ecchinswell . . . 46 D2
Ecclaw . . . 211 D4
Ecclefechan . . . 175 A4
Eccles
  Borders . . . 197 B6
  Gtr Man . . . 137 D6
  Kent . . . 51 C4
Ecclesall . . . 130 A3
Ecclesfield . . . 139 D6
Ecclesgreig . . . 233 B5
Eccleshall . . . 112 C2
Eccleshill . . . 147 D5
Ecclesmachan . . . 208 C3

Eccles on Sea . . . 121 C6
Eccles Road . . . 103 B6
Eccleston
  Ches W . . . 127 C4
  Lancs . . . 136 B4
  Mers . . . 136 D3
Eccleston Park . . . 136 D3
Eccup . . . 148 C1
Echt . . . 245 B5
Eckford . . . 187 A6
Eckington
  Derbys . . . 131 B4
  Worcs . . . 80 C2
Ecton . . . 83 A5
Edale . . . 129 A6
Edburton . . . 21 A5
Edderside . . . 174 D3
Edderton . . . 264 B3
Eddistone . . . 24 C3
Eddleston . . . 196 B1
Edenbridge . . . 36 B2
Edenfield . . . 137 B6
Edenhall . . . 164 B3
Edenham . . . 116 C3
Eden Park . . . 49 C6
Edensor . . . 130 C2
Edentaggart . . . 215 C6
Edenthorpe . . . 140 C4
Edentown . . . 175 C6
Ederline . . . 214 B1
Edern . . . 106 C2
Edgarley . . . 29 B5
Edgbaston . . . 96 C3
Edgcott
  Bucks . . . 66 A1
  Som . . . 26 B3
Edge . . . 94 A1
Edgebolton . . . 111 C4
Edge End . . . 62 B1
Edgefield . . . 120 B2
Edgefield Street . . . 120 B2
Edge Green . . . 127 D4
Edge Hill . . . 136 D2
Edgeside . . . 138 A1
Edgeworth . . . 63 C5
Edgmond . . . 111 D6
Edgmond Marsh . . . 111 C6
Edgton . . . 94 C1
Edgware . . . 68 D1
Edgworth . . . 137 B6
Edinample . . . 217 B5
Edinbane . . . 258 C3
Edinburgh . . . 209 C5
Edingale . . . 113 D6
Edingight House . . . 267 D6
Edingley . . . 131 D6
Edingthorpe . . . 121 B5
Edingthorpe Green . 121 B5
Edington
  Som . . . 28 B3
  Wilts . . . 44 D3
Edintore . . . 255 B5
Edithmead . . . 28 A3
Edith Weston . . . 99 A6
Edlesborough . . . 67 B4
Edlingham . . . 189 C4
Edlington . . . 134 B2
Edmondsham . . . 31 D4
Edmondsley . . . 167 A5
Edmondthorpe . . . 115 D6
Edmonstone . . . 282 E6
Edmonton . . . 68 D3
Edmundbyers . . . 178 D2
Ednam . . . 197 C6
Ednaston . . . 113 A6
Edradynate . . . 230 C2
Edrom . . . 198 A2
Edstaston . . . 111 B4
Edstone . . . 81 A4
Edvin Loach . . . 79 B4
Edwalton . . . 114 B3
Edwardstone . . . 87 C5
Edwinsford . . . 58 B3
Edwinstowe . . . 131 C6
Edworth . . . 84 C4
Edwyn Ralph . . . 79 B4
Edzell . . . 232 B3
Efail Isaf . . . 41 C5
Efailnewydd . . . 106 C3
Efailwen . . . 72 D4
Efenechtyd . . . 125 D6
Effingham . . . 35 A4
Effirth . . . 285 H5
Efford . . . 12 A3
Egdon . . . 80 B2
Egerton
  Gtr Man . . . 137 B6
  Kent . . . 37 B7
Egerton Forstal . . . 37 B6
Eggborough . . . 140 A3

Eggbuckland . . . 7 B4
Eggington . . . 67 A4
Egginton . . . 113 C6
Egglescliffe . . . 168 D2
Eggleston . . . 166 C2
Egham . . . 48 B3
Egleton . . . 99 A5
Eglingham . . . 189 B4
Egloshayle . . . 9 D5
Egloskerry . . . 10 C3
Eglwysbach . . . 124 B3
Eglwys-Brewis . . . 41 E5
Eglwys Cross . . . 110 A3
Eglwys Fach . . . 91 C4
Eglwyswen . . . 73 C3
Eglwyswrw . . . 72 C4
Egmanton . . . 132 C2
Egremont
  Cumb . . . 162 C3
  Mers . . . 136 D2
Egton . . . 159 A7
Egton Bridge . . . 159 A7
Eight Ash Green . . . 70 A3
Eignaig . . . 226 B2
Eil . . . 241 A6
Eilanreach . . . 238 C2
Eileanach Lodge . . . 264 D1
Eilean Darach . . . 262 B3
Einacleite . . . 288 E2
Eisgean . . . 288 F4
Eisingrug . . . 107 C6
Elan Village . . . 76 A3
Elberton . . . 43 A5
Elburton . . . 7 B4
Elcho . . . 219 B6
Elcombe . . . 45 A5
Eldernell . . . 101 B5
Eldersfield . . . 79 D6
Elderslie . . . 205 B4
Eldon . . . 167 C5
Eldrick . . . 181 C4
Eldroth . . . 146 A1
Eldwick . . . 147 C5
Elfhowe . . . 154 B3
Elford
  Northumb . . . 199 C5
  Staffs . . . 113 D5
Elgin . . . 266 C3
Elgol . . . 247 C4
Elham . . . 38 A3
Elie . . . 221 D4
Elim . . . 122 B3
Eling . . . 32 D2
Elishader . . . 259 B5
Elishaw . . . 188 D1
Elkesley . . . 132 B1
Elkstone . . . 63 B5
Ellan . . . 253 D4
Elland . . . 139 A4
Ellary . . . 202 A2
Ellastone . . . 113 A5
Ellemford . . . 211 D4
Ellenbrook . . . 152 D3
Ellenhall . . . 112 C2
Ellen's Green . . . 34 C3
Ellerbeck . . . 158 B3
Ellerburn . . . 160 C2
Ellerby . . . 169 D5
Ellerdine Heath . . . 111 C6
Ellerhayes . . . 13 A4
Elleric . . . 227 B5
Ellerker . . . 141 A7
Ellerton
  E Yorks . . . 149 D6
  Shrops . . . 111 C6
Ellesborough . . . 66 C3
Ellesmere . . . 110 B3
Ellesmere Port . . . 127 B4
Ellingham
  Norf . . . 105 B4
  Northumb . . . 189 A4
Ellingstring . . . 157 C5
Ellington
  Cambs . . . 100 D3
  Northumb . . . 189 D5
Elliot . . . 221 A6
Ellisfield . . . 33 A5
Ellistown . . . 114 D2
Ellon . . . 257 C4
Ellonby . . . 164 B2
Ellough . . . 105 C5
Elloughton . . . 142 A1
Ellwood . . . 62 C1
Elm . . . 101 A6
Elmbridge . . . 80 A2
Elmdon
  Essex . . . 85 D6
  W Mid . . . 97 C4
Elmdon Heath . . . 97 C4
Elmers End . . . 49 C6

Elmesthorpe . . . 98 B1
Elmfield . . . 19 B5
Elm Hill . . . 30 C2
Elmhurst . . . 113 D5
Elmley Castle . . . 80 C2
Elmley Lovett . . . 79 A6
Elmore . . . 62 B3
Elmore Back . . . 62 B3
Elm Park . . . 50 A2
Elmscott . . . 24 C3
Elmsett . . . 87 C6
Elmstead Market . . . 71 A4
Elmsted . . . 38 A3
Elmstone . . . 53 C4
Elmstone Hardwicke 63 A5
Elmswell
  E Yorks . . . 150 B2
  Suff . . . 87 A5
Elmton . . . 131 B5
Elphin . . . 271 C5
Elphinstone . . . 209 C6
Elrick . . . 245 B5
Elrig . . . 171 C5
Elsdon . . . 188 D2
Elsecar . . . 140 C1
Elsenham . . . 69 A5
Elsfield . . . 65 B6
Elsham . . . 142 B2
Elsing . . . 120 D2
Elslack . . . 146 C2
Elson . . . 110 B2
Elsrickle . . . 195 B5
Elstead . . . 34 B2
Elsted . . . 33 D7
Elsthorpe . . . 116 C3
Elstob . . . 167 C6
Elston
  Notts . . . 115 A5
  Wilts . . . 31 A4
Elstone . . . 26 D1
Elstow . . . 84 C2
Elstree . . . 68 D1
Elstronwick . . . 151 D5
Elswick . . . 144 D4
Elsworth . . . 85 A5
Elterwater . . . 154 A2
Eltham . . . 50 B1
Eltisley . . . 85 B4
Elton
  Cambs . . . 100 B2
  Ches W . . . 127 B4
  Derbys . . . 130 C2
  Glos . . . 62 B3
  Hereford . . . 94 D2
  Notts . . . 115 B5
  Stockton . . . 168 D2
Elton Green . . . 127 B4
Elvanfoot . . . 184 A2
Elvaston . . . 114 B2
Elveden . . . 103 D4
Elvingston . . . 210 C1
Elvington
  Kent . . . 53 D4
  York . . . 149 C5
Elwick
  Hrtlpl . . . 168 B2
  Northumb . . . 199 C5
Elworth . . . 128 C2
Elworthy . . . 27 B5
Ely
  Cambs . . . 102 C1
  Cardiff . . . 41 D6
Emberton . . . 83 C5
Embleton
  Cumb . . . 163 A4
  Northumb . . . 189 A5
Embo . . . 265 A4
Emborough . . . 43 D5
Embo Street . . . 265 A4
Embsay . . . 147 B4
Emersons Green . . . 43 B5
Emery Down . . . 18 A1
Emley . . . 139 B5
Emmbrook . . . 47 C5
Emmer Green . . . 47 B5
Emmington . . . 66 C2
Emneth . . . 101 A6
Emneth Hungate . . . 101 A7
Empingham . . . 99 A6
Empshott . . . 33 B6
Emstrey . . . 111 D4
Emsworth . . . 19 A6
Enborne . . . 46 C2
Enchmarsh . . . 94 B3
Enderby . . . 98 B2
Endmoor . . . 154 C4
Endon . . . 129 D4
Endon Bank . . . 129 D4
Enfield . . . 68 D3
Enfield Wash . . . 68 D3

Enford . . . 45 D5
Engamoor . . . 285 H4
Engine Common . . . 43 A5
Englefield . . . 47 B4
Englefield Green . . . 48 B2
Englesea-brook . . . 128 C2
English Bicknor . . . 62 B1
Englishcombe . . . 43 C6
English Frankton . . . 110 C3
Enham Alamein . . . 32 A2
Enmore . . . 28 B2
Ennerdale Bridge . . . 162 C3
Enoch . . . 183 B6
Enochdhu . . . 231 B4
Ensay . . . 224 B2
Ensbury . . . 17 B4
Ensdon . . . 110 D3
Ensis . . . 25 C6
Enstone . . . 65 A4
Enterkinfoot . . . 183 B6
Enterpen . . . 158 A3
Enville . . . 95 C6
Eolaigearraidh . . . 286 F3
Eorabus . . . 224 D2
Eòropaidh . . . 288 A6
Epperstone . . . 115 A4
Epping . . . 69 C4
Epping Green
  Essex . . . 68 C4
  Herts . . . 68 C2
Epping Upland . . . 68 C4
Eppleby . . . 167 D4
Eppleworth . . . 150 D3
Epsom . . . 49 C5
Epwell . . . 81 C6
Epworth . . . 141 C5
Epworth Turbary . . . 141 C5
Erbistock . . . 110 A2
Erbusaig . . . 249 D4
Erchless Castle . . . 251 B6
Erdington . . . 96 B4
Eredine . . . 214 B2
Eriboll . . . 277 C5
Ericstane . . . 184 A3
Eridge Green . . . 36 C3
Erines . . . 202 A3
Eriswell . . . 102 D3
Erith . . . 50 B2
Erlestoke . . . 44 D3
Ermine . . . 133 B4
Ermington . . . 7 B5
Erpingham . . . 120 B3
Errogie . . . 252 D1
Errol . . . 220 B2
Erskine . . . 205 A4
Erskine Bridge . . . 205 A4
Ervie . . . 170 A2
Erwarton . . . 88 D3
Erwood . . . 77 C4
Eryholme . . . 157 A7
Eryrys . . . 126 D2
Escomb . . . 167 C4
Escrick . . . 149 C5
Esgairdawe . . . 58 A3
Esgairgeiliog . . . 91 B5
Esh . . . 167 A4
Esher . . . 48 C4
Esholt . . . 147 C5
Eshott . . . 189 D5
Eshton . . . 146 B3
Esh Winning . . . 167 A4
Eskadale . . . 251 C6
Eskbank . . . 209 D6
Eskdale Green . . . 163 D4
Eskdalemuir . . . 185 C5
Eske . . . 150 C3
Eskham . . . 143 D5
Esk Valley . . . 159 A7
Esprick . . . 144 D4
Essendine . . . 116 D3
Essendon . . . 68 C2
Essich . . . 252 C2
Essington . . . 96 A2
Esslemont . . . 257 D4
Eston . . . 168 D3
Eswick . . . 285 H6
Etal . . . 198 C3
Etchilhampton . . . 44 C4
Etchingham . . . 37 D5
Etchinghill
  Kent . . . 38 B3
  Staffs . . . 112 D4
Ethie Castle . . . 233 D4
Ethie Mains . . . 233 D4
Etling Green . . . 120 D2
Eton . . . 48 B2
Eton Wick . . . 48 B2
Etteridge . . . 241 C4

Ettersgill 166 C1
Ettingshall 96 B2
Ettington 81 C5
Etton
  E Yorks 150 C2
  Pboro 100 A3
Ettrick 185 A5
Ettrickbridge 186 A5
Ettrickhill 185 A5
Etwall 113 B6
Euston 103 D4
Euximoor Drove . . .101 B6
Euxton 137 B4
Evanstown 41 C4
Evanton 264 D2
Evedon 116 A3
Evelix 264 A3
Evenjobb 77 A6
Evenley 82 D2
Evenlode 64 A3
Evenwood 167 C4
Evenwood Gate 167 C4
Everbay 282 E7
Evercreech 29 B6
Everdon 82 B2
Everingham 149 C7
Everleigh 45 D6
Everley 160 C3
Eversholt 84 D1
Evershot 15 A5
Eversley 47 C5
Eversley Cross 47 C5
Everthorpe 150 D2
Everton
  C Beds 84 B4
  Hants 18 B1
  Mers 136 D2
  Notts 141 D4
Evertown 175 A6
Evesbatch 79 C4
Evesham 80 C3
Evington 98 A3
Ewden Village 139 D5
Ewell 49 C5
Ewell Minnis 39 A4
Ewelme 66 D1
Ewen 63 D6
Ewenny 40 D4
Ewerby 116 A4
Ewerby Thorpe 116 A4
Ewes 185 C6
Ewesley 188 D3
Ewhurst 34 B3
Ewhurst Green
  E Sus 37 D5
  Sur 34 C3
Ewloe 126 C3
Ewloe Green 126 C2
Ewood 137 A5
Eworthy 11 B5
Ewshot 33 A7
Ewyas Harold 61 A5
Exbourne 11 A7
Exbury 18 B3
Exebridge 27 C4
Exelby 157 C6
Exeter 13 B4
Exford 26 B3
Exhall 80 B4
Exley Head 147 D4
Exminster 13 C4
Exmouth 13 C5
Exnaboe 285 M5
Exning 86 A2
Exton
  Devon 13 C4
  Hants 33 C5
  Rutland 116 D2
  Som 27 B4
Exwick 13 B4
Eyam 130 B2
Eydon 82 B2
Eye
  Hereford 78 A2
  Pboro 100 A4
  Suff 104 D2
Eye Green 100 A4
Eyemouth 211 D6
Eyeworth 85 C4
Eyhorne Street 37 A6
Eyke 88 B4
Eynesbury 84 B3
Eynort 246 B2
Eynsford 50 C2
Eynsham 65 C5
Eype 14 B4
Eyre
  Highld 248 C2

Eyre continued
  Highld 259 C4
Eythorne 39 A4
Eyton
  Hereford 78 A2
  Shrops 94 C1
  Wrex 110 A2
Eyton upon the Weald
  Moors 111 D5

F

Faccombe 46 D1
Faceby 158 A3
Facit 138 B1
Faddiley 127 D5
Fadmoor 159 C5
Faerdre 40 A1
Failand 43 B4
Failford 193 C4
Failsworth 138 C1
Fain 262 C3
Fairbourne 90 A4
Fairburn 140 A2
Fairfield
  Derbys 129 B5
  Stockton 168 D2
  Worcs 80 C3
  Worcs 96 D2
Fairford 64 C2
Fair Green 118 D3
Fairhaven 136 A2
Fair Hill 164 B3
Fairlie 204 C2
Fairlight 23 A6
Fairlight Cove 23 A6
Fairmile 13 B5
Fairmilehead 209 D5
Fairoak 111 B6
Fair Oak 32 D3
Fair Oak Green 47 C4
Fairseat 50 C3
Fairstead
  Essex 70 B1
  Norf 118 D3
Fairwarp 36 D2
Fairy Cottage 152 C4
Fairy Cross 25 C5
Fakenham 119 C6
Fakenham Magna . .103 D5
Fala 210 D1
Fala Dam 210 D1
Falahill 196 A2
Falcon 79 D4
Faldingworth 133 A5
Falfield 62 D2
Falkenham 88 D3
Falkirk 208 C1
Falkland 220 D2
Falla 187 B6
Fallgate 130 C3
Fallin 207 A5
Fallowfield 138 D1
Fallsidehill 197 B5
Falmer 21 B6
Falmouth 4 D3
Falsgrave 160 C4
Falstone 177 A5
Fanagmore 276 D2
Fangdale Beck 159 B4
Fangfoss 149 B6
Fankerton 207 B5
Fanmore 224 B3
Fannich Lodge 262 D4
Fans 197 B5
Far Bank 140 B4
Far Bletchley 83 D5
Farcet 100 B4
Far Cotton 83 B4
Farden 94 D3
Fareham 19 A4
Farewell 113 D4
Far Forest 95 D5
Farforth 134 B3
Faringdon 64 D3
Farington 136 A4
Farlam 176 D3
Farlary 273 D5
Far Laund 114 A1
Farleigh
  N Som 42 C3
  Sur 49 C6
Farleigh
  Hungerford 44 D2
Farleigh Wallop 33 A5
Farlesthorpe 135 B4
Farleton
  Cumb 154 C4
  Lancs 145 A5

Farley
  Shrops 94 A1
  Staffs 113 A4
  Wilts 31 C6
Farley Green 34 B3
Farley Hill
  Luton 67 A5
  Wokingham 47 C5
Farleys End 62 B3
Farlington 149 A5
Farlow 95 C4
Farmborough 43 C5
Farmcote
  Glos 63 A6
  Shrops 95 B5
Farmington 64 B2
Farmoor 65 C5
Farmtown 267 D6
Farnborough
  Hants 34 A1
  London 50 C1
  Warks 82 C1
  W Berks 46 A2
Farnborough
Green 34 A1
Farncombe 34 B2
Farndish 83 A6
Farndon
  Ches W 127 D4
  Notts 132 D2
Farnell 233 C4
Farnham
  Dorset 30 D3
  Essex 69 A4
  N Yorks 148 A2
  Suff 89 A4
  Sur 34 B1
Farnham Common . .48 A2
Farnham Green 69 A4
Farnham Royal 48 A2
Farnhill 147 C4
Farningham 50 C2
Farnley
  N Yorks 147 C6
  W Yorks 147 D6
Farnley Tyas 139 B4
Farnsfield 131 D6
Farnworth
  Gtr Man 137 C6
  Halton 127 A5
Farr
  Highld 241 B6
  Highld 252 C2
  Highld 278 B3
Farr House 252 C2
Farringdon 13 B5
Farrington Gurney . .43 D5
Far Sawrey 154 C2
Farsley 147 D6
Farthinghoe 82 D2
Farthingloe 39 A4
Farthingstone 82 B3
Fartown 139 B4
Farway 14 B1
Fasag 249 C6
Fascadale 235 C4
Faslane Port 215 D5
Fasnacloich 227 B5
Fasnakyle Ho 251 D5
Fassfern 237 B4
Fatfield 179 D5
Fattahead 268 D1
Faugh 176 D3
Fauldhouse 208 D2
Faulkbourne 70 B1
Faulkland 43 D6
Fauls 111 B4
Faversham 52 C2
Favillar 254 C3
Fawdington 158 D3
Fawfieldhead 129 C5
Fawkham Green 50 C2
Fawler 65 B4
Fawley
  Bucks 47 A5
  Hants 18 A3
  W Berks 46 A1
Fawley Chapel 62 A1
Faxfleet 141 A6
Faygate 35 C5
Fazakerley 136 D2
Fazeley 97 A5
Fearby 157 C5
Fearn 265 C4
Fearnan 229 D6
Fearnbeg 249 A4
Fearnhead 137 D5
Fearn Lodge 264 B2
Fearnmore 261 D4
Fearn Station 265 C4

Featherstone
  Staffs 96 A2
  W Yorks 140 A2
Featherwood 187 C7
Feckenham 80 A3
Feering 70 A2
Feetham 156 B3
Feizor 146 A1
Felbridge 35 C6
Felbrigg 120 B4
Felcourt 36 B1
Felden 67 C5
Felin-Crai 59 C5
Felindre
  Carms 58 B3
  Carms 58 C2
  Carms 59 C4
  Carms 73 C6
  Ceredig 75 C4
  Powys 93 C5
  Powys 93 D5
  Swansea 57 B6
Felindre Farchog . . .72 C4
Felinfach
  Ceredig 75 C4
  Powys 77 D4
Felinfoel 57 B5
Felingwm isaf 58 C2
Felingwm uchaf 58 C2
Felinwynt 73 A5
Felixkirk 158 C3
Felixstowe 88 D3
Felixstowe Ferry . . .88 D4
Felkington 198 B3
Felkirk 140 B1
Felling 179 C4
Fell Side 163 A6
Felmersham 84 B1
Felmingham 120 C4
Felpham 20 C2
Felsham 87 B5
Felsted 69 A6
Feltham 48 B4
Felthorpe 120 D3
Felton
  Hereford 78 C3
  Northumb 189 C4
  N Som 43 C4
Felton Butler 110 D2
Feltwell 102 B3
Fenay Bridge 139 B4
Fence 146 D2
Fence Houses 179 D5
Fen Ditton 85 A6
Fen Drayton 85 A5
Fen End 97 D5
Fengate
  Norf 120 C3
  Pboro 100 B4
Fenham 199 B4
Fenhouses 117 A5
Feniscliffe 137 A5
Feniscowles 137 A5
Feniton 13 B6
Fenlake 84 C2
Fenny Bentley 130 D1
Fenny Bridges 13 B6
Fenny Compton 81 B7
Fenny Drayton 97 B6
Fenny Stratford 83 D5
Fenrother 189 D4
Fen Side 134 D3
Fenstanton 85 A5
Fenton
  Cambs 101 D5
  Lincs 132 B3
  Lincs 132 D3
  Stoke 112 A6
Fenton Barns 210 B2
Fenton Town 198 C3
Fenwick
  E Ayrs 205 D4
  Northumb 178 B2
  Northumb 199 B4
  S Yorks 140 B3
Feochaig 190 D3
Feock 4 D3
Feolin Ferry 201 B4
Ferindonald 247 D5
Feriniquarrie 258 C1
Ferlochan 226 B4
Fern 232 B2
Ferndale 41 B5
Ferndown 17 A4
Ferness 253 B5
Ferney Green 154 B3
Fernham 64 D3
Fernhill Heath 79 B6
Fernhurst 34 D1
Fernie 220 C3
Ferniegair 194 A2

Fernilea 246 A2
Fernilee 129 B5
Ferrensby 148 A2
Ferring 20 B3
Ferrybridge 140 A2
Ferryden 233 C5
Ferryhill
  Aberdeen 245 B6
  Durham 167 B5
Ferry Hill 101 C5
Ferryhill Station . . .167 B6
Ferry Point 264 B3
Ferryside 56 A3
Fersfield 103 C6
Fersit 228 A2
Ferwig 73 B4
Feshiebridge 241 B6
Fetcham 35 A4
Fetterangus 269 D4
Fettercairn 233 A4
Fettes 252 A1
Fewcott 65 A6
Fewston 147 B5
Ffairfach 58 C3
Ffair-Rhos 75 B6
Ffaldybrenin 58 A3
Ffarmers 58 A3
Ffawyddog 60 B4
Fforest 57 B5
Fforest-fâch 57 C6
Ffostrasol 73 B6
Ffos-y-ffin 74 B3
Ffridd-Uchaf 107 A5
Ffrith 126 D2
Ffrwd 107 A4
Ffynnon ddrain 73 D7
Ffynnongroyw 125 A6
Ffynnon-oer 75 C4
Fidden 224 D2
Fiddes 245 D5
Fiddington
  Glos 80 D2
  Som 28 A2
Fiddleford 30 D2
Fiddlers Hamlet 69 C4
Field 112 B4
Field Broughton . . .154 C2
Field Dalling 120 B2
Field Head 98 A1
Fifehead Magdalen . 30 C1
Fifehead Neville . . .30 D1
Fifield
  Oxon 64 B3
  Wilts 45 D5
  Windsor 48 B2
Fifield Bavant 31 C4
Figheldean 31 A5
Filands 44 A3
Filby 121 D6
Filey 161 C5
Filgrave 83 C5
Filkins 64 C3
Filleigh
  Devon 26 C1
  Devon 26 D2
Fillingham 133 A4
Fillongley 97 C5
Filton 43 B5
Fimber 150 A1
Finavon 232 C2
Fincham 102 A2
Finchampstead 47 C5
Finchdean 33 D6
Finchingfield 86 D2
Finchley 68 D2
Findern 113 B7
Findhorn 265 D6
Findhorn Bridge . . .253 D4
Findochty 267 C5
Findo Gask 219 B5
Findon
  Aberds 245 C6
  W Sus 21 B4
Findon Mains 264 D2
Findrack House 244 B3
Finedon 99 D6
Fingal Street 88 A3
Fingask 256 D2
Fingerpost 95 D5
Fingest 66 D2
Finghall 157 C5
Fingland
  Cumb 175 C5
  Dumfries 183 A5
Finglesham 53 D5
Fingringhoe 71 A4
Finlarig 217 A5
Finmere 82 D3
Finnart 229 C4

Finningham 87 A6
Finningley 141 D4
Finnygaud 267 D6
Finsbury 49 A6
Finstall 80 A2
Finsthwaite 154 C2
Finstock 65 B4
Finstown 282 F4
Fintry
  Aberds 268 D2
  Dundee 220 A4
  Stirling 207 B4
Finzean 244 C3
Fionnphort 224 D2
Fionnsbhagh 287 F5
Firbeck 131 A5
Firby
  N Yorks 149 A6
  N Yorks 157 C6
Firgrove 138 B2
Firsby 135 C4
Firsdown 31 B5
First Coast 261 A6
Fir Tree 166 B4
Firby
Fishbourne
  IoW 19 B4
  W Sus 20 B1
Fishburn 167 B6
Fishcross 208 A1
Fisherford 256 C1
Fisher Place 163 C6
Fisher's Pond 32 C3
Fisherstreet 34 C2
Fisherton
  Highld 252 A3
  S Ayrs 192 D2
Fishguard
  = Abergwaun 72 C2
Fishlake 141 B4
Fishleigh Barton . . .25 C6
Fishponds 43 B5
Fishpool 62 A2
Fishtoft 117 A6
Fishtoft Drove 117 A6
Fishtown of Usan . .233 C5
Fishwick 198 A3
Fiskavaig 246 A2
Fiskerton
  Lincs 133 B5
  Notts 132 D2
Fitling 151 D5
Fittleton 31 A5
Fittleworth 20 A3
Fitton End 118 D1
Fitz 110 D3
Fitzhead 27 C6
Fitzwilliam 140 B2
Fiunary 225 B5
Five Acres 62 B1
Five Ashes 36 D3
Fivecrosses 127 B5
Fivehead 28 C3
Five Oak Green 36 B4
Five Oaks
  Jersey 6
  W Sus 34 D3
Five Roads 57 B4
Flack's Green 70 B1
Flackwell Heath 48 A1
Fladbury 80 C2
Fladdabister 285 K6
Flagg 129 C6
Flamborough 161 A4
Flamstead 67 B5
Flamstead End 68 C3
Flansham 20 B2
Flanshaw 139 A6
Flasby 146 B3
Flash 129 C5
Flashader 258 C3
Flask Inn 160 A3
Flaunden 67 C5
Flawborough 115 A5
Flawith 148 A3
Flax Bourton 43 C4
Flaxby 148 B2
Flaxholme 114 A1
Flaxley 62 B2
Flaxpool 27 B6
Flaxton 149 A5
Fleckney 98 B3
Flecknoe 82 A2
Fledborough 132 B3
Fleet
  Hants 19 A6
  Hants 47 D6
  Lincs 117 C6
Fleetham 189 A4
Fleet Hargate 117 C6
Fleetlands 19 A4

Fleetville 67 C6
Fleetwood 144 C3
Flemingston 41 D5
Flemington 205 C6
Flempton 87 A4
Fleoideabhagh 287 F5
Fletchertown 175 D5
Fletching 36 D2
Flexbury 10 A3
Flexford 34 B2
Flimby 162 A3
Flimwell 37 C5
Flint = Y Fflint 126 B2
Flintham 115 A5
Flint Mountain 126 B2
Flinton 151 D5
Flintsham 77 B7
Flitcham 119 C4
Flitton 84 D2
Flitwick 84 D2
Flixborough 141 B6
Flixborough
 Stather 141 B6
Flixton
 Gtr Man 137 D6
 N Yorks 160 D4
 Suff 104 C4
Flockton 139 B5
Flodaigh 286 A4
Flodden 198 C3
Flodigarry 259 A4
Flood's Ferry 101 B5
Flookburgh 154 D2
Florden 104 B2
Flore 82 A3
Flotterton 188 C2
Flowton 88 C1
Flush House 139 C4
Flushing
 Aberds 257 B5
 Corn 4 D3
Flyford Flavell 80 B2
Foals Green 104 D3
Fobbing 51 A4
Fochabers 266 D4
Fochriw 60 C3
Fockerby 141 B6
Fodderletter 254 D2
Fodderty 251 A4
Foel 109 D4
Foel-gastell 57 A5
Foffarty 232 D2
Foggathorpe 149 D6
Fogo 197 B6
Fogorig 198 B1
Foindle 276 D2
Folda 231 B5
Fole 112 B4
Foleshill 97 C6
Folke 29 D6
Folkestone 39 B4
Folkingham 116 B3
Folkington 22 B3
Folksworth 100 C3
Folkton 161 D4
Folla Rule 256 C2
Follifoot 148 B2
Folly Gate 11 B6
Fonthill Bishop 30 B3
Fonthill Gifford 30 B3
Fontmell Magna . . . 30 D2
Fontwell 20 B2
Foolow 130 B1
Foots Cray 50 B1
Forbestown 243 A6
Force Mills 154 B2
Forcett 167 D4
Ford
 Argyll 214 B1
 Bucks 66 C2
 Devon 25 C5
 Glos 64 A1
 Northumb 198 C3
 Shrops 110 D3
 Staffs 129 D5
 Wilts 44 B2
 W Sus 20 B2
Fordcombe 36 B3
Fordell 209 B4
Forden 93 A6
Ford End 69 B6
Forder Green 8 A1
Fordham
 Cambs 102 D2
 Essex 70 A3
 Norf 102 B2
Fordhouses 96 A2
Fordingbridge 31 D5
Fordon 160 D4
Fordoun 233 A5

Ford's Green 87 A6
Fordstreet 70 A3
Ford Street 27 D6
Fordwells 64 B4
Fordwich 52 D3
Fordyce 267 C6
Forebridge 112 C3
Forest 165 B6
Forest Becks 146 B1
Forestburn Gate . . . 188 D3
Foresterseat 266 D2
Forest Gate 49 A7
Forest Green 35 B4
Forest Hall 154 A4
Forest Head 176 D3
Forest Hill 65 C6
Forest Lane Head . . 148 B2
Forest Lodge
 Argyll 228 D1
 Highld 242 A3
 Perth 230 A3
Forest Mill 208 A2
Forest Row 36 C2
Forestside 33 D6
Forest Town 131 C5
Forfar 232 C2
Forgandenny 219 C5
Forge 91 C5
Forge Side 60 C4
Forgewood 194 A2
Forgie 267 D4
Forglen House 268 D1
Formby 136 C2
Forncett End 104 B2
Forncett St Mary . . . 104 B2
Forncett St Peter . . 104 B2
Forneth 231 D4
Fornham All Saints . . 87 A4
Fornham St Martin . . 87 A4
Forres 253 A6
Forrestfield 207 D6
Forrest Lodge 182 D3
Forsbrook 112 A3
Forse 275 A6
Forse House 275 A6
Forsinain 279 D5
Forsinard 279 D4
Forsinard Station . . 279 D4
Forston 15 B6
Fort Augustus 240 B1
Forteviot 219 C5
Fort George
 Guern 6
 Highld 252 A3
Forth 194 A4
Forthampton 79 D6
Forth Road Bridge . 208 C4
Fortingall 229 D6
Forton
 Hants 32 A3
 Lancs 145 B4
 Shrops 110 D3
 Som 14 A3
 Staffs 111 C6
Forton Heath 110 D3
Fortrie 256 B1
Fortrose 252 A3
Fortuneswell 15 D6
Fort William 237 B5
Forty Green 67 D4
Forty Hill 68 D3
Forward Green 88 B1
Fosbury 45 D7
Fosdyke 117 B6
Foss 230 C1
Foss Cross 63 C6
Fossebridge 64 B1
Fosterhouses 141 B4
Foster Street 69 C4
Foston
 Derbys 113 B5
 Lincs 115 A4
 N Yorks 149 A5
Foston on the
 Wolds 151 B4
Fotherby 143 D5
Fotheringhay 100 B2
Foubister 283 G6
Foulby 140 B1
Foulden
 Borders 198 A3
 Norf 102 B3
Foulis Castle 264 D1
Foul Mile 22 A4
Foulridge 146 C2
Foulsham 120 C2
Fountainhall 196 B3
Four Ashes
 Staffs 95 C6
 Suff 103 D6

Four Crosses
 Powys 93 A4
 Powys 110 D1
 Wrex 126 D2
Four Elms 36 B2
Four Forks 28 B2
Four Gotes 118 D1
Fourlane Ends 130 D3
Four Lane Ends 127 C5
Four Lanes 3 B4
Fourlanes End 128 D3
Four Marks 33 B5
Four Mile Bridge . . 122 C2
Four Oaks
 E Sus 37 D6
 W Mid 96 B4
 W Mid 97 C5
Fourpenny 265 A4
Four Roads
 Carms 57 B4
 IoM 152 E2
Fourstones 177 C6
Four Throws 37 D5
Fovant 31 C4
Foveran 257 D4
Fowey 5 B6
Fowley Common . . 137 D5
Fowlis 220 A3
Fowlis Wester 218 B4
Fowlmere 85 C6
Fownhope 78 D3
Foxbar 205 B4
Foxcombe Hill 65 C5
Fox Corner 34 A2
Foxdale 152 D2
Foxearth 87 C4
Foxfield 153 B3
Foxham 44 B3
Foxhole
 Corn 5 B4
 Swansea 57 C6
Foxholes 160 D4
Foxhunt Green 22 A3
Fox Lane 34 A1
Foxley
 Norf 120 C2
 Wilts 44 A2
Fox Street 71 A4
Foxt 112 A4
Foxton
 Cambs 85 C6
 Durham 167 C6
 Leics 99 B4
Foxup 156 D2
Foxwist Green 127 C6
Foxwood 95 D4
Foy 62 A1
Foyers 251 D6
Fraddam 2 B3
Fraddon 4 B4
Fradley 113 D5
Fradswell 112 B3
Fraisthorpe 151 A4
Framfield 36 D2
Framingham Earl . . 104 A3
Framingham Pigot . 104 A3
Framlingham 88 A3
Frampton
 Dorset 15 B6
 Lincs 117 B6
Frampton Cotterell . 43 A5
Frampton Mansell . . 63 C5
Frampton on Severn 62 C3
Frampton West
 End 117 A5
Framsden 88 B2
Framwellgate
 Moor 167 A5
Franche 95 D6
Frankby 126 A2
Frankley 96 C2
Frank's Bridge 77 B5
Frankton 98 D1
Frant 36 C3
Fraserburgh 269 C4
Frating Green 71 A4
Fratton 19 B5
Freathy 6 B3
Freckenham 102 D2
Freckleton 136 A3
Freeby 115 C6
Freehay 112 A4
Freeland 65 B5
Freester 285 H6
Freethorpe 105 A5
Freiston 117 A6
Fremington
 Devon 25 B6
 N Yorks 156 B4
Frenchay 43 B5

Frenchbeer 12 C1
Frenich 216 D4
Frensham 34 B1
Fresgoe 279 B5
Freshfield 136 C1
Freshford 44 C1
Freshwater 18 C2
Freshwater Bay 18 C2
Freshwater East . . . 55 E6
Fressingfield 104 D3
Freston 88 D2
Freswick 281 B5
Fretherne 62 C3
Frettenham 120 D4
Freuchie 220 D2
Freuchies 231 B6
Freystrop 55 C5
Friar's Gate 36 C2
Friarton 219 B6
Friday Bridge 101 A6
Friday Street 22 B4
Fridaythorpe 150 B1
Friern Barnet 68 D2
Friesland 223 B4
Friesthorpe 133 A5
Frieston 116 A2
Frieth 66 D2
Frilford 65 D5
Frilsham 46 B3
Frimley 34 A1
Frimley Green 34 A1
Frindsbury 51 B4
Fring 119 B4
Fringford 65 A7
Frinsted 37 A6
Frinton-on-Sea 71 A6
Friockheim 232 D3
Friog 90 A4
Frisby on the
 Wreake 115 D4
Friskney 135 D4
Friskney Eaudike . . 135 D4
Friskney Tofts 135 D4
Friston
 E Sus 22 C3
 Suff 89 A5
Fritchley 130 D3
Fritham 31 D6
Frith Bank 117 A6
Frith Common 79 A4
Frithelstock 25 D5
Frithelstock Stone . . 25 D5
Frithville 134 D3
Frittenden 37 B6
Frittiscombe 8 C2
Fritton
 Norf 104 B3
 Norf 105 A5
Fritwell 65 A6
Frizinghall 147 D5
Frizington 162 C3
Frocester 62 C3
Frodesley 94 A3
Frodingham 141 B6
Frodsham 127 B5
Frogden 187 A6
Froggatt 130 B2
Froghall 112 A4
Frogmore
 Devon 7 C6
 Hants 34 A1
Frognall 117 D4
Frogshail 121 B4
Frolesworth 98 B2
Frome 30 A1
Frome St Quintin . . . 15 A5
Fromes Hill 79 C4
Fron
 Denb 125 C5
 Gwyn 106 C3
 Gwyn 107 A5
 Powys 77 A4
 Powys 93 A6
 Powys 93 B5
Froncysyllte 110 A1
Frongoch 108 B4
Frostenden 105 C5
Frosterley 166 B3
Frotoft 282 E5
Froxfield 45 C7
Froxfield Green 33 C6
Froyle 33 A6
Fryerning 69 C6
Fryton 159 D5
Fulbeck 133 D4
Fulbourn 85 B7
Fulbrook 64 B3
Fulford
 Som 28 C2
 Staffs 112 B3

Fulford continued
 York 149 C5
Fulham 49 B5
Fulking 21 A5
Fullarton
 Glasgow 205 B6
 N Ayrs 192 B3
Fuller's Moor 127 D4
Fuller Street 70 B1
Fullerton 32 B2
Fulletby 134 B2
Full Sutton 149 B6
Fullwood 205 C4
Fulmer 48 A2
Fulmodestone 120 B1
Fulnetby 133 B5
Fulstow 143 D5
Fulwell 179 D5
Fulwood
 Lancs 145 D5
 S Yorks 130 A3
Fundenhall 104 B2
Fundenhall Street . . 104 B2
Funtington 19 A6
Funtley 19 A4
Funtullich 218 B2
Funzie 284 D8
Furley 14 A2
Furnace
 Argyll 214 B3
 Carms 57 B5
Furnace End 97 B5
Furneaux Pelham . . 68 A4
Furness Vale 129 A5
Furzehill 26 A2
Furze Platt 48 A1
Fyfett 28 D2
Fyfield
 Essex 69 C5
 Glos 64 C3
 Hants 32 A1
 Oxon 65 D5
 Wilts 45 C5
Fylingthorpe 160 A3
Fyvie 256 C2

G

Gabhsann bho
 Dheas 288 B5
Gabhsann bho
 Thuath 288 B5
Gablon 264 A3
Gabroc Hill 205 C4
Gaddesby 115 D4
Gadebridge 67 C5
Gaer 60 A3
Gaerllwyd 61 D6
Gaerwen 123 C4
Gagingwell 65 A5
Gaick Lodge 241 D5
Gailey 112 D3
Gainford 167 D4
Gainsborough
 Lincs 141 D6
 Suff 88 C2
Gainsford End 86 D3
Gairloch 261 C5
Gairlochy 239 D5
Gairney Bank 208 A4
Gairnshiel Lodge . . 243 B5
Gaisgill 155 A5
Gaitsgill 164 A1
Galashiels 196 C3
Galgate 145 B4
Galhampton 29 C6
Gallaberry 184 D2
Gallachoille 213 D5
Gallanach
 Argyll 223 A5
 Argyll 226 D3
Gallantry Bank 127 D5
Gallatown 209 A5
Galley Common . . . 97 B6
Galleyend 69 C7
Galley Hill 85 A5
Galleywood 69 C7
Gallin 229 D4
Gallowfauld 232 D2
Gallows Green 113 A4
Galltair 249 D5
Galmisdale 234 B3
Galmpton
 Devon 7 C5
 Torbay 8 B2
Galphay 157 D6
Galston 193 B5
Galtrigill 258 C1
Gamblesby 165 B4

Gamesley 138 D3
Gamlingay 84 B4
Gammersgill 157 C4
Gamston 132 B2
Ganarew 62 B1
Ganavan 226 C3
Gang 6 A2
Ganllwyd 108 C2
Gannochy
 Angus 232 A3
 Perth 219 B6
Gansclet 281 D5
Ganstead 151 D4
Ganthorpe 159 D5
Ganton 160 D3
Garbat 263 D6
Garbhallt 214 C3
Garboldisham 103 C6
Garden City 126 C3
Gardenstown 268 C2
Garden Village
 Wrex 126 D3
 W Yorks 148 D3
Garderhouse 285 J5
Gardham 150 C2
Gardin 284 G6
Gare Hill 30 A1
Garelochhead 215 C5
Garford 65 D5
Garforth 148 D3
Gargrave 146 B3
Gargunnock 207 A5
Garlic Street 104 C3
Garlieston 171 C6
Garlinge Green 52 D3
Garlogie 245 B4
Garmond 268 D3
Garmony 225 B5
Garmouth 266 C4
Garnant 58 D3
Garndiffaith 61 C4
Garndolbenmaen . . 107 B4
Garnedd 124 D2
Garnett Bridge 154 B4
Garnfadryn 106 C2
Garnkirk 207 D4
Garnlydan 60 B3
Garnswllt 57 B6
Garn-yr-erw 60 B4
Garrabost 288 D6
Garraron 213 B6
Garras 3 C5
Garreg 107 B6
Garrick 218 C3
Garrigill 165 A5
Garriston 157 B5
Garroch 182 D3
Garrogie Lodge . . . 240 A3
Garros 259 B4
Garrow 230 D2
Garryhorn 182 C3
Garsdale 155 C6
Garsdale Head 155 B6
Garsdon 44 A3
Garshall Green 112 B3
Garsington 65 C6
Garstang 145 C4
Garston 127 A4
Garswood 137 D4
Gartcosh 207 D4
Garth
 Bridgend 40 B3
 Gwyn 123 C5
 Powys 76 C3
 Shetland 285 H4
 Wrex 110 A1
Garthamlock 205 B6
Garthbrengy 76 D4
Garthdee 245 B6
Gartheli 75 C4
Garthmyl 93 B5
Garthorpe
 Leics 115 C6
 N Lincs 141 B6
Garth Row 154 B4
Gartly 255 C6
Gartmore 206 A3
Gartnagrenach . . . 202 C2
Gartness
 N Lanark 207 D5
 Stirling 206 B3
Gartocharn 206 B2
Garton 151 D5
Garton-on-the-
 Wolds 150 B2
Gartsherrie 207 D5
Gartymore 274 C4
Garvald 210 C2

Garvamore 240 C3
Garvard 212 C1
Garvault Hotel 273 A5
Garve 263 D5
Garvestone 103 A6
Garvock
  Aberds 233 A5
  Inylyd 204 A2
Garway 61 A6
Garway Hill 61 A6
Gaskan 236 B1
Gastard 44 C2
Gasthorpe 103 C5
Gatcombe 18 C3
Gateacre 127 A4
Gatebeck 154 C4
Gate Burton 132 A3
Gateford 131 A5
Gateforth 140 A4
Gatehead 192 B3
Gate Helmsley 149 B5
Gatehouse 177 A5
Gatehouse of Fleet .172 C4
Gatelawbridge 183 C7
Gateley 119 C6
Gatenby 158 C2
Gateshead 179 C4
Gatesheath 127 C4
Gateside
  Aberds 244 A3
  Angus 232 D2
  E Renf 205 C4
  Fife 219 D6
  N Ayrs 204 C3
Gathurst 136 C4
Gatley 128 A3
Gattonside 197 C4
Gatwick Airport 35 B5
Gaufron 76 A3
Gaulby 98 A3
Gauldry 220 B3
Gaunt's Common . . .17 A4
Gautby 134 B1
Gavinton 197 A6
Gawber 139 C6
Gawcott 82 D3
Gawsworth 128 C3
Gawthorpe 139 A5
Gawthrop 155 C5
Gawthwaite 153 B3
Gaydon 81 B6
Gayfield 282 B5
Gayhurst 83 C5
Gayle 156 C2
Gayles 157 A5
Gay Street 34 D3
Gayton
  Mers 126 A2
  Norf 119 D4
  Northants 83 B4
  Staffs 112 C3
Gayton le Marsh . . .135 A4
Gayton le Wold 134 A2
Gayton Thorpe 119 D4
Gaywood 118 C3
Gazeley 86 A3
Geanies House 265 C4
Gearraidh
  Bhailteas 286 D3
Gearraidh Bhaird . .288 E4
Gearraidh na h-
  Aibhne 288 D3
Gearraidh na
  Monadh 286 E3
Geary 258 B2
Geddes House 253 A4
Gedding 87 B5
Geddington 99 C5
Gedintailor 247 A4
Gedling 115 A4
Gedney 117 C7
Gedney Broadgate .117 C7
Gedney Drove End .118 C1
Gedney Dyke 117 C7
Gedney Hill 117 D6
Gee Cross 138 D2
Geilston 206 C1
Geirinis 286 B3
Geise 280 B3
Geisiadar 288 D2
Geldeston 105 B4
Gell 124 C3
Gelli
  Pembs 55 C6
  Rhondda 41 B4
Gellideg 60 C2
Gellifor 125 C6
Gelligaer 41 B6

Gellilydan 107 C6
Gellinudd 40 A2
Gellyburn 219 A5
Gellywen 73 D5
Gelston
  Dumfries 173 C5
  Lincs 116 A2
Gembling 151 B4
Gentleshaw 113 D4
Geocrab 288 H2
Georgefield 185 C5
George Green 48 A3
Georgeham 25 B5
George Nympton . . .26 C2
Georgetown 60 C3
Gerlan 123 D6
Germansweek 11 B5
Germoe 2 C3
Gerrans 4 D3
Gerrards Cross 48 A3
Gestingthorpe 87 D4
Geuffordd 109 D7
Gibbet Hill 98 C2
Gibbshill 173 A5
Gib Hill 127 B6
Gidea Park 50 A2
Gidleigh 12 C1
Giffnock 205 C5
Gifford 210 D2
Giffordland 204 D2
Giffordtown 220 C2
Giggleswick 146 A2
Gilberdyke 141 A6
Gilchriston 210 D1
Gilcrux 163 A4
Gildersome 139 A5
Gildingwells 131 A5
Gileston 41 E5
Gilfach 41 B6
Gilfach Goch 41 C4
Gilfachrheda 73 A7
Gillamoor 159 C5
Gillar's Green 136 D3
Gillen 258 C2
Gilling East 159 D5
Gillingham
  Dorset 30 C2
  Medway 51 C4
  Norf 105 B5
Gilling West 157 A5
Gillock 280 C4
Gillow Heath 128 D3
Gills 281 A5
Gill's Green 37 C5
Gilmanscleuch 196 D2
Gilmerton
  Edin 209 D5
  Perth 218 B3
Gilmonby 166 D2
Gilmorton 98 C2
Gilmourton 205 D6
Gilsland 176 C4
Gilsland Spa 176 C4
Gilston
  Borders 196 A3
  Herts 68 B4
Gilwern 60 B4
Gimingham 121 B4
Giosla 288 E2
Gipping 87 A6
Gipsey Bridge 117 A5
Girdle Toll 204 D3
Girlsta 285 H6
Girsby 158 A2
Girtford 84 B3
Girthon 172 C4
Girton
  Cambs 85 A6
  Notts 132 C3
Girvan 180 B3
Gisburn 146 C2
Gisleham 105 C6
Gislingham 104 D1
Gissing 104 C2
Gittisham 13 B6
Gladestry 77 B6
Gladsmuir 210 C1
Glais 40 A2
Glaisdale 159 A6
Glame 248 B2
Glamis 232 D1
Glan Adda 123 C5
Glanaman 57 A6
Glan Conwy 124 B3
Glandford 120 A2
Glan-Duar 58 A2
Glandwr 73 D4
Glan-Dwyfach 107 B4
Glandy Cross 72 D4
Glandyfi 91 C4

Glan Gors 123 C4
Glangrwyney 60 B4
Glanmule 93 B5
Glanrafon 90 D4
Glanrhyd
  Gwyn 106 C2
  Pembs 72 B4
Glan-rhyd 107 A4
Glanton 188 B3
Glanton Pike 188 B3
Glan-traeth 122 C2
Glanvilles Wootton . .15 A6
Glan-y-don 125 B6
Glan-y-nant 92 C3
Glan-yr-afon
  Anglesey 123 B6
  Gwyn 108 A4
  Gwyn 109 A5
Glan-y-wern 107 C6
Glapthorn 100 B2
Glapwell 131 C4
Glas-allt Shiel 243 D5
Glasbury 77 D5
Glaschoil 253 C6
Glascoed
  Denb 125 B4
  Mon 61 C5
  Powys 109 D6
Glascorrie 243 C6
Glascote 97 A5
Glascwm 77 B5
Glasdrum 227 B5
Glasfryn 125 D4
Glasgow 205 B5
Glashvin 259 B4
Glasinfryn 123 D5
Glasnacardoch 235 A5
Glasnakille 247 C4
Glasphein 258 D1
Glaspwll 91 C5
Glassburn 251 C5
Glasserton 171 D6
Glassford 194 B2
Glasshouse Hill 62 A3
Glasshouses 147 A5
Glasslie 220 D2
Glasson
  Cumb 175 B5
  Lancs 144 B4
Glassonby 164 B3
Glasterlaw 232 C3
Glaston 99 A5
Glastonbury 29 B5
Glatton 100 C3
Glazebrook 137 D5
Glazebury 137 D5
Glazeley 95 C5
Gleadless 130 A3
Gleadsmoss 128 C3
Gleann
  Tholàstaidh 288 C6
Gleaston 153 C3
Gleiniant 92 B3
Glemsford 87 C4
Glen
  Dumfries 172 C3
  Dumfries 173 A6
Glenamachrie 226 D4
Glen Auldyn 152 B4
Glenbarr 190 B2
Glenbeg
  Highld 235 D4
  Highld 253 D6
Glen Bernisdale . . .259 D4
Glenbervie 245 D4
Glenboig 207 D5
Glenborrodale 235 D5
Glenbranter 215 C4
Glenbreck 195 D5
Glenbrein Lodge . . .240 A2
Glenbrittle House . .246 B3
Glenbuchat Lodge .243 A6
Glenbuck 194 D2
Glenburn 205 B4
Glencalvie Lodge . . .263 B6
Glencanisp Lodge . .270 B4
Glencaple 174 B2
Glencarron Lodge . .250 A2
Glencarse 219 B6
Glencassley Castle . .272 D2
Glenceitlein 227 B6
Glencoe 237 D4
Glencraig 209 A4
Glencripesdale 225 A5
Glencrosh 183 D5
Glendavan House . .244 B1
Glendevon 219 D4
Glendoebeg 240 B2
Glendoe Lodge 240 B2
Glendoick 220 B2

Glendoll Lodge 231 A6
Glendoune 180 B3
Glenduckie 220 C2
Glendye Lodge 244 D3
Gleneagles Hotel . .218 C4
Gleneagles House . .218 D4
Glenegedale 200 C3
Glenelg 238 A2
Glenernie 253 B6
Glenfarg 219 C6
Glenfarquhar
  Lodge 245 D4
Glenferness House .253 B5
Glenfeshie Lodge . .241 C6
Glenfield 98 A2
Glenfinnan 238 D3
Glenfoot 219 C6
Glenfyne Lodge 215 A5
Glengap 173 C4
Glengarnock 204 C3
Glengorm Castle . . .224 A3
Glengrasco 259 D4
Glenhead Farm 231 B6
Glen Ho 196 C1
Glenhoul 182 D2
Glenhurich 236 C2
Glenkerry 185 A5
Glenkiln 173 A4
Glenkindie 244 A1
Glenlatterach 266 D2
Glenlee 182 D4
Glenlichorn 218 C2
Glenlivet 254 D2
Glenlochsie 231 A4
Glenloig 191 B5
Glenluce 171 B4
Glenmallan 215 C5
Glenmarksie 251 A5
Glenmassan 215 C4
Glenmavis 207 D5
Glenmaye 152 D2
Glenmidge 183 D6
Glen Mona 152 C4
Glenmore
  Argyll 213 A6
  Highld 259 D4
Glenmore Lodge . . .242 B2
Glenmoy 232 B2
Glen Nevis House . .237 B5
Glenogil 232 B2
Glen Parva 98 B2
Glenprosen Lodge .231 A6
Glenprosen Village .231 B1
Glenquiech 232 B2
Glenreasdell Mains .202 C3
Glenree 191 C5
Glenridding 164 D1
Glenrossal 272 D2
Glenrothes 220 D2
Glensanda 226 B3
Glensaugh 233 A4
Glenshero Lodge . . .240 C3
Glen Sluain 214 C3
Glenstockadale 170 A2
Glenstriven 203 A5
Glentaggart 194 D3
Glen Tanar House . .244 C1
Glentham 142 D2
Glentirranmuir 207 A4
Glenton 256 D1
Glentress 196 C1
Glentromie Lodge . .241 C5
Glen Trool Lodge . .181 C6
Glentrool Village . .181 D5
Glentruan 152 A4
Glentruim House . .241 C4
Glentworth 133 A4
Glenuig 235 C5
Glenurquhart 264 D3
Glen Village 208 C1
Glen Vine 152 D3
Glespin 194 D3
Gletness 285 H6
Glewstone 62 A1
Glinton 100 A3
Glooston 99 B4
Glororum 199 C5
Glossop 138 D3
Gloster Hill 189 C5
Gloucester 63 B4
Gloup 284 C7
Glusburn 147 C4
Glutt Lodge 274 A3
Glutton Bridge 129 C5
Glympton 65 A5
Glynarthen 73 B6
Glynbrochan 92 C3
Glyn-Ceiriog 109 B7
Glyncoch 41 B5
Glyncorrwg 40 B3

Glyn-cywarch 107 C6
Glynde 22 B2
Glyndebourne 22 A2
Glyndyfrdwy 109 A6
Glyn Ebwy
  =Ebbw Vale 60 C3
Glynedd
  =Glyn-neath 59 E5
Glyn-neath
  =Glynedd 59 E5
Glynogwr 41 C4
Glyntaff 41 C5
Glyntawe 59 D5
Gnosall 112 C2
Gnosall Heath 112 C2
Goadby 99 B4
Goadby Marwood . .115 C5
Goatacre 44 B4
Goathill 29 D6
Goathland 160 A2
Goathurst 28 B2
Goat Lees 38 A2
Gobernuisgach
  Lodge 277 D5
Gobhaig 287 D5
Gobowen 110 B2
Godalming 34 B2
Godley 138 D2
Godmanchester 100 D4
Godmanstone 15 B6
Godmersham 52 D2
Godney 29 A4
Godolphin Cross 3 B4
Godre'r-graig 59 E4
Godshill
  Hants 31 D5
  IoW 18 C4
Godstone 35 A6
Godwinscroft 17 B5
Goetre 61 C5
Goferydd 122 B2
Goff's Oak 68 C3
Gogar 209 C4
Goginan 91 D4
Golan 107 B5
Golant 5 B6
Golberdon 10 D4
Golborne 137 D5
Golcar 139 B4
Goldcliff 42 A2
Golden Cross 22 A3
Golden Green 36 B4
Golden Grove 57 A5
Goldenhill 128 D3
Golden Hill 17 B6
Golden Pot 33 A6
Golden Valley 63 A5
Golders Green 49 A5
Goldhanger 70 C3
Gold Hill 102 B1
Golding 94 A3
Goldington 84 B2
Goldsborough
  N Yorks 148 B2
  N Yorks 169 D6
Goldsithney 2 B3
Goldsworthy 25 C4
Goldthorpe 140 C2
Gollanfield 253 A4
Golspie 274 D2
Golval 279 B4
Gomeldon 31 B5
Gomersal 139 A5
Gomshall 34 B3
Gonalston 115 A4
Gonfirth 285 G5
Good Easter 69 B6
Gooderstone 102 A3
Goodleigh 25 B7
Goodmanham 150 C1
Goodnestone
  Kent 52 C2
  Kent 53 D4
Goodrich 62 B1
Goodrington 8 B2
Goodshaw 137 A7
Goodwick =Wdig . . .72 C2
Goodworth Clatford .32 A2
Goole 141 A5
Goonbell 4 C2
Goonhavern 4 B2
Goose Eye 147 C4
Goose Green
  Gtr Man 137 C4
  Norf 104 C2
  W Sus 21 A4
Gooseham 24 D3
Goosey 65 D4
Goosnargh 145 D5
Goostrey 128 B2

Gorcott Hill 80 A3
Gord 285 L6
Gordon 197 B5
Gordonbush 274 D2
Gordonsburgh 267 C5
Gordonstoun 266 C2
Gordonstown
  Aberds 256 C2
  Aberds 267 D6
Gore 53 D5
Gorebridge 209 D6
Gore Cross 44 D4
Gorefield 117 D7
Gore Pit 70 B2
Gorey 6
Gorgie 209 C5
Goring 47 A4
Goring-by-Sea 21 B4
Goring Heath 47 B4
Gorleston-on-Sea . .105 A6
Gornalwood 96 B2
Gorrachie 268 D2
Gorran Churchtown . . .5 C4
Gorran Haven 5 C5
Gorrenberry 186 D3
Gors 75 A5
Gorsedd 125 B6
Gorse Hill 45 A5
Gorseinon 57 C5
Gorseness 282 F5
Gorsgoch 74 C3
Gorslas 57 A5
Gorsley 62 A2
Gorstan 263 D5
Gorstanvorran 236 B2
Gorsteyhill 128 C2
Gorsty Hill 113 C5
Gortantaoid 200 A3
Gorton 138 D1
Gosbeck 88 B2
Gosberton 117 B5
Gosberton Clough . .117 C4
Gosfield 70 A1
Gosford 78 A3
Gosforth
  Cumb 162 D3
  T&W 179 C4
Gosmore 68 A1
Gosport 19 B5
Gossabrough 284 E7
Gossington 62 C3
Goswick 199 B4
Gotham 114 B3
Gotherington 63 A5
Gott 285 J6
Goudhurst 37 C5
Goulceby 134 B2
Gourdas 256 B2
Gourdon 233 A6
Gourock 204 A2
Govan 205 B5
Govanhill 205 B5
Goveton 7 C6
Govilon 61 B4
Gowanhill 269 C5
Gowdall 140 A4
Gowerton 57 C5
Gowkhall 208 B3
Gowthorpe 149 B6
Goxhill
  E Yorks 151 C4
  N Lincs 142 A3
Goxhill Haven 142 A3
Goytre 40 C2
Grabhair 288 F4
Graby 116 C3
Grade 3 D5
Graffham 20 A2
Grafham
  Cambs 84 A3
  Sur 34 B3
Grafton
  Hereford 78 D2
  N Yorks 148 A3
  Oxon 64 C3
  Shrops 110 D3
  Worcs 78 A3
Grafton Flyford 80 B2
Grafton Regis 83 C4
Grafton Underwood .99 C5
Grafty Green 37 B6
Graianrhyd 126 D2
Graig
  Conwy 124 B3
  Denb 125 B5
Graig-fechan 125 D6
Grain 51 B5
Grainsby 143 D4
Grainthorpe 143 D5
Grampound 4 C4

Grampound Road 4 B4
Gramsdal. 286 A4
Granborough 66 A2
Granby 115 B5
Grandborough. 82 A1
Grandtully. 230 C3
Grange
  Cumb 163 C5
  E Ayrs 193 C4
  Medway 51 C4
  Mers. 126 A2
  Perth. 220 B2
Grange Crossroads.267 D5
Grange Hall 265 D6
Grange Hill 68 D4
Grangemill 130 D2
Grange Moor 139 B5
Grangemouth. 208 B2
Grange of Lindores.220 C2
Grange-over-
  Sands 154 D3
Grangepans 208 B3
Grangetown
  Cardiff. 41 D6
  Redcar 168 C3
Grange Villa 179 D4
Granish 242 A2
Gransmoor 151 B4
Granston 55 A4
Grantchester 85 B6
Grantham 116 B2
Grantley. 147 A6
Grantlodge 245 A4
Granton
  Dumfries. 184 B3
  Edin. 209 C5
Grantown-on-
  Spey 253 D6
Grantshouse. 211 D5
Grappenhall 127 A6
Grasby 142 C2
Grasmere 154 A2
Grasscroft. 138 C2
Grassendale 126 A3
Grassholme 166 C2
Grassington 147 A4
Grassmoor 131 C4
Grassthorpe 132 C2
Grateley. 32 A1
Gratwich 112 B4
Graveley
  Cambs. 84 A4
  Herts. 68 A2
Gravelly Hill 96 B4
Gravels 94 A1
Graven 284 F6
Graveney 52 C2
Gravesend
  Herts. 68 A4
  Kent 50 B3
Grayingham 142 D1
Grayrigg 155 B4
Grays 50 B3
Grayshott 34 C1
Grayswood 34 C2
Graythorp 168 C3
Grazeley 47 C4
Greasbrough 140 D2
Greasby 126 A2
Great Abington 86 C1
Great Addington 99 D6
Great Alne 80 B4
Great Altcar 136 C2
Great Amwell 68 B3
Great Asby 165 D4
Great Ashfield 87 A5
Great Ayton. 168 D3
Great Baddow 70 C1
Great Bardfield 86 D2
Great Barford 84 B3
Great Barr 96 B3
Great Barrington 64 B3
Great Barrow 127 C4
Great Barton. 87 A4
Great Barugh 159 D6
Great Bavington . . .178 A1
Great Bealings 88 C3
Great Bedwyn 45 C6
Great Bentley 71 A5
Great Billing 83 A5
Great Bircham 119 B4
Great Blakenham 88 B2
Great Blencow 164 B2
Great Bolas 111 C5
Great Bookham 35 A4
Great Bourton 82 C1
Great Bowden 99 C4
Great Bradley 86 B2
Great Braxted. 70 B2
Great Bricett. 87 B6

Great Brickhill 83 D6
Great Bridge. 96 B2
Great Bridgeford. . .112 C2
Great Brington. 82 A3
Great Bromley 71 A4
Great Broughton
  Cumb 162 A3
  N Yorks 158 A4
Great Budworth 127 B6
Great Burdon 167 D6
Great Burgh 35 A5
Great Burstead 69 D6
Great Busby 158 A4
Great Canfield 69 B5
Great Carlton 135 A4
Great Casterton 100 A2
Great Chart. 38 A1
Great Chatwell 112 D1
Great Chesterford. . . .85 C7
Great Cheverell 44 D3
Great Chishill 85 D6
Great Clacton 71 B5
Great Cliff 139 B6
Great Clifton. 162 B3
Great Coates 143 C4
Great Comberton 80 C2
Great Corby 176 D2
Great Cornard 87 C4
Great Cowden 151 C5
Great Coxwell 64 D3
Great Crakehall 157 B6
Great Cransley 99 D5
Great Cressingham.103 A4
Great Crosby 136 D2
Great Cubley 113 B5
Great Dalby 115 D5
Great Denham 84 C2
Great Doddington . . .83 A5
Great Dunham 119 D5
Great Dunmow. 69 A6
Great Durnford 31 B5
Great Easton
  Essex 69 A6
  Leics 99 B5
Great Eccleston 144 C4
Great Edstone 159 C6
Great Ellingham 103 B6
Great Elm 30 A1
Greater Doward 62 B1
Great Eversden 85 B5
Great Fencote 157 B6
Great Finborough 87 B6
Greatford 116 D3
Great Fransham 119 D5
Great Gaddesden . . .67 B5
Greatgate 113 A4
Great Gidding 100 C3
Great Givendale. . . .149 B7
Great Glemham 88 A4
Great Glen 98 B3
Great Gonerby 116 B1
Great Gransden 85 B4
Great Green
  Norf 104 C3
  Suff. 87 B5
Great Habton 159 D6
Great Hale. 116 A4
Great Hallingbury . . .69 B5
Greatham
  Hants 33 B6
  Hrtlpl 168 C2
  W Sus 20 A3
Great Hampden 66 C3
Great Harrowden 99 D5
Great Harwood 146 D1
Great Haseley. 66 C1
Great Hatfield 151 C4
Great Haywood 112 C3
Great Heath 97 C6
Great Heck 140 A3
Great Henny 87 D4
Great Hinton. 44 D3
Great Hockham 103 B5
Great Holland. 71 B6
Great Horkesley. 87 D5
Great Hormead 68 A3
Great Horton 147 D5
Great Horwood 83 D4
Great Houghton
  Northants 83 B4
  S Yorks 140 C2
Great Hucklow 130 B1
Great Kelk 151 B4
Great Kimble 66 C3
Great Kingshill 66 D3
Great Langton 157 B6
Great Leighs 70 B1
Great Lever. 137 C6
Great Limber 142 C3
Great Linford 83 C5

Great Livermere 103 D4
Great Longstone 130 B2
Great Lumley 167 A5
Great Lyth 94 A2
Great Malvern 79 C5
Great Maplestead . . .87 D4
Great Marton 144 D3
Great Massingham .119 C4
Great Melton 104 A2
Great Milton 66 C1
Great Missenden 66 C3
Great Mitton 145 D7
Great Mongeham 53 D5
Great Moulton 104 B2
Great Munden 68 A3
Great Musgrave 165 D5
Great Ness 110 D2
Great Notley 70 A1
Great Oakley
  Essex 71 A5
  Northants 99 C5
Great Offley 67 A6
Great Ormside 165 D5
Great Orton 175 C6
Great Ouseburn 148 A3
Great Oxendon 99 C4
Great Oxney Green . . .69 C6
Great Palgrave 119 D5
Great Parndon 68 C4
Great Paxton 84 A4
Great Plumpton 144 D3
Great Plumstead . . .121 D5
Great Ponton 116 B2
Great Preston 140 A2
Great Raveley 101 C4
Great Rissington 64 B2
Great Rollright. 81 D6
Great Ryburgh 119 C6
Great Ryle 188 B3
Great Ryton 94 A2
Great Saling 69 A7
Great Salkeld 164 B3
Great Sampford 86 D2
Great Sankey 127 A5
Great Saxham 86 A3
Great Shefford 46 B1
Great Shelford 85 B6
Great Smeaton 158 A2
Great Snoring 119 B6
Great Somerford 44 A3
Great Stainton 167 C6
Great Stambridge . . .70 D2
Great Staughton 84 A3
Great Steeping 135 C4
Great Stonar 53 D5
Greatstone on Sea . . .38 C2
Great Strickland 164 C3
Great Stukeley 100 D4
Great Sturton 134 B2
Great Sutton
  Ches W 126 B3
  Shrops 94 C3
Great Swinburne . . .178 B1
Great Tew 65 A4
Great Tey 70 A2
Great Thurkleby 158 D3
Great Thurlow 86 B2
Great Torrington 25 D5
Great Tosson 188 C3
Great Totham
  Essex 70 B2
  Essex 70 B2
Great Tows 143 D4
Great Urswick 153 C3
Great Wakering 51 A6
Great Waldingfield . .87 C5
Great Walsingham .119 B6
Great Waltham 69 B6
Great Warley 69 D5
Great Washbourne . . .80 D2
Great Weldon 99 C6
Great Welnetham 87 B4
Great Wenham 87 D6
Great Whittington . . .178 B2
Great Wigborough . . .70 B3
Great Wilbraham 86 B1
Great Wishford 31 B4
Great Witcombe 63 B5
Great Witley 79 A5
Great Wolford 81 D5
Greatworth 82 C2
Great Wratting 86 C2
Great Wymondley . . .68 A2
Great Wyrley 96 A2
Great Wytheford 111 D4
Great Yarmouth 105 A6
Great Yeldham 86 D3
Greave 138 A1
Greeba 152 D2
Green 125 C5

Greenbank 284 C7
Greenburn 208 D2
Greendikes 188 A3
Green End 84 B3
Greenfield
  C Beds 84 D2
  Flint 126 B1
  Gtr Man 138 C2
  Highld 239 B6
  Oxon 66 D2
Greenford 48 A4
Greengairs 207 C5
Greenham 46 C2
Green Hammerton .148 B3
Greenhaugh 177 A5
Greenhead 177 C4
Greenhill
  Falk. 207 C6
  Kent 52 C3
  Leics 114 D2
  London 49 A4
Greenhills 204 C3
Greenhithe 50 B2
Greenholm 193 B5
Greenholme 155 A4
Greenhouse 187 A4
Greenhow Hill 147 A5
Greenigoe 283 G5
Greenland 280 B4
Greenlands 47 A5
Green Lane 93 B5
Greenlaw
  Aberds 268 D1
  Borders 197 B6
Greenlea 174 A3
Greenloaning 218 D3
Greenmount 137 B6
Greenmow 285 L6
Greenock 204 A2
Greenock West 204 A2
Greenodd 154 C2
Green Ore 43 D4
Greenrow 174 C4
Green St Green 50 C1
Greenside 178 C3
Greensidehill 188 A2
Greens Norton 82 C3
Greenstead Green . . .70 A2
Greensted 69 C5
Green Street 68 D1
Greenwich 49 B6
Greet 80 D3
Greete 94 D3
Greetham
  Lincs 134 B3
  Rutland 116 D2
Greetland 138 A3
Gregg Hall 154 B3
Gregson Lane 137 A4
Greinetobht 287 G3
Greinton 28 B4
Gremista 285 J6
Grenaby 152 D2
Grendon
  Northants 83 A5
  Warks 97 A5
Grendon Common . . .97 B5
Grendon Green 78 B3
Grendon
  Underwood 66 A1
Grenofen 11 D5
Grenoside 139 D6
Greosabhagh 288 H2
Gresford 126 D3
Gresham 120 B3
Greshornish 258 C3
Gressenhall 119 D6
Gressingham 145 A5
Gresty Green 128 D2
Greta Bridge. 166 D3
Gretna 175 B6
Gretna Green 175 B6
Gretton
  Glos 80 D3
  Northants 99 B5
  Shrops 94 B3
Grewelthorpe. 157 D6
Greygarth 157 D5
Grey Green 141 C5
Greynor 57 B5
Greysouthen. 162 B3
Greystoke 164 B2
Greystone
  Angus 232 D3
  Dumfries 174 A2
Greywell 47 D5
Griais 288 C5
Grianan 288 D5
Gribthorpe 149 D6
Gridley Corner 11 B4

Griff 97 C6
Griffithstown 61 D4
Grimbister 282 F4
Grimblethorpe. 134 A2
Grimeford Village . . .137 B5
Grimethorpe 140 C2
Griminis. 286 A3
Grimister. 284 D6
Grimley 79 A6
Grimoldby 134 A3
Grimpo 110 C2
Grimsargh 145 D5
Grimsbury 82 C1
Grimsby 143 B4
Grimscote 82 B3
Grimscott 10 A3
Grimsthorpe. 116 C3
Grimston
  E Yorks 151 D5
  Leics 115 C4
  Norf 119 C4
  York 149 B5
Grimstone 15 B6
Grinacombe Moor . . .11 B5
Grindale 161 D5
Grindigar 283 G6
Grindiscol 285 K6
Grindle. 95 A5
Grindleford 130 B2
Grindleton 146 C1
Grindley. 112 C4
Grindley Brook. 111 A4
Grindlow 130 B1
Grindon
  Northumb 198 B3
  Staffs 129 D5
Grindonmoor Gate .129 D5
Gringley on the
  Hill 141 D5
Grinsdale 175 C6
Grinshill 111 C4
Grinton 156 B4
Griomsidar 288 E4
Grishipoll 223 B4
Grisling Common . . .36 D2
Gristhorpe 161 C4
Griston 103 B5
Gritley 283 G6
Grittenham 44 A4
Grittleton 44 A2
Grizebeck 153 B3
Grizedale 154 B2
Grobister 282 E7
Groby 98 A2
Groes
  Conwy 125 C5
  Neath 40 C2
Groes-faen 41 C5
Groesffordd Marli .125 B5
Groeslon
  Gwyn. 107 A4
  Gwyn. 123 D5
Groes-lwyd 109 D7
Grogport 202 D3
Gromford 89 B4
Gronant 125 A5
Groombridge 36 C3
Grosmont
  Mon. 61 A6
  N Yorks 160 A2
Groton 87 C5
Grougfoot 208 C3
Grouville 6
Grove
  Dorset. 15 D7
  Kent 53 C4
  Notts. 132 B2
  Oxon 65 D5
Grove Park 49 B7
Grovesend. 57 B5
Grove Vale 96 B3
Grudie 263 D5
Gruids 272 D3
Gruinard House 261 A6
Grula 246 B2
Gruline 225 B4
Grunasound 285 K5
Grundisburgh. 88 B3
Grunsagill 146 B1
Gruting 285 J4
Grutness 285 N6
Gualachulain 227 B6
Gualin House 276 C4
Guardbridge 221 C4
Guarlford 79 C6
Guay 230 D4
Guestling Green 23 A6
Guestling Thorn 23 A6
Guestwick. 120 C2

Guestwick Green. . .120 C2
Guide 137 A6
Guide Post 179 A4
Guilden Morden 85 C4
Guilden Sutton 127 C4
Guildford 34 B2
Guildtown 219 A6
Guilsborough. 98 D3
Guilsfield 109 D7
Guilton. 53 D4
Guineaford 25 B6
Guisborough 168 D4
Guiseley. 147 C5
Guist 120 C1
Guith 282 D6
Guiting Power 64 A1
Gulberwick. 285 K6
Gullane 210 B1
Gulval. 2 B2
Gulworthy 11 D5
Gumfreston 55 D7
Gumley 98 B3
Gummow's Shop 4 B3
Gunby
  E Yorks 149 D6
  Lincs 116 C2
Gundleton 33 B5
Gun Hill 22 A3
Gunn 26 B1
Gunnerside 156 B3
Gunnerton 177 B7
Gunness 141 B6
Gunnislake 11 D5
Gunnista 285 J7
Gunthorpe
  Norf 120 B2
  Notts. 115 A4
  Pboro 100 A3
Gunville 18 C3
Gunwalloe 3 C4
Gurnard 18 B3
Gurnett 129 B4
Gurney Slade 29 A6
Gurnos 59 E4
Gussage All Saints . .31 D4
Gussage St Michael .30 D3
Guston 39 A5
Gutcher 284 D7
Guthrie 232 C3
Guyhirn 101 A5
Guyhirn Gull 101 A5
Guy's Head 118 C1
Guy's Marsh 30 C2
Guyzance 189 C5
Gwaenysgor 125 A5
Gwalchmai 122 C3
Gwaun-Cae-
  Gurwen 59 D4
Gwaun-Leision 59 D4
Gwbert. 73 B4
Gweek 3 C5
Gwehelog 61 C5
Gwenddwr 77 C4
Gwennap. 4 D2
Gwenter. 3 D5
Gwernaffield 126 C2
Gwernesney 61 C6
Gwernogle 58 B2
Gwernymynydd 126 C2
Gwersyllt. 126 D3
Gwespyr 125 A6
Gwithian 2 A3
Gwredog 123 B4
Gwyddelwern. 109 A5
Gwyddgrug. 58 B1
Gwydyr Uchaf. 124 C2
Gwynfryn. 126 D2
Gwystre 77 A4
Gwytherin 124 C3
Gyfelia 110 A2
Gyffin 124 B2
Gyre 283 G4
Gyrn-goch 107 B4

H

Habberley. 94 A1
Habergham 146 D2
Habrough 142 B3
Haceby 116 B3
Hacheston 88 B4
Hackbridge. 49 C5
Hackenthorpe 131 A4
Hackford 103 A6
Hackforth 157 B6
Hackland 282 E4
Hackleton 83 B5

Hackness
N Yorks 160 B3
Orkney 283 H4
Hackney 49 A6
Hackthorn 133 A4
Hackthorpe 164 C3
Haconby 116 C4
Hacton 50 A2
Hadden 198 C1
Haddenham
Bucks 66 C2
Cambs. 101 D6
Haddington
E Loth 210 C2
Lincs 133 C4
Haddiscoe 105 B5
Haddon
Cambs. 100 B3
Ches E. 129 C4
Hade Edge 139 C4
Hademore 97 A4
Hadfield 138 D3
Hadham Cross 68 B4
Hadham Ford 68 A4
Hadleigh
Essex 51 A5
Suff. 87 C6
Hadley 111 D5
Hadley End 113 C5
Hadlow 36 B4
Hadlow Down 36 D3
Hadnall 111 D4
Hadstock 86 C1
Hady 130 B3
Hadzor 80 A2
Haffenden Quarter . . 37 B6
Hafod-Dinbych 124 D3
Hafod-Iom 124 D3
Haggate 146 D2
Haggbeck 176 B2
Haggerston 198 B4
Haggrister 284 F5
Hagley
Hereford. 78 C3
Worcs. 96 C2
Hagworthingham . . 134 C3
Haigh
Gtr Man 137 C5
S Yorks 139 B5
Haigh Moor 139 A5
Haighton Green 145 D5
Haile 162 D3
Hailes 80 D3
Hailey
Herts 68 B3
Oxon 65 B4
Hailsham 22 B3
Hail Weston 84 A3
Haimer 280 B3
Hainault 69 D4
Hainford 120 D4
Hainton 134 A1
Hairmyres 205 C4
Haisthorpe 151 A4
Hakin 55 D4
Halam 132 C1
Halbeath 208 B4
Halberton 27 D5
Halcro 280 B4
Hale
Gtr Man 128 A2
Halton. 127 A4
Hants 31 D5
Hale Bank 127 A4
Halebarns 128 A2
Hales
Norf 105 B4
Staffs 111 B6
Halesfield 95 A5
Halesgate 117 C6
Halesowen 96 C2
Hales Place 52 D3
Hale Street 37 B4
Halesworth 105 D4
Halewood 127 A4
Halford
Shrops 94 C2
Warks 81 C5
Halfpenny Furze 56 A2
Halfpenny Green 95 B6
Halfway
Carms 58 B3
Carms 59 B5
W Berks 46 C2
Halfway Bridge 34 D2
Halfway House 110 D2
Halfway Houses 51 B6
Halifax 138 A3

Halket 205 C4
Halkirk 280 C3
Halkyn 126 B2
Halland 22 A2
Hallaton 99 B4
Hallatrow 43 D5
Hallbankgate 176 D3
Hall Dunnerdale 153 A3
Hallen 43 A4
Hall Green
W Mid 96 C4
W Yorks 139 B6
Hall Grove 68 B2
Halliburton 197 B5
Hallin 258 C2
Halling 51 C4
Hallington
Lincs 134 A3
Northumb 178 B1
Halliwell 137 B6
Hall of Tankerness . . 283 G6
Hall of the Forest . . 93 C6
Halloughton 132 D1
Hallow 79 B6
Hallrule 187 B4
Halls 210 C3
Hallsands 8 D2
Hall's Green 68 A2
Hallthwaites 153 B2
Hallworthy 10 C2
Hallyburton House . . 220 A2
Hallyne 195 B6
Halmer End 112 A1
Halmore 62 C2
Halmyre Mains 195 B6
Halnaker 20 B2
Halsall 136 B2
Halse
Northants 82 C2
Som. 27 C6
Halsetown 2 B3
Halsham 143 A4
Halsinger 25 B6
Halstead
Essex 87 D4
Kent 50 C1
Leics 99 A4
Halstock 15 A5
Haltham 134 C2
Haltoft End 117 A6
Halton
Bucks 66 B3
Halton. 127 A5
Lancs 145 A5
Northumb 178 C1
Wrex. 110 B2
W Yorks 148 D2
Halton East 147 B4
Halton Gill 156 D2
Halton Holegate . . . 135 C4
Halton Lea Gate . . . 176 D4
Halton West 146 B2
Haltwhistle 177 C5
Halvergate 105 A5
Halwell 8 B1
Halwill 11 B5
Halwill Junction 11 A5
Ham
Devon 14 A2
Glos 62 D2
Highld 280 A4
Kent 53 D5
London 49 B4
Shetland 285 K1
Wilts 46 C1
Hambleden 47 A5
Hambledon
Hants 33 D5
Sur 34 C2
Hamble-le-Rice 18 A3
Hambleton
Lancs 144 C3
N Yorks 149 D4
Hambridge 28 C3
Hambrook
S Glos 43 B5
W Sus 19 A6
Ham Common 30 C2
Hameringham 134 C3
Hamerton 100 D3
Hametoun 285 K1
Ham Green
Hereford. 79 C5
Kent 37 D6
Kent 51 C5
N Som 43 B4
Worcs. 80 A3
Hamilton 194 A2
Hammer 34 C1
Hammerpot 20 B3

Hammersmith 49 B5
Hammerwich 96 A3
Hammerwood 36 C2
Hammond Street 68 C3
Hammoon 30 D2
Hamnavoe
Shetland 284 E4
Shetland 284 E6
Shetland 284 F6
Shetland 285 K5
Hampden Park 22 B4
Hamperden End 86 D1
Hampnett 64 B1
Hampole 140 B3
Hampreston 17 B4
Hampstead 49 A5
Hampstead Norreys . . 46 B3
Hampsthwaite 147 B6
Hampton
London 48 C4
Shrops 95 C5
Worcs. 80 C3
Hampton Bishop 78 D3
Hampton Heath 110 A3
Hampton in Arden . . 97 C5
Hampton Loade 95 C5
Hampton Lovett 80 A1
Hampton Lucy 81 B5
Hampton on the Hill . 81 A5
Hampton Poyle 65 B6
Hamrow 119 C6
Hamsey 22 A2
Hamsey Green 35 A6
Hamstall Ridware . . 113 D5
Hamstead
IoW. 18 B3
W Mid 96 B3
Hamstead Marshall . 46 C2
Hamsterley
Durham 166 B4
Durham 178 D3
Hamstreet 38 B2
Ham Street 29 B6
Hamworthy 16 B3
Hanbury
Staffs 113 C5
Worcs. 80 A2
Hanbury Woodend . 113 C5
Hanby 116 B3
Hanchurch 112 A2
Handbridge 127 C4
Handcross 35 D5
Handforth 128 A3
Handley 127 D4
Handsacre 113 D4
Handsworth
S Yorks 131 A4
W Mid 96 B3
Handy Cross 25 C5
Hanford 112 A2
Hanging Langford . . . 31 B4
Hangleton 20 B3
Hanham 43 B5
Hankelow 111 A5
Hankerton 63 D5
Hankham 22 B4
Hanley 112 A2
Hanley Castle 79 C6
Hanley Child 79 A4
Hanley Swan 79 C6
Hanley William 79 A4
Hanlith 146 A3
Hanmer 110 B3
Hannah 135 B5
Hannington
Hants 46 D3
Northants 99 D5
Swindon 64 D2
Hannington Wick . . . 64 D2
Hansel Village 192 B3
Hanslope 83 C5
Hanthorpe 116 C3
Hanwell
London 49 A4
Oxon 82 C1
Hanwood 94 A2
Hanworth
London 48 B4
Norf 120 B3
Happendon 194 C3
Happisburgh 121 B5
Happisburgh
Common 121 C5
Hapsford 127 B4
Hapton
Lancs 146 D1
Norf 104 B2
Harberton 8 B1
Harbertonford 8 B1
Harbledown 52 D3

Harborne 96 C3
Harborough Magna . 98 D1
Harbottle 188 C2
Harbury 81 B6
Harby
Leics 115 B5
Notts 132 B3
Harcombe 13 B6
Harden
W Mid 96 A3
W Yorks 147 D4
Hardenhuish 44 B3
Hardgate 245 B4
Hardham 20 A3
Hardingham 103 A6
Hardingstone 83 B4
Hardington 43 D6
Hardington
Mandeville 29 D5
Hardington Marsh . . . 15 A5
Hardley 18 A3
Hardley Street 105 A4
Hardmead 83 C6
Hardrow 156 B2
Hardstoft 131 C4
Hardway
Hants 19 A5
Som. 29 B7
Hardwick
Bucks 66 B3
Cambs. 85 B5
Norf 104 C3
Norf 118 D3
Northants 83 A5
Oxon 65 A6
Oxon 65 C4
W Mid 96 B3
Hardwicke
Glos 62 B3
Glos 63 A5
Hereford 77 C6
Hardy's Green 70 A3
Hare Green 71 A4
Hare Hatch 47 B6
Harehills 148 D2
Harehope 188 A3
Haresceugh 165 A4
Harescombe 63 B4
Haresfield 63 B4
Hareshaw 207 D6
Hareshaw Head 177 A6
Hare Street 68 A3
Harewood 148 C2
Harewood End 62 A1
Harford
Carms 58 A3
Devon 7 B5
Hargate 104 B2
Hargatewall 129 B6
Hargrave
Ches W 127 C4
Northants 100 D2
Suff 86 B3
Harker 175 B6
Harkland 284 E6
Harkstead 88 D2
Harlaston 113 D6
Harlaw House 256 D2
Harlaxton 116 B1
Harlech 107 C5
Harlequin 115 B4
Harlescott 111 D4
Harlesden 49 A5
Harleston
Devon 8 C1
Norf 104 C3
Suff 87 B6
Harlestone 83 A4
Harle Syke 146 D2
Harley
Shrops 94 A3
S Yorks 139 D6
Harleyholm 194 C4
Harlington
C Beds 84 D2
London 48 B3
S Yorks 140 C2
Harlosh 258 D2
Harlow 69 B4
Harlow Hill
Northumb 178 C2
N Yorks 148 B1
Harlthorpe 149 D6
Harlton 85 B5
Harman's Cross 16 C3
Harmby 157 C5

Harmer Green 68 B2
Harmer Hill 110 C3
Harmondsworth 48 B3
Harmston 133 C4
Harnham 178 B2
Harnhill 63 C6
Harold Hill 69 D5
Haroldston West 55 C4
Haroldswick 284 B8
Harold Wood 69 D5
Harome 159 C5
Harpenden 67 B6
Harpford 13 B5
Harpham 150 A3
Harpley
Norf 119 C4
Worcs. 79 A4
Harpole 82 A3
Harpsdale 280 C3
Harpsden 47 A5
Harpswell 133 A4
Harpurhey 138 C1
Harpur Hill 129 B5
Harraby 175 C7
Harrapool 247 B5
Harrier 285 J1
Harrietfield 219 B4
Harrietsham 37 A6
Harrington
Cumb 162 B2
Lincs 134 B3
Northants 99 C4
Harringworth 99 B6
Harris 234 A2
Harrogate 148 B2
Harrold 83 B6
Harrow 49 A4
Harrowbarrow 6 A2
Harrowden 84 C2
Harrowgate Hill 167 D5
Harrow on the Hill . . 49 A4
Harrow Street 87 D5
Harrow Weald 67 D6
Harston
Cambs. 85 B6
Leics 115 B6
Harswell 150 C1
Hart 168 B2
Hartburn
Northumb 178 A2
Stockton 168 D2
Hart Common 137 C5
Hartest 87 B4
Hartfield 36 C2
Hartford
Cambs. 101 D4
Ches W 127 B6
Hartfordbridge 47 D5
Hartford End 69 B6
Harthill
Ches W 127 D5
N Lanark 208 D2
S Yorks 131 A4
Hart Hill 67 A6
Hartington 129 C6
Hartland 24 C3
Hartlebury 95 D6
Hartlepool 168 B3
Hartley
Cumb 155 A6
Kent 37 C5
Kent 50 C3
Northumb 179 B5
Hartley Westpall 47 D4
Hartley Wintney 47 D5
Hartlip 51 C5
Hartoft End 159 B6
Harton
N Yorks 149 A6
Shrops 94 C2
T&W 179 C5
Hartpury 62 A3
Hartshead 139 A4
Hartshill 97 B6
Hartshorne 113 C7
Hartsop 164 D2
Hart Station 168 B2
Hartwell 83 B4
Hartwood 194 A3
Harvieston 206 B3
Harvington 80 C3
Harvington Cross 80 C3
Harwell 46 A2
Harwich 88 D3
Harwood
Durham 165 B6
Gtr Man 137 B6
Harwood Dale 160 B3
Harworth 140 D4

Hasbury 96 C2
Hascombe 34 B2
Haselbech 99 D4
Haselbury Plucknett . 29 D4
Haseley 81 A5
Haselor 80 B4
Hasfield 63 A4
Hasguard 55 D4
Haskayne 136 C2
Hasketon 88 B3
Hasland 130 C3
Haslemere 34 C2
Haslingden 137 A6
Haslingfield 85 B6
Haslington 128 D2
Hassall 128 D2
Hassall Green 128 D2
Hassell Street 38 A2
Hassendean 186 A4
Hassingham 105 A4
Hassocks 21 A5
Hassop 130 B2
Hastigrow 281 B4
Hastingleigh 38 A2
Hastings 23 B6
Hastingwood 69 C4
Hastoe 67 C4
Haswell 167 A6
Haswell Plough 167 A6
Hatch
C Beds 84 C3
Hants 47 D4
Wilts 30 C3
Hatch Beauchamp . . . 28 C3
Hatch End 67 D6
Hatchet Gate 18 A2
Hatch Green 28 D3
Hatching Green 67 B6
Hatchmere 127 B5
Hatcliffe 143 C4
Hatfield
Hereford 78 B3
Herts 68 C2
S Yorks 141 C4
Worcs. 80 B1
Hatfield Broad Oak . . 69 B5
Hatfield Garden
Village 68 C2
Hatfield Heath 69 B5
Hatfield Hyde 68 B2
Hatfield Peverel 70 B1
Hatfield
Woodhouse 141 C4
Hatford 64 D4
Hatherden 46 D1
Hatherleigh 11 A6
Hathern 114 C2
Hatherop 64 C2
Hathersage 130 A2
Hathershaw 138 C2
Hatherton
Ches E. 111 A5
Staffs 112 D3
Hatley St George 85 B4
Hatt 6 A2
Hattingley 33 B5
Hatton
Aberds 257 C5
Derbys 113 C6
Lincs 134 B1
Shrops 94 B2
Warks 81 A5
Warr 127 A5
Hatton Castle 256 B2
Hattoncrook 256 D3
Hatton Heath 127 C4
Hatton of Fintray . . . 245 A5
Haugh
E Ayrs 193 C4
Gtr Man 138 B2
Lincs 135 B4
Haugham 134 A3
Haugh Head 188 A3
Haughley 87 A6
Haughley Green 87 A6
Haugh of Glass 255 C5
Haugh of Urr 173 B6
Haughs of
Clinterty 245 A5
Haughton
Notts 132 B1
Shrops 95 A5
Shrops 95 B4
Shrops 110 C2
Shrops 111 D4
Staffs 112 C2
Haughton Castle . . . 177 B7
Haughton Green . . . 138 D2
Haughton Moss 127 D5
Haultwick 68 A3

Haunn
Argyll 224 B2
W Isles. 286 E3
Haunton 113 D6
Hauxley 189 C5
Hauxton 85 B6
Havant 19 A6
Haven 78 B2
Haven Bank 134 D2
Haven Side 142 A3
Havenstreet 19 B4
Havercroft 140 B1
Haverfordwest
= Hwlffordd 55 C5
Haverhill 86 C2
Haverigg 153 C2
Havering-atte-
Bower. 69 D5
Haveringland 120 C3
Haversham 83 C5
Haverthwaite 154 C2
Haverton Hill 168 C2
Hawarden
= Penarlâg 126 C3
Hawcoat 153 C3
Hawen 73 B6
Hawes 156 C2
Hawes' Green 104 B3
Hawes Side. 144 D3
Hawford. 79 A6
Hawick 186 B4
Hawkchurch 14 A3
Hawkedon 86 B3
Hawkenbury
Kent 36 C3
Kent 37 B6
Hawkeridge 44 D2
Hawkerland 13 C5
Hawkesbury
S Glos 43 A6
Warks 97 C6
Hawkesbury Upton . .44 A1
Hawkes End 97 C6
Hawk Green 129 A4
Hawkhill 189 B5
Hawkhurst 37 C5
Hawkinge 39 B4
Hawkley 33 C6
Hawkridge 26 B3
Hawkshead 154 B2
Hawkshead Hill 154 B2
Hawksland 194 C3
Hawkswick 156 D3
Hawksworth
Notts. 115 A5
W Yorks 147 C5
W Yorks 147 D6
Hawkwell 70 D2
Hawley
Hants 34 A1
Kent 50 B2
Hawling 63 A6
Hawnby 158 C4
Haworth 147 D4
Hawstead 87 B4
Hawthorn
Durham. 168 A2
Rhondda 41 C6
Wilts 44 C2
Hawthorn Hill
Brack 48 B1
Lincs 134 D2
Hawthorpe 116 C3
Hawton 132 D2
Haxby 149 B5
Haxey 141 C5
Haydock 137 D4
Haydon 29 D6
Haydon Bridge 177 C6
Haydon Wick 45 A5
Haye. 6 A2
Hayes
London 48 A4
London 49 C7
Hayfield
Derbys 129 A5
Fife 209 A5
Hay Green 118 D2
Hayhill 182 A2
Hayhillock 232 D3
Hayle 2 B3
Haynes. 84 C2
Haynes
Church End 84 C2
Hay-on-Wye
= Y Gelli Gandryll . .77 C6
Hayscastle 55 B4
Hayscastle Cross . . .55 B5
Hayshead 233 D4
Hay Street 68 A3

Hayton
Aberdeen 245 B6
Cumb 174 D4
Cumb 176 D3
E Yorks 149 C7
Notts. 132 A2
Hayton's Bent. 94 C3
Haytor Vale 12 D2
Haywards Heath 35 D6
Haywood 140 B3
Haywood Oaks 131 D6
Hazelbank. 194 B3
Hazelbury Bryan . . .16 A1
Hazeley 47 D5
Hazel Grove 129 A4
Hazelhurst 138 C2
Hazelslade 112 D4
Hazel Street 37 C4
Hazelton 64 B1
Hazelton Walls 220 B3
Hazelwood 114 A1
Hazlemere 66 D3
Hazlerigg 179 B4
Hazlewood 147 B4
Hazon. 189 C4
Heacham 118 B3
Headbourne
Worthy 32 B3
Headbrook 77 B7
Headcorn 37 B6
Headingley 148 D1
Headington. 65 C6
Headlam 167 D4
Headless Cross 80 A3
Headley
Hants 33 B7
Hants 46 C3
Sur 35 A5
Head of Muir 207 B6
Headon 132 B2
Heads 194 B2
Heads Nook 176 D2
Heage. 130 D3
Healaugh
N Yorks 148 C3
N Yorks 156 B4
Heald Green 128 A3
Heale
Devon 26 A1
Som. 29 A6
Healey
Gtr Man 138 B1
Northumb 178 D2
N Yorks 157 C5
Healing 143 B4
Heamoor 2 B2
Heanish 222 C3
Heanor. 114 A2
Heanton
Punchardon 25 B6
Heapham 132 A3
Hearthstane 195 D6
Heasley Mill 26 B2
Heast 247 C5
Heath
Cardiff. 41 D6
Derbys 131 C4
Heath and Reach. . . .67 A4
Heathcote 129 C6
Heath End
Hants 46 C3
Sur 34 B1
Warks 81 A5
Heather 114 D1
Heatherfield. 259 D4
Heathfield
Devon 12 D3
E Sus. 36 D3
Som. 27 C6
Heathhall 174 A2
Heath Hayes 112 D4
Heath Hill 111 D6
Heath House 28 A4
Heathrow Airport . . .48 B3
Heathstock 14 A2
Heathton 95 B6
Heath Town 96 B2
Heatley 128 A2
Heaton
Lancs 144 A4
Staffs 129 C4
T&W 179 C4
W Yorks 147 D5
Heaton Moor 138 D1
Heaverham 36 A3
Heavitree 13 B4
Hebburn 179 C5
Hebden 147 A4
Hebden Bridge 138 A2

Hebron
Anglesey. 123 B4
Carms 73 D4
Northumb 178 A3
Heck. 184 D3
Heckfield. 47 C5
Heckfield Green . . .104 D2
Heckfordbridge 70 A3
Heckington 116 A4
Heckmondwike 139 A5
Heddington 44 C3
Heddle 282 F4
Heddon-on-the-
Wall 178 C3
Hedenham 104 B4
Hedge End 32 D3
Hedgerley 48 A2
Hedging. 28 C3
Hedley on the Hill . .178 D2
Hednesford 112 D3
Hedon 142 A3
Hedsor. 48 A2
Hedworth 179 C5
Hegdon Hill 78 B3
Heggerscales. 165 D6
Heglibister 285 H5
Heighington
Darl. 167 C5
Lincs 133 C5
Heights of Brae 263 D7
Heights of
Kinlochewe. 262 D2
Heilam 277 B5
Heiton 197 C6
Hele
Devon 13 A4
Devon 25 A6
Helensburgh 215 D5
Helford 3 C5
Helford Passage 3 C5
Helhoughton 119 C5
Helions Bumpstead . .86 C2
Hellaby 140 D3
Helland 10 D1
Hellesdon 120 D4
Hellidon 82 B2
Hellifield 146 B2
Hellingly 22 A3
Hellington 104 A4
Hellister. 285 J5
Helm. 189 D4
Helmdon 82 C2
Helmingham 88 B2
Helmington Row . . .167 B4
Helmsdale. 274 C4
Helmshore 137 A6
Helmsley 159 C5
Helperby 148 A3
Helperthorpe 160 D3
Helpringham 116 A4
Helpston 100 A3
Helsby 127 B4
Helsey 135 B5
Helston 3 C4
Helstone 10 C1
Helton 164 C3
Helwith Bridge. 146 A2
Hemblington 121 D5
Hemel Hempstead . .67 C5
Hemingbrough 149 D5
Hemingby 134 B2
Hemingford
Abbots 101 D4
Hemingford Grey. . .101 D4
Hemingstone 88 B2
Hemington
Leics 114 C2
Northants 100 C2
Som. 43 D6
Hemley 88 C3
Hemlington 168 D3
Hemp Green 89 A4
Hempholme 150 B3
Hempnall 104 B3
Hempnall Green . . .104 B3
Hempriggs House . .281 D5
Hempstead
Essex 86 D2
Medway 51 C4
Norf 120 B3
Norf 121 C6
Hempsted 63 B4
Hempton
Norf 119 C6
Oxon 82 D1
Hemsby 121 D6
Hemswell 142 D1
Hemswell Cliff 133 A4
Hemsworth 140 B2
Hemyock 27 D6

Henbury
Bristol. 43 B4
Ches E. 128 B3
Hendon
London 49 A5
T&W 179 D6
Hendre. 126 C1
Hendre-ddu 124 C3
Hendreforgan 41 C4
Hendy. 57 B5
Heneglwys 123 C4
Hen-feddau fawr . . .73 C5
Henfield 21 A5
Henford 11 B4
Henghurst 38 B1
Hengoed
Caerph 41 B6
Powys 77 B6
Shrops 110 B1
Hengrave 87 A4
Henham 69 A5
Heniarth 93 A5
Henlade 28 C2
Henley
Shrops 94 D3
Som. 28 B4
Suff 88 B2
W Sus 34 D1
Henley-in-Arden . . .81 A4
Henley-on-Thames . .47 A5
Henley's Down 23 A5
Henllan
Ceredig. 73 B6
Denb 125 C5
Henllan Amgoed 73 D4
Henllys 61 D4
Henlow 84 D3
Hennock 12 C3
Henny Street 87 D4
Henryd 124 B2
Henry's Moat 55 B6
Hensall 140 A3
Henshaw 177 C5
Hensingham 162 C2
Henstead 105 C5
Henstridge 30 D1
Henstridge Ash 29 C7
Henstridge Marsh . .30 C1
Henton
Oxon 66 C2
Som. 29 A4
Henwood. 10 D3
Heogan 285 J6
Heol-las 40 B1
Heol Senni 59 C6
Heol-y-Cyw 40 C4
Hepburn 188 A3
Hepple 188 C2
Hepscott 179 A4
Heptonstall 138 A2
Hepworth
Suff 103 D5
W Yorks 139 C4
Herbrandston. 55 D4
Hereford 78 C3
Heriot. 196 A2
Hermiston 209 C4
Hermitage
Borders. 186 D4
Dorset. 15 A6
W Berks 46 B3
W Sus 19 A6
Hermon
Anglesey. 122 D3
Carms 58 C3
Carms 73 C6
Pembs. 73 C5
Herne 52 C3
Herne Bay 52 C3
Herner 25 C6
Hernhill 52 C2
Herodsfoot 5 A7
Herongate. 69 D6
Heronsford 180 C3
Herriard 33 A5
Herringfleet 105 B5
Herringswell 102 D3
Hersden 53 C4
Hersham
Corn 10 A3
Sur 48 C4
Herstmonceux 22 A4
Herston 283 H5
Hertford. 68 B3
Hertford Heath 68 B3
Hertingfordbury 68 B3
Hesketh Bank 136 A3
Hesketh Lane 145 C6
Hesket Newmarket .163 A6
Heskin Green 136 B4

Hesleden 168 B2
Hesleyside 177 A6
Heslington 149 B5
Hessay 148 B4
Hessenford 6 B2
Hessett 87 A5
Hessle 142 A2
Hest Bank 145 A4
Heston 48 B4
Hestwall 282 F3
Heswall 126 A2
Hethe 65 A6
Hethersett. 104 A2
Hethersgill 176 C2
Hethpool 188 A1
Hett. 167 B5
Hetton 146 B3
Hetton-le-Hole 167 A6
Hetton Steads 198 C4
Heugh 178 B2
Heugh-head. 243 A6
Heveningham 104 D4
Hever 36 B2
Heversham 154 C3
Hevingham 120 C3
Hewas Water 5 C4
Hewelsfield 62 C1
Hewish
N Som 42 C3
Som. 14 A4
Heworth 149 B5
Hexham 178 C1
Hextable 50 B2
Hexton 84 D3
Hexworthy 12 D1
Hey 146 C2
Heybridge
Essex 69 D6
Essex 70 C2
Heybridge Basin . . .70 C2
Heybrook Bay 7 C4
Heydon
Cambs. 85 C6
Norf 120 C3
Heydour 116 B3
Heylipol 222 C2
Heylor 284 E4
Heysham 144 A4
Heyshott 20 A1
Heyside 138 C2
Heytesbury 30 A3
Heythrop 64 A4
Heywood
Gtr Man 138 B1
Wilts 44 D2
Hibaldstow 142 C1
Hickleton 140 C2
Hickling
Norf 121 C6
Notts. 115 C4
Hickling Green. 121 C6
Hickling Heath. 121 C6
Hickstead 35 D5
Hidcote Boyce 81 C4
High Ackworth. 140 B2
Higham
Derbys 130 D3
Kent 51 B4
Lancs 146 D2
Suff 86 A3
Suff 87 D6
Higham Dykes 178 B3
Higham Ferrers. 83 A6
Higham Gobion 84 D3
Higham on the Hill . .97 B6
Highampton 11 A5
Higham Wood 36 B3
High Angerton 178 A2
High Bankhill 164 A3
High Barnes 179 D5
High Beach 68 D4
High Bentham 145 A6
High Bickington 25 C7
High Birkwith 155 D6
High Blantyre 194 A1
High Bonnybridge . .207 C6
High Bradfield 139 D5
High Bray 26 B1
Highbridge
Highld 239 D5
Som. 28 A3
Highbrook 35 C6
High Brooms 36 B3
High Bullen 25 C6
Highburton 139 B4
Highbury 29 A6
High Buston 189 C5
High Callerton 178 B3
High Catton 149 B6
Highclere 46 C2

Highcliffe 17 B6
High Cogges. 65 C4
High Coniscliffe. . . .167 D5
High Cross
Hants 33 C6
Herts. 68 B3
High Easter 69 B6
High Eggborough . .140 A3
High Ellington 157 C5
Higher Ansty 16 A1
Higher Ashton 12 C3
Higher Ballam 144 D3
Higher Bartle 145 D5
Higher Boscaswell . . . 2 B1
Higher
Burwardsley 127 D5
High Ercall 111 D4
Higher Clovelly 24 C4
Higher End 136 C4
Higher Kinnerton . .126 C3
Higher
Penwortham. 136 A4
Higher Town Scilly . .P02 E4
Higher Walreddon . .11 D5
Higher Walton
Lancs 137 A4
Warr 127 A5
Higher Wheelton. . .137 A5
Higher Whitley. 127 A6
Higher Wincham . . .128 B1
Higher Wych 110 A3
High Etherley 167 C4
Highfield
E Yorks 149 D6
Gtr Man 137 C6
N Ayrs 204 C3
Oxon 65 A6
S Yorks 130 A3
T&W 178 D3
Highfields
Cambs. 85 B5
Northumb 198 A3
High Garrett 70 A1
Highgate 49 A5
High Grange 167 B4
High Green
Norf 104 A2
S Yorks 139 D6
Worcs 80 C1
High Halden 37 C6
High Halstow 51 B4
High Ham 28 B4
High Harrington . . .162 B3
High Hatton 111 C5
High Hawsker. 160 A3
High Hesket 164 A2
High Hesleden 168 B2
High Hoyland 139 B5
High Hunsley 150 D2
High Hurstwood 36 D2
High Hutton 149 A6
High Ireby 163 A5
High Kelling 120 A3
High Kilburn 158 D4
High Lands 166 C4
Highlane
Ches E. 128 C3
Derbys 131 A4
High Lane
Gtr Man 129 A4
Worcs 79 A4
High Laver 69 C5
Highlaws 174 D4
Highleadon 62 A3
High Legh 128 A2
Highleigh 20 C1
High Leven 168 D2
Highley 95 C5
High Littleton 43 D5
High Lorton 163 B4
High Marishes 159 D7
High Marnham 132 B3
High Melton 140 C3
High Mickley 178 C2
High Mindork. 171 B5
Highmoor Cross 47 A5
Highmoor Hill 42 A3
Highnam 62 B3
Highnam Green 62 A3
High Newton 154 C3
High Newton-by-the-
Sea 189 A5
High Nibthwaite . . .154 C1
High Offley 112 C1
High Ongar 69 C5
High Onn 112 D2
High Roding 69 B6
High Row 163 A6

312 Hig–Hot

High Salvington 21 B4
High Sellafield 162 D3
High Shaw 156 B2
High Spen 178 D3
Highsted 51 C6
High Stoop 166 A4
High Street
  Corn 5 B4
  Kent 37 C5
  Suff 87 C4
  Suff 89 B5
  Suff 105 D5
Highstreet Green 86 D3
High Street Green 87 B6
Hightae 174 A3
High Throston 168 B2
Hightown
  Ches E 128 C3
  Mers 136 C2
Hightown Green 87 B5
High Toynton 134 C2
High Trewhitt 188 C3
High Valleyfield 208 B3
Highway 44 B4
Highweek 12 D3
High Westwood 178 D3
Highworth 64 D3
High Wray 154 B2
High Wych 69 B4
High Wycombe 66 D3
Hilborough 103 A4
Hilcote 131 D4
Hilcott 45 D5
Hildenborough 36 B3
Hilden Park 36 B3
Hildersham 86 C1
Hilderstone 112 B3
Hilderthorpe 151 A4
Hilfield 15 A6
Hilgay 102 B2
Hill
  Pembs 55 D7
  S Glos 62 D2
  W Mid 96 B4
Hillam 140 A3
Hillbeck 165 D5
Hillborough 53 C4
Hillbrae
  Aberds 255 B7
  Aberds 256 D2
Hill Brow 33 C6
Hillbutts 16 A3
Hillclifflane 113 A6
Hillcommon 27 C6
Hill Dale 136 B3
Hill Dyke 117 A6
Hillend 208 B4
Hill End
  Durham 166 B3
  Fife 208 A3
  N Yorks 147 B4
Hillerton 12 B2
Hillesden 66 A1
Hillesley 43 A6
Hillfarance 27 C6
Hillhead
  Aberds 255 C6
  Devon 8 B3
  S Ayrs 182 A2
Hill Head
  Hants 18 A4
  Northumb 178 C1
Hillhead of Auchentumb 269 D4
Hillhead of Cocklaw 257 B5
Hillhouse 197 A4
Hilliclay 280 B3
Hillingdon 48 A3
Hillington
  Glasgow 205 B5
  Norf 119 C4
Hillmorton 98 D2
Hill Mountain 55 D5
Hillockhead
  Aberds 243 B6
  Aberds 244 A1
Hill of Beath 209 A4
Hill of Fearn 265 C4
Hill of Mountblairy 268 D1
Hill Ridware 113 D4
Hillside
  Aberds 245 C6
  Angus 233 B5
  Mers 136 B2
  Orkney 283 H5
  Shetland 285 G6
Hillswick 284 F4
Hill Top
  Durham 166 C2
  Hants 18 A3
  W Mid 96 B2
  W Yorks 139 B6
Hill View 16 B3
Hillway 19 C5
Hillwell 285 M5
Hilmarton 44 B4
Hilperton 44 D2
Hilsea 19 A5
Hilston 151 D5
Hilton
  Aberds 257 C4
  Cambs 85 A4
  Cumb 165 C5
  Derbys 113 B6
  Dorset 16 A1
  Durham 167 C4
  Highld 264 B3
  Shrops 95 B5
  Stockton 168 D2
Hilton of Cadboll 265 C4
Himbleton 80 B2
Himley 96 B1
Hincaster 154 C4
Hinckley 98 B1
Hinderclay 103 D6
Hinderton 126 B3
Hinderwell 169 D5
Hindford 110 B2
Hindhead 34 C1
Hindley 137 C5
Hindley Green 137 C5
Hindlip 80 B1
Hindolveston 120 C2
Hindon 30 B3
Hindringham 120 B1
Hingham 103 A6
Hinstock 111 C5
Hintlesham 88 C1
Hinton
  Hants 17 B6
  Hereford 78 D1
  Northants 82 B2
  S Glos 43 B6
  Shrops 94 A2
Hinton Ampner 33 C4
Hinton Blewett 43 D4
Hinton Charterhouse 43 D6
Hinton-in-the-Hedges 82 D2
Hinton Martell 17 A4
Hinton on the Green 80 C3
Hinton Parva 45 A6
Hinton St George 28 D4
Hinton St Mary 30 D1
Hinton Waldrist 65 D4
Hints
  Shrops 95 D4
  Staffs 97 A4
Hinwick 83 A6
Hinxhill 38 A2
Hinxton 85 C6
Hinxworth 84 C4
Hipperholme 139 A4
Hipswell 157 B5
Hirael 123 C5
Hiraeth 73 D4
Hirn 245 B4
Hirnant 109 C5
Hirst
  N Lanark 207 D6
  Northumb 179 A4
Hirst Courtney 140 A4
Hirwaen 125 C6
Hirwaun 59 E6
Hiscott 25 C6
Histon 85 A6
Hitcham 87 B5
Hitchin 68 A1
Hither Green 49 B6
Hittisleigh 12 B2
Hive 149 D7
Hixon 112 C4
Hoaden 53 D4
Hoaldalbert 61 A5
Hoar Cross 113 C5
Hoarwithy 62 A1
Hoath 53 C4
Hobarris 93 D7
Hobbister 283 G4
Hobkirk 187 B4
Hobson 178 D3
Hoby 115 D4
Hockering 120 D2
Hockerton 132 D2
Hockley 70 D2
Hockley Heath 97 D4
Hockliffe 67 A4
Hockwold cum Wilton 102 C3
Hockworthy 27 D5
Hoddesdon 68 C3
Hoddlesden 137 A6
Hoddomcross 175 A4
Hoddom Mains 175 A4
Hodgeston 55 E6
Hodley 93 B5
Hodnet 111 C5
Hodthorpe 131 B5
Hoe
  Hants 33 D4
  Norf 120 D1
Hoe Gate 33 D5
Hoff 165 D4
Hoggard's Green 87 B4
Hoggeston 66 A3
Hogha Gearraidh 287 G2
Hoghton 137 A5
Hognaston 130 D2
Hog Patch 34 B1
Hogsthorpe 135 B5
Holbeach 117 C6
Holbeach Bank 117 C6
Holbeach Clough 117 C6
Holbeach Drove 117 D6
Holbeach Hurn 117 C6
Holbeach St Johns 117 D6
Holbeach St Marks 117 B6
Holbeach St Matthew 117 B7
Holbeck
  Notts 131 B5
  W Yorks 148 D1
Holbeck Woodhouse 131 B5
Holberrow Green 80 B3
Holbeton 7 B5
Holborn 49 A6
Holbrook
  Derbys 114 A1
  Suff 88 D2
  S Yorks 131 A4
Holburn 198 C4
Holbury 18 A3
Holcombe
  Devon 13 D4
  Som 29 A6
Holcombe Rogus 27 D5
Holcot 83 A4
Holden 146 C1
Holdenby 82 A3
Holdenhurst 17 B5
Holdgate 94 C3
Holdingham 116 A3
Holditch 14 A3
Holefield 198 C2
Holehouses 128 B2
Hole-in-the-Wall 62 A2
Holemoor 11 A5
Holestane 183 C6
Holford 27 A6
Holgate 149 B4
Holker 154 D2
Holkham 119 A5
Hollacombe 11 A4
Holland
  Orkney 282 B5
  Orkney 282 E7
Holland Fen 117 A5
Holland-on-Sea 71 B6
Hollandstoun 282 B8
Hollee 175 B5
Hollesley 89 C4
Hollicombe 8 A2
Hollingbourne 37 A6
Hollington
  Derbys 113 B6
  E Sus 23 A5
  Staffs 113 B4
Hollington Grove 113 B6
Hollingworth 138 D3
Hollins 137 C7
Hollinsclough 129 C5
Hollins Green 137 D5
Hollins Lane 145 B4
Hollinwood
  Gtr Man 138 C2
  Shrops 111 B4
Hollocombe 26 D1
Holloway 130 D3
Hollowell 98 D3
Hollow Meadows 130 A2
Hollybush
  Caerph 41 A6
  E Ayrs 182 A1
  Worcs 79 D5
Holly End 101 A6
Holly Green 79 C6
Hollym 143 A5
Hollywood 96 D3
Holmbridge 139 C4
Holmbury St Mary 35 B4
Holmbush 5 B5
Holmcroft 112 C3
Holme
  Cambs 100 C3
  Cumb 154 D4
  Notts 132 D3
  N Yorks 158 C2
  W Yorks 139 C4
Holme Chapel 138 A1
Holme Green 149 C4
Holme Hale 103 A4
Holme Lacy 78 D3
Holme Marsh 78 B1
Holme next the Sea 119 A4
Holme-on-Spalding-Moor 149 D7
Holme on the Wolds 150 C2
Holme Pierrepont 115 B4
Holmer 78 C3
Holmer Green 67 D4
Holme St Cuthbert 174 D4
Holmes Chapel 128 C2
Holmesfield 130 B3
Holmeswood 136 B3
Holmewood 131 C4
Holme Wood 147 D5
Holmfirth 139 C4
Holmhead
  Dumfries 183 D5
  E Ayrs 193 C5
Holmisdale 258 D1
Holmpton 143 A5
Holmrook 153 A1
Holmsgarth 285 J6
Holmwrangle 164 A3
Holne 7 A6
Holnest 15 A6
Holsworthy 10 A4
Holsworthy Beacon 11 A4
Holt
  Dorset 17 A4
  Norf 120 B2
  Wilts 44 C2
  Worcs 79 A6
  Wrex 127 D4
Holtby 149 B5
Holt End
  Hants 33 B5
  Worcs 80 A3
Holt Fleet 79 A6
Holt Heath 79 A6
Holton
  Oxon 65 C7
  Som 29 C6
  Suff 105 D4
Holton cum Beckering 133 A6
Holton Heath 16 B3
Holton le Clay 143 C4
Holton le Moor 142 D2
Holton St Mary 87 D6
Holt Park 147 C6
Holwell
  Dorset 29 D7
  Herts 84 D3
  Leics 115 C5
  Oxon 64 C3
Holwick 166 C2
Holworth 16 C1
Holybourne 33 A6
Holy Cross 96 D2
Holyhead
  = *Caergybi* 122 B2
Holy Island 199 B5
Holymoorside 130 C3
Holyport 48 B1
Holystone 188 C2
Holytown 207 D5
Holywell
  Cambs 101 D5
  Corn 4 B2
  Dorset 15 A5
  E Sus 22 C3
  Northumb 179 B5
Holywell
  = *Treffynnon* 126 B1
Holywell Green 138 B3
Holywell Lake 27 C6
Holywell Row 102 D3
Holywood 184 D2
Homer 95 A4
Homersfield 104 C3
Hom Green 62 A1
Homington 31 C5
Honeyborough 55 D5
Honeybourne 80 C4
Honeychurch 12 A1
Honey Hill 52 C3
Honey Street 45 C5
Honey Tye 87 D5
Honiley 97 D5
Honing 121 C5
Honingham 120 D3
Honington
  Lincs 116 A2
  Suff 103 D5
  Warks 81 C5
Honiton 13 A6
Honley 139 B4
Hood Green 139 C6
Hooe
  E Sus 23 B4
  Plym 7 B4
Hooe Common 23 A4
Hoo Green 128 A2
Hook
  E Yorks 141 A5
  Hants 47 D5
  London 49 C4
  Pembs 55 C5
  Wilts 45 A4
Hooke 15 B5
Hookgate 111 B6
Hook Green
  Kent 37 C4
  Kent 50 C3
Hook Norton 81 D6
Hookway 12 B3
Hookwood 35 B5
Hoole 127 C4
Hooley 35 A5
Hoop 61 C7
Hoo St Werburgh 51 B4
Hooton 126 B3
Hooton Levitt 140 D3
Hooton Pagnell 140 C2
Hooton Roberts 140 D2
Hope
  Derbys 129 A6
  Devon 7 D5
  Highld 277 C5
  Powys 93 A6
  Shrops 94 A1
  Staffs 129 D6
Hope = *Yr Hôb* 126 D3
Hope Bagot 94 D3
Hope Bowdler 94 B2
Hope End Green 69 A5
Hope Green 129 A4
Hopeman 266 C2
Hope Mansell 62 B2
Hopesay 94 C1
Hope's Green 51 A4
Hope under Dinmore 78 B3
Hopley's Green 78 B1
Hopperton 148 B3
Hop Pole 117 D4
Hopstone 95 B5
Hopton
  Shrops 110 C2
  Shrops 111 C4
  Staffs 112 C3
  Suff 103 D5
Hopton Cangeford 94 C3
Hopton Castle 94 D1
Hoptonheath 94 D1
Hopton on Sea 105 A6
Hopton Wafers 95 D4
Hopwas 97 A4
Hopwood
  Gtr Man 138 C1
  Worcs 96 D3
Horam 22 A3
Horbling 116 B4
Horbury 139 B5
Horcott 64 C2
Horden 168 A2
Horderley 94 C2
Hordle 17 B6
Hordley 110 B2
Horeb
  Carms 57 B4
  Carms 58 C2
  Ceredig 73 B6
Horfield 43 B5
Horham 104 D3
Horkesley Heath 70 A3
Horkstow 142 B1
Horley
  Oxon 81 C7
  Sur 35 B5
Hornblotton Green 29 B5
Hornby
  Lancs 145 A5
  N Yorks 157 B6
  N Yorks 158 A2
Horncastle 134 C2
Hornchurch 50 A2
Horncliffe 198 B3
Horndean
  Borders 198 B2
  Hants 33 D6
Horndon 11 D6
Horndon on the Hill 50 A3
Horne 35 B6
Horniehaugh 232 B2
Horning 121 D5
Horninghold 99 B5
Horninglow 113 C6
Horningsea 85 A6
Horningsham 30 A2
Horningtoft 119 C6
Hornsby 176 D3
Horns Corner 37 D5
Horns Cross
  Devon 25 C4
  E Sus 37 D6
Hornsea 151 C5
Hornsea Bridge 151 C5
Hornsey 49 A6
Hornton 81 C6
Horrabridge 7 A4
Horringer 87 A4
Horringford 18 C4
Horsebridge
  Devon 11 D5
  Hants 32 B2
Horse Bridge 129 D4
Horsebrook 112 D2
Horsehay 95 A4
Horseheath 86 C2
Horsehouse 156 C4
Horsell 34 A2
Horseman's Green 110 A3
Horseway 101 C6
Horsey 121 C6
Horsford 120 D3
Horsforth 147 D6
Horsham
  Worcs 79 B5
  W Sus 35 C4
Horsham St Faith 120 D4
Horsington
  Lincs 134 C1
  Som 29 C7
Horsley
  Derbys 114 A1
  Glos 63 D4
  Northumb 178 C2
  Northumb 188 D1
Horsley Cross 71 A5
Horsleycross Street 71 A5
Horsleyhill 186 B4
Horsleyhope 166 A3
Horsley Woodhouse 114 A1
Horsmonden 37 B4
Horspath 65 C6
Horstead 121 D4
Horsted Keynes 36 D1
Horton
  Bucks 67 B4
  Dorset 17 A4
  Lancs 146 B2
  Northants 83 B5
  S Glos 43 A6
  Shrops 110 C3
  Som 28 D3
  Staffs 129 D4
  Swansea 57 D4
  Wilts 45 C4
  Windsor 48 B3
Horton-cum-Studley 65 B6
Horton Green 110 A3
Horton Heath 32 D3
Horton in Ribblesdale 155 D7
Horton Kirby 50 C2
Hortonlane 110 D3
Horwich 137 B5
Horwich End 129 A5
Horwood 25 C6
Hose 115 C5
Hoselaw 198 C2
Hoses 153 A3
Hosh 218 B3
Hosta 287 G2
Hoswick 285 L6
Hotham 150 D1
Hothfield 38 A1
Hoton 114 C3

Houbie 284 D8
Houdston 181 B3
Hough
  Ches E. 128 B3
  Ches E. 128 D2
Hougham 116 A1
Hough Green 127 A4
Hough-on-the-Hill 116 A2
Houghton
  Cambs. 101 D4
  Cumb 175 C7
  Hants 32 B2
  Pembs. 55 D5
  W Sus 20 A3
Houghton Conquest. 84 C2
Houghton Green
  E Sus. 37 D7
  Warr 137 D5
Houghton-le-Side .167 C5
Houghton-Le-
  Spring 167 A6
Houghton on the
  Hill 98 A3
Houghton Regis. . . . 67 A5
Houghton St Giles. .119 B6
Houlland
  Shetland 284 F7
  Shetland 285 H5
Houlsyke 159 A6
Hound 18 A3
Hound Green 47 D5
Houndslow 197 B5
Houndwood 211 D5
Hounslow 48 B4
Hounslow Green . . . 69 B6
Housay 284 F8
House of Daviot 252 B3
House of
  Glenmuick 243 C6
Housetter 284 E5
Houss 285 K5
Houston 205 B4
Houstry 275 A5
Houton 283 G4
Hove 21 B5
Hoveringham 115 A4
Hoveton 121 D5
Hovingham 159 D5
How 176 D3
Howbrook 139 D6
How Caple 79 D4
Howden
  Borders 187 A5
  E Yorks 141 A5
Howden-le-Wear . .167 B4
Howe
  Highld 281 B5
  Norf 104 A3
  N Yorks 158 C2
Howe Bridge 137 C5
Howe Green 70 C1
Howell 116 A4
How End 84 C2
Howe of Teuchar . . .256 B2
Howe Street
  Essex 69 B6
  Essex 86 D2
Howey 77 B4
Howgate 196 A1
How Green 36 B2
Howick 189 B5
Howle
  Durham 166 C3
  Telford 111 C5
Howlett End 86 D1
Howley 14 A2
Hownam 187 B6
Hownam Mains 187 A6
Howpasley 185 B6
Howsham
  N Lincs 142 C2
  N Yorks 149 A6
Howslack 184 B3
Howtel 198 C2
Howton 61 A6
Howtown. 164 D2
Howwood 204 B3
Hoxne 104 D2
Hoy 283 G3
Hoylake 126 A2
Hoyland 139 C6
Hoylandswaine 139 C5
Hubberholme 156 D3
Hubbert's Bridge. . .117 A5
Huby
  N Yorks 147 C6
  N Yorks 149 A4
Hucclecote 63 B4
Hucking 37 A6
Hucknall 114 A3

Huddersfield 139 B4
Huddington 80 B2
Hudswell 157 A5
Huggate. 150 B1
Hugglescote 114 D2
Hughenden Valley . . 66 D3
Hughley 94 B3
Hugh Town Scilly 2 E4
Huish
  Devon 25 D6
  Wilts 45 C5
Huish Champflower . 27 C5
Huish Episcopi 28 C4
Huisinis 287 C4
Hulcott. 66 B3
Hulland 113 A6
Hulland Ward 113 A6
Hullavington 44 A2
Hullbridge. 70 D2
Hulme 138 D1
Hulme End 129 D6
Hulme Walfield 128 C3
Hulverstone 18 C2
Hulver Street 105 C5
Humber 78 B3
Humber Bridge 142 A2
Humberston 143 C5
Humbie 210 D1
Humbleton
  E Yorks 151 D5
  Northumb 188 A2
Humby 116 B3
Hume 197 B6
Humshaugh 177 B7
Huna. 281 A5
Huncoat. 146 D1
Huncote 98 B2
Hundalee 187 B5
Hunderthwaite 166 C2
Hundleby 134 C3
Hundle Houses 134 D2
Hundleton 55 D5
Hundon 86 C3
Hundred Acres 33 D4
Hundred End 136 A3
Hundred House 77 B5
Hungarton 98 A3
Hungerford
  Hants 31 D5
  W Berks 46 C1
Hungerford
  Newtown. 46 B1
Hungerton 116 C1
Hungladder 258 A3
Hunmanby 161 D4
Hunmanby Moor . . .161 D5
Hunningham 81 A4
Hunny Hill 18 C3
Hunsdon 68 B4
Hunsingore 148 B3
Hunslet 148 D2
Hunsonby 164 B3
Hunspow 280 A4
Hunstanton 118 A3
Hunstanworth 166 A2
Hunsterson 111 A5
Hunston
  Suff. 87 A5
  W Sus 20 B1
Hunstrete 43 C5
Hunt End 80 A3
Hunter's Quay 203 A6
Hunthill Lodge 232 A2
Huntington
  E Loth 210 C1
  Hereford. 77 B6
  Staffs 112 D3
  York 149 B5
Huntingtower. 219 B5
Huntley 62 B3
Huntly 255 C6
Huntlywood 197 B5
Hunton
  Kent 37 B5
  N Yorks 157 B5
Hunt's Corner 103 C6
Hunt's Cross 127 A4
Huntsham 27 C5
Huntspill 28 A3
Huntworth 28 B3
Hunwick 167 B4
Hunworth 120 B2
Hurdsfield 129 B4
Hurley
  Warks 97 B5
  Windsor 47 A6
Hurlford. 193 B4

Hurliness. 283 J3
Hurn 17 B5
Hurn's End 118 A1
Hursley 32 C3
Hurst
  N Yorks 156 A4
  Som. 29 D4
  Wokingham 47 B5
Hurstbourne Priors . 32 A3
Hurstbourne
  Tarrant 46 D1
Hurst Green
  E Sus. 37 D5
  Lancs 145 D6
Hurstpierpoint 21 A5
Hurst Wickham 21 A5
Hurstwood 146 D2
Hurtmore 34 B2
Hurworth Place 157 A6
Hury 166 D2
Husabost. 258 C2
Husbands Bosworth . 98 C3
Husborne Crawley . . 83 D6
Husthwaite 158 D4
Hutchwns 40 D3
Huthwaite 131 D4
Huttoft 135 B5
Hutton
  Borders 198 A3
  Cumb 164 C2
  Essex 69 D6
  E Yorks 150 B3
  Lancs 136 A3
  N Som. 42 D2
Hutton Buscel 160 C3
Hutton Conyers 158 D2
Hutton Cranswick . .150 B3
Hutton End 164 B2
Hutton Gate 168 D3
Hutton Henry 168 B2
Hutton-le-Hole 159 B6
Hutton Magna 166 D4
Hutton Roof
  Cumb 155 D4
  Cumb 163 A6
Hutton Rudby 158 A3
Hutton Sessay 158 D3
Hutton Village 168 D3
Hutton Wandesley . .148 B4
Huxley 127 C5
Huxter
  Shetland 285 G7
  Shetland 285 H5
Huxton 211 D5
Huyton 136 D3
Hwlffordd
  =Haverfordwest. 55 C5
Hycemoor 153 B1
Hyde
  Glos 63 C4
  Gtr Man 138 D2
  Hants 31 D5
Hyde Heath 67 C4
Hyde Park 140 C3
Hydestile 34 B2
Hylton Castle 179 D5
Hyndford Bridge . . .194 B4
Hynish 222 D2
Hyssington 93 B7
Hythe
  Hants 18 A3
  Kent 38 B3
Hythe End 48 B3
Hythie 269 D5

I

Ibberton 16 A1
Ible 130 D2
Ibsley 17 A5
Ibstock 114 D2
Ibstone. 66 D2
Ibthorpe 46 D1
Ibworth 46 D3
Ichrachan 227 C5
Ickburgh 103 B4
Ickenham 48 A3
Ickford 66 C1
Ickham 53 D4
Ickleford 84 D3
Icklesham 23 A6
Ickleton 85 C6
Icklingham 102 D3
Ickwell Green 84 C3
Icomb 64 A3
Idbury 64 B3
Iddesleigh 11 A6
Ide 12 B3
Ideford 12 D3

Ide Hill 36 A2
Iden 37 D7
Iden Green
  Kent 37 C5
  Kent 37 C6
Idle 147 D5
Idlicote 81 C5
Idmiston 31 B5
Idole 57 A4
Idridgehay 113 A6
Idrigill 258 B3
Idstone 45 A6
Idvies 232 D3
Iffley 65 C6
Ifield 35 C5
Ifold 34 C3
Iford 22 B2
Ifton Heath 110 B2
Ightfield 111 B4
Ightham 36 A3
Iken 89 B5
Ilam 129 D6
Ilchester 29 C5
Ilderton 188 A3
Ilford 50 A1
Ilfracombe 25 A6
Ilkeston 114 A2
Ilketshall
  St Andrew 105 C4
Ilketshall
  St Lawrence 105 C4
Ilketshall
  St Margaret. 104 C4
Ilkley. 147 C5
Illey 96 C2
Illingworth 138 A3
Illogan 3 A4
Illston on the Hill. . . 99 B4
Ilmer. 66 C2
Ilmington 81 C5
Ilminster 28 D3
Ilsington 12 D2
Ilston 57 C5
Ilton
  N Yorks 157 D5
  Som. 28 D3
Imachar 202 D3
Imeraval 200 D3
Immingham 142 B3
Impington 85 A6
Ince. 127 B4
Ince Blundell 136 C2
Ince in Makerfield . .137 C4
Inchbare 233 B4
Inchberry 266 D4
Inchbraoch 233 C5
Incheril 262 D2
Inchgrundle 232 A2
Inchina. 261 A6
Inchinnan 205 B4
Inchkinloch 277 D6
Inchlaggan 239 B5
Inchlumpie 264 C1
Inchmore 251 B5
Inchnacardoch
  Hotel. 240 A1
Inchnadamph. 271 B5
Inch of Arnhall 233 A4
Inchree 237 C4
Inchture 220 B2
Inchyra. 219 B6
Indian Queens 4 B4
Inerval 200 D3
Ingatestone 69 D6
Ingbirchworth 139 C5
Ingestre 112 C3
Ingham
  Lincs 133 A4
  Norf 121 C5
  Suff 103 D4
Ingham Corner 121 C5
Ingleborough 118 D1
Ingleby
  Derbys 114 C1
  Lincs 132 B3
Ingleby Arncliffe . . .158 A3
Ingleby Barwick 168 D2
Ingleby Greenhow. .159 A4
Inglemire 150 D3
Inglesbatch. 43 C6
Inglesham 64 D3
Ingleton
  Durham 167 C4
  N Yorks 155 D4
Inglewhite 145 C5
Ingliston 208 C4
Ingoe 178 B2
Ingol 145 D5
Ingoldisthorpe. 118 B3
Ingoldmells 135 C5

Ingoldsby 116 B3
Ingon 81 B5
Ingram 188 B3
Ingrow 147 D4
Ings. 154 B3
Ingst 43 A4
Ingworth 120 C3
Inham's End 101 B4
Inkberrow 80 B3
Inkpen 46 C1
Inkstack 281 A4
Inn. 154 A3
Innellan 203 A6
Innerleithen 196 C2
Innerleven 220 D3
Innermessan 170 A2
Innerwick
  E Loth 211 C4
  Perth. 229 D4
Innis Chonain. 227 D6
Insch 256 D1
Insh. 241 B6
Inshore 276 B4
Inskip 145 D4
Instoneville. 140 B3
Instow 25 B5
Intake 140 C3
Inver
  Aberds 243 C5
  Highld 265 B4
  Perth. 230 D4
Inverailort 235 B6
Inveraldie 220 A4
Inveralligin 249 A5
Inverallochy 269 C5
Inveran 264 A1
Inveraray 214 B3
Inverarish 248 C2
Inverarity 232 D2
Inverarnan 215 A6
Inverasdale 261 B5
Inverbeg 206 A1
Inverbervie 233 A6
Inverboyndie 268 C1
Inverbroom 262 B3
Invercassley 272 D2
Invercauld House . .243 C4
Inverchaolain 203 A5
Invercharnan 227 B6
Inverchoran 251 A4
Invercreran 227 B5
Inverdruie 242 A2
Inverebrie 257 C4
Inveresk 209 C6
Inverey 242 D3
Inverfarigaig 251 D7
Invergarry 239 B7
Invergelder 243 C5
Invergeldie 218 B2
Invergordon 264 D3
Invergowrie 220 A3
Inverguseran 247 D6
Inverhadden 229 C5
Inverharroch 255 C4
Inverherive 216 B3
Inverie 247 E6
Inverinan 214 A2
Inverinate 249 D6
Inverkeilor 233 D4
Inverkeithing 208 B4
Inverkeithny 256 B1
Inverkip 204 A2
Inverkirkaig 270 C3
Inverlael 262 B3
Inverlochlarig 216 C4
Inverlochy
  Argyll 227 D6
  Highld 237 B5
Inverlussa 213 D4
Inver Mallie 239 D5
Invermark Lodge . .244 D1
Invermoidart 235 C5
Invermoriston 240 A2
Invernaver 278 B3
Inverneill 213 D6
Inverness 252 B2
Invernettie 257 B6
Invernoaden 215 C4
Inveroran Hotel 228 D1
Inverpolly Lodge . . .270 C3
Inverquharity 232 C2
Inverquhomery 257 B5
Inverroy 239 D6
Inversanda 236 D3
Invershiel 238 A3
Invershin 264 A1
Inversnaid Hotel . . .215 B6

Inverugie. 257 B6
Inveruglas 215 B6
Inveruglass 241 B6
Inverurie 256 D2
Invervar 229 D5
Inverythan. 256 B2
Inwardleigh 11 B6
Inworth 70 B2
Iochdar 286 B3
Iping 34 D1
Ipplepen 8 A2
Ipsden 47 A4
Ipsley 80 A3
Ipstones. 129 D5
Ipswich 88 C2
Irby 126 A2
Irby in the Marsh . . .135 C4
Irby upon Humber. .142 C3
Irchester 83 A6
Ireby
  Cumb 163 A5
  Lancs 155 D5
Ireland
  Orkney 283 G4
  Shetland 285 L5
Ireland's Cross. 111 A6
Ireleth 153 C3
Ireshopeburn 165 B6
Irlam. 137 D6
Irnham 116 C3
Iron Acton 43 A5
Ironbridge. 95 A4
Iron Cross 80 B3
Irongray. 173 A7
Ironmacannie. 173 A4
Ironside 268 D3
Ironville 131 D4
Irstead 121 C5
Irthington 176 C2
Irthlingborough. . . . 99 D6
Irton 160 C4
Irvine 192 B3
Isauld 279 B5
Isbister
  Orkney 282 E3
  Orkney 282 F4
  Shetland 284 D5
  Shetland 285 G7
Isfield. 22 A2
Isham 99 D5
Isle Abbotts 28 C3
Isle Brewers 28 C3
Isleham 102 D2
Isle of Whithorn. . . .171 D6
Isleornsay 247 C6
Islesburgh. 284 G5
Islesteps 174 A2
Isleworth 49 B4
Isley Walton 114 C2
Islibhig. 287 B4
Islington 49 A6
Islip
  Northants 100 D1
  Oxon 65 B6
Istead Rise 50 C3
Isycoed 127 D4
Itchen. 32 D3
Itchen Abbas 32 B4
Itchen Stoke 33 B4
Itchingfield 35 D4
Itchington 43 A5
Itteringham 120 B3
Itton 12 B1
Itton Common 61 D6
Ivegill 164 A2
Iver 48 A3
Iver Heath 48 A3
Iveston 178 D3
Ivinghoe 67 B4
Ivinghoe Aston 67 B4
Ivington 78 B2
Ivington Green 78 B2
Ivybridge 7 B5
Ivy Chimneys 68 C4
Ivychurch 38 C2
Ivy Cross 30 C2
Ivy Hatch 36 A3
Iwade 51 C6
Iwerne Courtney or
  Shroton 30 D2
Iwerne Minster 30 D2
Ixworth 103 D5
Ixworth Thorpe 103 D5

J

Jack Hill 147 B6
Jack in the Green . . . 13 B5
Jacksdale 131 D4
Jackstown 256 C2
Jacobstow 10 B2
Jacobstowe 11 A6
Jameston 55 E6
Jamestown
 Dumfries. 185 C6
 Highld. 251 A6
 W Dunb. 206 B1
Jarrow 179 C5
Jarvis Brook. 36 D3
Jasper's Green. 69 A7
Java 225 C6
Jawcraig 207 C6
Jaywick 71 B5
Jealott's Hill 47 B6
Jedburgh 187 A5
Jeffreyston 55 D6
Jellyhill 205 A6
Jemimaville 264 D3
Jersey Farm 67 C6
Jesmond 179 C4
Jevington 22 B3
Jockey End 67 B5
Johnby. 164 B2
John o' Groats 281 A5
John's Cross. 37 D5
Johnshaven 233 B5
Johnston 55 C5
Johnstone. 205 B4
Johnstonebridge . . 184 C3
Johnstown
 Carms 57 A4
 Wrex. 110 A2
Joppa
 Edin. 209 C6
 S Ayrs 182 A2
Jordans 67 D4
Jordanthorpe. 130 A3
Jump 140 C1
Jumpers Green 17 B5
Juniper Green 209 D4
Jurby East 152 B3
Jurby West 152 B3

K

Kaber 165 D5
Kaimend 195 B4
Kaimes. 209 D5
Kalemouth 187 A6
Kames
 Argyll 203 A4
 Argyll 213 A6
 E Ayrs 194 D1
Kea 4 C3
Keadby. 141 B6
Keal Cotes. 134 C3
Kearsley. 137 C6
Kearstwick 155 C5
Kearton 156 B3
Kearvaig 276 A3
Keasden. 145 A7
Keckwick. 127 A5
Keddington. 134 A3
Kedington 86 C3
Kedleston 113 A7
Keelby 142 B3
Keele 112 A2
Keeley Green 84 C2
Keeston 55 C5
Keevil 44 D3
Kegworth 114 C2
Kehelland 3 A4
Keig 244 A3
Keighley 147 C4
Keil 236 D3
Keilarsbrae. 208 A1
Keilhill 268 D2
Keillmore 213 D4
Keillor 231 D6
Keillour 219 B4
Keills 201 B4
Keils 201 B5
Keinton Mandeville . . 29 B5
Keir Mill. 183 C6
Keisby 116 C3
Keiss 281 B5
Keith. 267 D5
Keith Inch 257 B6
Keithock 233 B4

Kelbrook 146 C3
Kelby 116 A3
Keld
 Cumb 164 D3
 N Yorks 156 A2
Keldholme 159 C6
Kelfield
 N Lincs 141 C6
 N Yorks 149 D4
Kelham 132 D2
Kellan 225 B4
Kellas
 Angus 221 A4
 Moray 266 D2
Kellaton 8 D2
Kelleth 155 A5
Kelleythorpe 150 B2
Kelling 120 A2
Kellingley 140 A3
Kellington 140 A3
Kelloe 167 B6
Kelloholm 183 A5
Kelly 11 C4
Kelly Bray 11 C4
Kelmarsh 99 D4
Kelmscot 64 D3
Kelsale 89 A4
Kelsall 127 C5
Kelsall Hill 127 C5
Kelshall 85 D5
Kelsick 175 C4
Kelso 197 C6
Kelstedge 130 C3
Kelstern. 143 D4
Kelston 43 C6
Keltneyburn 229 D6
Kelton 174 A2
Kelty 208 A4
Kelvedon 70 B2
Kelvedon Hatch 69 D5
Kelvin 205 C6
Kelvinside 205 B5
Kelynack 2 B1
Kemback 220 C4
Kemberton 95 A5
Kemble 63 D5
Kemerton 80 D2
Kemeys Commander 61 C5
Kemnay 245 A4
Kempley 62 A2
Kempsey 79 C6
Kempsford 64 D2
Kemps Green 96 D4
Kempshott 47 D4
Kempston 84 C2
Kempston Hardwick. 84 C2
Kempton 94 C1
Kemp Town 21 B6
Kemsing 36 A3
Kemsley 51 C6
Kenardington 38 B1
Kenchester 78 C2
Kencot 64 C3
Kendal 154 B4
Kendon 182 D4
Kendray 139 C6
Kenfig 40 C3
Kenfig Hill 40 C3
Kenilworth 97 D5
Kenknock 217 A4
Kenley
 London 35 A6
 Shrops 94 A3
Kenmore
 Highld 249 A4
 Perth. 230 D1
Kenn
 Devon 13 C4
 N Som. 42 C1
Kennacley. 288 H2
Kennacraig 202 B3
Kennerleigh 12 A3
Kennet 208 A2
Kennethmont 255 D6
Kennett 86 A2
Kennford 13 C4
Kenninghall 103 C6
Kenninghall Heath .103 C6
Kennington
 Kent 38 A2
 Oxon 65 C6
Kennoway 220 D3
Kenny Hill 102 D2
Kennythorpe 149 A6
Kenovay 222 C2
Kensaleyre 259 C4
Kensington 49 B5
Kensworth 67 B5
Kensworth Common 67 B5
Kentallen. 237 D4

Kentchurch. 61 A6
Kentford 86 A3
Kentisbeare 13 A5
Kentisbury 25 A7
Kentisbury Ford. 25 A7
Kentmere 154 A3
Kenton
 Devon 13 C4
 Suff. 88 A2
 T&W 179 C4
Kenton Bankfoot. . . .179 C4
Kentra 235 D5
Kents Bank 154 D2
Kent's Green 62 A3
Kent's Oak. 32 C2
Kent Street
 E Sus. 23 A5
 Kent 37 A4
 W Sus. 35 D5
Kenwick. 110 B3
Kenwyn 4 C3
Keoldale 277 B4
Keppanach 237 C4
Keppoch 249 D6
Keprigan 190 D2
Kepwick. 158 B3
Kerchesters 197 C6
Keresley 97 C6
Kernborough 8 C1
Kerne Bridge 62 B1
Kerris 2 C2
Kerry 93 C5
Kerrycroy 203 B6
Kerrysdale 261 C5
Kerry's Gate 78 D1
Kersall 132 C2
Kersey 87 C6
Kershopefoot 176 A2
Kersoe 80 D2
Kerswell 13 A5
Kerswell Green 79 C6
Kesgrave. 88 C3
Kessingland 105 C6
Kessingland Beach .105 C6
Kessington 205 A5
Kestle. 5 C4
Kestle Mill. 4 B3
Keston 49 C7
Keswick
 Cumb 163 B5
 Norf. 104 A3
 Norf 121 B5
Ketley 111 D5
Ketley Bank 111 D5
Ketsby 134 B3
Kettering 99 D5
Ketteringham. 104 A2
Kettins 220 A2
Kettlebaston 87 B5
Kettlebridge 220 D3
Kettleburgh 88 A3
Kettlehill 220 D3
Kettleholm 174 A4
Kettleness 169 D6
Kettleshume. 129 B4
Kettlesing Bottom. . .147 B6
Kettlesing Head. . . .147 B6
Kettlestone 119 B6
Kettlethorpe 132 B3
Kettletoft 282 D7
Kettlewell 156 D3
Ketton 100 A1
Kew 49 B4
Kew Bridge 49 B4
Kewstoke 42 C2
Kexbrough 139 C6
Kexby
 Lincs 132 A3
 York 149 B6
Key Green 128 C3
Keyham 98 A3
Keyhaven 18 B2
Keyingham 143 A4
Keymer 21 A6
Keynsham 43 C5
Keysoe 84 A2
Keysoe Row 84 A2
Keyston 100 D2
Keyworth. 115 B4
Kibblesworth 179 D4
Kibworth
 Beauchamp 98 B3
Kibworth Harcourt . 98 B3
Kidbrooke 49 B7
Kiddemore Green . . . 95 A6
Kidderminster 95 D6
Kiddington 65 A5
Kidlington 65 B5
Kidmore End 47 B4
Kidsgrove 128 D3

Kidstones 156 C3
Kidwelly = Cydweli. . 57 B4
Kiel Crofts 226 C4
Kielder. 187 D5
Kierfiold Ho 282 F3
Kilbagie 208 B2
Kilbarchan 205 B4
Kilbeg 247 D5
Kilberry 202 B2
Kilbirnie 204 C3
Kilbride
 Argyll 226 D3
 Argyll 226 D4
 N Ayrs 191 C5
Kilburn
 Angus 232 B1
 Derbys 114 A1
 London 49 A5
 N Yorks 158 D4
Kilby 98 B3
Kilchamaig 202 B3
Kilchattan 212 C1
Kilchattan Bay 203 C6
Kilchenzie 190 C2
Kilcheran 226 C3
Kilchiaran 200 B2
Kilchoan
 Argyll 213 A5
 Highld 234 D3
Kilchoman 200 B2
Kilchrenan 227 D5
Kilconquhar 221 D4
Kilcot 62 A2
Kilcoy 252 A1
Kilcreggan 215 D5
Kildale 159 A5
Kildalloig 190 D3
Kildary 264 C3
Kildermorie Lodge .263 C7
Kildonan
 Highld 191 C6
Kildonan Lodge 274 B3
Kildonnan 234 B3
Kildrummy 244 A1
Kildwick 147 C4
Kilfinan 203 A4
Kilfinnan 239 C6
Kilgetty 56 B1
Kilgwrrwg
 Common 61 D6
Kilham
 E Yorks 150 A3
 Northumb 198 C2
Kilkenneth 222 C2
Kilkerran 190 D3
Kilkhampton 24 D3
Killamarsh 131 A4
Killay 57 C6
Killbeg 225 B5
Killean 202 D1
Killearn 206 B3
Killen 252 A2
Killerby 167 D4
Killichonan 229 C4
Killiechonate 239 D6
Killiechronan 225 B4
Killiecrankie. 230 B3
Killiemor 224 C3
Killiemore House . . .224 D3
Killilan 249 C6
Killimster 281 C5
Killin 217 A5
Killinallan 200 A3
Killinghall 148 B1
Killington 155 C5
Killingworth 179 B4
Killin Lodge 240 B3
Killmahumaig 213 C5
Killochyett 196 B3
Killocraw 190 B2
Killundine 225 B4
Kilmacolm 204 B3
Kilmaha 214 B2
Kilmahog 217 D6
Kilmalieu 236 D2
Kilmaluag 259 A4
Kilmany 220 B3
Kilmarie 247 C4
Kilmarnock 193 B4
Kilmaron Castle. . . .220 C3
Kilmartin 213 C6
Kilmaurs 205 D4
Kilmelford 213 A6
Kilmeny 200 B3
Kilmersdon 43 D5
Kilmeston 33 C4
Kilmichael 190 C2
Kilmichael
 Glassary 214 C1
Kilmichael of
 Inverlussa 213 D5

Kilmington
 Devon 14 B2
 Wilts 30 B1
Kilmonivaig 239 D5
Kilmorack 251 B6
Kilmore
 Argyll 226 D3
 Highld 247 D5
Kilmory
 Argyll 202 A2
 Highld 235 C4
 Highld 246 D2
 N Ayrs 191 C5
Kilmuir
 Highld 252 B2
 Highld 258 A3
 Highld 258 D2
 Highld 264 C3
Kilmun
 Argyll 214 A2
 Argyll 215 D4
Kilncadzow 194 B3
Kilndown 37 C5
Kilnhurst 140 D2
Kilninian 224 B2
Kilninver 226 D3
Kiln Pit Hill 178 D2
Kilnsea 143 B6
Kilnsey 146 A3
Kilnwick 150 C2
Kilnwick Percy 149 B7
Kiloran 212 C1
Kilpatrick 191 C5
Kilpeck 78 D2
Kilphedir 274 C3
Kilpin 141 A5
Kilpin Pike 141 A5
Kilrenny 221 D5
Kilsby 98 D2
Kilspindie 220 B2
Kilsyth 207 C5
Kiltarlity 251 B7
Kilton
 Notts 131 B5
 Som. 27 A6
Kilton Thorpe 169 D4
Kilvaxter 258 B3
Kilve 27 A6
Kilvington 115 A5
Kilwinning 204 D3
Kimberley
 Norf 103 A6
 Notts 114 A3
Kimber worth 140 D2
Kimblesworth 167 A5
Kimble Wick 66 C3
Kimbolton
 Cambs. 84 A2
 Hereford 78 A3
Kimcote 98 C2
Kimmeridge 16 D3
Kimmerston 198 C3
Kimpton
 Hants 32 A1
 Herts 68 B1
Kinbrace 274 A2
Kinbuck 218 D2
Kincaple 221 C4
Kincardine
 Fife 208 B2
 Highld 264 B2
Kincardine Bridge. . .208 B2
Kincardine O'Neil . .244 C2
Kinclaven 219 A6
Kincorth 245 B6
Kincorth House 265 D6
Kincraig 241 B6
Kincraigie 230 D3
Kindallachan 230 D3
Kineton
 Glos 64 A1
 Warks 81 B6
Kinfauns 219 B6
Kingairloch 236 D2
Kingarth 203 C5
Kingcoed 61 C6
King Edward 268 D2
Kingerby 142 D2
Kingham 64 A3
Kingholm Quay 174 A2
Kinghorn 209 B5
Kingie 239 B5
Kinglassie 209 A5
Kingoodie 220 B3
King's Acre 78 C2
Kingsand 6 B3
Kingsbarns 221 C5
Kingsbridge
 Devon 7 C6
 Som. 27 B4

King's Bromley 113 D5
Kingsburgh. 258 C3
Kingsbury
 London 49 A5
 Warks 97 B5
Kingsbury Episcopi. . 28 C4
King's Caple 62 A1
Kingsclere. 46 D3
King's Cliffe 100 B2
Kingscote 63 D4
Kingscott 25 D6
King's Coughton . . . 80 B3
Kingscross 191 C6
Kingsdon 29 C5
Kingsdown 39 A5
Kingseat 208 A4
Kingsey 66 C2
Kingsfold 35 C4
Kingsford
 E Ayrs 205 D4
 Worcs. 95 C6
Kingsforth 142 B2
Kingsgate 53 B5
Kingsheanton 25 B6
King's Heath 96 C5
Kings Hedges 85 A6
King's Hill 37 A4
Kingshouse Hotel . .237 D6
Kingside Hill 175 C4
Kingskerswell 8 A2
Kingskettle 220 D3
Kingsland
 Anglesey 122 B2
 Hereford. 78 A2
Kings Langley. 67 C5
Kingsley
 Ches W. 127 B5
 Hants 33 B6
 Staffs 112 A4
Kingsley Green 34 C1
Kingsley Holt 112 A4
Kingsley Park. 83 A4
King's Lynn 118 C3
King's Meaburn 165 C4
King's Mills 110 A2
Kingsmuir
 Angus 232 D2
 Fife 221 D5
Kings Muir 196 C1
King's Newnham . . . 98 D1
King's Newton 114 C1
Kingsnorth 38 B2
King's Norton
 Leics 98 A3
 W Mid 96 D3
King's Nympton 26 D1
King's Pyon 78 B2
King's Ripton 101 D4
King's Somborne . . . 32 B2
King's Stag 30 D1
King's Stanley 63 C4
King's Sutton 82 D1
Kingstanding 96 B3
Kingsteignton 12 D3
King Sterndale. 129 B5
King's Thorn. 78 D3
Kingsthorpe 83 A4
Kingston
 Cambs. 85 B5
 Devon 7 C5
 Dorset. 16 A1
 Dorset. 16 D3
 E Loth 210 B2
 Hants 17 A5
 IoW. 18 C3
 Kent 52 D3
 Moray 266 C4
Kingston Bagpuize . . 65 D5
Kingston Blount 66 D2
Kingston by Sea. . . . 21 B5
Kingston Deverill . . . 30 B2
Kingstone
 Hereford 78 D2
 Som. 28 D3
 Staffs 113 C4
Kingston Gorse 20 B3
Kingston Lisle 45 A7
Kingston Maurward . 15 B7
Kingston near
 Lewes. 22 B1
Kingston on Soar . . .114 C3
Kingston Russell . . . 15 B5
Kingston St Mary . . . 28 C2
Kingston Seymour . . 42 C3
Kingston Upon
 Hull 142 A2
Kingston upon
 Thames 49 C4
Kingston Vale. 49 B5
Kingstown. 175 C6

King's Walden	67 A6
Kingswear	8 B2
Kingswells	245 B5
Kingswinford	96 C1
Kingswood	
Bucks	66 B1
Glos	62 D3
Hereford	77 B6
Kent	37 A6
Powys	93 A6
S Glos	43 B5
Sur	35 A5
Warks	97 D4
Kings Worthy	32 B3
Kingthorpe	133 B6
Kington	
Hereford	77 B6
Worcs	80 B2
Kington Langley	44 B3
Kington Magna	30 C1
Kington St Michael	44 B3
Kingussie	241 B5
Kingweston	29 B5
Kininvie House	254 B4
Kinkell Bridge	218 C4
Kinknockie	257 B5
Kinlet	95 C5
Kinloch	
Fife	220 C2
Highld	234 B4
Highld	247 C5
Highld	271 A6
Perth	231 D5
Perth	231 D6
Kinlochan	236 C2
Kinlochard	217 D4
Kinlochbeoraid	238 D2
Kinlochbervie	276 C4
Kinlocheil	236 B3
Kinlochewe	262 D2
Kinloch Hourn	238 B3
Kinloch Laggan	240 D3
Kinlochleven	237 C5
Kinloch Lodge	277 C6
Kinlochmoidart	235 C6
Kinlochmorar	238 C2
Kinlochmore	237 C5
Kinloch Rannoch	229 C5
Kinlochspelve	225 D5
Kinloid	235 B5
Kinloss	265 D6
Kinmel Bay	125 A4
Kinmuck	256 E3
Kinmundy	245 A5
Kinnadie	257 B4
Kinnaird	220 B2
Kinnaird Castle	233 C4
Kinneff	233 A6
Kinnelhead	184 B3
Kinnell	233 C4
Kinnerley	110 C2
Kinnersley	
Hereford	78 C1
Worcs	79 C6
Kinnerton	77 A6
Kinnesswood	219 C6
Kinninvie	166 C3
Kinnordy	232 C1
Kinoulton	115 B4
Kinross	219 C6
Kinrossie	219 A6
Kinsbourne Green	67 B6
Kinsey Heath	111 A5
Kinsham	
Hereford	78 A1
Worcs	80 D2
Kinsley	140 B2
Kinson	17 B4
Kintbury	46 C1
Kintessack	265 D5
Kintillo	219 C6
Kintocher	244 B2
Kinton	
Hereford	94 D2
Shrops	110 D2
Kintore	245 A4
Kintour	201 C4
Kintra	
Argyll	200 D3
Argyll	224 D2
Kintraw	213 B6
Kinuachdrachd	213 C5
Kinveachy	242 A2
Kinver	95 C6
Kippax	148 D3
Kippen	207 A4
Kippford or Scaur	173 C6
Kirbister	
Orkney	282 E7
Orkney	283 G4

Kirbuster	282 E3
Kirby Bedon	104 A3
Kirby Bellars	115 D5
Kirby Cane	105 B4
Kirby Cross	71 A6
Kirby Grindalythe	150 A2
Kirby Hill	
N Yorks	148 A2
N Yorks	157 A5
Kirby Knowle	158 C3
Kirby-le-Soken	71 A6
Kirby Misperton	159 D6
Kirby Muxloe	98 A2
Kirby Row	105 B4
Kirby Sigston	158 B3
Kirby Underdale	149 B7
Kirby Wiske	158 C2
Kirdford	34 D3
Kirk	281 C4
Kirkabister	285 K6
Kirkandrews	172 D4
Kirkandrews upon	
Eden	175 C6
Kirkbampton	175 C6
Kirkbean	174 C2
Kirk Bramwith	140 B4
Kirkbride	175 C5
Kirkbuddo	232 D3
Kirkburn	
Borders	196 C1
E Yorks	150 B2
Kirkburton	139 B4
Kirkby	
Lincs	142 D2
Mers	136 D3
N Yorks	158 A4
Kirkby Fleetham	157 B6
Kirkby Green	133 D5
Kirkby In Ashfield	131 D5
Kirkby-in-Furness	153 B3
Kirkby la Thorpe	116 A4
Kirkby Lonsdale	155 D5
Kirkby Malham	146 A2
Kirkby Mallory	98 A1
Kirkby Malzeard	157 D6
Kirkby Mills	159 C6
Kirkbymoorside	159 C5
Kirkby on Bain	134 C2
Kirkby Overflow	148 C2
Kirkby Stephen	155 A6
Kirkby Thore	165 C4
Kirkby Underwood	116 C3
Kirkby Wharfe	148 C4
Kirkcaldy	209 A5
Kirkcambeck	176 C3
Kirkcarswell	173 D5
Kirkcolm	170 A2
Kirkconnel	183 A5
Kirkconnell	174 B2
Kirkcowan	171 A5
Kirkcudbright	173 C4
Kirkdale	136 D2
Kirk Deighton	148 B2
Kirk Ella	142 A2
Kirkfieldbank	194 B3
Kirkgunzeon	173 B6
Kirk Hallam	114 A2
Kirkham	
Lancs	144 D4
N Yorks	149 A6
Kirkhamgate	139 A5
Kirk Hammerton	148 B3
Kirkharle	178 A2
Kirkheaton	
Northumb	178 B2
W Yorks	139 B4
Kirkhill	
Angus	233 B4
Highld	252 B1
Midloth	209 D5
Moray	254 C3
Kirkhope	186 A2
Kirkhouse	196 C2
Kirkiboll	277 C6
Kirkibost	247 C4
Kirkinch	231 D7
Kirkinner	171 B6
Kirkintilloch	205 A6
Kirk Ireton	130 D2
Kirkland	
Cumb	162 C3
Cumb	165 B4
Dumfries	183 A5
Dumfries	183 C6
Kirk Langley	113 B6
Kirkleatham	168 C3
Kirklevington	158 A3
Kirkley	105 B6
Kirklington	
Notts	132 D1

Kirklington continued	
N Yorks	157 C7
Kirklinton	176 C2
Kirkliston	208 C4
Kirkmaiden	170 D3
Kirk Merrington	167 B5
Kirkmichael	
Perth	231 C4
S Ayrs	192 E3
Kirk Michael	152 B3
Kirkmuirhill	194 B2
Kirknewton	
Northumb	198 C3
W Loth	208 D4
Kirkney	255 C6
Kirk of Shotts	207 D6
Kirkoswald	
Cumb	164 A3
S Ayrs	192 E2
Kirkpatrick	
Durham	173 A5
Kirkpatrick-	
Fleming	175 A5
Kirk Sandall	140 C4
Kirksanton	153 B2
Kirk Smeaton	140 B3
Kirkstall	147 D6
Kirkstead	134 C1
Kirkstile	255 C6
Kirkstyle	281 A5
Kirkton	
Aberds	256 D1
Aberds	268 E1
Angus	220 A4
Angus	232 D2
Borders	186 B4
Dumfries	184 D2
Fife	220 B3
Highld	249 B6
Highld	249 D5
Highld	252 A3
Highld	265 A3
Perth	219 C4
S Lanark	194 D4
Stirling	217 D5
Kirktonhill	196 B4
Kirkton Manor	195 C7
Kirkton of Airlie	231 C7
Kirkton of	
Auchterhouse	220 A3
Kirkton of	
Auchterless	256 B2
Kirkton of Barevan	253 B4
Kirkton of Bourtie	256 D3
Kirkton of Collace	219 A6
Kirkton of Craig	233 C5
Kirkton of	
Culsalmond	256 C1
Kirkton of Durris	245 C4
Kirkton of	
Glenbuchat	243 A6
Kirkton of Glenisla	231 B6
Kirkton of	
Kingoldrum	232 C1
Kirkton of Largo	220 D4
Kirkton of	
Lethendy	231 D5
Kirkton of Logie	
Buchan	257 D4
Kirkton of	
Maryculter	245 C5
Kirkton of	
Menmuir	232 B3
Kirkton of Monikie	221 A5
Kirkton of Oyne	256 D1
Kirkton of Rayne	256 D1
Kirkton of Skene	245 B5
Kirkton of Tough	244 A3
Kirktown	269 D5
Kirktown of Alvah	268 C1
Kirktown of	
Deskford	267 C6
Kirktown of	
Fetteresso	245 D5
Kirktown of	
Mortlach	254 C4
Kirktown of Slains	257 D5
Kirkurd	195 B6
Kirkwall	282 F5
Kirkwhelpington	178 A1
Kirk Yetholm	188 A1
Kirmington	142 B3
Kirmond le Mire	142 D3
Kirn	203 A6
Kirriemuir	232 C1
Kirstead Green	104 B3
Kirtlebridge	175 A5
Kirtleton	185 D5
Kirtling	86 B2
Kirtling Green	86 B2

Kirtlington	65 B5
Kirtomy	278 B3
Kirton	
Lincs	117 B6
Notts	132 C1
Suff	88 D3
Kirton End	117 A5
Kirton Holme	117 A5
Kirton in Lindsey	142 D1
Kislingbury	82 B3
Kites Hardwick	82 A1
Kittisford	27 C5
Kittle	57 D5
Kitt's Green	97 C4
Kitt's Moss	128 A3
Kittybrewster	245 B6
Kitwood	33 B5
Kivernoll	78 D2
Kiveton Park	131 A4
Knaith	132 A3
Knaith Park	132 A3
Knap Corner	30 C2
Knaphill	34 A2
Knapp	
Perth	220 A2
Som	28 C3
Knapthorpe	132 D2
Knapton	
Norf	121 B5
York	149 B4
Knapton Green	78 B2
Knapwell	85 A5
Knaresborough	148 B2
Knarsdale	177 D4
Knauchland	267 D6
Knaven	256 B3
Knayton	158 C3
Knebworth	68 A2
Knedlington	141 A5
Kneesall	132 C2
Kneesworth	85 C5
Kneeton	115 A5
Knelston	57 D4
Knenhall	112 B3
Knettishall	103 C5
Knightacott	26 B1
Knightcote	81 B6
Knightley Dale	112 C2
Knighton	
Devon	7 C4
Leicester	98 A2
Staffs	111 A6
Staffs	111 C6
Knighton	
= Tref-y-Clawdd	93 D6
Knightswood	205 B5
Knightwick	79 B5
Knill	77 A6
Knipton	115 B6
Knitsley	166 A4
Kniveton	130 D2
Knock	
Argyll	225 C4
Cumb	165 C4
Moray	267 D6
Knockally	275 B5
Knockan	271 C5
Knockandhu	254 D3
Knockando	254 B2
Knockando House	254 B3
Knockbain	252 A2
Knockbreck	258 B2
Knockbrex	172 D3
Knockdee	280 B3
Knockdolian	180 C3
Knockenkelly	191 C6
Knockentiber	192 B3
Knockespock	
House	255 D6
Knockfarrel	251 A7
Knockglass	170 B2
Knockholt	36 A2
Knockholt Pound	36 A2
Knockie Lodge	240 A2
Knockin	110 C2
Knockinlaw	193 B4
Knocklearn	173 A5
Knocknaha	190 D2
Knocknain	170 A1
Knockrome	201 A5
Knocksharry	152 C2
Knodishall	89 A5
Knolls Green	128 B3
Knolton	110 B2
Knolton Bryn	110 B2
Knook	30 A3
Knossington	99 A5
Knott End-on-Sea	144 C3
Knotting	84 A2
Knotting Green	84 A2

Knottingley	140 A3
Knotts	
Cumb	164 C2
Lancs	146 B1
Knotty Ash	136 D3
Knotty Green	67 D4
Knowbury	94 D3
Knowe	181 D5
Knowehead	182 C4
Knowes of Elrick	267 D7
Knoweton	194 A2
Knowhead	269 D4
Knowle	
Bristol	43 B5
Devon	12 A2
Devon	13 C5
Devon	25 B5
Shrops	94 D3
W Mid	97 D4
Knowle Green	145 D6
Knowle Park	147 C4
Knowl Hill	47 B6
Knowlton	
Dorset	31 D4
Kent	53 D4
Knowsley	136 D3
Knowstone	26 C3
Knox Bridge	37 B5
Knucklas	93 D6
Knuston	83 A6
Knutsford	128 B2
Knutton	112 A2
Knypersley	128 D3
Kuggar	3 D5
Kyleakin	247 B6
Kyle of Lochalsh	249 D4
Kylerhea	247 B6
Kylesknoydart	238 C2
Kylesku	271 A5
Kylesmorar	238 C2
Kylestrome	271 A5
Kyllachy House	252 D3
Kynaston	110 C2
Kynnersley	111 D5
Kyre Magna	79 A4

L

Labost	288 C3
Lacasaidh	288 E4
Lacasdal	288 D5
Laceby	143 C4
Lacey Green	66 D3
Lach Dennis	128 B2
Lackford	102 D3
Lacock	44 C3
Ladbroke	81 B7
Laddingford	37 B4
Lade Bank	134 D3
Ladock	4 B3
Lady	282 C7
Ladybank	220 C3
Ladykirk	198 B2
Ladysford	269 C4
La Fontenelle	6
Laga	235 D5
Lagalochan	214 A1
Lagavulin	201 D4
Lagg	
Argyll	201 A5
N Ayrs	191 C5
Laggan	
Argyll	200 C2
Highld	235 C6
Highld	239 C6
Highld	241 C4
S Ayrs	181 C4
Lagganulva	224 B3
Laide	261 A5
Laigh Fenwick	205 D4
Laigh Glengall	192 C3
Laighmuir	205 D4
Laindon	50 A3
Lair	250 B2
Lairg	272 D3
Lairg Lodge	272 D3
Lairgmore	252 C1
Lairg Muir	272 D3
Laisterdyke	147 D5
Laithes	164 B2
Lake	
IoW	19 C4
Wilts	31 B5
Lakenham	104 A3
Lakenheath	102 C3
Lakesend	101 B7
Lakeside	154 C2
Laleham	48 C3

Kin–Lan 315	
Laleston	40 D3
Lamarsh	87 D4
Lamas	120 C4
Lambden	197 B6
Lamberhurst	37 C4
Lamberhurst	
Quarter	37 C4
Lamberton	198 A3
Lambeth	49 B6
Lambhill	205 B5
Lambley	
Northumb	177 D4
Notts	115 A4
Lamborough Hill	65 C5
Lambourn	46 B1
Lambourne End	69 D4
Lambs Green	35 C5
Lambston	55 C5
Lambton	179 D4
Lamerton	11 D5
Lamesley	179 D4
Laminess	282 D7
Lamington	
Highld	264 C3
S Lanark	195 C4
Lamlash	191 B6
Lamloch	182 C3
Lamonby	164 B2
Lamorna	2 C2
Lamorran	4 C3
Lampardbrook	88 A3
Lampeter = Llanbedr	
Pont Steffan	75 D4
Lampeter Velfrey	56 A1
Lamphey	55 D6
Lamplugh	162 B3
Lamport	99 D4
Lamyatt	29 B6
Lana	10 B4
Lanark	194 B3
Lancaster	145 A4
Lanchester	167 A4
Lancing	21 B4
Landbeach	85 A6
Landcross	25 C5
Landerberry	245 B4
Landford	31 D6
Landford Manor	31 D6
Landimore	57 C4
Landkey	25 B6
Landore	57 C6
Landrake	6 A2
Landscove	8 A1
Landshipping	55 C6
Landshipping Quay	55 C6
Landulph	6 A3
Landwade	86 A2
Lane	4 A3
Laneast	10 C3
Lane End	
Bucks	66 D3
Cumb	153 A2
Dorset	16 B2
Hants	33 C4
IoW	19 C5
Lancs	146 C2
Lane Ends	
Lancs	146 B1
Lancs	146 D1
N Yorks	146 C4
Laneham	132 B3
Lanehead	
Durham	165 A6
Northumb	177 A5
Lane Head	
Derbys	129 B6
Durham	166 D4
Gtr Man	137 D5
W Yorks	139 C4
Lanercost	176 C3
Laneshaw Bridge	146 C3
Lane Side	137 A6
Lanfach	41 B7
Langar	115 B5
Langbank	204 A3
Langbar	147 B4
Langburnshiels	186 C4
Langcliffe	146 A2
Langdale	278 D2
Langdale End	160 B3
Langdon	10 C4
Langdon Beck	165 B6
Langdon Hills	50 A3
Langdyke	220 D3
Langenhoe	71 B4
Langford	
C Beds	84 C3
Devon	13 A5

Langford continued
Essex 70 C2
Notts. 132 D3
Oxon 64 C3
Langford Budville . . .27 C6
Langham
Essex 87 D6
Norf 120 A2
Rutland 115 D6
Suff. 103 E5
Langhaugh 195 C7
Langho 145 D7
Langholm 185 D6
Langleeford 188 A2
Langley
Ches E. 129 B4
Hants 18 A3
Herts. 68 A2
Kent 37 A6
Northumb 177 C6
Slough 48 B3
Warks 81 A4
W Sus 33 C7
Langley Burrell 44 B3
Langley Common 113 B6
Langley Heath 37 A6
Langley Lower
Green 85 D6
Langley Marsh 27 C5
Langley Park 167 A5
Langley Street 105 A4
Langley Upper
Green 85 D6
Langney 22 B4
Langold 131 A5
Langore 10 C4
Langport 28 C4
Langrick 117 A5
Langridge 43 C6
Langridge Ford 25 C6
Langrigg 175 D4
Langrish 33 C6
Langsett 139 C5
Langshaw 197 C4
Langside 218 C2
Langskaill 282 C5
Langstone
Hants 19 A6
Newport 61 D5
Langthorne 157 B6
Langthorpe 148 A2
Langthwaite 156 A4
Langtoft
E Yorks 150 A3
Lincs 116 D4
Langton
Durham 167 D4
Lincs 134 B3
Lincs 134 C2
N Yorks 149 A6
Langton by Wragby 133 B6
Langton Green
Kent 36 C3
Suff 104 D2
Langton Herring 15 C6
Langton Matravers . . 17 D4
Langtree 25 D5
Langwathby 164 B3
Langwell House 275 D5
Langwell Lodge 271 D4
Langwith 131 C5
Langwith Junction .131 C5
Langworth 133 B5
Lanivet 5 A5
Lanlivery 5 B5
Lanner 4 D2
Lanreath 5 B6
Lansallos 5 B6
Lansdown 63 A5
Lanteglos Highway . . 5 B6
Lanton
Borders. 187 A5
Northumb 198 C3
Lapford 12 A2
Laphroaig 200 D3
La Planque 6
Lapley 112 D2
Lapworth 97 D4
Larachbeg 225 B5
Larbert 207 B6
Larden Green 127 C6
Largie 255 C7
Largiemore 214 D2
Largoward 221 D4
Largs 204 C2
Largybeg 191 C6
Largymore 191 C6
Larkfield 204 A2

Larkhall 194 A2
Larkhill 31 A5
Larling 103 C5
Larriston 186 D4
Lartington 166 D3
Lary 243 B6
Lasham 33 A5
Lashenden 37 B6
Lassington 62 A3
Lassodie 208 A4
Lastingham 159 B6
Latcham 29 A4
Latchford
Herts. 68 A3
Warr. 127 A6
Latchingdon 70 C2
Latchley 11 D5
Lately Common 137 D5
Lathbury 83 C5
Latheron 275 A5
Latheronwheel 275 A5
Latheronwheel
House. 275 A5
Lathones 221 D4
Latimer 67 D5
Latteridge 43 A5
Lattiford 29 C6
Latton 64 D1
Latton Bush 69 C4
Lauchintilly 245 A4
Lauder 197 B4
Laugharne 56 A3
Laughterton 132 B3
Laughton
E Sus. 22 A3
Leics 98 C3
Lincs 116 B3
Lincs 141 D6
Laughton Common .131 A5
Laughton en le
Morthen. 131 A5
Launcells. 10 A3
Launceston 10 C4
Launton 65 A7
Laurencekirk 233 A5
Laurieston
Dumfries 173 B4
Falk. 208 C2
Lavendon 83 B6
Lavenham 87 C5
Laverhay 185 C4
Laversdale 176 C2
Laverstock 31 B5
Laverstoke 32 A3
Laverton
Glos 80 D3
N Yorks 157 D6
Som. 44 D1
Lavister 126 D3
Law 194 A3
Lawers
Perth 217 A6
Perth 218 B2
Lawford 88 D1
Lawhitton 11 C4
Lawkland. 146 A1
Lawley 95 A4
Lawnhead 112 C2
Lawrenny 55 D6
Lawshall 87 B4
Lawton 78 B2
Laxey 152 C4
Laxfield 104 D3
Laxfirth
Shetland 285 H6
Shetland 285 J6
Laxford Bridge. 276 D3
Laxo 285 G6
Laxobigging 284 F6
Laxton
E Yorks 141 A5
Northants 99 B6
Notts. 132 C2
Laycock. 147 C4
Layer Breton. 70 B3
Layer de la Haye . . . 70 B3
Layer Marney. 70 B3
Layham 87 C6
Laylands Green 46 C1
Laytham 149 D6
Layton 144 D3
Lazenby 168 C3
Lazonby 164 B3
Lea
Derbys 130 D3
Hereford. 62 A2
Lincs 132 A3
Shrops 94 A2
Shrops 94 C1
Wilts. 44 A3

Leabrooks 131 D4
Leac a Li 288 H2
Leachkin 252 B2
Leadburn 196 A1
Leadenham 133 D4
Leaden Roding. 69 B5
Leadgate
Cumb 165 A5
Durham. 178 D3
T&W 178 D3
Leadhills 183 A6
Leafield 64 B4
Leagrave 67 A5
Leake 158 B3
Leake
Commonside. 134 D3
Lealholm 159 A6
Lealt
Argyll 213 C4
Highld 259 B5
Lea Marston 97 B5
Leamington
Hastings. 82 A1
Leamonsley 96 A4
Leamside. 167 A6
Leanaig 252 A1
Leargybreck 201 A5
Leasgill. 154 C3
Leasingham 116 A3
Leasingthorne 167 C5
Leasowe 136 D1
Leatherhead 35 A4
Leatherhead
Common 35 A4
Leathley 147 C6
Leaton 110 C3
Lea Town 145 D4
Leaveland 52 D2
Leavening 149 A6
Leaves Green 49 C7
Leazes 178 D3
Lebberston 161 C4
Lechlade-on-
Thames. 64 D3
Leck 155 D5
Leckford 32 B2
Leckfurin 278 C3
Leckgruinart 200 B2
Leckhampstead
Bucks 83 D4
W Berks 46 B2
Leckhampstead
Thicket. 46 B2
Leckhampton 63 B5
Leckie 262 D2
Leckmelm. 262 A3
Leckwith 41 D6
Leconfield 150 C3
Ledaig 226 C4
Ledburn 67 A4
Ledbury 79 D5
Ledcharrie 217 B5
Ledgemoor 78 B2
Ledicot. 78 A2
Ledmore 271 C5
Lednagullin 278 B3
Ledsham
Ches W 126 B3
W Yorks 140 A2
Ledston 140 A2
Ledston Luck 148 D3
Ledwell 65 A5
Lee
Argyll 224 D3
Devon 25 A5
Hants 32 D3
Lancs 145 B5
Shrops 110 B3
Leeans 285 J3
Leebotten 285 L6
Leebotwood 94 B2
Lee Brockhurst 111 C4
Leece 153 D3
Leechpool 55 C5
Lee Clump 67 C4
Leeds
Kent 37 A6
W Yorks 148 D1
Leedstown 3 B4
Leek 129 D4
Leekbrook 129 D4
Leek Wootton. 81 A5
Leeming 157 C6
Leeming Bar. 157 B6
Lee Moor. 7 A4
Lee-on-the-Solent . 19 A4
Lees
Derbys 113 B6
Gtr Man 138 C2

Lees continued
W Yorks 147 D4
Leeswood 126 C2
Legbourne 134 A3
Legerwood 197 B4
Legsby. 133 A6
Leicester 98 A2
Leicester Forest
East. 98 A2
Leigh
Dorset. 15 A6
Glos 63 A4
Gtr Man 137 C5
Kent 36 B3
Shrops 94 A1
Sur 35 B5
Wilts 63 D6
Worcs 79 B5
Leigh Beck 51 A5
Leigh Common 30 C1
Leigh Delamere. 44 B2
Leigh Green 37 C7
Leigh on Sea. 51 A5
Leigh Park 19 A6
Leigh Sinton 79 B5
Leighswood 96 A3
Leighterton. 63 D4
Leighton
N Yorks 157 D5
Powys 93 A6
Shrops 95 A4
Som. 29 A7
Leighton
Bromswold 100 D3
Leighton Buzzard . . . 67 A4
Leigh upon Mendip . 29 A6
Leigh Woods 43 B4
Leinthall Earls 78 A2
Leinthall Starkes. . . . 78 A2
Leintwardine 94 D2
Leire 98 B2
Leirinmore 277 B5
Leiston 89 A5
Leitfie. 231 D6
Leith 209 C5
Leitholm 198 B1
Lelant 2 B3
Lelley 151 D5
Lem Hill 95 D5
Lemington Hall 189 B4
Lempitlaw. 198 C1
Lenchwick 80 C3
Lendalfoot 180 C3
Lendrick Lodge. 217 D5
Lenham 37 A6
Lenham Heath 37 B7
Lennel 198 B2
Lennoxtown 205 A6
Lenton
Lincs 116 B3
Nottingham 114 B3
Lentran 252 B1
Lenwade 120 D2
Leny House 217 D6
Lenzie 205 A6
Leoch 220 A3
Leochel-Cushnie. . . .244 A2
Leominster 78 B2
Leonard Stanley 63 C4
Leorin 200 D3
Lepe 18 B3
Lephin 258 D1
Lephinchapel 214 C2
Lephinmore 214 C2
Le Planel 6
Leppington. 149 A6
Lepton 139 B5
Lerryn 5 B6
Lerwick 285 J6
Lesbury 189 B5
Le Skerne
Haughton. 167 D6
Leslie
Aberds 255 D6
Fife 220 D2
Lesmahagow 194 C3
Lesnewth. 10 B2
Lessendrum 255 B6
Lessingham 121 C5
Lessonhall 175 C5
Leswalt 170 A2
Letchmore Heath . . . 67 D6
Letchworth 84 D4
Letcombe Bassett. . . 46 A1
Letcombe Regis. 46 A1
Letham
Angus 232 D3
Falk. 208 B1
Fife 220 C3
Perth 219 B5

Letham Grange 233 D4
Lethenty 256 B3
Letheringham 88 B3
Letheringsett 120 B2
Lettaford 12 C2
Lettan 282 C8
Letterewe 261 C6
Letterfearn 249 D5
Letterfinlay 239 C6
Lettermorar 235 B6
Lettermore 224 B3
Letters 262 B3
Letterston 55 B5
Lettoch
Highld 242 A3
Highld 254 C1
Letton
Hereford. 78 C1
Hereford. 94 D1
Letton Green 103 A5
Letty Green 68 B2
Letwell 131 A5
Leuchars 221 B4
Leuchars House. 266 C3
Leumrabhagh 288 F4
Levan 204 A2
Levaneap. 285 G6
Levedale 112 D2
Leven
E Yorks 151 C4
Fife 220 D3
Levencorroch. 191 C6
Levens 154 C3
Levens Green 68 A3
Levenshulme 138 D1
Levenwick. 285 L6
Leverburgh
=An t-Ob 287 F5
Leverington 118 D1
Leverton 117 A7
Leverton Highgate .117 A7
Leverton
Lucasgate. 117 A7
Leverton Outgate .117 A7
Le Villocq 6
Levington 88 D3
Levisham 160 B2
Levishie 240 A2
Lew 64 C4
Lewannick 10 C3
Lewdown 11 C5
Lewes 22 A2
Leweston 55 B5
Lewisham 49 B6
Lewiston 251 D7
Lewistown 40 C4
Lewknor 66 D2
Leworthy
Devon 10 A4
Devon 26 B1
Lewtrenchard. 11 C5
Lexden 70 A3
Ley
Aberds 244 A2
Corn 5 A6
Leybourne 37 A4
Leyburn 157 B5
Leyfields 97 A5
Leyhill 67 C4
Leyland 136 A4
Leylodge 245 A4
Leymoor 139 B4
Leys
Aberds 269 D5
Perth. 220 A2
Leys Castle 252 B2
Leysdown-on-Sea . . 52 B2
Leysmill. 233 D4
Leys of Cossans 232 D1
Leysters Pole 78 A3
Leyton 49 A6
Leytonstone 49 A6
Lezant 10 D4
Leziate 118 D3
Lhanbryde. 266 C3
Liatrie 250 C4
Libanus 60 A1
Libberton 195 B4
Liberton 209 D5
Liceasto. 288 H2
Lichfield 96 A4
Lickey. 96 D2
Lickey End. 96 D2
Lickfold. 34 D2
Liddel 283 J5
Liddesdale 236 D1
Liddington 45 A6
Lidgate 86 B3
Lidget. 141 C4
Lidget Green 147 D5

Lidgett 131 C6
Lidlington. 84 D1
Lidstone 65 A4
Lieurary 279 B6
Liff 220 A3
Lifton 11 C4
Liftondown 11 C4
Lighthorne 81 B4
Lightwater 48 C2
Lightwood 112 A3
Lightwood Green
Ches E. 111 A5
Wrex. 110 A2
Lilbourne 98 D2
Lilburn Tower 188 A3
Lilleshall 111 D6
Lilley
Herts. 67 A6
W Berks 46 B2
Lilliesleaf 186 A4
Lillingstone
Dayrell 83 D4
Lillingstone Lovell . . 83 C4
Lillington
Dorset. 29 D6
Warks 81 A6
Lilliput 17 B4
Lilstock 27 A6
Lilyhurst 111 D6
Limbury 67 A5
Limebrook 78 A1
Limefield 137 B7
Limekilnburn 194 A2
Limekilns 208 B3
Limerigg 207 C6
Limerstone 18 C3
Limington 29 C5
Limpenhoe 105 A4
Limpley Stoke 44 C1
Limpsfield 36 A2
Limpsfield Chart . . . 36 A2
Linby 131 D5
Linchmere. 34 C1
Lincluden 174 A2
Lincoln. 133 B4
Lincomb 79 A6
Lincombe 7 B6
Lindale 154 C3
Lindal in Furness. . . .153 C3
Lindean 196 C3
Lindfield 35 D6
Lindford 33 B7
Lindifferon 220 C3
Lindley 139 B4
Lindley Green. 147 C6
Lindores 220 C2
Lindridge 79 A4
Lindsell 69 A6
Lindsey 87 C5
Linford
Hants 17 A5
Thurrock 50 B3
Lingague. 152 D2
Lingards Wood. 138 B3
Lingbob 147 D4
Lingdale 169 D4
Lingen 78 A1
Lingfield 36 B1
Lingreabhagh. 287 F5
Lingwood 105 A4
Linicro 258 B3
Linkenholt. 46 D1
Linkhill 37 D6
Linkinhorne. 10 D4
Linklater 283 J5
Linksness 283 G3
Linktown 209 A5
Linley 94 B1
Linley Green 79 B4
Linlithgow 208 C3
Linlithgow Bridge. . .208 C2
Linshiels 188 C1
Linsiadar 288 D3
Linsidemore 264 A1
Linslade 67 A4
Linstead Parva. 104 D4
Linstock 176 D2
Linthwaite 139 B4
Lintlaw 198 A2
Lintmill 267 C6
Linton
Borders. 187 A6
Cambs. 86 C1
Derbys 113 D6
Hereford. 62 A1
Kent 37 B5
Northumb 189 D5
N Yorks 146 A3
W Yorks 148 C2
Linton-on-Ouse 148 A3

Linwood
Hants . . . 17 A5
Lincs . . . 133 A6
Renfs . . . 205 B4
Lionacleit . . . 286 B3
Lional . . . 288 A6
Liphook . . . 34 C1
Liscard . . . 136 D2
Liscombe . . . 26 B3
Liskeard . . . 6 A1
L'Islet . . . 6
Liss . . . 33 C6
Lissett . . . 151 B4
Liss Forest . . . 33 C6
Lissington . . . 133 A6
Lisvane . . . 41 C6
Liswerry . . . 42 A2
Litcham . . . 119 D5
Litchborough . . . 82 B3
Litchfield . . . 46 D2
Litherland . . . 136 D2
Litlington
Cambs . . . 85 C5
E Sus . . . 22 B3
Little Abington . . . 86 C1
Little Addington . . . 99 D6
Little Alne . . . 80 A4
Little Altcar . . . 136 C2
Little Asby . . . 155 A5
Little Assynt . . . 271 B4
Little Aston . . . 96 A3
Little Atherfield . . . 18 C3
Little Ayre . . . 283 H4
Little-ayre . . . 285 G5
Little Ayton . . . 168 D3
Little Baddow . . . 70 C1
Little Badminton . . . 44 A2
Little Ballinluig . . . 230 C3
Little Bampton . . . 175 C5
Little Bardfield . . . 86 D2
Little Barford . . . 84 B3
Little Barningham . . . 120 B3
Little Barrington . . . 64 B3
Little Barrow . . . 127 B4
Little Barugh . . . 159 D6
Little Bavington . . . 178 B1
Little Bealings . . . 88 C3
Littlebeck . . . 160 A2
Little Bedwyn . . . 45 C6
Little Bentley . . . 71 A5
Little Berkhamsted . . . 68 C2
Little Billing . . . 83 A5
Little Birch . . . 78 D3
Little Blakenham . . . 88 C2
Little Blencow . . . 164 B2
Little Bollington . . . 128 A2
Little Bookham . . . 35 A4
Littleborough
Gtr Man . . . 138 B2
Notts . . . 132 A3
Littlebourne . . . 53 D4
Little Bowden . . . 99 C4
Little Bradley . . . 86 B2
Little Brampton . . . 94 C1
Little Brechin . . . 232 B3
Littlebredy . . . 15 C5
Little Brickhill . . . 83 D6
Little Brington . . . 82 A3
Little Bromley . . . 71 A4
Little Broughton . . . 162 A4
Little Budworth . . . 127 C5
Little Burstead . . . 69 D6
Littlebury . . . 85 D7
Littlebury Green . . . 85 D6
Little Bytham . . . 116 D3
Little Carlton
Lincs . . . 134 A3
Notts . . . 132 D2
Little Casterton . . . 100 A2
Little Cawthorpe . . . 134 A3
Little Chalfont . . . 67 D4
Little Chart . . . 38 A1
Little Chesterford . . . 85 C7
Little Cheverell . . . 44 D3
Little Chishill . . . 85 D6
Little Clacton . . . 71 B5
Little Clifton . . . 162 B3
Little Colp . . . 256 B2
Little Comberton . . . 80 C2
Little Common . . . 23 B5
Little Compton . . . 81 D5
Little Cornard . . . 87 D4
Little Cowarne . . . 79 B4
Little Coxwell . . . 64 D3
Little Crakehall . . . 157 B6
Little Cressingham . . . 103 B4
Little Crosby . . . 136 C2
Little Dalby . . . 115 D5
Little Dawley . . . 95 A4
Littledean . . . 62 B2

Little Dens . . . 257 B5
Little Dewchurch . . . 78 D3
Little Downham . . . 101 C7
Little Driffield . . . 150 B3
Little Dunham . . . 119 D5
Little Dunkeld . . . 230 D4
Little Dunmow . . . 69 A6
Little Easton . . . 69 A6
Little Eaton . . . 114 A1
Little Eccleston . . . 144 C4
Little Ellingham . . . 103 B6
Little End . . . 69 C5
Little Eversden . . . 85 B5
Little Faringdon . . . 64 C3
Little Fencote . . . 157 B6
Little Fenton . . . 148 D4
Littleferry . . . 265 A4
Little Finborough . . . 87 B6
Little Fransham . . . 119 D6
Little Gaddesden . . . 67 B4
Little Gidding . . . 100 C3
Little Glemham . . . 88 B4
Little Glenshee . . . 219 A4
Little Gransden . . . 85 B4
Little Green . . . 29 A7
Little Grimsby . . . 143 D5
Little Gruinard . . . 261 B6
Little Habton . . . 159 D6
Little Hadham . . . 68 A4
Little Hale . . . 116 A4
Little Hallingbury . . . 69 B4
Littleham
Devon . . . 13 C5
Devon . . . 25 C5
Little Hampden . . . 66 C3
Littlehampton . . . 20 B3
Little Harrowden . . . 99 D5
Little Haseley . . . 66 C1
Little Hatfield . . . 151 C4
Little Hautbois . . . 121 C4
Little Haven . . . 55 C4
Little Hay . . . 96 A4
Little Hayfield . . . 129 A5
Little Haywood . . . 112 C4
Little Heath . . . 97 C6
Littlehempston . . . 8 A2
Little Hereford . . . 78 A3
Little Horkesley . . . 87 D5
Little Horsted . . . 22 A2
Little Horton . . . 147 D5
Little Horwood . . . 83 D4
Littlehoughton . . . 189 B5
Little Houghton
Northants . . . 83 B5
S Yorks . . . 140 C2
Little Hucklow . . . 129 B6
Little Hulton . . . 137 C6
Little Humber . . . 142 A3
Little Hungerford . . . 46 B3
Little Irchester . . . 83 A6
Little Kimble . . . 66 C3
Little Kineton . . . 81 B6
Little Kingshill . . . 66 D3
Little Langdale . . . 154 A2
Little Langford . . . 31 B4
Little Laver . . . 69 C5
Little Leigh . . . 127 B6
Little Leighs . . . 69 B7
Little Lever . . . 137 C6
Little London
Bucks . . . 66 B1
E Sus . . . 22 A3
Hants . . . 32 A2
Hants . . . 47 D4
Lincs . . . 117 C5
Lincs . . . 118 C1
Norf . . . 120 C3
Powys . . . 92 C4
Little Longstone . . . 130 B1
Little Lynturk . . . 244 A2
Little Malvern . . . 79 C5
Little Maplestead . . . 87 D4
Little Marcle . . . 79 D4
Little Marlow . . . 47 A6
Little Marsden . . . 146 D2
Little Massingham . . . 119 C4
Little Melton . . . 104 A2
Littlemill
Aberds . . . 243 C6
E Ayrs . . . 182 A2
Highld . . . 253 A5
Northumb . . . 189 B5
Little Mill . . . 61 C5
Little Milton . . . 65 C7
Little Missenden . . . 67 D4
Littlemoor . . . 15 C6
Littlemore . . . 65 C6
Little Musgrave . . . 165 D5
Little Ness . . . 110 D3
Little Neston . . . 126 B2

Little Newcastle . . . 55 B5
Little Newsham . . . 166 D4
Little Oakley
Essex . . . 71 A6
Northants . . . 99 C5
Little Orton . . . 175 C6
Little Ouseburn . . . 148 A3
Littleover . . . 114 B1
Little Paxton . . . 84 A3
Little Petherick . . . 9 D5
Little Pitlurg . . . 255 B5
Little Plumpton . . . 144 D3
Little Plumstead . . . 121 D5
Little Ponton . . . 116 B2
Littleport . . . 102 C1
Little Raveley . . . 101 D4
Little Reedness . . . 141 A6
Little Ribston . . . 148 B2
Little Rissington . . . 64 B2
Little Ryburgh . . . 119 C6
Little Ryle . . . 188 B3
Little Salkeld . . . 164 B3
Little Sampford . . . 86 D2
Little Sandhurst . . . 47 C6
Little Saxham . . . 86 A3
Little Scatwell . . . 251 A5
Little Sessay . . . 158 D3
Little Shelford . . . 85 B6
Little Singleton . . . 144 D3
Little Skillymarno . . . 269 D4
Little Smeaton . . . 140 B3
Little Snoring . . . 119 B6
Little Sodbury . . . 43 A6
Little Somborne . . . 32 B2
Little Somerford . . . 44 A3
Little Stainforth . . . 146 A2
Little Stainton . . . 167 C6
Little Stanney . . . 127 B4
Little Staughton . . . 84 A3
Little Steeping . . . 135 C4
Little Stoke . . . 112 B3
Littlestone on Sea . . . 38 C2
Little Stonham . . . 88 A2
Little Stretton
Leics . . . 98 A3
Shrops . . . 94 B2
Little Strickland . . . 164 D3
Little Stukeley . . . 100 D4
Little Sutton . . . 126 B3
Little Tew . . . 65 A4
Little Thetford . . . 102 D1
Little Thirkleby . . . 158 D3
Littlethorpe
Leics . . . 98 B2
N Yorks . . . 148 A2
Little Thurlow . . . 86 B2
Little Thurrock . . . 50 B3
Littleton
Ches W . . . 127 C4
Hants . . . 32 B3
Perth . . . 220 A2
Som . . . 29 B4
Sur . . . 34 B2
Sur . . . 48 C3
Littleton Drew . . . 44 A2
Littleton-on-Severn . . . 43 A4
Littleton Pannell . . . 44 D4
Little Torboll . . . 264 A3
Little Torrington . . . 25 D5
Little Totham . . . 70 B2
Little Toux . . . 267 D6
Littletown . . . 167 A6
Little Town
Cumb . . . 163 C5
Lancs . . . 145 D6
Little Urswick . . . 153 C3
Little Wakering . . . 51 A6
Little Walden . . . 86 C1
Little Waldingfield . . . 87 C5
Little Walsingham . . . 119 B6
Little Waltham . . . 69 B7
Little Warley . . . 69 D6
Little Weighton . . . 150 D2
Little Weldon . . . 99 C6
Little Welnetham . . . 87 A4
Little Wenlock . . . 95 A4
Little Whittingham Green . . . 104 D3
Littlewick Green . . . 47 B6
Little Wilbraham . . . 86 B1
Little Wishford . . . 31 B4
Little Witley . . . 79 A5
Little Wittenham . . . 65 D6
Little Wolford . . . 81 D5
Littleworth
Bedford . . . 84 C2
Glos . . . 63 C4
Oxon . . . 64 D4
Staffs . . . 112 D4
Worcs . . . 80 B1

Little Wratting . . . 86 C2
Little Wymington . . . 83 A6
Little Wymondley . . . 68 A2
Little Wyrley . . . 96 A3
Little Yeldham . . . 86 D3
Litton
Derbys . . . 129 B6
N Yorks . . . 156 D3
Som . . . 43 D4
Litton Cheney . . . 15 B5
Liurbost . . . 288 E4
Liverpool . . . 136 D2
Liverpool Airport . . . 127 A4
Liversedge . . . 139 A5
Liverton
Devon . . . 12 D3
Redcar . . . 169 D5
Livingston . . . 208 D3
Livingston Village . . . 208 D3
Lixwm . . . 125 B5
Lizard . . . 3 D5
Llaingoch . . . 122 B2
Llaithddu . . . 93 C4
Llan . . . 91 B6
Llanaber . . . 90 A4
Llanaelhaearn . . . 106 B3
Llanafan . . . 75 A5
Llanafan-fawr . . . 76 B3
Llanallgo . . . 123 B4
Llanandras
=Presteigne . . . 77 A7
Llanarmon . . . 107 C4
Llanarmon Dyffryn Ceiriog . . . 109 B6
Llanarmon-yn-Ial . . . 126 D1
Llanarth
Ceredig . . . 73 A7
Mon . . . 61 B5
Llanarthne . . . 58 C2
Llanasa . . . 125 A6
Llanbabo . . . 122 B3
Llanbadarn Fawr . . . 90 D4
Llanbadarn Fynydd . . . 93 D5
Llanbadarn-y-Garreg . . . 77 C5
Llanbadoc . . . 61 C5
Llanbadrig . . . 122 A3
Llanbeder . . . 61 D5
Llanbedr
Gwyn . . . 107 D5
Powys . . . 60 A4
Powys . . . 77 C5
Llanbedr-Dyffryn-Clwyd . . . 125 D6
Llanbedrgoch . . . 123 B5
Llanbedrog . . . 106 C3
Llanbedr Pont Steffan
=Lampeter . . . 75 D4
Llanbedr-y-cennin . . . 124 C2
Llanberis . . . 123 D5
Llanbethery . . . 41 E5
Llanbister . . . 93 D5
Llanblethian . . . 41 D4
Llanboidy . . . 73 D5
Llanbradach . . . 41 B6
Llanbrynmair . . . 91 B6
Llancarfan . . . 41 D5
Llancayo . . . 61 C5
Llancloudy . . . 61 A6
Llancynfelyn . . . 90 C4
Llandaff . . . 41 D6
Llandanwg . . . 107 D5
Llandarcy . . . 40 B2
Llandawke . . . 56 A2
Llanddaniel Fab . . . 123 C4
Llanddarog . . . 57 A5
Llanddeiniol . . . 75 A4
Llanddeiniolen . . . 123 D5
Llandderfel . . . 109 B5
Llanddeusant
Anglesey . . . 122 B3
Carms . . . 59 C4
Llanddew . . . 77 D4
Llanddewi . . . 57 D4
Llanddewi-Brefi . . . 75 C5
Llanddewi'r Cwm . . . 76 C4
Llanddewi Rhydderch . . . 61 B5
Llanddewi Velfrey . . . 56 A1
Llanddoged . . . 124 C3
Llanddona . . . 123 C5
Llanddowror . . . 56 A2
Llanddulas . . . 125 B4
Llanddwywe . . . 107 D5
Llanddyfynan . . . 123 C5
Llandefaelog Fach . . . 76 D4
Llandefaelog-tre'r-graig . . . 77 E5
Llandefalle . . . 77 D5
Llandegai . . . 123 C5

Llandegfan . . . 123 C5
Llandegla . . . 126 D1
Llandegley . . . 77 A5
Llandegveth . . . 61 D5
Llandegwning . . . 106 C2
Llandeilo . . . 58 C3
Llandeilo Graban . . . 77 C4
Llandeilo'r Fan . . . 59 B5
Llandeloy . . . 55 B4
Llandenny . . . 61 C6
Llandevenny . . . 42 A3
Llandewednock . . . 3 D5
Llandewi Ystradenny . . . 77 A5
Llandinabo . . . 61 A7
Llandinam . . . 92 C4
Llandissilio . . . 55 B7
Llandogo . . . 62 C1
Llandough
V Glam . . . 41 D4
V Glam . . . 41 D6
Llandovery
=Llanymddyfri . . . 59 B4
Llandow . . . 40 D4
Llandre
Carms . . . 58 A3
Ceredig . . . 90 D4
Llandrillo . . . 109 B5
Llandrillo-yn-Rhos . . . 124 A3
Llandrindod
=Llandrindod Wells . . . 77 A4
Llandrindod Wells
=Llandrindod . . . 77 A4
Llandrinio . . . 110 D1
Llandudno . . . 124 A2
Llandudno Junction
=Cyffordd Llandudno . . . 124 B2
Llandwrog . . . 107 A4
Llandybie . . . 57 A6
Llandyfaelog . . . 57 A4
Llandyfan . . . 57 A6
Llandyfriog . . . 73 B6
Llandyfrydog . . . 123 B4
Llandygwydd . . . 73 B5
Llandynan . . . 109 A6
Llandyrnog . . . 125 C5
Llandysilio . . . 110 D1
Llandyssil . . . 93 B5
Llandysul . . . 73 B7
Llanedeyrn . . . 41 C7
Llanedi . . . 57 B5
Llaneglwys . . . 77 D4
Llanegryn . . . 90 B3
Llanegwad . . . 58 C2
Llaneilian . . . 123 A4
Llanelian-yn-Rhos . . . 124 B3
Llanelidan . . . 125 D6
Llanelieu . . . 77 D5
Llanellen . . . 61 B5
Llanelli . . . 57 C5
Llanelltyd . . . 91 A5
Llanelly . . . 60 B4
Llanelly Hill . . . 60 B4
Llanelwedd . . . 76 B4
Llanelwy =St Asaph . . . 125 B5
Llanenddwyn . . . 107 D5
Llanengan . . . 106 D2
Llanerchymedd . . . 123 B4
Llanerfyl . . . 92 A4
Llanfachraeth . . . 122 B3
Llanfachreth . . . 108 C2
Llanfaelog . . . 122 C3
Llanfaelrhys . . . 106 D2
Llanfaenor . . . 61 B6
Llanfaes
Anglesey . . . 123 C6
Powys . . . 60 A2
Llanfaethlu . . . 122 B3
Llanfaglan . . . 123 D4
Llanfair . . . 107 D5
Llanfair-ar-y-bryn . . . 59 B5
Llanfair Caereinion . . . 93 A5
Llanfair Clydogau . . . 75 C5
Llanfair-Dyffryn-Clwyd . . . 125 D6
Llanfairfechan . . . 124 B1
Llanfair Kilgheddin . . . 61 C5
Llanfair-Nant-Gwyn . . . 73 C4
Llanfairpwll-gwyngyll . . . 123 C5
Llanfair Talhaiarn . . . 125 B4
Llanfair Waterdine . . . 93 D6
Llanfair-ym-Muallt
=Builth Wells . . . 76 B4
Llanfairyneubwll . . . 122 C3
Llanfairynghornwy . . . 122 A3
Llanfallteg . . . 56 A1

Llanfaredd . . . 77 B4
Llanfarian . . . 75 A4
Llanfechain . . . 109 C6
Llanfechan . . . 76 B3
Llanfechell . . . 122 A3
Llanfendigaid . . . 90 B3
Llanferres . . . 126 C1
Llan Ffestiniog . . . 108 A2
Llanfflewyn . . . 122 B3
Llanfihangel-ar-arth . . . 58 B1
Llanfihangel-Crucorney . . . 61 A5
Llanfihangel Glyn Myfyr . . . 109 A4
Llanfihangel Nant Bran . . . 59 B6
Llanfihangel-nant-Melan . . . 77 B5
Llanfihangel Rhydithon . . . 77 A5
Llanfihangel Rogiet . . . 42 A3
Llanfihangel Tal-y-llyn . . . 60 A3
Llanfihangel-uwch-Gwili . . . 58 C1
Llanfihangel-y-Creuddyn . . . 75 A5
Llanfihangel-yn-Ngwynfa . . . 109 D5
Llanfihangel yn Nhowyn . . . 122 C3
Llanfihangel-y-pennant
Gwyn . . . 91 B5
Gwyn . . . 107 B5
Llanfihangel-y-traethau . . . 107 C5
Llanfilo . . . 77 D5
Llanfoist . . . 61 B4
Llanfor . . . 108 B4
Llanfrechfa . . . 61 D5
Llanfrothen . . . 107 B6
Llanfrynach . . . 60 A2
Llanfwrog
Anglesey . . . 122 B3
Denb . . . 125 D6
Llanfyllin . . . 109 D6
Llanfynydd
Carms . . . 58 C2
Flint . . . 126 D2
Llanfyrnach . . . 73 C5
Llangadfan . . . 109 D5
Llangadog . . . 59 C4
Llangadwaladr
Anglesey . . . 122 D3
Powys . . . 109 B6
Llangaffo . . . 123 D4
Llangain . . . 56 A3
Llangammarch Wells . . . 76 C3
Llangan . . . 41 D4
Llangarron . . . 62 A1
Llangasty Talyllyn . . . 60 A3
Llangathen . . . 58 C2
Llangattock . . . 60 B4
Llangattock Lingoed . . . 61 A5
Llangattock nigh Usk . . . 61 C5
Llangattock-Vibon-Avel . . . 61 B6
Llangedwyn . . . 109 C6
Llangefni . . . 123 C4
Llangeinor . . . 40 C4
Llangeitho . . . 75 C5
Llangeler . . . 73 C6
Llangelynin . . . 90 B3
Llangendeirne . . . 57 A4
Llangennech . . . 57 B5
Llangennith . . . 57 C4
Llangenny . . . 60 B4
Llangernyw . . . 124 C3
Llangian . . . 106 D2
Llanglydwen . . . 73 D4
Llangoed . . . 123 C6
Llangoedmor . . . 73 B4
Llangollen . . . 109 A7
Llangolman . . . 55 B7
Llangors . . . 60 A3
Llangovan . . . 61 C6
Llangower . . . 108 B4
Llangrannog . . . 73 A6
Llangristiolus . . . 123 C4
Llangrove . . . 62 B1
Llangua . . . 61 A5
Llangunllo . . . 93 D6
Llangunnor . . . 57 A4
Llanguryn . . . 92 D3
Llangwm
Conwy . . . 109 A4

Llangwm *continued*
Mon. 61 C6
Pembs. 55 D5
Llangwnnadl 106 C2
Llangwyfan 125 C6
Llangwyfan-isaf 122 C3
Llangwyllog 123 C4
Llangwyryfon 75 A4
Llangybi
Ceredig. 75 C5
Gwyn. 107 B4
Mon. 61 D5
Llangyfelach. 57 C6
Llangynhafal 125 C6
Llangynidr 60 B3
Llangynin 56 A2
Llangynog
Carms 56 A3
Powys. 109 C5
Llangynwyd 40 C3
Llanhamlach 60 A2
Llanharan 41 C5
Llanharry 41 C5
Llanhennock 61 D5
Llanhiledd
=Llanhilleth 41 A7
Llanhilleth
=Llanhiledd 41 A7
Llanidloes 92 C3
Llaniestyn 106 C2
Llanifyny 91 D6
Llanigon 77 D6
Llanilar 75 A5
Llanilid. 41 C4
Llanilltud Fawr
=Llantwit Major. 41 E4
Llanishen
Cardiff. 41 C6
Mon. 61 C6
Llanllawddog 58 C1
Llanllechid 123 D6
Llanllowell 61 D5
Llanllugan 93 A4
Llanllwch 56 A3
Llanllwchaiarn. 93 B5
Llanllwni 58 B1
Llanllyfni 107 A4
Llanmadoc 57 C4
Llanmaes 41 E4
Llanmartin 42 A2
Llanmihangel. 41 D4
Llanmorlais 57 C5
Llannefydd 125 B4
Llannon 57 B5
Llannor 106 C3
Llanon 75 B4
Llanover 61 C5
Llanpumsaint 73 D7
Llanreithan 55 B4
Llanrhaeadr 125 C5
Llanrhaeadr-ym-
Mochnant 109 C6
Llanrhian 54 A4
Llanrhidian 57 C4
Llanrhos 124 A2
Llanrhyddlad 122 B3
Llanrhystud 75 B4
Llanrosser 77 D6
Llanrothal 61 B6
Llanrug 123 D5
Llanrumney 41 C7
Llanrwst 124 C3
Llansadurnen. 56 A2
Llansadwrn
Anglesey. 123 C5
Carms 58 B3
Llansaint 56 B3
Llansamlet 40 B1
Llansannan 125 C4
Llansannor 41 D4
Llansantffraed
Ceredig. 75 B4
Powys. 60 A3
Llansantffraed
Cwmdeuddwr. 76 A3
Llansantffraed-in-
Elvel 77 B4
Llansantffraid-ym-
Mechain. 109 C7
Llansawel 58 B3
Llansilin. 109 C7
Llansoy 61 C6
Llanspyddid 60 A2
Llanstadwell. 55 D5
Llansteffan 56 A3
Llanstephan 77 C5
Llantarnam 61 D5
Llanteg 56 A1

Llanthony 61 A4
Llantilio Crossenny. . .61 B5
Llantilio Pertholey . . .61 B5
Llantood 73 B4
Llantrisant
Anglesey. 122 B3
Mon. 61 D5
Rhondda 41 C5
Llantrithyd 41 D5
Llantwit Fardre 41 C5
Llantwit Major
=Llanilltud Fawr 41 E4
Llanuwchllyn 108 B3
Llanvaches 61 D6
Llanvair Discoed 61 D6
Llanvapley. 61 B5
Llanvetherine. 61 B5
Llanveynoe 77 D7
Llanvihangel Gobion 61 C5
Llanvihangel-Ystern-
Llewern 61 B6
Llanwarne 61 A7
Llanwddyn 109 D5
Llanwenog 74 D3
Llanwern 42 A2
Llanwinio 73 D5
Llanwnda
Gwyn. 107 A4
Pembs. 72 C2
Llanwnnen 75 D4
Llanwnog 92 B4
Llanwrda 59 B4
Llanwrin 91 B5
Llanwrthwl 76 A3
Llanwrtud
=Llanwrtyd Wells . . .76 C2
Llanwrtyd 76 C2
Llanwrtyd Wells
=Llanwrtud 76 C2
Llanwyddelan. 93 A4
Llanyblodwel 110 C1
Llanybri 56 A3
Llanybydder 58 A2
Llanycefn 55 B6
Llanychaer 72 C2
Llanycil 108 B4
Llanycrwys 75 D5
Llanymawddwy 91 A7
Llanymddyfri
=Llandovery. 59 B4
Llanymynech 110 C1
Llanynghenedl. 122 B3
Llanynys 125 C6
Llan-y-pwll 126 D3
Llanyre. 76 A4
Llanystumdwy 107 C4
Llanywern 60 A3
Llawhaden 55 C6
Llawnt 110 B1
Llawr Dref. 106 D2
Llawryglyn 92 B3
Llay 126 D3
Llechcynfarwy 122 B3
Llecheiddior 107 B4
Llechfaen 60 A2
Llechryd
Caerph 60 C3
Ceredig. 73 B5
Llechrydau 110 B1
Lledrod 75 A5
Llenmerewig 93 B5
Llethrid 57 C5
Llidiad Nenog 58 B2
Llidiardau 108 B3
Llidiart-y-parc 109 A6
Lithfaen 106 B3
Llong 126 C2
Llowes 77 C5
Llundain-fach 75 C4
Llwydcoed 41 A4
Llwyn 93 C6
Llwyncelyn 74 C3
Llwyndafydd 73 A6
Llwynderw 93 A6
Llwyn-du 61 B4
Llwyndyrys 106 B3
Llwyngwril 90 B3
Llwyn-hendy 57 C5
Llwynmawr 110 B1
Llwyn-têg 57 B5
Llwyn-y-brain 56 A1
Llwyn-y-groes 75 C4
Llwynypia 41 B4
Llynclys 110 C1
Llynfaes 123 C4
Llysfaen 124 B3
Llyswen 77 D5
Llysworney 41 D4
Llys-y-frân 55 B6
Llywel 59 B5

Loan 208 C2
Loanend 198 A3
Loanhead 209 D5
Loans 192 B3
Loans of Tullich 265 C4
Lobb. 25 B5
Loch a Charnain 286 B4
Loch a'
Ghainmhich 288 E3
Lochailort 235 B6
Lochaline 225 B5
Lochanhully 253 D5
Lochans 170 C2
Locharbriggs 184 D2
Lochassynt Lodge . . .271 B4
Lochavich Ho 214 A2
Lochawe 227 D6
Loch Baghasdail
=Lochboisdale. 286 E3
Lochboisdale
=Loch Baghasdail . .286 E3
Lochbuie 225 D5
Lochcarron 249 C5
Loch Choire Lodge . . .273 D4
Lochdhu 279 D6
Lochdochart
House. 216 B4
Lochdon 225 C6
Lochdrum 263 C4
Lochead. 202 A2
Lochearnhead 217 B5
Lochee 220 A3
Lochend
Highld 252 C1
Highld 281 B5
Locherben 184 C2
Loch Euphoirt 287 H3
Lochfoot 173 A6
Lochgair 214 C2
Lochgarthside 240 A3
Lochgelly. 209 A4
Lochgilphead 214 D1
Lochgoilhead 215 B5
Loch Head. 171 C5
Lochhill 266 C3
Lochindorb Lodge 253 C6
Lochinver 270 B3
Lochlane 218 B3
Loch Loyal Lodge 277 D7
Lochluichart. 263 C5
Lochmaben. 184 D3
Lochmaddy =Loch nam
Madadh 287 H4
Lochmore Cottage .280 D2
Lochmore Lodge. 271 A5
Loch nam Madadh
=Lochmaddy 287 H4
Lochore 209 A4
Lochportain 287 G4
Lochranza 203 C4
Lochs Crofts 266 C4
Loch Sgioport 286 C4
Lochside
Aberds 233 B5
Highld 253 A4
Highld 274 A2
Highld 277 C5
Lochslin. 265 B4
Lochstack Lodge. 276 D3
Lochton 245 C4
Lochty
Angus 232 B3
Fife 221 D5
Perth. 219 B5
Lochuisge 236 D2
Lochurr 183 D5
Lochwinnoch 204 C3
Lochwood 184 C3
Lochyside 237 B5
Lockengate. 5 A5
Lockerbie 185 D4
Lockeridge. 45 C5
Lockerley 32 C1
Locking 42 D2
Lockinge 46 A2
Lockington
E Yorks 150 C2
Leics 114 C2
Lockleywood 111 C5
Locks Heath 18 A4
Lockton 160 B2
Lockwood 139 B4
Loddington
Leics 99 A4
Northants 99 D5
Loddiswell 7 C6
Loddon 105 B4
Lode 86 A1
Loders 15 B4
Lodsworth 34 D2

Lofthouse
N Yorks 157 D5
W Yorks 139 A6
Loftus 169 D5
Logan 193 C5
Loganlea 208 D2
Logan Mains 170 C2
Loggerheads 111 B6
Logie
Angus 233 B4
Fife 220 B4
Moray 253 A6
Logiealmond
Lodge 219 A4
Logie Coldstone 244 B1
Logie Hill. 264 C3
Logie Newton 256 C1
Logie Pert 233 B4
Logierait 230 C3
Login 73 D4
Lolworth 85 A5
Lonbain 248 A3
Londesborough 150 C1
London Colney 68 C1
Londonderry 157 C7
Londonthorpe 116 B2
Londubh 261 B5
Lonemore 264 B3
Long Ashton 43 B4
Longbar 204 C3
Long Bennington 115 A6
Longbenton 179 C4
Longborough 64 A2
Long Bredy 15 B5
Longbridge
Warks 81 A5
W Mid 96 D3
Longbridge
Deverill 30 A2
Long Buckby. 82 A3
Longburton. 29 D6
Long Clawson 115 C5
Longcliffe 130 D2
Long Common 32 D4
Long Compton
Staffs 112 C2
Warks 81 D5
Longcot 64 D3
Long Crendon 66 C1
Long Crichel 30 D3
Longcroft 207 C5
Longden 94 A2
Long Ditton 49 C4
Longdon
Staffs 113 D4
Worcs 79 D6
Longdon Green 113 D4
Longdon on Tern 111 D5
Longdown 12 B3
Longdowns 4 D2
Long Drax 141 A4
Long Duckmanton . .131 B4
Long Eaton 114 B2
Longfield
Kent 50 C3
Shetland 285 M5
Longford
Derbys 113 B6
Glos 63 A4
London 48 B3
Shrops 111 B5
Telford 111 D6
W Mid 97 C6
Longfordlane 113 B6
Longforgan 220 B3
Longformacus 197 A5
Longframlington. 189 C4
Long Green 79 D6
Longham
Dorset 17 B4
Norf 119 D6
Long Hanborough. . . .65 B5
Longhaven 257 C6
Longhill 269 D4
Longhirst. 179 A4
Longhope
Glos 62 B2
Orkney 283 H4
Longhorsley 189 D4
Longhoughton 189 B5
Long Itchington 81 A7
Longlane
Derbys 113 B6
W Berks 46 B2
Long Lawford 98 D1
Longlevens 63 A4
Longley 139 C4
Longley Green 79 B5
Long Load 29 C4
Longmanhill 268 C2

Long Marston
Herts 66 B3
N Yorks 148 B4
Warks 81 C4
Long Marton 165 C4
Long Melford 87 C4
Longmoor Camp 33 B6
Longmorn 266 D3
Long Newton 63 D5
Longnewton
Borders 187 A4
Stockton 167 D6
Long Newton 210 D2
Longney 62 B3
Longniddry 210 C1
Longnor
Shrops 94 A2
Staffs 129 C5
Longparish 32 A3
Longport 112 A2
Long Preston 146 B2
Longridge
Lancs 145 D6
Staffs 112 D3
W Loth 208 D2
Longriggend 207 C6
Long Riston 151 C4
Longsdon 129 D4
Longshaw 136 C4
Longside 257 B5
Long Sight 138 C2
Longstanton 85 A5
Longstock 32 B2
Longstone 56 B1
Longstowe 85 B5
Long Stratton 104 B2
Long Street 83 C4
Long Sutton
Hants 33 A6
Lincs 118 C1
Som. 29 C4
Longthorpe 100 B3
Long Thurlow 87 A6
Longthwaite 164 C2
Longton
Lancs 136 A3
Stoke 112 A3
Longtown
Cumb 175 B6
Hereford 61 A5
Longview. 136 D3
Longville in the Dale 94 B3
Long Whatton 114 C2
Longwick 66 C2
Long Wittenham 65 D6
Longwitton. 178 A2
Longwood 95 A4
Longworth 65 D4
Longyester 210 D2
Lonmay 269 D5
Lonmore 258 D2
Looe 6 B1
Loose 37 A5
Loosley Row 66 C3
Lopcombe Corner . . .31 B6
Lopen 28 D4
Loppington 110 C3
Lopwell 6 A3
Lorbottle 188 C3
Lorbottle Hall. 188 C3
Lornty 231 D5
Loscoe 114 A2
Losgaintir 287 E5
Lossiemouth 266 B3
Lossit 200 C1
Lostford 111 B5
Lostock Gralam 128 B1
Lostock Green 128 B1
Lostock Hall 136 A4
Lostock Junction . . .137 C5
Lostwithiel 5 B6
Loth 282 D7
Lothbeg 274 C3
Lothersdale 146 C3
Lothmore 274 C3
Loudwater 67 D4
Loughborough 114 D3
Loughor 57 C5
Loughton
Essex 68 D4
M Keynes 83 D5
Shrops 95 C4
Lound
Lincs 116 D3
Notts 132 A1
Suff. 105 B6
Lount 114 D1
Louth 134 A3
Love Clough 137 A7
Lovedean. 33 D5

Lover 31 C5
Loversall 140 D3
Loves Green 69 C6
Lovesome Hill 158 B2
Loveston 55 D6
Lovington 29 B5
Low Ackworth 140 B2
Low Barlings 133 B5
Low Bentham 145 A6
Low Bradfield 139 D5
Low Bradley 147 C4
Low Braithwaite 164 A2
Lowbridge House 154 A4
Low Brunton 177 B7
Low Burnham 141 C5
Low Burton 157 C6
Low Buston 189 C5
Lowca. 162 B2
Low Catton 149 B6
Low Clanyard 170 D3
Low Coniscliffe 167 D5
Low Crosby 176 D2
Low Dalby 160 C2
Low Dinsdale 167 D6
Lowdham 115 A4
Lowe. 111 B4
Lowe Hill 129 D4
Low Ellington 157 C6
Lower Aisholt. 28 B2
Lower Arncott 65 B7
Lower Ashton 12 C3
Lower Assendon 47 A5
Lower Badcall 276 D2
Lower Bartle 145 D4
Lower Basildon 47 B4
Lower Beeding 35 D5
Lower Benefield 100 C1
Lower Boddington . .82 B1
Lower Brailes 81 D6
Lower Breakish 247 B5
Lower Broadheath . .79 B6
Lower Bullingham . .78 D3
Lower Cam 62 C3
Lower Chapel 76 D4
Lower Chute 45 D7
Lower Cragabus 200 D3
Lower Crossings 129 A5
Lower
Cumberworth 139 C5
Lower Darwen 137 A5
Lower Dean 84 A2
Lower Diabaig 261 D4
Lower Dicker 22 A3
Lower Dinchope 94 C2
Lower Down 94 C1
Lower Drift 2 C2
Lower Dunsforth 148 A3
Lower Egleton 79 C4
Lower Elkstone 129 D5
Lower End. 67 A4
Lower Everleigh 45 D5
Lower Farringdon . . .33 B6
Lower Foxdale 152 D2
Lower Frankton 110 B2
Lower Froyle 33 A6
Lower Gledfield 264 A1
Lower Green 120 B1
Lower Hacheston 88 B4
Lower Halistra 258 C2
Lower Halstow 51 C5
Lower Hardres 52 D3
Lower Hawthwaite . .153 B3
Lower Heath. 128 C3
Lower Hempriggs . .266 C2
Lower Hergest 77 B6
Lower Heyford 65 A5
Lower Higham 51 B4
Lower Holbrook. 88 D2
Lower Hordley 110 C2
Lower Horsebridge . .22 A3
Lower Killeyan 200 D2
Lower Kingswood . . .35 A5
Lower Kinnerton 126 C3
Lower Langford 42 C3
Lower Largo 220 D4
Lower Leigh 112 B4
Lower Lemington 81 D5
Lower Lenie 251 D7
Lower Lydbrook 62 B1
Lower Lye 78 A2
Lower Machen 42 A1
Lower Maes-coed. . .78 D1
Lower Mayland 70 C3
Lower Midway 113 C7
Lower Milovaig 258 C1
Lower Moor 80 C2
Lower Nazeing 68 C3
Lower Netchwood. . .95 B4
Lower Ollach 247 A4
Lower Penarth 41 D6

Low–Mar 319

Lower Penn 95 B6
Lower Pennington 18 B2
Lower Peover 128 B2
Lower Pexhill 128 B3
Lower Place 138 B2
Lower Quinton 81 C4
Lower Rochford 79 A4
Lower Seagry 44 A3
Lower Shelton 84 C1
Lower Shiplake 47 B5
Lower Shuckburgh 82 A1
Lower Slaughter 64 A2
Lower Stanton St Quintin 44 A3
Lower Stoke 51 B5
Lower Stondon 84 D3
Lower Stow Bedon 103 B5
Lower Street
Norf 121 B4
Norf 121 D5
Lower Strensham 80 C2
Lower Stretton 127 A6
Lower Sundon 67 A5
Lower Swanwick 18 A3
Lower Swell 64 A2
Lower Tean 112 B4
Lower Thurlton 105 B5
Lower Tote 259 B5
Lower Town 72 C2
Lower Tysoe 81 C6
Lower Upham 32 D4
Lower Vexford 27 B6
Lower Weare 42 D3
Lower Welson 77 B6
Lower Whitley 127 B6
Lower Wield 33 A5
Lower Winchendon 66 B2
Lower Withington 128 C3
Lower Woodend 47 A6
Lower Woodford 31 B5
Lower Wyche 79 C5
Lowesby 99 A4
Lowestoft 105 B6
Loweswater 163 B4
Low Etherley 167 C4
Low Fell 179 D4
Lowford 32 D3
Low Fulney 117 C5
Low Garth 159 A6
Low Gate 177 C7
Lowgill
Cumb 155 B5
Lancs 145 A6
Low Grantley 157 D6
Low Habberley 95 D6
Low Ham 28 C4
Low Hesket 164 A2
Low Hesleyhurst 188 D3
Low Hutton 149 A6
Lowick
Northants 100 C1
Northumb 198 C4
Lowick Bridge 154 C1
Lowick Green 154 C1
Low Laithe 147 A5
Lowlands 61 D4
Low Leighton 129 A5
Low Lorton 163 B4
Low Marishes 159 D7
Low Marnham 132 C3
Low Mill 159 B5
Low Moor
Lancs 146 C1
W Yorks 139 A4
Lowmoor Row 165 C4
Low Moorsley 167 A6
Low Newton 154 C3
Low Newton-by-the-Sea 189 A5
Lownie Moor 232 D2
Low Row
Cumb 163 A6
Cumb 176 C3
N Yorks 156 B3
Low Salchrie 170 A2
Low Smerby 190 C3
Lowsonford 81 A4
Lowther 164 C3
Lowthorpe 150 A3
Lowton 137 D5
Lowton Common 137 D5
Low Torry 208 B3
Low Worsall 158 A2
Low Wray 154 A2
Loxbeare 27 D4
Loxhill 34 C3
Loxhore 25 B7
Loxley 81 B5
Loxton 42 D2
Loxwood 34 C3
Lubcroy 271 D6
Lubenham 99 C4
Luccombe 27 A4
Luccombe Village 19 D4
Lucker 199 C5
Luckett 11 D4
Luckington 44 A2
Lucklawhill 220 B4
Luckwell Bridge 27 B4
Lucton 78 A2
Ludag 286 E3
Ludborough 143 D4
Ludchurch 56 A1
Luddenden 138 A3
Luddenden Foot 138 A3
Luddesdown 50 C3
Luddington
N Lincs 141 B6
Warks 81 B4
Luddington in the Brook 100 C3
Lude House 230 B2
Ludford
Lincs 134 A2
Shrops 94 D3
Ludgershall
Bucks 66 B1
Wilts 45 D6
Ludgvan 2 B3
Ludham 121 D5
Ludlow 94 D3
Ludwell 30 C3
Ludworth 167 A6
Luffincott 10 B4
Lugar 193 C5
Luggate Burn 210 C3
Lugg Green 78 A2
Luggiebank 207 C5
Lugton 205 C4
Lugwardine 78 C3
Luib 247 B4
Lulham 78 C2
Lullenden 36 B2
Lullington
Derbys 113 D6
Som 44 D1
Lulsgate Bottom 43 C4
Lulsley 79 B5
Lumb 138 A3
Lumby 148 D3
Lumloch 205 B6
Lumphanan 244 B2
Lumphinnans 209 A4
Lumsdaine 211 D5
Lumsden 255 D5
Lunan 233 C4
Lunanhead 232 C2
Luncarty 219 B5
Lund
E Yorks 150 C2
N Yorks 149 D5
Shetland 284 C7
Lunderton 269 E6
Lundie
Angus 220 A2
Highld 239 A5
Lundin Links 220 D4
Lunga 213 B5
Lunna 284 G6
Lunning 284 G7
Lunnon 57 D5
Lunsford's Cross 23 A5
Lunt 136 C2
Luntley 78 B1
Luppitt 13 A6
Lupset 139 B6
Lupton 155 C4
Lurgashall 34 D2
Lusby 134 C3
Luson 7 C5
Luss 206 A1
Lussagiven 213 D4
Lusta 258 C2
Lustleigh 12 C2
Luston 78 A2
Luthermuir 233 B4
Luthrie 220 C3
Luton
Devon 13 D4
Luton 67 A5
Medway 51 C4
Lutterworth 98 C2
Lutton
Devon 7 B4
Lincs 118 C1
Northants 100 C3
Lutworthy 26 D2
Luxborough 27 B4
Luxulyan 5 B5
Lybster 275 A6
Lydbury North 94 C1
Lydcott 26 B1
Lydd 38 C2
Lydden 39 A4
Lyddington 99 B5
Lydd on Sea 38 C2
Lydeard St Lawrence 27 B6
Lyde Green 47 D5
Lydford 11 C6
Lydford-on-Fosse 29 B5
Lydgate 138 A2
Lydham 94 B1
Lydiard Green 45 A4
Lydiard Millicent 45 A4
Lydiate 136 C2
Lydlinch 30 D1
Lydney 62 C2
Lydstep 55 E6
Lye 96 C2
Lye Green
Bucks 67 C4
E Sus 36 C3
Lyford 65 D4
Lymbridge Green 38 A3
Lyme Regis 14 B3
Lyminge 38 A3
Lymington 18 B2
Lyminster 20 B3
Lymm 128 A1
Lymore 18 B1
Lympne 38 B3
Lympsham 42 D2
Lympstone 13 C4
Lynchat 241 B5
Lyndale House 258 C3
Lyndhurst 18 A2
Lyndon 99 A6
Lyne 48 C3
Lyneal 110 B3
Lyne Down 79 D4
Lyneham
Oxon 64 A3
Wilts 44 B4
Lynemore 253 D6
Lynemouth 189 D5
Lyne of Gorthleck 252 D1
Lyne of Skene 245 A4
Lyness 283 H4
Lyng
Norf 120 D2
Som 28 C3
Lynmouth 26 A2
Lynsted 51 C6
Lynton 26 A2
Lyon's Gate 15 A6
Lyonshall 78 B1
Lytchett Matravers 16 B3
Lytchett Minster 16 B3
Lyth 281 B4
Lytham 136 A2
Lytham St Anne's 136 A2
Lythe 169 D6
Lythes 283 J5

M

Mabe Burnthouse 4 D2
Mabie 174 A2
Mablethorpe 135 A5
Macclesfield 129 B4
Macclesfield Forest 129 B4
Macduff 268 C2
Mace Green 88 C2
Macharioch 190 E3
Machen 41 C7
Machrihanish 190 C2
Machynlleth 91 B5
Machynys 57 C5
Mackerel's Common 34 D3
Mackworth 113 B7
Macmerry 210 C1
Madderty 219 B4
Maddiston 208 C2
Madehurst 20 A2
Madeley
Staffs 111 A6
Telford 95 A4
Madeley Heath 112 A1
Madeley Park 112 A1
Madingley 85 A5
Madley 78 D2
Madresfield 79 C6
Madron 2 B2
Maenaddwyn 123 B4
Maenclochog 55 B6
Maendy 41 D5
Maentwrog 107 B6
Maen-y-groes 73 A6
Maer 112 B1
Maerdy
Conwy 109 A5
Rhondda 41 B4
Maesbrook 110 C1
Maesbury 110 C2
Maesbury Marsh 110 C2
Maesgwyn-Isaf 109 D6
Maesgwynne 73 D5
Maeshafn 126 C2
Maesllyn 73 B6
Maesmynis 76 C4
Maesteg 40 B3
Maestir 75 D4
Maes-Treylow 77 A6
Maesybont 57 A5
Maesycrugiau 58 A1
Maesy cwmmer 41 B6
Maesymeillion 73 B7
Magdalen Laver 69 C5
Maggieknockater 254 B4
Magham Down 22 A4
Maghull 136 C2
Magor 42 A3
Magpie Green 104 D1
Maiden Bradley 30 B2
Maidencombe 8 A3
Maidenhall 88 C2
Maidenhead 48 A1
Maiden Law 167 A4
Maiden Newton 15 B5
Maidens 192 E2
Maidensgrave 88 C3
Maiden's Green 48 B1
Maidenwell
Corn 10 D2
Lincs 134 B3
Maiden Wells 55 E5
Maidford 82 B3
Maids Moreton 83 D4
Maidstone 37 A5
Maidwell 99 D4
Mail 285 L6
Main 109 D6
Maindee 42 A2
Mainsforth 167 B6
Mains of Airies 170 A1
Mains of Allardice 233 A6
Mains of Annochie 257 B4
Mains of Ardestie 221 A5
Mains of Balhall 232 B3
Mains of Ballindarg 232 C2
Mains of Balnakettle 233 A4
Mains of Birness 257 C4
Mains of Burgie 266 D1
Mains of Clunas 253 B4
Mains of Crichie 257 B4
Mains of Dalvey 254 C2
Mains of Dellavaird 245 D4
Mains of Drum 245 C5
Mains of Edingight 267 D6
Mains of Fedderate 268 E3
Mains of Inkhorn 257 C4
Mains of Mayen 255 B6
Mains of Melgund 232 C3
Mains of Thornton 233 A4
Mains of Watten 281 C4
Mainsriddle 174 C2
Mainstone 93 C6
Maisemore 63 A4
Malacleit 287 G2
Malborough 7 D6
Malcoff 129 A5
Maldon 70 C2
Malham 146 A3
Maligar 259 B4
Mallaig 235 A5
Malleny Mills 209 D4
Malling 217 D5
Malltraeth 123 D4
Mallwyd 91 A6
Malmesbury 44 A3
Malmsmead 26 A2
Malpas
Ches W 110 A3
Corn 4 C3
Newport 61 D5
Malswick 62 A3
Maltby
Stockton 168 D2
S Yorks 140 D3
Maltby le Marsh 135 A4
Malting Green 70 A3
Maltman's Hill 37 B7
Malton 159 D6
Malvern Link 79 C5
Malvern Wells 79 C5
Mamble 95 D4
Manaccan 3 C5
Manafon 93 A5
Manar House 256 D2
Manaton 12 C2
Manby 134 A3
Mancetter 97 B6
Manchester 138 D1
Manchester Airport 128 A3
Mancot 126 C3
Mandally 239 B6
Manea 101 C6
Manfield 167 D5
Mangaster 284 F5
Mangotsfield 43 B5
Mangurstadh 287 A5
Mankinholes 138 A2
Manley 127 B5
Manmoel 41 A6
Mannal 222 C2
Mannerston 208 C3
Manningford Bohune 45 D5
Manningford Bruce 45 D5
Manningham 147 D5
Mannings Heath 35 D5
Mannington 17 A4
Manningtree 88 D1
Mannofield 245 B6
Manor 50 A1
Manorbier 55 E6
Manordeilo 58 C3
Manor Estate 130 A3
Manorhill 197 C5
Manorowen 72 C2
Manselfield 57 D5
Mansel Lacy 78 C2
Mansell Gamage 78 C1
Mansergh 155 C5
Mansfield
E Ayrs 182 A4
Notts 131 C5
Mansfield Woodhouse 131 C5
Mansriggs 154 C1
Manston
Dorset 30 D2
Kent 53 C5
W Yorks 148 D2
Manswood 16 A3
Manthorpe
Lincs 116 B2
Lincs 116 D3
Manton
N Lincs 142 C1
Notts 131 B5
Rutland 99 A5
Wilts 45 C5
Manuden 69 A4
Maperton 29 C6
Maplebeck 132 C2
Maple Cross 67 D5
Mapledurham 47 B4
Mapledurwell 47 D4
Maplehurst 35 D4
Maplescombe 50 C2
Mapleton 113 A5
Mapperley 114 A2
Mapperley Park 114 A3
Mapperton 15 B5
Mappleborough Green 80 A3
Mappleton 151 C5
Mappowder 16 A1
Maraig 288 G2
Marazanvose 4 B3
Marazion 2 B3
Marbhig 288 F5
Marbury 111 A4
March
Cambs 101 B6
S Lanark 184 A2
Marcham 65 D5
Marchamley 111 C4
Marchington 113 B5
Marchington Woodlands 113 C5
Marchroes 106 D3
Marchwiel 110 A2
Marchwood 32 D2
Marcross 40 E4
Marden
Hereford 78 C3
Kent 37 B5
T&W 179 B5
Wilts 45 D4
Marden Beech 37 B5
Marden Thorn 37 B5
Mardy 61 B5
Marefield 99 A4
Mareham le Fen 134 C2
Mareham on the Hill 134 C2
Marehay 114 A1
Marehill 20 A3
Maresfield 36 D2
Marfleet 142 A3
Marford 126 D3
Margam 40 C2
Margaret Marsh 30 D2
Margaret Roding 69 B5
Margaretting 69 C6
Margate 53 B5
Margnaheglish 191 B6
Margrove Park 169 D4
Marham 119 D4
Marhamchurch 10 A3
Marholm 100 A3
Mariandyrys 123 B6
Marianglas 123 B5
Mariansleigh 26 C2
Marionburgh 245 B4
Marishader 259 B4
Marjoriebanks 184 D3
Mark
Dumfries 170 B3
S Ayrs 180 D2
Som 28 A3
Markbeech 36 B2
Markby 135 B4
Mark Causeway 28 A3
Mark Cross
E Sus 22 A2
E Sus 36 C3
Market Bosworth 97 A7
Market Deeping 116 E4
Market Drayton 111 B5
Market Harborough 99 C4
Markethill 220 A2
Market Lavington 44 D4
Market Overton 116 D1
Market Rasen 133 A6
Market Stainton 134 B2
Market Warsop 131 C5
Market Weighton 150 C1
Market Weston 103 D5
Markfield 114 D2
Markham 41 A6
Markham Moor 132 B2
Markinch 220 D2
Markington 148 A1
Marksbury 43 C5
Marks Tey 70 A3
Markyate 67 B5
Marland 138 B1
Marlborough 45 C5
Marlbrook
Hereford 78 B3
Worcs 96 D2
Marlcliff 80 B3
Marldon 8 A2
Marlesford 88 B4
Marley Green 111 A4
Marley Hill 179 D4
Marley Mount 17 B6
Marlingford 104 A2
Mar Lodge 242 C3
Marloes 54 D3
Marlow
Bucks 47 A6
Hereford 94 D2
Marlow Bottom 47 A6
Marlpit Hill 36 B2
Marlpool 114 A2
Marnhull 30 D1
Marnoch 267 D6
Marnock 207 D5
Marple 129 A4
Marple Bridge 129 A4
Marr 140 C3
Marrel 274 C4
Marrick 157 B4
Marrister 285 G7
Marros 56 B2
Marsden
T&W 179 C5
W Yorks 138 B3
Marsett 156 C3
Marsh
Devon 28 D2
W Yorks 147 D4
Marshall's Heath 67 B6
Marshalsea 14 A3
Marshalswick 67 C6
Marsham 120 C3
Marshaw 145 B5

Marsh Baldon 65 D6
Marshborough 53 D5
Marshbrook 94 C2
Marshchapel 143 D5
Marshfield
  Newport 42 A1
  S Glos 44 B1
Marshgate 10 B2
Marsh Gibbon 66 A1
Marsh Green
  Devon 13 B5
  Kent 36 B2
  Staffs 128 D3
Marshland
  St James 101 A7
Marsh Lane 131 B4
Marshside 136 B2
Marsh Street 27 A4
Marshwood 14 B3
Marske 157 A5
Marske-by-the-
  Sea 168 C4
Marston
  Ches W 127 B6
  Hereford 78 B1
  Lincs 116 A1
  Oxon 65 C6
  Staffs 112 C3
  Staffs 112 D2
  Warks 97 B5
  Wilts 44 D3
Marston Doles 82 B1
Marston Green 97 C4
Marston Magna 29 C5
Marston Meysey 64 D2
Marston
  Montgomery 113 B5
Marston Moretaine . . 84 C1
Marston on Dove . . . 113 C6
Marston
  St Lawrence 82 C2
Marston Stannett 78 B3
Marston Trussell 98 C3
Marstow 62 B1
Marsworth 67 B4
Marten 45 D6
Marthall 128 B3
Martham 121 D6
Martin
  Hants 31 D4
  Kent 39 A5
  Lincs 133 D6
  Lincs 134 C2
Martin Dales 134 C1
Martin Drove End . . . 31 C4
Martinhoe 26 A1
Martinhoe Cross 26 A1
Martin Hussingtree . . 80 A1
Martin Mill 39 A5
Martinscroft 127 A6
Martinstown 15 C6
Martlesham 88 C3
Martlesham Heath . . 88 C3
Martletwy 55 C6
Martley 79 A5
Martock 29 D4
Marton
  Ches E 128 C3
  E Yorks 151 B4
  Lincs 132 A3
  Mbro 168 D3
  N Yorks 148 A3
  N Yorks 159 C6
  Shrops 93 A6
  Shrops 110 C3
  Warks 81 A7
Marton-le-Moor 158 D2
Martyr's Green 34 A3
Martyr Worthy 32 B4
Marwick 282 E3
Marwood 25 B6
Marybank 251 A6
Maryburgh 252 A1
Maryhill 205 B5
Marykirk 233 B4
Marylebone 137 C4
Marypark 254 C2
Maryport
  Cumb 162 A3
  Dumfries 170 D3
Mary Tavy 11 D6
Maryton 233 C4
Marywell
  Aberds 244 C2
  Aberds 245 C6
  Angus 233 D4
Masham 157 C6
Mashbury 69 B6

Masongill 155 D5
Masonhill 192 C3
Mastin Moor 131 B4
Mastrick 245 B5
Matching 69 B5
Matching Green 69 B5
Matching Tye 69 B5
Matfen 178 B2
Matfield 37 B4
Mathern 62 D1
Mathon 79 C5
Mathry 55 A4
Matlaske 120 B3
Matlock 130 C2
Matlock Bath 130 D2
Matson 63 B4
Matterdale End 164 C1
Mattersey 132 A1
Mattersey Thorpe . . 132 A1
Mattingley 47 D5
Mattishall 120 D2
Mattishall Burgh 120 D2
Mauchline 193 C4
Maud 257 B4
Maugersbury 64 A3
Maughold 152 B4
Mauld 251 C6
Maulden 84 D2
Maulds Meaburn . . . 165 D4
Maunby 158 C2
Maund Bryan 78 B3
Maundown 27 C5
Mautby 121 D6
Mavis Enderby 134 C3
Mawbray 174 D3
Mawdesley 136 B3
Mawdlam 40 C3
Mawgan 3 C5
Maw Green 128 D2
Mawla 4 C2
Mawnan 3 C5
Mawnan Smith 3 C5
Mawsley 99 D5
Maxey 100 A3
Maxstoke 97 C5
Maxton
  Borders 197 C5
  Kent 39 A5
Maxwellheugh 197 C6
Maxwelltown 174 A2
Maxworthy 10 B3
Mayals 57 C6
May Bank 112 A2
Maybole 192 E3
Mayfield
  E Sus 36 D3
  Midloth 209 D6
  Staffs 113 A5
  W Loth 208 D2
Mayford 34 A2
Mayland 70 C3
Maynard's Green . . . 22 A3
Maypole
  Mon 61 B6
  Scilly 2 E4
Maypole Green
  Essex 70 A3
  Norf 105 B4
  Suff 88 A3
Maywick 285 L5
Meadle 66 C3
Meadowtown 93 A7
Meaford 112 B2
Mealabost 288 D5
Mealabost Bhuirgh . . 288 B5
Meal Bank 154 B4
Mealsgate 175 D5
Meanwood 148 D1
Mearbeck 146 A2
Meare 29 A4
Meare Green 28 C3
Mears Ashby 83 A5
Measham 114 D1
Meath Green 35 B5
Meathop 154 C3
Meaux 150 D3
Meavy 7 A4
Medbourne 99 B4
Medburn 178 B3
Meddon 24 D3
Meden Vale 131 C5
Medlam 134 D3
Medmenham 47 A6
Medomsley 178 D3
Medstead 33 B5
Meerbrook 129 C4
Meer End 97 D5
Meers Bridge 135 A4
Meesden 85 D6
Meeth 11 A6

Meggethead 195 D6
Meidrim 73 D5
Meifod
  Denb 125 D5
  Powys 109 D6
Meigle
  N Ayrs 204 B1
  Perth 231 D6
Meikle Earnock 194 A2
Meikle Ferry 264 B3
Meikle Forter 231 B5
Meikle Gluich 264 B2
Meikleour 219 A6
Meikle Pinkerton . . . 211 C4
Meikle Strath 233 A4
Meikle Tarty 257 D4
Meikle Wartle 256 C2
Meinciau 57 A4
Meir 112 A3
Meir Heath 112 A3
Melbourn 85 C5
Melbourne
  Derbys 114 C1
  E Yorks 149 C6
  S Lanark 195 B5
Melbury Abbas 30 C2
Melbury Bubb 15 A5
Melbury Osmond . . . 15 A5
Melbury Sampford . . 15 A5
Melby 285 H3
Melchbourne 84 A2
Melcombe Bingham . 16 A1
Melcombe Regis 15 C6
Meldon
  Devon 11 B6
  Northumb 178 A3
Meldreth 85 C5
Meldrum House 256 D3
Melfort 213 A6
Melgarve 240 C2
Meliden 125 A5
Melinbyrhedyn 91 C6
Melincourt 40 A3
Melin-y-coed 124 C3
Melin-y-ddôl 93 A4
Melin-y-grug 93 A4
Melin-y-Wig 109 A5
Melkinthorpe 164 C3
Melkridge 177 C5
Melksham 44 C3
Melldalloch 203 A4
Melling
  Lancs 155 D4
  Mers 136 C2
Melling Mount 136 C3
Mellis 104 D2
Mellon Charles 261 A5
Mellon Udrigle 261 A5
Mellor
  Gtr Man 129 A4
  Lancs 145 D6
Mellor Brook 145 D6
Mells 30 A1
Melmerby
  Cumb 165 B4
  N Yorks 157 C4
  N Yorks 158 D2
Melplash 15 B4
Melrose 197 C4
Melsetter 283 J3
Melsonby 157 A5
Meltham 138 B4
Melton 88 B3
Meltonby 149 B6
Melton Constable . . . 120 B2
Melton Mowbray . . . 115 D5
Melton Ross 142 B2
Melvaig 261 B4
Melverley 110 D2
Melverley Green 110 D2
Melvich 279 B4
Membury 14 A2
Memsie 269 C4
Memus 232 C2
Menabilly 5 B5
Menai Bridge
  = Porthaethwy 123 C5
Mendham 104 C3
Mendlesham 88 A2
Mendlesham Green . 88 A1
Menheniot 6 A1
Mennock 183 B6
Menston 147 C5
Menstrie 207 A6
Menthorpe 149 D5
Mentmore 67 B4
Meoble 238 D1
Meole Brace 110 D3
Meols 136 D1
Meonstoke 33 D5

Meopham 50 C3
Meopham Station . . . 50 C3
Mepal 101 C6
Meppershall 84 D3
Merbach 77 C7
Mere
  Ches E 128 A2
  Wilts 30 B2
Mere Brow 136 B3
Mereclough 146 D2
Mere Green 96 B4
Mereside 144 D3
Mereworth 37 A4
Mergie 245 D4
Meriden 97 C5
Merkadale 246 A2
Merkland
  Dumfries 173 A5
  S Ayrs 181 B4
Merkland Lodge . . . 271 B7
Merley 17 B4
Merlin's Bridge 55 C5
Merrington 110 C3
Merrion 55 E5
Merriott 28 D4
Merrivale 11 D6
Merrow 34 A3
Merrymeet 6 A1
Mersham 38 B2
Merstham 35 A5
Merston 20 B1
Merstone 18 C4
Merther 4 C3
Merthyr 73 D6
Merthyr Cynog 76 D3
Merthyr-Dyfan 41 E6
Merthyr Mawr 40 D3
Merthyr Tudful
  = Merthyr Tydfil 60 C2
Merthyr Tydfil
  = Merthyr Tudful 60 C2
Merthyr Vale 41 B5
Merton
  Devon 25 D6
  London 49 B5
  Norf 103 B5
  Oxon 65 B6
Mervinslaw 187 B5
Meshaw 26 D2
Messing 70 B2
Messingham 141 C6
Metfield 104 C3
Metheringham 133 C5
Methil 209 A6
Methlem 106 C1
Methley 140 A1
Methlick 256 C3
Methven 219 B5
Methwold 102 B3
Methwold Hythe . . . 102 B3
Mettingham 105 C4
Mevagissey 5 C5
Mewith Head 145 A7
Mexborough 140 C2
Mey 281 A4
Meysey Hampton . . . 64 D2
Miabhag
  W Isles 287 D5
  W Isles 288 H2
Miabhig 287 A5
Michaelchurch 61 A7
Michaelchurch
  Escley 77 D7
Michaelchurch on
  Arrow 77 B6
Michaelston-le-Pit . 41 D6
Michaelston-y-
  Fedw 42 A1
Michaelstow 10 D1
Michealston-super-
  Ely 41 D6
Micheldever 32 B4
Michelmersh 32 C2
Mickfield 88 A2
Micklebring 140 D3
Mickleby 169 D6
Mickleham 35 A4
Mickleover 113 B7
Micklethwaite 147 C5
Mickleton
  Durham 166 C2
  Glos 81 C4
Mickletown 140 A1
Mickle Trafford 127 C4
Mickley 157 D6
Mickley Square 178 C2
Mid Ardlaw 269 C4
Mid Auchinleck 204 A3
Midbea 282 C5
Mid Beltie 244 B3

Mid Calder 208 D3
Mid Cloch Forbie . . 268 D2
Mid Clyth 275 A6
Middle Assendon . . . 47 A5
Middle Aston 65 A5
Middle Barton 65 A5
Middlebie 175 A5
Middle Cairncake . . 256 B3
Middle Claydon 66 A2
Middle Drums 232 C3
Middleforth Green . . 136 A4
Middleham 157 C5
Middle Handley 131 B4
Middlehope 94 C2
Middle Littleton 80 C3
Middle Maes-coed . . 78 D1
Middlemarsh 15 A6
Middle Mill 54 B4
Middlemuir 257 D4
Middle Rasen 133 A5
Middle Rigg 219 D5
Middlesbrough 168 C2
Middleshaw
  Cumb 155 C4
  Dumfries 174 A4
Middlesmoor 157 D4
Middlestone 167 B5
Middlestone Moor . . 167 B5
Middlestown 139 B5
Middlethird 197 B5
Middleton
  Aberds 245 A5
  Argyll 222 C2
  Cumb 155 C5
  Derbys 130 C1
  Derbys 130 D2
  Essex 87 D4
  Gtr Man 138 C1
  Hants 32 A3
  Hereford 78 A3
  Lancs 144 B4
  Midloth 196 A2
  Norf 118 D3
  Northants 99 C5
  Northumb 178 A5
  Northumb 199 C5
  N Yorks 147 C5
  N Yorks 159 C6
  Perth 219 D6
  Perth 231 D5
  Shrops 93 B6
  Shrops 94 D3
  Shrops 110 C2
  Suff 89 A5
  Swansea 57 D4
  Warks 97 B4
  W Yorks 139 A5
Middleton Cheney . . 82 C1
Middleton Green . . . 112 B3
Middleton Hall 188 A2
Middleton-in-
  Teesdale 166 C2
Middleton Moor 89 A5
Middleton One
  Row 167 D6
Middleton-on-
  Leven 158 A3
Middleton-on-Sea . . 20 B2
Middleton on the
  Hill 78 A3
Middleton-on-the-
  Wolds 150 C2
Middleton Priors . . . 95 B4
Middleton
  Quernham 158 D2
Middleton
  St George 167 D6
Middleton Scriven . . 95 C4
Middleton Stoney . . 65 A6
Middleton Tyas 157 A6
Middletown
  Cumb 162 D2
  Powys 110 D2
Middle Tysoe 81 C6
Middle Wallop 32 B1
Middlewich 128 C1
Middle Winterslow . . 31 B6
Middle Woodford . . . 31 B5
Middlewood Green . . 88 A1
Middlezoy 28 B3
Middridge 167 C5
Midfield 277 B6
Midge Hall 136 A4
Midgeholme 176 D4
Midgham 46 C3
Midgley
  W Yorks 138 A3
  W Yorks 139 B5
Midhopestones 139 D5
Midhurst 34 D1

Mid Lavant 20 B1
Midlem 186 A4
Mid Main 251 C6
Midmar 244 B3
Midsomer Norton . . . 43 D5
Midton 204 A2
Midtown
  Highld 261 B5
  Highld 277 B6
Midtown of
  Buchromb 254 B4
Mid Urchany 253 B4
Midville 134 D3
Mid Walls 285 H4
Midway 129 A4
Mid Yell 284 D7
Migdale 264 A3
Migvie 244 B1
Milarrochy 206 A2
Milborne Port 29 D6
Milborne St Andrew . 16 B1
Milborne Wick 29 C6
Milbourne 178 B3
Milburn 165 C4
Milbury Heath 62 D2
Milcombe 81 D7
Milden 87 C5
Mildenhall
  Suff 102 D3
  Wilts 45 C6
Milebrook 93 D7
Milebush 37 B5
Mile Cross 120 D4
Mile Elm 44 C3
Mile End
  Essex 70 A3
  Glos 62 B1
Mileham 119 D6
Mile Oak 21 B5
Milesmark 208 B3
Milfield 198 C3
Milford
  Derbys 114 A1
  Devon 24 C3
  Powys 93 B4
  Staffs 112 C3
  Sur 34 B2
  Wilts 31 C5
Milford Haven
  = Aberdaugleddau . . 55 D5
Milford on Sea 18 B1
Milkwall 62 C1
Milkwell 30 C3
Milland 34 D1
Millarston 205 B4
Millbank
  Aberds 257 B6
  Highld 280 B3
Mill Bank 138 A3
Millbeck 163 B5
Millbounds 282 D6
Millbreck 257 B5
Millbridge 34 B1
Millbrook
  C Beds 84 D2
  Corn 6 B3
  Soton 32 D2
Millburn 193 C4
Millcombe 8 C2
Mill Common 105 C5
Millcorner 37 D6
Milldale 129 D6
Millden Lodge 232 A3
Milldens 232 C3
Mill End
  Bucks 47 A5
  Herts 85 D5
Millerhill 209 D6
Miller's Dale 129 B6
Miller's Green 130 D2
Millgreen 111 C5
Mill Green
  Essex 69 C6
  Norf 104 C2
  Suff 87 C5
Millhalf 77 C6
Millhayes 14 A2
Millhead 154 D3
Millheugh 194 A2
Mill Hill 68 D2
Millholme 155 C4
Millhouse
  Argyll 203 A4
  Cumb 163 A6
Millhousebridge . . . 185 D4
Millhouse Green . . . 139 C5
Millhouses 130 A3
Millikenpark 205 B4
Millin Cross 55 C5
Millington 150 B1

Mill Lane 47 D5
Millmeece 112 B2
Mill of Kingoodie . .256 D3
Mill of Muiresk 256 B1
Mill of Sterin 243 C6
Mill of Uras 245 A6
Millom 153 B2
Millook 10 B2
Mill Place 142 C1
Millpool 10 D2
Millport 204 C1
Millquarter 182 D4
Mill Side 154 C3
Mill Street 120 D2
Millthorpe 116 B4
Millthrop 155 B5
Milltimber 245 B5
Milltown
    Corn 5 B6
    Derbys 130 C3
    Devon 25 B6
    Dumfries 175 A6
Milltown of
    Aberdalgie 219 B5
Milltown of
    Auchindoun 255 B4
Milltown of
    Craigston 268 D2
Milltown of
    Edinvillie 254 B3
Milltown of
    Kildrummy 244 A1
Milltown of
    Rothiemay 255 B6
Milltown of Towie . . .244 A1
Milnathort 219 D6
Milner's Heath 127 C4
Milngavie 205 A5
Milnrow 138 B2
Milnshaw 137 A6
Milnthorpe 154 C3
Milo 57 A5
Milson 95 D4
Milstead 37 A7
Milston 31 A5
Milton
    Angus 232 D1
    Cambs 85 A6
    Cumb 176 C3
    Derbys 113 C7
    Dumfries 171 B4
    Dumfries 173 A6
    Dumfries 183 D6
    Highld 251 A5
    Highld 251 C6
    Highld 252 B1
    Highld 264 C3
    Highld 281 C5
    Moray 267 C6
    Notts 132 B2
    N Som 42 C2
    Oxon 65 D5
    Oxon 82 D1
    Pembs 55 D6
    Perth 219 C4
    Ptsmth 19 B5
    Stirling 217 D5
    Stoke 129 D4
    W Dunb 205 A4
Milton Abbas 16 A2
Milton Abbot 11 D5
Milton Bridge 209 D5
Milton Bryan 83 D6
Milton Clevedon . . . 29 B6
Milton Coldwells . .257 C4
Milton Combe 6 A3
Milton Damerel 25 D4
Miltonduff 266 C2
Milton End 64 C2
Milton Ernest 84 B2
Milton Green 127 D4
Miltonhill 266 C1
Milton Hill 65 D5
Miltonise 180 D3
Milton Keynes 83 D5
Milton Keynes
    Village 83 D5
Milton Lilbourne 45 C5
Milton Malsor 83 B4
Milton Morenish 217 A6
Milton of
    Auchinhove 244 B2
Milton of Balgonie .220 D3
Milton of
    Buchanan 206 A2
Milton of
    Campfield 244 B3
Milton of Campsie . .205 A6
Milton of
    Corsindae 244 B3

Milton of Cushnie . .244 A2
Milton of Dalcapon .230 C3
Milton of Edradour .230 C3
Milton of
    Gollanfield 252 A3
Milton of Lesmore . .255 D5
Milton of Logie 244 B1
Milton of Murtle . . .245 B5
Milton of Noth 255 D6
Milton of Tullich . . .243 C6
Milton on Stour 30 C1
Milton Regis 51 C6
Milton under
    Wychwood 64 B3
Milverton
    Som 27 C6
    Warks 81 A6
Milwich 112 B3
Minard 214 C2
Minchinhampton . . . 63 C4
Mindrum 198 C2
Minehead 27 A4
Minera 126 D2
Minety 63 D6
Minffordd
    Gwyn 91 A5
    Gwyn 107 C5
    Gwyn 123 C5
Miningsby 134 C3
Minions 10 D3
Minishant 192 D3
Minllyn 91 A6
Minnes 257 D4
Minngearraidh 286 D3
Minnigaff 171 A6
Minnonie 268 C2
Minskip 148 A2
Minstead 32 D1
Minsted 34 D1
Minster
    Kent 51 B6
    Kent 53 C5
Minsterley 94 A1
Minster Lovell 64 B4
Minsterworth 62 B3
Minterne Magna . . . 15 A6
Minting 134 B3
Mintlaw 257 B5
Minto 187 A4
Minton 94 B2
Minwear 55 C6
Minworth 97 B4
Mirbister 282 E4
Mirehouse 162 C1
Mireland 281 B5
Mirfield 139 B5
Miserden 63 C5
Miskin 41 C5
Misson 141 D4
Misterton
    Leics 98 C2
    Notts 141 D5
    Som 15 A4
Mistley 88 D2
Mitcham 49 C5
Mitcheldean 62 B2
Mitchell 4 B3
Mitchel Troy 61 B6
Mitcheltroy
    Common 61 C6
Mitford 178 A3
Mithian 4 B2
Mitton 112 D2
Mixbury 82 D3
Moat 175 A7
Moats Tye 87 B6
Mobberley
    Ches E 128 B2
    Staffs 112 A4
Moccas 78 C1
Mochdre
    Conwy 124 B3
    Powys 93 C4
Mochrum 171 C5
Mockbeggar 17 A5
Mockerkin 162 B3
Modbury 7 B5
Moddershall 112 B3
Moelfre
    Anglesey 123 B5
    Powys 109 C6
Moffat 184 B3
Moggerhanger 84 C3
Moira 113 D7
Molash 52 D2
Mol-chlach 246 C3
Mold
    = Yr Wyddgrug 126 C2
Moldgreen 139 B4
Molehill Green 69 A5

Molescroft 150 C3
Molesden 178 A3
Molesworth 100 D2
Moll 247 A4
Molland 26 C3
Mollington
    Ches W 126 B3
    Oxon 82 C1
Mollinsburn 207 C5
Monachty 75 B4
Monachylemore . . .217 C4
Monar Lodge 250 B4
Monaughty 77 A6
Monboddo House . .233 A5
Mondynes 233 A5
Monevechadan 215 B4
Monewden 88 B3
Moneydie 219 B5
Moniaive 183 C5
Monifieth 221 A4
Monikie 221 A4
Monimail 220 C2
Monington 72 B4
Monk Bretton 139 C6
Monken Hadley 68 D2
Monk Fryston 140 A3
Monkhopton 95 B4
Monkland 78 B2
Monkleigh 25 C5
Monknash 40 D4
Monkokehampton . . 11 A6
Monkseaton 179 B5
Monks Eleigh 87 C5
Monk's Gate 35 D5
Monks Heath 128 B3
Monk Sherborne . . . 47 D4
Monkshill 256 B2
Monksilver 27 B5
Monks Kirby 98 C1
Monk Soham 88 A3
Monkspath 96 D4
Monks Risborough . . 66 C3
Monk Street 69 A6
Monkswood 61 C5
Monkton
    Devon 14 A1
    Kent 53 C4
    Pembs 55 D5
    S Ayrs 192 C3
Monkton Combe . . . 44 C1
Monkton Deverill . . . 30 B2
Monkton Farleigh . . . 44 C2
Monkton Heathfield . 28 C2
Monkton Up
    Wimborne 31 D4
Monkwearmouth . .179 D5
Monkwood 33 B5
Monmouth
    = Trefynwy 61 B7
Monmouth Cap 61 A6
Monnington on Wye . 78 C1
Monreith 171 C5
Monreith Mains . . .171 C5
Montacute 29 D4
Montcoffer House . .268 C1
Montford
    Argyll 203 B6
    Shrops 110 D3
Montford Bridge . . .110 D3
Montgarrie 244 A2
Montgomery
    = Trefaldwyn 93 B6
Montrave 220 D3
Montrose 233 C5
Mont Saint 6
Montsale 71 D4
Monxton 32 A2
Monyash 129 C6
Monymusk 244 A3
Monzie 218 B3
Monzie Castle 218 B3
Moodiesburn 207 C4
Moonzie 220 C3
Moor Allerton 148 D1
Moorby 134 C2
Moor Crichel 16 A3
Moordown 17 B4
Moore 127 A5
Moorend 62 C3
Moor End
    E Yorks 149 D7
    York 149 B5
Moorends 141 B4
Moorgate 140 D2
Moorgreen 114 A2
Moorhall 130 B3
Moorhampton 78 C1
Moorhead 147 D5
Moorhouse
    Cumb 175 C6

Moorhouse continued
    Notts 132 C2
Moorlinch 28 B3
Moor Monkton 148 B4
Moor of Granary . .253 A6
Moor of
    Ravenstone 171 C5
Moor Row 162 C3
Moorsholm 169 D4
Moorside 138 C2
Moor Street 51 C5
Moorthorpe 140 B2
Moortown
    Hants 17 A5
    IoW 18 C3
    Lincs 142 D2
Morangie 264 B3
Morar 235 A5
Morborne 100 B3
Morchard Bishop . . 12 A2
Morcombelake 14 B4
Morcott 99 A6
Morda 110 C1
Morden
    Dorset 16 B3
    London 49 C5
Mordiford 78 D3
Mordon 167 C6
More 94 B1
Morebath 27 C4
Morebattle 187 A6
Morecambe 144 A4
Morefield 262 A3
Moreleigh 7 B6
Morenish 217 A5
Moresby 162 B2
Moresby Parks 162 C2
Morestead 32 C4
Moreton
    Dorset 16 C2
    Essex 69 C5
    Mers 136 D1
    Oxon 66 C1
    Staffs 112 D1
Moreton Corbet 111 C4
Moretonhampstead . 12 C2
Moreton-in-Marsh . . 81 D5
Moreton Jeffries . . . 79 C4
Moreton Morrell . . . 81 B6
Moreton on Lugg . . 78 C3
Moreton Pinkney . . . 82 C2
Moreton Say 111 B5
Moreton Valence . . . 62 C3
Morfa
    Carms 57 A5
    Carms 57 C5
Morfa Bach 56 A3
Morfa Bychan 107 C5
Morfa Dinlle 107 A4
Morfa Glas 59 E5
Morfa Nefyn 106 B2
Morfydd 109 A6
Morgan's Vale 31 C5
Moriah 75 A5
Morland 164 C3
Morley
    Derbys 114 A1
    Durham 166 C4
    W Yorks 139 A5
Morley Green 128 A3
Morley St Botolph . .104 B1
Morningside
    Edin 209 C5
    N Lanark 194 A3
Morningthorpe 104 B3
Morpeth 179 A4
Morphie 233 B5
Morrey 113 D5
Morris Green 86 D3
Morriston 57 C6
Morston 120 A2
Mortehoe 25 A5
Mortimer 47 C4
Mortimer's Cross . . 78 A2
Mortimer West End . 47 C4
Mortlake 49 B5
Morton
    Cumb 175 C6
    Derbys 131 C4
    Lincs 116 C3
    Lincs 132 C3
    Lincs 141 D6
    Norf 120 D3
    Notts 132 D2
    S Glos 62 D2
    Shrops 110 C1
Morton Bagot 80 A4
Morton-on-Swale . .157 B7
Morvah 2 B2
Morval 6 B1

Morvich
    Highld 249 D6
    Highld 273 D5
Morville 95 B4
Morville Heath 95 B4
Morwenstow 24 D3
Mosborough 131 A4
Mosbrough 205 D4
Mosedale 163 A6
Moseley
    W Mid 96 B2
    W Mid 96 C3
    Worcs 79 B6
Moss
    Argyll 222 C2
    S Yorks 140 B3
    Wrex 126 D3
Mossat 244 A1
Mossbank 284 F6
Moss Bank 136 D4
Mossbay 162 B2
Mossblown 193 C4
Mossbrow 128 A2
Moss Edge 144 C4
Mossend 207 D5
Moss End 47 B6
Mosser 163 B4
Mossfield 264 C2
Mossgiel 193 C4
Mosside 232 C2
Mossley
    Ches E 128 C3
    Gtr Man 138 C2
Mossley Hill 126 A3
Moss of
    Barmuckity 266 C3
Moss Pit 112 C3
Moss-side 253 A4
Moss Side 144 D3
Mosstodloch 266 D4
Mosston 232 D3
Mossy Lea 136 B4
Mosterton 15 A4
Moston
    Gtr Man 138 C1
    Shrops 111 C4
Moston Green 128 C2
Mostyn 125 A6
Mostyn Quay 125 A6
Motcombe 30 C2
Mothecombe 7 C5
Motherby 164 C2
Motherwell 194 A2
Mottingham 49 B7
Mottisfont 32 C2
Mottistone 18 C3
Mottram in
    Longdendale 138 D2
Mottram
    St Andrew 128 B3
Mouilpied 6
Mouldsworth 127 B5
Moulin 230 C3
Moulsecoomb 21 B6
Moulsford 46 A3
Moulsoe 83 C6
Moulton
    Ches W 127 C6
    Lincs 117 C6
    Northants 83 A4
    N Yorks 157 A6
    Suff 86 A2
    V Glam 41 D5
Moulton Chapel 117 D5
Moulton Eaugate . . .117 D6
Moulton St Mary . . .105 A4
Moulton
    Seas End 117 C6
Mounie Castle 256 D2
Mount
    Corn 4 B2
    Corn 5 A6
    Highld 253 B5
Mountain 147 D4
Mountain Ash
    = Aberpennar 41 B5
Mountain Cross . . .195 B6
Mountain Water . . . 55 B5
Mountbenger 196 D2
Mount Bures 87 D5
Mount Canisp 264 C3
Mountfield 37 D5
Mountgerald 264 D1
Mount Hawke 4 C2
Mountjoy 4 A3
Mountnessing 69 D6
Mounton 61 D7

Mount Pleasant
    Ches E 128 D3
    Derbys 113 D6
    Derbys 114 A1
    Flint 126 B2
    Hants 18 B1
    W Yorks 139 A5
Mountsorrel 114 D3
Mount Sorrel 31 C4
Mount Tabor 138 A3
Mousehole 2 C2
Mousen 199 C5
Mouswald 174 A3
Mow Cop 128 D3
Mowhaugh 187 A7
Mowsley 98 C3
Moxley 96 B2
Moy
    Highld 240 D2
    Highld 252 C3
Moy Hall 252 C3
Moy House 265 D6
Moyles Court 17 A5
Moylgrove 72 B4
Moy Lodge 240 D2
Muasdale 202 D1
Muchalls 245 C6
Much Birch 78 D3
Much Cowarne 79 C4
Much Dewchurch . . 78 D2
Muchelney 28 C4
Much Hadham 68 B4
Much Hoole 136 A3
Muchlarnick 5 B7
Much Marcle 79 D4
Muchrachd 251 C4
Much Wenlock 95 A4
Muckernich 252 A1
Mucking 50 A3
Muckle ford 15 B6
Mucklestone 111 B6
Muckleton 111 C4
Muckletown 255 D6
Muckley Corner 96 A3
Muckton 134 A3
Mudale 272 A3
Muddiford 25 B6
Mudeford 17 B5
Mudford 29 D5
Mudgley 28 A4
Mugdock 205 A5
Mugeary 246 A3
Mugginton 113 A6
Muggleswick 166 A3
Muie 273 D4
Muir 242 D3
Muirden 268 D2
Muirdrum 221 A5
Muirhead
    Angus 220 A3
    Fife 220 D2
    N Lanark 207 D4
    S Ayrs 192 B3
Muirhouselaw 187 A5
Muirhouses 208 B3
Muirkirk 194 D1
Muirmill 207 B5
Muir of Fairburn . . .251 A6
Muir of Fowlis 244 A2
Muir of Ord 252 A1
Muir of Pert 220 A4
Muirshearlich 239 D5
Muirskie 245 C5
Muirtack 257 C4
Muirton
    Highld 264 D3
    Perth 218 C4
    Perth 219 B6
Muirton Mains 251 A6
Muirton of
    Ardblair 231 D5
Muirton of
    Ballochy 233 B4
Muiryfold 268 D2
Muker 156 B3
Mulbarton 104 A2
Mulben 267 D4
Mulindry 200 C3
Mullardoch House .250 C4
Mullion 3 D4
Mullion Cove 3 D4
Mumby 135 B5
Munderfield Row . . . 79 B4
Munderfield Stocks . 79 B4
Mundesley 121 B5
Mundford 103 B4
Mundham 104 B4
Mundon 70 C2

Mundurno 245 A6
Munerigie 239 B6
Muness 284 C8
Mungasdale 261 A6
Mungrisdale 163 A6
Munlochy 252 A2
Munsley 79 C4
Munslow 94 C3
Murchington 12 C1
Murcott 65 B6
Murkle 280 B3
Murlaggan
  Highld 238 C4
  Highld 239 D7
Murra 283 G3
Murrayfield 209 C5
Murrow 101 A5
Mursley 66 A3
Murthill 232 C2
Murthly 219 A5
Murton
  Cumb 165 C5
  Durham 167 A6
  Northumb 198 B3
  York 149 B5
Musbury 14 B2
Muscoates 159 C5
Musdale 226 D4
Musselburgh 209 C6
Muston
  Leics 115 B6
  N Yorks 161 D4
Mustow Green 95 D6
Mutehill 173 D4
Mutford 105 C5
Muthill 218 C3
Mutterton 13 A5
Muxton 111 D6
Mybster 280 C3
Myddfai 59 C4
Myddle 110 C3
Mydroilyn 74 C3
Myerscough 145 D4
Mylor Bridge 4 D3
Mynachlog-ddu 72 C4
Myndtown 94 C1
Mynydd Bach 75 A6
Mynydd-bach 61 D6
Mynydd Bodafon 123 B4
Mynydd Isa 126 C2
Mynyddygarreg 57 B4
Mynytho 106 C3
Myrebird 245 C4
Myrelandhorn 281 C4
Myreside 220 B2
Myrtle Hill 59 B4
Mytchett 34 A1
Mytholm 138 A2
Mytholmroyd 138 A3
Myton-on-Swale 148 A3
Mytton 110 D3

N

Naast 261 B5
Naburn 149 C4
Nackington 52 D3
Nacton 88 C3
Nafferton 150 B3
Na Gearrannan 288 C2
Nailbridge 62 B2
Nailsbourne 28 C2
Nailsea 42 B3
Nailstone 97 A7
Nailsworth 63 D4
Nairn 253 A4
Nalderswood 35 B5
Nancegollan 3 B4
Nancledra 2 B2
Nanhoron 106 C2
Nannau 108 C2
Nannerch 125 C6
Nanpantan 114 D3
Nanpean 5 B4
Nanstallon 5 A5
Nant-ddu 60 B2
Nanternis 73 A6
Nantgaredig 58 C1
Nantgarw 41 C6
Nant-glas 76 A3
Nantglyn 125 C5
Nantgwyn 92 D3
Nantlle 107 A5
Nantmawr 110 C1
Nantmel 76 A4
Nantmor 107 B6
Nant Peris 107 A6
Nant Uchaf 125 D5
Nantwich 127 D6
Nant-y-Bai 59 A4
Nant-y-cafn 59 E5
Nantycaws 57 A4
Nant-y-derry 61 C5
Nant-y-ffin 58 B2
Nantyffyllon 40 B3
Nantyglo 60 B3
Nant-y-moel 40 B4
Nant-y-pandy 124 B1
Naphill 66 D3
Nappa 146 B2
Napton on the Hill 82 A1
Narberth = *Arberth* 55 C7
Narborough
  Leics 98 B2
  Norf 119 D4
Nasareth 107 A4
Naseby 98 D3
Nash
  Bucks 83 D4
  Hereford 77 A7
  Newport 42 A2
  Shrops 95 D4
Nash Lee 66 C3
Nassington 100 B2
Nasty 68 A3
Nateby
  Cumb 155 A6
  Lancs 145 C4
Natland 154 C4
Naughton 87 C6
Naunton
  Glos 64 A2
  Worcs 80 D1
Naunton Beauchamp 80 B2
Navenby 133 D4
Navestock Heath 69 D5
Navestock Side 69 D5
Navidale 274 C4
Nawton 159 C5
Nayland 87 D5
Nazeing 68 C4
Neacroft 17 B5
Neal's Green 97 C6
Neap 285 H7
Near Sawrey 154 B2
Neasham 167 D6
Neath = *Castell-Nedd* 40 B2
Neath Abbey 40 B2
Neatishead 121 C5
Nebo
  Anglesey 123 A4
  Ceredig 75 B4
  Conwy 124 D3
  Gwyn 107 A4
Necton 103 A4
Nedd 270 A4
Nedderton 179 A4
Nedging Tye 87 C6
Needham 104 C3
Needham Market 88 B1
Needingworth 101 D5
Needwood 113 C5
Neen Savage 95 D4
Neen Sollars 95 D4
Neenton 95 C4
Nefyn 106 B3
Neilston 205 C4
Neinthirion 92 A3
Neithrop 82 C1
Nelly Andrews Green 93 A6
Nelson
  Caerph 41 B6
  Lancs 146 D2
Nelson Village 179 B4
Nemphlar 194 B3
Nempnett Thrubwell 43 C4
Nene Terrace 101 A4
Nenthall 165 A5
Nenthead 165 A5
Nenthorn 197 C5
Nerabus 200 C2
Nercwys 126 C2
Nerston 205 C6
Nesbit 198 C3
Ness 126 B3
Nesscliffe 110 D2
Neston
  Ches W 126 B2
  Wilts 44 C2
Nether Alderley 128 B3
Netheravon 31 A5
Nether Blainslie 197 B4
Nether Booth 129 A6
Netherbrae 268 D2
Netherbrough 282 F4
Nether Broughton 115 C4
Netherburn 194 B3
Nether Burrow 155 D5
Netherbury 15 B4
Netherby
  Cumb 175 A6
  N Yorks 148 C2
Nether Cerne 15 B6
Nether Compton 29 D5
Nethercote 82 A2
Nethercott 25 B5
Nether Crimond 256 D3
Nether Dalgliesh 185 B5
Nether Dallachy 267 C4
Netherend 62 C1
Nether Exe 13 A4
Netherfield 23 A5
Nether Glasslaw 268 D3
Netherhampton 31 C5
Nether Handwick 232 D1
Nether Haugh 140 D2
Nether Heage 130 D3
Nether Heyford 82 B3
Nether Hindhope 187 B6
Nether Howecleuch 184 A3
Nether Kellet 145 A5
Nether Kinmundy 257 B5
Nether Langwith 131 B5
Netherlaw 173 D5
Nether Leask 257 C5
Nether Lenshie 256 B1
Netherley
  Aberds 245 C5
  Mers 127 A4
Nethermill 184 D3
Nether Monynut 211 D4
Nethermuir 257 B4
Nether Padley 130 B2
Nether Park 269 D5
Netherplace 205 C5
Nether Poppleton 149 B4
Netherseal 113 D6
Nether Silton 158 B3
Nether Stowey 28 B1
Netherthird 182 A3
Netherthong 139 C4
Netherthorpe 131 A5
Netherton
  Angus 232 C3
  Devon 12 D3
  Hants 46 D1
  Mers 136 C2
  Northumb 188 C2
  Oxon 65 D5
  Perth 231 C5
  Stirling 205 A5
  W Mid 96 C2
  Worcs 80 C2
  W Yorks 139 B4
  W Yorks 139 B5
Nethertown
  Cumb 162 D2
  Highld 281 A5
Nether Urquhart 219 D6
Nether Wallop 32 B2
Nether Wasdale 163 D4
Nether Whitacre 97 B5
Netherwitton 189 D4
Netherwood 193 C6
Nether Worton 82 D1
Nethy Bridge 253 D6
Netley 18 A3
Netley Marsh 32 D2
Netteswell 69 B4
Nettlebed 47 A5
Nettlebridge 29 A6
Nettlecombe 15 B5
Nettleden 67 B5
Nettleham 133 B5
Nettlestead 37 A4
Nettlestead Green 37 A4
Nettlestone 19 B5
Nettlesworth 167 A5
Nettleton
  Lincs 142 C3
  Wilts 44 B2
Neuadd 58 C3
Nevendon 70 D1
Nevern 72 B3
New Abbey 174 B2
New Aberdour 268 C3
New Addington 49 C6
Newall 147 C5
New Alresford 33 B4
New Alyth 231 D6
Newark
  Orkney 282 C8
  Pboro 100 A4
Newark-on-Trent 132 D2
New Arley 97 C5
Newarthill 194 A2
New Ash Green 50 C3
New Barn 50 C3
New Barnetby 142 B2
Newbarns 153 C3
New Barton 83 A5
Newbattle 209 D6
New Bewick 188 A3
Newbiggin
  Cumb 153 A1
  Cumb 153 D3
  Cumb 164 A3
  Cumb 164 C2
  Cumb 165 C4
  Durham 166 C2
  N Yorks 156 B3
  N Yorks 156 C3
Newbiggin-by-the-Sea 179 A5
Newbigging
  Angus 220 A4
  Angus 221 A4
  Angus 231 D6
  S Lanark 195 B5
Newbiggin-on-Lune 155 A6
New Bilton 98 D1
Newbold
  Derbys 130 B3
  Leics 114 D2
Newbold on Avon 98 D1
Newbold on Stour 81 C5
Newbold Pacey 81 B5
Newbold Verdon 98 A1
New Bolingbroke 134 D3
Newborough
  Anglesey 123 D4
  Pboro 100 A4
  Staffs 113 C5
Newbottle
  Northants 82 D2
  T&W 179 D5
New Boultham 133 B4
Newbourne 88 C3
New Bradwell 83 C5
New Brancepeth 167 A5
Newbridge
  Caerph 41 B7
  Ceredig 75 C4
  Corn 2 B2
  Corn 6 A2
  Dumfries 174 A2
  Edin 208 C4
  Hants 32 D1
  IoW 18 C3
  Pembs 55 A5
New Bridge 110 A1
Newbridge Green 79 D6
Newbridge-on-Usk 61 D5
Newbridge on Wye 76 B4
New Brighton
  Flint 126 C2
  Mers 136 D2
New Brinsley 131 D4
Newbrough 177 C6
New Broughton 126 D3
New Buckenham 104 B1
Newbuildings 12 A2
Newburgh
  Aberds 257 D4
  Aberds 269 D4
  Borders 185 A6
  Fife 220 C2
  Lancs 136 B3
Newburn 178 C3
Newbury 46 C2
Newbury Park 50 A1
Newby
  Cumb 164 C3
  Lancs 146 C2
  N Yorks 155 D6
  N Yorks 160 B4
  N Yorks 168 D3
Newby Bridge 154 C2
Newby East 176 D2
New Byth 268 D3
Newby West 175 C6
Newby Wiske 158 C2
Newcastle
  Mon 61 B6
  Shrops 93 C6
Newcastle Emlyn = *Castell Newydd Emlyn* 73 B6
Newcastleton or Copshaw Holm 176 A2
Newcastle-under-Lyme 112 A2
Newcastle Upon Tyne 179 C4
New Catton 120 D4
Newchapel
  Pembs 73 C5
  Powys 92 C3
  Staffs 128 D3
  Sur 35 B6
New Cheriton 33 C4
Newchurch
  Carms 73 D6
  IoW 19 C4
  Kent 38 B2
  Lancs 146 D2
  Mon 61 D6
  Powys 77 B6
  Staffs 113 C5
New Costessey 120 D3
Newcott 14 A2
New Cowper 174 D4
Newcraighall 209 C6
New Cross
  Ceredig 75 A5
  London 49 B6
New Cumnock 182 A4
New Deer 256 B3
New Delaval 179 B4
Newdigate 35 B4
New Duston 83 A4
New Earswick 149 B5
New Edlington 140 D3
New Elgin 266 C3
New Ellerby 151 D4
Newell Green 48 B1
New Eltham 50 B1
New End 80 B3
Newenden 37 D6
Newent 62 A3
Newerne 62 C2
New Farnley 147 D6
New Ferry 126 A3
Newfield
  Durham 167 B5
  Highld 264 C3
Newford Scilly 2 E4
Newfound 46 D3
New Fryston 140 A2
Newgale 54 B4
New Galloway 172 A4
Newgate 120 A2
Newgate Street 68 C3
New Gilston 220 D4
New Grimsby Scilly 2 E3
New Hainford 120 D4
Newhall
  Ches E 111 A5
  Derbys 113 C6
Newhall House 264 D2
Newhall Point 264 D3
Newham 189 A4
Newham Hall 189 A4
New Hartley 179 B5
Newhaven
  Derbys 129 D6
  Edin 209 C5
  E Sus 22 B2
New Haw 48 C3
New Hedges 56 B1
New Herrington 179 D5
Newhey 138 B2
New Hinksey 65 C6
New Holkham 119 B5
New Holland 142 A2
Newholm 169 D6
New Houghton
  Derbys 131 C4
  Norf 119 C4
Newhouse 207 D5
New Houses 155 D7
New Humberstone 98 A3
New Hutton 155 B4
New Hythe 37 A5
Newick 36 D2
Newingreen 38 B3
Newington
  Kent 38 B3
  Kent 51 C5
  Kent 53 C5
  Notts 141 D4
  Oxon 65 D7
  Shrops 94 C2
New Inn
  Carms 58 B1
  Mon 61 C6
  Pembs 55 A6
  Torf 61 D5
New Invention
  Shrops 93 D6
  W Mid 96 A2
New Kelso 249 B6
New Kingston 114 C3
New Lanark 194 B3
Newland
  Glos 62 C1
  Hull 150 D3
  N Yorks 141 A4
  Worcs 79 C5
Newlandrig 209 D6
Newlands
  Borders 186 D4
  Highld 252 B3
  Moray 266 D4
  Northumb 178 D2
Newland's Corner 34 B3
Newlandsmuir 205 C6
Newlands of Geise 280 B2
Newlands of Tynet 267 C4
Newlands Park 122 B2
New Lane 136 B3
New Lane End 137 D5
New Leake 135 D4
New Leeds 269 D4
New Longton 136 A4
Newlot 282 F6
New Luce 170 A3
Newlyn 2 C2
Newmachar 245 A5
Newmains 194 A3
New Malden 49 C5
Newmarket
  Suff 86 A2
  W Isles 288 D5
New Marske 168 C4
New Marton 110 B2
New Micklefield 148 D3
Newmill
  Borders 186 B3
  Corn 2 B2
  Moray 267 D5
New Mill
  Aberds 245 D4
  Herts 67 B4
  Wilts 45 C5
  W Yorks 139 C4
Newmill of Inshewan 232 B2
New Mills
  Ches E 128 A2
  Corn 4 B3
  Derbys 129 A4
  Powys 93 A4
Newmills of Boyne 267 D6
Newmiln 219 A6
Newmilns 193 B5
New Milton 17 B6
New Moat 55 B6
Newnham
  Cambs 85 B6
  Glos 62 B2
  Hants 47 D5
  Herts 84 D4
  Kent 51 D6
  Northants 82 B2
Newnham Bridge 79 A4
New Ollerton 131 C6
New Oscott 96 B3
Newpark 221 C4
New Park 148 B1
New Pitsligo 268 D3
New Polzeath 9 D5
Newport
  Devon 25 B6
  Essex 85 D7
  E Yorks 150 D1
  Highld 275 B5
  IoW 18 C4
  Norf 121 D7
  Telford 111 D6
Newport = *Casnewydd* 42 A2
Newport = *Trefdraeth* 72 C3
Newport-on-Tay 220 B4
Newport Pagnell 83 C5
Newpound Common 34 D3
Newquay 4 A3
New Quay = *Ceinewydd* 73 A6
New Rackheath 121 D4
New Radnor 77 A6
New Rent 164 B2
New Ridley 178 D2
New Road Side 146 C3
New Romney 38 C2
New Rossington 140 D4
New Row
  Ceredig 75 A6
  Lancs 145 D6
  N Yorks 168 D4
New Sarum 31 B5

Newsbank.........128 C3
Newseat
　Aberds.........256 C2
　Aberds.........257 B5
Newsham
　Northumb.........179 B5
　N Yorks.........158 C2
　N Yorks.........166 D4
Newsholme
　E Yorks.........141 A5
　Lancs.........146 B2
New Silksworth....179 D5
Newsome.........139 B4
Newstead
　Borders.........197 C4
　Northumb.........189 A4
　Notts.........131 D5
New Stevenston....194 A2
New Street.........129 D5
New Street Lane...111 B5
New Swanage......17 C4
Newthorpe.........148 D3
Newton
　Argyll.........214 C3
　Borders.........187 B2
　Bridgend.........40 D3
　Cambs.........85 C6
　Cambs.........118 D1
　Cardiff.........42 B1
　Ches W.........127 B5
　Ches W.........127 C4
　Ches W.........127 D5
　Cumb.........153 C3
　Derbys.........131 D4
　Dorset.........30 D1
　Dumfries.........175 A5
　Dumfries.........185 C4
　Gtr Man.........138 D2
　Hereford.........78 B3
　Hereford.........78 D1
　Highld.........252 B3
　Highld.........264 D3
　Highld.........271 A5
　Highld.........281 D5
　Lancs.........144 D4
　Lancs.........145 B6
　Lancs.........155 C4
　Lincs.........116 B3
　Moray.........266 C2
　Norf.........119 D5
　Northants.........99 C5
　Northumb.........178 C2
　Notts.........115 A4
　Perth.........218 A3
　S Lanark.........194 C4
　S Lanark.........205 B6
　Staffs.........112 C4
　Suff.........87 C5
　Swansea.........57 D6
　S Yorks.........140 C4
　Warks.........98 D2
　Wilts.........31 C6
　W Loth.........208 C3
Newton Abbot......12 D3
Newtonairds.....183 D6
Newton Arlosh....175 C4
Newton Aycliffe...167 C5
Newton Bewley....168 C2
Newton Blossomville..83 B6
Newton Bromswold..84 A1
Newton Burgoland..97 A6
Newton by Toft...133 A6
Newton Ferrers...7 C4
Newton Flotman...104 B3
Newtongrange....209 D6
Newton Hall.....178 C2
Newton Harcourt...98 B3
Newton Heath....138 C1
Newtonhill
　Aberds.........245 C6
　Highld.........252 B1
Newton House....256 D1
Newton Kyme....148 C3
Newton-le-Willows
　Mers.........137 D4
　N Yorks.........157 C6
Newton Longville..83 D6
Newton Mearns...205 C5
Newtonmill.......233 B4
Newtonmore.....241 C6
Newton Morrell...157 A6
Newton Mulgrave.169 D5
Newton of Ardtoe..235 C5
Newton of Balcanquhal.219 C6
Newton of Falkland.220 D2
Newton on Ayr...192 C3
Newton on Ouse..148 B4

Newton-on-Rawcliffe.........159 B7
Newton-on-the-Moor.........189 C4
Newton on Trent..132 B3
Newton Park.....203 B6
Newton Poppleford..13 C5
Newton Purcell...82 D3
Newton Regis.....97 A5
Newton Reigny...164 B2
Newton St Cyres..12 B3
Newton St Faith..120 D4
Newton St Loe....43 C6
Newton St Petrock..25 D5
Newton Solney....113 C6
Newton Stacey....32 A3
Newton Stewart...171 A6
Newton Tony.....31 A6
Newton Tracey....25 C6
Newton under Roseberry.........168 D3
Newton upon Derwent.........149 C6
Newton Valence...33 B6
New Totley.........130 B3
Newtown
　Argyll.........214 B3
　BCP.........17 B4
　Ches W.........127 B5
　Corn.........3 C5
　Cumb.........174 D3
　Cumb.........176 C3
　Derbys.........129 A4
　Devon.........26 C2
　Glos.........62 C2
　Glos.........80 D2
　Hants.........18 A3
　Hants.........31 D6
　Hants.........32 C2
　Hants.........32 D4
　Hants.........33 D5
　Hants.........46 C2
　Hereford.........79 C4
　Highld.........240 B1
　IoM.........152 D3
　IoW.........18 B3
　Northumb.........188 A3
　Northumb.........188 C4
　Northumb.........198 C3
　Shrops.........110 B3
　Staffs.........129 C4
　Staffs.........129 C5
　Wilts.........30 C3
New Town.........210 C1
Newtown = Y Drenewydd......93 B5
Newtown Linford..98 A2
Newtown St Boswells.......197 C4
Newtown Unthank..98 A1
New Tredegar = Tredegar Newydd..41 A6
New Trows.........194 C3
Newtyle.........231 D6
New Ulva.........213 D5
New Walsoken....101 A6
New Waltham....143 C4
New Whittington..130 B3
New Wimpole....85 C5
New Winton.....210 C1
New Yatt.........65 B4
New York
　Lincs.........134 D2
　N Yorks.........147 A5
Neyland.........55 D5
Niarbyl.........152 D2
Nibley.........43 A5
Nibley Green....62 D3
Nibon.........284 F5
Nicholashayne...27 D6
Nicholaston.....57 D6
Nidd.........148 A2
Nigg
　Aberdeen.........245 B6
　Highld.........265 C4
Nigg Ferry.........264 D3
Nightcott.........26 C3
Nilig.........125 D5
Nine Ashes.........69 C5
Ninebanks.........177 D5
Nine Mile Burn...195 A6
Nine Wells.........54 B3
Ninfield.........23 A5
Ningwood.........18 C2
Nisbet.........187 A5
Nisthouse
　Orkney.........282 F4
　Shetland.........285 G7
Niton.........18 D4

Nitshill.........205 B5
Noak Hill.........69 D5
Noblethorpe.....139 C5
Nobottle.........82 A3
Nocton.........133 C5
Noke.........65 B6
Nolton.........55 C4
Nolton Haven....55 C4
No Man's Heath
　Ches W.........111 A4
　Warks.........97 A5
Nomansland
　Devon.........26 D3
　Wilts.........31 D6
Noneley.........110 C3
Nonikiln.........264 C2
Nonington.........53 D4
Noonsbrough....285 H4
Norbreck.........144 C3
Norbridge.........79 C5
Norbury
　Ches E.........111 A4
　Derbys.........113 A5
　Shrops.........94 B1
　Staffs.........112 C1
Nordelph.........102 A1
Norden.........138 B1
Norden Heath....16 C3
Nordley.........95 B4
Norham.........198 B3
Norley.........127 B5
Norleywood.....18 B2
Normanby
　N Lincs.........141 B6
　N Yorks.........159 C6
　Redcar.........168 D3
Normanby-by-Spital.........133 A5
Normanby by Stow.132 A3
Normanby le Wold.142 D3
Norman Cross....100 B3
Normandy.........34 A2
Norman's Bay....23 B4
Norman's Green..13 A5
Normanstone.....105 B6
Normanton
　Derby.........114 B1
　Leics.........115 A6
　Lincs.........116 A2
　Notts.........132 D2
　Rutland.........99 A6
　W Yorks.........140 A1
Normanton le Heath.........114 D1
Normanton on Soar.........114 C3
Normanton-on-the-Wolds.........115 B4
Normanton on Trent.........132 C2
Normoss.........144 D3
Norney.........34 B2
Norrington Common 44 C2
Norris Green.....136 D2
Norris Hill.........114 D1
Northacre.........103 B5
Northallerton.....158 B2
Northam
　Devon.........25 C5
　Soton.........32 D3
Northampton....83 A4
North Anston....131 A5
North Aston.....65 A5
Northaw.........68 C2
North Baddesley..32 D2
North Ballachulish.237 C4
North Barrow....29 C6
North Barsham...119 B6
Northbeck.........116 A3
North Benfleet...51 A4
North Bersted....20 B2
North Berwick....210 B2
North Boarhunt...33 D5
Northborough....100 A3
Northbourne....53 D5
North Bovey....12 C2
North Bradley....44 D2
North Brentor....11 C5
North Brewham...29 B7
Northbridge Street..37 D5
North Buckland..25 A5
North Burlingham.121 D5
North Cadbury....29 C6
North Cairn.....180 D1
North Carlton....133 B4
North Carrine....190 E2
North Cave.........150 D1
North Cerney....63 C6
Northchapel.....34 D2
North Charford...31 D5

North Charlton....189 A4
North Cheriton...29 C6
Northchurch.........67 C4
North Cliff.........151 C5
North Cliffe.....150 D1
North Clifton....132 B3
North Cockerington.143 D5
North Coker.....29 D5
North Collafirth..284 E5
North Common....36 D1
North Connel....226 C4
North Cornelly...40 C3
North Cotes.....143 C5
Northcott.........10 B4
North Cove.........105 C5
North Cowton....157 A6
North Crawley....83 C6
North Cray.........50 B1
North Creake....119 B5
North Curry.....28 C3
North Dalton....150 B2
North Dawn.....283 G5
North Deighton..148 B2
Northdown.........53 B5
North Duffield...149 D5
Northdyke.........282 E3
North Elkington..143 D4
North Elmham...120 C1
North Elmsall...140 B2
Northend
　Bath.........44 C1
　Bucks.........66 D2
　Warks.........81 B6
North End
　Bucks.........66 A3
　Essex.........69 B6
　E Yorks.........151 D5
　Hants.........46 C2
　Lincs.........117 A5
　N Som.........42 C3
　Ptsmth.........19 A5
　Som.........28 C2
　W Sus.........21 B4
Northenden.....137 D7
North Erradale..261 B4
North Fambridge..70 D2
North Fearns....248 C2
North Featherstone.140 A2
North Ferriby....142 A1
Northfield
　Aberdeen.........245 B6
　Borders.........211 D6
　E Yorks.........142 A2
　W Mid.........96 D3
Northfields.....100 A2
Northfleet.........50 B3
North Frodingham.151 B4
Northgate.........117 C4
North Gluss.....284 F5
North Gorley....31 D5
North Green
　Norf.........104 C3
　Suff.........89 A4
North Greetwell..133 B5
North Grimston..150 A1
North Halley....283 G6
North Halling....51 C4
North Hayling....19 A6
North Hazelrigg..199 C4
North Heasley...26 B2
North Heath....34 D3
North Hill
　Cambs.........101 D6
　Corn.........10 D3
North Hinksey...65 C5
North Holmwood..35 B4
Northhouse.....186 C3
North Howden...149 D6
North Huish.....7 B6
North Hykeham..133 C4
Northiam.........37 D6
Northill.........84 C3
Northington.....33 B4
North Johnston..55 C5
North Kelsey....142 C2
North Kelsey Moor.142 C2
North Kessock...252 B2
North Killingholme.142 B3
North Kilvington.158 C3
North Kilworth..98 C3
North Kirkton...269 D6
North Kiscadale..191 C6
North Kyme.....133 D6
North Lancing...21 B4
Northlands.....134 D3
Northlea.........179 D6
Northleach.....64 B2
North Lee.........66 C3

Northleigh.........14 B1
North Leigh.....65 B4
North Leverton with Habblesthorpe..132 A2
Northlew.........11 B6
North Littleton...80 C3
North Lopham...103 C6
North Luffenham..99 A6
North Marden...33 D7
North Marston...66 A2
North Middleton
　Midloth.........196 A2
　Northumb.........188 A3
North Molton....26 C2
Northmoor.........65 C5
Northmoor Green or Moorland.........28 B3
North Moreton...46 A3
Northmuir.........232 C1
North Mundham..20 B1
North Muskham...132 D2
North Newbald...150 D2
North Newington..81 D7
North Newnton...45 D5
North Newton....28 B2
Northney.........19 A6
North Nibley....62 D3
North Oakley....46 D3
North Ockendon..50 A2
Northolt.........48 A4
Northop.........126 C2
Northop Hall....126 C2
North Ormesby..168 C3
North Ormsby....143 D4
Northorpe
　Lincs.........116 D3
　Lincs.........117 B5
　Lincs.........141 D6
North Otterington.158 C2
Northover
　Som.........29 B4
　Som.........29 C5
North Owersby...142 D2
Northowram....139 A4
North Perrott...15 A4
North Petherton..28 B2
North Petherwin..10 C3
North Pickenham.103 A4
North Piddle....80 B2
North Poorton...15 B5
North Port.........227 D5
Northpunds.....285 L6
North Queensferry.208 B4
North Radworthy..26 B2
North Rauceby...116 A3
Northrepps.....120 B4
North Reston....134 A3
North Rigton....148 C1
North Rode.....128 C3
North Roe.........284 E5
North Runcton..118 D3
North Sandwick..284 D7
North Scale.....153 D2
North Scarle....132 C3
North Seaton...179 A4
North Shian....226 B4
North Shields...179 C5
North Shoebury..51 A6
North Shore....144 D3
North Side
　Cumb.........162 B3
　Pboro.........101 B4
North Skelton...169 D4
North Somercotes.143 D6
North Stainley..157 D6
North Stainmore.165 D6
North Stifford..50 A3
North Stoke
　Bath.........43 C6
　Oxon.........47 A4
　W Sus.........20 A3
North Street
　Hants.........33 B5
　Kent.........52 D2
　Medway.........51 B5
　W Berks.........47 B4
North Sunderland.199 C6
North Tamerton..10 B4
North Tawton...12 A1
North Thoresby..143 D4
North Tidworth..31 A6
North Togston...189 C5
Northtown.........283 H5
North Tuddenham.120 D2
North Walbottle..178 C3
North Walsham..121 B4
North Waltham..33 A4
North Warnborough.47 D5

North Water Bridge.........233 B4
North Watten....280 C4
Northway.........80 D2
North Weald Bassett 69 C4
North Wheatley..132 A2
North Whilborough..8 A2
Northwich.........127 B6
Northwick.........43 A4
North Wick.........43 C4
North Willingham.133 A6
North Wingfield..131 C5
North Witham...116 C2
Northwold.........102 B3
Northwood
　Derbys.........130 C2
　IoW.........18 B3
　Kent.........53 C5
　London.........67 D5
　Shrops.........110 B3
Northwood Green..62 B3
North Woolwich..50 B1
North Wootton
　Dorset.........29 C6
　Norf.........118 C3
　Som.........29 A5
North Wraxall...44 B2
North Wroughton.45 A5
Norton
　E Sus.........22 B2
　Glos.........63 A4
　Halton.........127 A5
　Herts.........84 D4
　IoW.........18 C2
　Mon.........61 B6
　Northants.........82 A3
　Notts.........131 B5
　Powys.........77 A7
　Shrops.........94 A3
　Shrops.........94 C2
　Shrops.........95 A5
　Stockton.........168 C2
　Suff.........87 A5
　S Yorks.........140 B3
　Wilts.........44 A2
　Worcs.........80 B1
　Worcs.........80 B2
　W Sus.........20 B2
　W Sus.........20 C1
Norton Bavant...30 A3
Norton Bridge...112 B2
Norton Canes....96 A3
Norton Canon....78 C1
Norton Corner...120 C2
Norton Disney...132 C3
Norton East.....96 A3
Norton Ferris...30 B1
Norton Fitzwarren.28 C2
Norton Green...18 C2
Norton Hawkfield.43 C4
Norton Heath....69 C6
Norton in Hales..111 B6
Norton-in-the-Moors.........128 D3
Norton-Juxta-Twycross.........97 A6
Norton-le-Clay..158 D3
Norton Lindsey..81 A5
Norton Malreward.43 C5
Norton Mandeville.69 C5
Norton-on-Derwent.........159 D6
Norton St Philip..43 D6
Norton sub Hamdon.29 D4
Norton Woodseats.130 A3
Norwell.........132 C2
Norwell Woodhouse.........132 C2
Norwich.........104 A3
Norwick.........284 B8
Norwood.........131 A4
Norwood Hill....35 B5
Norwoodside....101 B6
Noseley.........99 B4
Noss.........285 M5
Noss Mayo.........7 C4
Nosterfield.....157 C6
Nostie.........249 D5
Notgrove.........64 A2
Nottage.........40 D3
Nottingham.....114 B3
Nottington.....15 C6
Notton
　Wilts.........44 C3
　W Yorks.........139 B6
Nounsley.........70 B1
Noutard's Green..79 A5
Novar House....264 D2

Nox 110 D3
Nuffield 47 A4
Nunburnholme 150 C1
Nuncargate 131 D5
Nuneaton 97 B6
Nuneham Courtenay 65 D6
Nun Hills 138 A1
Nun Monkton 148 B4
Nunney 30 A1
Nunnington 159 D5
Nunnykirk 188 D3
Nunsthorpe 143 C4
Nunthorpe
  Mbro 168 D3
  York 149 B5
Nunton 31 C5
Nunwick 157 D7
Nupend 62 C3
Nursling 32 D2
Nursted 33 C6
Nutbourne
  W Sus 19 A6
  W Sus 20 A3
Nutfield 35 A6
Nuthall 114 A3
Nuthampstead 85 D6
Nuthurst 35 D4
Nutley
  E Sus 36 D2
  Hants 33 A5
Nutwell 140 C4
Nybster 281 B5
Nyetimber 20 C1
Nyewood 33 C7
Nymet Rowland 12 A2
Nymet Tracey 12 A2
Nympsfield 63 C4
Nynehead 27 C6
Nyton 20 B2

O

Oadby 98 A3
Oad Street 51 C5
Oakamoor 113 A4
Oakbank 208 D3
Oak Cross 11 B6
Oakdale 41 B6
Oake 27 C6
Oaken 95 A6
Oakenclough 145 C5
Oakengates 111 D6
Oakenholt 126 B2
Oakenshaw
  Durham 167 B5
  W Yorks 139 A4
Oakerthorpe 130 D3
Oakes 139 B4
Oakfield 61 D5
Oakford
  Ceredig 74 C3
  Devon 27 C4
Oakfordbridge 27 C4
Oakgrove 129 C4
Oakham 99 A5
Oakhanger 33 B6
Oakhill 29 A6
Oakhurst 36 A4
Oakington 85 A6
Oaklands
  Herts 68 B2
  Powys 76 B4
Oakle Street 62 B3
Oakley
  BCP 17 B4
  Bedford 84 B2
  Bucks 66 B1
  Fife 208 B3
  Hants 46 D3
  Oxon 66 C2
  Suff 104 D2
Oakley Green 48 B2
Oakley Park 92 C3
Oakmere 127 C5
Oakridge
  Glos 63 C5
  Hants 47 D4
Oaks 94 A2
Oaksey 63 D5
Oaks Green 113 B5
Oakthorpe 113 D7
Oakwoodhill 35 C4
Oakworth 147 D4
Oape 272 D2
Oare
  Kent 52 C2
  Som 26 A3

Oare continued
  W Berks 46 B3
  Wilts 45 C5
Oasby 116 B3
Oathlaw 232 C2
Oatlands 148 B2
Oban
  Argyll 226 D3
  Highld 238 D2
Oborne 29 D6
Obthorpe 116 D3
Occlestone Green . .128 C1
Occold 104 D2
Ochiltree 193 C5
Ochtermuthill 218 C3
Ochtertyre 218 B3
Ockbrook 114 B2
Ockham 34 A3
Ockle 235 C4
Ockley 35 C4
Ocle Pychard 78 C3
Octon 150 A3
Octon Cross Roads .150 A3
Odcombe 29 D5
Odd Down 43 C6
Oddendale 164 D3
Odder 133 B4
Oddingley 80 B2
Oddington
  Glos 64 A3
  Oxon 65 B6
Odell 83 B6
Odie 282 E7
Odiham 47 D5
Odstock 31 C5
Odstone 97 A6
Offchurch 81 A6
Offenham 80 C3
Offham
  E Sus 22 A1
  Kent 37 A4
  W Sus 20 B3
Offord Cluny 84 A4
Offord Darcy 84 A4
Offton 87 C6
Offwell 14 B1
Ogbourne Maizey . . 45 B5
Ogbourne
  St Andrew 45 B5
Ogbourne St George 45 B6
Ogil 232 B2
Ogle 178 B3
Ogmore 40 D3
Ogmore-by-Sea 40 D3
Ogmore Vale 40 B4
Okeford Fitzpaine . . 30 D2
Okehampton 11 B6
Okehampton Camp . . 11 B6
Okraquoy 285 K6
Old 99 D4
Old Aberdeen 245 B6
Old Alresford 33 B4
Oldany 270 A4
Old Arley 97 B5
Old Basford 114 A3
Old Basing 47 D4
Oldberrow 80 A4
Old Bewick 188 A4
Old Bolingbroke . . .134 C3
Oldborough 12 A2
Old Bramhope 147 C6
Old Brampton 130 B3
Old Bridge of Tilt . .230 B2
Old Bridge of Urr . .173 B5
Old Buckenham . . .103 B6
Old Burghclere 46 D2
Oldbury
  Shrops 95 B5
  Warks 97 B6
  W Mid 96 C2
Oldbury-on-Severn . 62 D2
Oldbury on the Hill . . 44 A2
Old Byland 159 C4
Old Cassop 167 B6
Oldcastle
  Bridgend 40 D4
  Mon 61 A5
Old Castleton 186 D4
Old Catton 120 D4
Old Clee 143 C4
Old Cleeve 27 A5
Old Clipstone 131 C6
Old Colwyn 124 B3
Oldcotes 131 A5
Old Coulsdon 35 A6
Old Crombie 267 D6
Old Dailly 181 B4
Old Dalby 115 C4
Old Deer 257 B4
Old Denaby 140 D2

Old Edlington 140 D3
Old Eldon 167 C5
Old Ellerby 151 D4
Oldfallow 112 D3
Old Felixstowe 88 D4
Oldfield 79 A6
Old Fletton 100 B3
Oldford 44 D1
Old Glossop 138 D3
Old Goole 141 A5
Old Hall 91 D7
Oldham 138 C2
Oldhamstocks 211 C1
Old Heath 71 A4
Old Heathfield 36 D3
Old Hill 96 C2
Old Hunstanton 118 A3
Old Hurst 101 D4
Old Hutton 155 C4
Old Kea 4 C3
Old Kilpatrick 205 A4
Old Kinnernie 245 B4
Old Knebworth 68 A2
Oldland 43 B5
Old Langho 145 D7
Old Laxey 152 C4
Old Leake 135 D4
Old Malton 159 D6
Oldmeldrum 256 D3
Old Micklefield 148 D3
Old Milton 17 B6
Old Milverton 81 A5
Old Monkland 207 D5
Old Netley 18 A3
Old Philpstoun 208 C3
Old Quarrington . . .167 B6
Old Radnor 77 B6
Old Rattray 269 D5
Old Rayne 256 D1
Old Romney 38 C2
Oldshore Beg 276 C2
Oldshoremore 276 C3
Old Sodbury 43 A6
Old Somerby 116 B2
Oldstead 158 C4
Old Stratford 83 C4
Old Thirsk 158 C3
Oldtown 255 D6
Old Town
  Cumb 155 C4
  Cumb 164 A2
  Northumb 188 D1
  Scilly 2 E4
Oldtown of Ord . .267 D7
Old Trafford 137 D7
Old Tupton 130 C3
Old Warden 84 C3
Oldway 57 D5
Oldways End 26 C3
Old Weston 100 D2
Oldwhat 268 D3
Old Whittington . . .130 B3
Old Wick 281 C5
Old Windsor 48 B2
Old Wives Lees 52 D2
Old Woking 34 A3
Old Woodhall 134 C2
Olgrinmore 280 C2
Oliver's Battery 32 C3
Ollaberry 284 E5
Ollerton
  Ches E 128 B2
  Notts 131 C6
  Shrops 111 C5
Olmarch 75 C5
Olney 83 B5
Olrig House 280 B3
Olton 96 C4
Olveston 43 A5
Olwen 75 D4
Ombersley 79 A6
Ompton 132 C1
Onchan 152 D3
Onecote 129 D5
Onen 61 B6
Ongar Hill 118 C2
Ongar Street 78 A1
Onibury 94 D2
Onich 237 C4
Onllwyn 59 D5
Onneley 111 A6
Onslow Village 34 B2
Onthank 205 D4
Openwoodgate 114 A1
Opinan
  Highld 261 A5
  Highld 261 C4
Orange Lane 198 B1
Orange Row 118 C2
Orasaigh 288 F4

Orbliston 266 D4
Orbost 258 D2
Orby 135 C4
Orchard Hill 25 C5
Orchard Portman . . 28 C2
Orcheston 31 A4
Orcop 61 A6
Orcop Hill 61 A6
Ord 247 C5
Ordhead 244 A3
Ordie 244 B1
Ordiequish 266 D4
Ordsall 132 A1
Ore 23 A6
Oreton 95 C4
Orford
  Suff 89 C5
  Warr 137 D5
Orgreave 113 D5
Orlestone 38 B1
Orleton
  Hereford 78 A2
  Worcs 79 A4
Orlingbury 99 D5
Ormesby 168 D3
Ormesby
  St Margaret 121 D6
Ormesby
  St Michael 121 D6
Ormiclate Castle . . .286 C3
Ormiscaig 261 A5
Ormiston 209 D7
Ormsaigbeg 234 D3
Ormsaigmore 234 D3
Ormsary 202 A2
Ormsgill 153 C2
Ormskirk 136 C3
Orpington 50 C1
Orrell
  Gtr Man 136 C4
  Mers 136 D2
Orrisdale 152 B3
Orroland 173 D5
Orsett 50 A3
Orslow 112 D2
Orston 115 A5
Orthwaite 163 A5
Ortner 145 B5
Orton
  Cumb 155 A5
  Northants 99 D5
Orton Longueville . .100 B3
Orton-on-the-Hill . . 97 A6
Orton Waterville . . .100 B3
Orwell 85 B5
Osbaldeston 145 D6
Osbaldwick 149 B5
Osbaston 110 C2
Osbournby 116 B3
Oscroft 127 C5
Ose 258 D3
Osgathorpe 114 D2
Osgodby
  Lincs 142 D2
  N Yorks 149 D5
  N Yorks 161 C4
Oskaig 248 C2
Oskamull 224 B3
Osmaston
  Derby 114 B1
  Derbys 113 A6
Osmington 16 C1
Osmington Mills . . 16 C1
Osmotherley 158 B3
Ospisdale 264 B3
Ospringe 52 C2
Ossett 139 A5
Ossington 132 C2
Ostend 70 D3
Oswaldkirk 159 D4
Oswaldtwistle 137 A6
Oswestry 110 C1
Otford 36 A3
Otham 37 A5
Othery 28 B3
Otley
  Suff 88 B3
  W Yorks 147 C6
Otterbourne 32 C3
Otterburn
  Northumb 188 D1
  N Yorks 146 B2
Otterburn Camp . . .188 D1
Otter Ferry 214 D2
Otterham 10 B2
Otterhampton 28 A2
Ottershaw 48 C3
Otterswick 284 E7
Otterton 13 C5
Ottery St Mary 13 B6

Ottinge 38 A3
Ottringham 143 A4
Oughterby 175 C5
Oughtershaw 156 C2
Oughterside 174 D4
Oughtibridge 139 D6
Oughtrington 128 A1
Oulston 158 D4
Oulton
  Cumb 175 C5
  Norf 120 C3
  Staffs 112 B3
  Suff 105 B6
  W Yorks 139 A6
Oulton Broad 105 B6
Oulton Street 120 C3
Oundle 100 C2
Ousby 165 B4
Ousdale 275 B4
Ousden 86 B3
Ousefleet 141 A6
Ouston
  Durham 179 D4
  Northumb 178 B2
Outertown 282 F3
Outgate 154 B2
Outhgill 155 A6
Outlane 138 B3
Out Newton 143 A5
Out Rawcliffe 144 C4
Outwell 101 A7
Outwick 31 D5
Outwood
  Sur 35 B6
  W Yorks 139 A6
Outwoods 112 D1
Ovenden 138 A3
Ovenscloss 196 C3
Over
  Cambs 101 D5
  Ches W 127 C6
  S Glos 43 A4
Overbister 282 C7
Overbury 80 D2
Overcombe 15 C6
Over Compton 29 D5
Overgreen 130 B3
Over Green 97 B4
Over Haddon 130 C2
Over Hulton 137 C5
Over Kellet 154 D4
Over Kiddington . . . 65 A5
Over Knutsford 128 B2
Overleigh 29 B4
Overley Green 80 B3
Over Monnow 61 B7
Over Norton 64 A4
Over Peover 128 B2
Overpool 126 B3
Overscaig Hotel . . .271 B7
Overseal 113 D6
Over Silton 158 B3
Oversland 52 D2
Overstone 83 A5
Over Stowey 28 B1
Overstrand 120 A4
Over Stratton 28 D4
Over Tabley 128 A2
Overthorpe 82 C1
Overton
  Aberdeen 245 A5
  Ches W 127 B5
  Dumfries 174 B2
  Hants 32 A4
  Lancs 144 B4
  N Yorks 149 B4
  Shrops 94 D3
  Swansea 57 D4
  W Yorks 139 B5
Overton = Owrtyn . . .110 A2
Overton Bridge 110 A2
Overtown 194 A3
Over Wallop 32 B1
Over Whitacre 97 B5
Over Worton 65 A5
Oving
  Bucks 66 A2
  W Sus 20 B2
Ovingdean 21 B6
Ovingham 178 C2
Ovington
  Durham 166 D4
  Essex 86 C3
  Hants 33 B4
  Norf 103 A5
  Northumb 178 C2
Ower 32 D2
Owermoigne 16 C1
Owlbury 93 B7
Owler Bar 130 B2

Owlerton 130 A3
Owl's Green 88 A3
Owlswick 66 C2
Owmby 142 C2
Owmby-by-Spital . .133 A5
Owrtyn = Overton . . .110 A2
Owslebury 32 C4
Owston
  Leics 99 A4
  S Yorks 140 B5
Owston Ferry 141 C6
Owstwick 151 D5
Owthorne 143 A5
Owthorpe 115 B4
Oxborough 102 A3
Oxcombe 134 B3
Oxenholme 154 C4
Oxenhope 147 D4
Oxen Park 154 C2
Oxenton 80 D2
Oxenwood 45 D7
Oxford 65 C6
Oxhey 67 D6
Oxhill 81 C6
Oxley 96 A2
Oxley Green 70 B3
Oxley's Green 37 D4
Oxnam 187 B2
Oxshott 48 C4
Oxspring 139 C5
Oxted 36 A1
Oxton
  Borders 196 A3
  Notts 131 D6
Oxwich 57 D4
Oxwick 119 C6
Oykel Bridge 271 D6
Oyne 256 D1

P

Pabail Iarach 288 D6
Pabail Uarach 288 D6
Pace Gate 147 B5
Packington 114 D1
Padanaram 232 C2
Padbury 83 D4
Paddington 49 A5
Paddlesworth 38 B3
Paddockhaugh 266 D3
Paddockhole 185 D5
Paddock Wood 37 B4
Padfield 138 D3
Padiham 146 D1
Padog 124 D3
Padside 147 B5
Padstow 9 D5
Padworth 47 C4
Page Bank 167 B5
Pagham 20 C1
Paglesham
  Churchend 70 D3
Paglesham Eastend 70 D3
Paibeil 287 H2
Paible 287 E5
Paignton 8 A2
Pailton 98 C1
Painscastle 77 C5
Painshawfield 178 C2
Painsthorpe 149 B7
Painswick 63 C4
Pairc Shiaboist 288 C3
Paisley 205 B4
Pakefield 105 B6
Pakenham 87 A5
Pale 109 B4
Palestine 31 A6
Paley Street 47 B6
Palfrey 96 B3
Palgowan 181 C5
Palgrave 104 D2
Pallion 179 D5
Palmarsh 38 B3
Palnackie 173 C6
Palnure 171 A6
Palterton 131 C4
Pamber End 47 D4
Pamber Green 47 D4
Pamber Heath 47 C4
Pamphill 16 A3
Pampisford 85 C6
Pan 283 H4
Panbride 221 A5
Pancrasweek 10 A3
Pandy
  Gwyn 90 B4
  Mon 61 A4
  Powys 91 B7
  Wrex 109 B6

Pandy Tudur 124 C3
Panfield 70 A1
Pangbourne 47 B4
Pannal 148 B2
Panshanger 68 B2
Pant 110 C1
Pant-glas
  Carms 58 C2
  Gwyn 107 B4
Pant-glâs 91 C5
Pant-glas 110 B1
Pantgwyn
  Carms 58 C2
  Ceredig 73 B5
Pant-lasau 57 C6
Pant Mawr 91 D6
Panton 134 B1
Pantperthog 91 B5
Pant-teg 58 C1
Pant-y-Caws 73 D4
Pant-y-dwr 92 D3
Pant-y-ffridd 93 A5
Pantyffynnon 57 A6
Pantymwyn 126 C1
Pant-yr-awel 40 C4
Pant-y-Wacco 125 B6
Panxworth 121 D5
Papcastle 163 A4
Papigoe 281 C5
Papil 285 K5
Papley 283 H5
Papple 210 C2
Papplewick 131 D5
Papworth Everard . . . 85 A4
Papworth St Agnes . . 85 A4
Par 5 B5
Parbold 136 B3
Parbrook
  Som 29 B5
  W Sus 34 D3
Parc 108 B3
Parcllyn 73 A4
Parc-Seymour 61 D6
Parc-y-rhôs 75 D4
Pardshaw 162 B3
Parham 88 A4
Park 183 C7
Park Corner
  Oxon 47 A4
  Windsor 47 A6
Parkend 62 C2
Park End
  Mbro 168 D3
  Northumb 177 B6
Parkeston 88 D3
Parkgate
  Ches W 126 B2
  Dumfries 184 D3
  Kent 37 C6
  Sur 35 B5
Park Gate 18 A4
Parkham 25 C4
Parkham Ash 25 C4
Park Hill
  Notts 132 D1
  N Yorks 148 A2
Parkhill House 245 A5
Parkhouse 61 C6
Parkhouse Green . . . 131 C6
Parkhurst 18 B3
Parkmill 57 D5
Parkneuk 233 A5
Parkstone 17 B4
Park Street 35 C4
Parley Cross 17 B4
Parracombe 26 A1
Parrog 72 C3
Parsley Hay 129 C6
Parsonage Green 69 C7
Parsonby 163 A4
Parson Cross 139 D6
Parson Drove 101 A5
Parson's Heath 71 A4
Partick 205 B5
Partington 137 D6
Partney 135 C4
Parton
  Cumb 162 B2
  Dumfries 173 A4
  Glos 63 A4
Partridge Green 21 A4
Parwich 130 D1
Passenham 83 D4
Paston 121 B5
Patchacott 11 B5
Patcham 21 B6
Patching 20 B3
Patchole 25 A7
Patchway 43 A4
Pateley Bridge 147 A5

Paternoster Heath . . 70 B3
Pathe 28 B3
Pathhead
  Aberds 233 B5
  E Ayrs 182 A4
  Fife 209 A5
  Midloth 209 D6
Path of Condie 219 C5
Pathstruie 219 C5
Patna 182 A2
Patney 45 D4
Patrick 152 C2
Patrick Brompton . . 157 B6
Patrington 143 A5
Patrixbourne 52 D3
Patterdale 164 D1
Pattingham 95 B6
Pattishall 82 B3
Pattiswick Green . . . 70 A2
Patton Bridge 155 B4
Paul 2 C2
Paulerspury 83 C4
Paull 142 A3
Pavenham 84 B1
Pawlett 28 A3
Pawston 198 C2
Paxford 81 D4
Paxton 198 A3
Payhembury 13 A5
Paythorne 146 B2
Peacehaven 22 B2
Peak Dale 129 B5
Peak Forest 129 B6
Peakirk 100 A3
Pearsie 232 C1
Peasedown St John . 43 D6
Peasemore 46 B2
Peasenhall 89 A4
Pease Pottage 35 C5
Peaslake 34 B3
Peasley Cross 136 D4
Peasmarsh 37 D6
Peaston 210 D1
Peastonbank 210 D1
Peathill 269 C4
Peat Inn 221 D4
Peatling Magna 98 B2
Peatling Parva 98 C2
Peaton 94 C3
Peats Corner 88 A2
Pebmarsh 87 D4
Pebworth 80 C4
Pecket Well 138 A2
Peckforton 127 D5
Peckham 49 B6
Peckleton 98 A1
Pedlinge 38 B3
Pedmore 96 C2
Pedwell 28 B4
Peebles 196 B1
Peel 152 C2
Peel Common 19 A4
Peel Park 205 C6
Peening Quarter 37 D6
Pegsdon 84 D3
Pegswood 179 A4
Pegwell 53 C5
Peinchorran 247 A4
Peinlich 259 C4
Pelaw 179 C4
Pelcomb Bridge 55 C5
Pelcomb Cross 55 C5
Peldon 70 B3
Pellon 138 A3
Pelsall 96 A3
Pelton 179 D4
Pelutho 174 D4
Pelynt 5 B7
Pemberton 137 C4
Pembrey 57 B4
Pembridge 78 B1
Pembroke = Penfro . . 55 D5
Pembroke Dock
  = Doc Penfro 55 D5
Pembury 36 B4
Penallt 61 B7
Penally 55 E7
Penalt 62 A1
Penare 5 C4
Penarlâg
  = Hawarden 126 C3
Penarth 41 D6
Pen-bont
  Rhydybeddau 91 D4
Penbryn 73 A5
Pencader 58 B1
Pencaenewydd 107 B4
Pencaitland 210 D1
Pencarnisiog 122 C3

Pencarreg 75 D4
Pencelli 60 A2
Pen-clawdd 57 C5
Pencoed 41 C4
Pencombe 78 B3
Pencoyd 61 A7
Pencraig
  Hereford 62 A1
  Powys 109 C5
Pendeen 2 B1
Penderyn 59 E6
Pendine 56 B2
Pendlebury 137 C6
Pendleton 146 D1
Pendock 79 D5
Pendoggett 9 D6
Pendomer 29 D5
Pendoylan 41 D5
Pendre 40 C4
Penegoes 91 B5
Pen-ffordd 55 B6
Pengam 41 B6
Penge 49 B6
Pengenffordd 77 D5
Pengorffwysfa 123 A4
Pengover Green 6 A1
Pen-groes-oped 61 C5
Penhale
  Corn 3 D4
  Corn 4 B4
Penhalvaen 4 D2
Penhill 45 A5
Penhow 61 D6
Penhurst 23 A4
Peniarth 90 B4
Penicuik 209 D5
Peniel
  Carms 58 C1
  Denb 125 C5
Penifiler 259 D4
Peninver 190 C3
Penisarwaun 123 D5
Penistone 139 C5
Penjerrick 4 D2
Penketh 127 A5
Penkill 181 B4
Penkridge 112 D3
Penley 110 B3
Penllergaer 57 C6
Penllyn 41 D4
Pen-llyn 122 B3
Pen-lon 123 D4
Penmachno 124 D2
Penmaen 57 D5
Penmaenan 124 B2
Penmaenmawr 124 B2
Penmaenpool 91 A4
Penmark 41 E5
Penmarth 4 D2
Penmon 123 B6
Penmore Mill 224 A3
Penmorfa
  Ceredig 73 A6
  Gwyn 107 B5
Penmynydd 123 C5
Penn
  Bucks 67 D4
  W Mid 96 B1
Pennal 91 B5
Pennan 268 C3
Pennant
  Ceredig 75 B4
  Denb 109 B5
  Denb 125 D5
  Powys 91 C6
Pennant
  Melangell 109 C5
Pennar 55 D5
Pennard 57 D5
Pennerley 94 B1
Pennington
  Cumb 153 C3
  Gtr Man 137 D5
  Hants 18 B2
Penn Street 67 D4
Penny Bridge 154 C2
Pennycross 225 D4
Pennygate 121 C5
Pennygown 225 B4
Pennymoor 26 D3
Pennywell 179 D5
Penparc
  Ceredig 73 B5
  Pembs 55 A4
Penparcau 90 D3
Penperlleni 61 C5
Penpillick 5 B5
Penpol 4 D3
Penpoll 5 B6

Penpont
  Dumfries 183 C6
  Powys 59 C6
Penrherber 73 C5
Penrhiwceiber 41 B5
Penrhiw goch 57 A5
Penrhiw-llan 73 B6
Penrhiw-pâl 73 B6
Penrhos 106 C3
Penrhôs 61 B6
Penrhosfeilw 122 B2
Penrhyn Bay 124 A3
Penrhyn-coch 90 D4
Penrhyndeudraeth . . 107 C6
Penrhynside 124 A3
Penrice 57 D4
Penrith 164 B3
Penrose 9 D4
Penruddock 164 C2
Penryn 4 D2
Pensarn
  Carms 57 A4
  Gwyn 125 B4
Pen-sarn
  Gwyn 107 B4
  Gwyn 107 D5
Pensax 79 A5
Pensby 126 A2
Penselwood 30 B1
Pensford 43 C5
Penshaw 179 D5
Penshurst 36 B3
Pensilva 6 A1
Penston 210 C1
Pentewan 5 C5
Pentir 123 D5
Pentire 4 A2
Pentlow 87 C4
Pentney 119 D4
Penton Mewsey 32 A2
Pentraeth 123 C5
Pentre
  Carms 57 A5
  Powys 93 B6
  Powys 93 C4
  Rhondda 41 B4
  Shrops 110 D2
  Wrex 109 B6
  Wrex 110 A1
Pentrebach
  M Tydf 41 A5
  Swansea 57 B6
Pentre-bâch 75 D4
Pentre-bach 59 B6
Pentrebeirdd 109 D6
Pentre Berw 123 C4
Pentre-bont 124 D2
Pentrecagal 73 B6
Pentre-celyn
  Denb 125 D6
  Powys 91 B6
Pentre-chwyth 57 C6
Pentre-cwrt 73 C6
Pentre Dolau-
  Honddu 76 C3
Pentredwr 109 A6
Pentre-dwr 40 B1
Pentrefelin
  Carms 58 C2
  Ceredig 75 D5
  Conwy 124 B3
  Gwyn 107 C5
Pentrefoelas 124 D3
Pentre-galar 73 C4
Pentregat 73 A6
Pentre-Gwenlais 57 A6
Pentre Gwynfryn . . . 107 D5
Pentre Halkyn 126 B2
Pentreheyling 93 B6
Pentre-Isaf 124 C3
Pentre Llanrhaeadr 125 C5
Pentre-llwyn-ll yd . . 76 B3
Pentre-llyn 75 A5
Pentre-llyn
  cymmer 125 D4
Pentre Meyrick 41 D4
Pentre-poeth 42 A1
Pentre'r Felin 124 C3
Pentre'r-felin 59 B6
Pentre-rhew 75 C5
Pentre-tafarn-y-
  fedw 124 C2
Pentre-ty-gwyn 59 B5
Pentrich 130 D3
Pentridge 31 D4
Pen-twyn 61 C7
Pentyrch 41 C6
Penuchadre 40 D3
Penuwch 75 B4

Penwithick 5 B5
Penwyllt 59 D5
Penybanc 57 A6
Pen-y-banc 58 C3
Penybont 77 A5
Pen-y-bont
  Carms 73 D6
  Gwyn 91 B5
  Gwyn 107 B6
  Powys 109 C7
Pen-y-bont ar Ogwr
  = Bridgend
  Bridgend 40 D4
Penybontfawr 109 C5
Pen-y-bryn
  Gwyn 91 A4
  Pembs 73 B4
Penycae 110 A1
Pen-y-cae 59 D5
Pen-y-cae-mawr . . . 61 D6
Pen-y-cefn 125 B6
Pen-y-clawdd 61 C6
Pen-y-coedcae 41 C5
Penycwm 54 B4
Pen-y-fai 40 C3
Penyffordd 126 C3
Penyffridd 107 A5
Pen-y-garn
  Carms 58 B2
  Ceredig 90 D4
Penygarnedd 109 C6
Pen-y-garnedd 123 C5
Pen-y-gop 108 A4
Penygraig 41 B4
Pen-y-graig 106 C1
Penygroes
  Gwyn 107 A4
  Pembs 73 C4
Pen-y-groes 57 A5
Pen-y-groeslon 106 C2
Pen-y-Gwryd
  Hotel 107 A6
Penyrheol 41 C6
Pen-yr-heol 61 B6
Pen-yr-Heolgerrig . . 60 C2
Penysarn 123 A4
Pen-y-stryt 126 D1
Penywaun 41 A4
Penzance 2 B2
Peopleton 80 B2
Peover Heath 128 B2
Peper Harow 34 B2
Perceton 204 D3
Percie 244 C2
Percyhorner 269 C4
Periton 27 A4
Perivale 49 A4
Perkinsville 179 D4
Perlethorpe 131 B6
Perranarworthal 4 D2
Perranporth 4 B2
Perranuthnoe 2 C3
Perranzabuloe 4 B2
Perry Barr 96 B3
Perryfoot 129 A6
Perry Green
  Herts 68 B4
  Wilts 44 A3
Perry Street 50 B3
Pershall 112 B2
Pershore 80 C2
Pert 233 B4
Pertenhall 84 A2
Perth 219 B6
Perthy 110 B2
Perton 95 B6
Pertwood 30 B2
Peterborough 100 B3
Peterburn 261 B4
Peterchurch 78 D1
Peterculter 245 B5
Peterhead 257 B6
Peterlee 168 A2
Petersfield 33 C6
Peter's Green 67 B6
Peters Marland 25 D5
Peterstone
  Wentlooge 42 A1
Peterstone super-Ely . 41 D5
Peterstow 62 A1
Peter Tavy 11 D6
Petertown 283 G4
Petham 52 D3
Petrockstow 11 A6
Pett 23 A6
Pettaugh 88 B2
Petteridge 37 B4
Pettinain 195 B4
Pettistree 88 B3

Petton
  Devon 27 C5
  Shrops 110 C3
Petts Wood 50 C1
Petty 256 C2
Pettycur 209 B5
Pettymuick 257 C4
Petworth 34 D2
Pevensey 22 B4
Pevensey Bay 23 B4
Pewsey 45 C5
Philham 24 C3
Philiphaugh 186 A3
Phillack 2 B3
Philleigh 4 D3
Philpstoun 208 C3
Phocle Green 62 A2
Phoenix Green 47 D5
Pica 162 B3
Piccotts End 67 C5
Pickering 159 C6
Picket Piece 32 A2
Picket Post 17 A5
Pickhill 158 C2
Picklescott 94 B2
Pickletillem 220 B4
Pickmere 128 B1
Pickney 28 C1
Pickstock 111 C6
Pickwell
  Devon 25 A5
  Leics 115 D5
Pickworth
  Lincs 116 B3
  Rutland 116 D2
Picton
  Ches W 127 B4
  Flint 125 A6
  N Yorks 158 A3
Piddinghoe 22 B2
Piddington
  Northants 83 B5
  Oxon 66 B1
Piddlehinton 15 B7
Piddletrenthide 15 B7
Pidley 101 D5
Piercebridge 167 D5
Pierowall 282 C5
Pigdon 178 A3
Pikehall 130 D1
Pilgrims Hatch 69 D5
Pilham 141 D6
Pill 43 B4
Pillaton 6 A2
Pillerton Hersey 81 C6
Pillerton Priors 81 C5
Pilleth 77 A6
Pilley
  Hants 18 B2
  S Yorks 139 C6
Pilling 144 C4
Pilling Lane 144 C3
Pillowell 62 C2
Pillwell 30 D1
Pilning 43 A4
Pilsbury 129 C6
Pilsdon 14 B4
Pilsgate 100 A2
Pilsley
  Derbys 130 B2
  Derbys 131 C4
Pilton
  Devon 25 B6
  Northants 100 C2
  Rutland 99 A6
  Som 29 A5
Pilton Green 57 D4
Pimperne 16 A3
Pinchbeck 117 C5
Pinchbeck Bars 117 C4
Pinchbeck West 117 C5
Pincheon Green 141 B4
Pinehurst 45 A5
Pinfold 136 B2
Pinged 57 B4
Pinhoe 13 B4
Pinkneys Green 47 A6
Pinley 97 D6
Pin Mill 88 D3
Pinminnoch 180 B3
Pinmore 181 B4
Pinmore Mains 181 B4
Pinner 48 A4
Pinvin 80 C2
Pinwherry 180 C3
Pinxton 131 D4
Pipe and Lyde 78 C3
Pipe Gate 111 A6

Piperhill 253 A4
Piper's Pool 10 C3
Pipewell 99 C5
Pippacott 25 B6
Pipton 77 D5
Pirbright 34 A2
Pirnmill 202 D3
Pirton
Herts. 84 D3
Worcs. 80 C1
Pisgah
Ceredig. 75 A5
Stirling 218 D2
Pishill 47 A5
Pistyll 106 B3
Pitagowan. 230 B2
Pitblae. 269 C4
Pitcairngreen. 219 B5
Pitcalnie 265 C4
Pitcaple 256 D2
Pitchcombe 63 C4
Pitchcott. 66 A2
Pitchford. 94 A3
Pitch Green 66 C2
Pitch Place 34 A2
Pitcombe 29 B6
Pitcorthie 221 D5
Pitcox. 210 C3
Pitcur 220 A2
Pitfichie 244 A3
Pitforthie 233 A6
Pitgrudy 264 A3
Pitkennedy 232 C3
Pitkevy 220 D2
Pitkierie 221 D5
Pitlessie. 220 D3
Pitlochry 230 C3
Pitmachie 256 D1
Pitmain 241 B5
Pitmedden 256 D3
Pitminster 28 D2
Pitmuies 232 D3
Pitmunie 244 A3
Pitney. 29 C4
Pitscottie 220 C4
Pitsea. 51 A4
Pitsford 83 A4
Pitsmoor 130 A3
Pitstone 67 B4
Pitstone Green. 67 B4
Pittendreich. 266 C2
Pittentrail 273 D5
Pittenweem 221 D5
Pittington 167 A6
Pittodrie 256 D1
Pitton. 31 B6
Pittswood 36 B4
Pittulie 269 C4
Pityme 9 D5
Pity Me. 167 A5
Pityoulish 242 A2
Pixey Green 104 D3
Pixham. 35 C4
Pixley 79 D4
Place Newton. 160 D2
Plaidy. 268 D2
Plains. 207 D5
Plaish. 94 B3
Plaistow 34 C3
Plaitford 32 D1
Plank Lane 137 D5
Plas-canol 90 A3
Plas Gogerddan. 90 D4
Plas Llwyngwern 91 B5
Plas Nantyr 109 B6
Plastow Green 46 C3
Plas-yn-Cefn 125 B5
Platt 36 A4
Platt Bridge 137 C5
Platts Common 139 C6
Plawsworth 167 A5
Plaxtol 36 A4
Playden 37 D7
Playford 88 C3
Play Hatch 47 B5
Playing Place 4 C3
Playley Green 79 D5
Plealey. 94 A2
Plean 207 B6
Pleasington 137 A5
Pleasley. 131 C5
Pleckgate 145 D6
Plenmeller 177 C5
Pleshey 69 B6
Plockton 249 C6
Plocrapol 288 H2
Ploughfield 78 C1
Plowden 94 C1

Ploxgreen 94 A1
Pluckley. 38 A1
Pluckley Thorne. . . .37 B7
Plumbland 163 A4
Plumley 128 B2
Plumpton
Cumb 164 B2
E Sus. 21 A6
Plumpton Green 21 A6
Plumpton Head 164 B3
Plumstead
London 50 B1
Norf 120 B3
Plumtree 115 B4
Plungar 115 B5
Plush 15 A7
Plwmp 73 A6
Plymouth. 6 B3
Plympton. 7 B4
Plymstock 7 B4
Plymtree 13 A5
Pockley 159 C5
Pocklington 149 C7
Pode Hole 117 C5
Podimore 29 C5
Podington 83 A6
Podmore 112 B1
Point Clear 71 B4
Pointon 116 B4
Pokesdown 17 B5
Pol a Charra 286 E3
Polbae 181 D4
Polbain 270 C2
Polbathic. 6 B2
Polbeth 208 D3
Polchar 242 B1
Polebrook 100 C2
Pole Elm 79 C6
Polegate 22 B3
Poles 264 A3
Polesworth 97 A5
Polgigga 2 C1
Polglass. 270 D3
Polgooth 5 B4
Poling 20 B3
Polkerris 5 B5
Polla. 277 C4
Pollington 140 B4
Polloch 236 C1
Pollok 205 B5
Pollokshields 205 B5
Polmassick 5 C4
Polmont 208 C2
Polnessan 182 A2
Polnish 235 B6
Polperro 5 B7
Polruan 5 B6
Polsham 29 A5
Polstead 87 D5
Poltalloch 213 C6
Poltimore 13 B4
Polton 209 D5
Polwarth 197 A6
Polyphant 10 C3
Polzeath 9 D5
Pondersbridge. 101 B4
Ponders End. 68 D3
Pondtail. 34 A1
Ponsanooth 4 D2
Ponsworthy 12 D2
Pont Aber 59 C4
Pont Aber-Geirw. . . .108 C2
Pontamman 57 A6
Pontantwn 57 A4
Pontardawe 40 A2
Pontarddulais 57 B5
Pont-ar-gothi 58 C2
Pont ar Hydfer 59 C5
Pont-ar-llechau 59 C4
Pontarsais 58 C1
Pontblyddyn 126 C2
Pontbren Araeth 58 C3
Pontbren Llwyd 59 E6
Pont Cwm Pydew . . .109 B5
Pont Cyfyng 124 D2
Pont Cysyllte 110 A1
Pont Dolydd Prysor .108 B2
Pontefract. 140 A2
Ponteland 178 B3
Pontesbury. 94 A1
Pontesford 94 A1
Pontfadog. 110 B1
Pontfaen 55 A6
Pont-faen 76 D3
Pont Fronwydd 108 C3
Pont-gareg. 72 B4
Pontgarreg 73 A6
Pont-Henri 57 B4
Ponthir 61 D5
Ponthirwaun 73 B5

Pontllanfraith 41 B6
Pontlliw 57 B6
Pont-Llogel 109 D5
Pontllyfni 107 A4
Pontlottyn 60 C3
Pontneddfechan 59 E6
Pontnewydd 61 D4
Pont Pen-y-
benglog 123 D6
Pont Rhyd-goch . . .124 C1
Pont-Rhyd-sarn . . .108 C3
Pont Rhyd-y-cyff . . .40 C3
Pontrhydfendigaid . .75 B6
Pontrhydfen 40 B2
Pont-rhyd-y-groes . .75 A6
Pontrilas 61 A5
Pontrobert 109 D6
Pont-rug. 123 D5
Pont Senni
= Sennybridge 59 C6
Ponts Green 23 A4
Pontshill 62 A2
Pont-siân 74 D3
Pontsticill 60 B2
Pontwgan 124 B2
Pontyates 57 B4
Pontyberem 57 A5
Pontyclun 41 C5
Pontycymer 40 B4
Pontyglasier 72 C4
Pont-y-gwaith. 41 B5
Pont-y-pant 124 D2
Pont y Pennant 108 C4
Pontypool
= Pont-Y-Pŵl 61 C4
Pontypridd 41 C5
Pont-Y-Pŵl
= Pontypool 61 C4
Pont yr Afon-Gam. .108 A2
Pont-yr-hafod 55 B5
Pontywaun 41 B7
Pooksgreen 32 D2
Pool
Corn 3 A4
W Yorks 147 C6
Poole 17 B4
Poole Keynes 63 D5
Poolend 129 D4
Poolewe 261 B5
Pooley Bridge 164 C2
Poolfold. 128 D3
Poolhill 62 A3
Pool o' Muckhart. . . .219 D5
Pool Quay 110 D1
Poolsbrook 131 B4
Pootings 36 B2
Pope Hill 55 C5
Popeswood 47 C6
Popham. 33 A4
Poplar 49 A6
Popley 47 D4
Porchester 114 A3
Porchfield 18 B3
Porin 251 A5
Poringland 104 A3
Porkellis 3 B4
Porlock 26 A3
Porlock Weir 26 A3
Portachoillan 202 C2
Port Ann 214 D2
Port Appin 226 B4
Port Arthur 285 K5
Port Askaig. 201 B4
Portavadie 203 B4
Port Bannatyne 203 B5
Portbury 43 B4
Port Carlisle 175 B5
Port Charlotte 200 C2
Portchester 19 A5
Portclair 240 A1
Port Clarence. 168 C2
Port Driseach. 203 A4
Port Ellen 200 D3
Port Elphinstone . . .256 E2
Portencalzie. 180 D2
Portencross 204 D1
Port Erin 152 E1
Port Erroll 257 C5
Portesham 15 C6
Portessie 267 C5
Port e Vullen 152 B4
Port-Eynon 57 D4
Portfield Gate 55 C5
Portgate 11 C5
Port Gaverne 9 C6
Port Glasgow 204 A3
Portgordon 267 C4
Portgower 274 C4
Porth
Corn 4 A3

Porth continued
Rhondda 41 B5
Porthaethwy
= Menai Bridge. 123 C5
Porthallow
Corn 3 C5
Corn 6 B1
Porthcawl. 40 D3
Porthcothan. 9 D4
Porthcurno 2 C1
Port Henderson. 261 C4
Porthgain 54 A4
Porthill 110 D3
Porthkerry 41 E5
Porthleven 3 C4
Porthllechog 123 A4
Porthmadog 107 C5
Porthmeor 2 B2
Porth Navas 3 C5
Portholland 5 C4
Porthoustock 3 C6
Porthpean. 5 B5
Porthtowan 3 A4
Porth Tywyn
= Burry Port 57 B4
Porthyrhyd
Carms 57 A5
Carms 59 B4
Porth-y-waen 110 C1
Portincaple. 215 C5
Portington 149 D6
Portinnisherrich 214 A2
Portinscale 163 B5
Port Isaac 9 C5
Portishead 42 B3
Portkil 215 D5
Portknockie 267 C5
Port Lamont 203 A5
Portlethen 245 C6
Portling 173 C6
Port Lion 55 D5
Portloe 4 D4
Port Logan 170 C2
Portmahomack 265 B5
Portmeirion 107 C5
Portmellon 5 C5
Port Mholair 288 D6
Port Mor 234 C3
Portmore 18 B2
Port Mulgrave 169 D5
Portnacroish 226 B4
Portnahaven. 200 C1
Portnaluchaig 235 B5
Portnancon 277 B5
Port Nan Giùran . . .288 D6
Port nan Long 287 G3
Portnellan. 216 B4
Port Nis 288 A6
Portobello. 209 C6
Port of Menteith . . .217 D5
Porton 31 B5
Portpatrick 170 B2
Port Quin. 9 C5
Port Ramsay 226 B3
Portreath 3 A4
Portree 259 D4
Port St Mary 152 E2
Portscatho 4 D3
Portsea 19 A5
Portskerra 279 B4
Portskewett 43 A4
Portslade 21 B5
Portslade-by-Sea. . . .21 B5
Portsmouth
Ptsmth 19 A5
W Yorks 138 A2
Portsonachan 227 D5
Portsoy 267 C6
Port Sunlight 126 A3
Portswood 32 D3
Port Talbot 40 B2
Porttanachy 267 C4
Port Tennant 57 C6
Portuairk. 234 D3
Portway
Hereford. 78 D2
Worcs 96 D3
Port Wemyss 200 C1
Port William 171 C5
Portwrinkle 6 B2
Poslingford. 86 C3
Postbridge. 12 D1
Postcombe 66 D2
Postling 38 B3
Postwick 104 A3
Potholm. 185 D6
Potsgrove 67 A4
Potten End 67 C5
Potter Brompton . . .160 D3

Potterhanworth. . . .133 C5
Potterhanworth
Booths 133 C5
Potter Heigham 121 D6
Potterne 44 D3
Potterne Wick 44 D4
Potternewton. 148 D2
Potters Bar 68 C2
Potter's Cross 95 C6
Potterspury 83 C4
Potter Street 69 C4
Potterton
Aberds 245 A6
W Yorks 148 D3
Potto 158 A3
Potton 84 C4
Pott Row 119 C4
Pott Shrigley 129 B4
Poughill
Corn 10 A3
Devon 12 A3
Poulshot 44 D3
Poulton
Glos 64 C2
Mers 136 D2
Poulton-le-Fylde . . .144 D3
Pound Bank 95 D5
Poundfield 36 C3
Pound Green
E Sus 36 D3
IoW 18 C2
Worcs 95 D5
Pound Hill 35 C5
Poundland 180 C3
Poundon 66 A1
Poundsgate 12 D2
Poundstock 10 B3
Powburn 188 B3
Powderham 13 C4
Powerstock 15 B5
Powfoot 174 B4
Powick 79 B6
Powmill 208 A3
Poxwell 16 C1
Poyle 48 B3
Poynings 21 A5
Poyntington 29 D6
Poynton 129 A4
Poynton Green. 111 D4
Poystreet Green 87 B5
Praa Sands 2 C3
Pratt's Bottom 50 C1
Praze 2 B3
Praze-an-Beeble 3 B4
Predannack Wollas. . .3 D4
Prees 111 B4
Preesall 144 C3
Prees Green 111 B4
Preesgweene 110 B1
Prees Heath 111 B4
Prees Higher
Heath 111 B4
Prees Lower Heath . .111 B4
Prenderguest. 198 A3
Prendwick. 188 B3
Prengwyn 73 B7
Prenteg 107 B5
Prenton 126 A3
Prescot. 136 D3
Prescott. 110 C3
Pressen 198 C2
Prestatyn 125 A5
Prestbury
Ches E. 129 B4
Glos 63 A5
Presteigne
= Llanandras. 77 A7
Presthope 94 B3
Prestleigh 29 A6
Preston
Borders 198 A1
Brighton 21 B6
Devon 12 D3
Dorset 15 C7
E Loth 210 C2
E Yorks 151 D4
Glos 63 C6
Glos 79 D4
Herts. 68 A1
Kent 52 C2
Kent 53 C4
Lancs 136 A4
Northumb 189 A4
Rutland 99 A5
Shrops 111 D4
Wilts 44 B4
Wilts 45 B6
Preston Bagot 81 A4
Preston Bissett 66 A1
Preston Bowyer 27 C6

Preston
Brockhurst 111 C4
Preston Brook 127 A5
Preston Candover. . .33 A5
Preston Capes 82 B2
Preston Crowmarsh .65 D7
Preston Gubbals . . .110 D3
Prestonmill. 174 C2
Preston on Stour. . . .81 C5
Preston on the Hill .127 A5
Preston on Wye 78 C1
Prestonpans. 209 C6
Preston Plucknett. . .29 D5
Preston St Mary. 87 B5
Preston-under-
Scar 157 B4
Preston upon the Weald
Moors. 111 D5
Preston Wynne 78 C3
Prestwich 137 C7
Prestwick
Northumb 178 B3
S Ayrs 192 C3
Prestwood 66 C3
Price Town 40 B4
Prickwillow 102 C1
Priddy 43 D4
Priesthaugh 186 C3
Priest Hutton 154 D4
Priest Weston. 93 B6
Primethorpe. 98 B2
Primrose Green 120 D2
Primrosehill 67 C5
Primrose Valley 161 D5
Princes Gate. 56 A1
Princes Risborough . .66 C3
Princethorpe 97 D7
Princetown
Caerph 60 B3
Devon 11 D6
Prion 125 C5
Prior Muir. 221 C5
Prior Park 198 A3
Priors Frome 78 D3
Priors Hardwick 82 B1
Priorslee 111 D6
Priors Marston 82 B1
Priory Wood 77 C6
Priston. 43 C5
Pristow Green 104 C2
Prittlewell 51 A5
Privett 33 C5
Prixford 25 B6
Probus 4 C3
Proncy 264 A3
Prospect 174 D4
Prudhoe 178 C2
Ptarmigan Lodge . .215 B5
Pubil 228 D3
Puckeridge 68 A3
Puckington 28 D3
Pucklechurch 43 B5
Pucknall 32 C2
Puckrup. 80 D1
Puddinglake. 128 C2
Puddington
Ches W. 126 B3
Devon 26 D3
Puddledock 103 B6
Puddletown 16 B1
Pudleston 78 B3
Pudsey. 147 D6
Pulborough 20 A3
Puleston 111 C6
Pulford 126 D3
Pulham 15 A7
Pulham Market 104 C2
Pulham St Mary. . . .104 C3
Pulloxhill 84 D2
Pumpherston 208 D3
Pumsaint 58 A3
Puncheston 55 B6
Puncknowle. 15 C5
Punnett's Town 36 D4
Purbrook 19 A5
Purewell 17 B5
Purfleet. 50 B2
Puriton 28 A3
Purleigh 70 C2
Purley
London 49 C6
W Berks 47 B4
Purlogue 93 D6
Purls Bridge 101 C6
Purse Caundle 29 D6
Purslow 94 C1
Purston Jaglin 140 B2
Purton
Glos 62 C2
Glos 62 C2

Purton *continued*
Wilts 45 A4
Purton Stoke 64 D1
Pury End 83 C4
Pusey 65 D4
Putley 79 D4
Putney 49 B5
Putsborough 25 A5
Puttenham
  Herts 66 B3
  Sur 34 B2
Puxton 42 C3
Pwll 57 B4
Pwllcrochan 55 D5
Pwll-glas 125 D6
Pwllgloyw 76 D4
Pwllheli 106 C3
Pwllmeyric 61 D7
Pwll-trap 56 A2
Pwll-y-glaw 40 B2
Pyecombe 21 A5
Pye Corner 42 A2
Pye Green 112 D3
Pyewipe 143 B4
Pyle 18 D3
Pyle = *Y Pîl* 40 C3
Pylle 29 B6
Pymoor 101 C6
Pyrford 34 A3
Pyrton 66 D1
Pytchley 99 D5
Pyworthy 10 A4

Q

Quabbs 93 C6
Quadring 117 B5
Quainton 66 B2
Quarley 31 A6
Quarndon 114 A1
Quarrier's Homes . . 204 B3
Quarrington 116 A3
Quarrington Hill . . 167 B6
Quarry Bank 96 C2
Quarryford 210 D2
Quarryhill 264 B3
Quarrywood 266 C2
Quarter 194 A2
Quatford 95 B5
Quatt 95 C5
Quebec 167 A4
Quedgeley 63 B4
Queen Adelaide . . . 102 C1
Queenborough 51 B6
Queen Camel 29 C5
Queen Charlton . . . 43 C5
Queen Dart 26 D3
Queenhill 79 D6
Queen Oak 30 B1
Queensbury 147 D5
Queensferry
  Edin 208 C4
  Flint 126 C3
Queensferry
  Crossing 208 C4
Queen's Head 110 C2
Queen's Park
  Bedford 84 C2
  Northants 83 A4
Queenstown 144 D3
Queen Street
  Kent 37 B4
  Wilts 44 A4
Queenzieburn 207 C4
Quemerford 44 C4
Quendale 285 M5
Quendon 85 D7
Queniborough 115 D4
Quenington 64 C2
Quernmore 145 B5
Quethiock 6 A2
Quholm 282 F3
Quicks Green 46 B3
Quidenham 103 C6
Quidhampton
  Hants 46 D3
  Wilts 31 B5
Quilquox 257 C4
Quina Brook 111 B4
Quindry 283 H5
Quinton
  Northants 83 B4
  W Mid 96 C2
Quintrell Downs 4 A3
Quixhill 113 A5
Quoditch 11 B5
Quoig 218 B3
Quorndon 114 D3
Quothquan 195 C4

Quoyloo 282 E3
Quoyness 283 G3
Quoys
  Shetland 284 B8
  Shetland 285 G6

R

Raasay House 248 C2
Rabbit's Cross 37 B5
Raby 126 B3
Rachan Mill 195 C6
Rachub 123 D6
Rackenford 26 D3
Rackham 20 A3
Rackheath 121 D4
Racks 174 A3
Rackwick
  Orkney 282 C5
  Orkney 283 H3
Radbourne 113 B6
Radcliffe
  Gtr Man 137 C6
  Northumb 189 C5
Radcliffe on Trent . 115 B4
Radclive 82 D3
Radcot 64 D3
Raddery 252 A3
Radernie 221 D4
Radford Semele . . . 81 A6
Radipole 15 C6
Radlett 67 D6
Radley 65 D6
Radmanthwaite . . . 131 C5
Radmoor 111 C5
Radmore Green . . . 127 D5
Radnage 66 D2
Radstock 43 D5
Radstone 82 C2
Radway 81 C6
Radway Green 128 D2
Radwell
  Bedford 84 B2
  Herts 84 D4
Radwinter 86 D2
Radyr 41 C6
Rafford 253 A6
Ragdale 115 D4
Raglan 61 C6
Ragnall 132 B3
Rahane 215 D5
Rainford 136 C3
Rainford Junction . 136 C3
Rainham
  London 50 A2
  Medway 51 C5
Rainhill 136 D3
Rainhill Stoops . . . 136 D4
Rainow 129 B4
Rainton 158 D2
Rainworth 131 D5
Raisbeck 155 A5
Raise 165 A5
Rait 220 B2
Raithby
  Lincs 134 A3
  Lincs 134 C3
Rake 33 C7
Rakewood 138 B2
Ram 75 D4
Ramasaig 258 D1
Rame
  Corn 4 D2
  Corn 6 C3
Rameldry Mill
  Bank 220 D3
Ram Lane 38 A1
Ramnageo 284 C8
Rampisham 15 A5
Rampside 153 D3
Rampton
  Cambs 85 A6
  Notts 132 B2
Ramsbottom 137 B6
Ramsbury 45 B6
Ramscraigs 275 B5
Ramsdean 33 C6
Ramsdell 46 D3
Ramsden 65 B4
Ramsden Bellhouse . 69 D7
Ramsden Heath . . . 69 D7
Ramsey
  Cambs 101 C4
  Essex 88 D3
  IoM 152 B4
Ramseycleuch 185 A4
Ramsey Forty Foot . 101 C5
Ramsey Heights . . . 101 C4
Ramsey Island 70 C3

Ramsey Mereside . . 101 C4
Ramsey St Mary's . . 101 C4
Ramsgate 53 C5
Ramsgill 157 D5
Ramshorn 113 A4
Ramsnest Common . 34 C2
Ranais 288 E5
Ranby
  Lincs 134 B2
  Notts 131 A6
Rand 133 B6
Randwick 63 C4
Ranfurly 204 B3
Rangag 280 D3
Rangemore 113 C5
Rangeworthy 43 A5
Rankinston 182 A2
Ranmoor 130 A3
Ranmore Common . 35 A4
Rannerdale 163 C4
Rannoch Station . . 228 C3
Ranochan 238 D2
Ranskill 131 A6
Ranton 112 C2
Ranworth 121 D5
Raploch 207 A5
Rapness 282 C6
Rascal Moor 149 D7
Rascarrel 173 D5
Rashiereive 257 D4
Raskelf 158 D3
Rassau 60 B3
Rastrick 139 A4
Ratagan 238 A3
Ratby 98 A2
Ratcliffe Culey 97 B6
Ratcliffe on Soar . . 114 C2
Ratcliffe on the
  Wreake 115 D4
Rathen 269 C5
Rathillet 220 B3
Rathmell 146 B2
Ratho 208 C4
Ratho Station 208 C4
Rathven 267 C5
Ratley 81 C6
Ratlinghope 94 B2
Rattar 281 A4
Ratten Row 144 C4
Rattery 7 A6
Rattlesden 87 B5
Rattray 231 D5
Raughton Head . . . 164 A1
Raunds 100 D1
Ravenfield 140 D2
Ravenglass 153 A1
Raveningham 105 B4
Ravenscar 160 A3
Ravenscraig 204 A2
Ravensdale 152 B3
Ravensden 84 B2
Ravenseat 156 A2
Ravenshead 131 D5
Ravensmoor 127 D6
Ravensthorpe
  Northants 98 D3
  W Yorks 139 A5
Ravenstone
  Leics 114 D2
  M Keynes 83 B5
Ravenstonedale . . . 155 A6
Ravenstown 154 D2
Ravenstruther 194 B4
Ravensworth 157 A5
Raw 160 A3
Rawcliffe
  E Yorks 141 A4
  York 149 B4
Rawcliffe Bridge . . 141 A4
Rawdon 147 D6
Rawmarsh 140 D2
Rawreth 70 D1
Rawridge 14 A2
Rawtenstall 137 A7
Raxton 256 C3
Raydon 87 D6
Raylees 188 D2
Rayleigh 70 D2
Rayne 70 A1
Rayners Lane 48 A4
Raynes Park 49 C5
Reach 86 A1
Read 146 D1
Reading 47 B5
Reading Street 37 C7
Reagill 165 D4
Rearquhar 264 A3
Rearsby 115 D4
Reaster 281 B4
Reawick 285 J5

Reay 279 B5
Rechullin 249 A5
Reculver 53 C4
Redberth 55 D6
Redbourn 67 B6
Redbourne 142 D1
Redbrook
  Mon 62 B1
  Wrex 111 A4
Redburn
  Highld 253 B5
  Highld 264 D1
  Northumb 177 C5
Redcar 168 C4
Redcastle
  Angus 233 C4
  Highld 252 B1
Redcliff Bay 42 B3
Red Dial 175 D5
Redding 208 C2
Reddingmuirhead . . 208 C2
Reddish 138 D1
Redditch 80 A3
Rede 87 B4
Redenhall 104 C3
Redesdale Camp . . 187 D7
Redesmouth 177 A6
Redford
  Aberds 233 A5
  Angus 232 D3
  Durham 166 B3
Redfordgreen 185 A6
Redgorton 219 B5
Redgrave 103 D6
Redhill
  Aberds 245 B4
  Aberds 256 C1
  N Som 42 C3
  Sur 35 A5
Red Hill 79 B6
Redhouse 202 B3
Redhouses 200 B3
Red Houses 6
Redisham 105 C5
Redland
  Bristol 43 B4
  Orkney 282 E4
Redlingfield 104 D2
Red Lodge 102 D2
Redlynch
  Som 29 B7
  Wilts 31 C6
Redmarley D'Abitot . 79 D5
Redmarshall 167 C6
Redmile 115 B5
Redmire 156 B4
Redmoor 5 A5
Rednal 110 C2
Redpath 197 C4
Redpoint 261 D4
Red Rail 62 A1
Red Rock 137 C4
Red Roses 56 A2
Red Row 189 D5
Redruth 3 A4
Red Street 128 D3
Redvales 137 C7
Red Wharf Bay . . . 123 B5
Redwick
  Newport 42 A3
  S Glos 43 A4
Redworth 167 C5
Reed 85 D5
Reedham 105 A5
Reedness 141 A5
Reeds Beck 134 C2
Reepham
  Lincs 133 B5
  Norf 120 C2
Reeth 156 B4
Regaby 152 B4
Regoul 253 A4
Reiff 270 C2
Reigate 35 A5
Reighton 161 D5
Reighton Gap 161 D5
Reinigeadal 288 G3
Reiss 281 C5
Rejerrah 4 B2
Releath 3 B4
Relubbus 2 B3
Relugas 253 B5
Remenham 47 A5
Remenham Hill . . . 47 A5
Remony 229 D6
Rempstone 114 C3
Rendcomb 63 C6
Rendham 88 A4
Rendlesham 88 B4
Renfrew 205 B4

Renhold 84 B2
Renishaw 131 B4
Rennington 189 B5
Renton 206 C1
Renwick 164 A3
Repps 121 D6
Repton 113 C7
Reraig 249 D5
Rescobie 232 C3
Resipole 235 D6
Resolis 264 D2
Resolven 40 A3
Reston 211 D5
Reswallie 232 C3
Retew 4 B4
Retford 132 A2
Rettendon 70 D1
Rettendon Place . . . 70 D1
Revesby 134 C2
Revesby Bridge . . . 134 C3
Rewe 13 B4
Rew Street 18 B3
Rexare 11 D4
Reydon 105 D5
Reydon Smear 105 D5
Reymerston 103 A6
Reynalton 55 D6
Reynoldston 57 C4
Rezare 11 D4
Rhaeadr Gwy
  = *Rhayader* 76 A3
Rhandirmwyn 59 A4
Rhayader
  = *Rhaeadr Gwy* . . 76 A3
Rhedyn 106 C2
Rhemore 225 A4
Rhencullen 152 B3
Rhes-y-cae 126 B1
Rhewl
  Denb 109 A6
  Denb 125 C6
Rhian 272 C3
Rhicarn 270 B3
Rhiconich 276 C3
Rhicullen 264 C2
Rhidorroch House . 262 A3
Rhifail 278 D3
Rhigos 59 E6
Rhilochan 273 D5
Rhiroy 262 B3
Rhisga = *Risca* . . . 60 D4
Rhiw 106 D2
Rhiwabon
  = *Ruabon* 110 A2
Rhiwbina 41 C6
Rhiwbryfdir 107 B6
Rhiwderin 42 A1
Rhiwlas
  Gwyn 108 B4
  Gwyn 123 D5
  Powys 109 B6
Rhodes 138 C1
Rhodesia 131 B5
Rhodes Minnis 38 A3
Rhodiad 54 B3
Rhondda 41 B4
Rhonehouse or Kelton
  Hill 173 C5
Rhoose = *Y Rhws* . . 41 E5
Rhôs
  Carms 73 C6
  Neath 40 A2
Rhosaman 59 D4
Rhosbeirio 122 A3
Rhoscefnhir 123 C5
Rhoscolyn 122 C2
Rhoscrowther 55 D5
Rhosesmor 126 C2
Rhos-fawr 106 C3
Rhosgadfan 107 A5
Rhosgoch 123 B4
Rhos-goch 77 C5
Rhos-hill 73 B4
Rhoshirwaun 106 D1
Rhoslan 107 B4
Rhoslefain 90 B3
Rhosllanerchrugog 110 A1
Rhosmaen 58 C3
Rhosmeirch 123 C4
Rhosneigr 122 C2
Rhosnesni 126 D3
Rhos-on-Sea 124 A3
Rhosrobin 126 D3
Rhossili 57 D4
Rhosson 54 B3
Rhostryfan 107 A4
Rhostyllen 110 A2
Rhosybol 123 B4
Rhos-y-brithdir . . . 109 C6
Rhos-y-garth 75 A5

Rhos-y-gwaliau . . . 108 B4
Rhos-y-llan 106 C2
Rhos-y-Madoc 110 A2
Rhos-y-meirch 77 A6
Rhu
  Argyll 202 B3
  Argyll 215 D5
Rhuallt 125 B5
Rhuddall Heath . . . 127 C5
Rhuddlan
  Ceredig 58 A1
  Denb 125 B5
Rhue 262 A2
Rhulen 77 B5
Rhunahaorine 202 D2
Rhuthun = *Ruthin* . . 125 D6
Rhyd
  Gwyn 107 B6
  Powys 92 A3
Rhydaman
  = *Ammanford* . . . 57 A6
Rhydargaeau 58 C1
Rhydcymerau 58 B2
Rhydd 79 C6
Rhyd-Ddu 107 A5
Rhydding 40 B2
Rhydfudr 75 B4
Rhydlewis 73 B6
Rhydlios 106 C1
Rhydlydan 124 D3
Rhyd-moel-ddu . . . 93 D4
Rhydness 77 C5
Rhydowen 74 D3
Rhyd-Rosser 75 B4
Rhydspence 77 C6
Rhydtalog 126 D2
Rhyd-uchaf 108 B4
Rhyd-wen 91 A5
Rhydwyn 122 B3
Rhyd-y-clafdy 106 C3
Rhydycroesau 110 B1
Rhydyfelin
  Ceredig 75 A4
  Rhondda 41 C5
Rhyd-y-fro 59 E4
Rhyd-y-gwin 57 B5
Rhydymain 108 C3
Rhyd-y-meirch 61 C5
Rhyd-y-meudwy . . 125 D6
Rhydymwyn 126 C2
Rhyd-y-pandy 57 B6
Rhyd-yr-onen 90 B4
Rhyd-y-sarn 107 B6
Rhyl = *Y Rhyl* 125 A5
Rhymney = *Rhymni* . 60 C3
Rhymni = *Rhymney* . 60 C3
Rhynd
  Fife 221 B4
  Perth 219 B6
Rhynie
  Aberds 255 D5
  Highld 265 C4
Ribbesford 95 D5
Ribblehead 155 D6
Ribbleton 145 D5
Ribchester 145 D6
Ribigill 277 C6
Riby 142 C3
Riby Cross Roads . . 142 C3
Riccall 149 D5
Riccarton 193 B4
Richards Castle . . . 78 A2
Richings Park 48 B3
Richmond
  London 49 B4
  N Yorks 157 A5
Rickarton 245 D5
Rickinghall 103 D6
Rickleton 179 D4
Rickling 85 D6
Rickmansworth . . . 67 D5
Riddings
  Cumb 175 A7
  Derbys 131 D4
Riddlecombe 25 D7
Riddlesden 147 C4
Riddrie 205 B6
Ridge
  Dorset 16 C3
  Hants 32 D2
  Wilts 30 B3
Ridgebourne 77 A4
Ridge Green 35 B6
Ridgehill 43 C4
Ridge Lane 97 B5
Ridgeway Cross . . . 79 C5
Ridgewell 86 C3
Ridgewood 22 A2

Ridgmont 84 D1
Riding Mill 178 C2
Ridleywood. 127 D4
Ridlington
  Norf 121 B5
  Rutland 99 A5
Ridsdale 177 D4
Riechip 231 D4
Riemore. 230 D4
Rienachait 270 A3
Rievaulx. 159 C4
Rift House 168 B2
Rigg 175 B5
Riggend. 207 C5
Rigsby 135 B4
Rigside. 194 C3
Riley Green 137 A5
Rileyhill 113 D5
Rilla Mill 10 D3
Rillington 160 D2
Rimington 146 C2
Rimpton. 29 C6
Rimswell 143 A5
Rinaston 55 B5
Ringasta 285 M5
Ringford 173 C4
Ringinglow 130 A2
Ringland 120 D3
Ringles Cross 36 D2
Ringmer 22 A2
Ringmore 7 C5
Ringorm 254 B3
Ring's End 101 A5
Ringsfield 105 C5
Ringsfield Corner . . .105 C5
Ringshall
  Herts. 67 B4
  Suff. 87 B6
Ringshall Stocks . . . 87 B6
Ringstead
  Norf 119 A4
  Northants 100 D1
Ringwood 17 A5
Ringwould 39 A5
Rinmore 243 A7
Rinnigill 283 H4
Rinsey 2 C5
Riof 288 D2
Ripe 22 A3
Ripley
  Derbys 130 D3
  Hants 17 B5
  N Yorks 148 A1
  Sur 34 A3
Riplingham 150 D2
Ripon 157 D7
Rippingale 116 C3
Ripple
  Kent 39 A5
  Worcs 79 D6
Ripponden 138 B3
Rireavach 262 A2
Risabus 200 D3
Risbury 78 B3
Risby 86 A3
Risca = Rhisga 60 D4
Rise. 151 C4
Riseden. 36 C4
Risegate 117 C5
Riseholme 133 B4
Riseley
  Bedford. 84 A2
  Wokingham 47 C5
Rishangles 88 A2
Rishton 146 D1
Rishworth 138 B3
Rising Bridge 137 A6
Risley
  Derbys 114 B2
  Warr 137 D5
Risplith 147 A6
Rispond 277 B5
Rivar 45 C7
Rivenhall End 70 B2
River Bank 86 A1
Riverhead 36 A3
Rivington 137 B5
Roachill 26 C3
Roade. 83 B4
Road Green. 104 B3
Roadhead 176 B3
Roadmeetings 194 B3
Roadside 280 B3
Roadside of
  Catterline. 233 A6
Roadside of
  Kinneff. 233 A6
Roadwater 27 B5

Roag. 258 D2
Roa Island 153 D3
Roath 41 D6
Roberton
  Borders. 186 B3
  S Lanark 194 D4
Robertsbridge 37 D5
Roberttown 139 A4
Robeston Cross 55 D4
Robeston Wathen . . . 55 C6
Robin Hood 139 A6
Robin Hood's Bay . .160 A3
Roborough
  Devon 7 A4
  Devon 25 D6
Roby 136 D3
Roby Mill 136 C4
Rocester 113 B5
Roch 55 B4
Rochdale 138 B1
Roche 5 A4
Rochester
  Medway 51 C4
  Northumb 188 D1
Rochford 70 D2
Roch Gate 55 B4
Rock
  Corn 9 D5
  Northumb 189 A5
  Worcs 95 D5
  W Sus 21 A4
Rockbeare 13 B5
Rockbourne 31 D5
Rockcliffe
  Cumb 175 B6
  Dumfries 173 C6
Rock Ferry 126 A3
Rockfield
  Highld 265 B5
  Mon 61 B6
Rockford 17 A5
Rockhampton 62 D2
Rockingham 99 B5
Rockland All Saints 103 B5
Rockland St Mary . .104 A4
Rockland St Peter. . .103 B5
Rockley 45 B5
Rockwell End 47 A5
Rockwell Green 27 C6
Rodborough 63 C4
Rodbourne
  Swindon 45 A5
  Wilts 44 A3
Rodbourne Cheney . . 45 A5
Rodd. 77 A7
Roddam 188 A3
Rodden 15 C6
Rode 44 D2
Rodeheath 128 C3
Rode Heath 128 D3
Roden 111 D4
Rodhuish 27 B5
Rodington 111 D4
Rodley
  Glos 62 B3
  W Yorks 147 D6
Rodmarton 63 D5
Rodmell 22 B2
Rodmersham 51 C6
Rodney Stoke 42 D3
Rodsley 113 A6
Rodway 28 B2
Rodwell 15 D6
Roecliffe 148 A2
Roe Green 85 D5
Roehampton 49 B5
Roesound 284 G5
Roffey 35 C4
Rogart 273 D5
Rogart Station 273 D5
Rogate 33 C7
Rogerstone 42 A1
Roghadal 287 F5
Rogiet 42 A3
Rogue's Alley 101 A5
Roke 66 D1
Roker 179 D6
Rollesby 121 D6
Rolleston
  Leics 99 A4
  Notts. 132 D2
Rolleston-on-Dove 113 C6
Rolston 151 C5
Rolvenden 37 C6
Rolvenden Layne . . . 37 C6
Romaldkirk 166 C2
Romanby 158 B2
Romannobridge 195 B6
Romansleigh 26 C2
Romford 50 A2

Romiley 138 D2
Romsey 32 C2
Romsey Town 85 B6
Romsley
  Shrops 95 C5
  Worcs 96 D2
Ronague 152 D2
Rookhope 166 A2
Rookley 18 C4
Rooks Bridge 42 D2
Roos 151 D5
Roosebeck 153 D3
Rootham's Green . . . 84 B3
Rootpark 195 A4
Ropley 33 B5
Ropley Dean 33 B5
Ropsley 116 B3
Rora 269 D5
Rorandle 244 A3
Rorrington 93 A7
Roscroggan 3 A4
Rose 4 B2
Roseacre
  Kent 37 A5
  Lancs 144 D4
Rose Ash 26 C2
Rosebank 194 B3
Rosebrough 189 A4
Rosebush 55 B6
Rosecare 10 B2
Rosedale Abbey 159 B6
Roseden 188 A3
Rosefield 253 A4
Rose Green 20 C2
Rose Grove 146 D2
Rosehall 272 D2
Rosehaugh Mains . .252 A2
Rosehearty 269 C4
Rosehill 111 B5
Rose Hill
  E Sus. 22 A2
  Lancs 146 D2
  Suff. 88 C1
Roseisle 266 C2
Roselands 22 B4
Rosemarket 55 D5
Rosemarkie 252 A3
Rosemary Lane 27 D6
Rosemount 231 D5
Rosenannon 5 A4
Rosewell 209 D5
Roseworth 168 C2
Roseworthy 3 B4
Rosgill 164 D3
Roshven 235 C6
Roskhill 258 D2
Roskill House 252 A2
Rosley 175 D6
Roslin 209 D5
Rosliston 113 D6
Rosneath 215 D5
Ross
  Dumfries 172 D4
  Northumb 199 C5
  Perth. 218 B2
Rossett. 126 D3
Rossett Green 148 B2
Rossie Ochill 219 C5
Rossie Priory 220 A2
Rossington 140 D4
Rosskeen 264 D2
Rossland 205 A4
Ross-on-Wye 62 A2
Roster 281 E4
Rostherne 128 A2
Rosthwaite 163 C5
Roston 113 A5
Rosyth 208 B4
Rothbury 188 C3
Rotherby 115 D4
Rotherfield 36 D3
Rotherfield Greys . . 47 A5
Rotherfield Peppard 47 A5
Rotherham 140 D2
Rothersthorpe 83 B4
Rotherwick 47 D5
Rothes 254 B3
Rothesay 203 B5
Rothiebrisbane 256 C2
Rothienorman 256 C2
Rothiesholm 282 E7
Rothley
  Leics 114 D3
  Northumb 178 A2
Rothley Shield East .188 D3
Rothmaise 256 C1
Rothwell
  Lincs 142 D3
  Northants 99 C5
  W Yorks 139 A6

Rothwell Haigh 139 A6
Rotsea 150 B3
Rottal 232 B1
Rotten End 89 A4
Rottingdean 21 B6
Rottington 162 C2
Roud 18 C4
Rougham
  Norf 119 C5
  Suff. 87 A5
Rougham Green . . . 87 A5
Roughburn 240 D1
Rough Close 112 B3
Rough Common 52 D3
Roughlee 146 C2
Roughley 96 B4
Roughsike 176 B3
Roughton
  Lincs 134 C2
  Norf 120 B4
  Shrops 95 B5
Roughton Moor 134 C2
Roundhay 148 D2
Roundstonefoot . . .185 B4
Roundstreet
  Common 34 D3
Roundway 44 C4
Rousdon 14 B2
Rous Lench 80 B3
Routenburn 204 B1
Routh 150 C3
Row
  Corn 10 D1
  Cumb 154 C3
Rowanburn 175 A4
Rowardennan 206 A1
Rowde 44 C3
Rowen 124 B2
Rowfoot 177 C4
Row Heath 71 B5
Rowhedge. 71 A4
Rowhook 35 C4
Rowington 81 A5
Rowland 130 B2
Rowlands Castle . . . 33 D6
Rowlands Gill 178 D3
Rowledge 33 A7
Rowlestone 61 A5
Rowley
  E Yorks 150 D2
  Shrops 93 A7
Rowley Hill 139 B4
Rowley Regis 96 C2
Rowly 34 B3
Rowney Green 96 D3
Rownhams 32 D2
Rowrah 162 C3
Rowsham 66 B3
Rowsley 130 C2
Rowstock 46 A3
Rowston 133 D5
Rowton
  Ches W 127 C4
  Shrops 110 D2
  Telford 111 D5
Roxburgh 197 C6
Roxby
  N Lincs 141 B7
  N Yorks 169 D5
Roxton 84 B3
Roxwell 69 C6
Royal Leamington
  Spa 81 A6
Royal Oak
  Darl. 167 C5
  Lancs 136 C3
Royal Tunbridge
  Wells 36 C3
Royal Wootton
  Bassett. 45 A4
Roybridge 239 D6
Roydhouse 139 B5
Roydon
  Essex 68 C4
  Norf 104 C1
  Norf 119 C4
Roydon Hamlet 68 C4
Royston
  Herts. 85 C5
  S Yorks 139 B6
Royton 138 C2
Rozel 6
Ruabon
  = Rhiwabon 110 A2
Ruaig 222 C3
Ruan Lanihorne 4 C3
Ruan Minor 3 D5
Ruarach 249 D6
Ruardean 62 B2
Ruardean Woodside. 62 B2

Rubery 96 D2
Ruckcroft 164 A3
Ruckhall 78 D2
Ruckinge 38 B2
Ruckland 134 B3
Ruckley 94 A3
Rudbaxton 55 B5
Rudby. 158 A3
Ruddington 114 B3
Rudford 62 A3
Rudge
  Shrops 95 B6
  Som. 44 D2
Rudgeway 43 A5
Rudgwick 34 C3
Rudhall 62 A2
Rudheath 128 B1
Rudley Green 70 C2
Rudry 41 C6
Rudston 150 A3
Rudyard 129 D4
Rufford 136 B3
Rufforth 148 B4
Rugby 98 D2
Rugeley 112 D4
Ruglen 181 A4
Ruilick 251 B7
Ruishton 28 C2
Ruisigearraidh. 287 F4
Ruislip 48 A3
Ruislip Common . . . 48 A3
Rumbling Bridge . . .208 A3
Rumburgh 104 C4
Rumford 9 D4
Rumney 41 D7
Runcorn 127 A5
Runcton 20 B1
Runcton Holme 102 A2
Rundlestone 11 D6
Runfold 34 B1
Runhall 103 A6
Runham
  Norf 105 A6
  Norf 121 D6
Runnington. 27 C6
Runsell Green 70 C1
Runswick Bay. 169 D6
Runwell 70 D1
Ruscombe 47 B5
Rushall
  Hereford. 79 D4
  Norf 104 C2
  Wilts 45 D5
  W Mid 96 A3
Rushbrooke 87 A4
Rushbury. 94 B3
Rushden
  Herts. 85 D5
  Northants 83 A6
Rushenden 51 B6
Rushford 103 C5
Rush Green. 50 A2
Rush-head 256 B3
Rushlake Green 22 A4
Rushmere 105 C5
Rushmere
  St Andrew 88 C3
Rushmoor. 34 B1
Rushock 96 D1
Rusholme 138 D1
Rushton
  Ches W 127 C5
  Northants 99 C5
  Shrops 95 A4
Rushton Spencer . . .129 C4
Rushwick 79 B6
Rushyford 167 C5
Ruskie 217 D6
Ruskington 133 D5
Rusland 154 C2
Rusper 35 C5
Ruspidge 62 B2
Russell's Water 47 A5
Russel's Green 104 D3
Rusthall 36 C3
Rustington 20 B3
Ruston 160 C3
Ruston Parva 150 A3
Ruswarp 160 A2
Rutherford 197 C5
Rutherglen 205 B6
Ruthernbridge 5 A5
Ruthin = Rhuthun. . .125 D6
Ruthrieston 245 B6
Ruthven
  Aberds 255 B6
  Angus 231 D6
  Highld 241 C5
  Highld 253 C4
Ruthven House 231 D7

Ruthvoes 4 A4
Ruthwell 174 B3
Ryton-XI-Towns . . .110 C2
Ryal 178 B2
Ryal Fold 137 A5
Ryall 14 B4
Ryarsh 37 A4
Rydal 154 A2
Ryde 19 B4
Rye 37 D7
Ryecroft Gate 129 C4
Rye Foreign 37 D6
Rye Harbour 38 D1
Ryehill 143 A4
Rye Park 68 C3
Rye Street 79 D5
Ryhall 116 D3
Ryhill 140 B1
Ryhope 179 D6
Rylstone 146 B3
Ryme Intrinseca . . . 29 D5
Ryther 149 D4
Ryton
  Glos 79 D5
  N Yorks 159 D6
  Shrops 95 A5
  T&W 178 C3
Ryton-on-
  Dunsmore 97 D6

S

Sabden 146 D1
Sacombe 68 B3
Sacriston 167 A5
Sadberge 167 D6
Saddell 190 B3
Saddington 98 B3
Saddle Bow 118 D3
Saddlescombe. 21 A5
Sadgill 154 A3
Saffron Walden 86 D1
Sageston 55 D6
Saham Hills 103 A5
Saham Toney 103 A5
Saighdinis 287 H3
Saighton 127 C4
St Abbs 211 D6
St Abb's Haven 211 D6
St Agnes
  Corn 4 B2
  Scilly 2 F3
St Albans 67 C6
St Allen 4 B3
St Andrews 221 C5
St Andrew's Major . 41 D6
St Anne 7
St Annes 136 A2
St Ann's 184 C3
St Ann's Chapel
  Corn 11 D5
  Devon 7 C5
St Anthony-in-
  Meneage 3 C5
St Anthony's Hill . . . 22 B4
St Arvans 61 D7
St Asaph
  = Llanelwy 125 B5
St Athan 41 E5
St Aubin 6
St Austell 5 B5
St Bees 162 C2
St Blazey 5 B5
St Boswells 197 C4
St Brelade 6
St Breock 9 D5
St Breward 10 D1
St Briavels 62 C1
St Bride's 54 C4
St Brides Major . . . 40 D3
St Bride's
  Netherwent. 42 A3
St Brides super Ely . 41 D5
St Brides Wentlooge 42 A1
St Budeaux 6 B3
Saintbury 80 D4
St Buryan 2 C2
St Catherine 44 B1
St Catherine's 215 B4
St Clears = Sanclêr. . 56 A2
St Cleer 6 A1
St Clement 4 C3
St Clements 6
St Clether 10 C3
St Colmac 203 B5
St Columb Major . . . 4 A4
St Columb Minor . . . 4 A4
St Columb Road . . . 4 B4
St Combs. 269 C5

St Cross South
  Elmham 104 C3
St Cyrus 233 B5
St David's 218 B4
St David's = Tyddewi . 54 B3
St Day 4 C2
St Dennis 4 B4
St Devereux 78 D2
St Dogmaels 73 B4
St Dogwells 55 B5
St Dominick 6 A3
St Donat's 40 E4
St Edith's 44 C3
St Endellion 9 D5
St Enoder 4 B3
St Erme 4 B3
St Erney 6 B2
St Erth 2 B3
St Ervan 9 D4
St Eval 4 A3
St Ewe 5 C4
St Fagans 41 D6
St Fergus 269 D5
St Fillans 217 B6
St Florence 55 D6
St Genny's 10 B2
St George 125 B4
St George's 41 D5
St Germans 6 B2
St Giles 133 B4
St Giles in the Wood .25 D6
St Giles on the
  Heath 11 B4
St Harmon 92 D3
St Helena 97 A5
St Helen Auckland .167 C4
St Helens
  IoW 19 C5
  Mers 136 D4
St Helen's 23 A6
St Helier
  Jersey 6
  London 49 C5
St Hilary
  Corn 2 B3
  V Glam 41 D5
Saint Hill 36 C1
St Illtyd 41 A7
St Ippollytts 68 A1
St Ishmael's 54 D4
St Issey 9 D5
St Ive 6 A2
St Ives
  Cambs 101 D5
  Corn 2 A3
  Dorset 17 A5
St James South
  Elmham 104 C4
St Jidgey 9 E5
St John 6 B3
St John's
  IoM 152 C2
  Jersey 6
  Sur 34 A2
  Worcs 79 B6
St John's Chapel .166 B1
St John's Fen End .118 D2
St John's Highway .118 D2
St John's Town of
  Dalry 182 D4
St Judes 152 B3
St Just 2 B1
St Just in Roseland . . . 4 D3
St Katherine's 256 C2
St Keverne 3 C5
St Kew 9 D6
St Kew Highway 9 D6
St Keyne 6 A1
St Lawrence
  Corn 5 A5
  Essex 70 C3
  IoW 18 D4
St Leonards
  Dorset 17 A5
  E Sus 23 B5
St Leonard's 67 C4
Saint Leonards 205 C6
St Levan 2 C1
St Lythans 41 D6
St Mabyn 9 D6
St Madoes 219 B6
St Margarets 68 B3
St Margaret's 78 D1
St Margaret's at
  Cliffe 39 A5
St Margaret's Hope 283 H5
St Margaret South
  Elmham 104 C4
St Mark's 152 D2
St Martin 6 B1

St Martins
  Corn 3 C5
  Perth 219 A6
St Martin's
  Jersey 6
  Shrops 110 B2
St Mary Bourne . . .46 D2
St Mary Church . . .41 D5
St Mary Cray 50 C1
St Mary Hill 41 D4
St Mary Hoo 51 B5
St Mary in the
  Marsh 38 C2
St Mary's
  Jersey 6
  Orkney 283 G5
St Mary's Bay 38 C2
St Maughans 61 B6
St Mawes 4 D3
St Mawgan 4 A3
St Mellion 6 A2
St Mellons 42 A1
St Merryn 9 D4
St Mewan 5 B4
St Michael Caerhays . 5 C4
St Michael Penkevil . 4 C3
St Michaels 78 A3
St Michael's 37 C6
St Michael's on
  Wyre 145 C4
St Michael South
  Elmham 104 C4
St Minver 9 D5
St Monans 221 D5
St Neot 5 A6
St Neots 84 A3
St Newlyn East 4 B3
St Nicholas
  Pembs 72 C1
  V Glam 41 D5
St Nicholas at Wade .53 C4
St Ninians 207 C6
St Osyth 71 B5
St Osyth Heath 71 B5
St Ouens 6
St Owens Cross 62 A1
St Paul's Cray 50 C1
St Paul's Walden . . .68 A1
St Peter Port 6
St Peter's
  Jersey 6
  Kent 53 C5
St Petrox 55 E5
St Pinnock 5 A7
St Quivox 192 C3
St Ruan 3 D5
St Sampson 6
St Stephen 4 B4
St Stephens
  Corn 6 B3
  Herts 67 C6
St Stephen's 10 C4
St Teath 9 C6
St Thomas 13 B4
St Tudy 9 D6
St Twynnells 55 E5
St Veep 5 B6
St Vigeans 233 D4
St Wenn 5 A4
St Weonards 61 A6
Salcombe 7 D6
Salcombe Regis 13 C6
Salcott 70 B3
Sale 137 D6
Saleby 135 B4
Sale Green 80 B2
Salehurst 37 D5
Salem
  Carms 58 C3
  Ceredig 91 D4
Salen
  Argyll 225 B4
  Highld 235 D5
Salesbury 145 D6
Salford
  C Beds 83 D6
  Gtr Man 137 D7
  Oxon 64 A3
Salford Priors 80 B3
Salfords 35 B5
Salhouse 121 D5
Saline 208 A3
Salisbury 31 C5
Sallachan 236 C3
Sallachy
  Highld 249 C6
  Highld 272 D2
Salle 120 C3
Salmonby 134 B3
Salmond's Muir . . .221 A5

Salperton 64 A1
Salph End 84 B2
Salsburgh 207 D6
Salt 112 C3
Saltaire 147 D5
Saltash 6 B3
Saltburn 264 D3
Saltburn-by-the-
  Sea 169 C4
Saltby 115 C6
Saltcoats
  Cumb 153 A1
  N Ayrs 204 D2
Saltdean 22 B1
Salt End 142 A3
Salter 145 A6
Salterforth 146 C2
Salterswall 127 C6
Saltfleet 143 D6
Saltfleetby All
  Saints 143 D6
Saltfleetby
  St Clements 143 D6
Saltfleetby
  St Peter 135 A4
Saltford 43 C5
Salthouse 120 A2
Saltmarshe 141 A5
Saltney 126 C3
Salton 159 D6
Saltwick 178 B3
Saltwood 38 B3
Salum 222 C3
Salvington 21 B4
Salwarpe 80 A1
Salwayash 15 B4
Sambourne 80 A3
Sambrook 111 C6
Samhla 287 H2
Samlesbury 145 D5
Samlesbury
  Bottoms 137 A5
Sampford Arundel . .27 D6
Sampford Brett 27 A5
Sampford Courtenay 12 A1
Sampford Peverell . .27 D5
Sampford Spiney 11 D6
Sampool Bridge . . .154 C2
Samuelston 210 C1
Sanachan 249 B5
Sanaigmore 200 A2
Sanclêr = St Clears . . .56 A2
Sancreed 2 C2
Sancton 150 D2
Sand
  Highld 261 A6
  Shetland 285 J5
Sandaig 247 D6
Sandale 175 D5
Sandal Magna 139 B6
Sandbach 128 C2
Sandbank 215 D4
Sandbanks 17 C4
Sandend 267 C6
Sanderstead 49 C6
Sandfields 63 A5
Sandford
  Cumb 165 D5
  Devon 12 A3
  Dorset 16 C3
  IoW 18 C4
  N Som 42 D3
  Shrops 111 B4
  S Lanark 194 B2
Sandfordhill 257 B6
Sandford on
  Thames 65 C6
Sandford Orcas 29 C6
Sandford St Martin .65 A5
Sandgate 38 B3
Sandgreen 172 C3
Sandhaven 269 C4
Sandhead 170 C2
Sandhills 34 C2
Sandhoe 178 C1
Sand Hole 149 D7
Sandholme
  E Yorks 150 D1
  Lincs 117 B6
Sandhurst
  Brack 47 C6
  Glos 63 A4
  Kent 37 D5
Sandhurst Cross 37 D5
Sandhutton 158 C2
Sand Hutton 149 B5
Sandiacre 114 B2
Sandilands
  Lincs 135 A5
  S Lanark 194 C3

Sandiway 127 B6
Sandleheath 31 D5
Sandling 37 A5
Sandlow Green 128 C2
Sandness 285 H3
Sandon
  Essex 70 C1
  Herts 85 D5
  Staffs 112 B3
Sandown 19 C4
Sandplace 6 B1
Sandridge
  Herts 67 B6
  Wilts 44 C3
Sandringham 118 C3
Sandsend 169 D6
Sandside House 279 B5
Sandsound 285 J5
Sandtoft 141 C5
Sandway 37 A6
Sandwell 96 C3
Sandwich 53 D5
Sandwick
  Cumb 164 D2
  Orkney 283 J5
  Shetland 285 L6
Sandwith 162 C2
Sandy
  Carms 57 B4
  C Beds 84 C3
Sandy Bank 134 D2
Sandycroft 126 C3
Sandyford
  Dumfries 185 C5
  Stoke 128 D3
Sandygate 152 B3
Sandy Haven 55 D4
Sandyhills 173 C6
Sandylands 144 A4
Sandy Lane
  Wilts 44 C3
  Wrex 110 A2
Sandypark 12 C2
Sandysike 175 B6
Sangobeg 277 B5
Sangomore 277 B5
Sanna 234 D3
Sanndabhaig
  W Isles 286 B4
  W Isles 288 D5
Sannox 203 D5
Sanquhar 183 B5
Santon 142 B1
Santon Bridge 163 D4
Santon Downham . .103 C4
Sapcote 98 B1
Sapey Common 79 A5
Sapiston 103 D5
Sapley 100 D4
Sapperton
  Glos 63 C5
  Lincs 116 B3
Saracen's Head 117 C6
Sarclet 281 D5
Sardis 57 B5
Sarn
  Bridgend 40 C4
  Powys 93 B6
Sarnau
  Carms 56 A3
  Ceredig 73 A6
  Gwyn 109 B4
  Powys 76 D4
  Powys 110 D1
Sarn Bach 106 D3
Sarnesfield 78 B1
Sarn Meyllteyrn . . .106 C2
Saron
  Carms 57 A6
  Carms 73 C6
  Denb 125 C5
  Gwyn 107 A4
  Gwyn 123 D5
Sarratt 67 D5
Sarre 53 C4
Sarsden 64 A3
Sarsgrum 277 B4
Satley 166 A4
Satron 156 B3
Satterleigh 26 C1
Satterthwaite 154 B2
Satwell 47 A5
Sauchen 244 A3
Saucher 219 A6
Sauchie 208 A1
Sauchieburn 233 B4
Saughall 126 B3
Saughtree 187 D4
Saul 62 C3
Saundby 132 A2

Saundersfoot 56 B1
Saunderton 66 C2
Saunton 25 B5
Sausthorpe 134 C2
Saval 272 D3
Savary 225 B5
Savile Park 138 A3
Sawbridge 82 A2
Sawbridgeworth . . .69 B4
Sawdon 160 C3
Sawley
  Derbys 114 B2
  Lancs 146 C1
  N Yorks 147 A6
Sawston 85 C6
Sawtry 100 C3
Saxby
  Leics 115 D6
  Lincs 133 A5
Saxby All Saints . . .142 B1
Saxelbye 115 B4
Saxham Street 88 A1
Saxilby 132 B3
Saxlingham 120 B2
Saxlingham Green .104 B3
Saxlingham
  Nethergate 104 B3
Saxlingham Thorpe .104 B3
Saxmundham 89 A4
Saxondale 115 B4
Saxon Street 86 B2
Saxtead 88 A3
Saxtead Green 88 A3
Saxthorpe 120 B3
Saxton 148 D3
Sayers Common . . .21 A5
Scackleton 159 D5
Scadabhagh 288 H2
Scaftworth 141 D4
Scagglethorpe 160 D2
Scaitcliffe 137 A6
Scalasaig 212 C1
Scalby
  E Yorks 141 A6
  N Yorks 160 B4
Scaldwell 99 D4
Scaleby 176 C2
Scaleby Hill 176 C2
Scale Houses 164 A3
Scales
  Cumb 153 C3
  Cumb 163 B6
  Lancs 145 D4
Scalford 115 C5
Scaling 169 D5
Scallastle 225 C5
Scalloway 285 K6
Scalpay 288 H3
Scalpay House 247 B5
Scalpsie 203 C5
Scamadale 235 A6
Scamblesby 134 B2
Scamodale 236 B2
Scampston 160 D2
Scampton 133 B4
Scapa 283 G5
Scapegoat Hill 138 B3
Scar 282 C7
Scarborough 160 C4
Scarcliffe 131 C4
Scarcroft 148 C2
Scarcroft Hill 148 C2
Scardroy 250 A4
Scarff 284 E4
Scarfskerry 281 A4
Scargill 166 D3
Scarinish 222 C3
Scarisbrick 136 B2
Scarning 119 D6
Scarrington 115 A5
Scartho 143 C4
Scarwell 282 E3
Scatness 285 M5
Scatraig 252 C3
Scawby 142 C1
Scawsby 140 C3
Scawton 158 C4
Scayne's Hill 35 D6
Scethrog 60 A3
Scholar Green 128 D3
Scholes
  W Yorks 139 A4
  W Yorks 139 C4
  W Yorks 148 D2
School Green 127 C6
Scleddau 55 A5
Scofton 131 B6
Scole 104 D2
Scolpaig 287 G2
Scone 219 B6

Sconser 247 A4
Scoonie 220 D3
Scoor 224 E3
Scopwick 133 D5
Scoraig 262 A2
Scorborough 150 C3
Scorrier 4 C2
Scorton
  Lancs 145 C5
  N Yorks 157 A6
Sco Ruston 121 C4
Scotbheinn 286 A4
Scotby 176 D2
Scotch Corner 157 A6
Scotforth 145 B4
Scothern 133 B5
Scotland Gate 179 A4
Scotlandwell 219 D6
Scotsburn 264 C3
Scotscalder
  Station 280 C2
Scotscraig 220 B4
Scots' Gap 178 A2
Scotston
  Aberds 233 A5
  Perth 230 D3
Scotstoun 205 B5
Scotstown 236 C2
Scotswood 178 C3
Scottas 247 D6
Scotter 141 C6
Scotterthorpe 141 C6
Scottlethorpe 116 C3
Scotton
  Lincs 141 D6
  N Yorks 148 B2
  N Yorks 157 B5
Scottow 121 C4
Scoughall 210 B3
Scoulag 203 C6
Scoulton 103 A5
Scourie 276 D2
Scourie More 276 D2
Scousburgh 285 M5
Scrabster 280 B2
Scrafield 134 C3
Scrainwood 188 C2
Scrane End 117 A6
Scraptoft 98 A3
Scratby 121 D7
Scrayingham 149 A6
Scredington 116 A3
Scremby 135 C4
Scremerston 198 B4
Screveton 115 A5
Scrivelsby 134 C2
Scriven 148 B2
Scrooby 141 D4
Scropton 113 B5
Scrub Hill 134 D2
Scruton 157 B6
Sculcoates 150 D3
Sculthorpe 119 B5
Scunthorpe 141 B6
Scurlage 57 D4
Seaborough 14 A4
Seacombe 136 D2
Seacroft
  Lincs 135 C5
  W Yorks 148 D2
Seadyke 117 B6
Seafield
  S Ayrs 192 C3
  W Loth 208 D3
Seaford 22 C2
Seaforth 136 D2
Seagrave 115 D4
Seaham 168 A2
Seahouses 199 C6
Seal 36 A3
Sealand 126 C3
Seale 34 B1
Seamer
  N Yorks 160 C4
  N Yorks 168 D2
Seamill 204 D2
Sea Palling 121 C6
Searby 142 C2
Seasalter 52 C2
Seascale 162 D3
Seathorne 135 C5
Seathwaite
  Cumb 153 A3
  Cumb 163 C5
Seatoller 163 C5
Seaton
  Corn 6 B2
  Cumb 162 A3

Seaton continued
Devon 14 B2
Durham 179 D5
E Yorks 151 C4
Northumb 179 B5
Rutland 99 B6
Seaton Burn 179 B4
Seaton Carew 168 C3
Seaton Delaval 179 B5
Seaton Ross 149 C6
Seaton Sluice 179 B5
Seatown
Aberds 267 C6
Dorset 14 B4
Seave Green 159 A4
Seaview 19 B5
Seaville 175 A4
Seavington St Mary . 28 D3
Seavington
St Michael 28 D4
Sebergham 164 A1
Seckington 97 A5
Second Coast 261 A6
Sedbergh 155 B5
Sedbury 62 D1
Sedbusk 156 B2
Sedgeberrow 80 D3
Sedgebrook 115 B6
Sedgefield 167 C6
Sedgeford 119 B4
Sedgehill 30 C2
Sedgley 96 B2
Sedgwick 154 C4
Sedlescombe 23 A5
Sedlescombe Street . 23 A5
Seend 44 C3
Seend Cleeve 44 C3
Seer Green 67 D4
Seething 104 B4
Sefton 136 C2
Seghill 179 B4
Seifton 94 C2
Seighford 112 C2
Seilebost 287 E5
Seion 123 D5
Seisdon 95 B6
Seisiadar 288 D6
Selattyn 110 B1
Selborne 33 B6
Selby 149 D5
Selham 34 D2
Selhurst 49 C6
Selkirk 186 A3
Sellack 62 A1
Sellafirth 284 D7
Sellibister 282 C8
Sellindge 38 B2
Sellindge Lees 38 B3
Selling 52 D2
Sells Green 44 C3
Selly Oak 96 C3
Selmeston 22 B3
Selsdon 49 C6
Selsey 20 C1
Selsfield Common . . 35 C6
Selsted 39 A4
Selston 131 D4
Selworthy 27 A4
Semblister 285 H5
Semer 87 C5
Semington 44 C2
Semley 30 C2
Send 34 A3
Send Marsh 34 A3
Senghenydd 41 B6
Sennen 2 C1
Sennen Cove 2 C1
Sennybridge
=Pont Senni 59 C2
Serlby 131 A6
Sessay 158 D3
Setchey 118 D3
Setley 18 A2
Setter
Shetland 284 E6
Shetland 285 H5
Shetland 285 J7
Settiscarth 282 F4
Settle 146 A2
Settrington 160 D2
Sevenhampton 63 A6
Seven Kings 50 A1
Sevenoaks 36 A3
Sevenoaks Weald . . . 36 A3
Seven Sisters 59 E5
Severn Beach 43 A4
Severnhampton 64 D3
Severn Stoke 79 C6

Sevington 38 A2
Sewards End 86 D1
Sewardstone 68 D3
Sewardstonebury . . 68 D3
Sewerby 151 A4
Seworgan 4 D2
Sewstern 116 C1
Sezincote 81 D4
Sgarasta Mhor . . . 287 E5
Sgiogarstaigh 288 A6
Shabbington 66 C1
Shackerstone 97 A6
Shackleford 34 B2
Shade 138 A2
Shadforth 167 A6
Shadingfield 105 C5
Shadoxhurst 38 B1
Shadsworth 137 A6
Shadwell
Norf 103 C5
W Yorks 148 D2
Shaftesbury 30 C2
Shafton 140 B1
Shalbourne 45 C7
Shalcombe 18 C2
Shalden 33 A5
Shaldon 13 D4
Shalfleet 18 C3
Shalford
Essex 69 A7
Sur 34 B3
Shalford Green 69 A7
Shallowford 26 A2
Shalmsford Street . . 52 D2
Shalstone 82 D3
Shamley Green 34 B3
Shandon 215 D5
Shandwick 265 C4
Shangton 99 B4
Shankhouse 179 B4
Shanklin 19 C4
Shanquhar 255 C6
Shanzie 231 C6
Shap 164 D3
Shapwick
Dorset 16 A3
Som 28 B4
Shardlow 114 B2
Shareshill 96 A2
Sharlston 140 B1
Sharlston Common . 140 B1
Sharnbrook 84 B1
Sharnford 98 B1
Sharoe Green 145 D5
Sharow 158 D2
Sharpenhoe 84 D2
Sharperton 188 C2
Sharpness 62 C2
Sharp Street 121 C5
Sharpthorne 35 C6
Sharrington 120 B2
Shatterford 95 C5
Shaugh Prior 7 A4
Shavington 128 D2
Shaw
Gtr Man 138 C2
W Berks 46 C2
Wilts 44 C2
Shawbury 111 C4
Shawdon Hall 188 B3
Shawell 98 C2
Shawford 32 C3
Shawforth 138 A1
Shaw Green 136 B4
Shawhead 173 A6
Shawhill 175 B5
Shaw Mills 147 A6
Shawton 194 B1
Shawtonhill 194 B1
Shear Cross 30 A2
Shearington 174 B3
Shearsby 98 B3
Shebbear 11 A5
Shebdon 111 C6
Shebster 279 B6
Sheddens 205 C5
Shedfield 33 D4
Sheen 129 C6
Sheepscar 148 D2
Sheepscombe 63 B4
Sheepstor 7 A4
Sheepwash 11 A5
Sheepway 42 B3
Sheepy Magna 97 A6
Sheepy Parva 97 A6
Sheering 69 B5
Sheerness 51 B6
Sheet 33 C6
Sheffield 130 A3
Sheffield Bottom . . . 47 C4

Sheffield Green 36 D2
Shefford 84 D3
Shefford Woodlands . 46 B1
Sheigra 276 B2
Sheinton 95 A4
Shelderton 94 D1
Sheldon
Derbys 129 C6
Devon 13 A6
W Mid 97 C4
Sheldwich 52 D2
Shelf 139 A4
Shelfanger 104 C2
Shelfield
Warks 80 A4
W Mid 96 A3
Shelford 115 A4
Shellacres 198 B2
Shelley
Essex 69 C5
Suff 87 D6
W Yorks 139 B5
Shellingford 64 D4
Shellow Bowells 69 C5
Shelsley Beauchamp 79 A5
Shelsley Walsh 79 A5
Shelthorpe 114 D3
Shelton
Bedford 84 A2
Norf 104 B3
Notts 115 A5
Shrops 110 D3
Shelton Green 104 B3
Shelve 94 B1
Shelwick 78 C3
Shenfield 69 D6
Shenington 81 C6
Shenley 68 C1
Shenley Brook End . . 83 D5
Shenleybury 68 C1
Shenley Church End . 83 D5
Shenmore 78 D1
Shennanton 171 A5
Shenstone
Staffs 96 A4
Worcs 95 D6
Shenton 97 A6
Shenval
Highld 251 D6
Moray 254 D3
Shepeau Stow 117 D6
Shephall 68 A2
Shepherd's Green . . 47 A5
Shepherd's Port . . . 118 B3
Shepherdswell 39 A4
Shepley 139 C4
Shepperdine 62 D2
Shepperton 48 C3
Shepreth 85 C5
Shepshed 114 D2
Shepton
Beauchamp 28 D4
Shepton Mallet 29 A6
Shepton Montague . 29 B6
Shepway 37 A5
Sheraton 168 B2
Sherborne
Dorset 29 D6
Glos 64 B2
Sherborne St John . 47 D4
Sherbourne 81 A5
Sherburn
Durham 167 A6
N Yorks 160 D3
Sherburn Hill 167 A6
Sherburn in Elmet . 148 D3
Shere 34 B3
Shereford 119 C5
Sherfield English . . . 32 C1
Sherfield on Loddon . 47 D4
Sherford 8 C1
Sheriffhales 111 D6
Sheriff Hutton 149 A5
Sheringham 120 A3
Sherington 83 C5
Shernal Green 80 A2
Shernborne 119 B4
Sherrington 30 B3
Sherston 44 A2
Sherwood Green . . . 25 C6
Shettleston 205 B6
Shevington 136 C4
Shevington Moor . . 136 B4
Shevington Vale . . . 136 C4
Sheviock 6 B2
Shide 18 C3
Shiel Bridge 238 A3
Shieldaig
Highld 249 A5
Highld 261 C5

Shieldhill
Dumfries 184 D3
Falk 208 C1
S Lanark 195 B5
Shielfoot 235 D5
Shielhill
Angus 232 C2
Invclyd 204 A2
Shifford 65 C4
Shifnal 95 A5
Shilbottle 189 C4
Shildon 167 C5
Shillingford
Devon 27 C4
Oxon 65 D6
Shillingford
St George 13 C4
Shillingstone 30 D2
Shillington 84 D3
Shillmoor 188 C1
Shilton
Oxon 64 C3
Warks 97 C7
Shilvington 178 A3
Shimpling
Norf 104 C2
Suff 87 B4
Shimpling Street . . . 87 B4
Shincliffe 167 A5
Shiney Row 179 D5
Shinfield 47 C5
Shingham 102 A3
Shingle Street 89 C4
Shinner's Bridge 8 A1
Shinness 272 C3
Shipbourne 36 A3
Shipdham 103 A5
Shipham 42 D3
Shiphay 8 A2
Shiplake 47 B5
Shipley
Derbys 114 A2
Northumb 189 B4
Shrops 95 B6
W Sus 35 D4
W Yorks 147 D5
Shipley Shiels 187 D6
Shipmeadow 105 C4
Shippea Hill
Station 102 C2
Shippon 65 D5
Shipston-on-Stour . . 81 C5
Shipton
Glos 63 B6
N Yorks 149 B4
Shrops 94 B3
Shipton Bellinger . . . 31 A6
Shipton Gorge 15 B4
Shipton Green 19 A7
Shipton Moyne 44 A2
Shipton on Cherwell 65 B5
Shipton Solers 63 B6
Shiptonthorpe 150 C1
Shipton-under-
Wychwood 64 B3
Shirburn 66 D1
Shirdley Hill 136 B2
Shirebrook 131 C5
Shiregreen 139 D6
Shirehampton 43 B4
Shiremoor 179 B5
Shirenewton 61 D6
Shireoaks 131 A5
Shirkoak 38 B1
Shirland 130 D3
Shirley
Derbys 113 A6
London 49 C6
Soton 32 D3
W Mid 96 D4
Shirl Heath 78 B2
Shirrell Heath 33 D4
Shirwell 25 B6
Shirwell Cross 25 B6
Shiskine 191 C5
Shobdon 78 A2
Shobrooke 12 A3
Shoby 115 D4
Shocklach 110 A3
Shoeburyness 51 A6
Sholden 53 D5
Sholing 32 D3
Shoot Hill 110 D3
Shop
Corn 9 D4
Corn 24 D3
Shop Corner 88 D3
Shoreditch 49 A6
Shoreham 50 C2

Shoreham-By-Sea . . 21 B5
Shore Mill 264 D3
Shoresdean 198 B3
Shoreswood 198 B3
Shoreton 264 D2
Shorncote 63 D6
Shorne 50 B3
Shortacombe 11 C6
Shortgate 22 A2
Short Heath 96 A2
Shortlanesend 4 C3
Shortlees 193 B4
Shortstown 84 C2
Shorwell 18 C3
Shoscombe 43 D6
Shotatton 110 C2
Shotesham 104 B3
Shotgate 70 D1
Shotley 88 D3
Shotley Bridge 178 D2
Shotleyfield 178 D2
Shotley Gate 88 D3
Shottenden 52 D2
Shottermill 34 C1
Shottery 81 B4
Shotteswell 81 C7
Shottisham 88 C4
Shottle 113 A7
Shottlegate 113 A7
Shotton
Durham 168 B2
Flint 126 C3
Northumb 198 C2
Shotton Colliery . . . 167 A6
Shotts 207 D6
Shotwick 126 B3
Shouldham 102 A2
Shouldham Thorpe . 102 A2
Shoulton 79 B6
Shover's Green 37 C4
Shrawardine 110 D3
Shrawley 79 A6
Shrewley Common . . 81 A5
Shrewsbury 110 D3
Shrewton 31 A4
Shripney 20 B2
Shrivenham 45 A6
Shropham 103 B5
Shrub End 70 A3
Shucknall 78 C3
Shudy Camps 86 C2
Shulishadermor . . . 259 D4
Shurdington 63 B5
Shurlock Row 47 B6
Shurrery 279 C6
Shurrery Lodge . . . 279 C6
Shurton 28 A2
Shustoke 97 B5
Shute
Devon 12 A3
Devon 14 B2
Shutford 81 C6
Shuthonger 80 D1
Shutlanger 83 B4
Shuttington 97 A5
Shuttlewood 131 B4
Siabost bho Dheas . 288 C3
Siabost bho
Thuath 288 C3
Siadar 288 B4
Siadar Iarach 288 B4
Siadar Uarach 288 B4
Sibbaldbie 185 D4
Sibbertoft 98 C3
Sibdon Carwood . . . 94 C2
Sibford Ferris 81 D6
Sibford Gower 81 D6
Sible Hedingham . . . 86 D3
Sibsey 134 D3
Sibson
Cambs 100 B2
Leics 97 A6
Sibthorpe 115 A5
Sibton 89 A4
Sibton Green 105 D4
Sicklesmere 87 A4
Sicklinghall 148 C2
Sid 13 C6
Sidbury
Devon 13 B6
Shrops 95 C4
Sidcot 42 D3
Sidcup 50 B1
Siddick 162 A3
Siddington
Ches E 128 B3
Glos 63 D6
Sidemoor 96 D2
Sidestrand 121 B4
Sidford 13 B6

Sidlesham 20 C1
Sidley 23 B5
Sidlow 35 B5
Sidmouth 13 C6
Sigford 12 D2
Sigglesthorne 151 C4
Sighthill 209 C4
Sigingstone 41 D4
Signet 64 B3
Silchester 47 C4
Sildinis 288 F3
Sileby 114 D3
Silecroft 153 B2
Silfield 104 B2
Silian 75 C4
Silkstone 139 C5
Silkstone Common . 139 C5
Silk Willoughby . . . 116 A3
Silloth 174 C4
Sills 188 C1
Sillyearn 267 D6
Siloh 59 B4
Silpho 160 B3
Silsden 147 C4
Silsoe 84 D2
Silverburn 209 D5
Silverdale
Lancs 154 D3
Staffs 112 A2
Silver End 70 B2
Silvergate 120 C3
Silverhill 23 A5
Silverstone 82 C3
Silverton 13 A4
Silvington 95 C4
Silwick 285 J4
Simmondley 138 D3
Simonburn 177 B6
Simonsbath 26 B2
Simonstone 146 D1
Simprim 198 B2
Simpson 83 D5
Simpson Cross 55 C4
Sinclair's Hill 198 A2
Sinclairston 182 A2
Sinderby 158 C2
Sinderhope 177 D6
Sindlesham 47 C5
Singdean 187 C4
Singleborough 83 D4
Singleton
Lancs 144 D3
W Sus 20 A1
Singlewell 50 B3
Sinkhurst Green . . . 37 B6
Sinnahard 244 A1
Sinnington 159 C6
Sinton Green 79 A6
Sipson 48 B3
Sirhowy 60 B3
Sisland 104 B4
Sissinghurst 37 C5
Sisterpath 197 B6
Siston 43 B5
Sithney 3 C4
Sittingbourne 51 C5
Six Ashes 95 C5
Sixhills 133 A6
Six Hills 115 C4
Six Mile Bottom . . . 86 B1
Sixpenny Handley . . 30 D3
Sizewell 89 A5
Skail 278 D3
Skaill
Orkney 282 D5
Orkney 282 F3
Orkney 283 G6
Skares 182 A3
Skateraw 211 C4
Skaw 284 G7
Skeabost 259 D4
Skeabrae 282 E3
Skeeby 157 A6
Skeffington 99 A4
Skeffling 143 B5
Skegby 131 C4
Skegness 135 C5
Skelberry 285 M5
Skelbo 264 A3
Skelbrooke 140 B3
Skeldyke 117 B6
Skellingthorpe 133 B4
Skellister 285 H6
Skellow 140 B3
Skelmanthorpe 139 B5
Skelmersdale 136 C3
Skelmonae 256 C3
Skelmorlie 204 B1
Skelmuir 257 B4

Skelpick........278 C3
Skelton
  Cumb.........164 B2
  E Yorks.......141 A5
  N Yorks.......157 A4
  Redcar........169 D4
  York..........149 B4
Skelton-on-Ure..148 A2
Skelwick.......282 C5
Skelwith Bridge..154 A2
Skendleby......135 C4
Skene House....245 B4
Skenfrith......61 A6
Skerne.........150 B3
Skeroblingarry..190 C3
Skerray........278 B2
Skerton........145 A4
Sketchley......98 B1
Sketty.........57 C6
Skewen.........40 B2
Skewsby........159 D5
Skeyton........120 C4
Skiag Bridge...271 B5
Skibo Castle...264 B3
Skidbrooke.....143 D6
Skidbrooke North
  End...........143 D6
Skidby.........150 D3
Skilgate.......27 C4
Skillington....116 C1
Skinburness....174 C4
Skinflats......208 B2
Skinidin.......258 D2
Skinnet........277 B6
Skinningrove...169 C5
Skipness.......202 C3
Skippool.......144 C3
Skipsea........151 B4
Skipsea Brough...151 B4
Skipton........146 B3
Skipton-on-Swale.158 D2
Skipwith.......149 D5
Skirbeck.......117 A6
Skirbeck Quarter..117 A6
Skirlaugh......151 D4
Skirling.......195 C5
Skirmett.......47 A5
Skirpenbeck....149 B6
Skirwith.......165 B4
Skirza.........281 B5
Skulamus.......247 B5
Skullomie......277 B7
Skyborry Green..93 D6
Skye of Curr...253 D5
Skyreholme.....147 A4
Slackhall......129 A5
Slackhead......267 C5
Slad...........63 C4
Slade
  Devon.........25 A6
  Pembs.........55 C5
Slade Green....50 B2
Slaggyford.....177 D4
Slaidburn......145 B7
Slaithwaite....138 B3
Slaley.........178 D1
Slamannan......207 C6
Slapton
  Bucks.........67 A4
  Devon.........8 C2
  Northants.....82 C3
Slatepit Dale..130 C3
Slattocks......138 C1
Slaugham.......35 D5
Slaughterford..44 B2
Slawston.......99 B4
Sleaford
  Hants.........33 B7
  Lincs.........116 A3
Sleagill.......164 D3
Sleapford......111 D5
Sledge Green...79 D6
Sledmere.......150 A2
Sleightholme...166 D2
Sleights.......160 A2
Slepe..........16 B3
Slickly........281 B4
Sliddery.......191 C5
Sligachan Hotel..246 B3
Slimbridge.....62 C3
Slindon
  Staffs........112 B2
  W Sus.........20 B2
Slinfold.......35 C4
Sling..........123 D6
Slingsby.......159 D5
Slioch.........255 C6
Slip End
  C Beds........67 B5
  Herts.........85 D4

Slipton........99 D6
Slitting Mill..112 D4
Slochd.........253 D4
Slockavullin...213 C6
Sloley.........121 C5
Sloothby.......135 B4
Slough.........48 B2
Slough Green...35 D5
Sluggan........253 D4
Slumbay........249 C5
Slyfield.......34 A2
Slyne..........145 A4
Smailholm......197 C5
Smallbridge....138 B2
Smallburgh.....121 C5
Smallburn
  Aberds........257 B5
  E Ayrs........194 D1
Small Dole.....21 A5
Smalley........114 A2
Smallfield.....35 B6
Small Hythe....37 C6
Smallridge.....14 A3
Smannell.......32 A2
Smardale.......155 A6
Smarden........37 B6
Smarden Bell...37 B6
Smeatharpe.....28 D1
Smeeth.........38 B2
Smeeton Westerby..98 B3
Smercleit......286 E3
Smerral........275 A5
Smethwick......96 C3
Smirisary......235 C5
Smisby.........114 D1
Smithfield.....176 C2
Smith Green....145 B4
Smithincott....27 D5
Smith's Green...69 A5
Smithstown.....261 C4
Smithton.......252 B3
Smithy Green...128 B2
Smockington....98 C1
Smoogro........283 G4
Smythe's Green...70 B3
Snaigow House..231 D4
Snailbeach.....94 A1
Snailwell......86 A2
Snainton.......160 C3
Snaith.........140 A4
Snape
  N Yorks.......157 C6
  Suff..........89 B4
Snape Green....136 B2
Snarestone.....97 A6
Snarford.......133 A5
Snargate.......38 C1
Snave..........38 C2
Snead..........93 B7
Sneath Common..104 C2
Sneaton........160 A2
Sneatonthorpe..160 A3
Snelland.......133 A5
Snelston.......113 A5
Snettisham.....118 B3
Sniseabhal.....286 C3
Snitter........188 C3
Snitterby......142 D1
Snitterfield...81 B5
Snitton........94 D3
Snodhill.......77 C7
Snodland.......51 C4
Snowden Hill...139 C5
Snowdown.......53 D4
Snowshill......80 D3
Snydale........140 B2
Soar
  Anglesey......122 C3
  Carms.........58 C3
  Devon.........7 D6
Soar-y-Mynydd..76 B1
Soberton.......33 D5
Soberton Heath..33 D5
Sockbridge.....164 C3
Sockburn.......158 A2
Soham..........102 D1
Soham Cotes....102 D1
Solas..........287 G3
Soldon Cross...24 D4
Soldridge......33 B5
Sole Street
  Kent..........38 A2
  Kent..........50 C3
Solihull.......97 D4
Sollers Dilwyn..78 B2
Sollers Hope...79 D4
Sollom.........136 B3
Solva..........54 B3
Somerby
  Leics.........115 D5

Somerby *continued*
  Lincs.........142 C2
Somercotes.....131 D4
Somerford......17 B5
Somerford Keynes..63 D6
Somerley.......19 B7
Somerleyton....105 B5
Somersal Herbert..113 B5
Somersby.......134 B3
Somersham
  Cambs.........101 D5
  Suff..........88 C1
Somerton
  Oxon..........65 A5
  Som...........29 C4
Sompting.......21 B4
Sonning........47 B5
Sonning Common..47 A5
Sonning Eye....47 B5
Sontley........110 A2
Sopley.........17 B5
Sopwell........67 C6
Sopworth.......44 A2
Sorbie.........171 C6
Sordale........280 B3
Sorisdale......223 A5
Sorn...........193 C5
Sornhill.......193 B5
Sortat.........281 B4
Sotby..........134 B2
Sots Hole......133 C6
Sotterley......105 C5
Soudley........111 C6
Soughton.......126 C2
Soulbury.......66 A3
Soulby.........165 D5
Souldern.......82 D2
Souldrop.......84 A1
Sound
  Ches E........111 A5
  Shetland......285 H5
  Shetland......285 J6
Sound Heath....111 A5
Soundwell......43 B5
Sourhope.......188 A1
Sourin.........282 D5
Sourton........11 B6
Soutergate....153 B3
South Acre.....119 D5
Southall.......48 A4
South Allington..8 D1
South Alloa....208 A1
Southam
  Glos..........63 A5
  Warks.........81 A7
South Ambersham..34 D2
Southampton....32 D3
South Anston...131 A5
South Ascot....48 C2
South Ballachulish.237 D4
South Balloch..181 B5
South Bank.....168 C3
South Barrow...29 C6
South Beach....106 C3
South Benfleet..51 A4
South Bersted..20 B2
Southborough...36 B3
Southbourne
  BCP...........17 B5
  W Sus.........19 A6
South Brent....7 A5
South Brewham..29 B7
South Broomhill..189 D5
Southburgh.....103 A5
South Burlingham..105 A4
Southburn......150 B2
South Cadbury..29 C6
South Cairn....170 A1
South Carlton..133 B4
South Cave.....150 D2
South Cerney...63 D6
South Chard....14 A3
South Charlton..189 A4
South Cheriton..29 C6
Southchurch....51 A6
South Cliffe...150 D1
South Clifton..132 B3
South
  Cockerington..134 A3
South Cornelly..40 C3
Southcott......45 D5
Southcourt.....66 B3
South Cove.....105 C5
South Creagan..227 B4
South Creake...119 B5
South Croxton..115 D4
South Croydon..49 C6
South Dalton...150 C2
South Darenth..50 C2
Southdean......187 C5

Southdene......136 D3
South Duffield..149 D5
Southease......22 B2
South Elkington..134 A2
South Elmsall..140 B2
Southend
  Argyll........190 E2
  W Berks.......46 B3
  Wilts.........45 B5
South End
  Bucks.........66 A3
  Cumb..........153 D3
  N Lincs.......142 A3
Southend-on-Sea..51 A5
Southernden....37 B6
Southerndown...40 D3
Southerness....174 C2
South Erradale..261 C4
Southery.......102 B2
South Fambridge..70 D2
South Fawley...46 A1
South Ferriby..142 A1
Southfield.....179 B4
Southfleet.....50 B3
South Garth....284 D7
South Garvan...236 B3
Southgate
  Ceredig.......75 A4
  London........68 D2
  Norf..........120 C3
  Swansea.......57 D5
South Glendale..286 E3
South Godstone..35 B6
South Gorley...31 D5
South Green
  Essex.........69 D6
  Kent..........51 C5
South-haa......284 E5
South Ham......47 D4
South Hanningfield..70 D1
South Harting..33 D6
South Hatfield..68 C2
South Hayling..19 B6
South Hazelrigg..199 C4
South Heath....67 C4
South Heighton..22 B2
South Hetton...167 A6
South Hiendley..140 B1
South Hill.....10 D4
South Hinksey..65 C6
South Hole.....24 C3
South Holme....159 D5
South Holmwood..35 B4
South Hornchurch..50 A2
South Hykeham..133 C4
South Hylton...179 D5
Southill.......84 C3
South Kelsey...142 D2
South Kessock..252 B2
South Killingholme.142 B3
South Kilvington..158 C3
South Kilworth..98 C3
South Kirkby...140 B2
South Kirkton..245 B4
South Kiscadale..191 C6
South Kyme.....117 A4
South Lancing..21 B4
Southleigh.....14 B2
South Leigh....65 C4
South Leverton..132 A2
South Littleton..80 C3
South Lopham...103 C6
South Luffenham..99 A6
South Malling..22 A2
South Marston..45 A5
South Middleton..188 A2
South Milford..148 D3
South Millbrex..256 B3
South Milton...7 C6
South Mimms....68 C2
Southminster...70 D3
South Molton...26 C2
Southmoor......65 D4
South Moreton..46 A3
South Mundham..20 B1
South Muskham..132 D2
South Newbald..150 D2
South Newington..81 D7
South Newton...31 B4
South Normanton.131 D4
South Norwood..49 C6
South Nutfield..35 B6
South Ockendon..50 A2
Southoe........84 A3
Southolt.......88 A2
South Ormsby...134 B3
Southorpe......100 A2
South Otterington.158 C2
South Owersby..142 D2
Southowram.....139 A4

South Oxhey....67 D6
South Perrott..15 A4
South Petherton..28 D4
South Petherwin..10 C4
South Pickenham..103 A4
South Pool.....7 C6
Southport......136 B2
South Port.....227 D5
Southpunds.....285 L6
South Radworthy..26 B2
South Rauceby..116 A3
South Raynham..119 C5
Southrepps.....121 B4
South Reston...135 A4
Southrey.......133 C6
Southrop.......64 C2
Southrope......33 A5
South Runcton..102 A2
South Scarle...132 C3
Southsea.......19 B5
South Shian....226 B4
South Shields..179 C5
South Shore....144 D3
South Somercotes.143 D6
South Stainley..148 A2
South Stainmore.165 D6
South Stifford..50 B3
Southstoke.....43 C6
South Stoke
  Oxon..........46 A3
  W Sus.........20 B3
South Street
  E Sus.........22 A1
  Kent..........52 C3
  Kent..........52 D2
  London........36 A2
South Tawton...12 B1
South Thoresby..135 B4
South Tidworth..31 A6
Southtown
  Norf..........105 A6
  Orkney........283 H5
South Town.....33 B5
South View.....47 D4
Southwaite.....164 A2
South Walsham..121 D5
Southwark......49 B6
South Warnborough.33 A6
Southwater.....35 D4
Southwater Street..35 D4
Southway.......29 A5
South Weald....69 D5
Southwell
  Dorset........15 D6
  Notts.........132 D1
South Weston...66 D2
South Wheatley
  Corn..........10 B3
  Notts.........132 A2
South Whiteness..285 J5
Southwick
  Hants.........19 A5
  Northants.....100 B2
  T&W...........179 D5
  Wilts.........44 D2
  W Sus.........21 B5
South Widcombe..43 D4
South Wigston..98 B2
South Willingham.134 A1
South Wingfield..130 D3
South Witham...116 D2
Southwold......105 D6
South Wonston..32 B3
Southwood
  Norf..........105 A4
  Som...........29 B5
South Woodham
  Ferrers.......70 D2
South Wootton..118 C3
South Wraxall..44 C2
South Zeal.....12 B1
Soval Lodge....288 E4
Sowber Gate....158 C2
Sowerby
  N Yorks.......158 C3
  W Yorks.......138 A3
Sowerby Bridge..138 A3
Sowerby Row....164 B3
Sowood.........138 B3
Sowton.........13 B4
Soyal..........264 A1
Spacey Houses..148 B2
Spa Common....121 B4
Spadeadam Farm..176 B3
Spalding.......117 C5
Spaldington....149 D6
Spaldwick......100 D3
Spalford.......132 C3
Spanby.........116 B3
Sparham........120 D2

Spark Bridge...154 C2
Sparkford......29 C6
Sparkhill......96 C3
Sparkwell......7 B4
Sparrow Green..119 D6
Sparrowpit.....129 A5
Sparsholt
  Hants.........32 B3
  Oxon..........46 A1
Spartylea......165 A6
Spaunton.......159 C6
Spaxton........28 B2
Spean Bridge...239 D6
Spear Hill.....21 A4
Speen
  Bucks.........66 D3
  W Berks.......46 C2
Speeton........161 D5
Speke..........127 A4
Speldhurst.....36 B3
Spellbrook.....69 B4
Spelsbury......64 A4
Spelter........40 B3
Spencers Wood..47 C5
Spennithorne...157 C5
Spennymoor.....167 B5
Spetchley......80 B1
Spetisbury.....16 A3
Spexhall.......105 C4
Spey Bay.......267 C4
Speybridge.....253 D6
Speyview.......254 B3
Spilsby........135 C4
Spindlestone...199 C5
Spinkhill......131 B4
Spinningdale...264 B2
Spirthill......44 B3
Spital Hill....140 D4
Spital in the Street.133 A4
Spithurst......22 A2
Spittal
  Dumfries......171 B5
  E Loth........210 C1
  Highld........280 C3
  Northumb......198 A4
  Pembs.........55 B5
  Stirling......206 B3
Spittalfield...231 D5
Spittal of
  Glenmuick.....243 D6
Spittal of Glenshee.231 A5
Spixworth......120 D4
Splayne's Green..36 D2
Spofforth......148 B2
Spondon........114 B2
Spon End.......97 D6
Spon Green.....126 C2
Spooner Row....104 B1
Sporle.........119 D5
Spott..........210 C3
Spratton.......99 D4
Spreakley......34 B1
Spreyton.......12 B1
Spridlington...133 A5
Springburn.....205 B6
Springfield
  Dumfries......175 B6
  Essex.........69 C2
  Fife..........220 C3
  Moray.........253 A6
  W Mid.........96 C3
Springhill.....96 A2
Springholm.....173 B6
Springkell.....175 A5
Springside.....192 B3
Springthorpe...132 A3
Spring Vale....139 C5
Spring Valley..152 D3
Springwell.....179 D4
Sproatley......151 D4
Sproston Green..128 C2
Sprotbrough....140 C3
Sproughton....88 C2
Sprouston......197 C6
Sprowston......120 D4
Sproxton
  Leics.........115 C6
  N Yorks.......159 C5
Spurstow.......127 D5
Spynie.........266 C3
Squires Gate...144 D3
Srannda........287 F5
Sronphadruig
  Lodge.........229 A6
Stableford
  Shrops........95 B5
  Staffs........112 B2
Stacey Bank....139 D5

Stackhouse........146 A2
Stackpole.........55 E5
Staddiscombe......7 B4
Staddlethorpe.....141 A6
Stadhampton.......65 D7
Stadhlaigearraidh.286 C3
Staffield.........164 A3
Staffin...........259 B4
Stafford..........112 C3
Stagsden..........84 C1
Stainburn
 Cumb............162 B3
 N Yorks.........147 C6
Stainby...........116 C2
Staincross........139 B6
Staindrop.........166 C4
Staines-upon-
 Thames..........48 B3
Stainfield
 Lincs...........116 C3
 Lincs...........133 B6
Stainforth
 N Yorks.........146 A2
 S Yorks.........140 B4
Staining..........144 D3
Stainland.........138 B3
Stainsacre........160 A3
Stainsby..........131 C4
Stainton
 Cumb............154 C4
 Cumb............164 C2
 Durham..........166 D3
 Mbro............168 D2
 N Yorks.........157 B5
 S Yorks.........140 D3
Stainton by
 Langworth.......133 B5
Staintondale......160 B3
Stainton le Vale..142 D3
Stainton with
 Adgarley........153 C3
Stair
 Cumb............163 B5
 E Ayrs..........193 C4
Stairhaven........171 B4
Staithes..........169 D5
Stakeford.........179 A4
Stake Pool........144 C4
Stalbridge........30 D1
Stalbridge Weston.29 D7
Stalham...........121 C5
Stalham Green.....121 C5
Stalisfield Green..51 D6
Stallingborough...142 B3
Stalling Busk.....156 C3
Stalmine..........144 C3
Stalybridge.......138 D2
Stambourne........86 D3
Stambourne Green..86 D3
Stamford..........100 A2
Stamford Bridge
 Ches W..........127 C4
 E Yorks.........149 B6
Stamfordham.......178 B2
Stanah............163 C6
Stanborough.......68 B2
Stanbridge
 C Beds..........67 A4
 Dorset..........17 A4
Stanbrook.........79 C6
Stanbury..........147 D4
Stand
 Gtr Man.........137 C6
 N Lanark........207 D5
Standburn.........208 C2
Standeford........96 A2
Standen...........37 B6
Standford.........33 B7
Standingstone.....162 A3
Standish..........137 B4
Standlake.........65 C4
Standon
 Hants...........32 C3
 Herts...........68 A3
 Staffs..........112 B2
Stane.............194 A3
Stanfield.........119 C6
Stanford
 C Beds..........84 C3
 Kent............38 B3
Stanford Bishop...79 B4
Stanford Bridge...79 A5
Stanford Dingley..46 B3
Stanford in the Vale..64 D4
Stanford-le-Hope..50 A3
Stanford on Avon..98 D2
Stanford on Soar..114 C3
Stanford on Teme..79 A5

Stanford Rivers...69 C5
Stanfree..........131 B4
Stanghow..........169 D4
Stanground........100 B4
Stanhoe...........119 B5
Stanhope
 Borders.........195 D6
 Durham..........166 B2
Stanion...........99 C6
Stanley
 Derbys..........114 A2
 Durham..........178 D3
 Lancs...........136 C3
 Perth...........219 A6
 Staffs..........129 D4
 W Yorks.........139 A6
Stanley Common....114 A2
Stanley Gate......136 C3
Stanley Hill......79 C4
Stanlow...........127 B4
Stanmer...........21 B6
Stanmore
 Hants...........32 C3
 London..........67 D6
 W Berks.........46 B2
Stannergate.......220 A4
Stanningley.......147 D6
Stannington
 Northumb........179 B4
 S Yorks.........130 A3
Stansbatch........78 A1
Stansfield........86 B3
Stanstead.........87 C4
Stanstead Abbotts.68 B3
Stansted..........50 C3
Stansted Airport..69 A5
Stansted
 Mountfitchet....69 A5
Stanton
 Glos............80 D3
 Mon.............61 A4
 Northumb........178 A3
 Staffs..........113 A5
 Suff............103 D5
Stanton by Bridge.114 C1
Stanton-by-Dale...114 B2
Stanton Drew......43 C4
Stanton Fitzwarren.64 D2
Stanton Harcourt..65 C5
Stanton Hill......131 C4
Stanton in Peak...130 C2
Stanton Lacy......94 D2
Stanton Long......94 B3
Stanton-on-the-
 Wolds...........115 B4
Stanton Prior.....43 C5
Stanton St Bernard.45 C4
Stanton St John...65 C6
Stanton St Quintin.44 B3
Stanton Street....87 A5
Stanton under
 Bardon..........114 D2
Stanton upon Hine
 Heath...........111 C4
Stanton Wick......43 C5
Stanwardine in the
 Fields..........110 C3
Stanwardine in the
 Wood............110 C3
Stanway
 Essex...........70 A3
 Glos............80 D3
Stanway Green.....104 D3
Stanwell..........48 B3
Stanwell Moor.....48 B3
Stanwick..........100 D1
Stanwick-St-John..167 D4
Stanwix...........175 C7
Stanydale.........285 H4
Staoinebrig.......286 C3
Stape.............159 B6
Stapehill.........17 A4
Stapeley..........111 A5
Stapenhill........113 C6
Staple
 Kent............53 D4
 Som.............27 A6
Staple Cross......37 D5
Staplefield.......35 D5
Staple Fitzpaine..28 D2
Stapleford
 Cambs...........85 B6
 Herts...........68 B3
 Leics...........115 D6
 Lincs...........132 D3
 Notts...........114 B2
 Wilts...........31 B4
Stapleford Abbotts.69 D5
Stapleford Tawney.69 D5
Staplegrove.......28 C2

Staplehay.........28 C2
Staplehurst.......37 B5
Staplers..........18 C4
Stapleton
 Bristol.........43 B5
 Cumb............176 B3
 Hereford........78 A1
 Leics...........98 B1
 N Yorks.........167 D5
 Shrops..........94 A2
 Som.............29 C4
Stapley...........28 D1
Staploe...........84 A3
Staplow...........79 C4
Star
 Fife............220 D3
 Pembs...........73 C5
 Som.............42 D3
Stara.............282 E3
Starbeck..........148 B2
Starbotton........156 D3
Starcross.........13 C4
Stareton..........97 D6
Starkholmes.......130 D3
Starlings Green...85 D6
Starston..........104 C3
Startforth........166 D3
Startley..........44 B3
Stathe............28 C3
Stathern..........115 B5
Station Town......168 B2
Staughton Green...84 A3
Staughton Highway.84 A3
Staunton
 Glos............62 A3
 Glos............62 B1
Staunton in the
 Vale............115 A6
Staunton on Arrow.78 A1
Staunton on Wye...78 C1
Staveley
 Cumb............154 B3
 Cumb............154 C2
 Derbys..........131 B4
 N Yorks.........148 A2
Staverton
 Devon...........8 A1
 Glos............63 A4
 Northants.......82 A2
 Wilts...........44 C2
Staverton Bridge..63 A4
Stawell...........28 B3
Staxigoe..........281 C4
Staxton...........160 D4
Staylittle........91 C6
Staynall..........144 C3
Staythorpe........132 D2
Stean.............157 D4
Stearsby..........159 D5
Steart............28 A2
Stebbing..........69 A6
Stebbing Green....69 A6
Stedham...........34 D1
Steele Road.......186 D4
Steen's Bridge....78 B3
Steep.............33 C6
Steeple
 Dorset..........16 C3
 Essex...........70 C3
Steeple Ashton....44 D3
Steeple Aston.....65 A5
Steeple Barton....65 A5
Steeple Bumpstead.86 C2
Steeple Claydon...66 A1
Steeple Gidding...100 C3
Steeple Langford..31 B4
Steeple Morden....85 C4
Steep Marsh.......33 C6
Steeton..........147 C4
Stein............258 C2
Steinmanhill.....256 B2
Stelling Minnis...38 A3
Stemster.........280 B3
Stemster House...280 B3
Stenalees.........5 B5
Stenhousemuir....207 B6
Stenigot.........134 A2
Stenness.........284 F4
Stenscholl.......259 B4
Stenso...........282 E4
Stenson..........114 C1
Stenton
 E Loth.........210 C3
 Fife...........209 A5
Stenwith.........115 B6
Stepaside.........56 B1
Stepping Hill....129 A4
Steppingley......84 D2
Stepps...........205 B6
Sterndale Moor...129 C6

Sternfield........89 A4
Sterridge.........25 A6
Stert.............44 D4
Stetchworth.......86 B2
Stevenage.........68 A2
Stevenston........204 D2
Steventon
 Hants...........32 A4
 Oxon............65 D5
Stevington........84 B1
Stewartby.........84 C2
Stewarton
 Argyll..........190 D2
 E Ayrs..........205 D4
Stewkley..........66 A3
Stewton...........134 A3
Steyne Cross......19 C5
Steyning..........21 A4
Steynton..........55 D5
Stibb.............24 D3
Stibbard..........120 C1
Stibb Cross.......25 D5
Stibb Green.......45 C6
Stibbington.......100 B2
Stichill..........197 C6
Sticker...........5 B4
Stickford.........134 D3
Sticklepath.......12 B1
Stickney..........134 D3
Stiffkey..........119 A6
Stifford's Bridge.79 C5
Stillingfleet.....149 C4
Stillington
 N Yorks.........149 A4
 Stockton........167 C6
Stilton...........100 C3
Stinchcombe.......62 D3
Stinsford.........15 B7
Stirchley.........95 A5
Stirkoke House....281 C5
Stirling
 Aberds..........257 B6
 Stirling........207 A5
Stisted...........70 A1
Stithians.........4 D2
Stittenham.......264 C2
Stivichall........97 D6
Stixwould........134 C1
Stoak............127 B4
Stobieside.......193 B6
Stobo............195 C6
Stoborough.......16 C3
Stoborough Green..16 C3
Stobshiel........210 D1
Stobswood........189 D5
Stock............69 D6
Stockbridge......32 B2
Stockbury........51 C5
Stockcross.......46 C2
Stockdalewath....164 A1
Stock Green......80 B2
Stockheath.......19 A6
Stockiemuir......206 B3
Stockingford.....97 B6
Stocking Pelham..69 A4
Stockland........14 A2
Stockland Bristol.28 A2
Stockleigh English.12 A3
Stockleigh Pomeroy.12 A3
Stockley.........44 C4
Stocklinch.......28 D3
Stockport........138 D1
Stocksbridge.....139 D5
Stocksfield......178 C2
Stockton
 Hereford.......78 A3
 Norf...........105 B4
 Shrops.........93 A6
 Shrops.........95 B5
 Warks..........82 A1
 Wilts..........30 B3
Stockton Heath...127 A6
Stockton-on-Tees.168 D2
Stockton on Teme..79 A5
Stockton on the
 Forest.........149 B5
Stock Wood.......80 B3
Stodmarsh........53 C4
Stody............120 B2
Stoer............270 B3
Stoford
 Som............29 D5
 Wilts..........31 B4
Stogumber........27 B5
Stogursey........28 A1
Stoke
 Devon..........24 C3
 Hants..........19 A6
 Hants..........46 D2

Stoke continued
 Medway.........51 B5
 Suff...........88 C2
Stoke Abbott.....15 A4
Stoke Albany.....99 C5
Stoke Ash........104 D2
Stoke Bardolph...115 A4
Stoke Bliss......79 A4
Stoke Bruerne....83 C4
Stoke by Clare...86 C3
Stoke-by-Nayland.87 D5
Stoke Canon......13 B4
Stoke Charity....32 B3
Stoke Climsland...11 D4
Stoke D'Abernon..35 A4
Stoke Doyle......100 C2
Stoke Dry........99 B5
Stoke Farthing...31 C4
Stoke Ferry......102 B3
Stoke Fleming....8 C2
Stokeford........16 C2
Stoke Gabriel....8 B2
Stoke Gifford....43 B5
Stoke Golding....97 B6
Stoke Goldington.83 C5
Stoke Green......48 A2
Stokeham.........132 B2
Stoke Hammond...66 A3
Stoke Heath......111 C5
Stoke Holy Cross.104 A3
Stokeinteignhead.13 D4
Stoke Lacy.......79 C4
Stoke Lyne.......65 A6
Stoke Mandeville..66 B3
Stoke Newington..49 A6
Stokenchurch.....66 D2
Stokenham........8 C2
Stoke on Tern....111 C5
Stoke-on-Trent...112 A2
Stoke Orchard....63 A5
Stoke Poges......48 A2
Stoke Prior
 Hereford.......78 B3
 Worcs..........80 A2
Stoke Rivers.....26 B1
Stoke Rochford...116 C2
Stoke Row........47 A4
Stoke St Gregory..28 C3
Stoke St Mary....28 C2
Stoke St Michael..29 A6
Stoke St Milborough 94 C3
Stokesay.........94 C2
Stokesby.........121 D6
Stokesley........158 A4
Stoke sub Hamdon..29 D4
Stoke Talmage....66 D1
Stoke Trister....30 C1
Stoke Wake.......16 A1
Stolford.........28 A2
Stondon Massey...69 C5
Stone
 Bucks..........66 B2
 Glos...........62 D2
 Kent...........38 C1
 Kent...........50 B1
 Staffs.........112 B3
 S Yorks........131 A5
 Worcs..........95 D6
Stone Allerton...42 D3
Ston Easton......43 D5
Stone Bridge
 Corner.........101 A4
Stonebroom......131 D4
Stone Chair......139 A4
Stone Cross
 E Sus..........22 B4
 Kent...........53 D5
Stone-edge Batch..42 B3
Stoneferry......151 D4
Stonefield......194 A1
Stonegate
 E Sus..........37 D4
 N Yorks........159 A6
Stonegrave......159 D5
Stonehaugh......177 B5
Stonehaven......245 D5
Stonehouse
 Glos...........63 C4
 Northumb.......177 D4
 S Lanark.......194 B2
Stone House.....155 C6
Stoneleigh......97 D6
Stonely.........84 A3
Stoner Hill......33 C6
Stonesby........115 C6
Stonesfield......65 B4
Stone's Green....71 A5
Stone Street
 Kent...........36 A3
 Suff...........87 D5

Stone Street continued
 Suff...........105 C4
Stonethwaite.....163 C5
Stoneybreck......285 R4
Stoneyburn......208 D2
Stoney Cross.....31 D6
Stoneygate
 Aberds.........257 C5
 Leicester......98 A3
Stoneyhills......70 D3
Stoneykirk......170 B2
Stoney Middleton.130 B2
Stoney Stanton...98 B1
Stoney Stoke.....29 B6
Stoney Stratton..29 B6
Stoney Stretton..94 A1
Stoneywood
 Aberdeen.......245 A5
 Falk...........207 B5
Stonganess......284 C7
Stonham Aspal....88 B2
Stonnall.........96 A3
Stonor...........47 A5
Stonton Wyville..99 B4
Stony Cross......79 C5
Stonyfield......264 C2
Stony Stratford..83 C4
Stoodleigh.......27 C4
Stopes..........130 A3
Stopham.........20 A3
Stopsley........67 A6
Stores Corner....89 C4
Storeton........126 A3
Stornoway.......288 D5
Storridge.......79 C5
Storrington.....20 A3
Storrs..........154 B2
Storth..........154 C3
Storwood........149 C6
Stotfield.......266 B3
Stotfold........84 D4
Stottesdon......95 C4
Stoughton
 Leics..........98 A3
 Sur............34 A2
 W Sus..........33 D7
Stoul...........235 A6
Stoulton........80 C2
Stourbridge.....96 C2
Stourpaine......16 A2
Stourport on Severn.95 D6
Stour Provost....30 C1
Stour Row.......30 C2
Stourton
 Staffs.........95 C6
 Warks..........81 D5
 Wilts..........30 B1
Stourton Caundle.29 D7
Stove
 Orkney.........282 D7
 Shetland.......285 L6
Stoven..........105 C5
Stow
 Borders........196 B3
 Lincs..........116 B3
 Lincs..........132 A3
Stow Bardolph...102 A2
Stow Bedon......103 B5
Stowbridge......102 A2
Stow cum Quy.....85 A7
Stowe...........93 D7
Stowe-by-Chartley 112 C4
Stowe Green......62 C1
Stowell.........29 C6
Stowford........11 C5
Stowlangtoft.....87 A5
Stow Longa......100 D3
Stow Maries......70 D2
Stowmarket......87 B6
Stow-on-the-Wold.64 A2
Stowting.........38 A3
Stowupland......87 B6
Straad..........203 B5
Strachan........244 C3
Stradbroke......104 D3
Stradishall......86 B3
Stradsett.......102 A2
Stragglethorpe...133 D4
Straid..........180 B3
Straith.........183 D7
Straiton
 Edin...........209 D5
 S Ayrs.........181 A5
Straloch
 Aberds.........256 D3
 Perth..........230 B4
Stramshall......113 B4
Strang..........152 D3
Stranraer.......170 A2
Stratfield Mortimer.47 C4

Stratfield Saye......47 C4
Stratfield Turgis......47 D4
Stratford.........49 A6
Stratford St Andrew.89 A4
Stratford St Mary...87 C6
Stratford Sub Castle.31 B5
Stratford Tony......31 C4
Stratford-upon-
  Avon...........81 B4
Strath
  Highld..........261 C4
  Highld..........281 C4
Strathan
  Highld..........238 C3
  Highld..........270 B3
  Highld..........277 B6
Strathaven.......194 B2
Strathblane......205 A5
Strathcanaird...271 C4
Strathcarron.....249 B6
Strathcoil.......225 C5
Strathdon.......243 A6
Strathellie......269 C5
Strathkinness...221 C4
Strathmashie
  House..........240 C3
Strathmiglo......220 C2
Strathmore Lodge.280 D3
Strathpeffer.....251 A6
Strathrannoch...263 C5
Strathtay.......230 C3
Strathvaich Lodge.263 C5
Strathwhillan...191 B6
Strathy.........279 B4
Strathyre.......217 C5
Stratton
  Corn...........10 A3
  Dorset.........15 B6
  Glos...........63 C6
Stratton Audley.....65 A7
Stratton on the
  Fosse..........43 D5
Stratton
  St Margaret......45 A5
Stratton St Michael 104 B3
Stratton Strawless.120 C4
Stravithie.......221 C5
Streat.........21 A6
Streatham......49 B6
Streatley
  C Beds.........67 A5
  W Berks.........46 A3
Street
  Lancs.........145 B5
  N Yorks........159 A6
  Som...........29 B4
Street Dinas.....110 B2
Street End
  Kent...........52 D3
  W Sus.........20 C1
Street Gate......179 D4
Streethay.......113 D5
Streetlam.......157 B7
Streetly.........96 B3
Streetly End.....86 C2
Strefford.......94 C2
Strelley.........114 A3
Strensall.......149 A5
Stretcholt.......28 A2
Strete.........8 C2
Stretford.......137 D7
Strethall.......85 D6
Stretham.......101 D7
Strettington.....20 B1
Stretton
  Ches W........127 D4
  Derbys.........130 C3
  Rutland........116 D2
  Staffs.........112 D2
  Staffs.........113 C6
  Warr.........127 A6
Stretton Grandison..79 C4
Stretton-on-
  Dunsmore......97 D7
Stretton-on-Fosse.81 D5
Stretton Sugwas....78 C2
Stretton under
  Fosse..........98 C1
Stretton Westwood..94 B3
Strichen.........269 D4
Strines.........129 A4
Stringston......28 A1
Strixton.........83 A6
Stroat.........62 D1
Stromeferry.....249 C5
Stromemore.....249 C5
Stromness.......283 G3
Stronaba.......239 D6
Stronachlachar...216 C4

Stronchreggan...237 B4
Stronchrubie.....271 C5
Strone
  Argyll..........215 D4
  Highld.........239 D5
  Highld.........252 D1
  Invclyd........204 A2
Stronmilchan.....227 D6
Strontian.......236 C2
Strood.........51 C4
Strood Green
  Sur...........35 B5
  W Sus.........34 D3
  W Sus.........35 C4
Stroud
  Glos...........63 C4
  Hants.........33 C6
Stroud Green.....70 D2
Stroxton.......116 B2
Struan
  Highld.........246 A2
  Perth.........230 B2
Strubby.........135 A4
Strumpshaw.....104 A4
Strutherhill......194 B2
Struy.........251 C5
Stryt-issa.......110 A1
Stuartfield......257 B4
Stubbington.....19 A4
Stubbins.......137 B6
Stubbs Cross......38 B1
Stubbs Green.....105 B4
Stubb's Green....104 B3
Stubhampton.....30 D3
Stub Place.......153 A1
Stubton.......115 A6
Stuckgowan.....215 B6
Stuckton.......31 D5
Stud Green......48 B1
Studham.......67 B5
Studland.......17 C4
Studley
  Warks.........80 A3
  Wilts.........44 B3
Studley Roger.....157 D6
Stump Cross......85 C7
Stuntney.......102 D1
Sturbridge......112 B2
Sturmer.......86 C2
Sturminster
  Marshall.......16 A3
Sturminster Newton.30 D1
Sturry.........52 C3
Sturton.........142 C1
Sturton by Stow...132 A3
Sturton le Steeple..132 A2
Stuston.......104 D2
Stutton
  N Yorks........148 C3
  Suff.........88 D2
Styal.........128 A3
Styrrup.......140 D4
Suainebost......288 A4
Suardail.......288 D5
Succoth
  Aberds........255 C5
  Argyll.........215 B5
Suckley.........79 B5
Suckquoy.......283 J5
Sudborough.....99 C6
Sudbourne......89 B5
Sudbrook
  Lincs.........116 A2
  Mon.........43 A4
Sudbrooke......133 B5
Sudbury
  Derbys.........113 B5
  London........49 A4
  Suff.........87 C4
Suddie.........252 A2
Sudgrove.......63 C5
Suffield
  Norf.........120 B4
  N Yorks........160 B3
Sugnall.......112 B1
Sugwas Pool.....78 C2
Suladale.......258 C3
Sulaisiadar......288 D6
Sulby.........152 B3
Sulgrave.......82 C2
Sulham.........47 B4
Sulhamstead......47 C4
Sulland.......282 C6
Sullington......20 A3
Sullom.........284 F5
Sullom Voe Oil
  Terminal.......284 F5
Sully.........41 E6
Sumburgh.......285 N6
Summer Bridge...147 A6
Summercourt......4 B3

Summerfield.....119 B4
Summergangs...151 D4
Summer-house...167 D5
Summerleaze......42 A3
Summersdale.....20 B1
Summerseat......137 B6
Summertown......65 C6
Summit.........138 C2
Sunbury-on-
  Thames........48 C4
Sundaywell......183 D6
Sunderland
  Argyll.........200 B2
  Cumb.........163 A4
  T&W.........179 D5
Sunderland Bridge.167 B5
Sundhope.......196 D2
Sundon Park......67 A5
Sundridge.......36 A2
Sunipol.........224 A2
Sunk Island.......143 B4
Sunningdale......48 C2
Sunninghill......48 C2
Sunningwell......65 C5
Sunniside
  Durham........166 B4
  T&W.........179 D4
Sunnyhurst......137 A5
Sunnylaw.......207 A5
Sunnyside.......36 C1
Sunton.........45 D6
Surbiton.......49 C4
Surby.........152 D2
Surfleet.......117 C5
Surfleet Seas End..117 C5
Surlingham.......104 A4
Sustead.......120 B3
Susworth.......141 C6
Sutcombe.......24 D4
Suton.........104 B1
Sutors of
  Cromarty.......265 D4
Sutterby.......134 B3
Sutterton.......117 B5
Sutton
  Cambs.........101 D6
  C Beds.........84 C4
  Kent.........39 A5
  London........49 C5
  Mers.........136 D4
  Norf.........121 C5
  Notts.........115 B5
  Notts.........132 A1
  N Yorks........140 A2
  Oxon.........65 C5
  Pboro.........100 B2
  Shrops.........95 C5
  Shrops.........111 B5
  Som.........29 B6
  Staffs.........111 C6
  Suff.........88 C4
  Sur.........34 B4
  S Yorks........140 B3
  W Sus.........20 A3
Sutton at Hone....50 B2
Sutton Bassett.....99 B4
Sutton Benger.....44 B3
Sutton Bonington.114 C3
Sutton Bridge.....118 C1
Sutton Cheney.....97 A7
Sutton Coldfield....96 B4
Sutton Courtenay...65 D6
Sutton Crosses....118 C1
Sutton Grange.....157 D6
Sutton Green......34 A3
Sutton Howgrave...157 D7
Sutton In Ashfield.131 D4
Sutton-in-Craven..147 C4
Sutton Ings.......151 D4
Sutton in the Elms..98 B2
Sutton Lane Ends..129 B4
Sutton Leach.....136 D4
Sutton Maddock...95 A5
Sutton Mallet.....28 B3
Sutton Mandeville..30 C3
Sutton Manor.....136 D4
Sutton Montis.....29 C6
Sutton on Hull....151 D4
Sutton on Sea....135 A5
Sutton-on-the-
  Forest.........149 A4
Sutton on the Hill.113 B6
Sutton on Trent...132 C2
Sutton St Edmund.117 D6
Sutton St James...117 D6
Sutton St Nicholas.78 C3
Sutton Scarsdale..131 C4
Sutton Scotney....32 B3
Sutton under
  Brailes.........81 D6

Sutton-under-White-
  stonecliffe......158 C3
Sutton upon
  Derwent........149 C6
Sutton Valence....37 B6
Sutton Veny.......30 A2
Sutton Waldron....30 D2
Sutton Weaver....127 B5
Sutton Wick......43 C5
Swaby.........134 B3
Swadlincote.......113 D7
Swaffham.......103 A4
Swaffham Bulbeck..86 A1
Swaffham Prior...86 A1
Swafield.......121 B4
Swainby.......158 A3
Swainshill......78 C2
Swainsthorpe......104 A3
Swainswick......43 C6
Swalcliffe......81 D6
Swalecliffe......52 C3
Swallow.......142 C3
Swallowcliffe......30 C3
Swallowfield......47 C5
Swallownest......131 A4
Swallows Cross....69 D6
Swanage.......17 D4
Swanbister......283 G4
Swanbourne.......66 A3
Swan Green
  Ches W........128 B2
  Suff.........104 D3
Swanland.......142 A1
Swanley.......50 C2
Swanley Village....50 C2
Swanmore.......33 D4
Swannington
  Leics.........114 D2
  Norf.........120 D3
Swanscombe.......50 B3
Swansea
  =Abertawe.......57 C6
Swanton Abbott...121 C4
Swanton Morley...120 D2
Swanton Novers...120 B2
Swanton Street....37 A6
Swanwick
  Derbys.........131 D4
  Hants.........18 A4
Swarby.........116 A3
Swardeston.......104 A3
Swarister.......284 E7
Swarkestone......114 C1
Swarland.......189 C4
Swarland Estate...189 C4
Swarthmoor......153 C3
Swathwick......130 C3
Swaton.........116 B4
Swavesey.......85 A5
Sway.........18 B1
Swayfield.......116 C2
Swaythling......32 D3
Sweet Green......79 A4
Sweetham.......12 B3
Sweethouse......5 A5
Sweffling.......88 A4
Swepstone.......114 D1
Swerford.......81 D6
Swettenham.......128 C3
Swetton.......157 D5
Swffryd.........60 D4
Swiftsden.......37 D5
Swilland.......88 B2
Swillington......148 D2
Swimbridge......25 C7
Swimbridge
  Newland.......25 B7
Swinbrook......64 B3
Swinderby......132 C3
Swindon
  Glos.........63 A5
  Staffs.........95 B6
  Swindon........45 A5
Swine.........151 D4
Swinefleet......141 A5
Swineshead
  Bedford........84 A2
  Lincs.........117 A5
Swineshead Bridge 117 A5
Swiney.........275 A6
Swinford
  Leics.........98 D2
  Oxon.........65 C5
Swingate.......114 A2
Swingfield Minnis..39 A4
Swingfield Street...39 A4
Swinhoe.......189 A5
Swinhope.......143 D4
Swining.........284 G6
Swinithwaite.....156 C4

Swinnow Moor....147 D6
Swinscoe.......113 A5
Swinside Hall.....187 B6
Swinstead.......116 C3
Swinton
  Borders........198 B2
  Gtr Man........137 C6
  N Yorks........157 D6
  N Yorks........159 D6
  S Yorks........140 D2
Swintonmill......198 B2
Swithland.......114 D3
Swordale.......264 D1
Swordland.......238 C1
Swordly.........278 B3
Sworton Heath....128 A1
Swyddffynnon....75 B5
Swynnerton......112 B2
Swyre.........15 C5
Sychtyn.......92 A3
Syde.........63 B5
Sydenham
  London........49 B6
  Oxon.........66 C2
Sydenham Damerel.11 D5
Syderstone.......119 B5
Sydling St Nicholas..15 B6
Sydmonton......46 D2
Syerston.......115 A5
Syke.........138 B1
Sykehouse.......140 B4
Sykes.........145 B6
Syleham.......104 D3
Sylen.........57 B5
Symbister.......285 G7
Symington
  S Ayrs.........192 B3
  S Lanark........195 C4
Symondsbury......14 B4
Symonds Yat......62 B1
Synod Inn.......73 A7
Syre.........278 D2
Syreford.......63 A6
Syresham.......82 C3
Syston
  Leics.........115 D4
  Lincs.........116 A2
Sytchampton.....79 A6
Sywell.........83 A5

T

Taagan.........262 D2
Tàbost.........288 A6
Tabost.........288 F4
Tackley.........65 A5
Tacleit.........288 D2
Tacolneston......104 B2
Tadcaster......148 C3
Taddington......129 B6
Taddiport.......25 D5
Tadley.........47 C4
Tadlow.........85 C4
Tadmarton......81 D6
Tadworth.......35 A5
Tafarnau-bach....60 B3
Tafarn-y-gelyn...126 C1
Taff's Well......41 C6
Tafolwern......91 B6
Tai.........124 C2
Taibach.......40 C2
Tai-bach.......109 C6
Taigh a Ghearraidh.287 G2
Tai-mawr.......109 A4
Tain
  Highld.........264 B3
  Highld.........280 B4
Tainant.......110 A1
Tainlon.......107 A4
Tairbeart = Tarbert.288 G2
Tai'r-Bull.......60 A1
Tairgwaith......59 D4
Tai-Ucha.......125 D5
Takeley.......69 A5
Takeley Street.....69 A5
Talachddu......77 D4
Talacre.......125 A6
Talardd.......108 C3
Talaton.........13 B5
Talbenny.......54 C4
Talbot Green......41 C5
Talbot Village.....17 B4
Tale.........13 B5
Talerddig......92 A3
Talgarreg.......74 C3
Talgarth.......77 D5
Talisker.......246 A2
Talke.........128 D3
Talkin.........176 D3

Str–Tar 333

Talladale.......261 C6
Talla Linnfoots....195 D6
Tallarn Green.....110 A3
Tallentire.......163 A4
Talley.........58 B3
Tallington......100 A2
Talmine.......277 B6
Talog.........73 D6
Talsarn.........59 C4
Tal-sarn.......75 C4
Talsarnau.......107 C4
Talskiddy.......4 A4
Talwrn
  Anglesey........123 C4
  Wrex.........110 A1
Tal-y-bont
  Ceredig........91 D4
  Conwy.........124 C2
  Gwyn.........107 D5
  Gwyn.........123 C6
Tal-y-bont-on-Usk..60 A3
Tal-y-cafn.......124 B2
Talygarn.......41 C5
Talyllyn.......60 A3
Tal-y-llyn.......91 B5
Talysarn.......107 A4
Talywain.......61 C4
Tal-y-wern......91 B6
Tame Bridge.....158 A4
Tamerton Foliot....6 A3
Tamworth.......97 A5
Tandem.......139 B4
Tanden.........37 C2
Tandridge.......35 A6
Tanerdy.......73 D7
Tanfield.......178 D3
Tanfield Lea......178 D3
Tangasdal.......286 G2
Tangiers.......55 C5
Tangley.......46 D1
Tanglwst.......73 C6
Tangmere.......20 B2
Tangwick.......284 F4
Tan Hinon.......91 D6
Tankersley.......139 C6
Tankerton.......52 C3
Tan-lan
  Conwy.........124 C2
  Gwyn.........107 B6
Tannach.......281 D5
Tannachie.......245 D4
Tannadice.......232 C2
Tannington......88 A3
Tansley.........130 D3
Tansley Knoll.....130 C3
Tansor.........100 B2
Tantobie.......178 D3
Tanton.........158 A3
Tanworth-in-Arden.96 D4
Tan-y-bwlch.....107 B6
Tan-y-fron......125 C4
Tan-y-graig
  Anglesey........123 C5
  Gwyn.........106 C3
Tanygrisiau......107 B6
Tan-y-groes......73 B5
Tan-y-pistyll.....109 C5
Tan-yr-allt......107 A4
Tanyrhydiau......75 B6
Taobh a Chaolais..286 E3
Taobh a' Ghlinne...288 F4
Taobh a Thuath Loch
  Aineort.........286 D3
Taobh a Tuath Loch Bag-
  hasdail.........286 D3
Taobh Tuath......287 F4
Taplow.........48 A2
Tapton.........130 B3
Tarbat House.....264 C3
Tarbert
  Argyll.........202 B3
  Argyll.........202 C1
  Argyll.........213 D4
Tarbert = Tairbeart..288 G2
Tarbet
  Argyll.........215 B6
  Highld.........238 C1
  Highld.........276 D2
Tarbock Green....127 A4
Tarbolton.......193 C4
Tarbrax.......195 A5
Tardebigge......80 A3
Tarfside.......232 A2
Tarland.......244 B1
Tarleton.......136 A3
Tarlogie.......264 B3
Tarlscough......136 B3
Tarlton.........63 D5

Tarnbrook........145 B5
Tarporley.........127 C5
Tarr..............27 B6
Tarrant Crawford....16 A3
Tarrant Gunville.....30 D3
Tarrant Hinton......30 D3
Tarrant Keyneston...16 A3
Tarrant Launceston..16 A3
Tarrant Monkton...16 A3
Tarrant Rawston....16 A3
Tarrant Rushton....16 A3
Tarrel...........265 B4
Tarring Neville......22 B2
Tarrington.........79 C4
Tarsappie.........219 B6
Tarskavaig.......247 D4
Tarves..........256 C3
Tarvie
  Highld........251 A6
  Perth..........230 B4
Tarvin...........127 C4
Tasburgh.........104 B3
Tasley............95 B4
Taston............65 A4
Tatenhill.........113 C6
Tathall End.......83 C5
Tatham..........145 A6
Tathwell.........134 A3
Tatling End.......48 A3
Tatsfield..........36 A2
Tattenhall.......127 D4
Tattenhoe.........83 D5
Tatterford.......119 C5
Tattersett.......119 B5
Tattershall.......134 D2
Tattershall Bridge..134 D1
Tattershall Thorpe..134 D2
Tattingstone.......88 D2
Tatworth..........14 A3
Taunton...........28 C2
Taverham........120 D3
Tavernspite.......56 A1
Tavistock.........11 D5
Taw Green.........12 B1
Tawstock.........25 C6
Taxal...........129 B5
Tay Bridge.......220 B4
Tayinloan........202 D1
Taymouth Castle..230 D1
Taynish.........213 D5
Taynton
  Glos...........62 A3
  Oxon..........64 B3
Taynuilt.........227 C5
Tayport.........221 B4
Tayvallich.......213 D5
Tealby..........142 D3
Tealing.........220 A4
Teangue.........247 D5
Teanna Mhachair..287 H2
Tebay...........155 A5
Tebworth.........67 A4
Tedburn St Mary...12 B3
Teddington
  Glos...........80 D2
  London.........49 B4
Tedstone Delamere..79 B4
Tedstone Wafre....79 B4
Teeton...........98 D3
Teffont Evias......30 B3
Teffont Magna......30 B3
Tegryn...........73 C5
Teigh...........115 D6
Teigncombe.......12 C1
Teigngrace........12 D3
Teignmouth.......13 D4
Telford..........95 A4
Telham...........23 A5
Tellisford........44 D2
Telscombe.........22 B2
Telscombe Cliffs...22 B1
Templand........184 D3
Temple
  Corn..........10 D2
  Glasgow.......205 B5
  Midloth.......196 A2
Temple Balsall....97 D5
Temple Bar
  Carms.........57 A5
  Ceredig........75 C4
Temple Cloud......43 D5
Temple Combe......29 C7
Temple Ewell......39 A4
Temple Grafton....80 B4
Temple Guiting....64 A1
Templehall......209 A5
Temple Herdewyke..81 B6
Temple Hirst.....140 A4

Temple
  Normanton.....131 C4
Temple Sowerby...165 C4
Templeton
  Devon.........26 D3
  Pembs.........55 C7
Templeton Bridge..26 D3
Templetown......178 D3
Tempsford.........84 B3
Tenbury Wells......78 A3
Tenby =
  Dinbych-y-Pysgod...56 B1
Tendring.........71 A5
Tendring Green.....71 A5
Ten Mile Bank.....102 B2
Tenston.........282 F3
Tenterden.........37 C6
Terling..........70 B1
Ternhill.........111 B5
Terregles Banks....174 A2
Terrick..........66 C3
Terrington.......159 D5
Terrington
  St Clement......118 D2
Terrington St John..118 D2
Teston...........37 A5
Testwood.........32 D2
Tetbury..........63 D4
Tetbury Upton.....63 D4
Tetchill........110 B2
Tetcott...........10 B4
Tetford.........134 B3
Tetney..........143 C5
Tetney Lock......143 C5
Tetsworth.........66 C1
Tettenhall........96 B1
Teuchan.........257 C5
Teversal.........131 C4
Teversham.........85 B6
Teviothead.......186 C3
Tewel...........245 D5
Tewin............68 B2
Tewkesbury.......80 D1
Thackthwaite.....163 B4
Thainston.......233 A4
Thakeham.........21 A4
Thame...........66 C2
Thames Ditton.....49 C4
Thames Haven.....51 A4
Thamesmead.......50 A1
Thanington........52 D3
Thankerton......195 C4
Tharston........104 B2
Thatcham.........46 C3
Thatto Heath.....136 D4
Thaxted..........86 D2
The Aird........259 C4
Theakston.......157 C7
Thealby.........141 B6
Theale
  Som...........29 A4
  W Berks........47 B4
The Arms........103 B4
Thearne.........150 D3
The Bage.........77 C6
The Balloch......218 C3
The Barony......282 E3
Theberton.........89 A5
The Bog..........94 B1
The Bourne.......33 A7
The Braes.......247 A5
The Broad.........78 A2
The Butts.........30 A1
The Camp
  Glos..........63 C5
  Herts.........67 C6
The Chequer......110 A3
The City.........66 D2
The Common.......31 B6
The Craigs......263 A6
The Cronk.......152 B3
Theddingworth....98 C3
Theddlethorpe All
  Saints........135 A4
Theddlethorpe
  St Helen......135 A4
The Dell........105 B5
The Den.........204 C3
The Eals........177 A6
The Eaves........62 C2
The Flatt.......176 B3
The Four Alls....111 B5
The Garths......284 B8
The Green
  Cumb..........153 B2
  Wilts.........30 B2
The Grove.......174 A2
The Hall........284 D8
The Haven........34 C3

The Heath
  Norf..........120 C3
  Suff...........88 D2
The Hill........153 B2
The Howe
  Cumb.........154 C3
  IoM..........152 E1
The Hundred......78 A3
Thelbridge Barton..26 D2
The Lee..........67 C4
The Lhen.......152 A3
Thelnetham......103 D6
Thelveton.......104 C2
Thelwall........127 A6
The Marsh
  Powys..........93 B7
  Wilts..........45 A4
Themelthorpe....120 C2
The Middles.....179 D4
The Moor.........37 D5
The Mumbles
  = Y Mwmbwls...57 D6
The Murray......205 C6
The Neuk.......245 C4
Thenford.........82 C2
The Oval.........43 C6
The Pole of Itlaw..268 C1
The Quarry.......62 D3
Therfield........85 D5
The Rhos.........55 C6
The Rock.........95 A4
The Ryde.........68 C2
The Sands........34 B1
The Stocks.......37 D7
Thetford
  Lincs........116 D4
  Norf.........103 C4
The Throat.......47 C6
The Vauld........78 C3
The Wyke.........95 A5
Theydon Bois.....68 D4
Thickwood.........44 B2
Thimbleby
  Lincs........134 C2
  N Yorks......158 B3
Thingwall.......126 A2
Thirdpart.......204 D1
Thirlby.........158 C3
Thirlestane.....197 B4
Thirn...........157 C6
Thirsk.........158 C3
Thirtleby.......151 D4
Thistleton
  Lancs........144 D4
  Rutland......116 D2
Thistley Green...102 D2
Thixendale......150 A1
Thockrington....178 B1
Tholomas Drove...101 A5
Tholthorpe......148 A3
Thomas Chapel....55 D7
Thomas Close....164 A2
Thomastown.....255 C6
Thompson.......103 B5
Thomshill......266 D3
Thong............50 B3
Thongsbridge....139 C4
Thoralby.......156 C4
Thoresway......142 D3
Thorganby
  Lincs........143 D4
  N Yorks......149 C5
Thorgill........159 B6
Thorington......105 D5
Thorington Street..87 D6
Thorlby........146 B3
Thorley..........69 B4
Thorley Street
  Herts.........69 B4
  IoW..........18 C2
Thormanby......158 D3
Thornaby-on-Tees..168 D2
Thornage.......120 B2
Thornborough
  Bucks.........83 D4
  N Yorks......157 D6
Thornbury
  Devon.........11 A5
  Hereford......79 B4
  S Glos.........62 D2
  W Yorks......147 D5
Thornby..........98 D3
Thorncliffe.....129 D5
Thorncombe
  Dorset.........14 A3
  Dorset.........16 A2
Thorncombe Street..34 B3
Thorncote Green...84 C3
Thorncross.......18 C3
Thorndon.........88 A2

Thorndon Cross....11 B6
Thorne.........141 B4
Thorner........148 C2
Thorne St Margaret..27 C5
Thorney
  Notts........132 B3
  Pboro........101 A4
Thorney Crofts...143 A4
Thorney Green.....87 A6
Thorney Hill......17 B5
Thorney Toll.....101 A5
Thornfalcon.......28 C2
Thornford........29 D6
Thorngumbald....143 A4
Thornham........119 A4
Thornham Magna...104 D2
Thornham Parva...104 D2
Thornhaugh......100 A2
Thornhill
  Cardiff........41 C6
  Cumb.........162 D3
  Derbys........130 A1
  Dumfries......183 C6
  Soton..........32 D3
  Stirling.......207 A4
  W Yorks......139 B5
Thornhill Edge...139 B5
Thornhill Lees...139 B5
Thornholme......151 A4
Thornley
  Durham.......166 B4
  Durham.......167 B6
Thornliebank....205 C5
Thorns..........86 B3
Thornsett......129 A5
Thorns Green....128 A2
Thornthwaite
  Cumb.........163 B5
  N Yorks......147 B5
Thornton
  Angus........232 D1
  Bucks........83 D4
  E Yorks......149 C6
  Fife.........209 A5
  Lancs........144 C3
  Leics.........98 A1
  Lincs........134 C2
  Mbro.........168 D2
  Mers.........136 C2
  Northumb......198 B3
  Pembs.........55 D5
  W Yorks......147 D5
Thornton Curtis..142 B2
Thorntonhall....205 C5
Thornton Heath....49 C6
Thornton Hough...126 A3
Thornton in Craven 146 C3
Thornton-le-Beans 158 B2
Thornton-le-Clay..149 A5
Thornton-le-Dale..160 C2
Thornton le Moor..142 D2
Thornton-le-Moor..158 C2
Thornton-le-
  Moors.........127 B4
Thornton-le-
  Street........158 C3
Thorntonloch....211 C4
Thorntonpark....198 B3
Thornton Rust....156 C3
Thornton Steward..157 C5
Thornton Watlass..157 C6
Thornwood
  Common.......69 C4
Thornydykes....197 B5
Thoroton.......115 A5
Thorp Arch.....148 C3
Thorpe
  Derbys.......129 D6
  E Yorks......150 C2
  Lincs........135 A4
  Norf.........105 B5
  Notts........115 A5
  N Yorks......147 A4
  Sur..........48 C3
Thorpe Abbotts..104 D2
Thorpe Acre.....114 C3
Thorpe Arnold...115 C5
Thorpe Audlin...140 B2
Thorpe Bassett..160 D2
Thorpe Bay.......51 A6
Thorpe by Water...99 B5
Thorpe Common....88 D3
Thorpe Constantine 97 A5
Thorpe Culvert..135 C4
Thorpe End......121 D5
Thorpe Fendykes..135 C4
Thorpe Green
  Essex.........71 A5
  Suff..........87 B5
Thorpe Hesley...140 D1

Thorpe in Balne...140 B3
Thorpe in the
  Fallows........133 A4
Thorpe Langton...99 B4
Thorpe Larches...167 C6
Thorpe-le-Soken...71 A5
Thorpe le Street..150 C1
Thorpe Malsor.....99 D5
Thorpe Mandeville..82 C2
Thorpe Market....120 B4
Thorpe Marriot...120 D3
Thorpe Morieux...87 B5
Thorpeness........89 B5
Thorpe on the Hill..133 C4
Thorpe St Andrew..104 A3
Thorpe St Peter..135 C4
Thorpe Salvin...131 A5
Thorpe Satchville..115 D5
Thorpe Thewles...168 C2
Thorpe Tilney...133 D6
Thorpe Underwood 148 B3
Thorpe Waterville..100 C2
Thorpe Willoughby..149 D4
Thorrington......71 A4
Thorverton.......13 A4
Thrandeston.....104 D2
Thrapston......100 D1
Thrashbush.......207 D5
Threapland
  Cumb.........163 A4
  N Yorks......146 A3
Threapwood
  Ches W........110 A3
  Staffs.......112 A4
Three Ashes......61 A7
Three Bridges....35 C5
Three Burrows.....4 C2
Three Chimneys...37 C6
Three Cocks......77 D5
Three Crosses....57 C5
Three Cups Corner..36 D4
Threehammer
  Common.......121 D5
Three Holes.....101 A7
Threekingham...116 B3
Three Leg Cross...37 C4
Three Legged Cross 17 A4
Threemile Cross...47 C5
Threemilestone.....4 C2
Threemiletown...208 C3
Three Oaks.......23 A6
Threlkeld.......163 B6
Threshfield.....146 A3
Thrigby.........121 D6
Thringarth......166 C2
Thringstone.....114 D2
Thrintoft.......157 B7
Thriplow.........85 C6
Throckenholt....101 A5
Throcking........85 D5
Throckley......178 C3
Throckmorton....80 C2
Throphill......178 A3
Thropton.......188 C3
Throsk.........207 A6
Throwleigh.......12 B1
Throwley.........52 D1
Thrumpton......114 B3
Thrumster......281 D5
Thrunton......188 B3
Thrupp
  Glos..........63 C4
  Oxon..........65 B5
Thrushelton......11 C5
Thrussington....115 D4
Thruxton
  Hants.........32 A1
  Hereford......78 D2
Thrybergh......140 D2
Thulston.......114 B2
Thundergay.....202 D3
Thundersley......51 A4
Thundridge.......68 B3
Thurcaston.....114 D3
Thurcroft.......131 A4
Thurgarton
  Norf.........120 B3
  Notts........115 A4
Thurgoland......139 C5
Thurlaston
  Leics.........98 B2
  Warks.........98 D1
Thurlbear........28 C2
Thurlby
  Lincs........116 D4
  Lincs........133 C4
Thurleigh........84 B2
Thurlestone.......7 C5
Thurloxton.......28 B2
Thurlstone.....139 C5

Thurlton.......105 B5
Thurlwood......128 D3
Thurmaston......98 A3
Thurnby..........98 A3
Thurne.........121 D6
Thurnham
  Kent..........37 A6
  Lancs........145 B4
Thurning
  Norf.........120 C2
  Northants.....100 C2
Thurnscoe......140 C2
Thurnscoe East..140 C2
Thursby.........175 C6
Thursford......120 B1
Thursley.........34 C2
Thurso.........280 B3
Thurso East.....280 B3
Thurstaston....126 A2
Thurston........87 A5
Thurstonfield...175 C6
Thurstonland...139 B4
Thurton........104 A4
Thurvaston.....113 B6
Thuxton........103 A6
Thwaite
  N Yorks......156 B2
  Suff..........88 A2
Thwaites.......147 C4
Thwaite St Mary..104 B4
Thwaites Brow...147 C4
Thwing.........160 D4
Tibbermore.....219 B5
Tibberton
  Glos..........62 A3
  Telford......111 C5
  Worcs.........80 B2
Tibenham......104 C2
Tibshelf.......131 C4
Tibthorpe......150 B2
Ticehurst........37 C4
Tichborne.......33 B4
Tickencote.....100 A1
Tickenham.......42 B3
Tickhill.......140 D3
Ticklerton......94 B2
Ticknall.......114 C1
Tickton........150 C3
Tidcombe........45 D6
Tiddington
  Oxon.........66 C1
  Warks.........81 B5
Tidebrook........36 D4
Tideford..........6 B2
Tideford Cross....6 A2
Tidenham........62 D1
Tideswell......129 B6
Tidmarsh.........47 B4
Tidmington......81 D5
Tidpit..........31 D4
Tidworth.........31 A6
Tiers Cross......55 C5
Tiffield.........82 B3
Tifty..........256 B2
Tigerton.......232 B3
Tigh-na-Blair...218 C2
Tighnabruaich...203 A4
Tighnafiline....261 B5
Tigley...........7 A6
Tilbrook........84 A2
Tilbury..........50 B3
Tilbury Juxta Clare..86 C3
Tile Cross.......97 C4
Tile Hill........97 D5
Tilehurst........47 B4
Tilford..........34 B1
Tilgate..........35 C5
Tilgate Forest Row..35 C5
Tillathrowie....255 C5
Tilley.........111 C4
Tillicoultry....208 A2
Tillingham.......70 C3
Tillington
  Hereford......78 C2
  W Sus.........34 D2
Tillington Common..78 C2
Tillyarblet.....232 B3
Tillybirloch....244 B3
Tillycorthie....257 D4
Tillydrine......244 C3
Tillyfour......244 A2
Tillyfourie.....244 A3
Tillygarmond...244 C3
Tillygreig.....256 D3
Tillykerrie....256 D3
Tilmanstone.....53 D5
Tilney All Saints..118 D2
Tilney High End...118 D2
Tilney St Lawrence.118 D2
Tilshead.........31 A4

Tilstock 111 B4
Tilston 127 D4
Tilstone Fearnall . . .127 C5
Tilsworth 67 A4
Tilton on the Hill . . .99 A4
Timberland 133 D6
Timbersbrook 128 C3
Timberscombe 27 A4
Timble 147 B5
Timperley 128 A2
Timsbury
 Bath 43 D5
 Hants 32 C2
Timsgearraidh 287 A5
Timworth Green . . .87 A4
Tincleton 16 B1
Tindale 176 D4
Tingewick 82 D3
Tingley 139 A5
Tingrith 84 D2
Tingwall 282 E4
Tinhay 11 C4
Tinshill 147 D6
Tinsley 140 D2
Tintagel 9 C6
Tintern Parva 62 C1
Tintinhull 29 D5
Tintwistle 138 D3
Tinwald 184 D3
Tinwell 100 A2
Tipperty 257 D4
Tipsend 101 B7
Tipton 96 B2
Tipton St John . . .13 B5
Tiptree 70 B2
Tirabad 59 A5
Tiraghoil 224 D2
Tirley 63 A4
Tirphil 41 A6
Tirril 164 C3
Tir-y-dail 57 A6
Tisbury 30 C3
Tisman's Common . .34 C3
Tissington 130 D1
Titchberry 24 C3
Titchfield 18 A4
Titchmarsh 100 D2
Titchwell 119 A4
Tithby 115 B4
Titley 78 A1
Titlington 189 B4
Titsey 36 A2
Tittensor 112 B2
Tittleshall 119 C5
Tiverton
 Ches W 127 C5
 Devon 27 D4
Tivetshall
 St Margaret 104 C2
Tivetshall St Mary . .104 C2
Tividale 96 B2
Tivy Dale 139 C5
Tixall 112 C3
Tixover 99 A6
Toab
 Orkney 283 G6
 Shetland 285 M5
Toadmoor 130 D3
Tobermory 225 A4
Toberonochy 213 B5
Tobha Mor 286 C3
Tobhtarol 288 D2
Tobson 288 D2
Tocher 256 C1
Tockenham 44 B4
Tockenham Wick . . .44 A4
Tockholes 137 A5
Tockington 43 A5
Tockwith 148 B3
Todber 30 C2
Todding 94 D2
Toddington
 C Beds 67 A5
 Glos 80 D3
Todenham 81 D5
Todhills 175 B6
Todlachie 244 A3
Todmorden 138 A2
Todrig 186 B3
Todwick 131 A4
Toft
 Cambs 85 B5
 Lincs 116 D3
Toft Hill
 Durham 167 C4
 Lincs 134 C2
Toft Monks 105 B5
Toft next Newton . .133 A5
Toftrees 119 C5
Tofts 281 B5

Toftwood 120 D1
Togston 189 C5
Tokavaig 247 C5
Tokers Green . . .47 B5
Tolastadh a
 Chaolais 288 D2
Tolastadh bho
 Thuath 288 C6
Tolland 27 B6
Tollard Royal 30 D3
Toll Bar 140 C2
Tollbar End 97 D6
Toll End 96 B2
Toller Fratrum 15 B5
Toller Porcorum 15 B5
Tollerton
 Notts 115 B4
 N Yorks 148 A4
Tollesbury 70 B3
Tolleshunt D'Arcy . . .70 B3
Tolleshunt Major . . .70 B3
Toll of Birness . . .257 C5
Tolm 288 D5
Tolpuddle 16 B1
Tolvah 241 C6
Tolworth 49 C4
Tomatin 253 D4
Tombreck 252 C2
Tomchrasky 239 A6
Tomdoun 239 B5
Tomich
 Highld 251 D5
 Highld 264 C2
Tomich House 252 B1
Tomintoul
 Aberds 242 C4
 Moray 243 A4
Tomnaven 255 C5
Tomnavoulin 254 D3
Tonbridge 36 B3
Tondu 40 C3
Tonfanau 90 B3
Tong
 Shrops 95 A5
 W Yorks 147 D6
Tonge 114 C2
Tongham 34 B1
Tongland 173 C4
Tong Norton 95 A5
Tongue 277 C6
Tongue End 117 D4
Tongwynlais 41 C6
Tonna 40 B2
Ton-Pentre 41 B4
Tonwell 68 B3
Tonypandy 41 B4
Tonyrefail 41 C5
Toot Baldon 65 C6
Toothill 32 C2
Toot Hill 69 C5
Topcliffe 158 D3
Topcroft 104 B3
Topcroft Street . . .104 B3
Top of Hebers 138 C1
Toppesfield 86 D3
Toppings 137 B6
Topsham 13 C4
Torbay 8 B3
Torbeg 191 C5
Torboll Farm 264 A3
Torbrex 207 A5
Torbryan 8 A2
Torcross 8 C2
Tore 252 A2
Torinturk 202 B3
Torksey 132 B3
Torlum 286 A3
Torlundy 237 B5
Tormarton 43 B6
Tormisdale 200 C1
Tormitchell 181 B4
Tormore 191 B4
Tornagrain 252 B3
Tornahaish 243 B5
Tornaveen 244 B3
Torness 252 D1
Toronto 167 B4
Torpenhow 163 A4
Torphichen 208 C2
Torphins 244 B3
Torpoint 6 B3
Torquay 8 A3
Torquhan 196 B3
Torran
 Argyll 214 B1
 Highld 248 B2
 Highld 264 C3
Torrance 205 A6
Torrans 224 D3
Torranyard 204 D3

Torre 8 A3
Torridon 249 A6
Torridon House . . .249 A5
Torrin 247 B4
Torrisdale 278 B2
Torrisdale-Square . .190 B3
Torrish 274 C3
Torrisholme 145 A4
Torroble 272 D3
Torry
 Aberdeen 245 B6
 Aberds 255 C5
Torryburn 208 B3
Torterston 257 B5
Torthorwald 174 A3
Tortington 20 B3
Tortworth 62 D3
Torvaig 259 D4
Torver 154 B1
Torwood 207 B6
Torworth 131 A6
Tosberry 24 C3
Toscaig 249 C4
Toseland 84 A4
Tosside 146 B1
Tostock 87 A5
Totaig
 Highld 249 D5
 Highld 258 C2
Tote 259 D4
Totegan 279 B4
Tothill 135 A4
Totland 18 C2
Totnes 8 A2
Toton 114 B3
Totronald 223 B4
Totscore 258 B3
Tottenham 68 D3
Tottenhill 118 D3
Tottenhill Row 118 D3
Totteridge 68 D2
Totternhoe 67 A4
Tottington 137 B6
Totton 32 D2
Touchen End 48 B1
Tournaig 261 B5
Toux 269 D4
Tovil 37 A5
Toward 203 B6
Towcester 82 C3
Towednack 2 B2
Tower End 118 D3
Towersey 66 C2
Towie
 Aberds 244 A1
 Aberds 268 C2
Towiemore 255 B4
Tow Law 166 B4
Townend 205 A4
Town End
 Cambs 101 B6
 Cumb 154 C3
Towngate 116 D4
Townhead
 Cumb 164 B3
 Dumfries 173 D4
 S Ayrs 181 A4
 S Yorks 139 C5
Townhead of
 Greenlaw 173 B5
Townhill 208 B4
Town Row 36 C3
Townsend
 Bucks 66 C2
 Herts 67 C6
Townshend 2 B3
Town Yetholm . . .187 A7
Towthorpe 149 B5
Towton 148 D3
Towyn 125 B4
Toxteth 126 A3
Toynton All Saints . .134 C3
Toynton Fen Side . .134 C3
Toynton St Peter . . .135 C4
Toy's Hill 36 A2
Trabboch 193 C4
Traboe 3 C5
Tradespark
 Highld 253 A4
 Orkney 283 G5
Trafford Park 137 D6
Trallong 59 C6
Tranent 209 C7
Tranmere 126 A3
Trantlebeg 279 C4
Trantlemore 279 C4
Tranwell 178 A3
Trapp 57 A6
Traprain 210 C2
Traquair 196 C2

Trawden 146 D3
Trawsfynydd 108 B2
Trealaw 41 B5
Treales 144 D4
Trearddur 122 C2
Treaslane 258 C3
Trebanog 41 B5
Trebanos 40 A2
Trebartha 10 D3
Trebarwith 9 C6
Trebetherick 9 D5
Treborough 27 B5
Trebudannon 4 A3
Trebullett 10 D4
Treburley 10 D4
Trebyan 5 A5
Trecastle 59 C5
Trecenydd 41 C6
Trecwn 55 A5
Trecynon 41 A4
Tredavoe 2 C2
Treddiog 55 B4
Tredegar 60 C3
Tredegar Newydd
 = New Tredegar 41 A6
Tredington
 Glos 63 A5
 Warks 81 C5
Tredinnick 9 D5
Tredomen 77 D5
Tredunnock 61 D5
Tredustan 77 D5
Treen 2 C1
Treeton 131 A4
Trefaldwyn
 = Montgomery 93 B6
Trefasser 72 C1
Trefdraeth 123 C4
Trefdraeth
 = Newport 72 C3
Trefecca 77 D5
Trefechan 90 D3
Trefeglwys 92 B3
Trefenter 75 B5
Treffgarne 55 B5
Treffynnon 54 B4
Treffynnon
 = Holywell 126 B1
Trefgarn Owen . . .55 B4
Trefil 60 B3
Trefilan 75 C4
Trefin 54 A4
Treflach 110 C1
Trefnanney 109 D7
Trefnant 125 B5
Trefonen 110 C1
Trefor
 Anglesey 122 B3
 Gwyn 106 B3
Treforest 41 C5
Trefriw 124 C2
Tref-y-Clawdd
 = Knighton
 Powys 93 D6
 Powys 93 D6
Trefynwy
 = Monmouth 61 B7
Tregadillett 10 C3
Tregaian 123 C4
Tregare 61 B6
Tregaron 75 C5
Tregarth 123 D6
Tregeare 10 C3
Tregeiriog 109 B6
Tregele 122 A3
Tre-Gibbon 60 C1
Tregidden 3 C5
Treglemais 54 B4
Tregole 10 B2
Tregonetha 5 A4
Tregony 4 C4
Tregoss 5 A4
Tregoyd 77 D6
Tregroes 73 B7
Tregurrian 4 A3
Tregynon 93 B4
Trehafod 41 B5
Treharris 41 B5
Treherbert 40 B4
Trekenner 10 D4
Treknow 9 C6
Trelan 3 D5
Trelash 10 B2
Trelassick 4 B3
Trelawnyd 125 B5
Trelech 73 C5
Treleddyd-fawr . . .54 B3
Trelewis 41 B6
Treligga 9 C6
Trelights 9 D5

Trelill 9 D6
Trelissick 4 D3
Trellech 61 C7
Trelleck Grange . . .61 C6
Trelogan 125 A6
Trelystan 93 A6
Tremadog 107 B5
Tremail 10 C2
Tremain 73 B5
Tremaine 10 C3
Tremar 6 A1
Trematon 6 B2
Tremeirchion 125 B5
Trenance 4 A3
Trenarren 5 C5
Trench 111 D5
Treneglos 10 C3
Trenewan 5 B6
Trent 29 D5
Trentham 112 A2
Trentishoe 26 A1
Trent Vale 112 A2
Treoes 40 C4
Treorchy = Treorci . .41 B4
Treorci = Treorchy . .41 B4
Tre'r-ddôl 91 C4
Trerulefoot 6 B2
Tresaith 73 A5
Tresawle 4 C3
Trescott 95 B6
Trescowe 2 B3
Tresham 62 D3
Tresillian 4 C3
Tresinwen 72 B1
Treskinnick Cross . .10 B3
Tresmeer 10 C3
Tresparrett 10 B2
Tresparrett Posts . .10 B2
Tressait 230 B2
Tresta
 Shetland 284 D8
 Shetland 285 H5
Treswell 132 B2
Tre-Taliesin 91 C4
Trethosa 4 B4
Trethurgy 5 B5
Tretio 54 B3
Tretire 62 A1
Tretower 60 A3
Treuddyn 126 D2
Trevalga 10 C1
Trevalyn 126 D3
Trevanson 9 D5
Trevarren 4 A4
Trevarrian 4 A3
Trevarrick 5 C4
Trevaughan 56 A1
Tre-vaughan 73 D7
Treveighan 9 D6
Trevellas 4 B2
Treverva 4 D2
Trevethin 61 C4
Trevigro 6 A2
Treviscoe 4 B4
Trevone 9 D4
Trewarmett 9 C6
Trewassa 10 C2
Trewellard 2 B1
Trewen 10 C3
Trewennack 3 C4
Trewern 110 D1
Trewethern 9 D6
Trewidland 6 B1
Trewint
 Corn 10 B2
 Corn 10 C3
Trewithian 4 D3
Trewoofe 2 C2
Trewoon 5 B4
Treworga 4 C3
Treworlas 4 D3
Tre-wyn 61 A5
Treyarnon 9 D4
Treyford
 W Sus 20 A1
 W Sus 33 D7
Trezaise 5 B4
Ty'r-felin-isaf 124 C3
Triangle 138 A3
Triffleton 55 B5
Trimdon 167 B6
Trimdon Colliery . . .167 B6
Trimdon Grange . . .167 B6
Trimingham 121 B4
Trimley Lower
 Street 88 C2
Trimley St Martin . .88 C2
Trimley St Mary . . .88 C2
Trimpley 95 D5
Trimsaran 57 B4

Trimstone 25 A5
Trinafour 229 B6
Trinant 41 A7
Tring 67 B4
Tring Wharf 67 B4
Trinity
 Angus 233 B4
 Jersey 6
Trisant 75 A6
Trislaig 237 B4
Trispen 4 B3
Tritlington 189 D5
Trochry 230 D3
Trodigal 190 C2
Troed-rhiwdalar . . .76 B3
Troedyraur 73 B6
Troedyrhiw 41 A5
Tromode 152 D3
Trondavoe 284 F5
Troon
 Corn 3 B4
 S Ayrs 192 B3
Trosaraidh 286 E3
Trossachs Hotel . . .217 D5
Troston 103 D4
Trottiscliffe 50 C3
Trotton 34 D1
Troutbeck
 Cumb 154 A3
 Cumb 164 C1
Troutbeck Bridge . .154 A3
Trowbridge 44 D2
Trowell 114 B2
Trow Green 62 C1
Trowle Common . . .44 D2
Trowley Bottom . . .67 B5
Trows 197 C5
Trowse Newton . . .104 A3
Trudoxhill 30 A1
Trull 28 C2
Trumaisgear-
 raidh 287 G3
Trumpan 258 B2
Trumpet 79 D4
Trumpington 85 B6
Trunch 121 B4
Trunnah 144 C3
Truro 4 C3
Trusham 12 C3
Trusley 113 B6
Trusthorpe 135 A4
Trysull 95 B6
Tubney 65 D5
Tuckenhay 8 B2
Tuckhill 95 C5
Tuckingmill 3 A4
Tuddenham 102 D3
Tuddenham
 St Martin 88 C2
Tudeley 36 B4
Tudhoe 167 B5
Tudorville 62 A1
Tudweiliog 106 C2
Tuesley 34 B2
Tuffley 63 B4
Tufton
 Hants 32 A3
 Pembs 55 B6
Tugby 99 A4
Tugford 94 C3
Tullibardine 218 C2
Tullibody 207 A6
Tullich
 Argyll 214 A3
 Highld 252 D2
Tullich Muir 264 C3
Tulliemet 230 C3
Tulloch
 Aberds 233 A5
 Aberds 256 C3
 Perth 219 B5
Tulloch Castle . . .264 D1
Tullochgorm 214 C2
Tulloes 232 D3
Tullybannocher . . .218 B2
Tullybelton 219 A5
Tullyfergus 231 D6
Tullymurdoch 231 C5
Tullynessle 244 A2
Tumble 57 A5
Tumby Woodside . .134 D2
Tummel Bridge . . .229 C6
Tunga 288 D5
Tunstall
 E Yorks 151 D6
 Kent 51 C5
 Lancs 155 D5
 Norf 105 A5

Tunstall *continued*
N Yorks 157 B6
Stoke 128 D3
Suff 89 B4
T&W 179 D5
Tunstead
Derbys 129 B6
Gtr Man 138 C3
Norf 121 C4
Tunworth 33 A5
Tupsley 78 C3
Tupton 130 C3
Turgis Green 47 D4
Turin 232 C3
Turkdean 64 B2
Tur Langton 99 B4
Turleigh 44 C2
Turn 137 B7
Turnastone 78 D1
Turnberry 192 E2
Turnditch 113 A6
Turners Hill 35 C6
Turners Puddle 16 B2
Turnford 68 C3
Turnhouse 209 C4
Turnworth 16 A2
Turriff 268 D2
Turton Bottoms 137 B6
Turves 101 B5
Turvey 83 B6
Turville 66 D2
Turville Heath 66 D2
Turweston 82 D3
Tushielaw 185 A6
Tutbury 113 C6
Tutnall 96 D2
Tutshill 62 D1
Tuttington 120 C4
Tutts Clump 46 B3
Tuxford 132 B2
Twatt
Orkney 282 E3
Shetland 285 H5
Twechar 207 C4
Tweedmouth 198 A3
Tweedsmuir 195 D5
Twelve Heads 4 C2
Twemlow Green 128 C2
Twenty 117 C4
Twerton 43 C6
Twickenham 49 B4
Twigworth 63 A4
Twineham 21 A5
Twinhoe 43 D6
Twinstead 87 D4
Twinstead Green 87 D4
Twiss Green 137 D5
Twiston 146 C2
Twitchen
Devon 26 B2
Shrops 94 D1
Two Bridges 11 D7
Two Dales 130 C2
Two Mills 126 B3
Twycross 97 A6
Twyford
Bucks 66 A1
Derbys 114 C1
Hants 32 C3
Leics 115 D5
Lincs 116 C2
Norf 120 C2
Wokingham 47 B5
Twyford Common 78 D3
Twynholm 173 C4
Twyning 80 D1
Twyning Green 80 D2
Twynllanan 59 C4
Twynmynydd 57 A6
Twyn-y-Sheriff 61 C6
Twywell 99 D6
Tyberton 78 D1
Tyburn 96 B4
Tycroes 57 A6
Tycrwyn 109 D6
Tyddewi = *St David's* 54 B3
Tydd Gote 118 D1
Tydd St Giles 118 D1
Tydd St Mary 118 D1
Tyddyn-mawr 107 B5
Ty-draw 124 D3
Tye Green
Essex 69 C4
Essex 70 A1
Essex 86 D1
Ty-hen
Carms 73 D6
Gwyn 106 C1

Tyldesley 137 C5
Tyler Hill 52 C3
Tylers Green 67 D4
Tylorstown 41 B5
Tylwch 92 C3
Ty-mawr 123 B4
Ty Mawr 58 A2
Ty Mawr Cwm 108 A4
Ty-nant
Conwy 109 A4
Gwyn 108 C4
Tyncelyn 75 B5
Tyndrum 216 A3
Tyneham 16 C2
Tynehead 196 A2
Tynemouth 179 C5
Tyne Tunnel 179 C5
Tynewydd 40 B4
Tyninghame 210 C3
Tynron 183 C6
Tyn-y-celyn 109 B6
Tyn-y-coed 110 C1
Tyn-y-fedwen 109 B6
Tyn-y-ffridd 109 B6
Tynygongl 123 B5
Tynygraig 75 B5
Tyn-y-graig 76 B4
Ty'n-y-groes 124 B2
Tyn-y-maes 123 D6
Tyn-y-pwll 123 B4
Ty'n-yr-eithin 75 B5
Tyrie 269 C4
Tyringham 83 C5
Tythecott 25 D5
Tythegston 40 D3
Tytherington
Ches E. 129 B4
S Glos 43 A5
Som 30 A1
Wilts 30 A3
Tytherleigh 14 A3
Ty-uchaf 109 C5
Tywardreath 5 B5
Tywyn
Conwy 124 B2
Gwyn 90 B3

U
Uachdar 286 A3
Uags 249 C4
Ubbeston Green 104 D4
Ubley 43 D4
Uckerby 157 A6
Uckfield 36 D2
Uckington 63 A5
Uddingston 207 D4
Uddington 194 C3
Udimore 23 A6
Udny Green 256 D3
Udny Station 257 D4
Udston 194 A1
Udstonhead 194 B2
Uffcott 45 B5
Uffculme 27 D5
Uffington
Lincs 100 A2
Oxon 45 A7
Shrops 111 D4
Ufford
Pboro 100 A2
Suff 88 B3
Ufton 81 A6
Ufton Nervet 47 C4
Ugadale 190 C3
Ugborough 7 B5
Uggeshall 105 C5
Ugglebarnby 160 A2
Ughill 139 D5
Ugley 69 A5
Ugley Green 69 A5
Ugthorpe 169 D5
Uidh 286 G2
Uig
Argyll 215 D4
Highld 258 B3
Highld 258 C1
Uigen 287 A5
Uigshader 259 D4
Uisken 224 E2
Ulbster 281 D5
Ulceby
Lincs 135 B4
N Lincs 142 B3
Ulceby Skitter 142 B3
Ulcombe 37 B6
Uldale 163 A5
Uley 62 D3
Ulgham 189 D5

Ullapool 262 A3
Ullenhall 80 A4
Ullenwood 63 B5
Ulleskelf 148 C4
Ullesthorpe 98 C2
Ulley 131 A4
Ullingswick 78 C3
Ullinish 246 A2
Ullock 162 B3
Ulnes Walton 136 B4
Ulpha 153 A2
Ulrome 151 B4
Ulsta 284 E6
Ulva House 224 C3
Ulverston 154 D1
Ulwell 17 C4
Umberleigh 25 C7
Unapool 271 A5
Unasary 286 D3
Underbarrow 154 B3
Undercliffe 147 D5
Underhoull 284 C7
Underriver 36 A3
Underwood 131 D4
Undy 42 A3
Unifirth 285 H4
Union Cottage 245 C5
Union Mills 152 D3
Union Street 37 C5
Unstone 130 B3
Unstone Green 130 B3
Unthank
Cumb 164 B2
Cumb 165 A4
Unthank End 164 B2
Upavon 45 D5
Up Cerne 15 A6
Upchurch 51 C5
Upcott 78 B1
Upend 86 B2
Up Exe 13 A4
Upgate 120 D3
Uphall 208 C3
Uphall Station 208 C3
Upham
Devon 12 A3
Hants 32 C4
Uphampton 79 A6
Up Hatherley 63 A5
Uphill 42 D2
Up Holland 136 C4
Uplawmoor 205 C4
Upleadon 62 A3
Upleatham 168 D4
Uplees 52 C1
Uploders 15 B5
Uplowman 27 D5
Uplyme 14 B3
Up Marden 33 D6
Upminster 50 A2
Up Nately 47 D4
Upnor 51 B4
Upottery 14 A2
Upper Affcot 94 C2
Upper Ardchronie 264 B2
Upper Arley 95 C5
Upper Arncott 65 B7
Upper Astrop 82 D2
Upper Badcall 276 D2
Upper Basildon 46 B3
Upper Beeding 21 A4
Upper Benefield 100 C1
Upper Bighouse 279 C4
Upper Boddington 82 B1
Upper Borth 90 D4
Upper Boyndlie 269 C4
Upper Brailes 81 D6
Upper Breakish 247 B5
Upper Breinton 78 C2
Upper Broadheath 79 B6
Upper Broughton 115 C4
Upper Bucklebury 46 C3
Upper Burnhaugh 245 C5
Upperby 175 C7
Upper Caldecote 84 C3
Upper Catesby 82 B2
Upper Chapel 76 D4
Upper Church Village 41 C5
Upper Chute 45 D6
Upper Clatford 32 A2
Upper Clynnog 107 B4
Upper Cumberworth 139 C5
Upper Cwmbran 61 D4
Upper Dallachy 267 C4
Upper Dean 84 A2
Upper Denby 139 C5
Upper Denton 176 C4
Upper Derraid 253 C6

Upper Dicker 22 B3
Upper Dovercourt 88 D3
Upper Druimfin 225 A4
Upper Dunsforth 148 A3
Upper Eathie 264 D3
Upper Elkstone 129 D5
Upper End 129 B5
Upper Farringdon 33 B6
Upper Framilode 62 B3
Upper Glenfintaig 239 D6
Upper Gornal 96 B2
Upper Gravenhurst 84 D3
Upper Green
Mon. 61 B5
W Berks 46 C1
Upper Grove Common 62 A1
Upper Hackney 130 C2
Upper Hale 34 B1
Upper Halistra 258 C2
Upper Halling 50 C3
Upper Hambleton 99 A5
Upper Hardres Court 52 D3
Upper Hartfield 36 C2
Upper Haugh 140 D2
Upper Heath 94 C3
Upper Hellesdon 120 D4
Upper Helmsley 149 B5
Upper Hergest 77 B6
Upper Heyford
Northants 82 B3
Oxon 65 A5
Upper Hill 78 B2
Upper Hopton 139 B4
Upper Horsebridge 22 A3
Upper Hulme 129 C5
Upper Inglesham 64 D3
Upper Inverbrough 253 C4
Upper Killay 57 C5
Upper Knockando 254 B2
Upper Lambourn 45 A7
Upper Leigh 112 B4
Upper Lenie 251 D7
Upper Lochton 244 C3
Upper Longdon 113 D4
Upper Lybster 275 A6
Upper Lydbrook 62 B2
Upper Maes-coed 78 D1
Upper Midway 113 C6
Uppermill 138 C2
Upper Milovaig 258 D1
Upper Minety 63 D6
Upper Mitton 95 D6
Upper North Dean 66 D3
Upper Obney 219 A5
Upper Ollach 247 A4
Upper Padley 130 B2
Upper Pollicott 66 B2
Upper Poppleton 149 B4
Upper Quinton 81 C4
Upper Ratley 32 C2
Upper Rissington 64 B3
Upper Rochford 79 A4
Upper Sandaig 238 A1
Upper Sanday 283 G6
Upper Sapey 79 A4
Upper Saxondale 115 B4
Upper Seagry 44 A3
Upper Shelton 84 C1
Upper Sheringham 120 A3
Upper Skelmorlie 204 B2
Upper Slaughter 64 A2
Upper Soudley 62 B2
Uppersound 285 J6
Upper Stondon 84 D3
Upper Stowe 82 B3
Upper Stratton 45 A5
Upper Street
Hants 31 D5
Norf 121 D5
Norf 121 D5
Suff 88 D2
Upper Strensham 80 D2
Upper Sundon 67 A5
Upper Swell 64 A2
Upper Tean 112 B4
Upperthong 139 C4
Upperthorpe 141 C5
Upper Tillyrie 219 D6
Upperton 34 D2
Upper Tooting 49 B5
Upper Tote 259 C5
Uppertown
Derbys 130 C3
Highld 281 A5
Orkney 283 H5
Upper Town 43 C4
Upper Treverward 93 D6
Upper Tysoe 81 C6

Upper Upham 45 B6
Upper Wardington 82 C1
Upper Weald 83 D4
Upper Weedon 82 B3
Upper Wield 33 B5
Upper Winchendon 66 B2
Upper Witton 96 B3
Upper Woodend 244 A3
Upper Woodford 31 B5
Upper Wootton 46 D3
Upper Wyche 79 C5
Uppingham 99 B5
Uppington 95 A4
Upsall 158 C3
Upshire 68 C4
Up Somborne 32 B2
Upstreet 53 C4
Up Sydling 15 A6
Upthorpe 103 D5
Upton
Cambs 100 D3
Ches W 127 C4
Corn 10 A3
Dorset 16 B3
Dorset 16 C1
Hants 32 D2
Hants 46 D1
Leics 97 B6
Lincs 132 A3
Mers 126 A2
Norf 121 D6
Northants 83 A4
Notts 132 A3
Notts 132 D2
Oxon 46 A3
Pboro 100 A3
Slough 48 B2
Som. 27 C4
W Yorks 140 B2
Upton Bishop 62 A2
Upton Cheyney 43 C5
Upton Cressett 95 B4
Upton Cross 10 D3
Upton Grey 33 A5
Upton Hellions 12 A3
Upton Lovell 30 A3
Upton Magna 111 D4
Upton Noble 29 B7
Upton Pyne 13 B4
Upton St Leonard's 63 B4
Upton Scudamore 30 A2
Upton Snodsbury 80 B2
Upton upon Severn 79 C6
Upton Warren 80 A2
Upwaltham 20 A2
Upware 102 D1
Upwell 101 A6
Upwey 15 C6
Upwood 101 C4
Uradale 285 K6
Urafirth 284 F5
Urchfont 44 D4
Urdimarsh 78 C3
Ure 284 F4
Ure Bank 157 D7
Urgha 288 H2
Urishay Common 77 D7
Urlay Nook 167 D6
Urmston 137 D6
Urpeth 179 D4
Urquhart
Highld 252 A1
Moray 266 C3
Urra 159 A4
Urray 251 A7
Ushaw Moor 167 A5
Usk = *Brynbuga* 61 C5
Usselby 142 D2
Usworth 179 D5
Utkinton 127 C5
Utley 147 C4
Uton 12 B3
Utterby 143 D5
Uttoxeter 113 B4
Uwchmynydd 106 D1
Uxbridge 48 A3
Uyeasound 284 C7
Uzmaston 55 C5

V
Valley 122 C2
Valleyfield 173 C4
Valley Truckle 10 C1
Valsgarth 284 B8
Valtos 259 B5
Van 92 C3
Vange 51 A4
Varteg 61 C4

Vatten 258 D2
Vaul 222 C3
Vaynor 60 B2
Veensgarth 285 J6
Velindre 77 D5
Vellow 27 B5
Veness 282 E6
Venn Green 25 D4
Vennington 94 A1
Venn Ottery 13 B5
Venny Tedburn 12 B3
Ventnor 19 D4
Vernham Dean 46 D1
Vernham Street 46 D1
Vernolds Common 94 C2
Verwood 17 A4
Veryan 4 D4
Vicarage 14 C2
Vickerstown 153 D2
Victoria
Corn 5 A4
S Yorks 139 C4
Vidlin 284 G6
Viewpark 207 D5
Vigo Village 50 C3
Vinehall Street 37 D5
Vine's Cross 22 A3
Viney Hill 62 C2
Virginia Water 48 C2
Virginstow 11 B4
Vobster 29 A7
Voe
Shetland 284 E5
Shetland 285 G6
Vowchurch 78 D1
Voxter 284 F5
Voy 282 F3

W
Wackerfield 167 C4
Wacton 104 B2
Wadbister 285 J6
Wadborough 80 C2
Waddesdon 66 B2
Waddingham 142 D1
Waddington
Lancs 146 C1
Lincs 133 C4
Wadebridge 9 D5
Wadeford 28 D3
Wadenhoe 100 C2
Wadesmill 68 B3
Wadhurst 36 C4
Wadshelf 130 B3
Wadsley 139 D6
Wadsley Bridge 139 D6
Wadworth 140 D3
Waen
Denb 125 C4
Denb 125 C6
Waen Fach 109 D7
Waen Goleugoed 125 B5
Wag 274 B4
Wainfleet All Saints 135 D4
Wainfleet Bank 135 D4
Wainfleet St Mary 135 D5
Wainfleet Tofts 135 D4
Wainhouse Corner 10 B2
Wainscott 51 B4
Wainstalls 138 A3
Waitby 155 A6
Waithe 143 C4
Wakefield 139 A6
Wake Lady Green 159 B5
Wakerley 99 B6
Wakes Colne 70 A2
Walberswick 105 D5
Walberton 20 B2
Walbottle 178 C3
Walcot
Lincs 116 B3
N Lincs 141 A6
Shrops 94 C1
Swindon 45 A5
Telford 111 D4
Walcote
Leics 98 C2
Warks 80 B4
Walcot Green 104 C2
Walcott
Lincs 133 D6
Norf 121 B5
Walden 156 C4
Walden Head 156 C3
Walden Stubbs 140 B3
Waldersey 101 A6
Walderslade 51 C4

Walderton 33 D6
Walditch 15 B4
Waldley 113 B5
Waldridge 179 D4
Waldringfield 88 C3
Waldringfield Heath . 88 C3
Waldron 22 A3
Wales 131 A4
Walesby
  Lincs 142 D3
  Notts 132 B1
Walford
  Hereford 62 A1
  Hereford 94 D1
  Shrops 110 C3
Walford Heath 110 D3
Walgherton 111 A5
Walgrave 99 D5
Walhampton 18 B2
Walkden 137 C6
Walker 179 C4
Walker Barn 129 B4
Walkerburn 196 C2
Walker Fold 145 C6
Walkeringham 141 D5
Walkerith 141 D5
Walkern 68 A2
Walker's Green 78 C3
Walkerville 157 B6
Walkford 17 B6
Walkhampton 7 A4
Walkington 150 D2
Walkley 130 A3
Walk Mill 146 D2
Wall
  Northumb 177 C7
  Staffs 96 A4
Wallaceton 183 D6
Wallacetown
  S Ayrs 181 A4
  S Ayrs 192 C3
Wallands Park 22 A2
Wallasey 136 D2
Wall Bank 94 B3
Wallcrouch 37 C4
Wall Heath 96 C1
Wallingford 47 A4
Wallington
  Hants 19 A4
  Herts 85 D4
  London 49 C5
Wallis 55 B6
Walliswood 35 C4
Walls 285 J4
Wallsend 179 C4
Wallston 41 D6
Wall under
  Heywood 94 B3
Wallyford 209 C6
Walmer 53 D5
Walmer Bridge 136 A3
Walmersley 137 B7
Walmley 96 B4
Walpole 105 D4
Walpole Cross
  Keys 118 D2
Walpole Highway . . 118 D2
Walpole Marsh 118 D1
Walpole St Andrew . 118 D2
Walpole St Peter . . 118 D2
Walsall 96 B3
Walsall Wood 96 A3
Walsden 137 B6
Walsgrave on Sowe . 97 C6
Walsham le
  Willows 103 D5
Walshaw 137 B6
Walshford 148 B3
Walsoken 118 D1
Walston 195 B5
Walsworth 84 D4
Walters Ash 66 D3
Walterston 41 D5
Walterstone 61 A5
Waltham
  Kent 38 A3
  NE Lincs 143 C4
Waltham Abbey 68 C3
Waltham Chase 33 D4
Waltham Cross 68 C3
Waltham on the
  Wolds 115 C6
Waltham
  St Lawrence 47 B6
Walthamstow 49 A6
Walton
  Cumb 176 C3
  Derbys 130 C3
  Leics 98 C2
  Mers 136 D2

Walton continued
  M Keynes 83 D5
  Pboro 100 A3
  Powys 77 B6
  Som 29 B4
  Staffs 112 B2
  Suff 88 D3
  Telford 111 D4
  Warks 81 B5
  W Yorks 139 B6
  W Yorks 148 C3
Walton Cardiff 80 D2
Walton East 55 B6
Walton-in-Gordano . 42 B3
Walton-le-Dale 137 A4
Walton-on-Thames . 48 C4
Walton on the Hill
  Staffs 112 C3
  Sur 35 A5
Walton-on-the-
  Naze 71 A6
Walton on the
  Wolds 114 D3
Walton-on-Trent . . 113 D6
Walton West 55 C4
Walwen 126 B2
Walwick 177 B7
Walworth 167 D5
Walworth Gate 167 C5
Walwyn's Castle . . . 55 C4
Wambrook 14 A2
Wanborough
  Sur 34 B2
  Swindon 45 A6
Wandsworth 49 B5
Wangford 105 D5
Wanlockhead 183 A6
Wansford
  E Yorks 150 B3
  Pboro 100 B2
Wanstead 49 A7
Wanstrow 29 A7
Wanswell 62 C2
Wantage 46 A1
Wapley 43 B6
Wappenbury 81 A6
Wappenham 82 C3
Warbleton 22 A4
Warblington 19 A6
Warborough 65 D6
Warboys 101 C5
Warbreck 144 D3
Warbstow 10 B3
Warburton 128 A2
Warcop 165 D5
Warden
  Kent 52 B2
  Northumb 177 C7
Ward End 96 C4
Ward Green 87 A6
Wardhill 282 E7
Wardington 82 C1
Wardlaw 185 A4
Wardle
  Ches E. 127 D6
  Gtr Man 138 B2
Wardley 99 A5
Wardlow 130 B1
Wardy Hill 101 C6
Ware
  Herts 68 B3
  Kent 53 C4
Wareham 16 C3
Warehorne 38 B1
Warenford 189 A4
Waren Mill 199 C5
Warenton 199 C5
Wareside 68 B3
Waresley
  Cambs 84 B4
  Worcs 95 D6
Warfield 48 B1
Warfleet 8 B2
Wargrave 47 B5
Warham 119 A6
Warhill 138 D2
Wark
  Northumb 177 B6
  Northumb 198 C2
Warkleigh 26 C1
Warkton 99 D5
Warkworth
  Northants 82 C1
  Northumb 189 C5
Warlaby 158 B2
Warland 138 A2
Warleggan 5 A6
Warlingham 35 A6
Warmfield 140 A1
Warmingham 128 C2

Warmington
  Northants 100 B2
  Warks 81 C7
Warminster 30 A2
Warmlake 37 A6
Warmley 43 B5
Warmley Tower 43 B5
Warmonds Hill 83 A6
Warmsworth 140 C3
Warmwell 16 C1
Warndon 80 B1
Warnford 33 C5
Warnham 35 C4
Warninglid 35 D5
Warren
  Ches E. 128 B3
  Pembs 55 E5
Warren Heath 88 C3
Warren Row 47 A6
Warren Street 51 D6
Warrington
  M Keynes 83 B5
  Warr 127 A6
Warsash 18 A3
Warslow 129 D5
Warter 150 B1
Warthermarske . . . 157 D6
Warthill 149 B5
Wartling 23 B4
Wartnaby 115 C5
Warton
  Lancs 136 A3
  Lancs 154 D3
  Northumb 188 C3
  Warks 97 A5
Warwick 81 A5
Warwick Bridge . . . 176 D2
Warwick on Eden . . 176 D2
Wasbister 282 D4
Wasdale Head 163 D4
Washaway 5 A5
Washbourne 8 B1
Wash Common 46 C2
Washfield 27 D4
Washfold 157 A4
Washford 27 A5
Washford Pyne 26 D3
Washingborough . . 133 B5
Washington
  T&W 179 D5
  W Sus 21 A4
Wasing 46 C3
Waskerley 166 A3
Wasperton 81 B5
Wasps Nest 133 C5
Wass 159 D4
Watchet 27 A5
Watchfield
  Oxon 64 D3
  Som 28 A3
Watchgate 154 B4
Watchhill 175 D4
Watcombe 8 A3
Watendlath 163 C5
Water
  Devon 12 C2
  Lancs 138 A1
Waterbeach 85 A6
Waterbeck 175 A5
Waterden 119 B5
Water End
  E Yorks 149 D6
  Herts 67 B5
  Herts 68 C2
Waterfall 129 D5
Waterfoot
  E Renf 205 C5
  Lancs 138 A1
Waterford
  Hants 18 B2
  Herts 68 B3
Waterhead
  Cumb 154 A2
  Dumfries 185 C4
Waterheads 196 A1
Waterhouses
  Durham 167 A4
  Staffs 129 D5
Wateringbury 37 A4
Waterloo
  BCP 17 B4
  Gtr Man 138 C2
  Highld 247 B5
  Mers 136 D2
  N Lanark 194 A3
  Norf 120 D4
  Perth 219 A5
  Shrops 111 B4
Waterloo Port . . . 123 D4
Waterlooville 19 A5

Watermeetings . . . 184 A2
Watermillock 164 C2
Water Newton 100 B3
Water Orton 97 B4
Waterperry 66 C1
Waterrow 27 C5
Watersfield 20 A3
Waterside
  Aberds 257 D5
  Blackburn 137 A6
  E Ayrs 182 B3
  E Ayrs 205 D4
  E Dunb 207 C4
  E Renf 205 C5
Water's Nook 137 C5
Waterstock 66 C1
Waterston 55 D5
Water Stratford . . . 82 D3
Waters Upton 111 D5
Water Yeat 154 C1
Watford
  Herts 67 D6
  Northants 82 A3
Watford Gap 96 A4
Wath
  N Yorks 147 A5
  N Yorks 157 D7
  N Yorks 159 D5
Wath Brow 162 C3
Wath upon Dearne . 140 C2
Watley's End 43 A5
Watlington
  Norf 118 D3
  Oxon 66 D1
Watnall 114 A3
Watten 280 C4
Wattisfield 103 D6
Wattisham 87 B6
Wattlesborough
  Heath 110 D2
Watton
  E Yorks 150 B3
  Norf 103 A6
Watton at Stone . . . 68 B3
Wattston 207 C5
Wattstown 41 B5
Wauchan 238 D3
Waulkmill Lodge . . 283 G4
Waun 91 B6
Waunarlwydd 57 C6
Waunclunda 58 B3
Waunfawr 107 A5
Waungron 57 B5
Waunlwyd 60 C3
Waun-y-clyn 57 B4
Wavendon 83 D6
Waverbridge 175 D5
Waverton
  Ches W 127 C4
  Cumb 175 D5
Wavertree 126 A3
Wawne 150 D3
Waxham 121 C6
Waxholme 143 A5
Way 53 C5
Wayfield 51 C4
Wayford 14 A4
Waymills 111 A4
Wayne Green 61 B6
Way Village 26 D3
Wdig =Goodwick . . 72 C2
Weachyburn 268 D1
Weald 64 C4
Wealdstone 49 A4
Weardley 148 C1
Weare 42 D3
Weare Giffard 25 C5
Wearhead 165 B6
Weasdale 155 A5
Weasenham All
  Saints 119 C5
Weasenham
  St Peter 119 C5
Weatherhill 35 B6
Weaverham 127 B6
Weaverthorpe . . . 160 D3
Webheath 80 A3
Wedderlairs 256 C3
Wedderlie 197 A5
Weddington 97 B6
Wedhampton 45 D4
Wedmore 28 A4
Wednesbury 96 B2
Wednesfield 96 A2
Weedon 66 B3
Weedon Bec 82 B3
Weedon Lois 82 C3
Weeford 96 A4
Week 26 D2

Weeke 32 B3
Weekley 99 C5
Week St Mary 10 B3
Weel 150 D3
Weeley 71 A5
Weeley Heath 71 A5
Weem 230 D2
Weeping Cross . . . 112 C3
Weethley Gate 80 B3
Weeting 102 C3
Weeton
  E Yorks 143 A5
  Lancs 144 D3
  N Yorks 148 C1
Weetwood Hall . . 188 A3
Weir 138 A1
Weir Quay 6 A3
Welborne 120 E2
Welbourn 133 D4
Welburn
  N Yorks 149 A6
  N Yorks 159 C5
Welbury 158 A2
Welby 116 B2
Welches Dam . . . 101 C6
Welcombe 24 D3
Weld Bank 137 B4
Weldon 189 D4
Welford
  Northants 98 C3
  W Berks 46 B2
Welford-on-Avon . . 81 B4
Welham
  Leics 99 B4
  Notts 132 A2
Welham Green 68 C2
Well
  Hants 33 A6
  Lincs 135 B4
  N Yorks 157 C6
Welland 79 C5
Wellbank 221 A4
Welldale 175 B4
Well End 48 A1
Wellesbourne 81 B5
Well Heads 147 D4
Well Hill 50 C1
Welling 50 B1
Wellingborough . . 83 A5
Wellingham 119 C5
Wellingore 133 D4
Wellington
  Cumb 162 D3
  Hereford 78 C2
  Som 27 C6
  Telford 111 D5
Wellington Heath . . 79 C5
Wellington Hill . . 148 D2
Wellow
  Bath 43 D6
  IoW 18 C2
  Notts 131 C6
Wellpond Green . . 68 A4
Wells 29 A5
Wellsborough 97 A6
Wells Green 128 D1
Wells-Next-The-
  Sea 119 A6
Wellswood 8 A3
Well Town 13 A4
Wellwood 208 B3
Welney 102 B1
Welshampton . . . 110 B3
Welsh Bicknor . . . 62 B1
Welsh End 111 B4
Welsh Frankton . . 110 B2
Welsh Hook 55 B5
Welsh Newton . . . 61 B6
Welshpool
  =Y Trallwng 93 A6
Welsh St Donats . . 41 D5
Welton
  Cumb 164 A1
  E Yorks 142 A1
  Lincs 133 B5
  Northants 82 A2
Welton Hill 133 A5
Welton le Marsh . . 135 C4
Welton le Wold . . 134 A2
Welwick 143 A5
Welwyn 68 B2
Welwyn Garden City 68 B2
Wem 111 C4
Wembdon 28 B2
Wembley 49 A4
Wembury 7 C4
Wembworthy 12 A1
Wemyss Bay . . . 204 B1
Wenallt
  Ceredig 75 A5

Wenallt continued
  Gwyn 109 A4
Wendens Ambo . . 85 D7
Wendlebury 65 B6
Wendling 119 D6
Wendover 66 C3
Wendron 3 B4
Wendy 85 C5
Wenfordbridge . . 10 D1
Wenhaston 105 D5
Wennington
  Cambs 100 D4
  Lancs 155 D5
  London 50 A2
Wensley
  Derbys 130 C2
  N Yorks 157 C4
Wentbridge 140 B2
Wentnor 94 B1
Wentworth
  Cambs 101 D6
  S Yorks 140 D1
Wenvoe 41 D6
Weobley 78 B2
Weobley Marsh . . 78 B2
Wereham 102 A2
Wergs 95 A6
Wern
  Powys 109 D4
  Powys 110 D1
Wernffrwd 57 C5
Wernyrheolydd . . 61 B5
Werrington
  Corn 10 C4
  Pboro 100 A3
  Staffs 112 A3
Wervin 127 B4
Wesham 144 D4
Wessington . . . 130 D3
Westacott 25 D4
West Acre 119 D4
West Adderbury . 82 D1
West Allerdean . 198 B3
West Alvington . . 7 C6
West Amesbury . 31 A5
West Anstey . . . 26 C3
West Ashby . . . 134 B2
West Ashling . . . 19 A7
West Ashton . . . 44 D2
West Auckland . 167 C4
West Ayton . . . 160 C3
West Bagborough . 27 B6
West Barkwith . 133 A6
West Barnby . . 169 D6
West Barns . . . 210 C3
West Barsham . 119 B6
West Bay 15 B4
West Beckham . 120 B3
West Bedfont . . 48 B3
West Benhar . . 208 D1
Westbere 52 C3
West Bergholt . . 70 A3
West Bexington . 15 C5
West Bilney . . . 119 D4
West Blatchington . 21 B5
Westborough . . 115 A6
Westbourne
  BCP 17 B4
  Suff 88 C2
  W Sus 19 A6
West Bowling . . 147 D5
West Bradford . 146 C1
West Bradley . . 29 B5
West Bretton . . 139 B5
West Bridgford . 114 B3
West Bromwich . 96 B3
Westbrook 46 B2
West Buckland
  Devon 26 B1
  Som 28 C1
West Burrafirth . 285 H4
West Burton
  N Yorks 156 C4
  W Sus 20 A2
Westbury
  Bucks 82 D3
  Shrops 94 A1
  Wilts 44 D2
Westbury Leigh . 44 D2
Westbury-on-
  Severn 62 B3
Westbury on Trym . 43 B4
Westbury-sub-
  Mendip 29 A5
West Butterwick . 141 C6
Westby 144 D3
West Byfleet . . . 48 C3
West Caister . . 121 D7

West Calder 208 D3
West Camel. 29 C5
West Challow 46 A1
West Chelborough . . 15 A5
West Chevington. . .189 D5
West Chiltington . . . 20 A3
West Chiltington
Common 20 A3
West Chinnock. 29 D4
West Chisenbury . . . 45 D5
West Clandon 34 A3
West Cliffe 39 A5
Westcliff-on-Sea . . . 51 C6
West Clyne 274 D2
West Clyth 275 A6
West Coker 29 D5
Westcombe. 29 B6
West Compton
  Dorset. 15 B5
  Som. 29 A5
Westcote 64 A3
Westcott
  Bucks 66 B2
  Devon 13 A5
  Sur 35 B4
Westcott Barton . . . 65 A5
West Cowick. 140 A4
West Cranmore 29 A6
West Cross 57 D6
West Cullery 245 B4
West Curry 10 B3
West Curthwaite . .175 D6
West Darlochan . . .190 C2
Westdean 22 C3
West Dean
  Wilts 31 C6
  W Sus 20 A1
West Deeping. 100 A3
Westdene 21 B5
West Derby 136 D2
West Dereham 102 A2
West Didsbury 138 D1
West Ditchburn . . .189 A4
West Down 25 A6
West Drayton
  London 48 B3
  Notts. 132 B2
West Ella. 142 A2
West End
  Bedford. 84 B1
  E Yorks 150 D2
  E Yorks 151 D4
  Hants 32 D3
  Lancs 137 A6
  Norf 103 A5
  Norf 121 D7
  N Som. 42 C3
  N Yorks 147 B5
  Oxon 65 C5
  S Lanark 195 B4
  Suff. 105 C5
  Sur 48 C2
  S Yorks 141 C4
  Wilts 30 C3
  Wilts 44 B3
  W Sus 21 A5
West End Green . . . 47 C4
Wester
  Aberchalder 252 D1
Wester Balgedie . . .219 D6
Wester Culbeuchly .268 C1
Westerdale
  Highld 280 C3
  N Yorks 159 A5
Wester Dechmont . .208 D3
Wester Denoon . . .232 D1
Westerfield
  Shetland 285 H5
  Suff 88 C2
Wester Fintray 245 A5
Westergate 20 B2
Wester Gruinards . .263 A7
Westerham 36 A2
Westerhope 178 C3
Wester Lealty 264 C2
Westerleigh 43 B6
Wester Milton 253 A6
Wester Newburn . .220 D4
Wester Quarff 285 K6
Wester Skeld 285 J4
Westerton
  Angus 233 C4
  Durham 167 B5
  W Sus 20 B1
Westerwick 285 J4
West Farleigh. 37 A5
West Felton 110 C2
West Fenton 210 B1

West Ferry. 221 A4
Westfield
  Cumb 162 B2
  E Sus 23 A6
  Hereford 79 C5
  Highld 279 B6
  N Lanark 207 C5
  Norf 103 A5
  W Loth 208 C2
Westfields 15 A7
Westfields of
Rattray. 231 D5
West Firle 22 B2
Westgate
  Durham 166 B2
  N Lincs 141 C5
  Norf 119 A5
  Norf 119 A6
Westgate on Sea . . 53 B5
West Ginge 46 A2
West Grafton 45 C6
West Green 47 D5
West Greenskares .268 C2
West Grimstead . . . 31 C6
West Grinstead . . . 35 D4
West Haddlesey . . .140 A3
West Haddon 98 D3
West Hagbourne . . 46 A3
West Hagley 96 C2
Westhall
  Aberds 256 D1
  Suff 105 C5
West Hall 176 C3
West Hallam 114 A2
West Halton 141 A7
Westham
  Dorset. 15 D6
  E Sus 22 B4
  Som. 28 A4
West Ham 49 A7
Westhampnett 20 B1
West Handley 130 B3
West Hanney 65 D5
West Hanningfield . . 70 D1
West Hardwick 140 B2
West Harnham 31 C5
West Harptree 43 D4
West Hatch 28 C2
Westhay 28 A4
Westhead 136 C3
West Head. 102 A1
West Heath
  Ches E. 128 C3
  Hants 34 A1
  Hants 46 D3
West Helmsdale . . .274 C4
West Hendred 46 A2
West Heslerton . . .160 D3
Westhide. 78 C3
Westhill
  Aberds 245 B5
  Highld 252 B3
West Hill
  Devon 13 B5
  E Yorks 151 A4
  N Som. 42 B3
West Hoathly 35 C5
West Holme 16 C2
Westhope
  Hereford 78 B2
  Shrops 94 C2
West Horndon 50 A3
Westhorpe
  Lincs 117 B5
  Suff 87 A6
West Horrington . . . 29 A5
West Horsley 34 A3
West Horton 198 C4
West Hougham 39 A4
Westhoughton 137 C5
West Houlland 285 H4
Westhouse 155 D5
Westhouses 131 D4
Westhumble 35 A4
West Huntington . .149 B5
West Hythe 38 B3
West Ilsley 46 A2
Westing 284 C7
West Itchenor. 19 A6
West Keal 134 C3
West Kennett 45 C5
West Kilbride 204 D2
West Kingsdown . . . 50 C2
West Kington 44 B2
West Kinharrachie .257 C4
West Kirby. 126 A2
West Knapton 160 D2
West Knighton 16 C1
West Knoyle 30 B2
West Kyloe 199 B4

Westlake 7 B5
West Lambrook . . . 28 D4
West Langdon 39 A5
West Langwell 273 D4
West Lavington
  Wilts 44 D4
  W Sus 34 D1
West Layton 157 A5
West Lea 168 A2
West Leake 114 C3
West Learmouth . .198 C2
Westleigh
  Devon 25 C5
  Devon 27 D5
  Gtr Man 137 C5
West Leigh 12 A1
Westleton 89 A5
West Lexham 119 D5
Westley
  Shrops 94 A1
  Suff 87 A4
Westley Waterless . 86 B2
West Lilling 149 A5
Westlington 66 B2
Westlinton 175 B6
West Linton 195 A6
West Liss 33 C6
West Littleton 43 B6
West Looe 6 B1
West Luccombe . . . 26 A3
West Lulworth 16 C2
West Lutton 150 A2
West Lydford 29 B5
West Lyng 28 C3
West Lynn 118 C3
West Malling 37 A4
West Malvern 79 C5
West Marden 33 D6
West Marina 23 B5
West Markham. . . .132 B2
Westmarsh 53 C4
West Marsh 143 B4
West Marton 146 B2
West Meon 33 C5
West Mersea 71 B4
Westmeston 21 A6
Westmill 68 A3
West Milton 15 B5
Westminster 49 B6
West Minster 51 B6
West Molesey 48 C4
West Monkton 28 C2
West Moors 17 A4
West Morriston 197 B5
Westmuir 232 C1
West Muir 232 B3
Westness 282 E4
West Ness 159 D5
West Newham 178 B2
Westnewton
  Cumb 174 D4
  Northumb 198 C3
West Newton
  E Yorks 151 D4
  Norf 118 C3
West Norwood 49 B6
Westoe 179 C5
West Ogwell 12 D3
Weston
  Bath 43 C6
  Ches E. 128 D2
  Devon 13 C6
  Dorset. 15 D6
  Halton 127 A5
  Hants 33 C6
  Herts 85 D4
  Lincs 117 C5
  Northants 82 C2
  Notts. 132 C2
  N Yorks 147 C5
  Shrops 94 B3
  Shrops 111 C4
  Staffs 112 C3
  W Berks 46 B1
Weston Beggard . . . 78 C3
Westonbirt 44 A2
Weston by Welland . 99 B4
Weston Colville . . . 86 B2
Westoncommon . . .110 C3
Weston Coyney . . .112 A3
Weston Favell 83 A4
Weston Green
  Cambs. 86 B2
  Norf 120 D3
Weston Heath 112 D1
Weston Hills 117 C5
Westoning. 84 D2
Weston-in-Gordano 42 B3
Weston Jones 111 C6
Weston Longville . .120 D3

Weston
Lullingfields 110 C3
Weston-on-the-
Green 65 B6
Weston-on-Trent . .114 C2
Weston Patrick . . . 33 A5
Weston Rhyn 110 B1
Weston-Sub-Edge . 80 C4
Weston-super-Mare 42 C2
Weston Turville . . . 66 B3
Weston under
Lizard. 112 D2
Weston under
Penyard 62 A2
Weston under
Wetherley 81 A6
Weston Underwood
  Derbys 113 A6
  M Keynes 83 B5
Westonzoyland . . . 28 B3
West Orchard 30 D2
West Overton 45 C5
Westow 149 A6
West Park 168 B2
West Parley 17 B4
West Peckham 36 A4
West Pelton 179 D4
West Pennard 29 B5
West Pentire 4 A2
West Perry 84 A3
Westport
  Argyll 190 C2
  Som. 28 D3
West Putford 25 D4
West Quantoxhead . 27 A6
West Rainton 167 A6
West Rasen 133 A5
West Raynham 119 C5
West Retford 132 A1
Westrigg 208 D2
West Rounton 158 A3
West Row 102 D2
West Rudham 119 C5
West Runton 120 A3
Westruther 197 B5
Westry 101 B5
West Saltoun 210 D1
West Sandwick 284 E6
West Scrafton 157 C4
West Sleekburn . . .179 A4
West Somerton . . .121 D6
West Stafford 16 C1
West Stockwith . . .141 D5
West Stoke 20 B1
West Stonesdale . .156 A2
West Stoughton . . 28 A4
West Stour 30 C1
West Stourmouth . . 53 C4
West Stow 103 D4
West Stowell 45 C5
West Strathan 277 B6
West Stratton 32 A4
West Street 37 A7
West Tanfield 157 D6
West Taphouse. 5 A6
West Tarbert 202 B3
West Thirston 189 D4
West Thorney 19 A6
West Thurrock 50 B2
West Tilbury 50 B3
West Tisted 33 C5
West Tofts
  Norf 103 B4
  Perth 219 A6
West Torrington . . .133 A6
West Town
  Hants 19 B6
  N Som. 42 C3
West Tytherley . . . 32 C1
West Tytherton . . . 44 B3
Westville 114 A3
West Walton 118 D1
West Walton
Highway. 118 D1
Westward 175 D5
Westward Ho! 25 C5
Westwell
  Kent 38 A1
  Oxon 64 C3
Westwell Leacon . . 38 A1
West Wellow 32 D1
West Wemyss 209 A6
Westwick
  Cambs. 85 A6
  Durham 166 D3
  Norf 121 C5
West Wick 42 C2
West Wickham
  Cambs. 86 C2
  London 49 C6

West Williamston . . 55 D6
West Willoughby . .116 A2
West Winch. 118 D3
West Winterslow . . 31 B6
West Wittering . . . 19 B6
West Witton 157 C4
Westwood
  Devon 13 B5
  Wilts 44 D2
West Woodburn . . .177 A6
West Woodhay 46 C1
West Woodlands . . 30 A1
Westwoodside 141 D5
West Worldham . . . 33 B6
West Worlington . . 26 D2
West Worthing 21 B4
West Wratting 86 B2
West Wycombe . . . 66 D3
West Wylam 178 C3
West Yell 284 E6
Wetheral 176 D2
Wetherby 148 C3
Wetherden 87 A6
Wetheringsett 88 A2
Wethersfield 86 D3
Wethersta 284 G5
Wetherup Street . . 88 A2
Wetley Rocks 112 A3
Wettenhall 127 C6
Wetton 129 D6
Wetwang 150 B2
Wetwood 111 B6
Wexcombe 45 C6
Wexham Street . . . 48 A2
Weybourne 120 A3
Weybread 104 C3
Weybridge 48 C3
Weycroft 14 B3
Weydale 280 B3
Weyhill 32 A2
Weymouth 15 D6
Whaddon
  Bucks 83 D5
  Cambs. 85 C5
  Glos 63 B4
  Wilts 31 C5
Whale. 164 C3
Whaley. 131 B5
Whaley Bridge 129 A5
Whaley Thorns 131 B5
Whaligoe 281 D5
Whalley 146 D1
Whalton 178 A3
Wham. 146 A1
Whaplode 117 C6
Whaplode Drove . .117 D6
Whaplode
St Catherine 117 C6
Wharfe. 146 A1
Wharles. 144 D4
Wharncliffe Side . .139 D5
Wharram le Street .150 A1
Wharton 127 C6
Wharton Green . . .127 C6
Whashton 157 A5
Whatcombe 16 A2
Whatcote 81 C6
Whatfield 87 C6
Whatley
  Som. 14 A3
  Som. 30 A1
Whatlington 23 A5
Whatstandwell 130 D3
Whatton 115 B5
Whauphill 171 C6
Whaw. 156 A3
Wheatacre 105 B5
Wheatcroft 130 D3
Wheathampstead . . 68 B1
Wheathill 95 C4
Wheatley
  Devon 13 B4
  Hants 33 A6
  Oxon 65 C6
  S Yorks 140 C3
  W Yorks 138 A3
Wheatley Hill 167 B6
Wheaton Aston . . .112 D2
Wheddon Cross . . . 27 B4
Wheedlemont 255 D5
Wheelerstreet 34 B2
Wheelock 128 D2
Wheelock Heath . .128 D2
Wheelton 137 A5
Wheen 232 A1
Wheldrake 149 C5
Whelford 64 D2
Whelpley Hill 67 C4
Whempstead 68 A3
Whenby 149 A5

Whepstead 87 B4
Wherstead 88 C2
Wherwell. 32 A2
Wheston 129 B6
Whetsted 37 B4
Whetstone 98 B2
Whicham 153 B2
Whichford 81 D6
Whiddon Down . . . 12 B1
Whigstreet 232 D2
Whilton 82 A3
Whimble 11 A4
Whim Farm 195 A4
Whimple 13 B5
Whimpwell Green . .121 C5
Whinburgh 103 A6
Whinnieliggate . . .173 C5
Whinnyfold 257 C5
Whippingham 18 B4
Whipsnade 67 B5
Whipton 13 B4
Whirlow 130 A3
Whisby 133 C4
Whissendine 115 D6
Whissonsett 119 C6
Whistlefield
  Argyll 215 C4
  Argyll 215 C5
Whistley Green . . . 47 B5
Whiston
  Mers 136 D3
  Northants 83 A5
  Staffs 112 A4
  Staffs 112 D2
  S Yorks 131 A4
Whitbeck 153 B2
Whitbourne 79 B5
Whitburn
  T&W 179 C6
  W Loth 208 D2
Whitburn Colliery . .179 C6
Whitby
  Ches W 126 B3
  N Yorks 169 D6
Whitbyheath. 126 B3
Whitchurch
  Bath 43 C5
  Bucks 66 A2
  Cardiff 41 C6
  Devon 11 D5
  Hants 32 A3
  Hereford 62 B1
  Oxon 47 B4
  Pembs. 54 B3
  Shrops 111 A4
Whitchurch
Canonicorum 14 B3
Whitchurch Hill . . . 47 B4
Whitcombe. 15 C7
Whitcott Keysett . . 93 C6
Whiteacen 254 B3
Whiteacre Heath . . 97 C5
Whitebridge 240 A2
Whitebrook 62 C1
Whiteburn 197 B4
Whitecairn 171 B4
Whitecairns 245 A6
Whitecastle 195 B5
Whitechapel 145 C5
Whitecleat 283 G6
White Coppice 137 B5
Whitecraig 209 C6
Whitecroft 62 C2
Whitecross
  Corn 9 D5
  Falk. 208 C2
  Staffs 112 C2
Whiteface 264 B3
Whitefarland 202 D3
Whitefaulds 192 E2
Whitefield
  Gtr Man 137 C7
  Perth. 219 A6
Whiteford 256 D2
Whitegate 127 C6
Whitehall
  Blackburn 137 A5
  W Sus 35 D4
Whitehall Village . .282 E7
Whitehaven 162 C2
Whitehill 33 B6
Whitehills
  Aberds 268 C1
  S Lanark 205 C6
Whitehough 129 A5
Whitehouse
  Aberds 244 A3
  Argyll 202 B3
Whiteinch 205 B5

Whitekirk 210 B2
White Lackington . . . 15 B7
White Ladies Aston . . 80 B2
Whitelaw 205 D6
Whiteleas 179 C5
Whiteley Bank 19 C4
Whiteley Green 129 B4
Whiteley Village 48 C3
White Lund 144 A4
Whitemans Green . . . 35 D6
White Mill 58 C1
Whitemire 253 A5
Whitemoor 5 B4
Whitemore 128 C3
Whitenap 32 C2
White Ness 285 J5
White Notley 70 B1
Whiteoak Green 64 B4
Whiteparish 31 C6
White Pit 134 B3
White Post 131 D6
Whiterashes 256 D3
White Rocks 61 A6
White Roding 69 B5
Whiterow 281 D5
Whiteshill 63 C4
Whiteside
  Northumb 177 C5
  W Loth 208 D2
Whitesmith 22 A3
Whitestaunton 28 D2
Whitestone
  Devon 12 B3
  Devon 25 A5
  Warks 97 C6
Whitestones 268 D3
Whitestreet Green . . 87 D5
Whitewall Corner . . 159 D6
White Waltham 47 B6
Whiteway
  Glos 63 B5
  Glos 63 D4
Whitewell
  Aberds 269 C4
  Lancs 145 C6
Whitewell Bottom . . 138 A1
Whiteworks 11 D7
Whitfield
  Kent 39 A5
  Northants 82 D3
  Northumb 177 D5
  S Glos 62 D2
Whitford
  Devon 14 B2
  Flint 125 B6
Whitgift 141 A6
Whitgreave 112 C2
Whithorn 171 C6
Whiting Bay 191 C6
Whitkirk 148 D2
Whitland 56 A1
Whitletts 192 C3
Whitley
  N Yorks 140 A3
  Reading 47 B5
  Wilts 44 C2
Whitley Bay 179 B5
Whitley Chapel 178 D1
Whitley Lower 139 B5
Whitley Row 36 A2
Whitlock's End 96 D4
Whitminster 62 C3
Whitmore 112 A2
Whitnage 27 D5
Whitnash 81 A6
Whitney-on-Wye . . . 77 C6
Whitrigg
  Cumb 163 A5
  Cumb 175 C5
Whitsbury 31 D5
Whitsome 198 A2
Whitson 42 A2
Whitstable 52 C3
Whitstone 10 B3
Whittingham 188 B3
Whittingslow 94 C2
Whittington
  Glos 63 A6
  Lancs 155 D5
  Norf 102 B3
  Shrops 110 B2
  Staffs 95 C6
  Staffs 97 A4
  Worcs 80 B1
Whittlebury 82 C3
Whittle-le-Woods . . 137 A4
Whittlesey 101 B4
Whittlesford 85 C6
Whittlestone
  Head 137 B6

Whitton
  Borders 187 A6
  N Lincs 141 A7
  Northumb 188 C3
  Powys 77 A6
  Shrops 94 D3
  Stockton 167 C6
  Suff 88 C2
Whittonditch 45 B6
Whittonstall 178 D2
Whitway 46 D2
Whitwell
  Derbys 131 B5
  Herts 68 A1
  IoW 18 D4
  N Yorks 157 B6
  Rutland 99 A6
Whitwell-on-the-
  Hill 149 A6
Whitwell Street . . . 120 C3
Whitwick 114 D2
Whitwood 140 A2
Whitworth 138 B1
Whixall 111 B4
Whixley 148 B3
Whoberley 97 D6
Whorlton
  Durham 166 D4
  N Yorks 158 A3
Whygate 177 B5
Whyle 78 A3
Whyteleafe 35 A6
Wibdon 62 D1
Wibsey 147 D5
Wibtoft 98 C1
Wichenford 79 A5
Wichling 37 A7
Wick
  BCP 17 B5
  Devon 13 A6
  Highld 281 C5
  S Glos 43 B6
  Shetland 285 K6
  V Glam 40 D4
  Wilts 31 C5
  Worcs 80 C2
  W Sus 20 B3
Wicken
  Cambs 102 D1
  Northants 83 D4
Wicken Bonhunt . . . 85 D6
Wickenby 133 A5
Wicken Green
  Village 119 B5
Wickersley 140 D2
Wickford 70 D1
Wickham
  Hants 33 D4
  W Berks 46 B1
Wickham Bishops . . 70 B2
Wickhambreaux 53 D4
Wickhambrook 86 B3
Wickhamford 80 C3
Wickham Market . . . 88 B4
Wickhampton 105 A5
Wickham St Paul . . . 87 D4
Wickham Skeith . . . 88 A1
Wickham Street
  Suff 86 B3
  Suff 88 A1
Wick Hill 47 C5
Wicklewood 104 A1
Wickmere 120 B3
Wick St Lawrence . . 42 C2
Wickwar 43 A6
Widdington 86 D1
Widdrington 189 D5
Widdrington
  Station 189 D5
Widecombe in the
  Moor 12 D2
Widegates 6 B1
Widemouth Bay 10 A3
Wide Open 179 B4
Widewall 283 H5
Widford
  Essex 69 C6
  Herts 68 B4
Widham 45 A4
Widmer End 66 D3
Widmerpool 115 C4
Widnes 127 A5
Wigan 137 C4
Wiggaton 13 B6
Wiggenhall
  St Germans 118 D2
Wiggenhall St Mary
  Magdalen 118 D2
Wiggenhall St Mary the
  Virgin 118 D2

Wigginton
  Herts 67 B4
  Oxon 81 D6
  Staffs 97 A5
  York 149 B4
Wigglesworth 146 B2
Wiggonby 175 C5
Wiggonholt 20 A3
Wighill 148 C3
Wighton 119 B6
Wigley 32 D2
Wigmore
  Hereford 78 A2
  Medway 51 C5
Wigsley 132 B3
Wigsthorpe 100 C2
Wigston 98 B3
Wigthorpe 131 A5
Wigtoft 117 B5
Wigton 175 D5
Wigtown 171 B6
Wigtwizzle 139 D5
Wike 148 C2
Wike Well End 141 B4
Wilbarston 99 C5
Wilberfoss 149 B6
Wilberlee 138 B3
Wilburton 101 D6
Wilby
  Norf 103 C6
  Northants 83 A5
  Suff 104 D3
Wilcot 45 C5
Wilcott 110 D2
Wilcrick 42 A3
Wilday Green 130 B3
Wildboarclough . . . 129 C4
Wilden
  Bedford 84 B2
  Worcs 95 D6
Wildhern 46 D1
Wildhill 68 C2
Wildmoor 96 D2
Wildsworth 141 D6
Wilford 114 B3
Wilkesley 111 A5
Wilkhaven 265 B5
Wilkieston 208 D4
Willand 27 D5
Willaston
  Ches E 128 D1
  Ches W 126 B3
Willen 83 C5
Willenhall
  W Mid 96 B2
  W Mid 97 D6
Willerby
  E Yorks 150 D3
  N Yorks 160 D4
Willersey 80 D4
Willersley 77 C7
Willesborough 38 A2
Willesborough
  Lees 38 A2
Willesden 49 A5
Willett 27 B6
Willey
  Shrops 95 B4
  Warks 98 C1
Willey Green 34 A2
Williamscott 82 C1
Willian 84 D4
Willingale 69 C5
Willingdon 22 B3
Willingham 101 D6
Willingham by
  Stow 132 A3
Willington
  Bedford 84 C3
  Derbys 113 C6
  Durham 167 B4
  T&W 179 C5
  Warks 81 D5
Willington Corner . . 127 C5
Willisham Tye 87 B6
Willitoft 149 D6
Williton 27 A5
Willoughbridge . . . 111 A6
Willoughby
  Lincs 135 B4
  Warks 82 A2
Willoughby-on-
  the-Wolds 115 C4
Willoughby
  Waterleys 98 B2
Willoughton 142 D1
Willows Green 69 B7
Willsbridge 43 B5
Willsworthy 11 C6
Wilmcote 81 B4

Wilmington
  Devon 14 B2
  E Sus 22 B3
  Kent 50 B2
Wilminstone 11 D5
Wilmslow 128 A3
Wilnecote 97 A5
Wilpshire 145 D6
Wilsden 147 D4
Wilsford
  Lincs 116 A3
  Wilts 31 B5
  Wilts 45 D5
Wilsill 147 A5
Wilsley Pound 37 C5
Wilsom 33 B6
Wilson 114 C2
Wilsontown 195 A4
Wilstead 84 C2
Wilsthorpe 116 D3
Wilstone 67 B4
Wilton
  Borders 186 B3
  Cumb 162 C3
  N Yorks 160 C2
  Redcar 168 D3
  Wilts 31 B4
  Wilts 45 C6
Wimbish 86 D1
Wimbish Green 86 D2
Wimblebury 112 D4
Wimbledon 49 B5
Wimblington 101 B6
Wimborne Minster . 17 B4
Wimborne St Giles . 31 D4
Wimbotsham 102 A2
Wimpson 32 D2
Wimpstone 81 C5
Wincanton 29 C7
Wincham 128 B1
Winchburgh 208 C3
Winchcombe 63 A6
Winchelsea 23 A7
Winchelsea Beach . . 23 A7
Winchester 32 C3
Winchet Hill 37 B5
Winchfield 47 D5
Winchmore Hill
  Bucks 67 D4
  London 68 D3
Wincle 129 C4
Wincobank 140 D1
Windermere 154 B3
Winderton 81 C6
Windhill 252 B1
Windhouse 284 D6
Windlehurst 129 A4
Windlesham 48 C2
Windley 113 A7
Windmill Hill
  E Sus 22 A4
  Som 28 D3
Windrush 64 B2
Windsor
  N Lincs 141 B5
  Windsor 48 B2
Windsoredge 63 C4
Windygates 220 D3
Windyknowe 208 D2
Windywalls 197 C6
Wineham 35 D5
Winestead 143 A4
Winewall 146 C3
Winfarthing 104 C2
Winford
  IoW 19 C4
  N Som 43 C4
Winforton 77 C6
Winfrith Newburgh . . 16 C2
Wing
  Bucks 66 A3
  Rutland 99 A5
Wingate 168 B2
Wingates
  Gtr Man 137 C5
  Northumb 189 D4
Wingerworth 130 C3
Wingfield
  C Beds 67 A4
  Suff 104 D3
  Wilts 44 D2
Wingham 53 D4
Wingmore 38 A3
Wingrave 66 B3
Winkburn 132 D2
Winkfield 48 B2
Winkfield Row 48 B1
Winkhill 129 D5
Winklebury 47 D4
Winkleigh 12 A1

Winksley 157 D6
Winkton 17 B5
Winlaton 178 C3
Winless 281 C5
Winmarleigh 145 C4
Winnal 78 D2
Winnall 32 C3
Winnersh 47 B5
Winscales 162 B3
Winscombe 42 D3
Winsford
  Ches W 127 C6
  Som 27 B4
Winsham 14 A3
Winshill 113 C6
Winskill 164 B3
Winslade 33 A5
Winsley 44 C2
Winslow 66 A2
Winson 64 C1
Winson Green 96 C3
Winsor 32 D2
Winster
  Cumb 154 B3
  Derbys 130 C2
Winston
  Durham 166 D4
  Suff 88 A2
Winstone 63 C5
Winston Green 88 A2
Winswell 25 D5
Winterborne
  Clenston 16 A2
Winterborne
  Herringston 15 C6
Winterborne
  Houghton 16 A2
Winterborne
  Kingston 16 B2
Winterborne
  Monkton 15 C6
Winterborne
  Stickland 16 A2
Winterborne
  Whitechurch 16 A2
Winterborne Zelston 16 B2
Winterbourne
  S Glos 43 A5
  W Berks 46 B2
Winterbourne Abbas 15 B6
Winterbourne
  Bassett 45 B5
Winterbourne
  Dauntsey 31 B5
Winterbourne Down 43 B5
Winterbourne Earls . 31 B5
Winterbourne
  Gunner 31 B5
Winterbourne
  Monkton 45 B5
Winterbourne
  Steepleton 15 C6
Winterbourne Stoke . 31 A4
Winterburn 146 B3
Winter Gardens 51 A4
Winteringham 142 A1
Winterley 128 D2
Wintersett 140 B1
Wintershill 32 D4
Winterton 142 A1
Winterton-on-Sea . 121 D6
Winthorpe
  Lincs 135 C5
  Notts 132 D3
Winton
  BCP 17 B4
  Cumb 165 D5
  N Yorks 158 B3
Wintringham 160 D2
Winwick
  Cambs 100 C3
  Northants 98 D3
  Warr 137 D5
Wirksworth 130 D2
Wirksworth Moor . . 130 D3
Wirswall 111 A4
Wisbech 101 A6
Wisbech St Mary . . 101 A6
Wisborough Green . 34 D3
Wiseton 132 A2
Wishaw
  N Lanark 194 A2
  Warks 97 B4
Wisley 34 A3
Wispington 134 B2
Wissenden 37 B7
Wissett 105 D4
Wistanstow 94 C2
Wistanswick 111 C5
Wistaston 128 D1

Wistaston Green . . . 128 D1
Wiston
  Pembs 55 C6
  S Lanark 195 C4
  W Sus 21 A4
Wistow
  Cambs 101 C4
  N Yorks 149 D4
Wiswell 146 D1
Witcham 101 C6
Witchampton 16 A3
Witchford 101 D7
Witham 70 B2
Witham Friary 30 A1
Witham on the Hill . 116 D3
Withcall 134 A2
Withdean 21 B6
Witherenden Hill . . . 36 D4
Witheridge 26 D3
Witherley 97 B6
Withern 135 A4
Withernsea 143 A5
Withernwick 151 C4
Withersdale Street . 104 C3
Withersfield 86 C2
Witherslack 154 C3
Withiel 5 A4
Withiel Florey 27 B4
Withington
  Glos 63 B6
  Gtr Man 138 D1
  Hereford 78 C3
  Shrops 111 D4
  Staffs 112 B4
Withington Green . . 128 B3
Withleigh 27 D4
Withnell 137 A5
Withybrook 98 C1
Withycombe 27 A5
Withycombe Raleigh 13 C5
Withyham 36 C2
Withypool 26 B3
Witley 34 C2
Witnesham 88 B2
Witney 65 B4
Wittering 100 A2
Wittersham 37 D6
Witton
  Angus 232 A3
  Worcs 80 A1
Witton Bridge 121 B5
Witton Gilbert 167 A5
Witton-le-Wear . . . 166 B4
Witton Park 167 B4
Wiveliscombe 27 C5
Wivelrod 33 B5
Wivelsfield 35 D6
Wivelsfield Green . . 35 D6
Wivenhoe 71 A4
Wivenhoe Cross . . . 71 A4
Wiveton 120 A2
Wix 71 A5
Wixford 80 B3
Wixhill 111 C4
Wixoe 86 C3
Woburn 83 D6
Woburn Sands 83 D6
Wokefield Park 47 C4
Woking 34 A3
Wokingham 47 C6
Wolborough 12 D3
Woldingham 35 A6
Wold Newton
  E Yorks 160 D4
  NE Lincs 143 D4
Wolfclyde 195 C5
Wolferton 118 C3
Wolfhill 219 A6
Wolf's Castle 55 B5
Wolfsdale 55 B5
Woll 186 A3
Wollaston
  Northants 83 A6
  Shrops 110 D2
Wollaton 114 B3
Wollerton 111 B5
Wollescote 96 C2
Wolsingham 166 B3
Wolstanton 112 A2
Wolston 97 D7
Wolvercote 65 C5
Wolverhampton . . . 96 B2
Wolverley
  Shrops 110 B3
  Worcs 95 D6
Wolverton
  Hants 46 D3
  M Keynes 83 C5

Wolverton continued
Warks......81 A5
Wolverton Common .46 D3
Wolvesnewton......61 D6
Wolvey......98 C1
Wolviston......168 C2
Wombleton......159 C5
Wombourne......95 B6
Wombwell......140 C1
Womenswold......53 D4
Womersley......140 B3
Wonastow......61 B6
Wonersh......34 B3
Wonson......12 C1
Wonston......32 B3
Wooburn......48 A2
Wooburn Green......48 A2
Woodacott......11 A4
Woodale......156 D4
Woodbank......190 D2
Woodbastwick......121 D5
Woodbeck......132 B2
Woodborough
Notts......115 A4
Wilts......45 D5
Woodbridge
Dorset......29 D7
Suff......88 C3
Woodbury......13 C5
Woodbury Salterton.13 C5
Woodchester......63 C4
Woodchurch
Kent......38 B1
Mers......126 A2
Woodcombe......27 A4
Woodcote......47 A4
Woodcott......46 D2
Woodcroft......62 D1
Woodcutts......30 D3
Wood Dalling......120 C2
Woodditton......86 B2
Woodeaton......65 B6
Woodend
Cumb......153 A2
Northants......82 C3
W Sus......19 A7
Wood End
Herts......68 A3
Warks......96 D4
Warks......97 B5
Wood Enderby......134 C2
Woodend Green....82 C3
Woodfalls......31 C5
Woodfield
Oxon......65 A6
S Ayrs......192 C3
Wood Field......35 A4
Woodford
Corn......24 D3
Devon......8 B1
Glos......62 D2
Gtr Man......128 A3
London......68 D4
Northants......99 D6
Woodford Bridge..68 D4
Woodford Halse....82 B2
Woodgate
Norf......120 D2
W Mid......96 C2
Worcs......80 A2
W Sus......20 B2
Woodgreen......31 D5
Wood Green......68 D3
Woodhall
Herts......68 B2
Invclyd......204 A3
N Yorks......156 B3
Woodhall Spa....134 C1
Woodham......48 C3
Woodham Ferrers..70 D1
Woodham Mortimer.70 C2
Woodham Walter...70 C2
Woodhaven......220 B4
Wood Hayes......96 A2
Woodhead......256 C2
Woodhey......137 B6
Woodhill......95 C5
Woodhorn......179 A4
Woodhouse
Leics......114 D3
N Lincs......141 C5
S Yorks......131 A4
W Yorks......140 A1
W Yorks......148 D1
Woodhouse Eaves..114 D3
Woodhouselee..209 D5
Woodhouselees...175 A6
Woodhouse Park..128 A3

Woodhouses......113 D5
Woodhurst......101 D5
Woodingdean......21 B6
Woodkirk......139 A5
Woodland
Devon......8 A1
Durham......166 C3
Woodlands
Aberds......245 C4
Dorset......17 A4
Hants......32 D2
Highld......264 D1
N Yorks......148 B2
S Yorks......140 C3
Woodlands Park....47 B6
Woodlands St Mary.46 B1
Woodlane......113 C5
Wood Lanes......129 A4
Woodleigh......7 C6
Woodlesford......139 A6
Woodley
Gtr Man......138 D2
Wokingham......47 B5
Woodmancote
Glos......62 D3
Glos......63 A5
Glos......63 C6
W Sus......19 A6
W Sus......21 A5
Woodmancott......33 A4
Woodmansey......150 D3
Woodmansterne...35 A5
Woodminton......31 C4
Woodnesborough...53 D5
Woodnewton......100 B2
Wood Norton......120 C2
Woodplumpton....145 D5
Woodrising......103 A5
Woodseaves
Shrops......111 B5
Staffs......112 C1
Woodsend......45 B6
Woodsetts......131 A5
Woodsford......16 B1
Wood's Green......36 C4
Woodside
Aberdeen......245 B6
Aberds......257 B5
Brack......48 B2
Fife......220 D4
Hants......18 B2
Herts......68 C2
Perth......220 A2
Woodside of
Arbeadie......245 C4
Woodstock
Oxon......65 B5
Pembs......55 B6
Wood Street
Norf......121 C5
Sur......34 A2
Woodthorpe
Derbys......131 B4
Leics......114 D3
Lincs......135 A4
York......149 C4
Woodton......104 B3
Woodtown
Devon......25 C5
Devon......25 C5
Woodvale......136 B2
Woodville......113 D7
Wood Walton......100 C4
Woodyates......31 D4
Woofferton......78 A3
Wookey......29 A5
Wookey Hole......29 A5
Wool......16 C2
Woolacombe......25 A5
Woolage Green......39 A4
Woolaston......62 D1
Woolavington......28 A3
Woolbeding......34 D1
Wooldale......139 C4
Wooler......188 A2
Woolfardisworthy
Devon......12 A3
Devon......24 C4
Woolfords
Cottages......195 A5
Woolhampton......46 C3
Woolhope......79 D4
Woolhope
Cockshoot......79 D4
Woolland......16 A1
Woollaton......25 D5
Woolley
Bath......43 C6
Cambs......100 D3
Corn......24 D3

Woolley continued
Derbys......130 C3
W Yorks......139 B6
Woolmere Green....80 A2
Woolmer Green....68 B2
Woolpit......87 A5
Woolscott......82 A1
Woolsington......178 C3
Woolstanwood......128 D1
Woolstaston......94 B2
Woolsthorpe
Lincs......115 B6
Lincs......116 C2
Woolston
Devon......7 C6
Shrops......94 C2
Shrops......110 C2
Soton......32 D3
Warr......127 A6
Woolstone
M Keynes......83 D5
Oxon......45 A6
Woolton......127 A4
Woolton Hill......46 C2
Woolverstone......88 D2
Woolverton......44 D1
Woolwich......50 B1
Woolwich Ferry......50 B1
Woonton......78 B1
Wooperton......188 A3
Woore......111 A6
Wootten Green......104 D3
Wootton
Bedford......84 C2
Hants......17 B6
Hereford......78 B1
Kent......39 A4
N Lincs......142 B2
Northants......83 B4
Oxon......65 B5
Oxon......65 C5
Shrops......94 C2
Shrops......110 C2
Staffs......112 C2
Staffs......113 A5
Wootton Bridge....18 B4
Wootton Common...18 B4
Wootton Courtenay.27 A4
Wootton Fitzpaine.14 B3
Wootton Rivers....45 C5
Wootton
St Lawrence......46 D3
Wootton Wawen...81 A4
Worcester......79 B6
Worcester Park....49 C5
Wordsley......96 C1
Worfield......95 B5
Work......282 F5
Workington......162 B2
Worksop......131 B5
Worlaby......142 B2
World's End......46 B2
Worle......42 C2
Worleston......127 D6
Worlingham......105 C5
Worlington......102 D2
Worlingworth......88 A3
Wormald Green....148 A2
Wormbridge......78 D2
Wormegay......118 D3
Wormelow Tump...78 D2
Wormhill......129 B6
Wormingford......87 D5
Worminghall......66 C1
Wormington......80 D3
Worminster......29 A5
Wormit......220 B3
Wormleighton......82 B1
Wormley
Herts......68 C3
Sur......34 C2
Wormley West End..68 C3
Wormshill......37 A6
Wormsley......78 C2
Worplesdon......34 A2
Worrall......139 D6
Worsbrough......139 C6
Worsbrough
Common......139 C6
Worsley......137 C6
Worstead......121 C5
Worsthorne......146 D2
Worston......146 C1
Worswell......7 C4
Worth
Kent......53 D5
W Sus......35 C6
Wortham......104 D1
Worthen......94 A1
Worthenbury......110 A3

Worthing
Norf......120 D1
W Sus......21 B4
Worthington......114 C2
Worth Matravers....16 D3
Worting......47 D4
Wortley
S Yorks......139 D6
W Yorks......147 D6
Worton
N Yorks......156 B3
Wilts......44 D3
Wortwell......104 C3
Wotherton......93 A6
Wotter......7 A4
Wotton......35 B4
Wotton-under-Edge 62 D3
Wotton Underwood .66 B1
Woughton on the
Green......83 D5
Wouldham......51 C4
Wrabness......88 D2
Wrafton......25 B5
Wragby
Lincs......133 B6
W Yorks......140 B2
Wragholme......143 D5
Wramplingham....104 A2
Wrangbrook......140 B2
Wrangham......256 C1
Wrangle......135 D4
Wrangle Bank......135 D4
Wrangle Lowgate...135 D4
Wrangway......27 D6
Wrantage......28 C3
Wrawby......142 C2
Wraxall
Dorset......15 A5
N Som......42 B3
Som......29 B6
Wray......145 A6
Wraysbury......48 B3
Wrayton......155 D5
Wrea Green......144 D3
Wreay
Cumb......164 A2
Cumb......164 C2
Wrecclesham......34 B1
Wrecsam
=Wrexham......126 D3
Wrekenton......179 D4
Wrelton......159 C6
Wrenbury......111 A4
Wrench Green......160 C3
Wreningham......104 B2
Wrentham......105 C5
Wrenthorpe......139 A6
Wrentnall......94 A2
Wressle
E Yorks......149 D6
N Lincs......142 C1
Wrestlingworth....85 C4
Wretham......103 C5
Wretton......102 B2
Wrexham
=Wrecsam......126 D3
Wrexham Industrial
Estate......110 A2
Wribbenhall......95 D5
Wrightington Bar .136 B4
Wrinehill......111 A6
Wrington......42 C3
Writhlington......43 D6
Writtle......69 C6
Wrockwardine....111 D5
Wroot......141 C5
Wrotham......36 A4
Wrotham Heath....36 A4
Wroughton......45 A5
Wroxall
IoW......19 D4
Warks......97 D5
Wroxeter......94 A3
Wroxham......121 D5
Wroxton......81 C7
Wyaston......113 A5
Wyberton......117 A6
Wyboston......84 B3
Wybunbury......111 A6
Wychbold......80 A2
Wych Cross......36 C2
Wyck......33 B6
Wyck Rissington...64 A2
Wycoller......146 D3
Wycomb......115 C5
Wycombe Marsh...66 D3
Wyddial......85 D5
Wye......38 A2
Wyesham......61 B7
Wyfordby......115 D5

Wyke
Dorset......30 C1
Shrops......95 A4
Sur......34 A2
W Yorks......139 A4
Wykeham
N Yorks......159 D7
N Yorks......160 C3
Wyken......97 C6
Wyke Regis......15 D6
Wykey......110 C2
Wylam......178 C3
Wylde Green......96 B4
Wyllie......41 B6
Wylye......31 B4
Wymering......19 A5
Wymeswold......115 C4
Wymington......83 A6
Wymondham
Leics......115 D6
Norf......104 A2
Wyndham......40 B4
Wynford Eagle......15 B5
Wyng......283 H4
Wynyard Village...168 C2
Wyre Piddle......80 C2
Wysall......115 C4
Wythall......96 D3
Wytham......65 C5
Wythburn......163 C6
Wythenshawe....128 A3
Wythop Mill......163 B4
Wyton......101 D4
Wyverstone......87 A6
Wyverstone Street .87 A6
Wyville......116 C1
Wyvis Lodge......263 C6

Y
Yaddlethorpe......141 C6
Yafford......18 C3
Yafforth......158 B2
Yalding......37 A4
Yanworth......63 B6
Yapham......149 B6
Yapton......20 B2
Yarburgh......143 D5
Yarcombe......14 A2
Yard......27 B5
Yardley......96 C4
Yardley Gobion....83 C4
Yardley Hastings...83 B5
Yardro......77 B6
Yarkhill......79 C4
Yarlet......112 C3
Yarlington......29 C6
Yarlside......153 D3
Yarm......168 D2
Yarmouth......18 C2
Yarnbrook......44 D2
Yarnfield......112 B2
Yarnscombe......25 C6
Yarnton......65 B5
Yarpole......78 A2
Yarrow......196 D2
Yarrow Feus......196 D2
Yarsop......78 C2
Yarwell......100 B2
Yate......43 A6
Yateley......47 C6
Yatesbury......45 B4
Yattendon......46 B3
Yatton
Hereford......78 A2
N Som......42 C3
Yatton Keynell......44 B2
Yaverland......19 C5
Yaxham......120 D2
Yaxley
Cambs......100 B3
Suff......104 D2
Yazor......78 C2
Y Bala =Bala......108 B4
Y Barri =Barry......41 E6
Y Bont-Faen
=Cowbridge......41 D4
Y Drenewydd
=Newtown......93 B5
Yeading......48 A4
Yeadon......147 C6
Yealand Conyers...154 D4
Yealand Redmayne.154 D4
Yealmpton......7 B4
Yearby......168 C4
Yearsley......159 D4
Yeaton......110 D3
Yeaveley......113 A5
Yedingham......160 D2

Yeldon......84 A2
Yelford......65 C4
Yelland......25 B5
Yelling......85 A4
Yelvertoft......98 D2
Yelverton
Devon......7 A4
Norf......104 A3
Yenston......29 C7
Yeoford......12 B2
Yeolmbridge......10 C4
Yeo Mill......26 C3
Yeovil......29 D5
Yeovil Marsh......29 D5
Yeovilton......29 C5
Yerbeston......55 D6
Yesnaby......282 F3
Yetlington......188 C3
Yetminster......29 D5
Yettington......13 C5
Yetts o' Muckhart..219 D5
Y Felinheli......123 D5
Y Fenni
=Abergavenny....61 B4
Y Fflint =Flint......126 B2
Y Ffôr......106 C3
Y-Ffrith......125 A5
Y Gelli Gandryll
=Hay-on-Wye....77 C6
Yieldshields......194 A3
Yiewsley......48 A3
Y Mwmbwls
=The Mumbles....57 D6
Ynysboeth......41 B5
Ynysddu......41 B6
Ynysgyfflog......90 A4
Ynyshir......41 B5
Ynyslas......90 C4
Ynys-meudwy......59 E4
Ynystawe......40 A1
Ynysybwl......41 B5
Yockenthwaite....156 D3
Yockleton......110 D2
Yokefleet......141 A6
Yoker......205 B5
Yonder Bognie....255 B6
York......149 B4
Yorkletts......52 C2
Yorkley......62 C2
York Town......47 C6
Yorton......111 C4
Youlgreave......130 C2
Youlstone......24 D3
Youlthorpe......149 B6
Youlton......148 A3
Young's End......70 B1
Young Wood......133 B6
Yoxall......113 D5
Yoxford......89 A4
Y Pîl =Pyle......40 C3
Yr Hôb =Hope......126 D3
Y Rhws =Rhoose....41 E5
Y Rhyl =Rhyl......125 A5
Yr Wyddgrug
=Mold......126 C2
Ysbyty-Cynfyn......75 A6
Ysbyty Ifan......108 A3
Ysbyty Ystwyth....75 A6
Ysceifiog......125 B6
Yspitty......57 C5
Ystalyfera......59 E4
Ystrad......41 B4
Ystrad Aeron......75 C4
Ystradfellte......59 D6
Ystradffin......76 C1
Ystradgynlais......59 D4
Ystradmeurig......75 B6
Ystrad-mynach....41 B6
Ystradowen
Carms......59 D4
V Glam......41 D5
Ystumtuen......75 A6
Ythanbank......257 C4
Ythanwells......256 C1
Ythsie......256 C3
Y Trallwng
=Welshpool......93 A6

Z
Zeal Monachorum ..12 A2
Zeals......30 B1
Zelah......4 B3
Zennor......2 B2